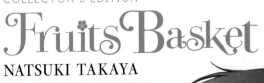

COLLECTOR'S EDITION

Fruits Basket

NATSUKI TAKAYA

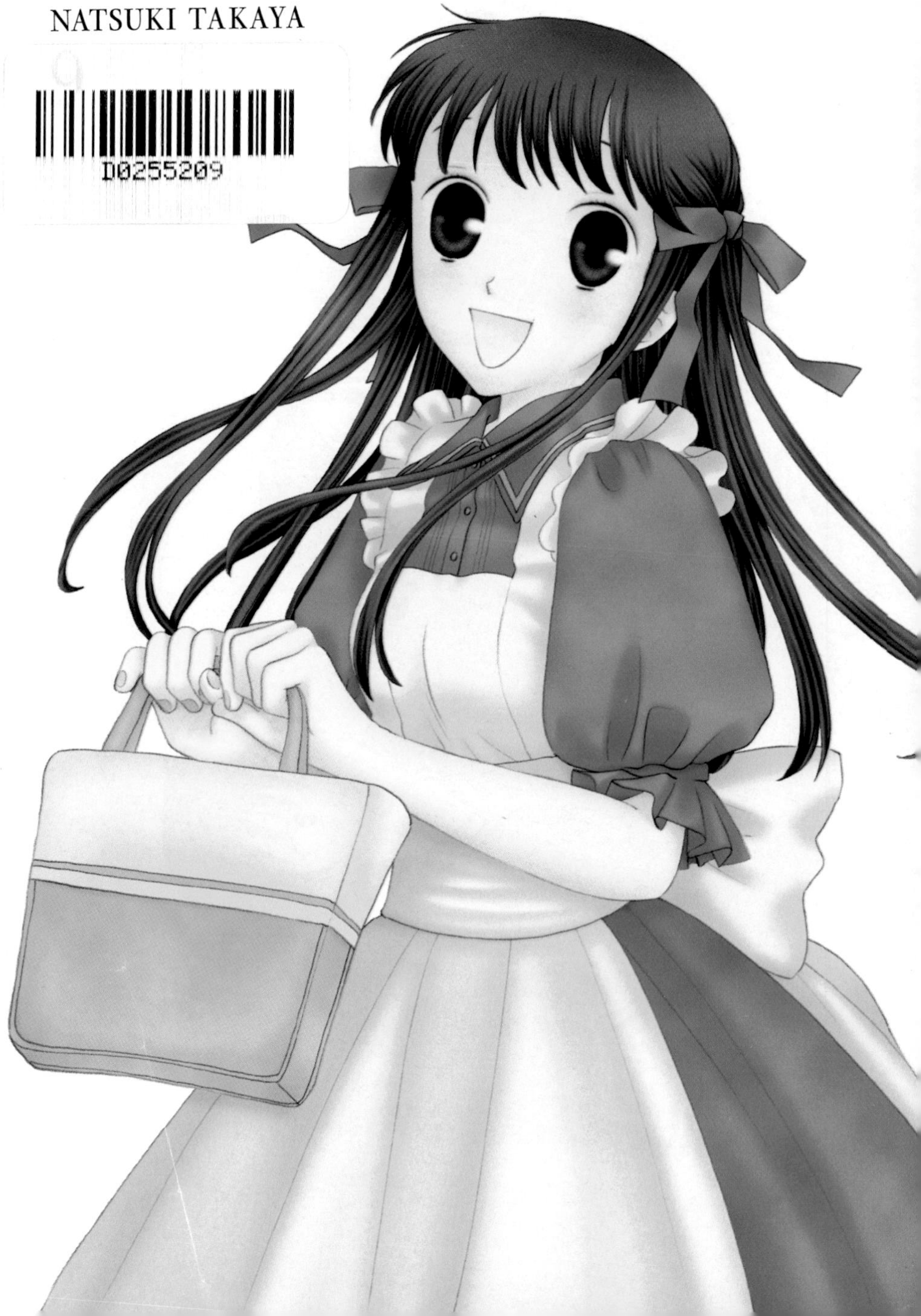

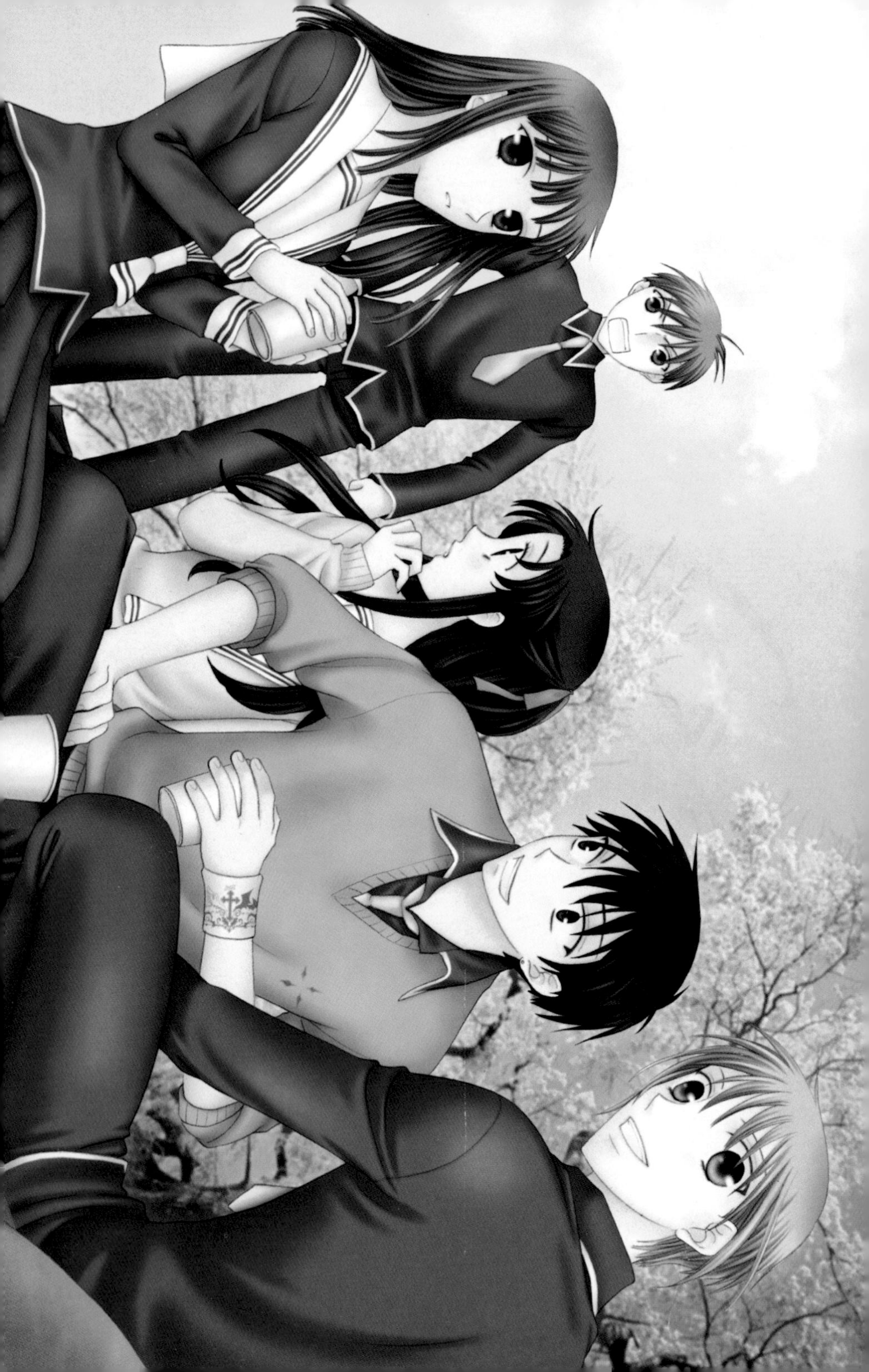

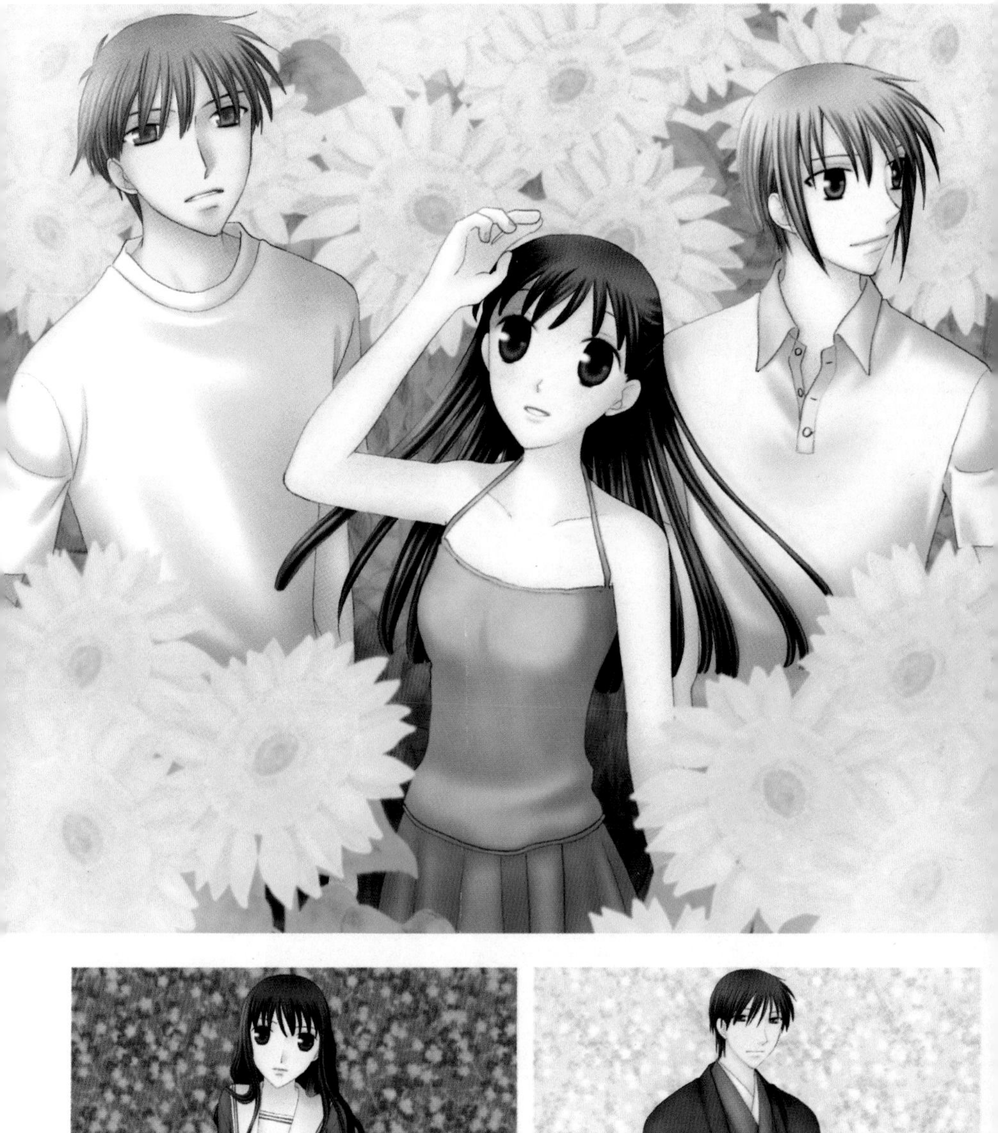
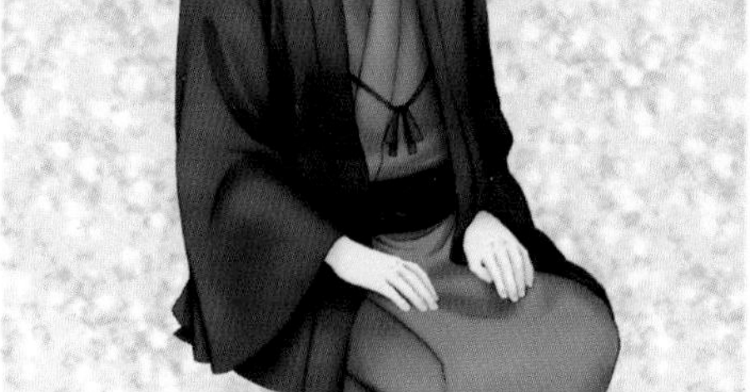
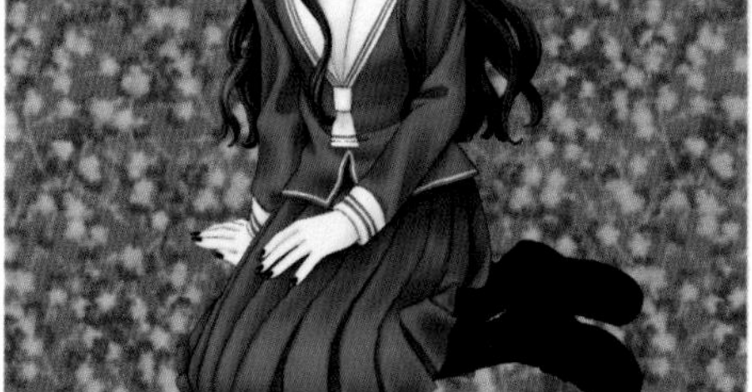

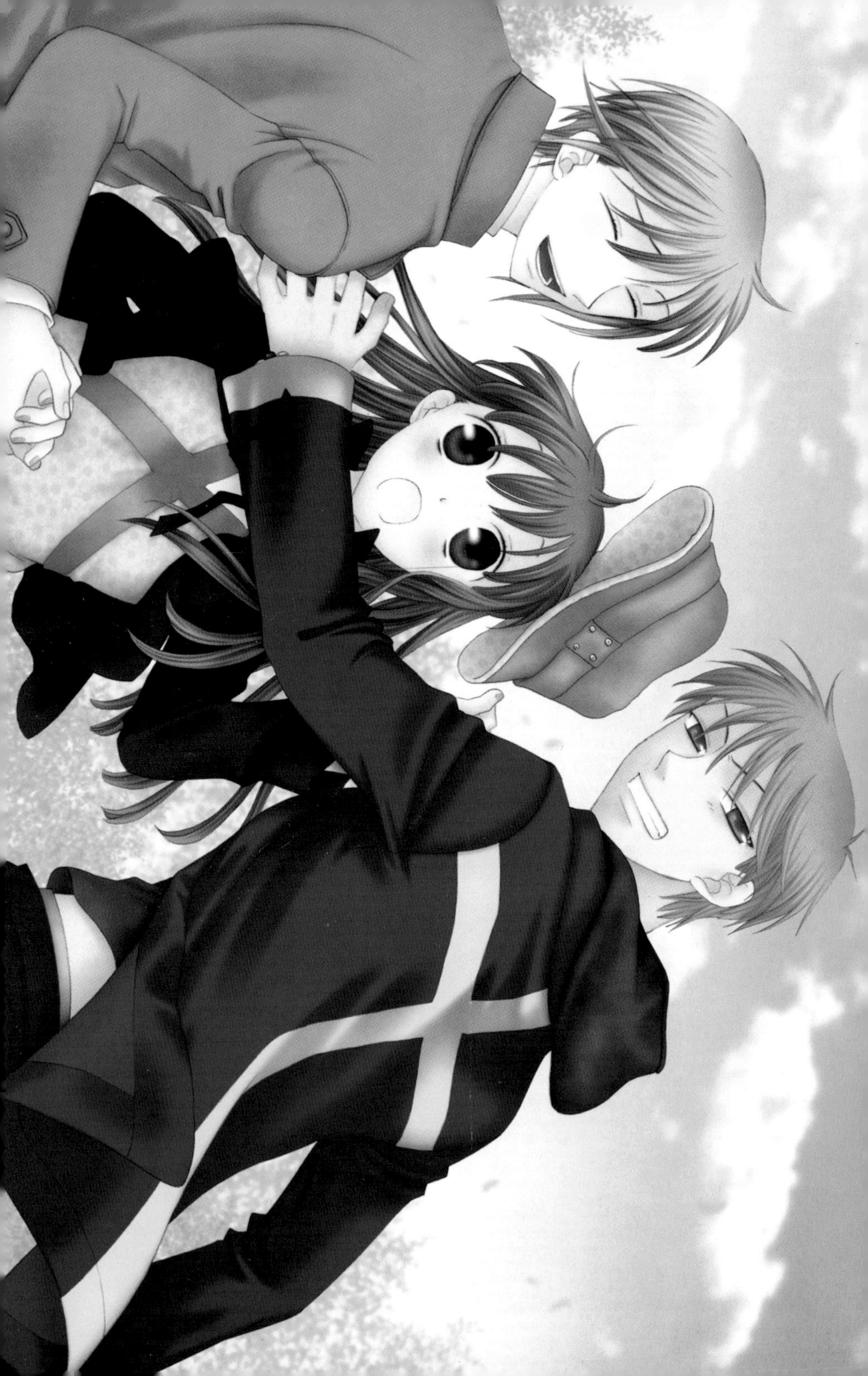

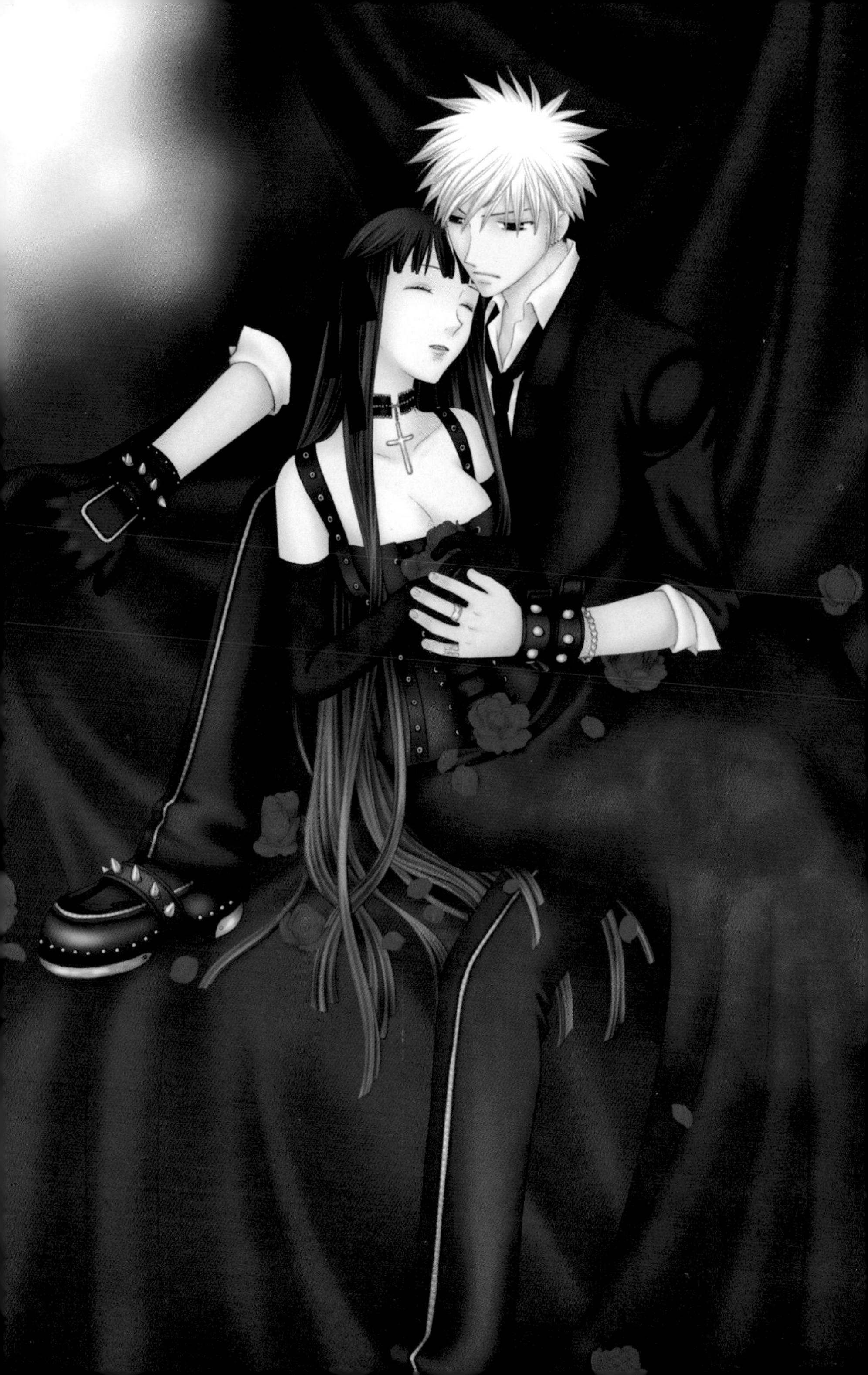

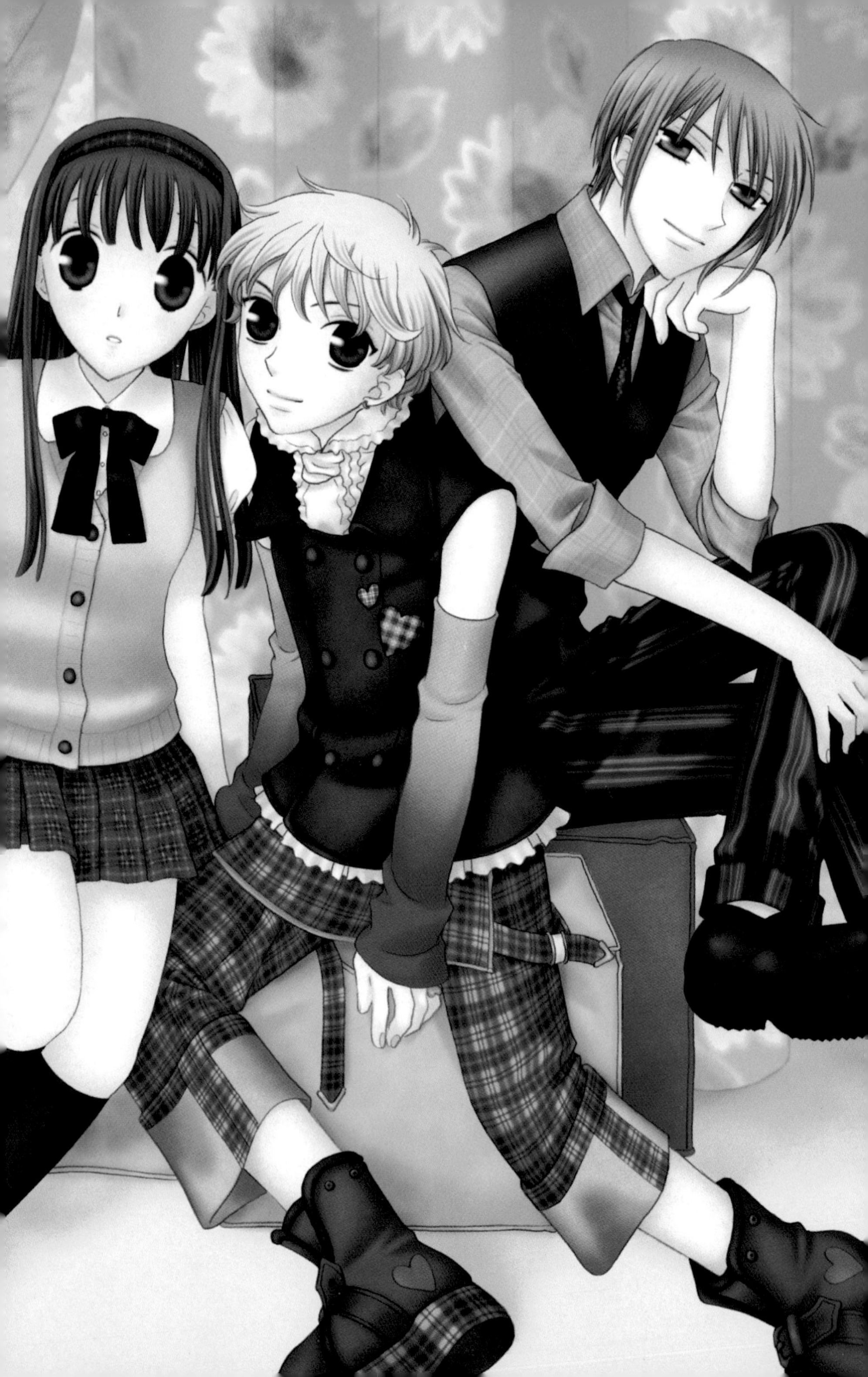

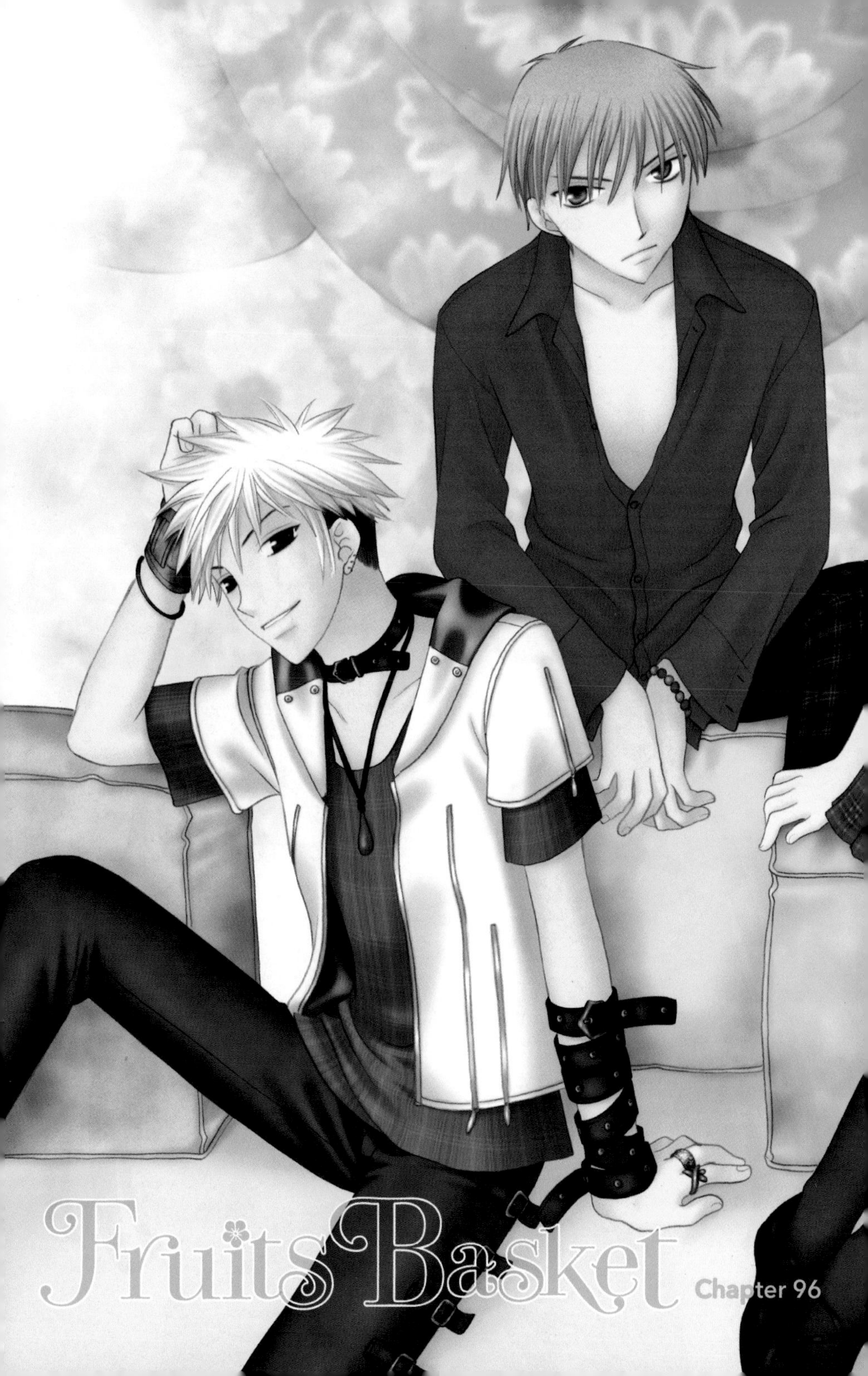
Fruits Basket
Chapter 96

TABLE OF CONTENTS

COLLECTOR'S EDITION

Fruits Basket 9

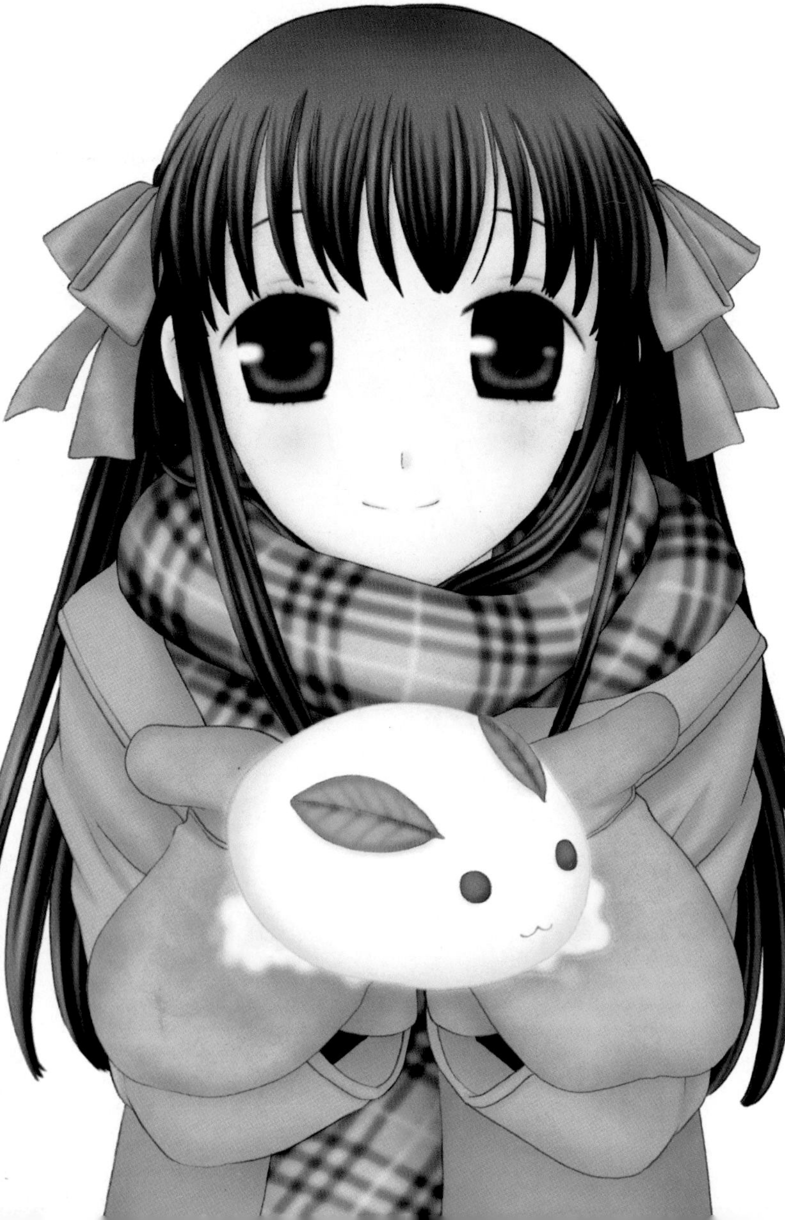

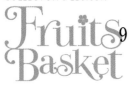

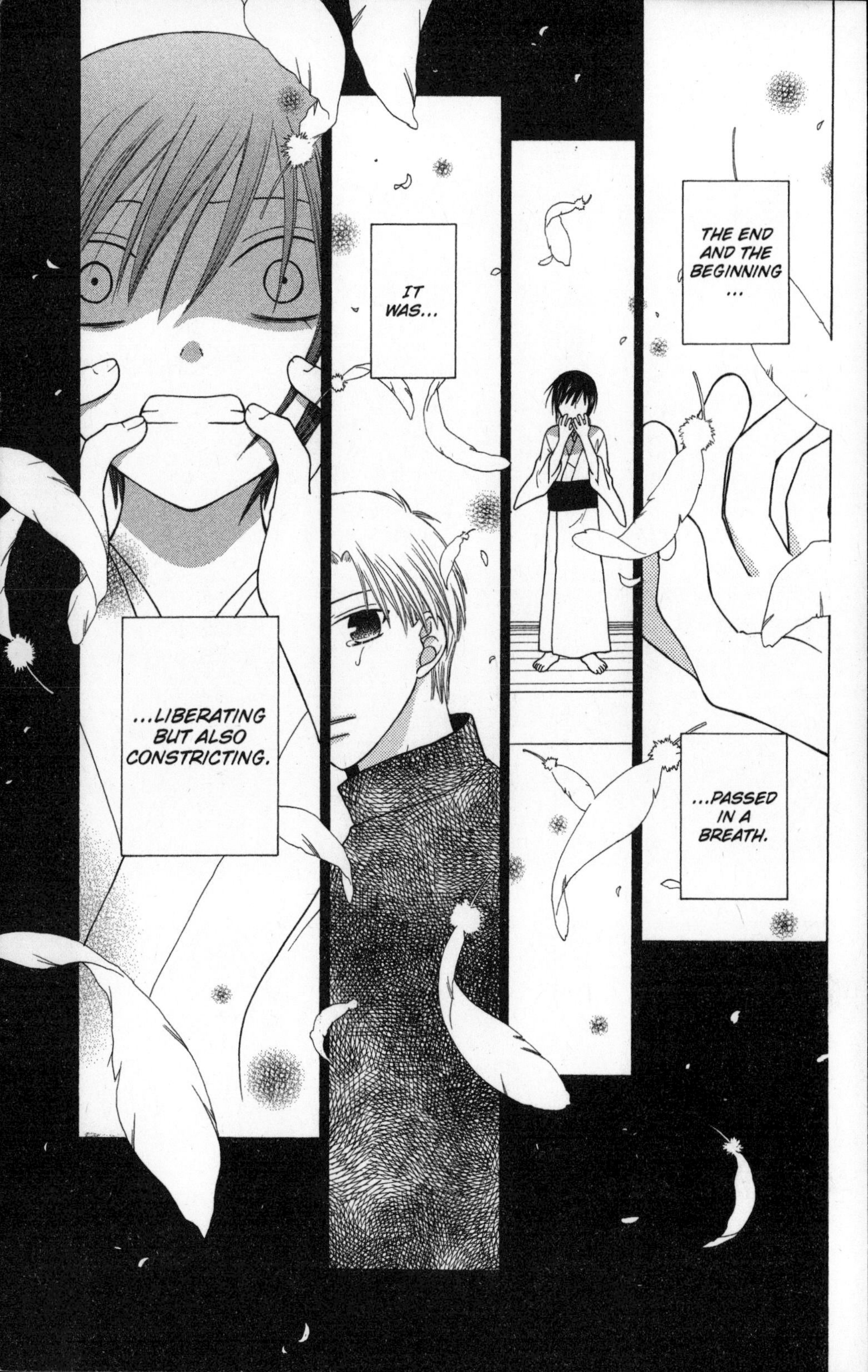
THE END AND THE BEGINNING ...
...PASSED IN A BREATH.
IT WAS...
...LIBERATING BUT ALSO CONSTRICTING.

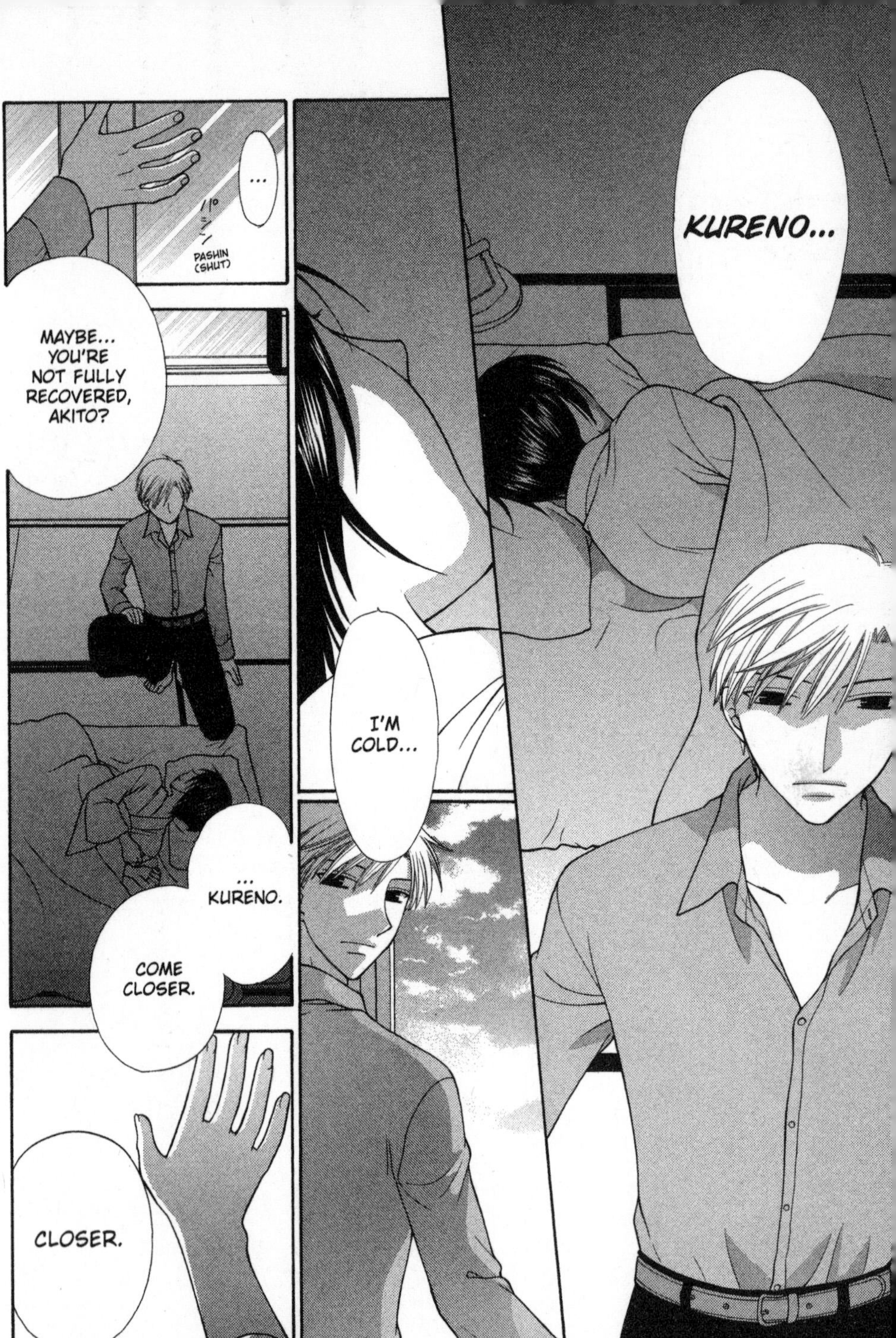
KURENO...
I'M COLD...
...
PASHIN (SHUT)
MAYBE... YOU'RE NOT FULLY RECOVERED, AKITO?
... KURENO.
COME CLOSER.
CLOSER.

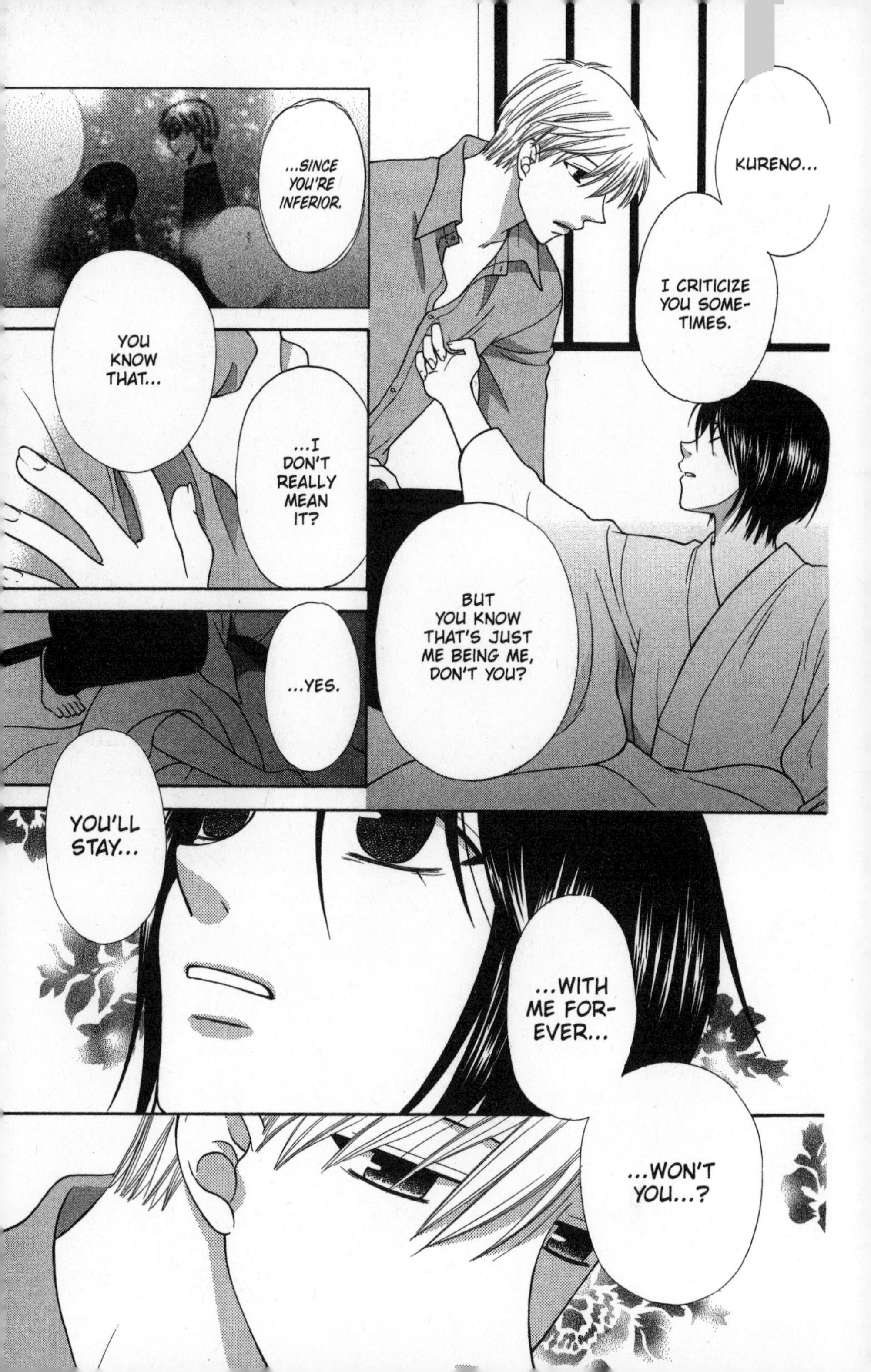
KURENO...
I CRITICIZE YOU SOMETIMES.
BUT YOU KNOW THAT'S JUST ME BEING ME, DON'T YOU?
...SINCE YOU'RE INFERIOR.
YOU KNOW THAT...
...I DON'T REALLY MEAN IT?
...YES.
YOU'LL STAY...
...WITH ME FOREVER...
...WON'T YOU...?

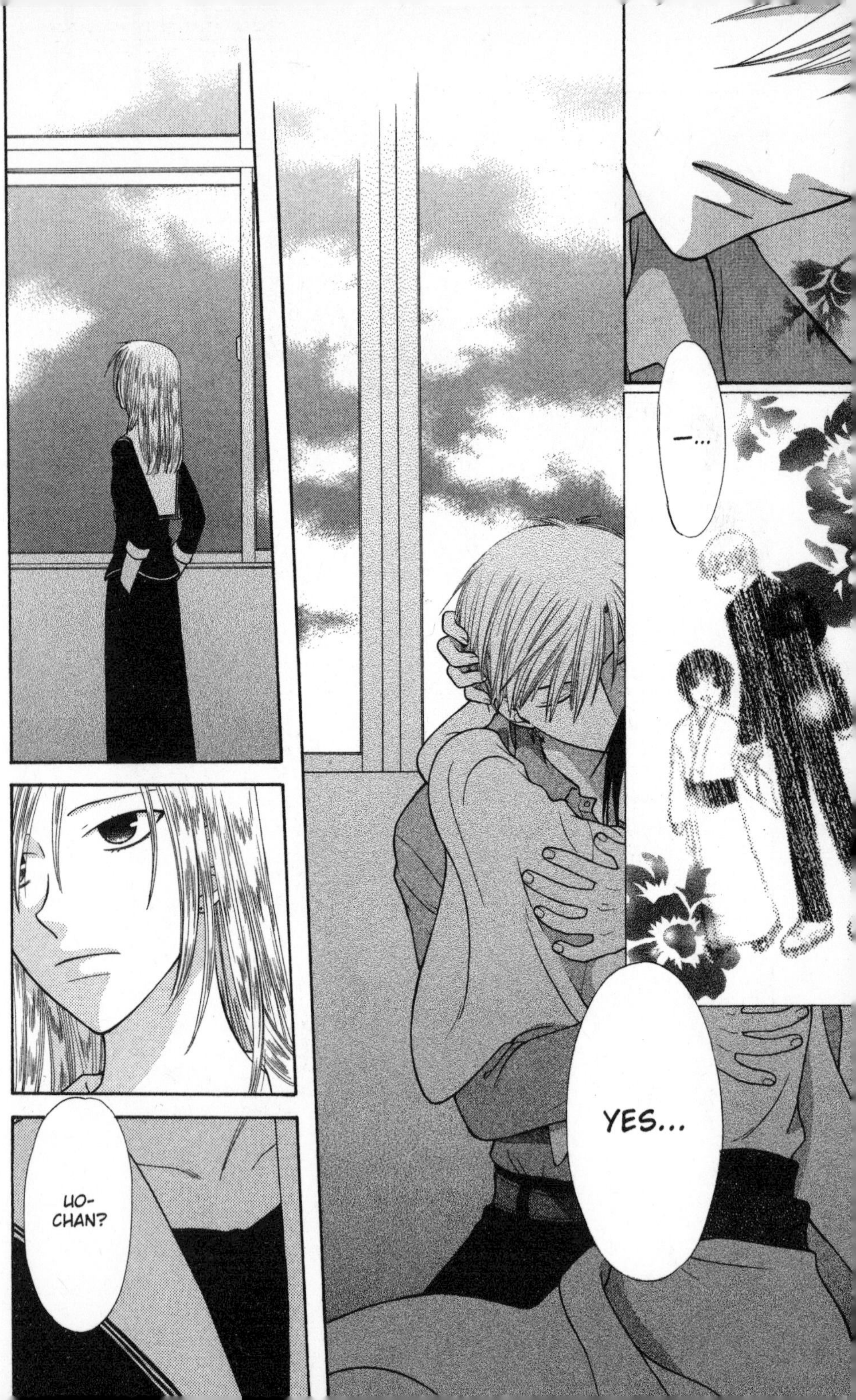
—...
YES...
UO-CHAN?

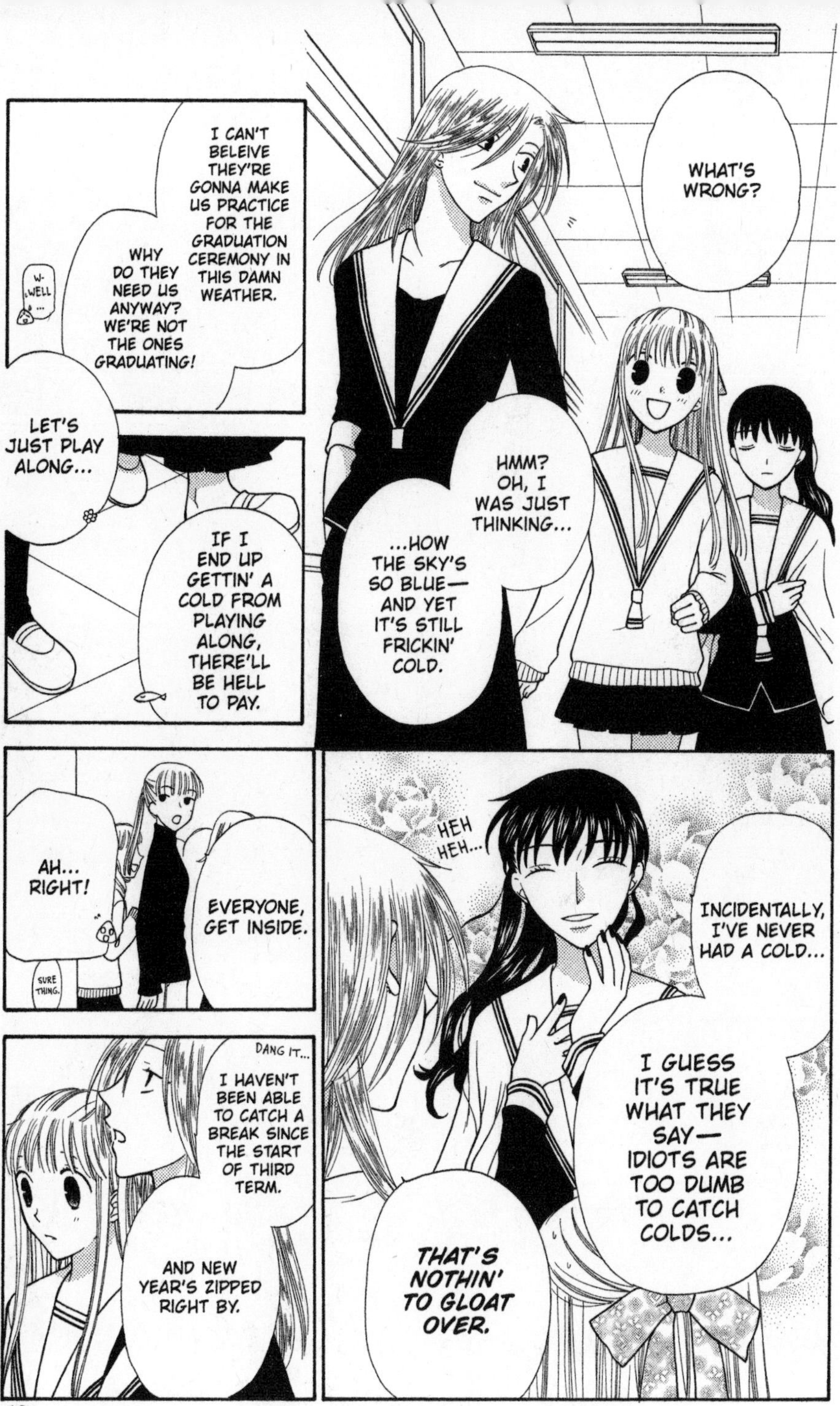
WHAT'S WRONG?
HMM? OH, I WAS JUST THINKING...
...HOW THE SKY'S SO BLUE—AND YET IT'S STILL FRICKIN' COLD.
I CAN'T BELEIVE THEY'RE GONNA MAKE US PRACTICE FOR THE GRADUATION CEREMONY IN THIS DAMN WEATHER.
WHY DO THEY NEED US ANYWAY? WE'RE NOT THE ONES GRADUATING!
W-WELL...
LET'S JUST PLAY ALONG...
IF I END UP GETTIN' A COLD FROM PLAYING ALONG, THERE'LL BE HELL TO PAY.
HEH HEH...
INCIDENTALLY, I'VE NEVER HAD A COLD...
I GUESS IT'S TRUE WHAT THEY SAY—IDIOTS ARE TOO DUMB TO CATCH COLDS...
THAT'S NOTHIN' TO GLOAT OVER.
EVERYONE, GET INSIDE.
AH... RIGHT!
SURE THING.
DANG IT...
I HAVEN'T BEEN ABLE TO CATCH A BREAK SINCE THE START OF THIRD TERM.
AND NEW YEAR'S ZIPPED RIGHT BY.

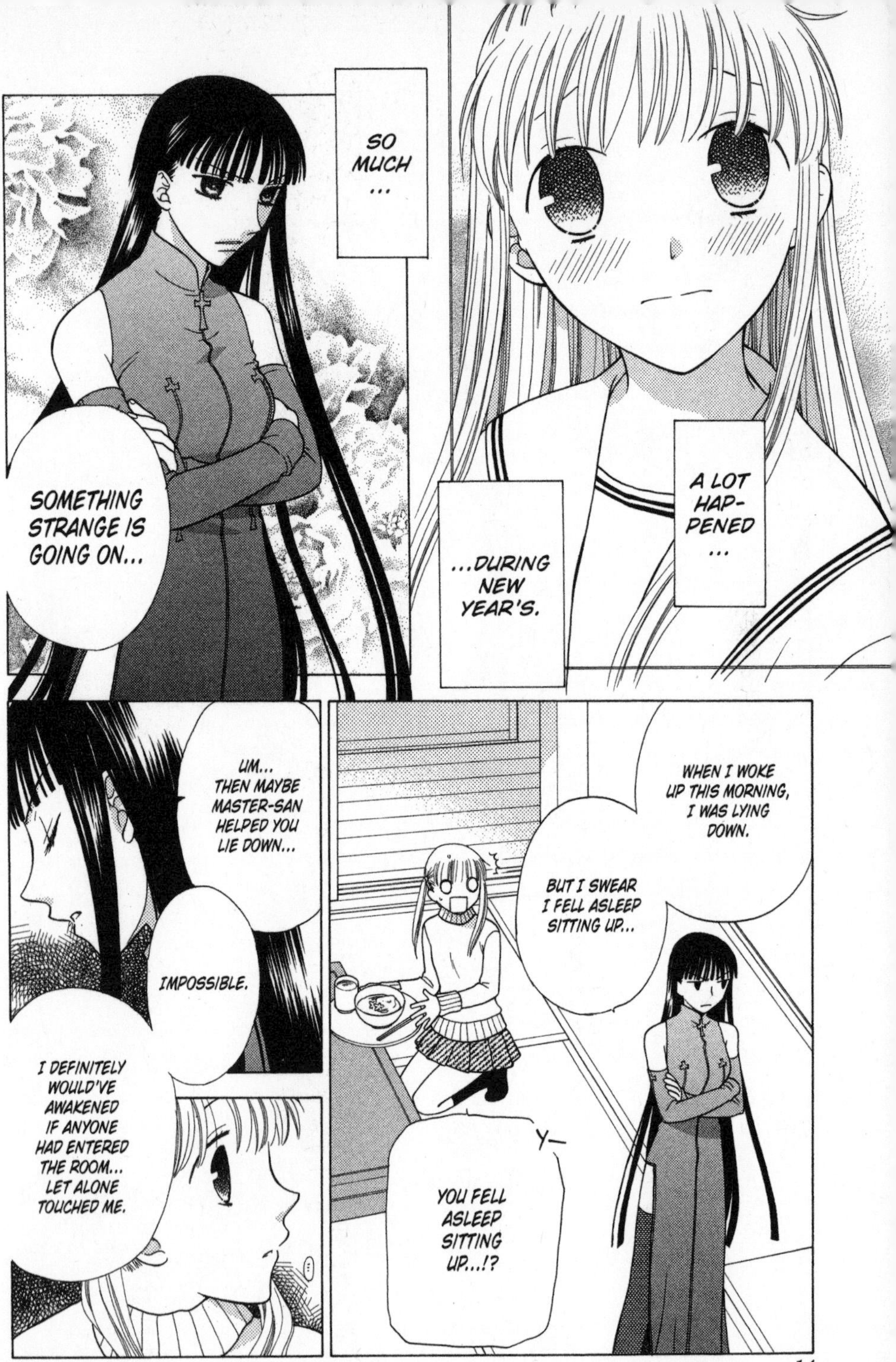
SO MUCH...
A LOT HAP-PENED...
...DURING NEW YEAR'S.
SOMETHING STRANGE IS GOING ON...
WHEN I WOKE UP THIS MORNING, I WAS LYING DOWN.
BUT I SWEAR I FELL ASLEEP SITTING UP...
Y—
YOU FELL ASLEEP SITTING UP...!?
UM... THEN MAYBE MASTER-SAN HELPED YOU LIE DOWN...
IMPOSSIBLE.
I DEFINITELY WOULD'VE AWAKENED IF ANYONE HAD ENTERED THE ROOM... LET ALONE TOUCHED ME.
...

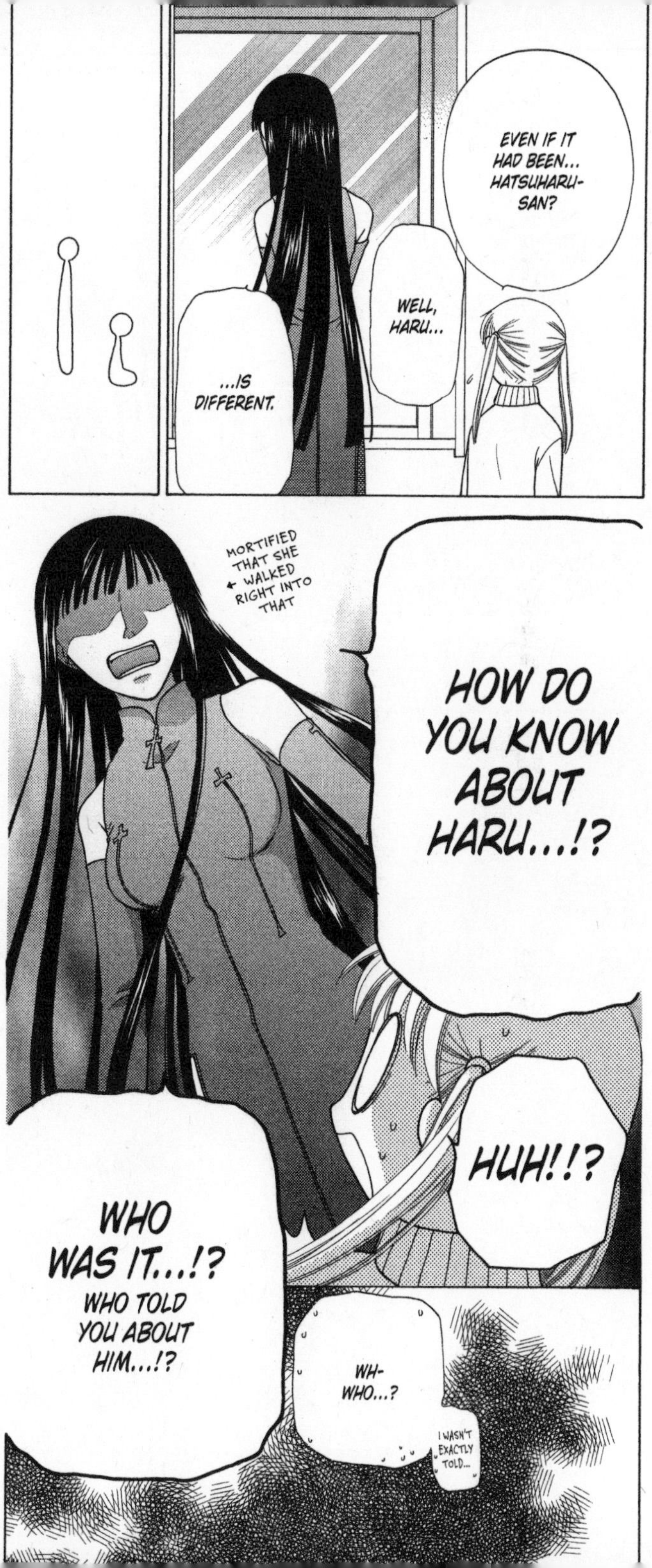
EVEN IF IT HAD BEEN... HATSUHARU-SAN?
WELL, HARU...
...IS DIFFERENT.
HOW DO YOU KNOW ABOUT HARU...!?
MORTIFIED THAT SHE WALKED RIGHT INTO THAT
HUH!!?
WHO WAS IT...!?
WHO TOLD YOU ABOUT HIM...!?
WH- WHO...?
I WASN'T EXACTLY TOLD...
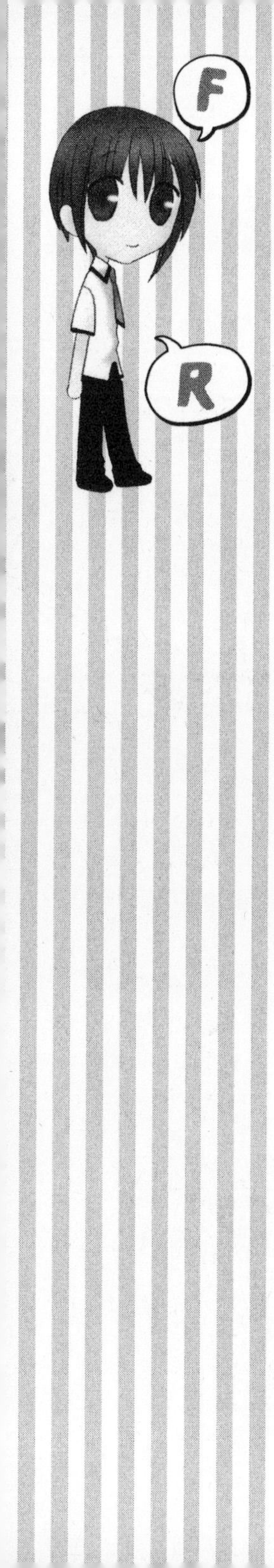
F
R

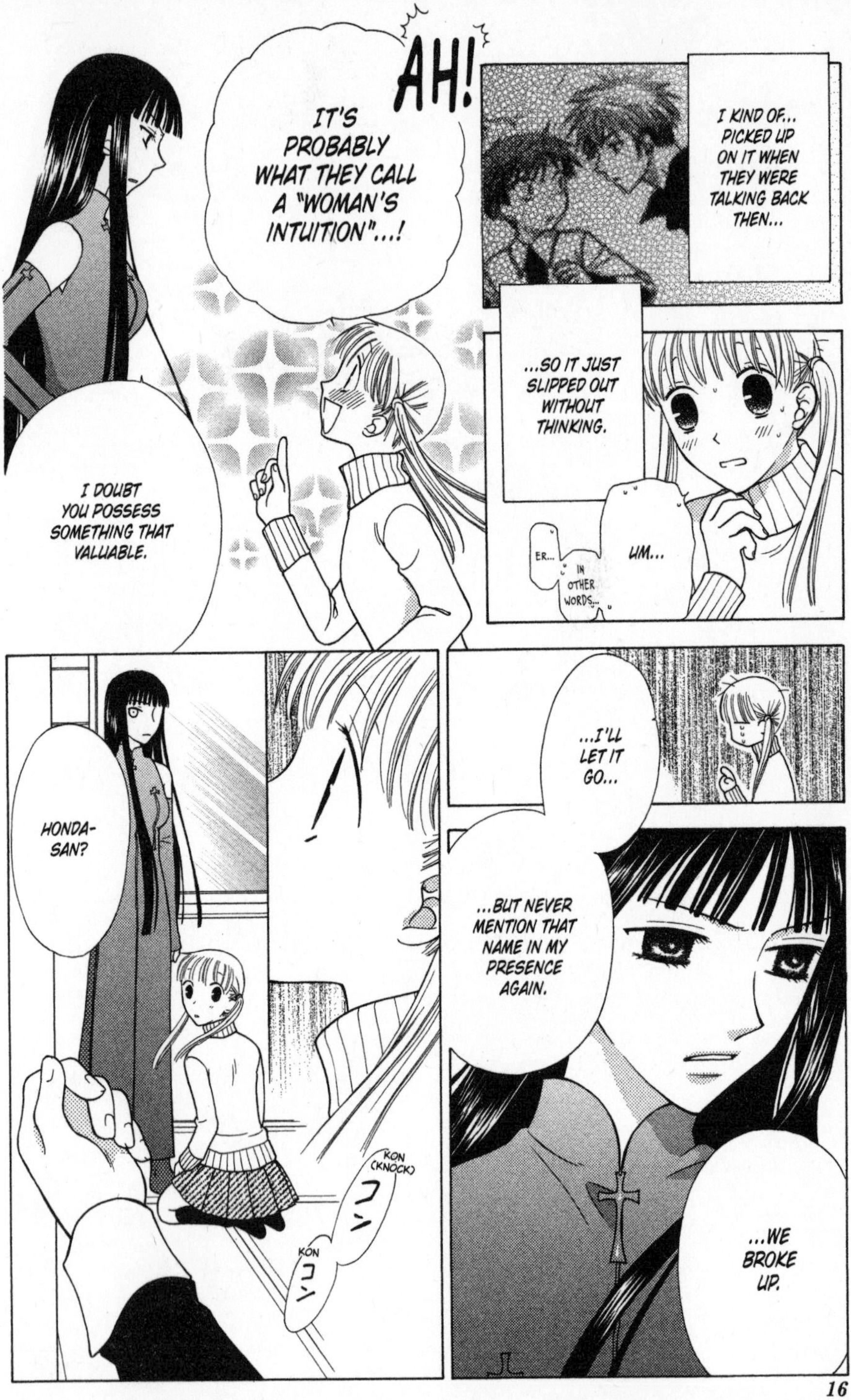
I KIND OF... PICKED UP ON IT WHEN THEY WERE TALKING BACK THEN...
...SO IT JUST SLIPPED OUT WITHOUT THINKING.
UM...
ER... IN OTHER WORDS...
AH!
IT'S PROBABLY WHAT THEY CALL A "WOMAN'S INTUITION"...!
I DOUBT YOU POSSESS SOMETHING THAT VALUABLE.
...I'LL LET IT GO...
...BUT NEVER MENTION THAT NAME IN MY PRESENCE AGAIN.
...WE BROKE UP.
KON (KNOCK)
コン
KON
コン
HONDA-SAN?

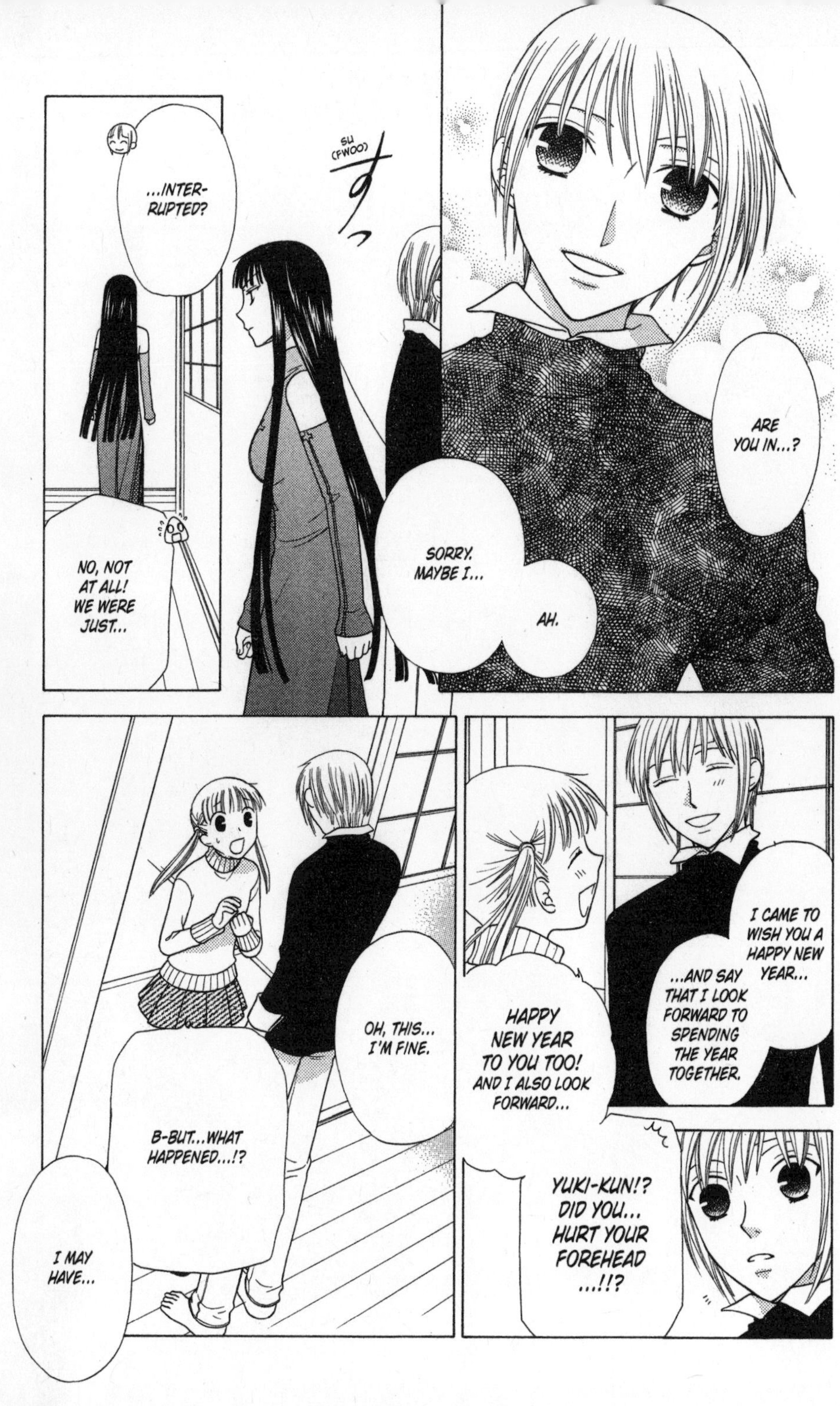
ARE YOU IN...?
SORRY. MAYBE I...
AH.
SU (FWOO)
...INTER-RUPTED?
NO, NOT AT ALL! WE WERE JUST...
I CAME TO WISH YOU A HAPPY NEW YEAR...
...AND SAY THAT I LOOK FORWARD TO SPENDING THE YEAR TOGETHER.
HAPPY NEW YEAR TO YOU TOO! AND I ALSO LOOK FORWARD...
YUKI-KUN!? DID YOU... HURT YOUR FOREHEAD ...!!?
OH, THIS... I'M FINE.
B-BUT...WHAT HAPPENED...!?
I MAY HAVE...

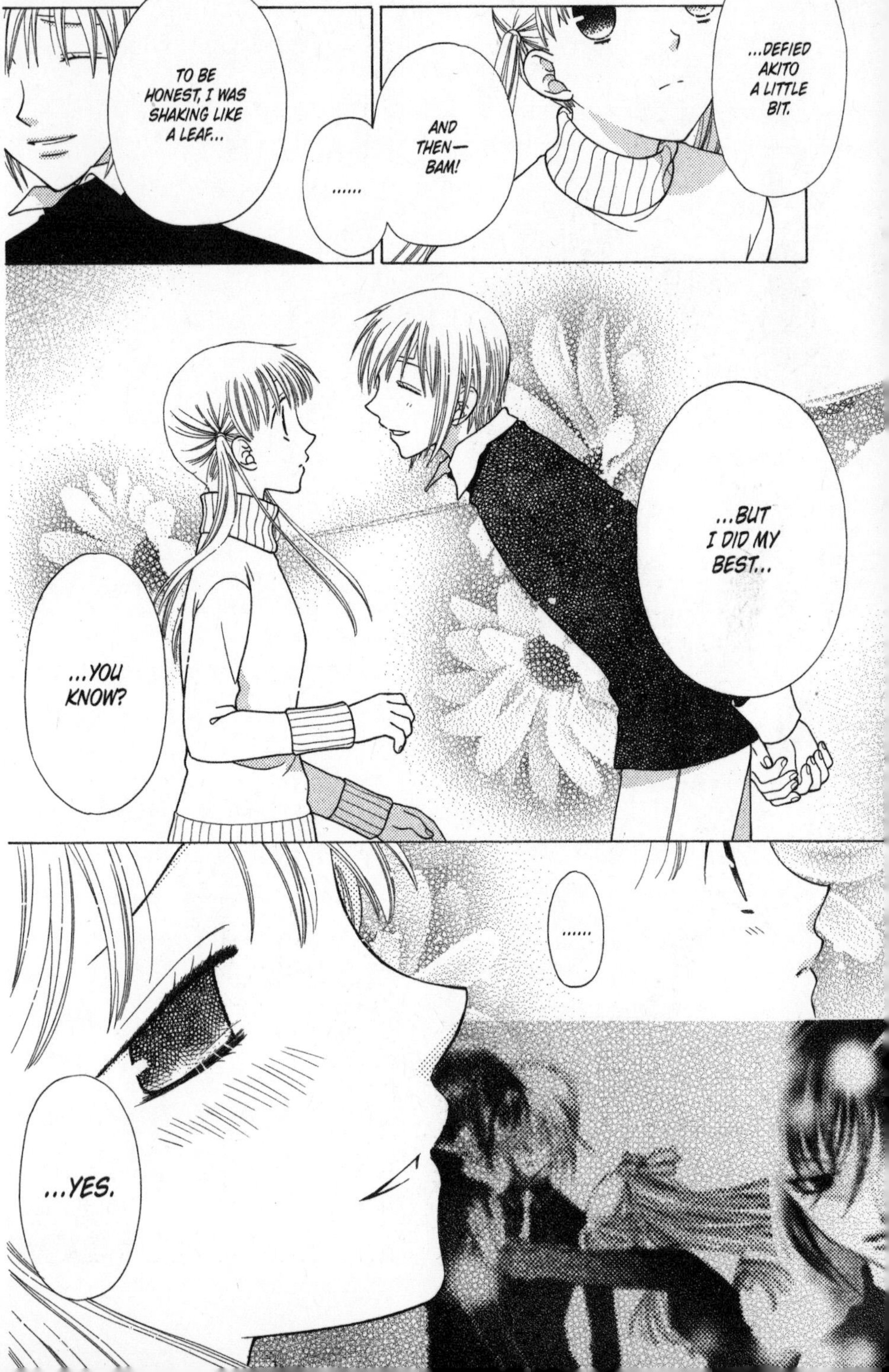
...DEFIED AKITO A LITTLE BIT.
AND THEN— BAM!
......
TO BE HONEST, I WAS SHAKING LIKE A LEAF...
...BUT I DID MY BEST...
...YOU KNOW?
......
...YES.

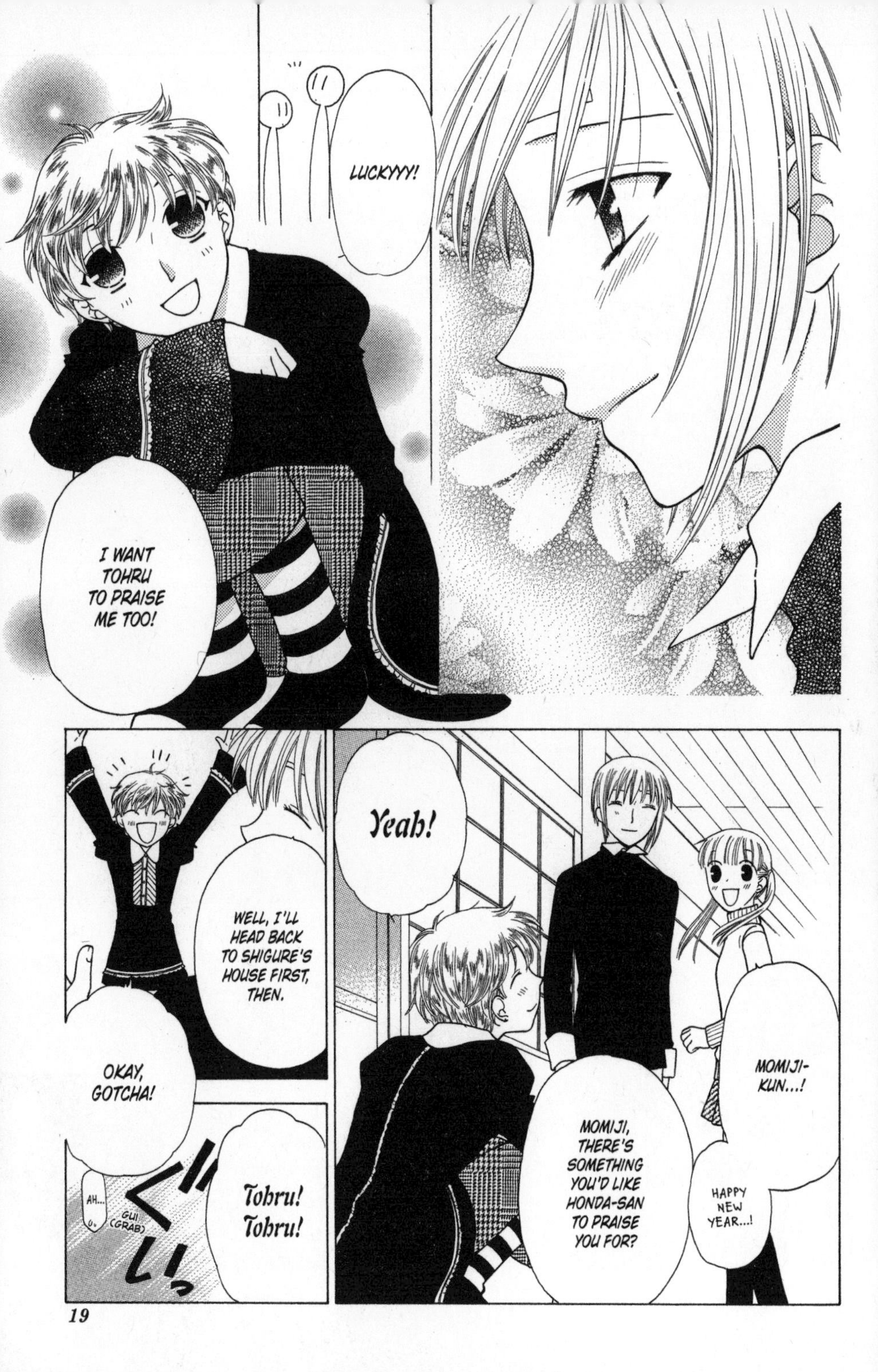
LUCKYYY!
I WANT TOHRU TO PRAISE ME TOO!
Yeah!
MOMIJI-KUN...!
HAPPY NEW YEAR...!
MOMIJI, THERE'S SOMETHING YOU'D LIKE HONDA-SAN TO PRAISE YOU FOR?
WELL, I'LL HEAD BACK TO SHIGURE'S HOUSE FIRST, THEN.
OKAY, GOTCHA!
Tohru! Tohru!
GUI (GRAB)
AH...

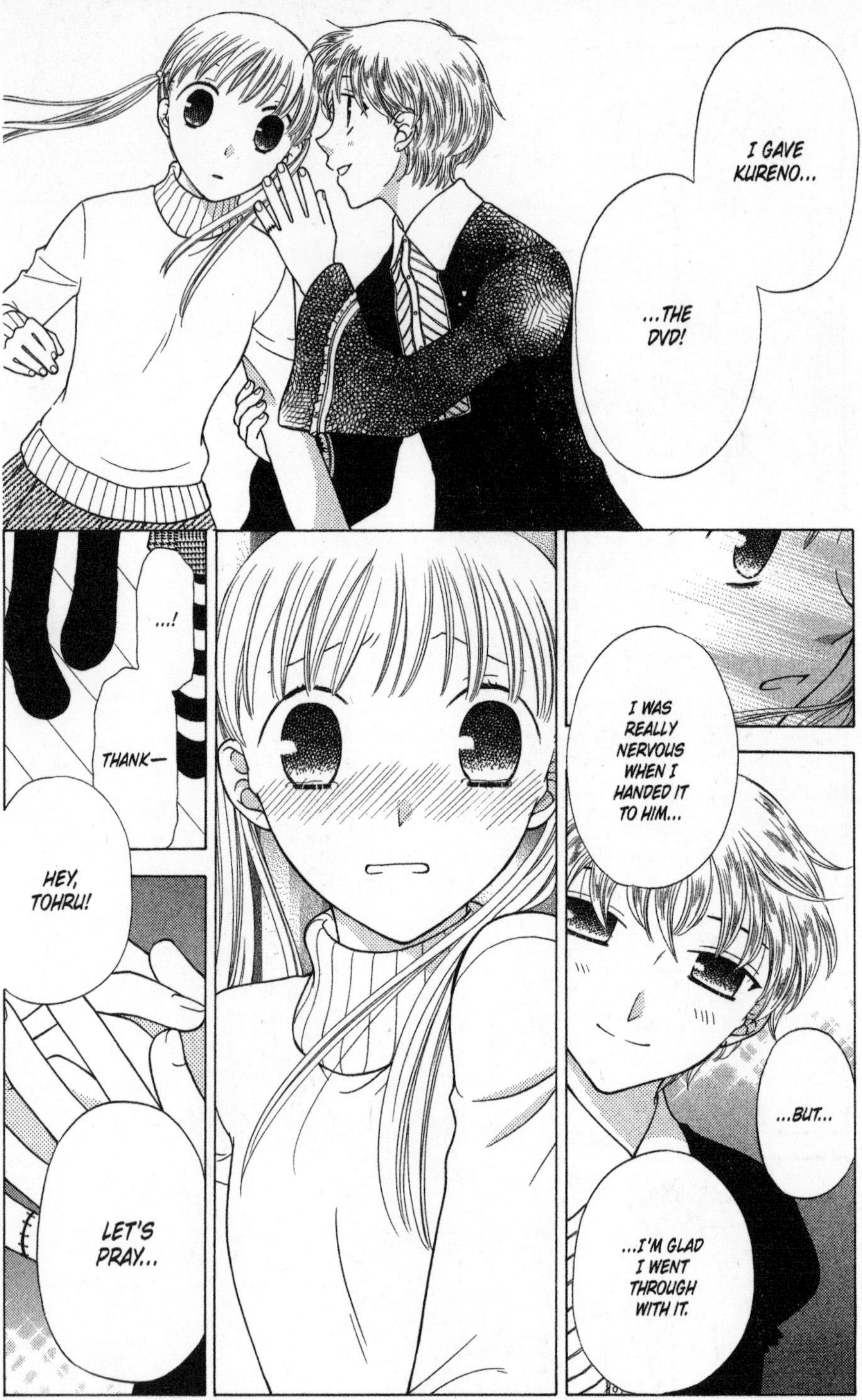
I GAVE KURENO...
...THE DVD!
I WAS REALLY NERVOUS WHEN I HANDED IT TO HIM...
...BUT...
...I'M GLAD I WENT THROUGH WITH IT.
...!
THANK—
HEY, TOHRU!
LET'S PRAY...

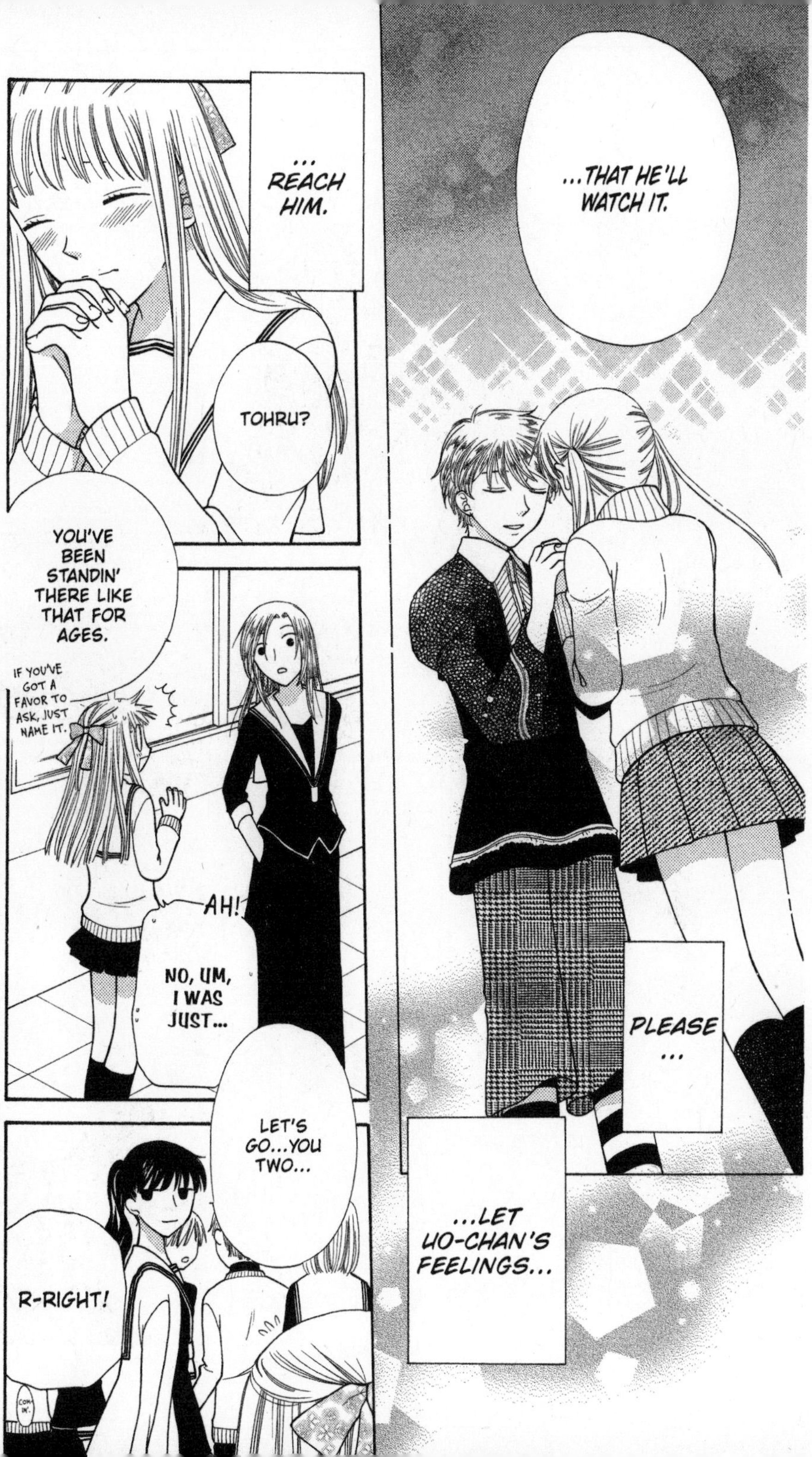
...THAT HE'LL WATCH IT.
PLEASE ...
...LET UO-CHAN'S FEELINGS...
... REACH HIM.
TOHRU?
YOU'VE BEEN STANDIN' THERE LIKE THAT FOR AGES.
IF YOU'VE GOT A FAVOR TO ASK, JUST NAME IT.
AH!
NO, UM, I WAS JUST...
LET'S GO...YOU TWO...
R-RIGHT!
COM-IN'.

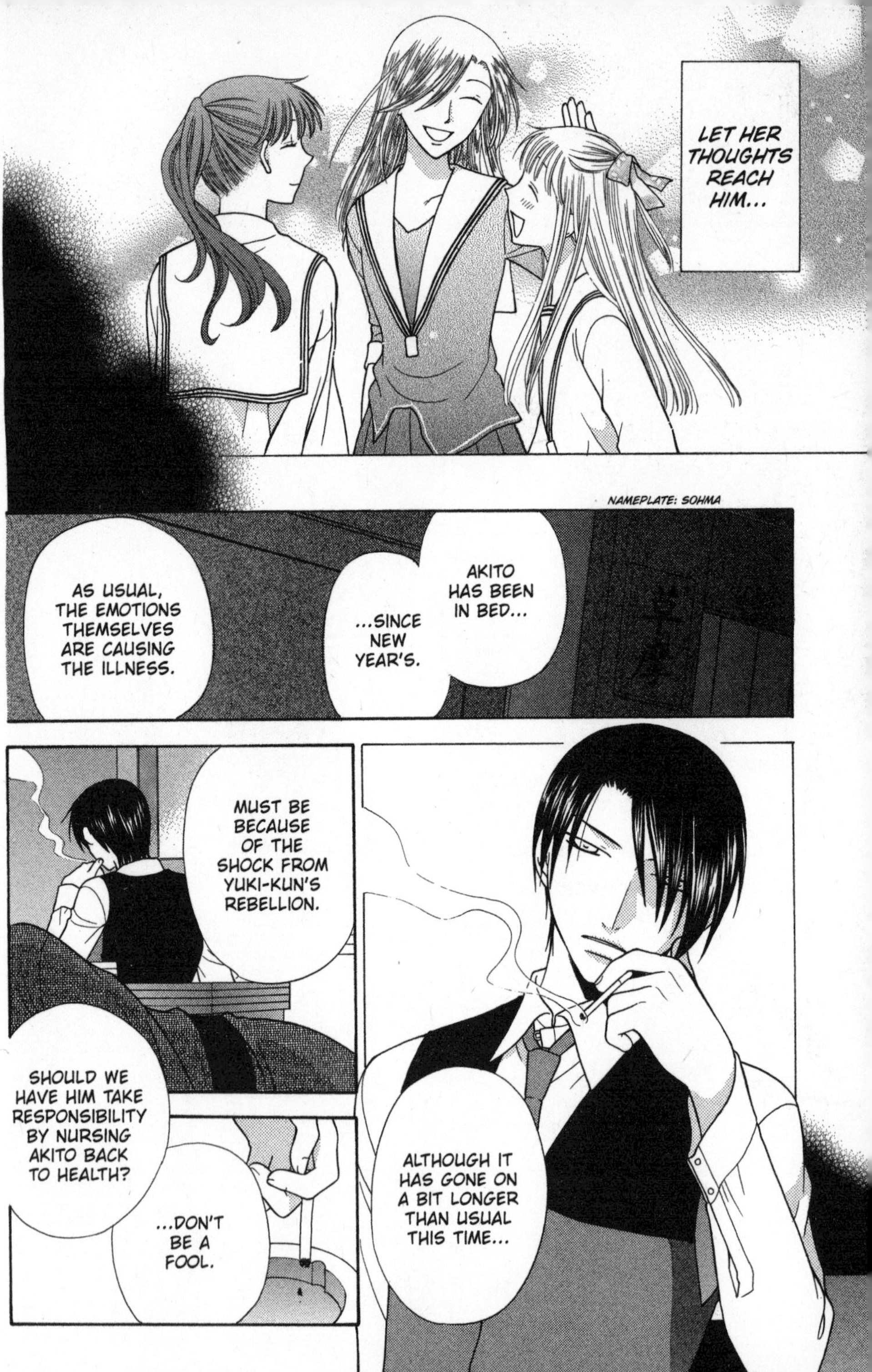
LET HER THOUGHTS REACH HIM...
NAMEPLATE: SOHMA
AKITO HAS BEEN IN BED...
...SINCE NEW YEAR'S.
AS USUAL, THE EMOTIONS THEMSELVES ARE CAUSING THE ILLNESS.
ALTHOUGH IT HAS GONE ON A BIT LONGER THAN USUAL THIS TIME...
MUST BE BECAUSE OF THE SHOCK FROM YUKI-KUN'S REBELLION.
SHOULD WE HAVE HIM TAKE RESPONSIBILITY BY NURSING AKITO BACK TO HEALTH?
...DON'T BE A FOOL.

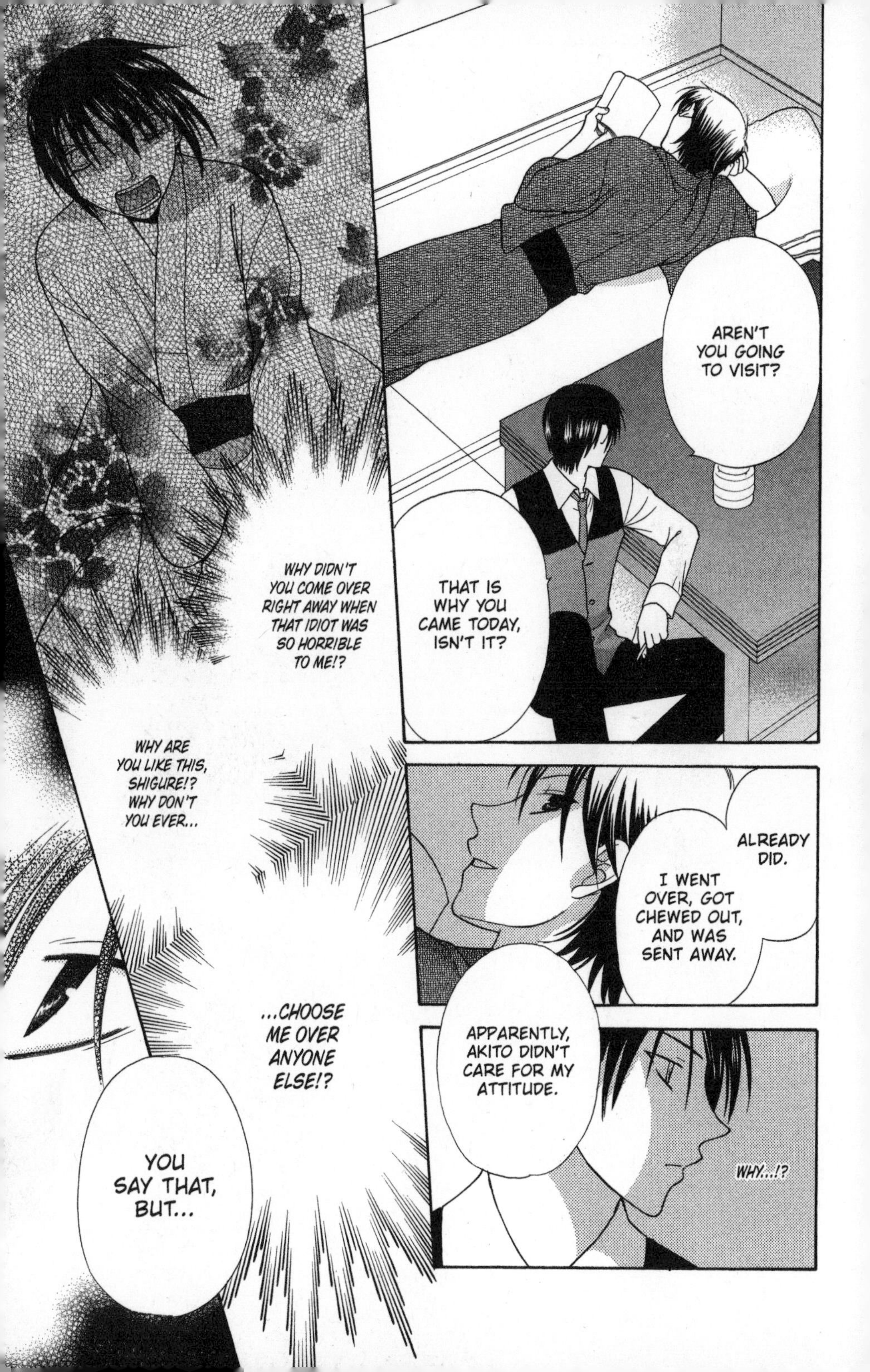
AREN'T YOU GOING TO VISIT?
THAT IS WHY YOU CAME TODAY, ISN'T IT?
ALREADY DID.
I WENT OVER, GOT CHEWED OUT, AND WAS SENT AWAY.
APPARENTLY, AKITO DIDN'T CARE FOR MY ATTITUDE.
WHY...!?
WHY DIDN'T YOU COME OVER RIGHT AWAY WHEN THAT IDIOT WAS SO HORRIBLE TO ME!?
WHY ARE YOU LIKE THIS, SHIGURE!? WHY DON'T YOU EVER...
...CHOOSE ME OVER ANYONE ELSE!?
YOU SAY THAT, BUT...

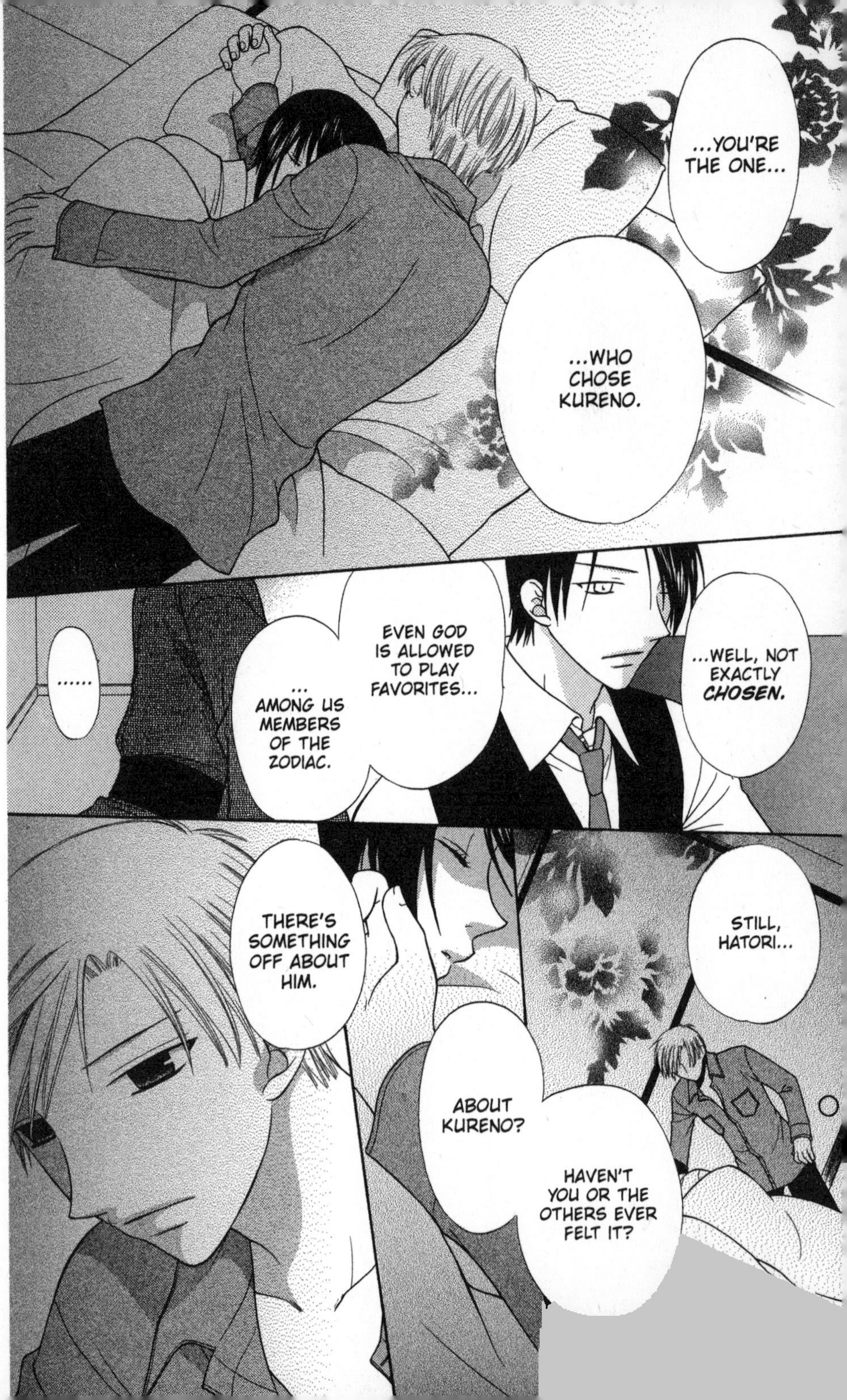
...YOU'RE THE ONE...
...WHO CHOSE KURENO.
...WELL, NOT EXACTLY *CHOSEN.*
EVEN GOD IS ALLOWED TO PLAY FAVORITES...
... AMONG US MEMBERS OF THE ZODIAC.
......
STILL, HATORI...
THERE'S SOMETHING OFF ABOUT HIM.
ABOUT KURENO?
HAVEN'T YOU OR THE OTHERS EVER FELT IT?

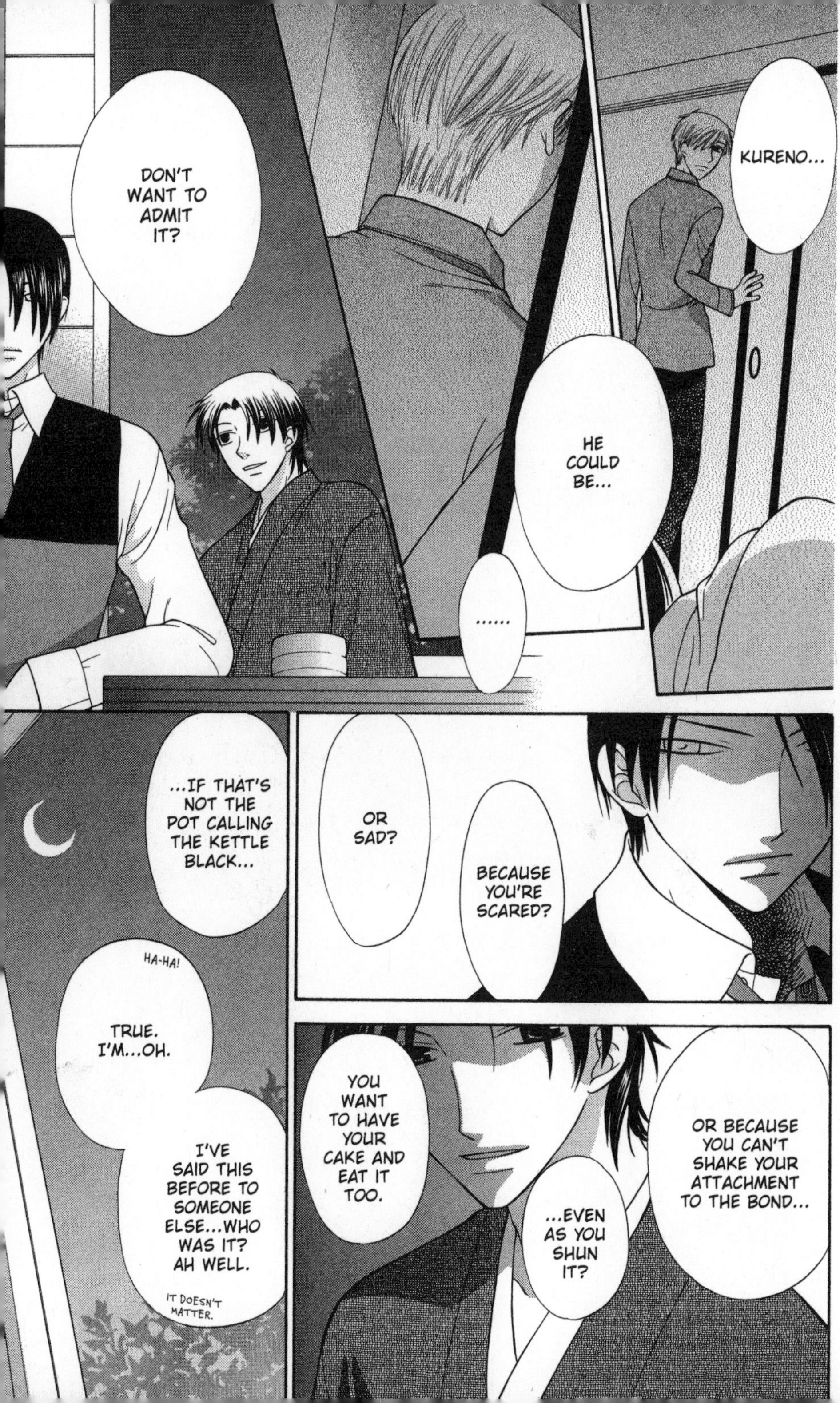
KURENO...
HE COULD BE...
DON'T WANT TO ADMIT IT?
......
BECAUSE YOU'RE SCARED?
OR SAD?
OR BECAUSE YOU CAN'T SHAKE YOUR ATTACHMENT TO THE BOND...
...EVEN AS YOU SHUN IT?
YOU WANT TO HAVE YOUR CAKE AND EAT IT TOO.
...IF THAT'S NOT THE POT CALLING THE KETTLE BLACK...
HA-HA!
TRUE. I'M...OH.
I'VE SAID THIS BEFORE TO SOMEONE ELSE...WHO WAS IT? AH WELL.
IT DOESN'T MATTER.

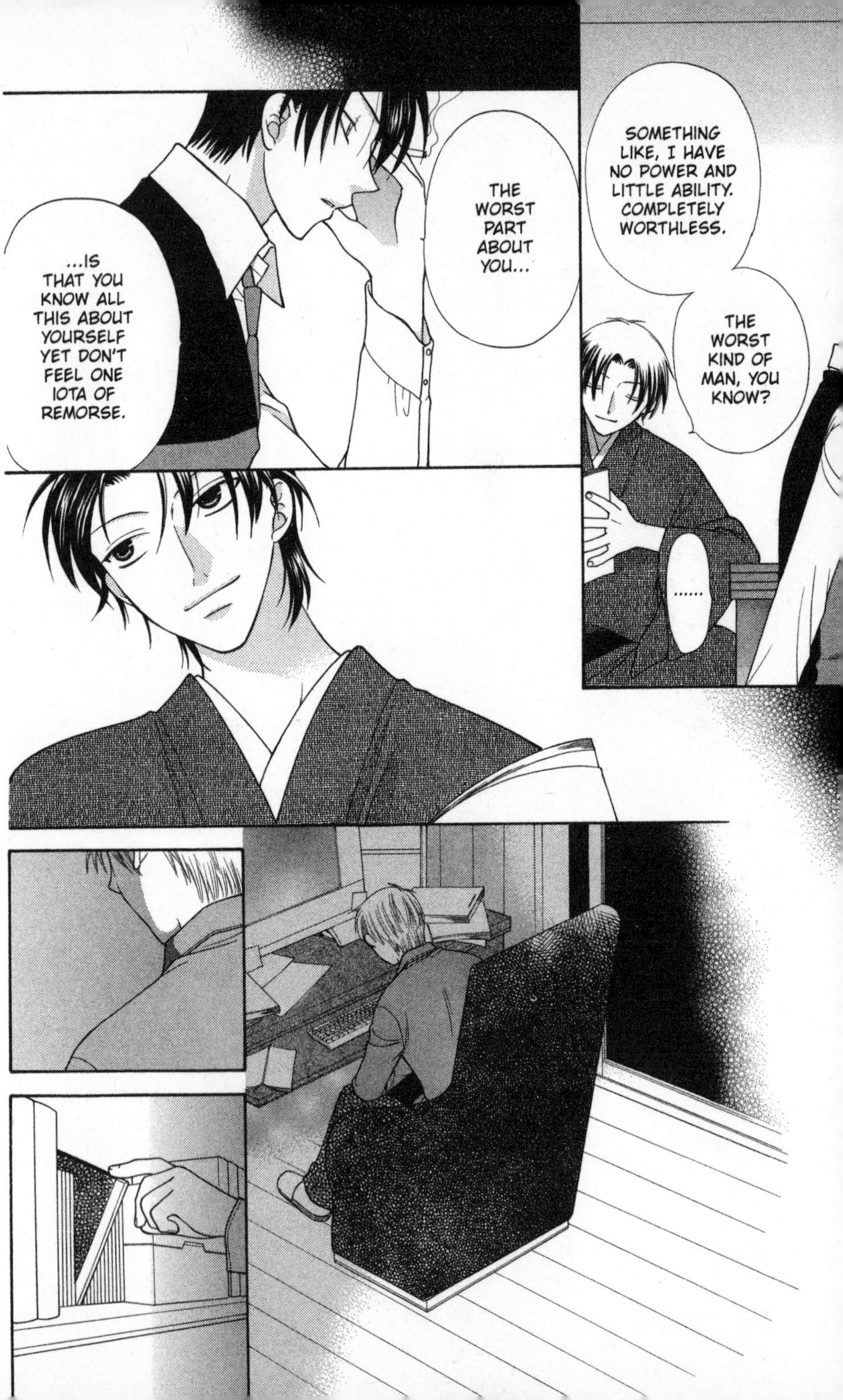
SOMETHING LIKE, I HAVE NO POWER AND LITTLE ABILITY. COMPLETELY WORTHLESS.
THE WORST KIND OF MAN, YOU KNOW?
......
THE WORST PART ABOUT YOU...
...IS THAT YOU KNOW ALL THIS ABOUT YOURSELF YET DON'T FEEL ONE IOTA OF REMORSE.

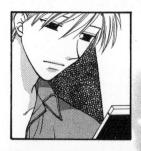

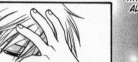

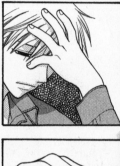

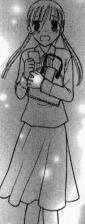

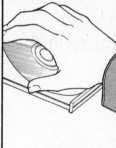

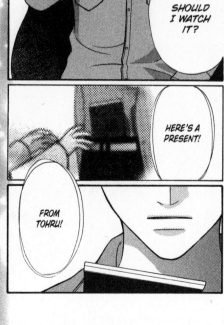

Watch this when you're alone!
I WONDER ...
...WHAT'S ON IT.
SHOULD I WATCH IT?
HERE'S A PRESENT!
FROM TOHRU!
AS LONG AS...
...YOU'RE ALIVE...
...YOU'LL ALWAYS HAVE SOMETHING TO WISH FOR...
...HEY.
TELL ME, KURENO...

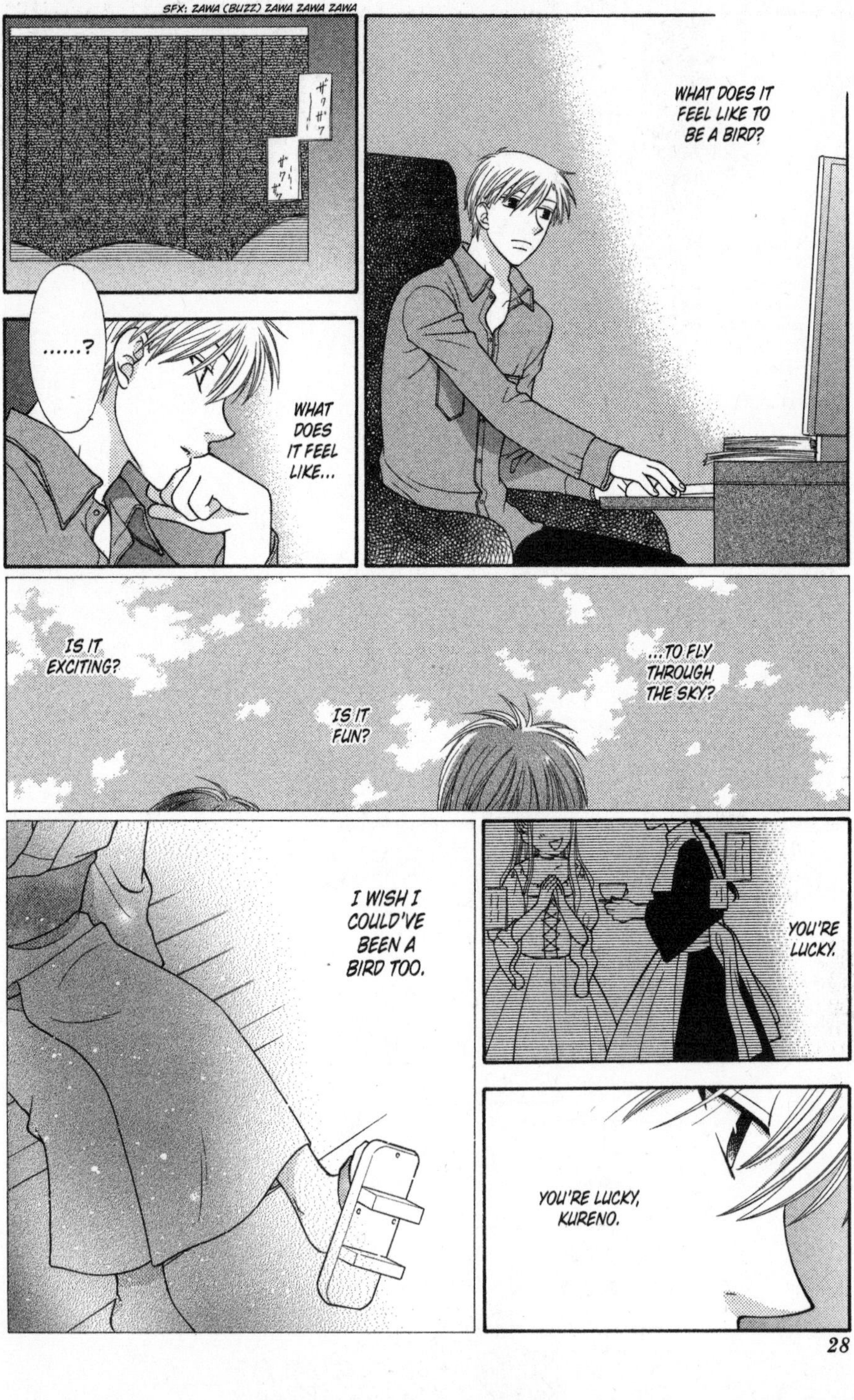
WHAT DOES IT FEEL LIKE TO BE A BIRD?
SFX: ZAWA (BUZZ) ZAWA ZAWA ZAWA
......?
WHAT DOES IT FEEL LIKE...
...TO FLY THROUGH THE SKY?
IS IT FUN?
IS IT EXCITING?
YOU'RE LUCKY.
YOU'RE LUCKY, KURENO.
I WISH I COULD'VE BEEN A BIRD TOO.

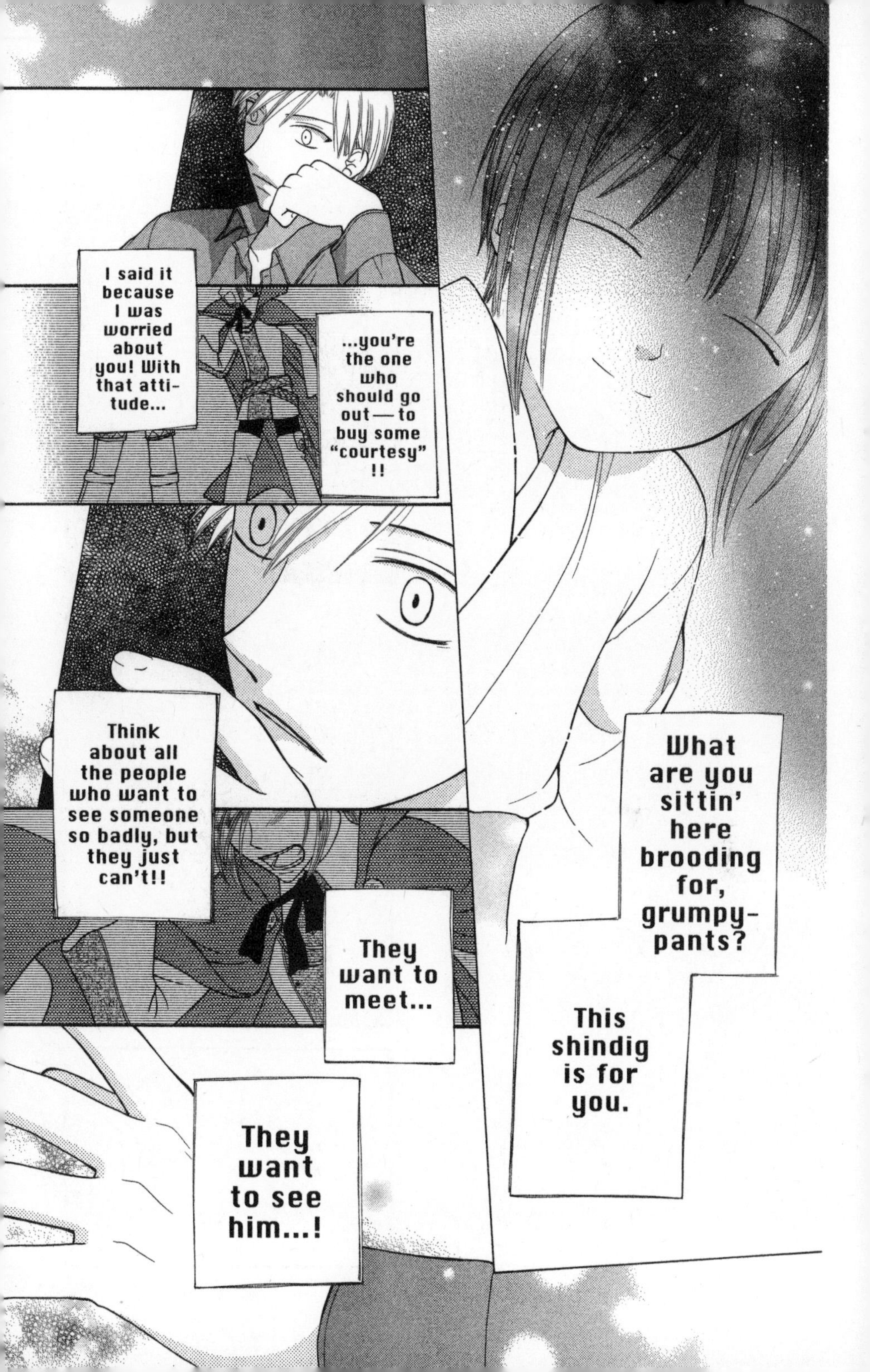
What are you sittin' here brooding for, grumpy-pants?
This shindig is for you.
I said it because I was worried about you! With that atti-tude...
...you're the one who should go out—to buy some "courtesy" !!
Think about all the people who want to see someone so badly, but they just can't!!
They want to meet...
They want to see him...!

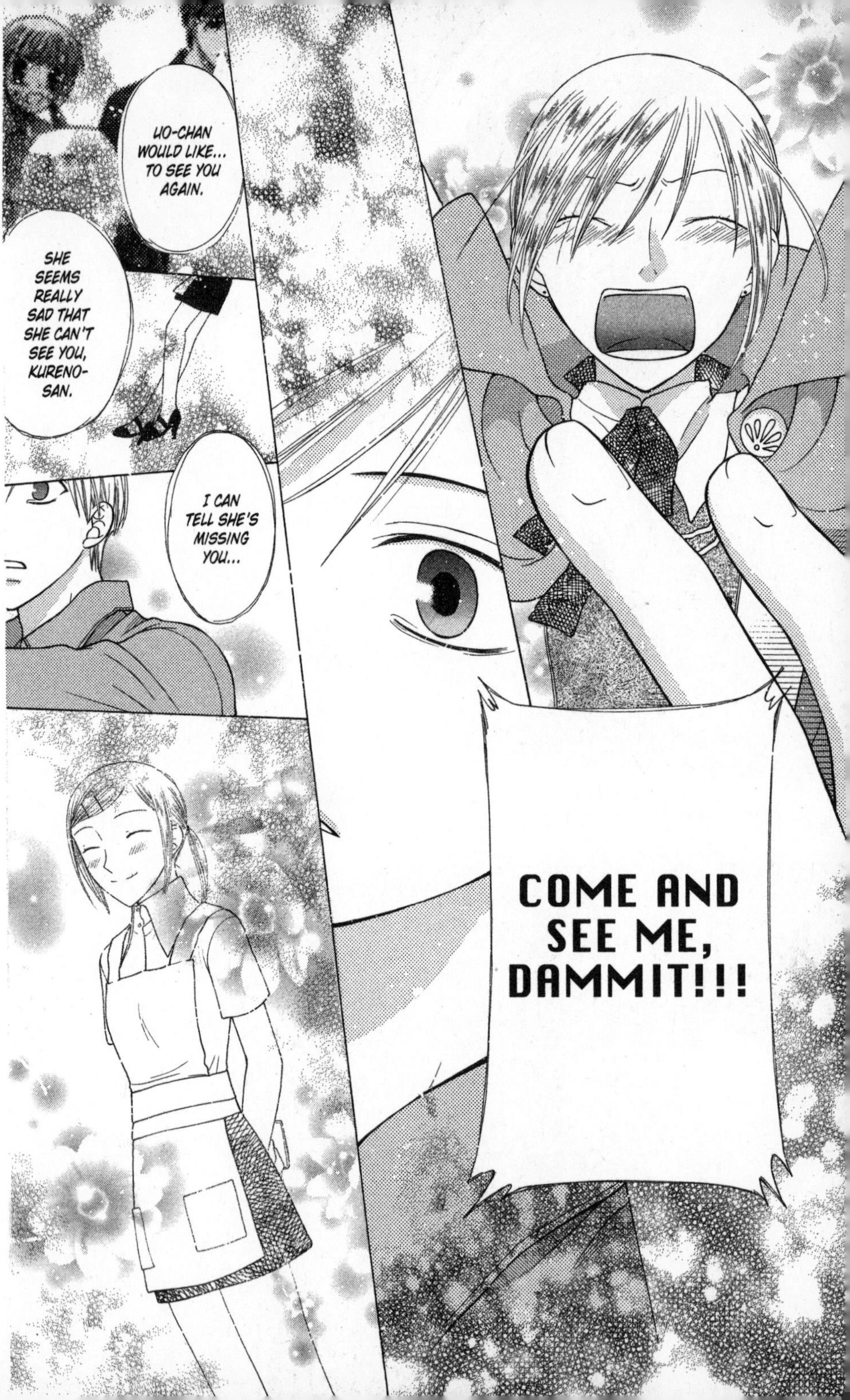
COME AND SEE ME, DAMMIT!!!
UO-CHAN WOULD LIKE... TO SEE YOU AGAIN.
SHE SEEMS REALLY SAD THAT SHE CAN'T SEE YOU, KURENO-SAN.
I CAN TELL SHE'S MISSING YOU...

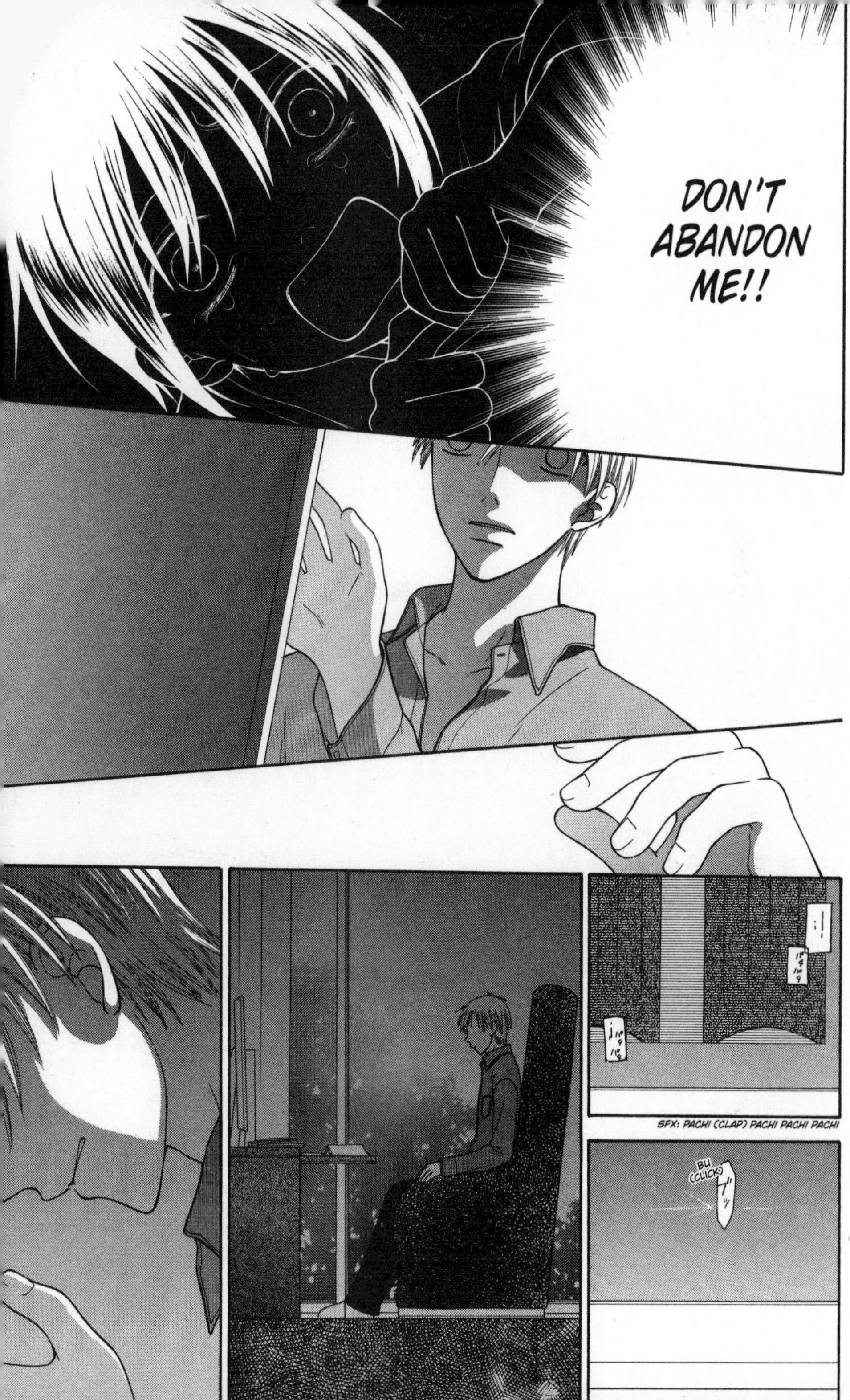
DON'T ABANDON ME!!
SFX: PACHI (CLAP) PACHI PACHI PACHI
BU (CLICK)

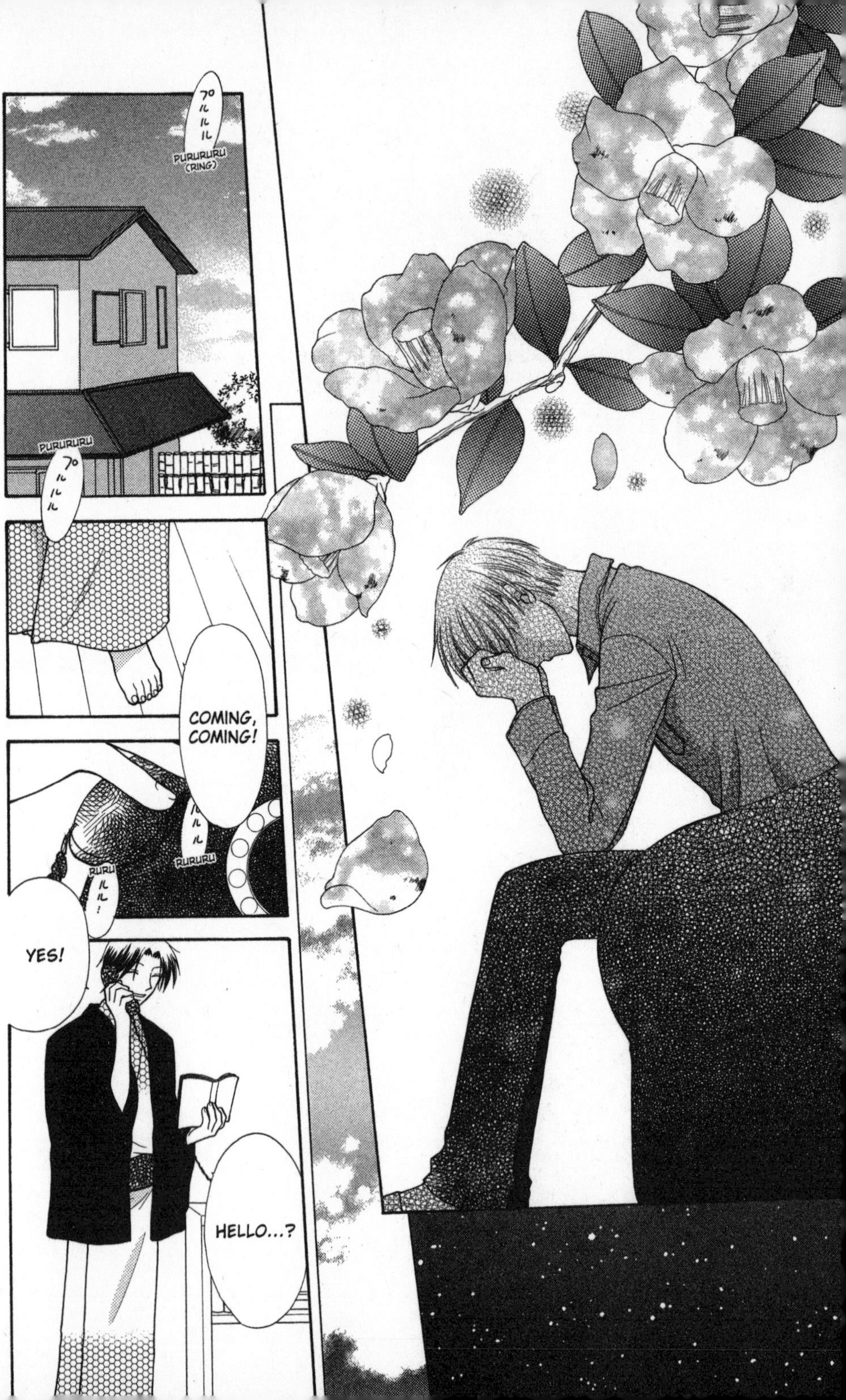

プルルル
PURURURU (RING)
PURURURU
プルルル
COMING, COMING!
ルルル
RURURU
RURU
ルル…!
YES!
HELLO...?

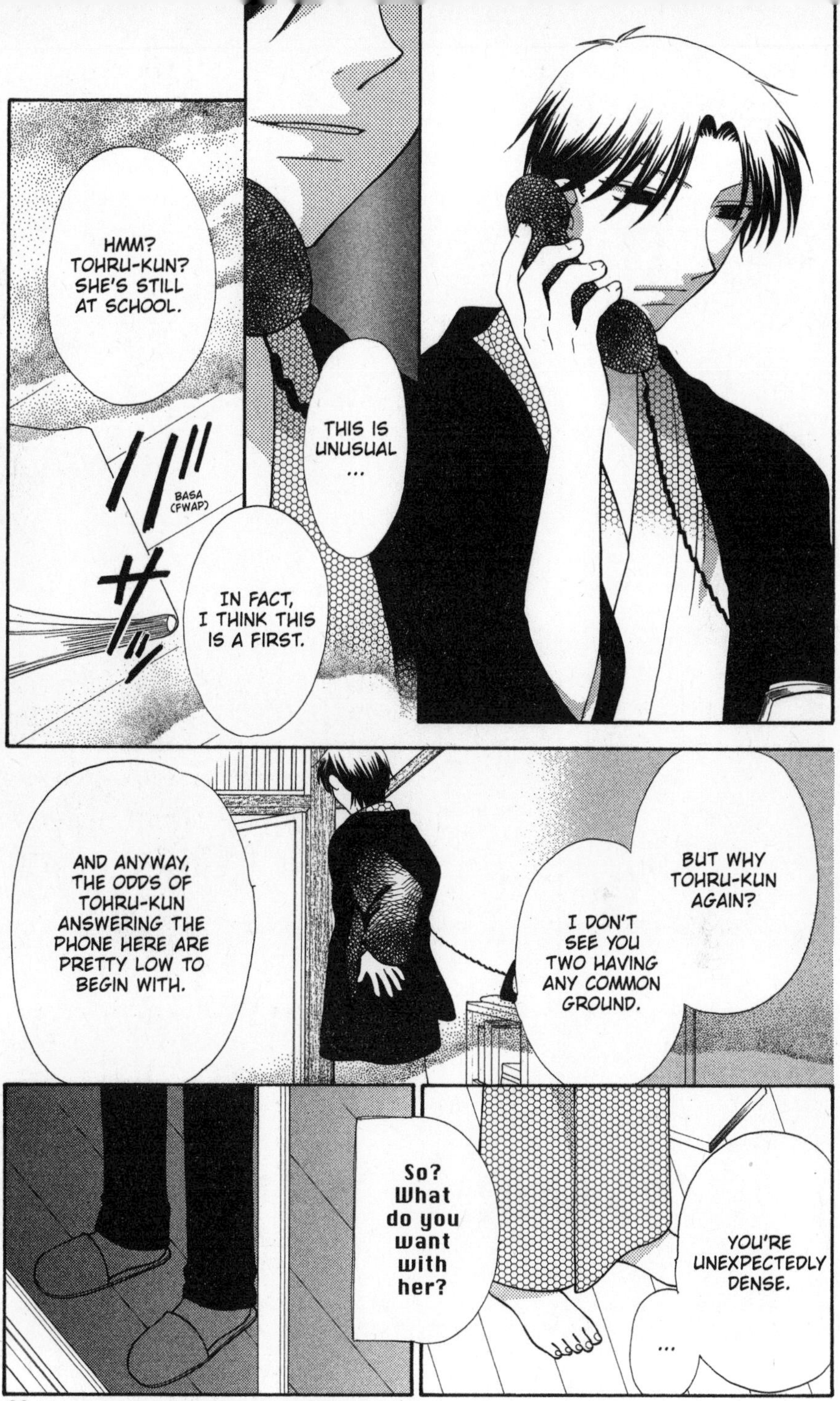
THIS IS UNUSUAL ...
IN FACT, I THINK THIS IS A FIRST.
HMM? TOHRU-KUN? SHE'S STILL AT SCHOOL.
BASA (FWAP)
BUT WHY TOHRU-KUN AGAIN?
I DON'T SEE YOU TWO HAVING ANY COMMON GROUND.
AND ANYWAY, THE ODDS OF TOHRU-KUN ANSWERING THE PHONE HERE ARE PRETTY LOW TO BEGIN WITH.
YOU'RE UNEXPECTEDLY DENSE.
...
So? What do you want with her?

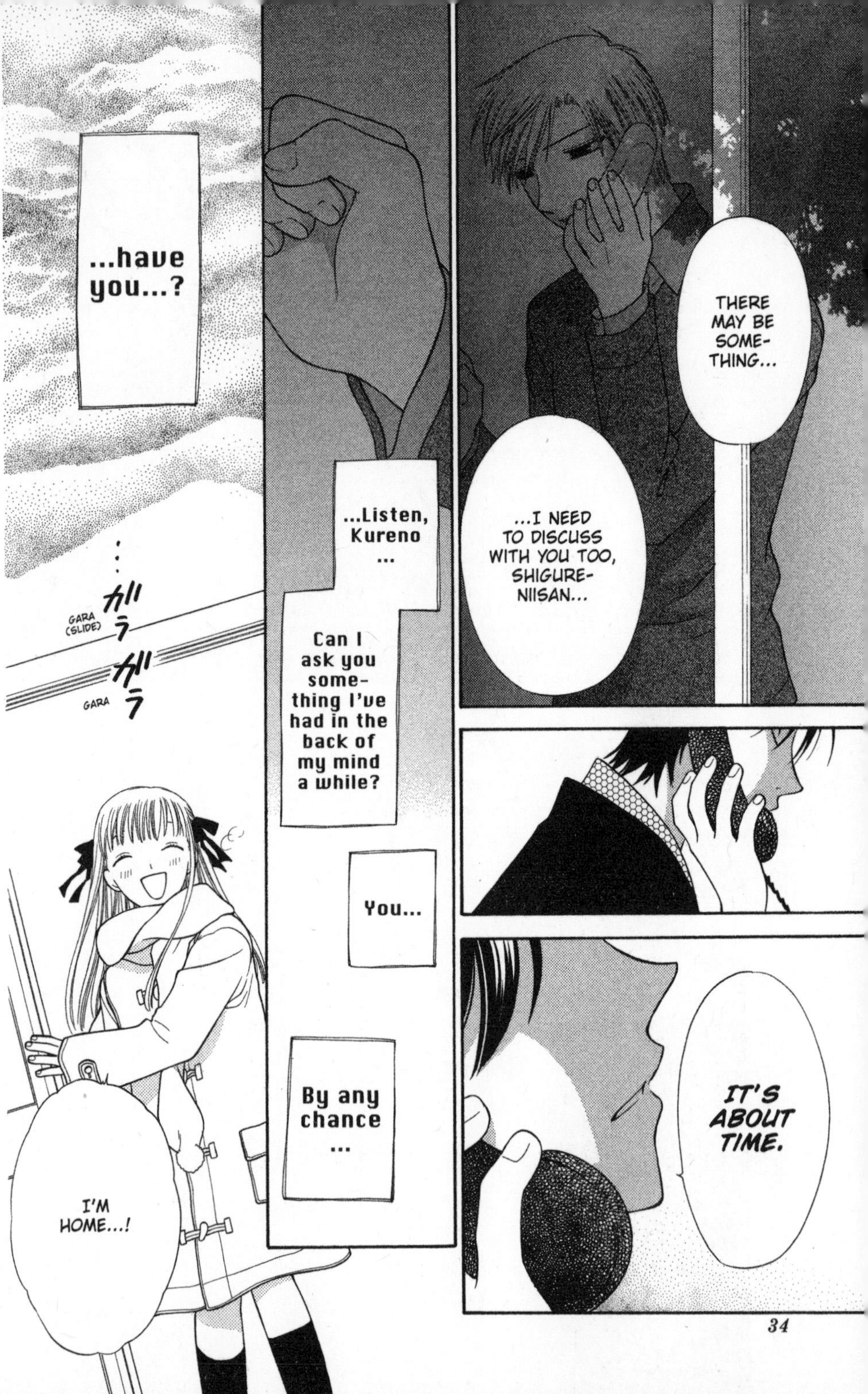
THERE MAY BE SOMETHING...
...I NEED TO DISCUSS WITH YOU TOO, SHIGURE-NIISAN...
IT'S ABOUT TIME.
...Listen, Kureno ...
Can I ask you something I've had in the back of my mind a while?
You...
By any chance ...
...have you...?
ガラ
GARA (SLIDE)
ガラ
GARA
I'M HOME...!

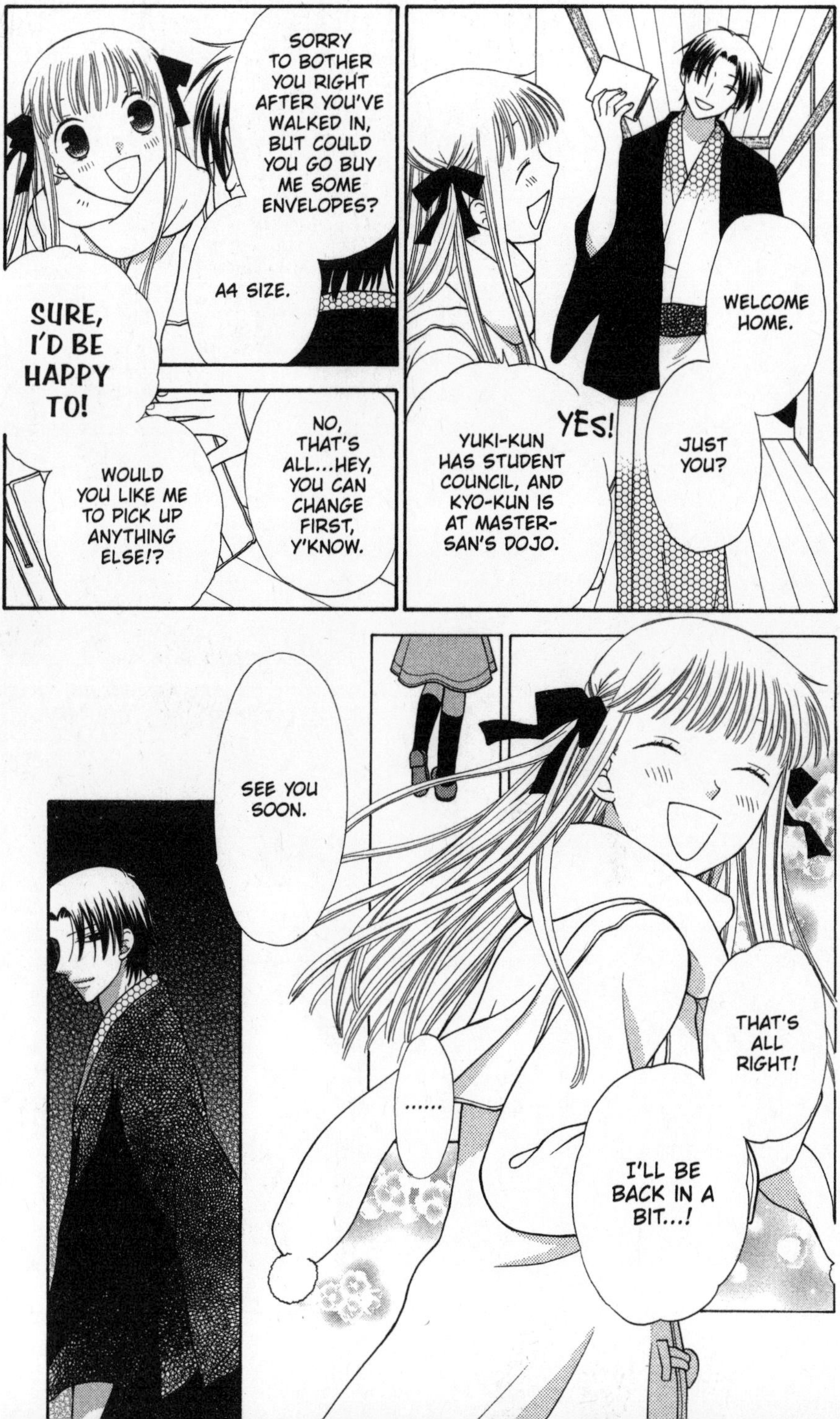
WELCOME HOME.
JUST YOU?
YES!
YUKI-KUN HAS STUDENT COUNCIL, AND KYO-KUN IS AT MASTER-SAN'S DOJO.
SORRY TO BOTHER YOU RIGHT AFTER YOU'VE WALKED IN, BUT COULD YOU GO BUY ME SOME ENVELOPES?
A4 SIZE.
SURE, I'D BE HAPPY TO!
WOULD YOU LIKE ME TO PICK UP ANYTHING ELSE!?
NO, THAT'S ALL...HEY, YOU CAN CHANGE FIRST, Y'KNOW.
THAT'S ALL RIGHT!
I'LL BE BACK IN A BIT...!
SEE YOU SOON.
......

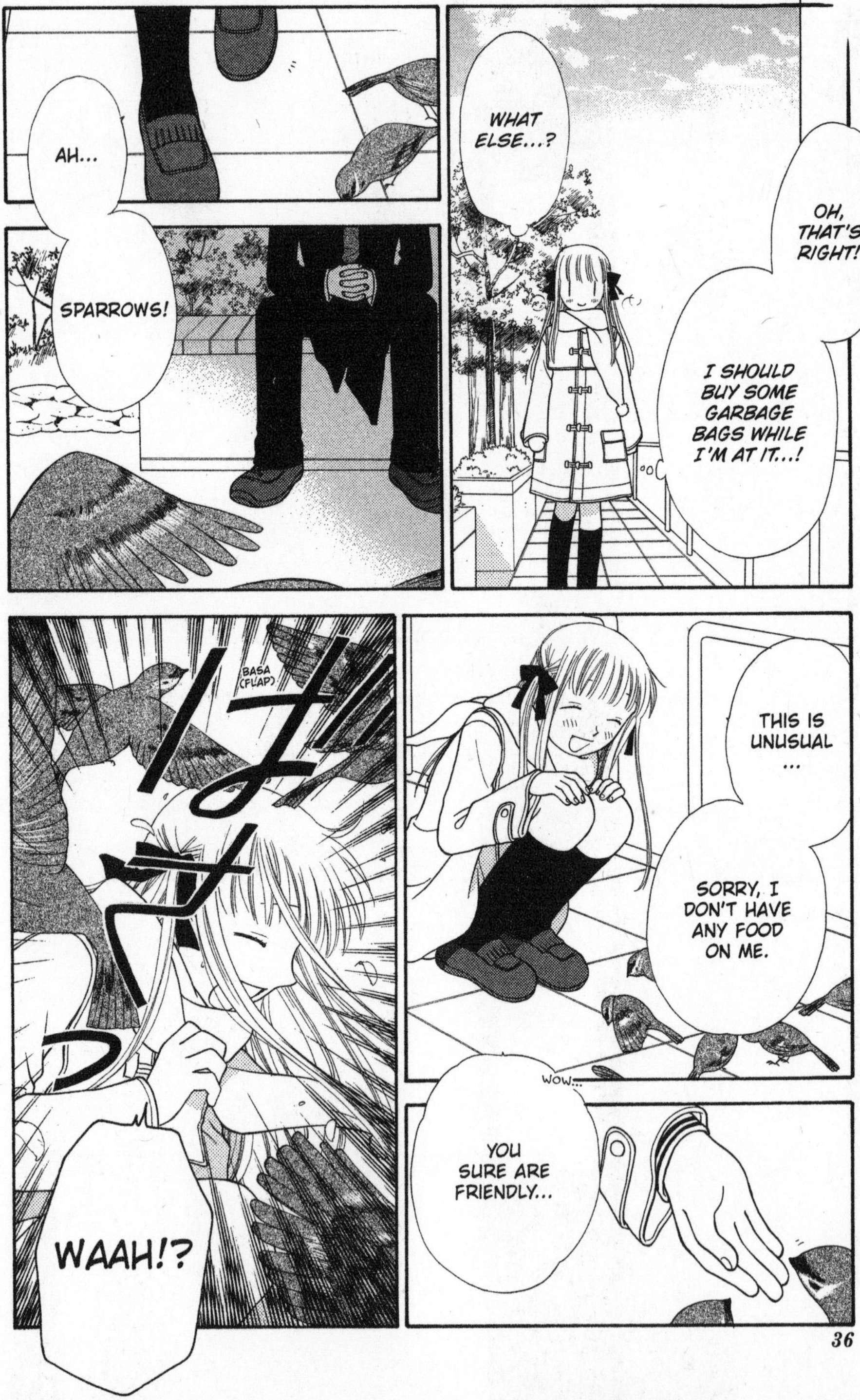
WHAT ELSE...?
OH, THAT'S RIGHT!
I SHOULD BUY SOME GARBAGE BAGS WHILE I'M AT IT...!
AH...
SPARROWS!
THIS IS UNUSUAL...
SORRY, I DON'T HAVE ANY FOOD ON ME.
WOW...
YOU SURE ARE FRIENDLY...
BASA (FLAP)
WAAH!?

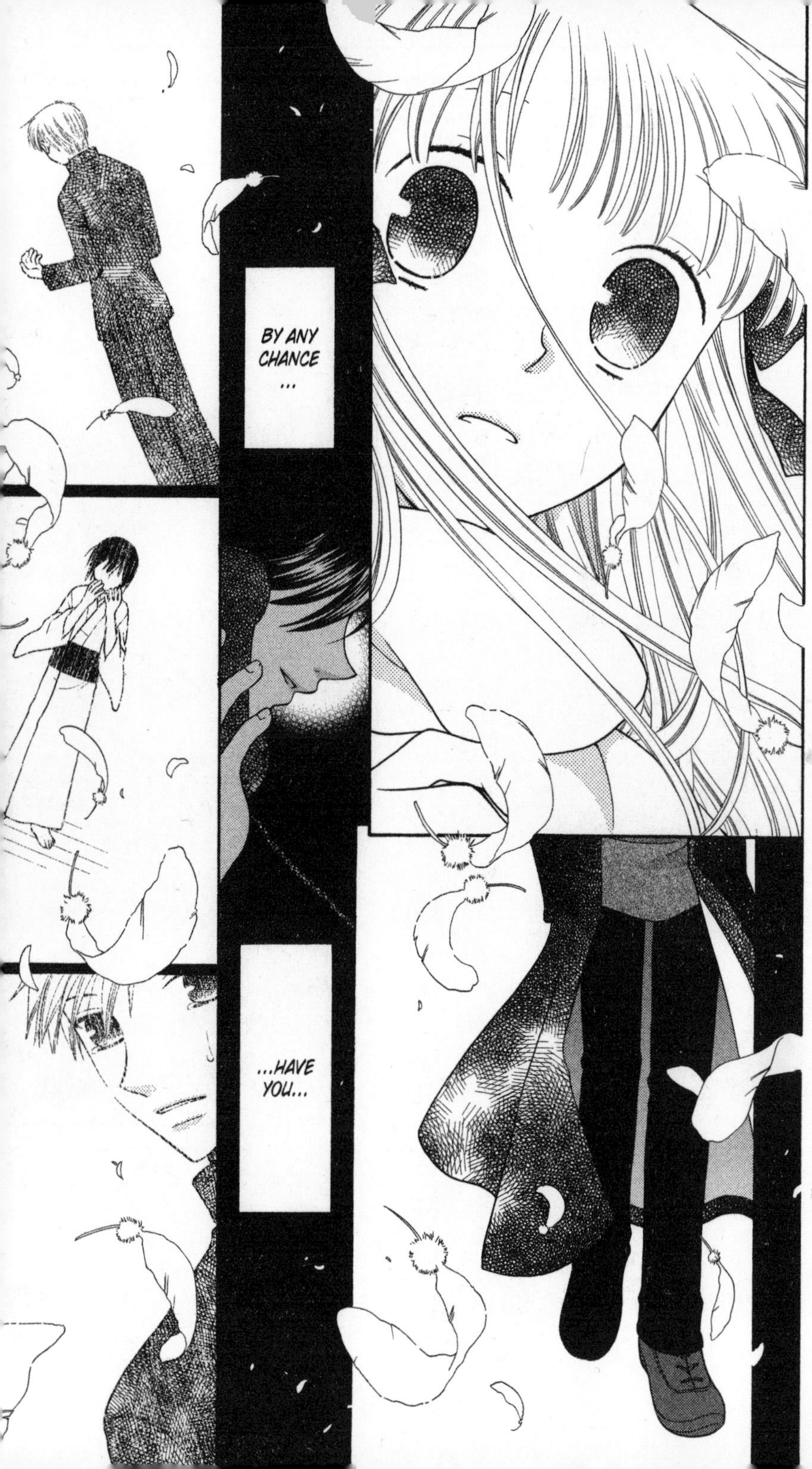
BY ANY CHANCE ...
...HAVE YOU...

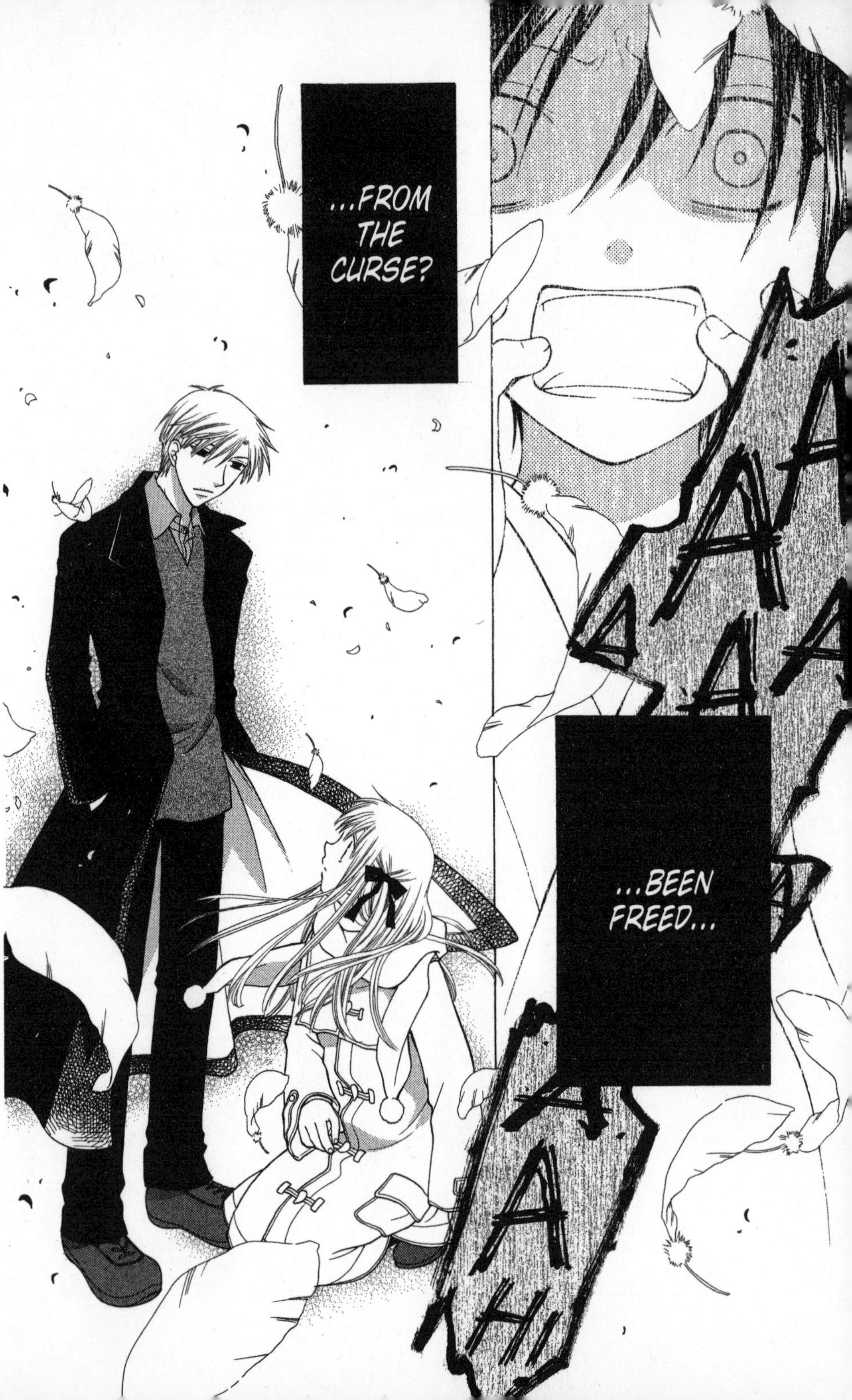
...BEEN FREED...
...FROM THE CURSE?

Chapter 97

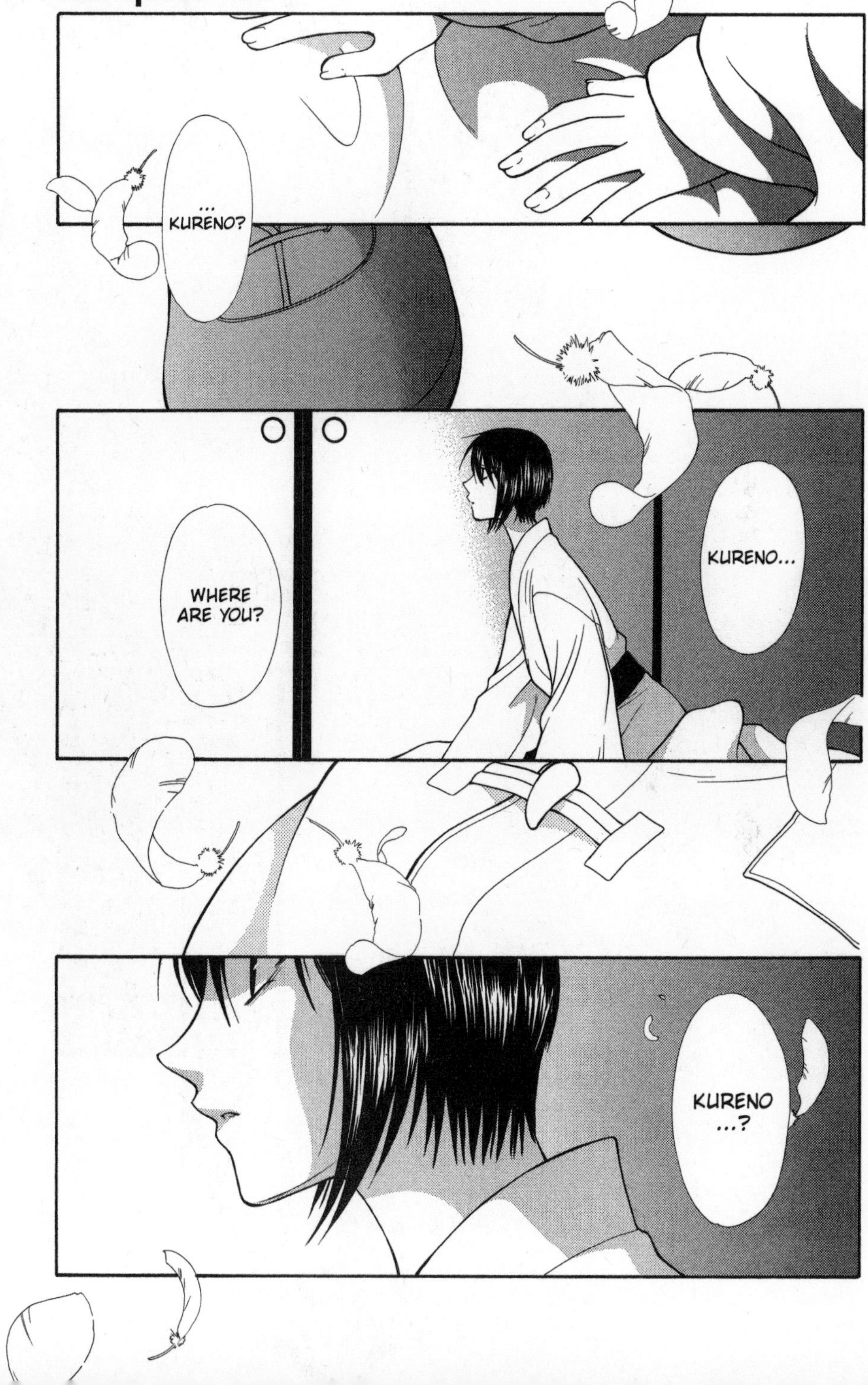

... KURENO?
KURENO...
WHERE ARE YOU?
KURENO ...?

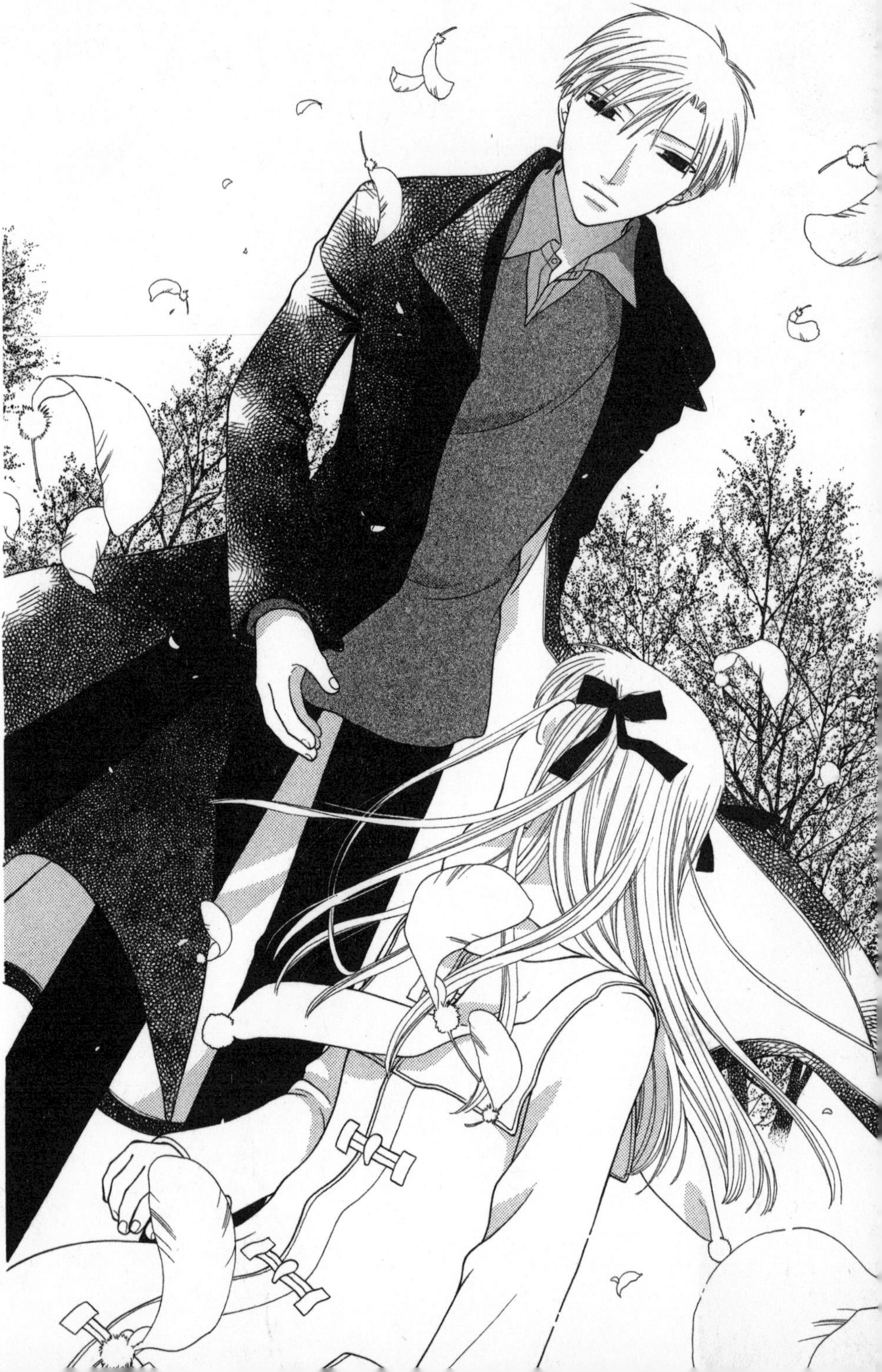

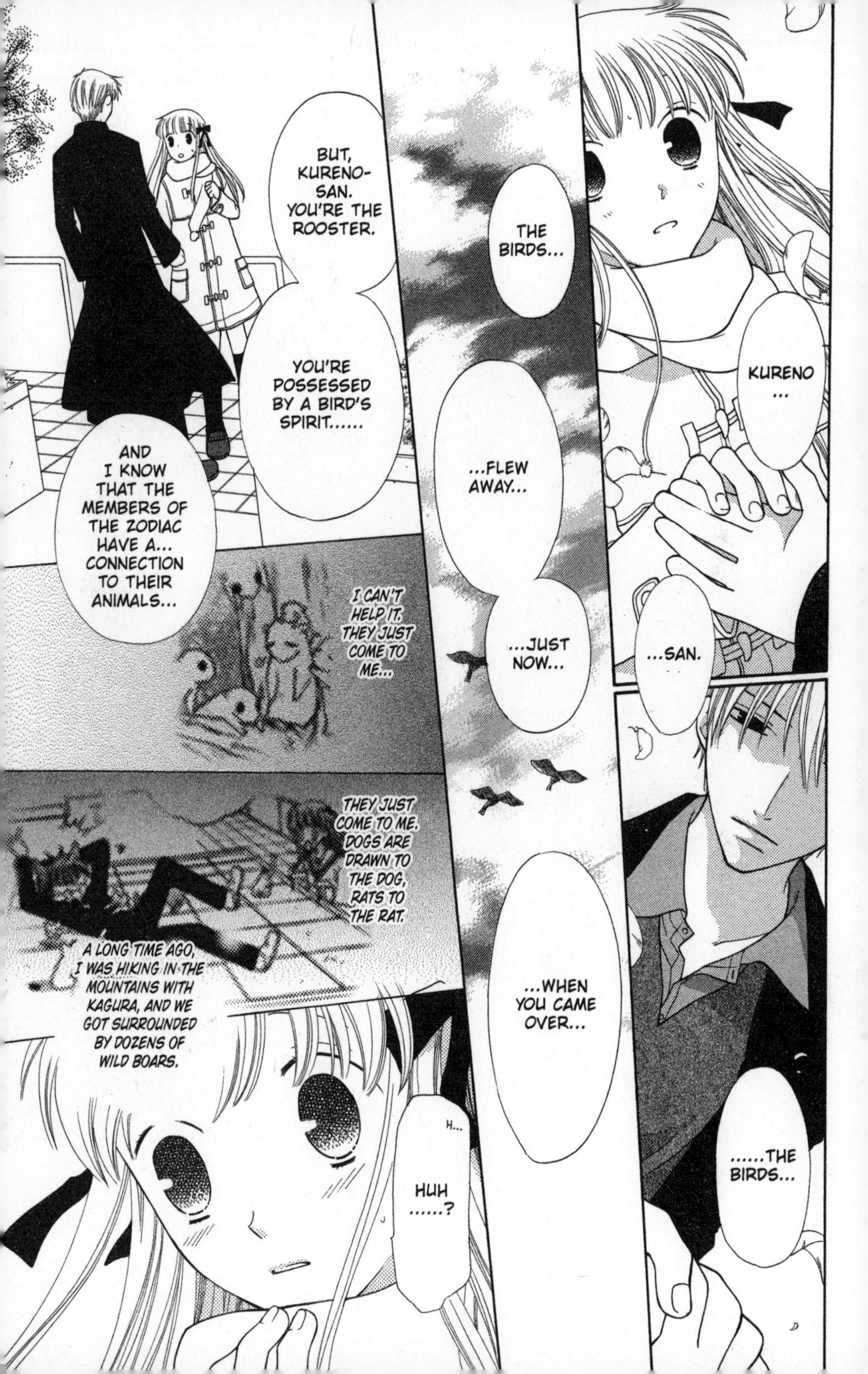
KURENO ...
...SAN.
......THE BIRDS...
...WHEN YOU CAME OVER...
THE BIRDS...
...FLEW AWAY...
...JUST NOW...
BUT, KURENO-SAN. YOU'RE THE ROOSTER.
YOU'RE POSSESSED BY A BIRD'S SPIRIT......
AND I KNOW THAT THE MEMBERS OF THE ZODIAC HAVE A... CONNECTION TO THEIR ANIMALS...
I CAN'T HELP IT. THEY JUST COME TO ME...
THEY JUST COME TO ME. DOGS ARE DRAWN TO THE DOG, RATS TO THE RAT.
A LONG TIME AGO, I WAS HIKING IN THE MOUNTAINS WITH KAGURA, AND WE GOT SURROUNDED BY DOZENS OF WILD BOARS.
H...
HUH ......?

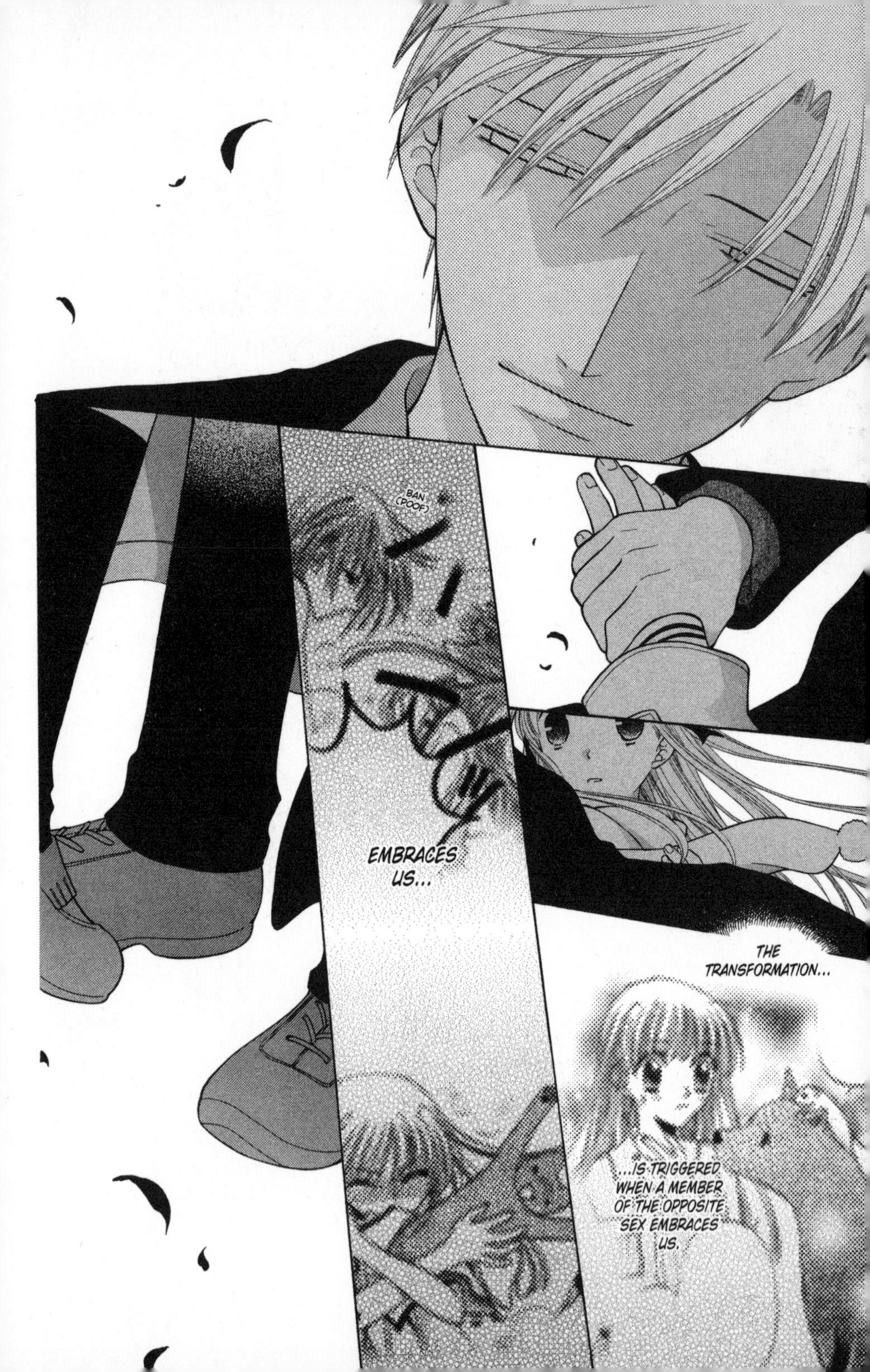
THE TRANSFORMATION...
...IS TRIGGERED WHEN A MEMBER OF THE OPPOSITE SEX EMBRACES US.
BAN (POOF)
EMBRACES US...

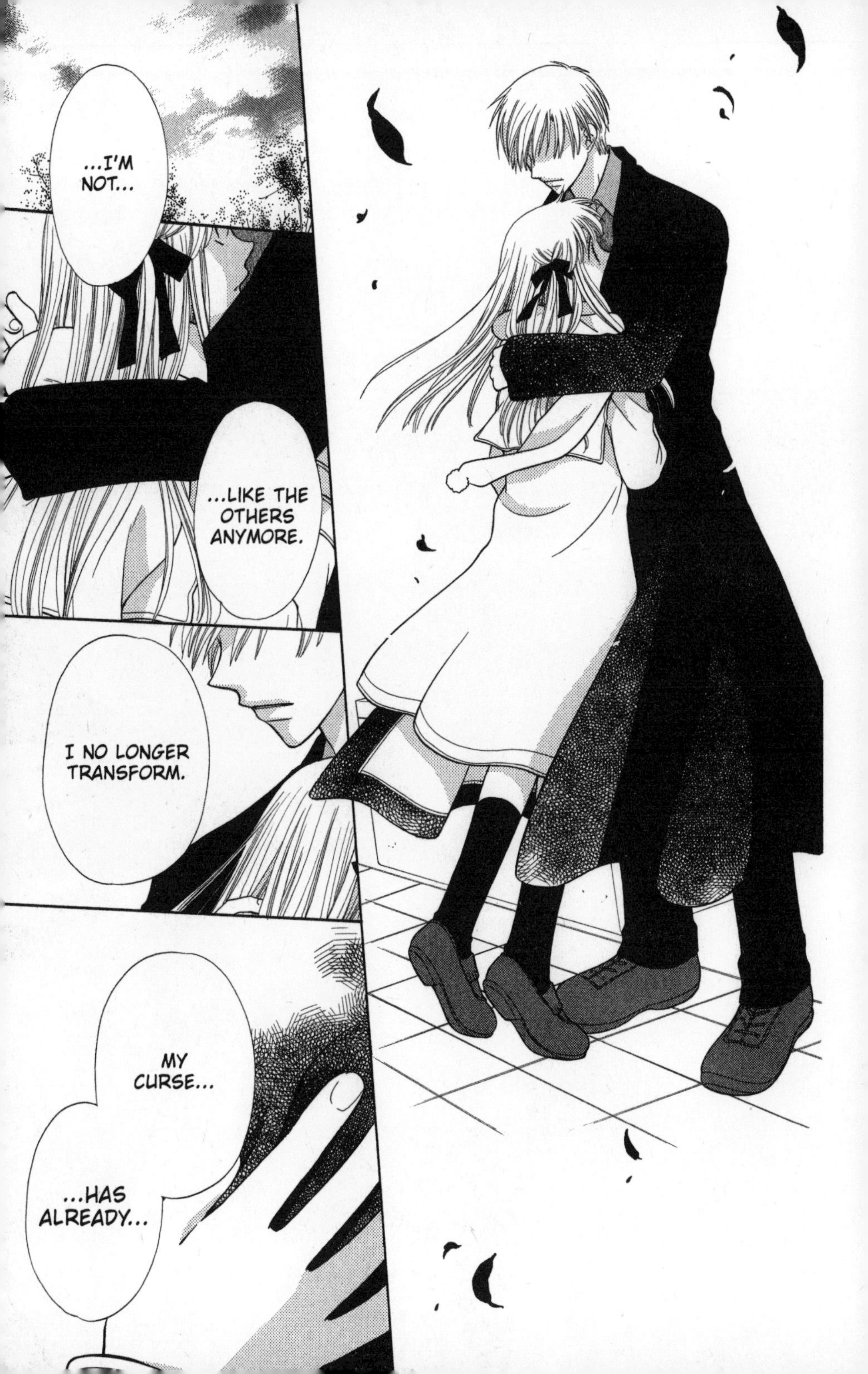
...I'M NOT...
...LIKE THE OTHERS ANYMORE.
I NO LONGER TRANSFORM.
MY CURSE...
...HAS ALREADY...

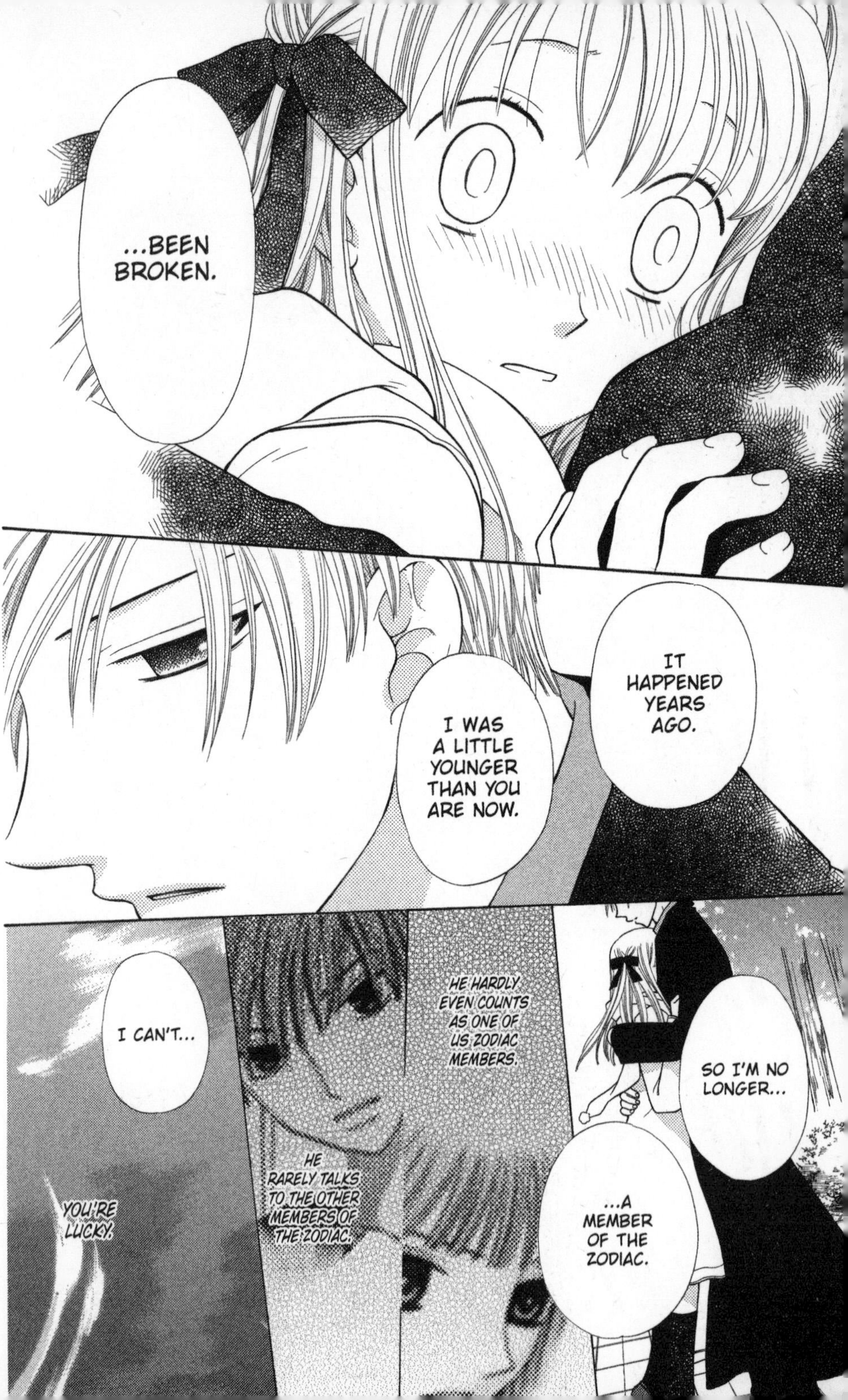
...BEEN BROKEN.
IT HAPPENED YEARS AGO.
I WAS A LITTLE YOUNGER THAN YOU ARE NOW.
SO I'M NO LONGER...
...A MEMBER OF THE ZODIAC.
HE HARDLY EVEN COUNTS AS ONE OF US ZODIAC MEMBERS.
HE RARELY TALKS TO THE OTHER MEMBERS OF THE ZODIAC.
I CAN'T...
YOU'RE LUCKY.

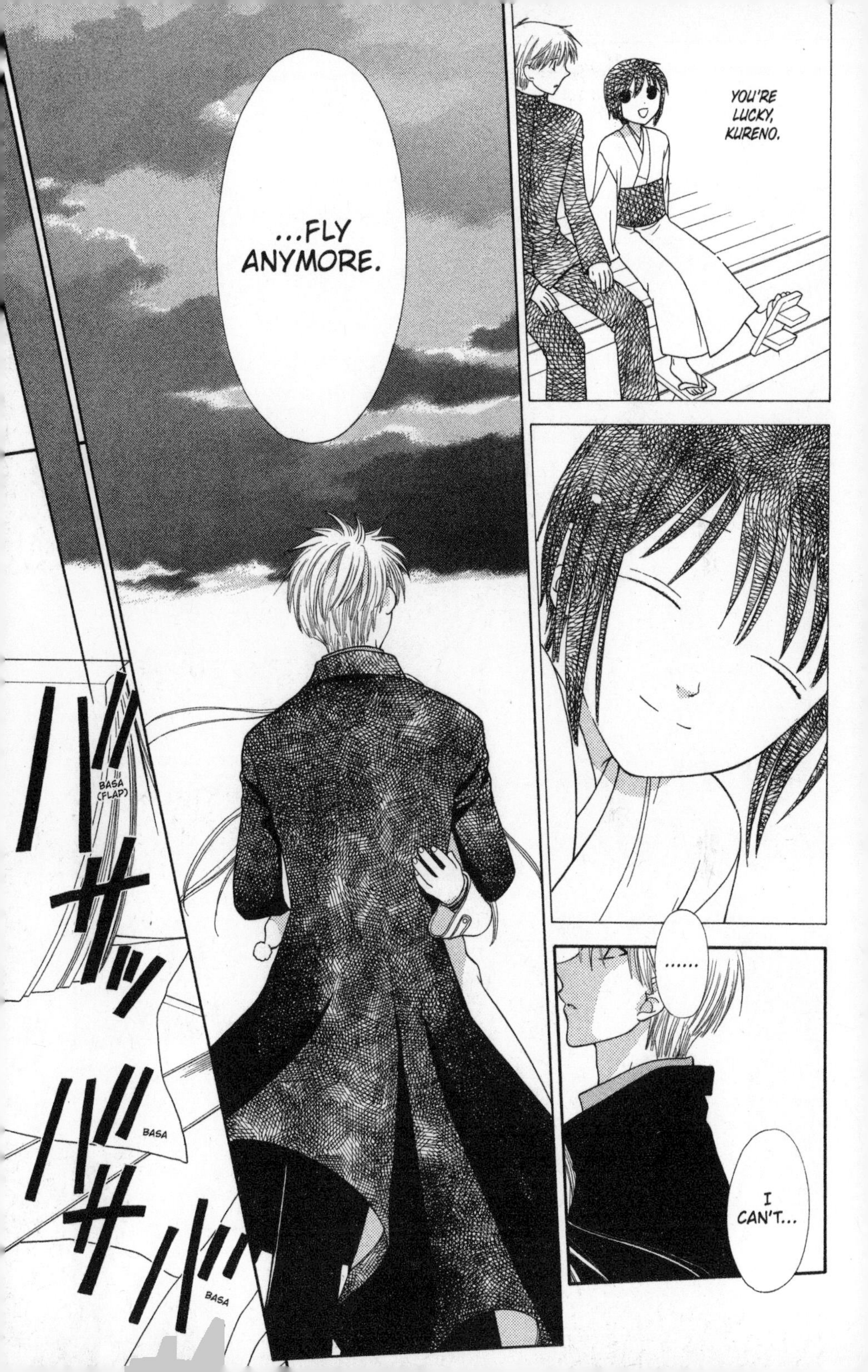
YOU'RE LUCKY, KURENO.
......
I CAN'T...
...FLY ANYMORE.
BASA (FLAP)
BASA
BASA

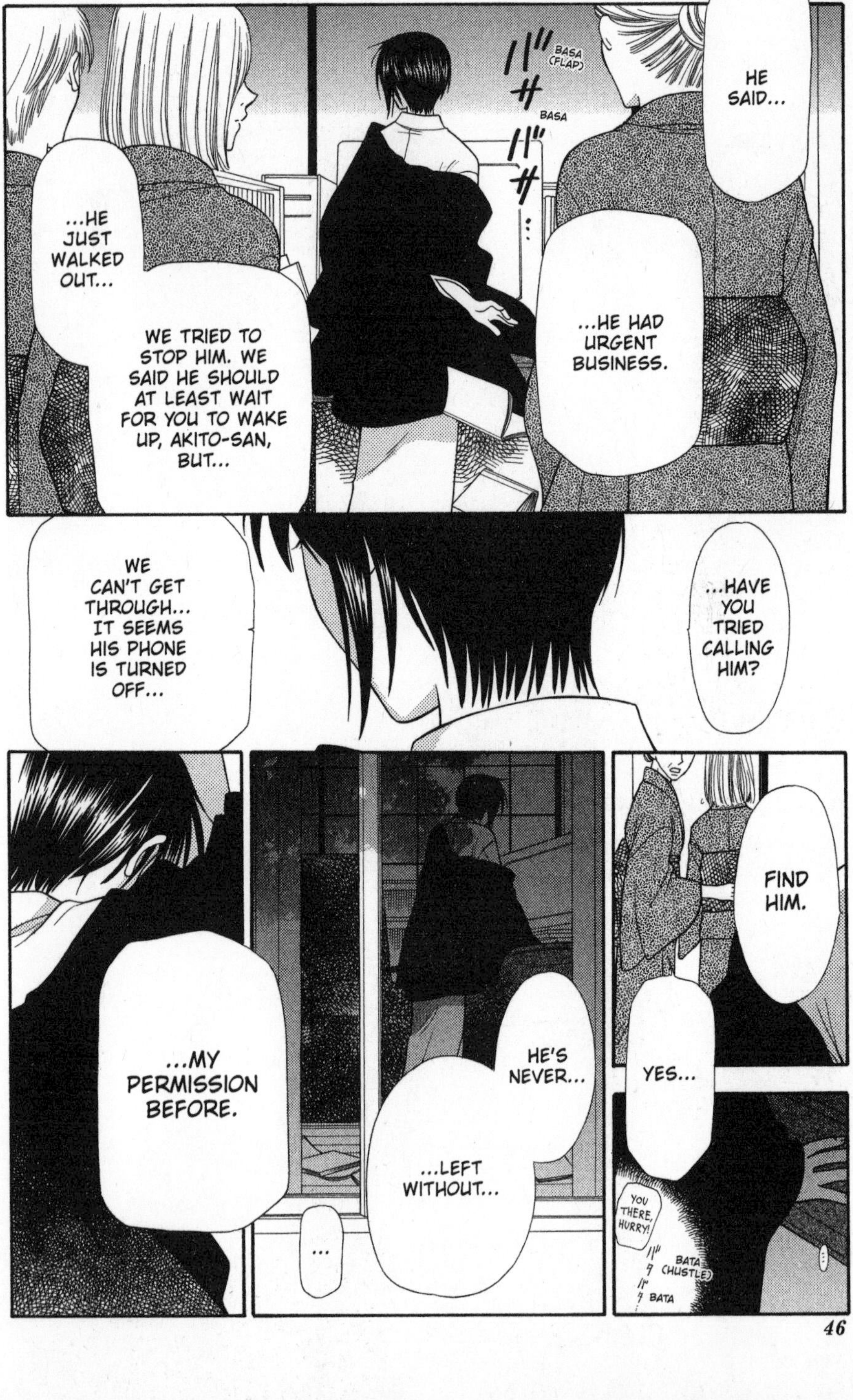
HE SAID...
...HE HAD URGENT BUSINESS.
BASA (FLAP)
BASA
...HE JUST WALKED OUT...
WE TRIED TO STOP HIM. WE SAID HE SHOULD AT LEAST WAIT FOR YOU TO WAKE UP, AKITO-SAN, BUT...
...HAVE YOU TRIED CALLING HIM?
WE CAN'T GET THROUGH... IT SEEMS HIS PHONE IS TURNED OFF...
FIND HIM.
YES...
YOU THERE, HURRY!
BATA (HUSTLE)
BATA
...
HE'S NEVER...
...LEFT WITHOUT...
...
...MY PERMISSION BEFORE.

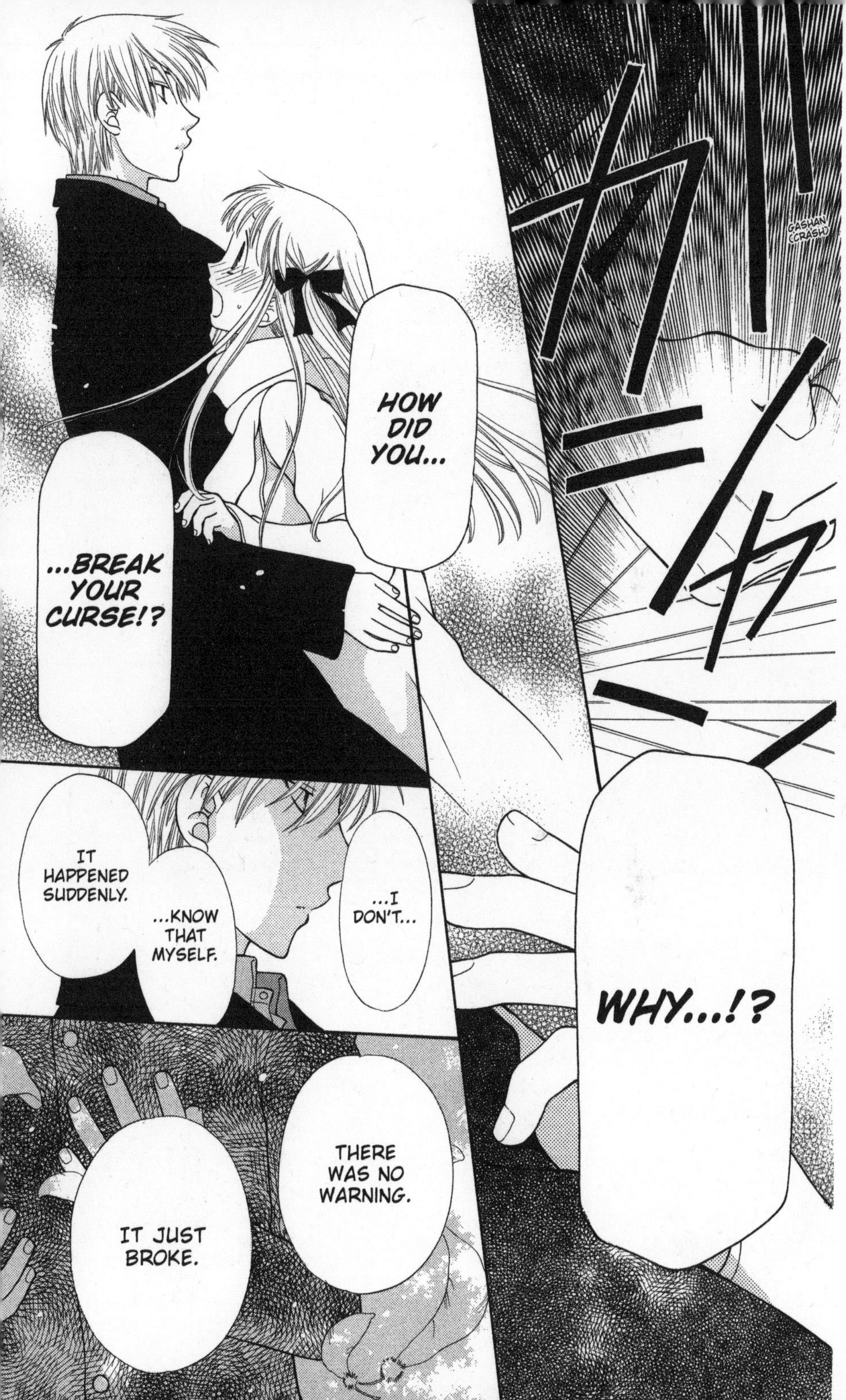
GASHAN (CRASH)
WHY...!?
HOW DID YOU...
...BREAK YOUR CURSE!?
...I DON'T...
...KNOW THAT MYSELF.
IT HAPPENED SUDDENLY.
THERE WAS NO WARNING.
IT JUST BROKE.

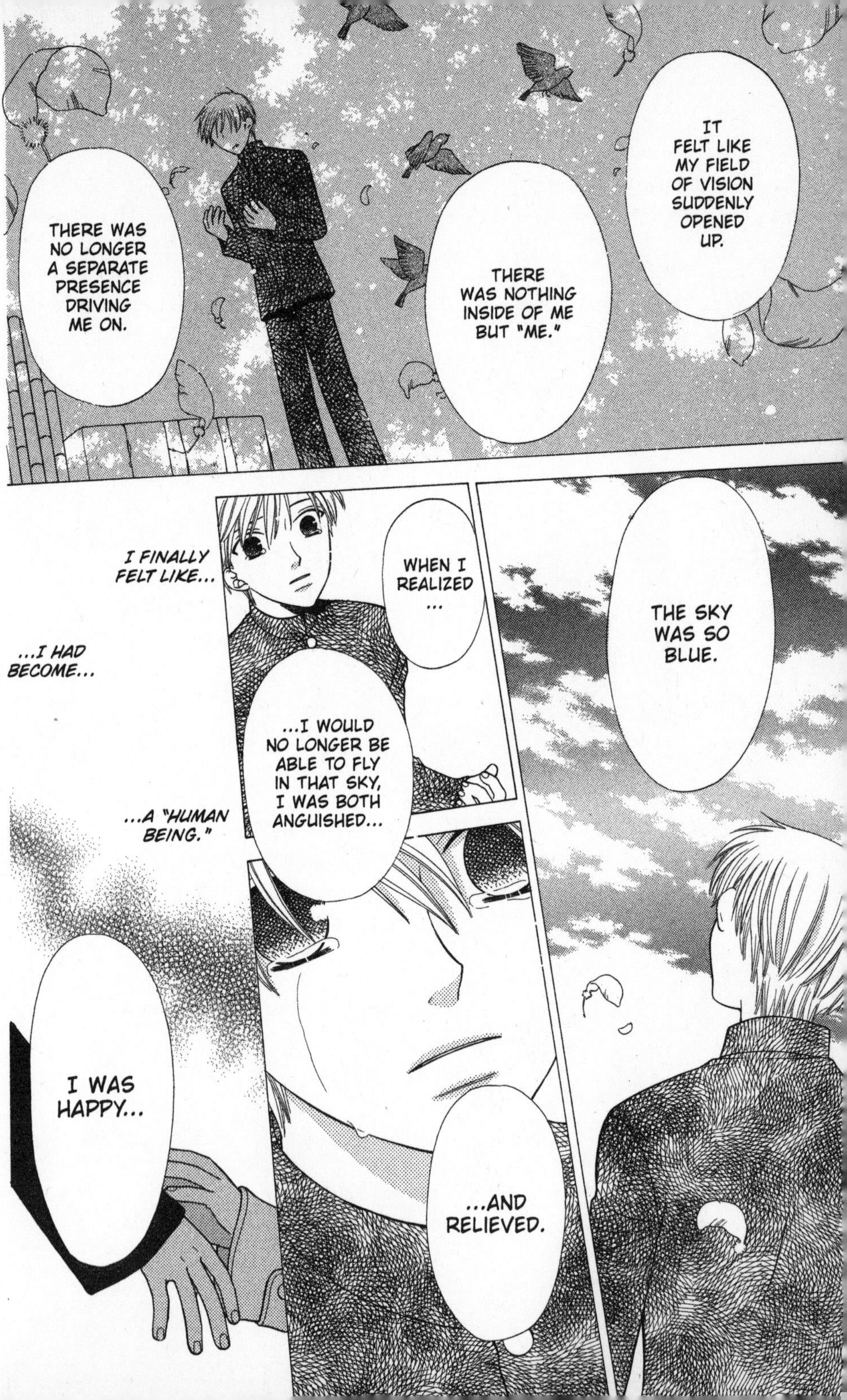
IT FELT LIKE MY FIELD OF VISION SUDDENLY OPENED UP.
THERE WAS NOTHING INSIDE OF ME BUT "ME."
THERE WAS NO LONGER A SEPARATE PRESENCE DRIVING ME ON.
THE SKY WAS SO BLUE.
WHEN I REALIZED ...
...I WOULD NO LONGER BE ABLE TO FLY IN THAT SKY, I WAS BOTH ANGUISHED...
...AND RELIEVED.
I FINALLY FELT LIKE...
...I HAD BECOME...
...A "HUMAN BEING."
I WAS HAPPY...

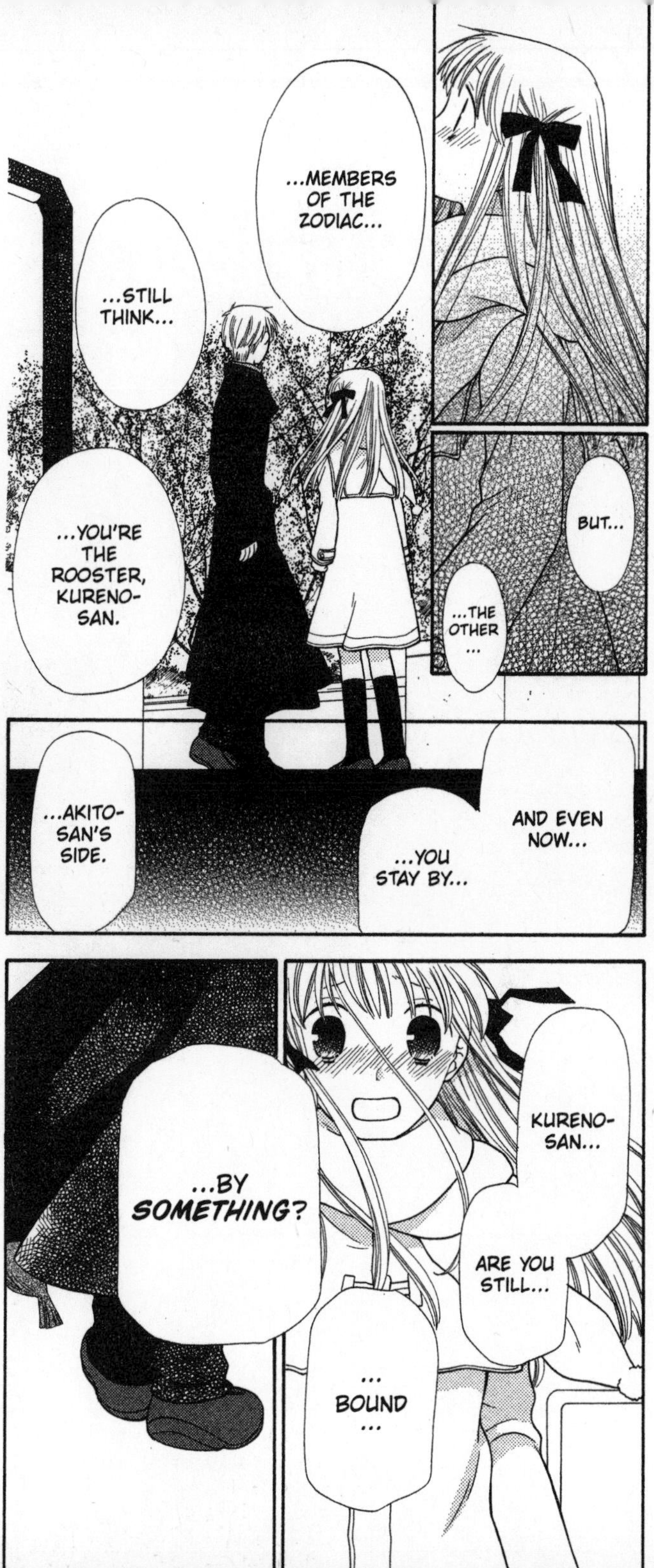
BUT...
...THE OTHER...
...MEMBERS OF THE ZODIAC...
...STILL THINK...
...YOU'RE THE ROOSTER, KURENO-SAN.
AND EVEN NOW...
...YOU STAY BY...
...AKITO-SAN'S SIDE.
KURENO-SAN...
ARE YOU STILL...
...BOUND...
...BY *SOMETHING?*
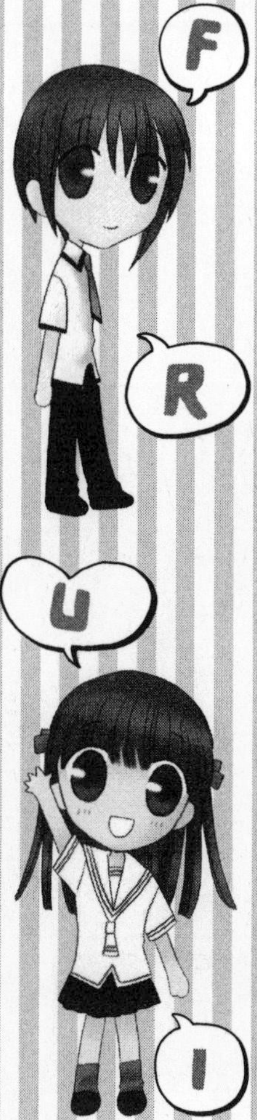
F
R
U
I

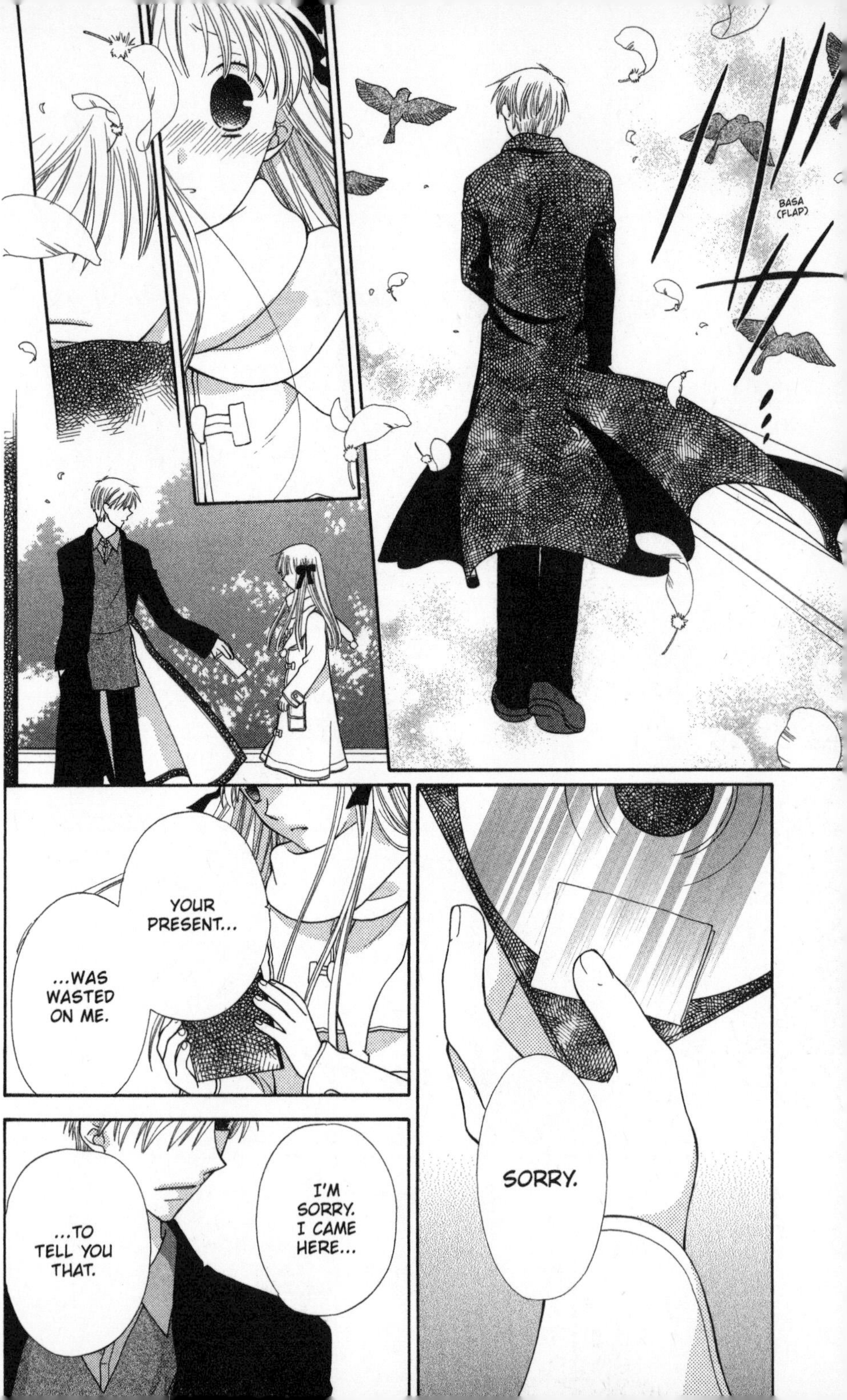
BASA (FLAP)
SORRY.
YOUR PRESENT...
...WAS WASTED ON ME.
I'M SORRY. I CAME HERE...
...TO TELL YOU THAT.

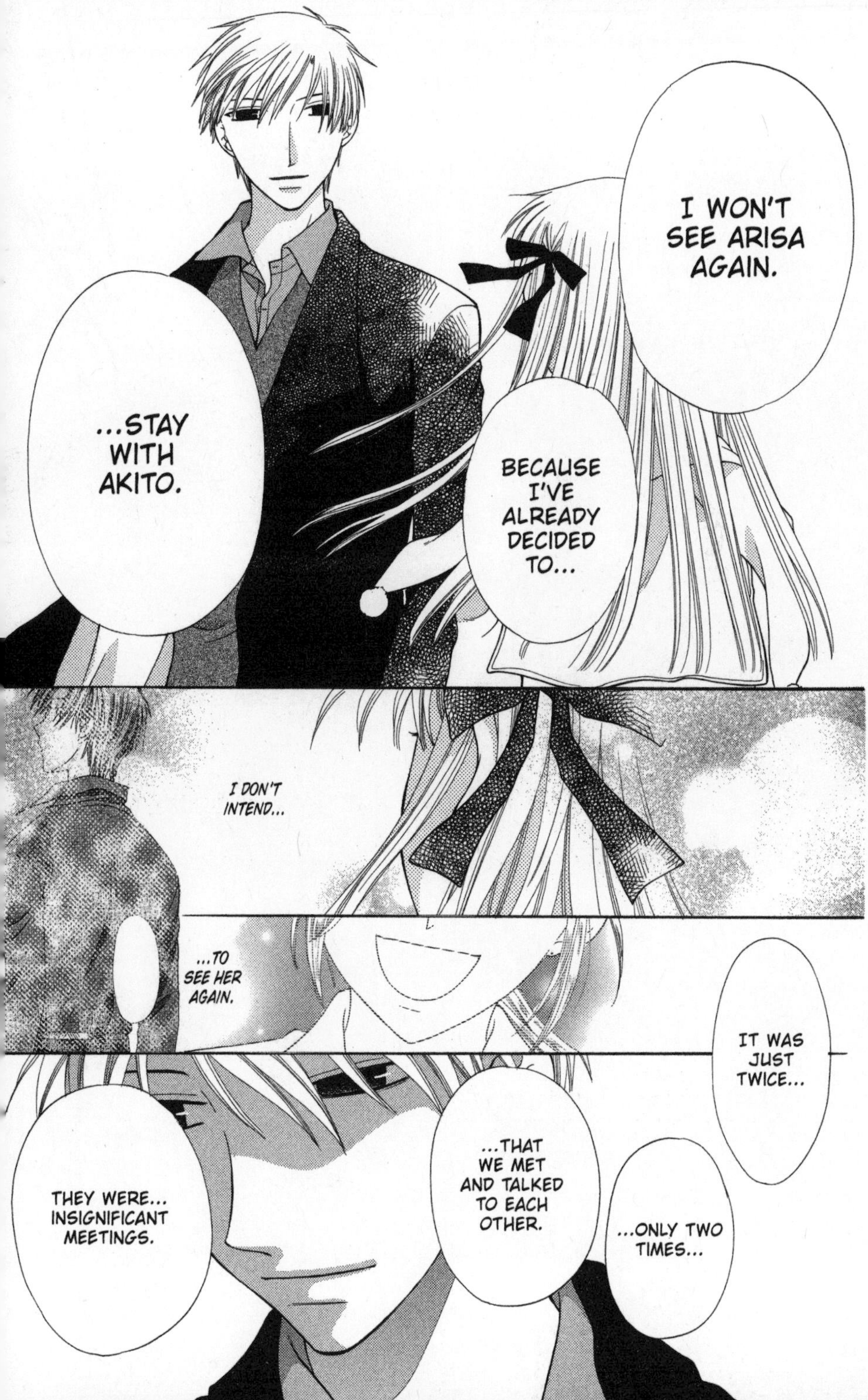
I WON'T SEE ARISA AGAIN.
BECAUSE I'VE ALREADY DECIDED TO...
...STAY WITH AKITO.
I DON'T INTEND...
...TO SEE HER AGAIN.
IT WAS JUST TWICE...
...ONLY TWO TIMES...
...THAT WE MET AND TALKED TO EACH OTHER.
THEY WERE... INSIGNIFICANT MEETINGS.

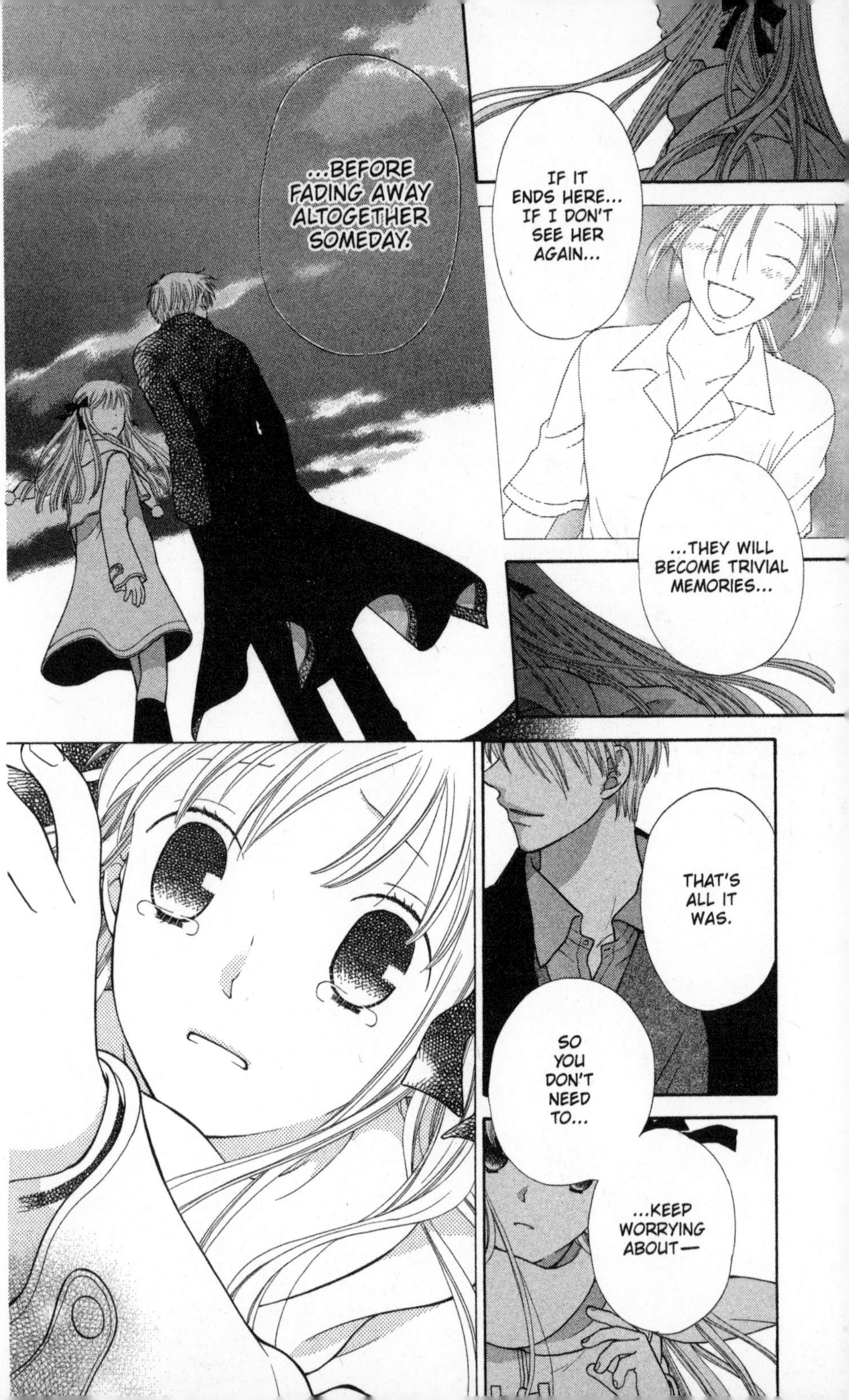
IF IT ENDS HERE... IF I DON'T SEE HER AGAIN...
...THEY WILL BECOME TRIVIAL MEMORIES...
...BEFORE FADING AWAY ALTOGETHER SOMEDAY.
THAT'S ALL IT WAS.
SO YOU DON'T NEED TO...
...KEEP WORRYING ABOUT—

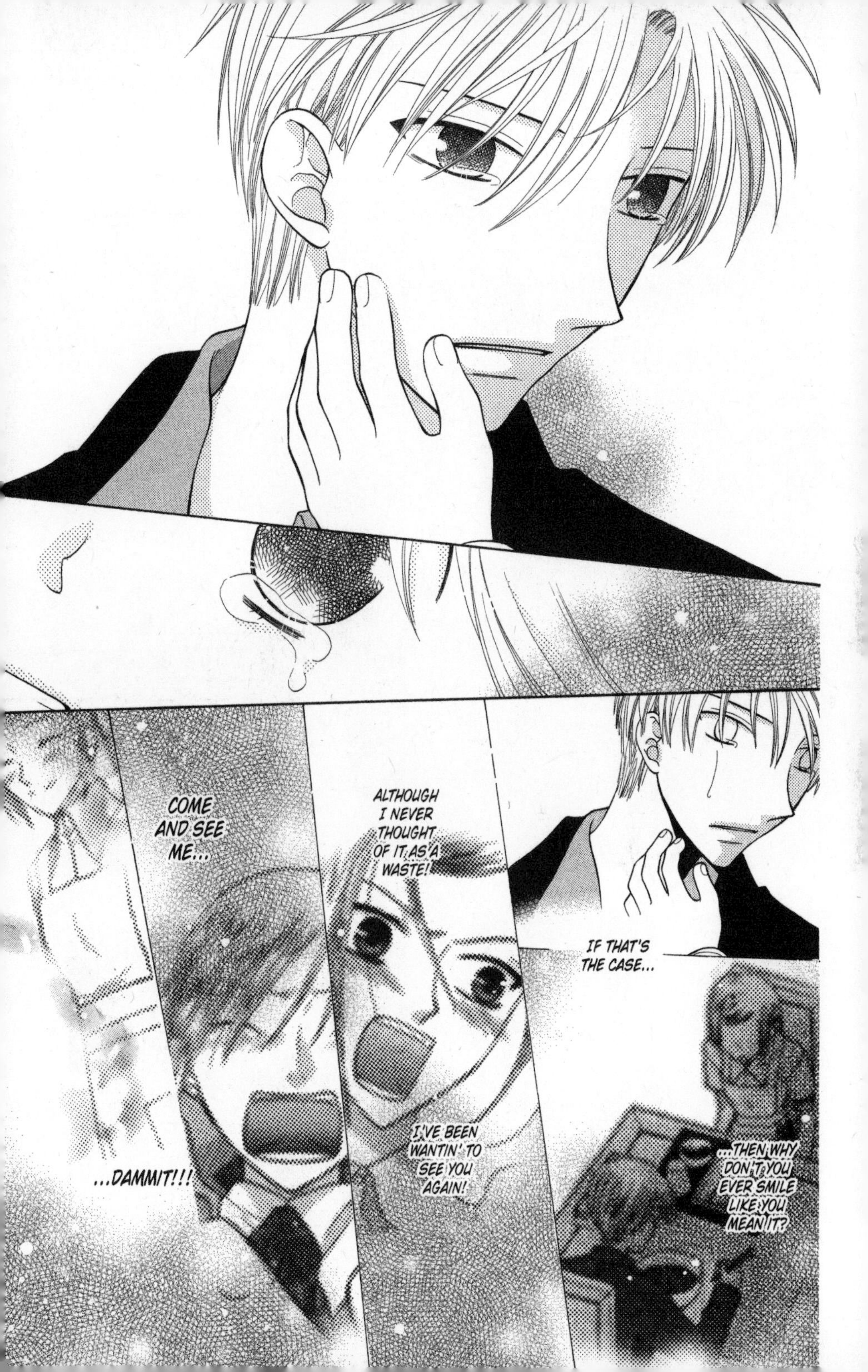
IF THAT'S THE CASE...
...THEN WHY DON'T YOU EVER SMILE LIKE YOU MEAN IT?
ALTHOUGH I NEVER THOUGHT OF IT AS A WASTE!
I'VE BEEN WANTIN' TO SEE YOU AGAIN!
COME AND SEE ME...
...DAMMIT!!!

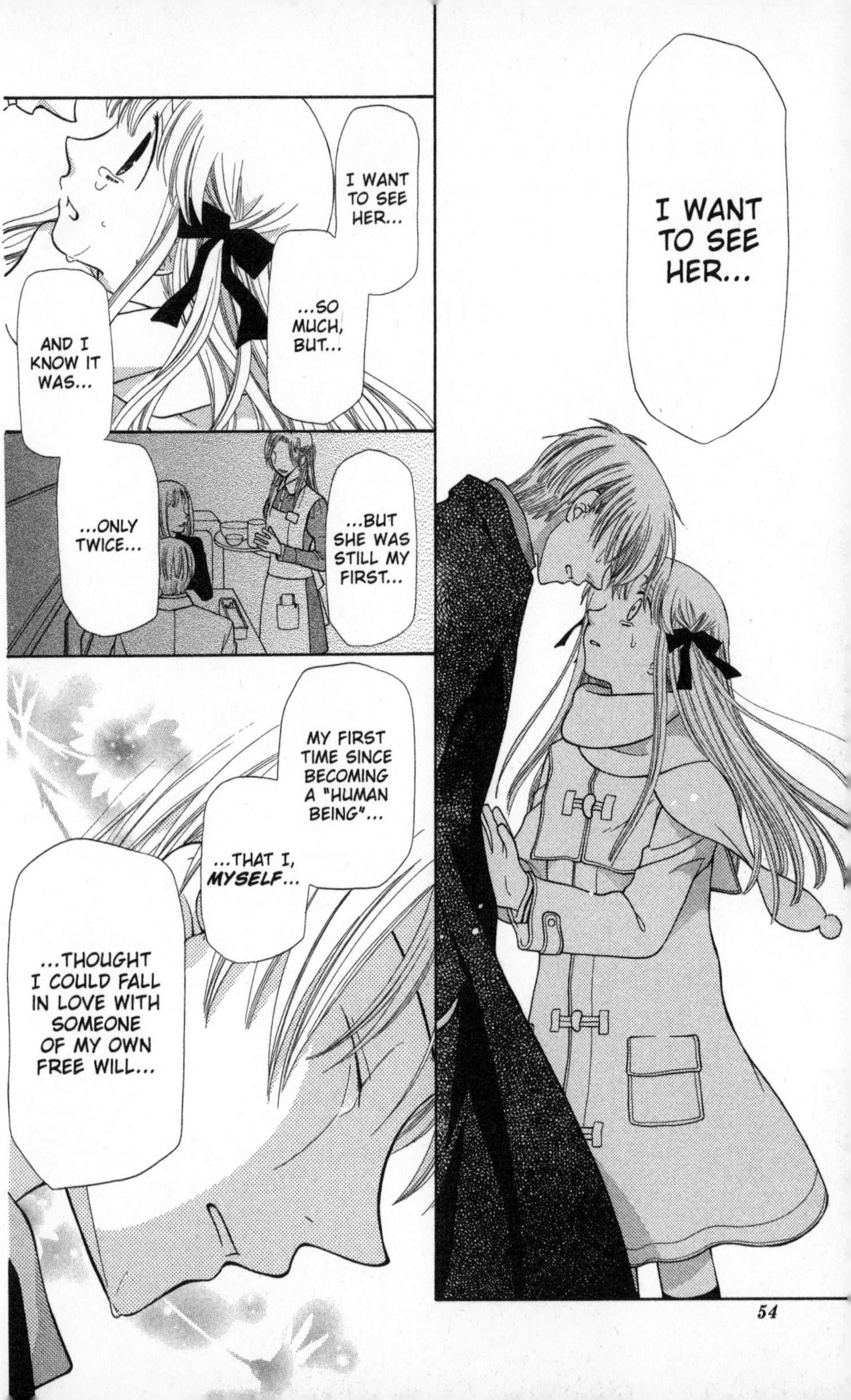
I WANT TO SEE HER...
I WANT TO SEE HER...
...SO MUCH, BUT...
AND I KNOW IT WAS...
...ONLY TWICE...
...BUT SHE WAS STILL MY FIRST...
MY FIRST TIME SINCE BECOMING A "HUMAN BEING"...
...THAT I, ***MYSELF***...
...THOUGHT I COULD FALL IN LOVE WITH SOMEONE OF MY OWN FREE WILL...

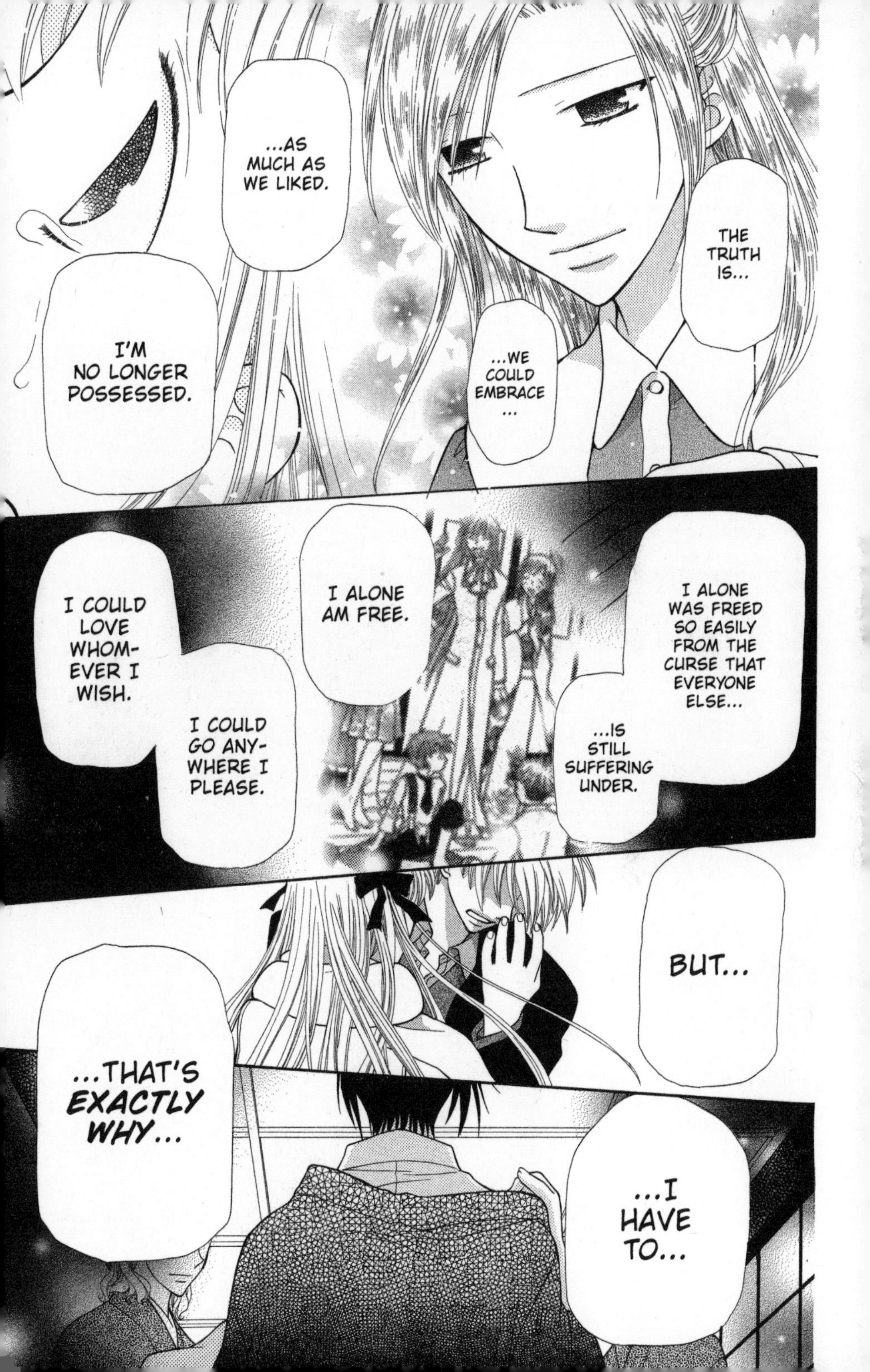
THE TRUTH IS...
...WE COULD EMBRACE ...
...AS MUCH AS WE LIKED.
I'M NO LONGER POSSESSED.
I ALONE WAS FREED SO EASILY FROM THE CURSE THAT EVERYONE ELSE...
...IS STILL SUFFERING UNDER.
I ALONE AM FREE.
I COULD LOVE WHOM-EVER I WISH.
I COULD GO ANY-WHERE I PLEASE.
BUT...
...THAT'S *EXACTLY* *WHY*...
...I HAVE TO...

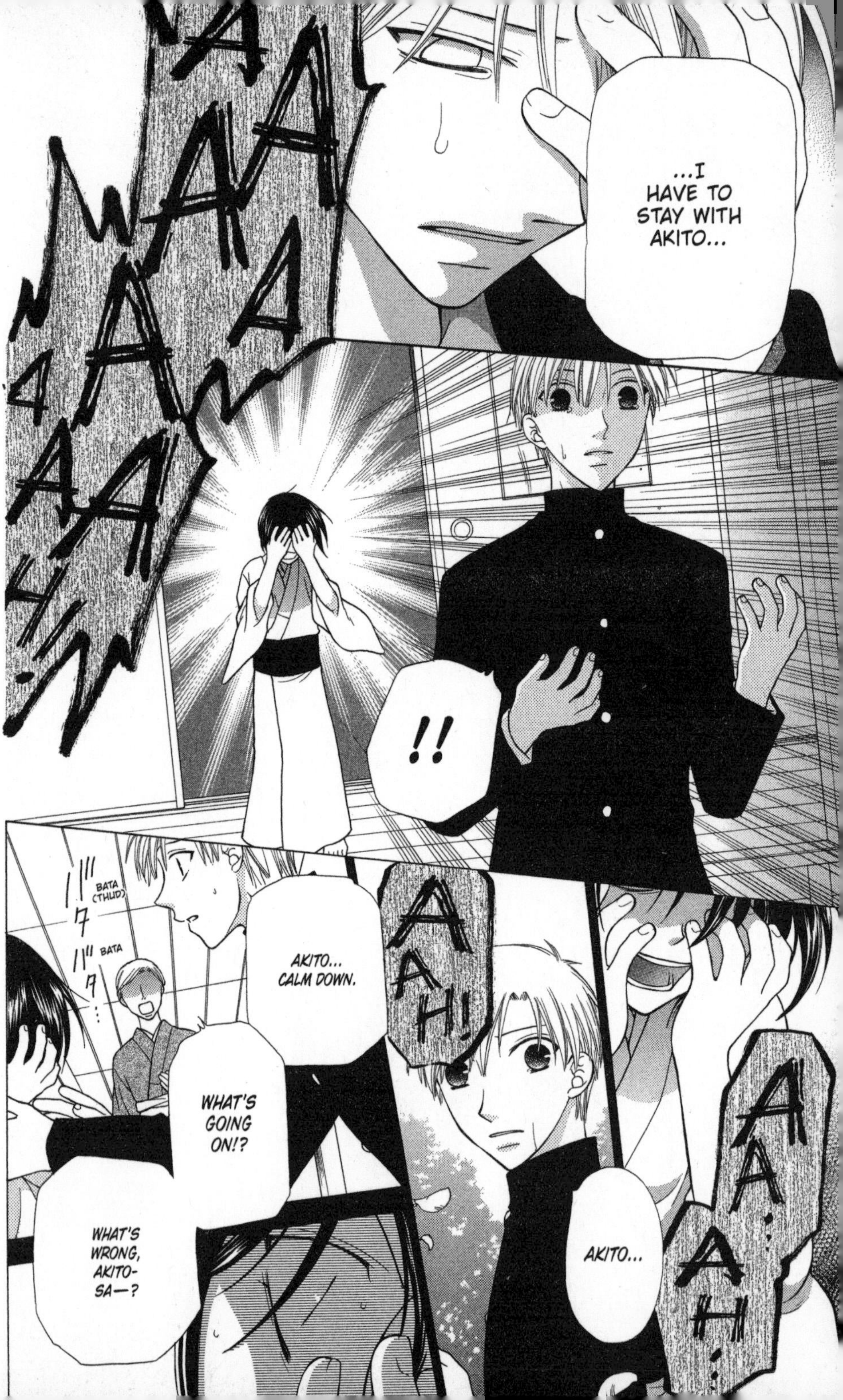
...I HAVE TO STAY WITH AKITO...
!!
AAAAH...
AKITO...
AAH!
AKITO... CALM DOWN.
BATA (THUD)
BATA
WHAT'S GOING ON!?
WHAT'S WRONG, AKITO-SA—?

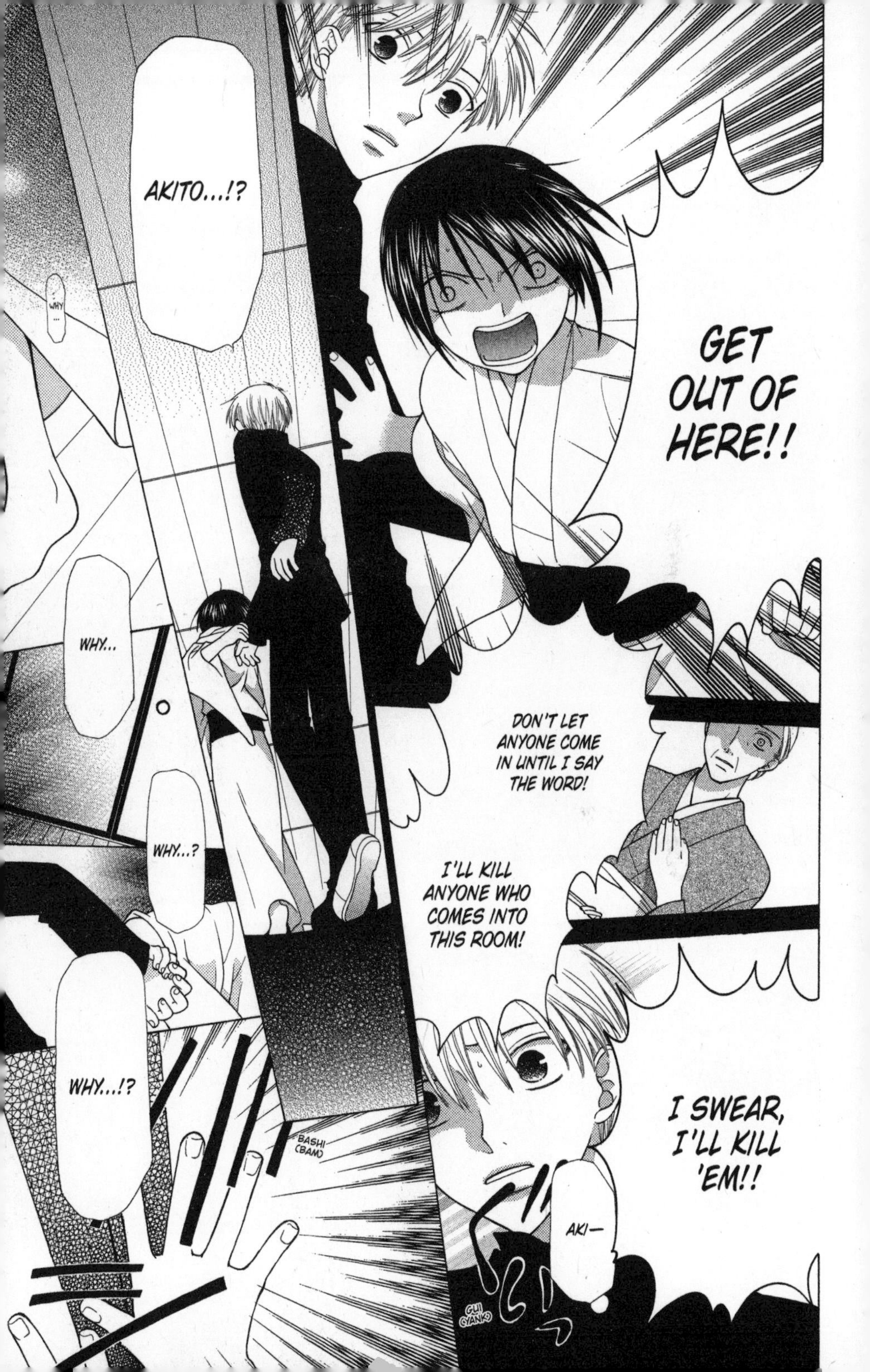
GET OUT OF HERE!!
AKITO...!?
WHY...
DON'T LET ANYONE COME IN UNTIL I SAY THE WORD!
I'LL KILL ANYONE WHO COMES INTO THIS ROOM!
I SWEAR, I'LL KILL 'EM!!
AKI—
GUI (YANK)
WHY...
WHY...?
BASHI (BAM)
WHY...!?

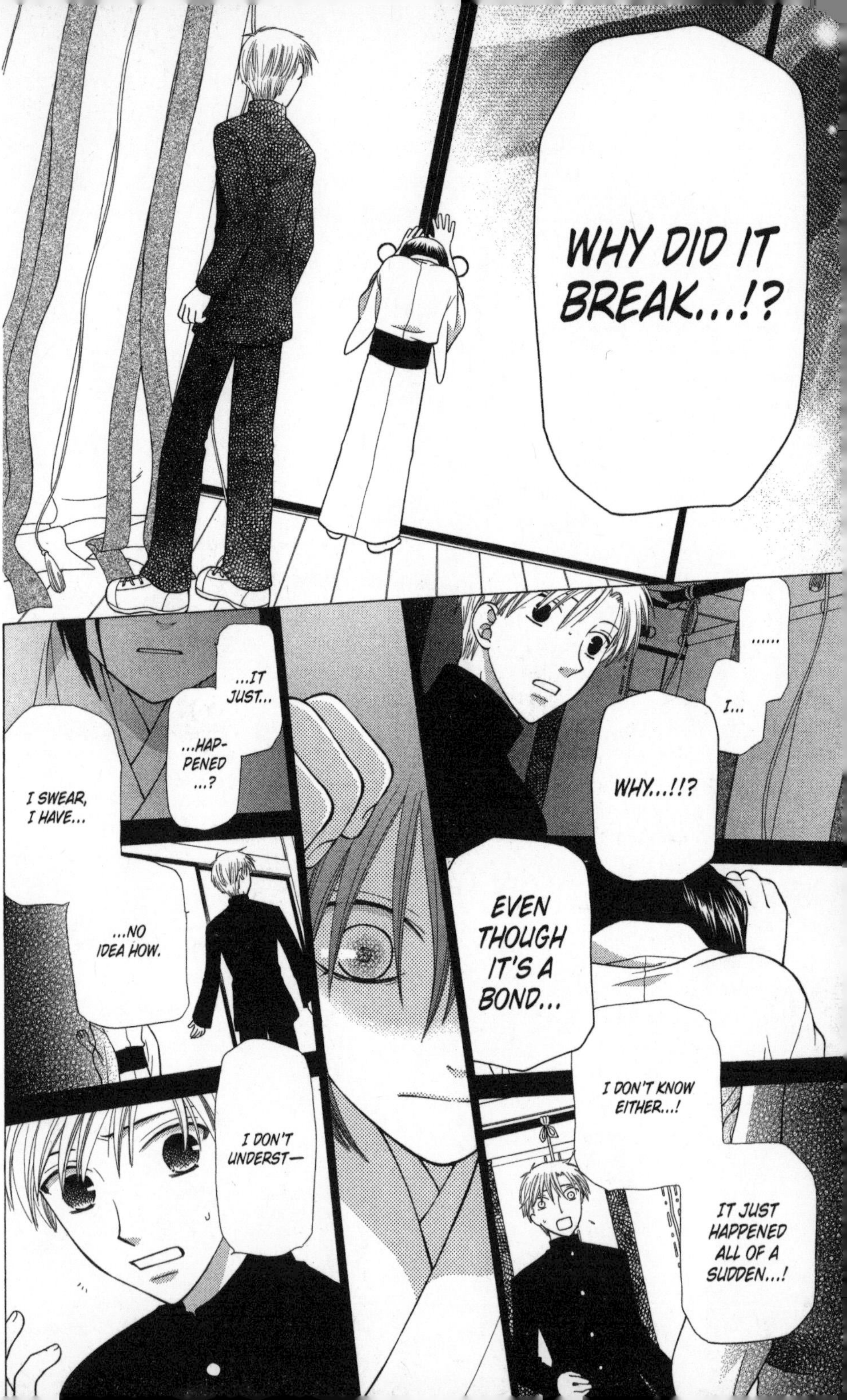
WHY DID IT BREAK...!?
......
I...
WHY...!!?
EVEN THOUGH IT'S A BOND...
I DON'T KNOW EITHER...!
IT JUST HAPPENED ALL OF A SUDDEN...!
...IT JUST...
...HAP-PENED...?
I SWEAR, I HAVE...
...NO IDEA HOW.
I DON'T UNDERST—

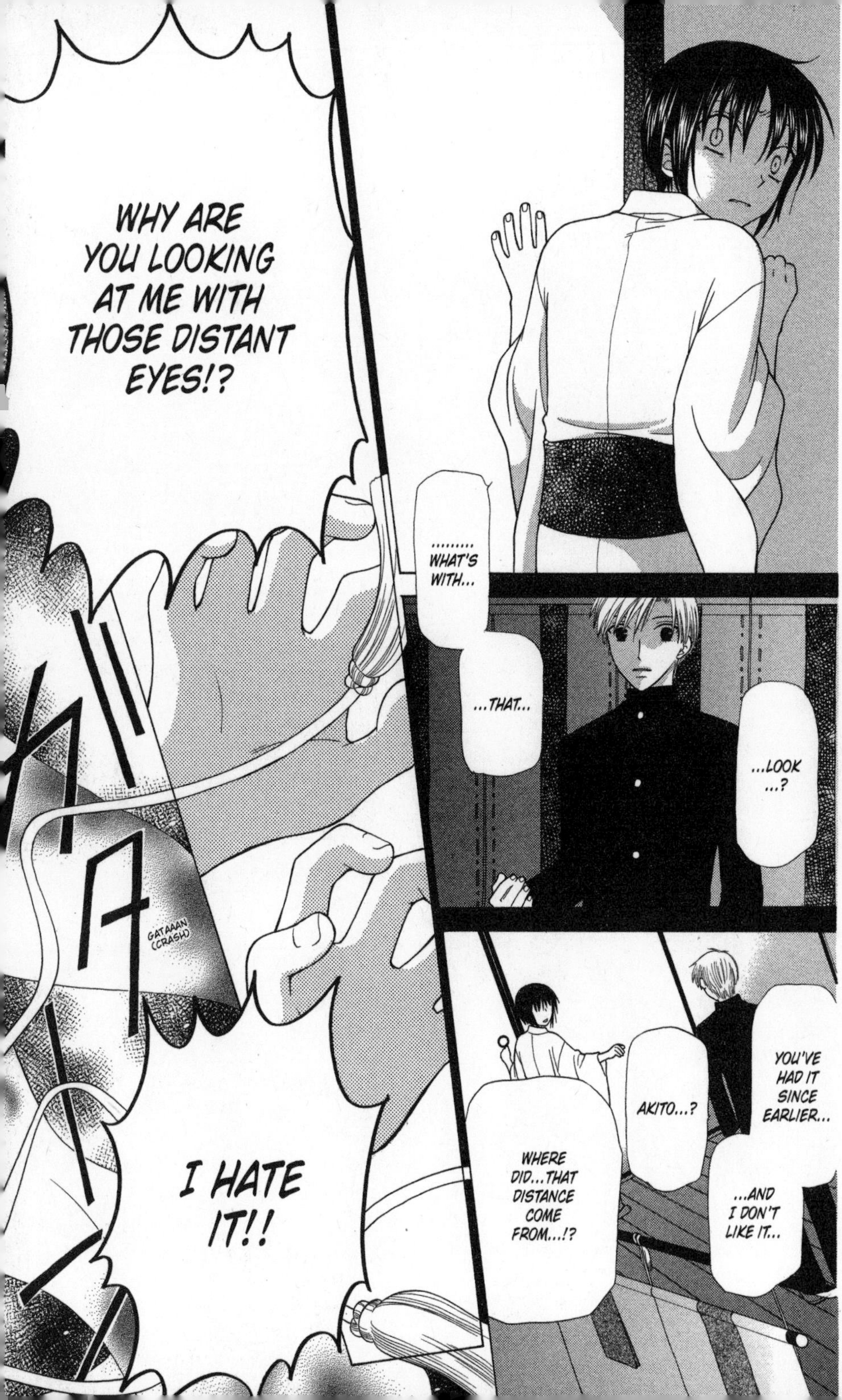

.... WHAT'S WITH...
...THAT...
...LOOK ...?
YOU'VE HAD IT SINCE EARLIER...
...AND I DON'T LIKE IT...
AKITO...?
WHERE DID...THAT DISTANCE COME FROM...!?
WHY ARE YOU LOOKING AT ME WITH THOSE DISTANT EYES!?
GATAAAN (CRASH)
I HATE IT!!

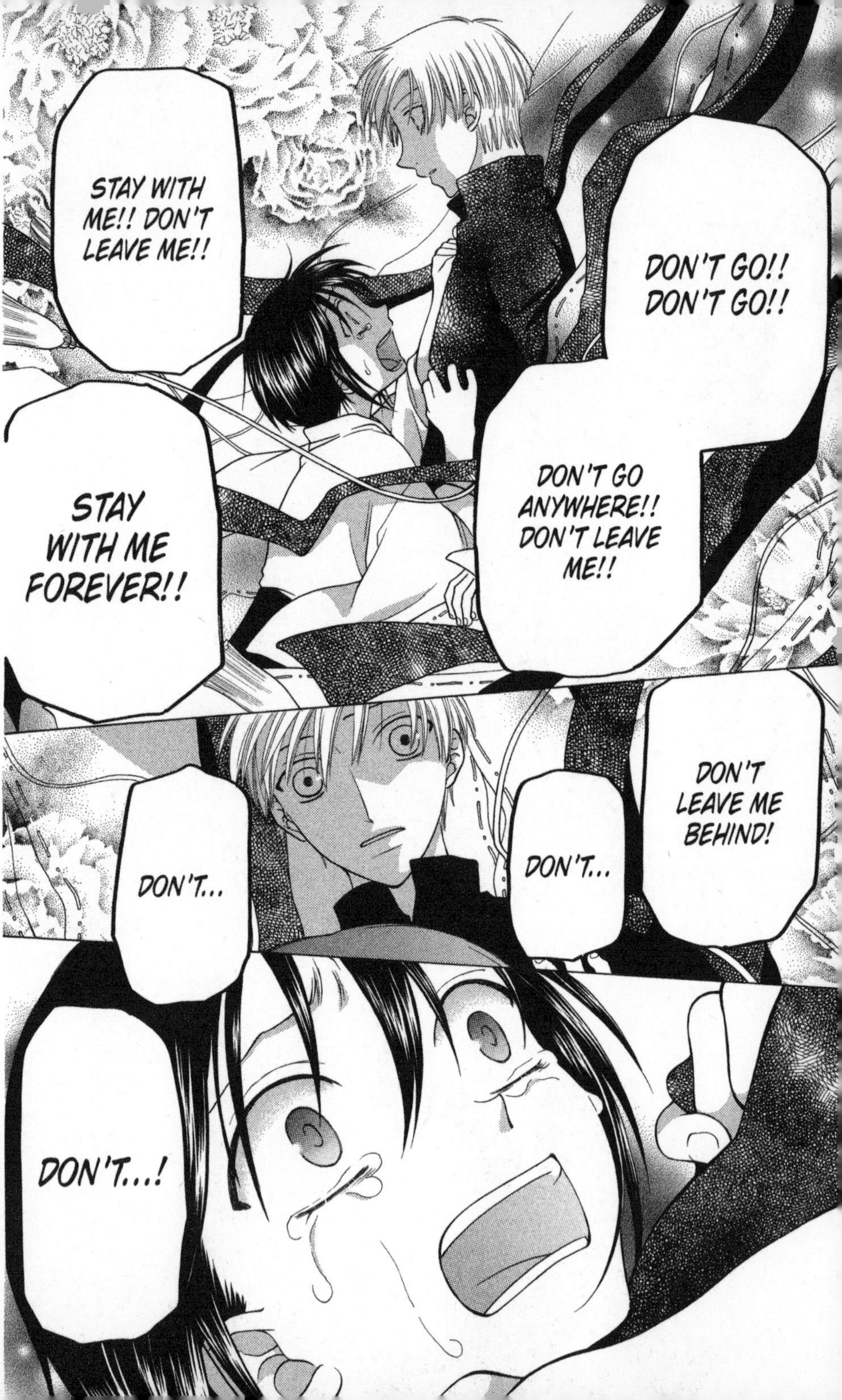
DON'T GO!! DON'T GO!!
STAY WITH ME!! DON'T LEAVE ME!!
DON'T GO ANYWHERE!! DON'T LEAVE ME!!
STAY WITH ME FOREVER!!
DON'T LEAVE ME BEHIND!
DON'T...
DON'T...
DON'T...!

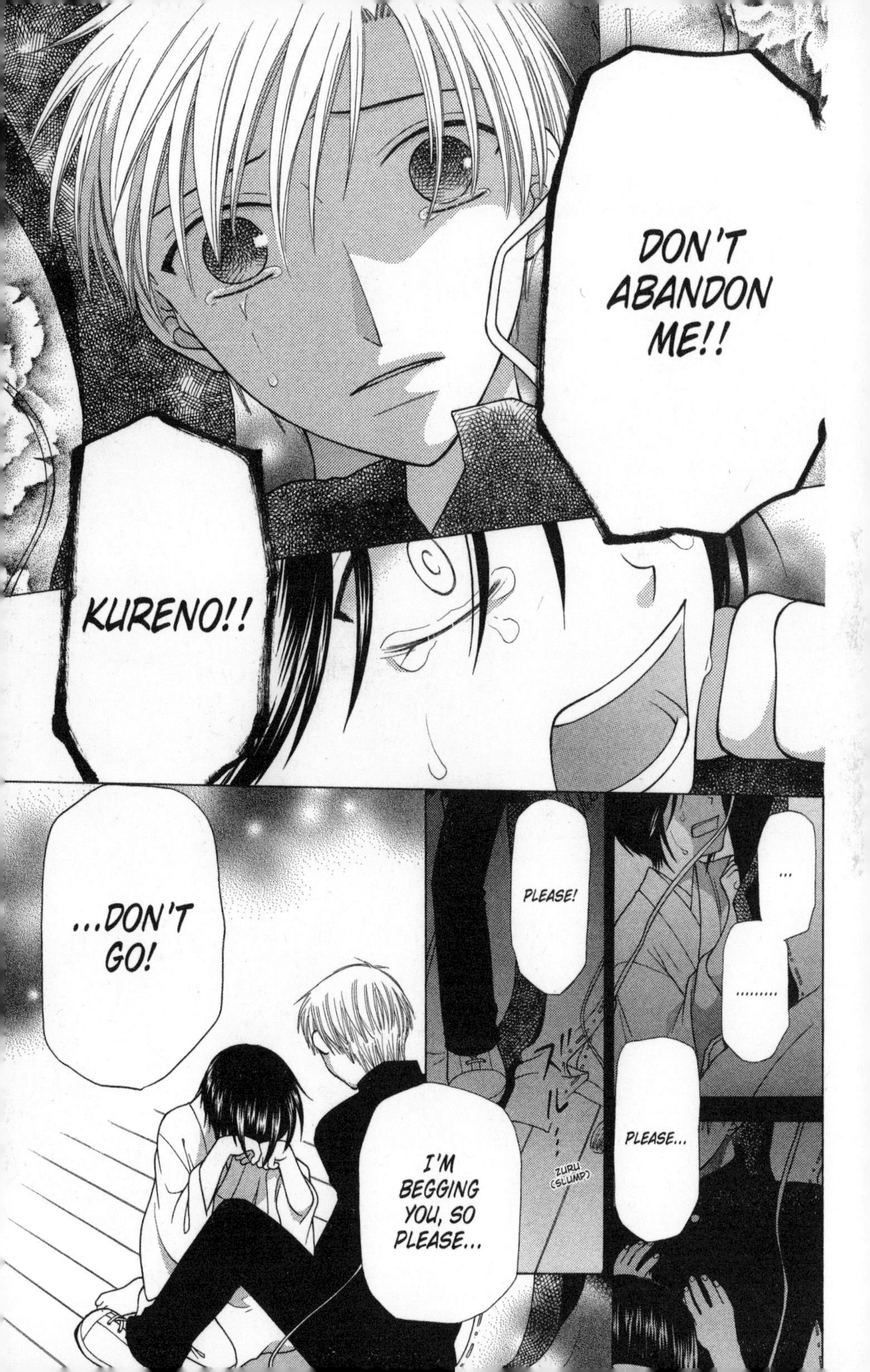
DON'T ABANDON ME!!
KURENO!!
...
....
PLEASE...
PLEASE!
ZURU (SLUMP)
...DON'T GO!
I'M BEGGING YOU, SO PLEASE...

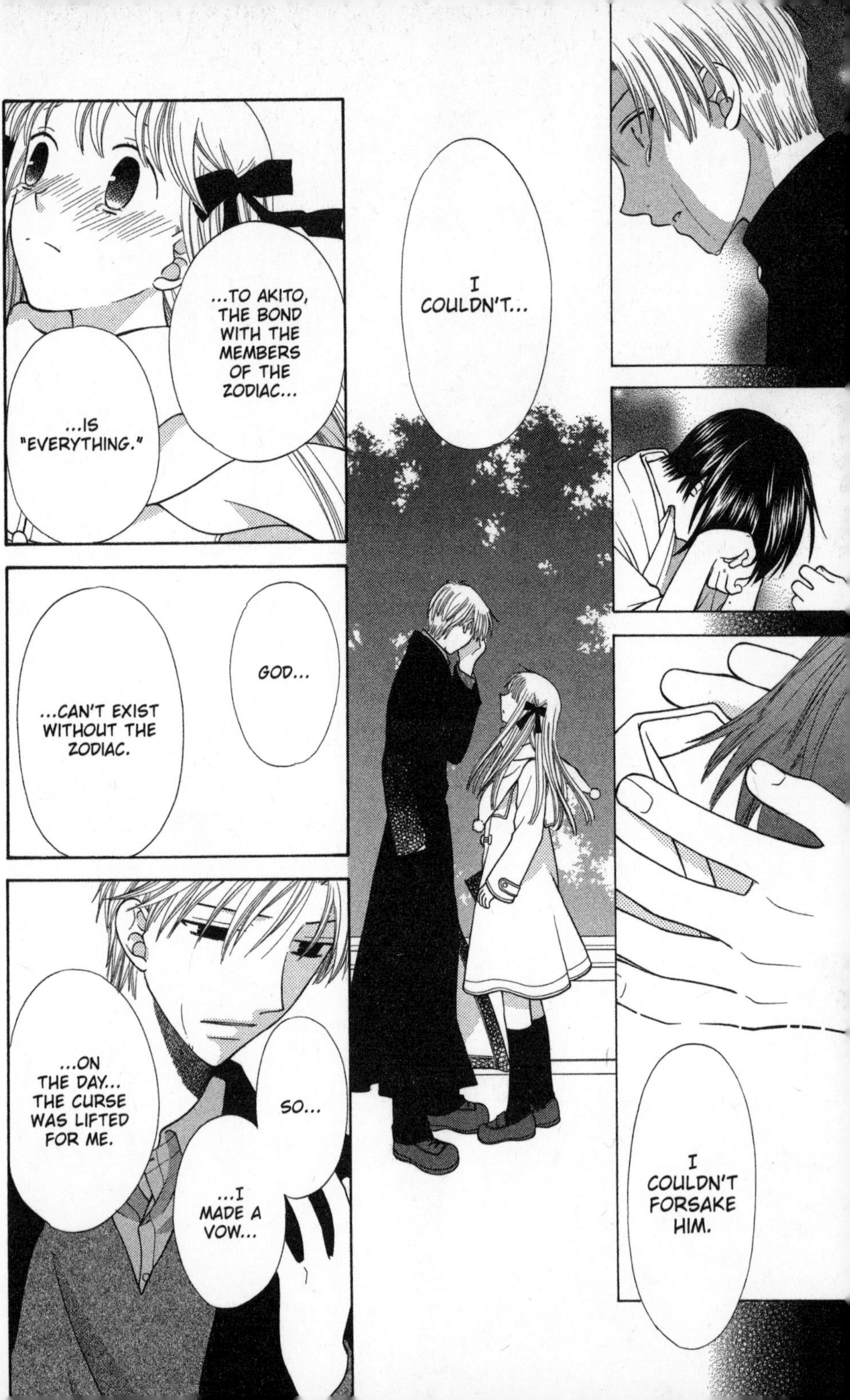
I COULDN'T FORSAKE HIM.
I COULDN'T...
...TO AKITO, THE BOND WITH THE MEMBERS OF THE ZODIAC...
...IS "EVERYTHING."
GOD...
...CAN'T EXIST WITHOUT THE ZODIAC.
SO...
...I MADE A VOW...
...ON THE DAY... THE CURSE WAS LIFTED FOR ME.

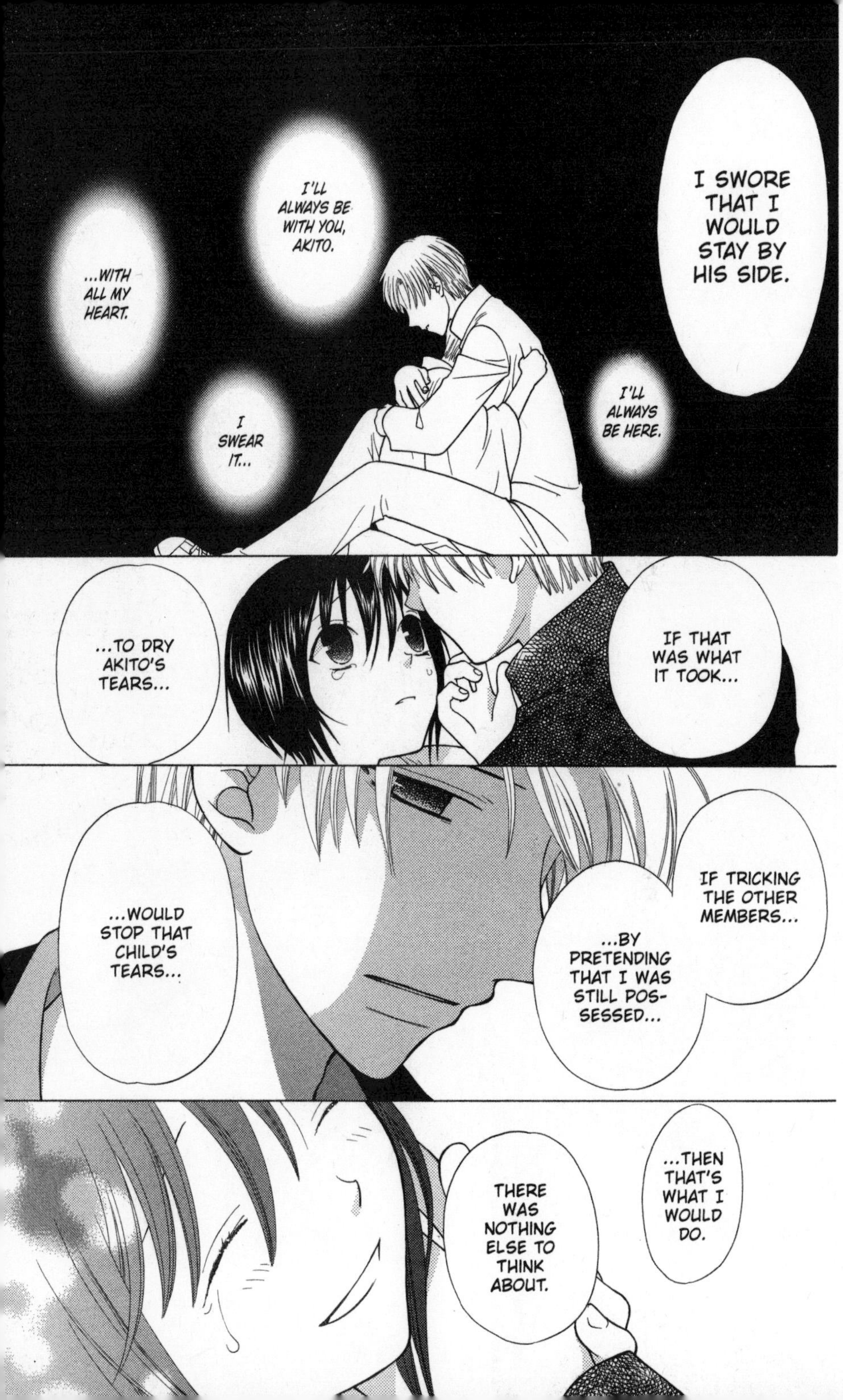
I SWORE THAT I WOULD STAY BY HIS SIDE.
I'LL ALWAYS BE HERE.
I'LL ALWAYS BE WITH YOU, AKITO.
I SWEAR IT...
...WITH ALL MY HEART.
IF THAT WAS WHAT IT TOOK...
...TO DRY AKITO'S TEARS...
IF TRICKING THE OTHER MEMBERS...
...BY PRETENDING THAT I WAS STILL POS-SESSED...
...WOULD STOP THAT CHILD'S TEARS...
...THEN THAT'S WHAT I WOULD DO.
THERE WAS NOTHING ELSE TO THINK ABOUT.

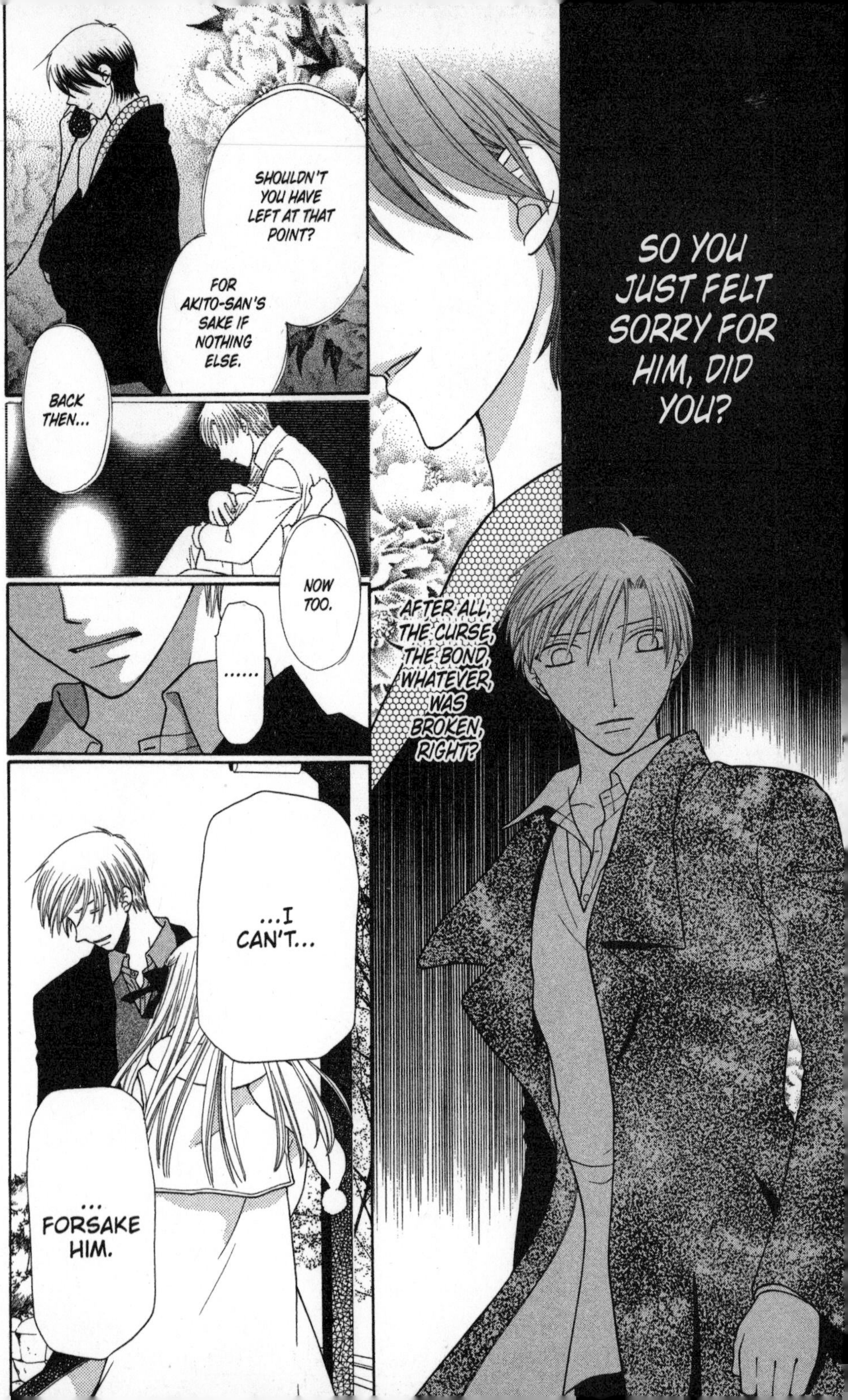
SO YOU JUST FELT SORRY FOR HIM, DID YOU?
AFTER ALL, THE CURSE, THE BOND, WHATEVER, WAS BROKEN, RIGHT?
SHOULDN'T YOU HAVE LEFT AT THAT POINT?
FOR AKITO-SAN'S SAKE IF NOTHING ELSE.
BACK THEN...
NOW TOO.
......
...I CAN'T...
...FORSAKE HIM.

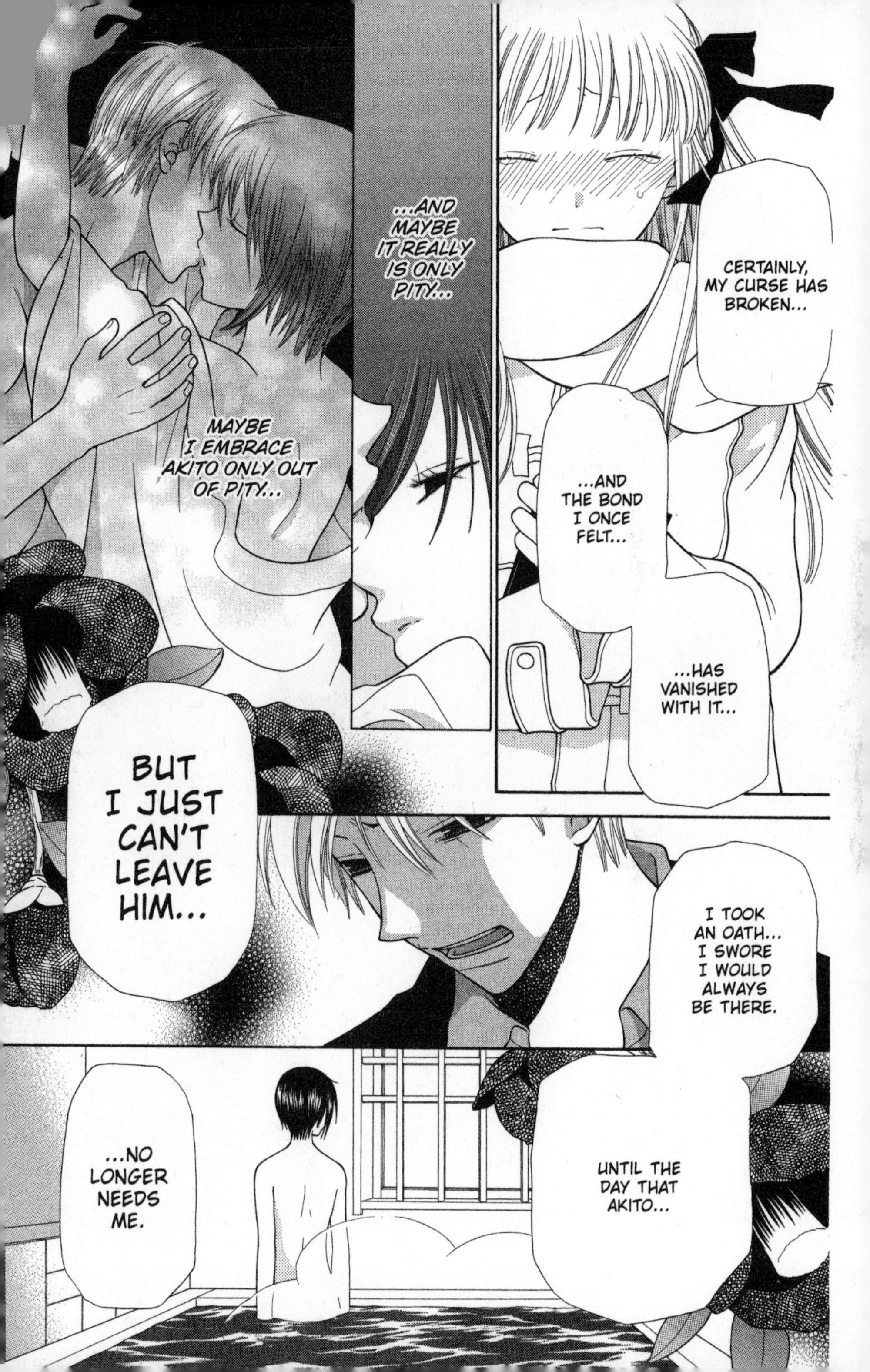
CERTAINLY, MY CURSE HAS BROKEN...
...AND THE BOND I ONCE FELT...
...HAS VANISHED WITH IT...
...AND MAYBE IT REALLY IS ONLY PITY...
MAYBE I EMBRACE AKITO ONLY OUT OF PITY...
BUT I JUST CAN'T LEAVE HIM...
I TOOK AN OATH... I SWORE I WOULD ALWAYS BE THERE.
UNTIL THE DAY THAT AKITO...
...NO LONGER NEEDS ME.

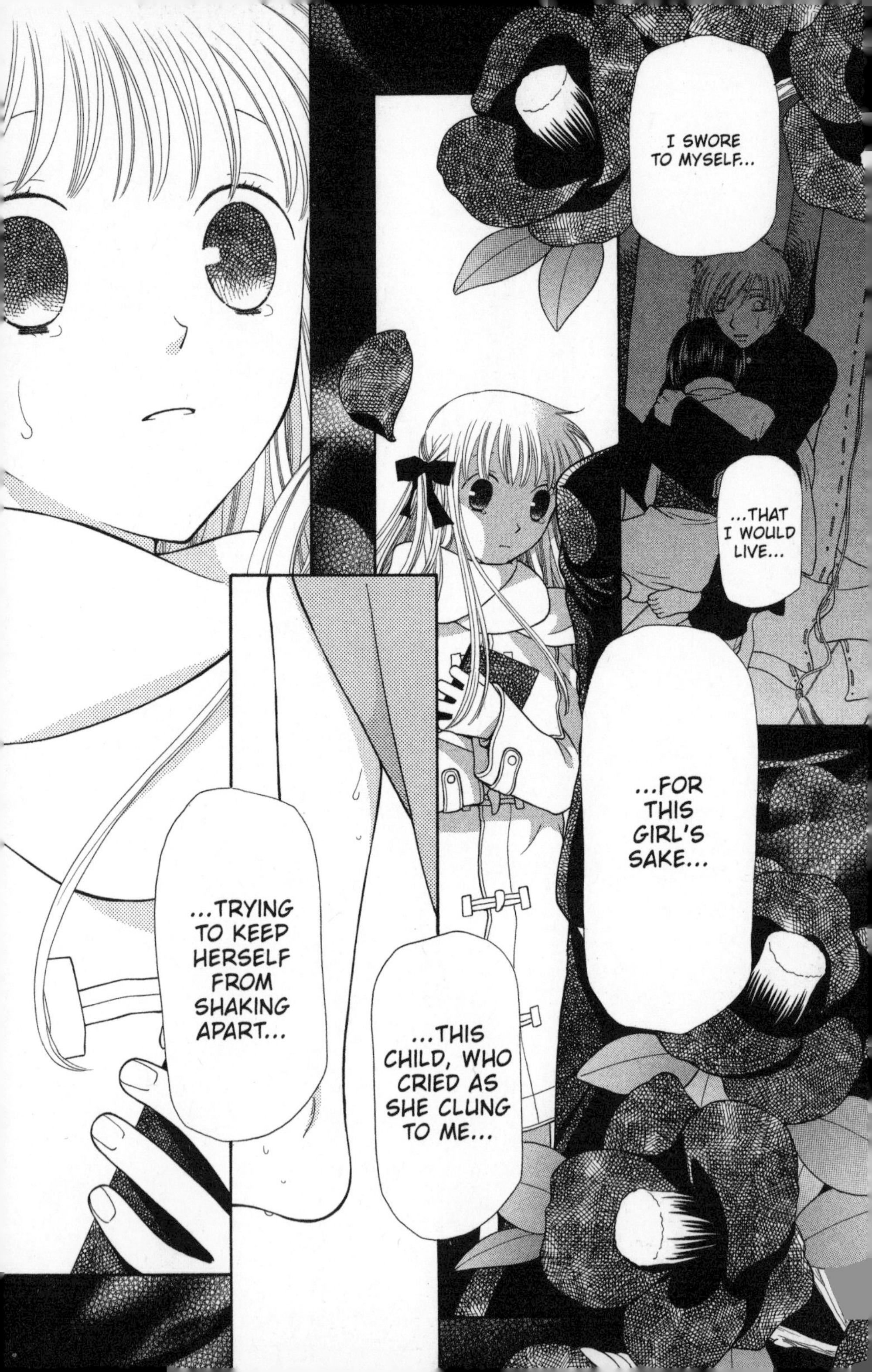
I SWORE TO MYSELF...
...THAT I WOULD LIVE...
...FOR THIS GIRL'S SAKE...
...THIS CHILD, WHO CRIED AS SHE CLUNG TO ME...
...TRYING TO KEEP HERSELF FROM SHAKING APART...

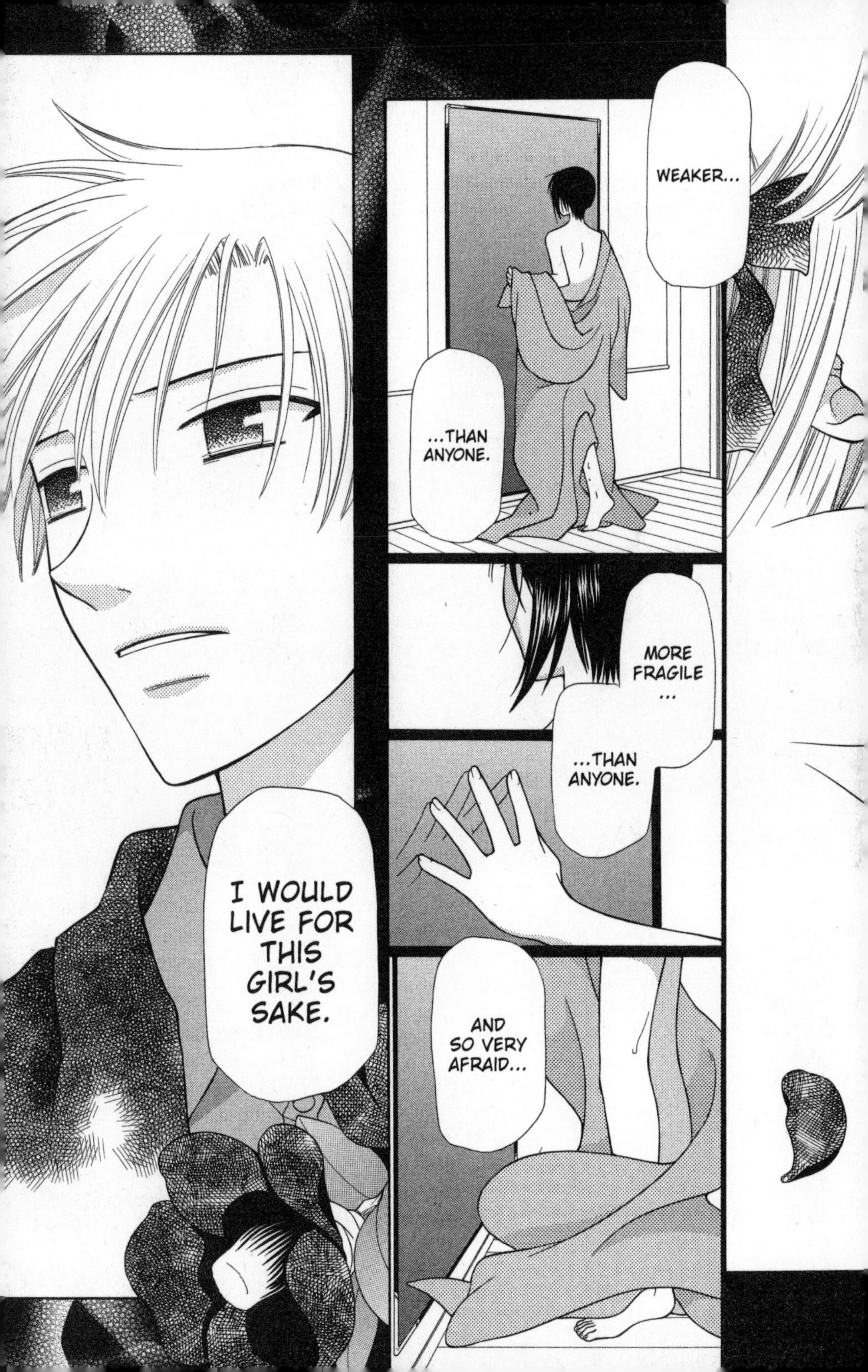
WEAKER...
...THAN ANYONE.
MORE FRAGILE ...
...THAN ANYONE.
AND SO VERY AFRAID...
I WOULD LIVE FOR THIS GIRL'S SAKE.

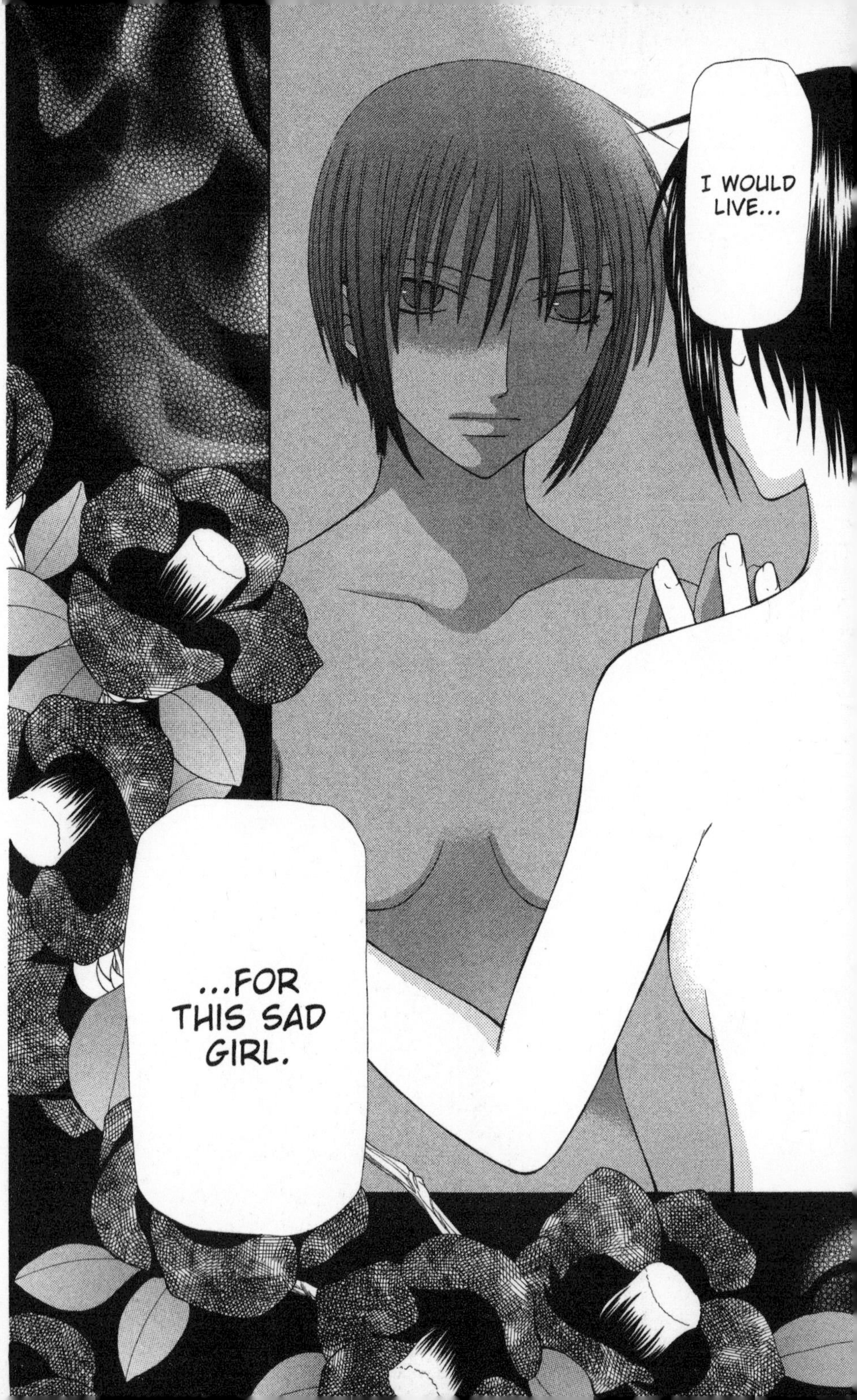
I WOULD LIVE...
...FOR THIS SAD GIRL.

Chapter 98

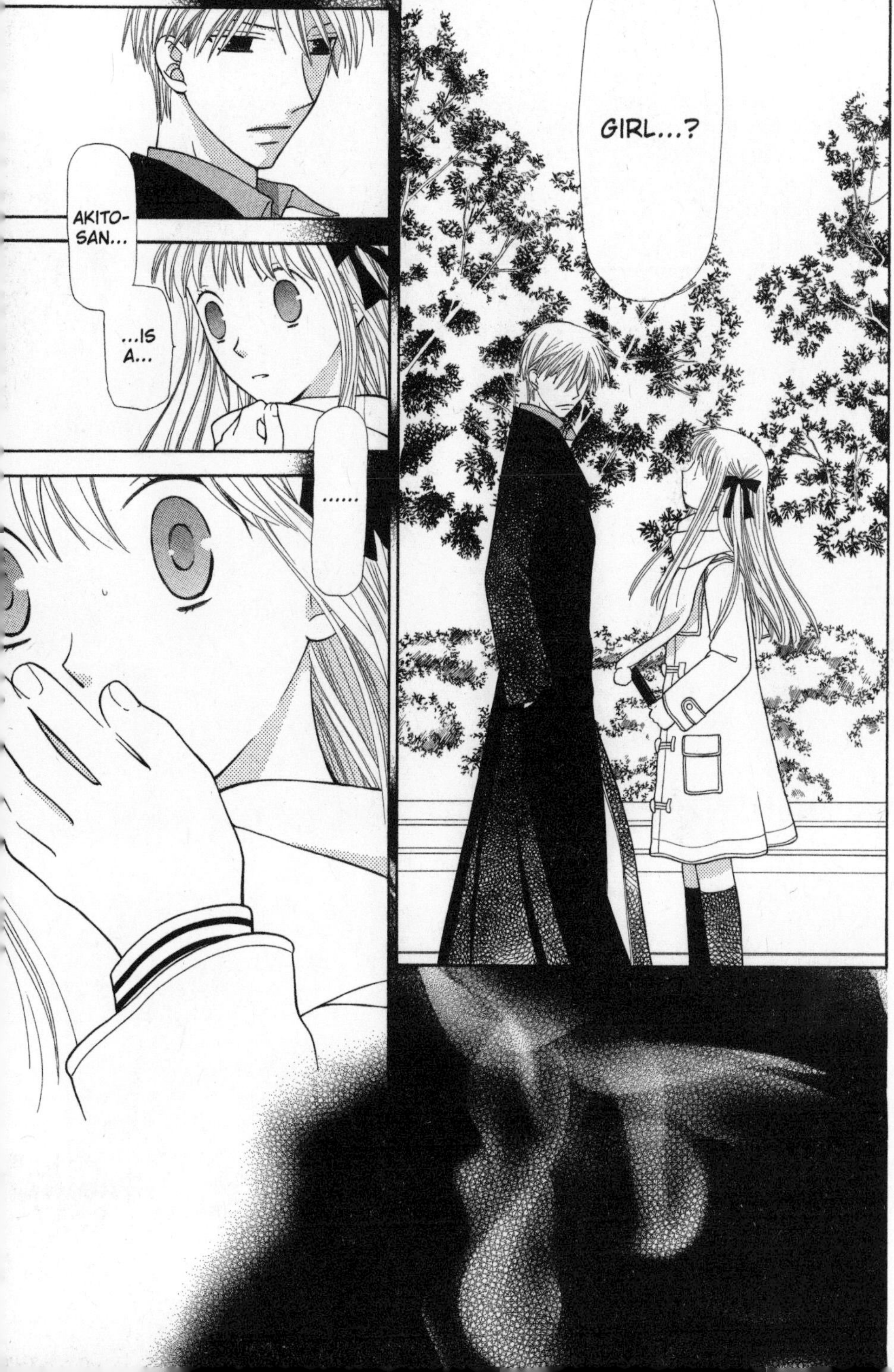
GIRL...?
AKITO-SAN...
...IS A...
......

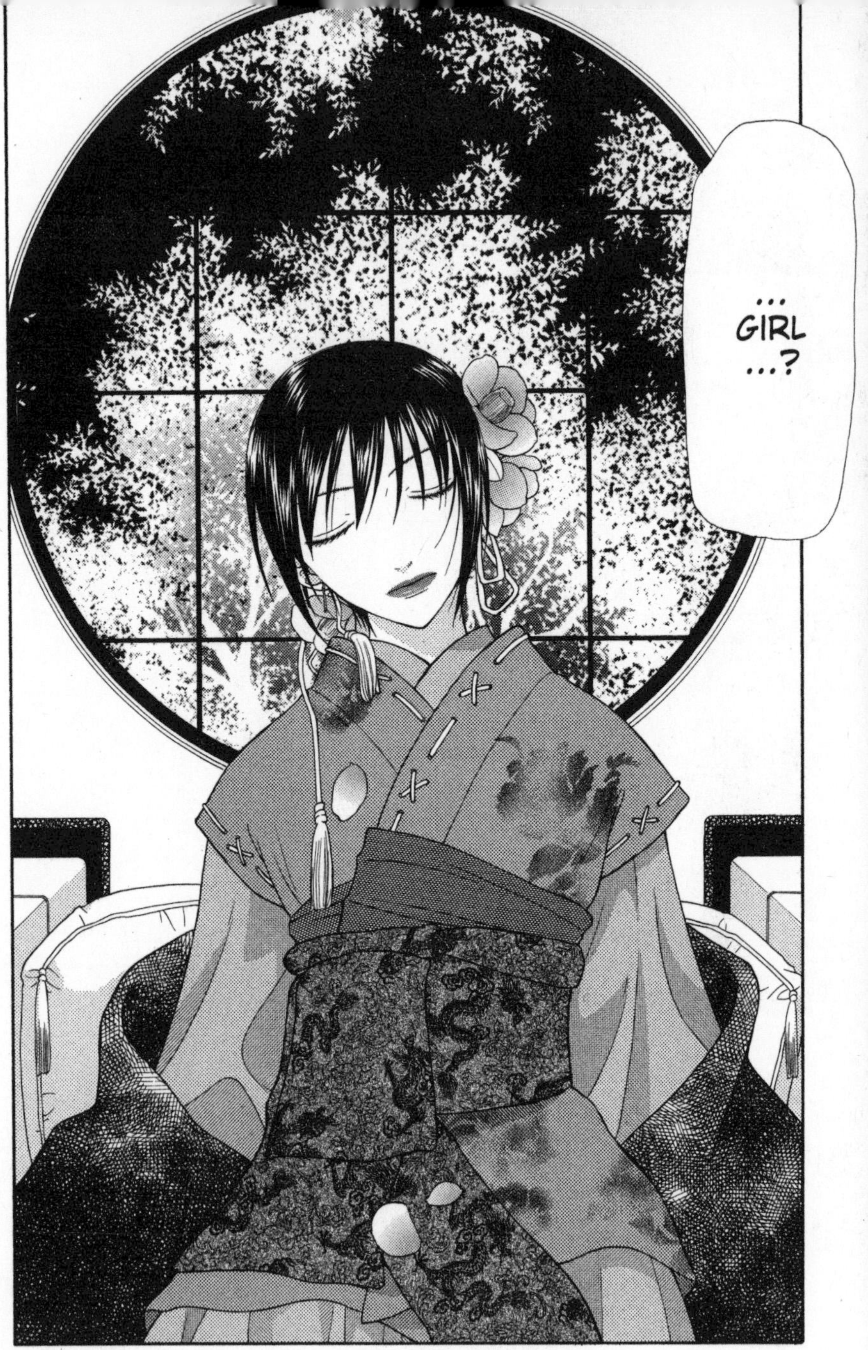
... GIRL ...?

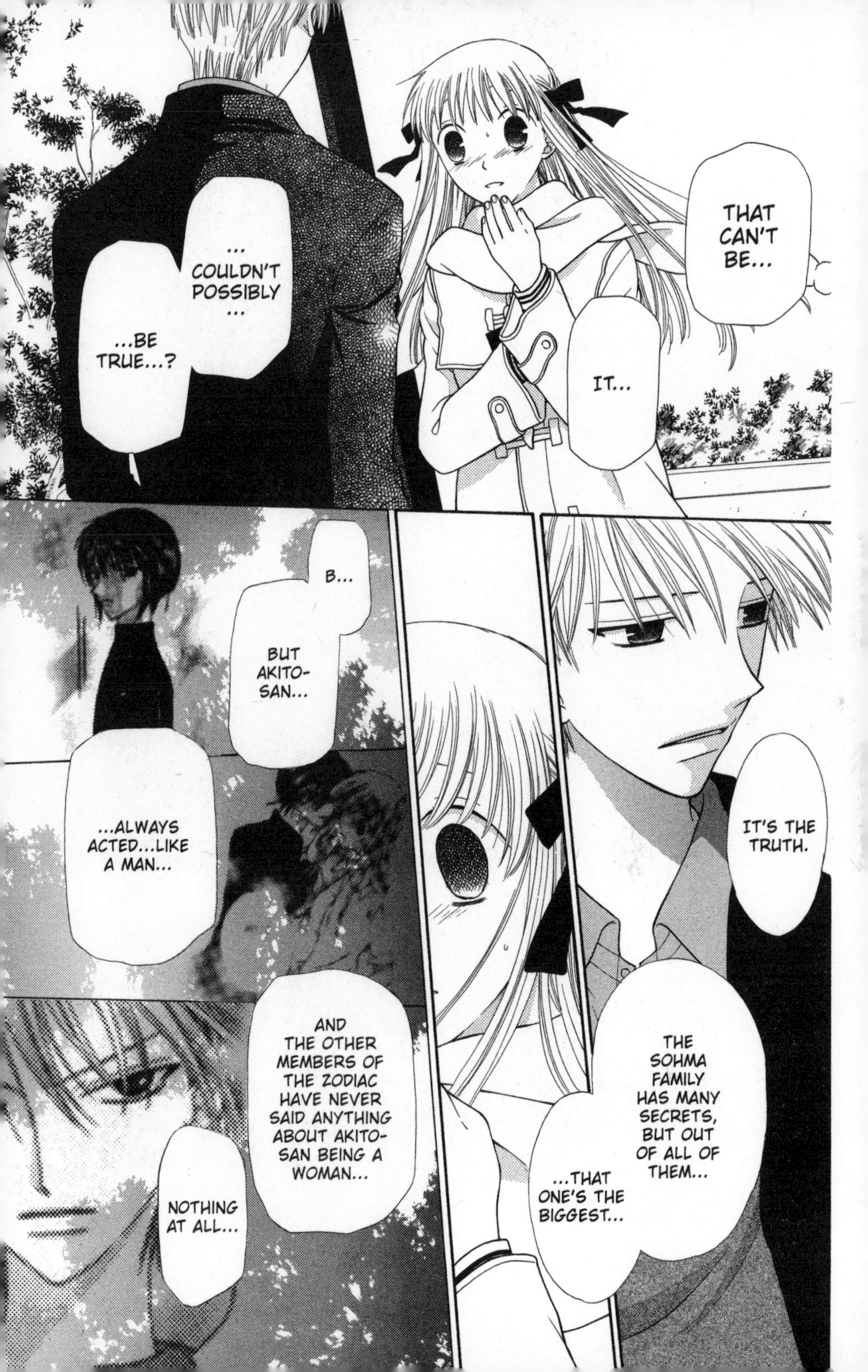
THAT CAN'T BE...
IT...
... COULDN'T POSSIBLY ...
...BE TRUE...?
IT'S THE TRUTH.
THE SOHMA FAMILY HAS MANY SECRETS, BUT OUT OF ALL OF THEM...
...THAT ONE'S THE BIGGEST...
B...
BUT AKITO-SAN...
...ALWAYS ACTED...LIKE A MAN...
AND THE OTHER MEMBERS OF THE ZODIAC HAVE NEVER SAID ANYTHING ABOUT AKITO-SAN BEING A WOMAN...
NOTHING AT ALL...

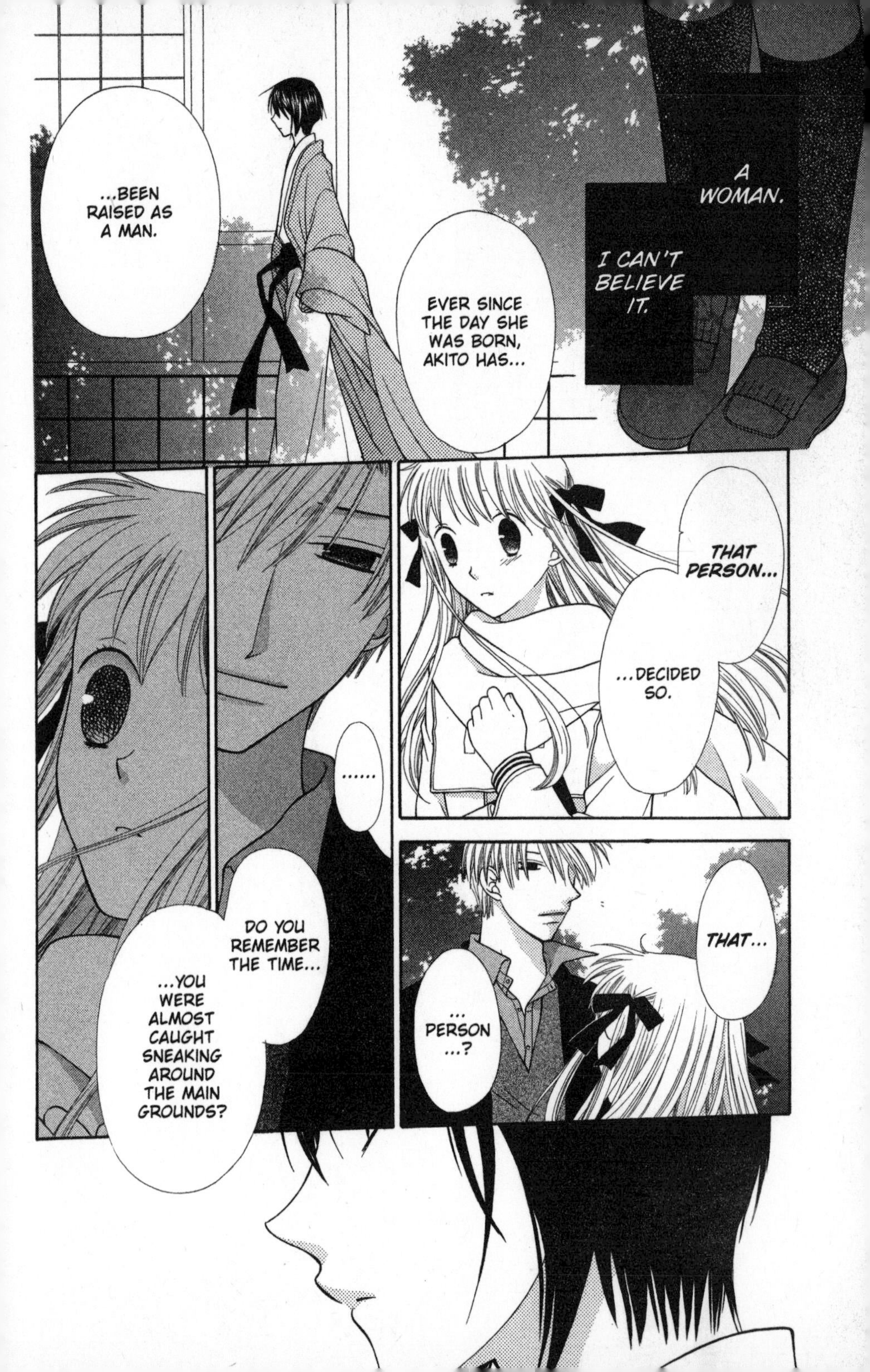
A WOMAN.
I CAN'T BELIEVE IT.
EVER SINCE THE DAY SHE WAS BORN, AKITO HAS...
...BEEN RAISED AS A MAN.
THAT PERSON...
...DECIDED SO.
THAT...
...PERSON...?
......
DO YOU REMEMBER THE TIME...
...YOU WERE ALMOST CAUGHT SNEAKING AROUND THE MAIN GROUNDS?

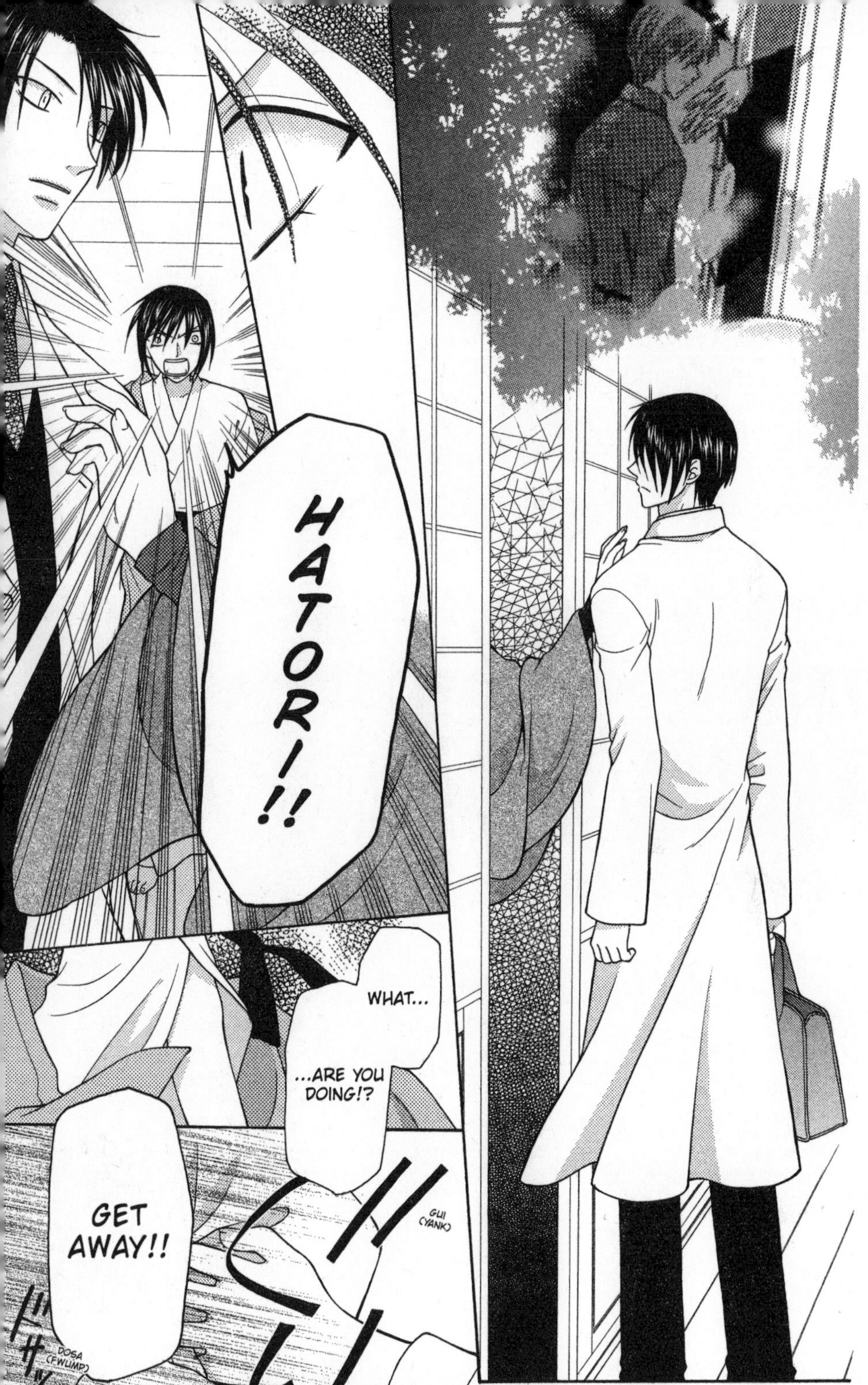
HATORI!!
WHAT...
...ARE YOU DOING!?
GUI (YANK)
GET AWAY!!
DOSA (FWUMP)

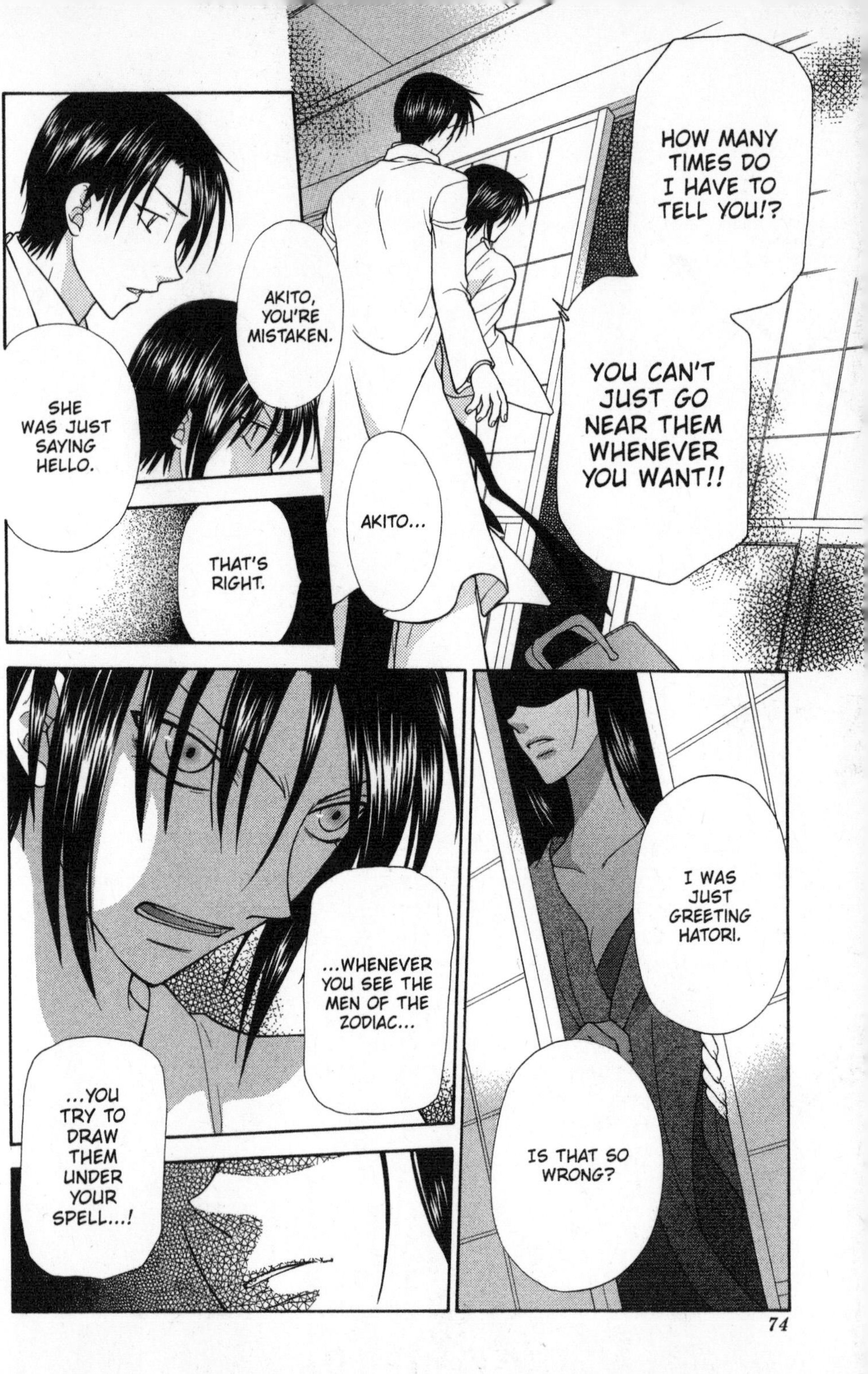

HOW MANY TIMES DO I HAVE TO TELL YOU!?
YOU CAN'T JUST GO NEAR THEM WHENEVER YOU WANT!!
AKITO, YOU'RE MISTAKEN.
AKITO...
SHE WAS JUST SAYING HELLO.
THAT'S RIGHT.
I WAS JUST GREETING HATORI.
IS THAT SO WRONG?
...WHENEVER YOU SEE THE MEN OF THE ZODIAC...
...YOU TRY TO DRAW THEM UNDER YOUR SPELL...!

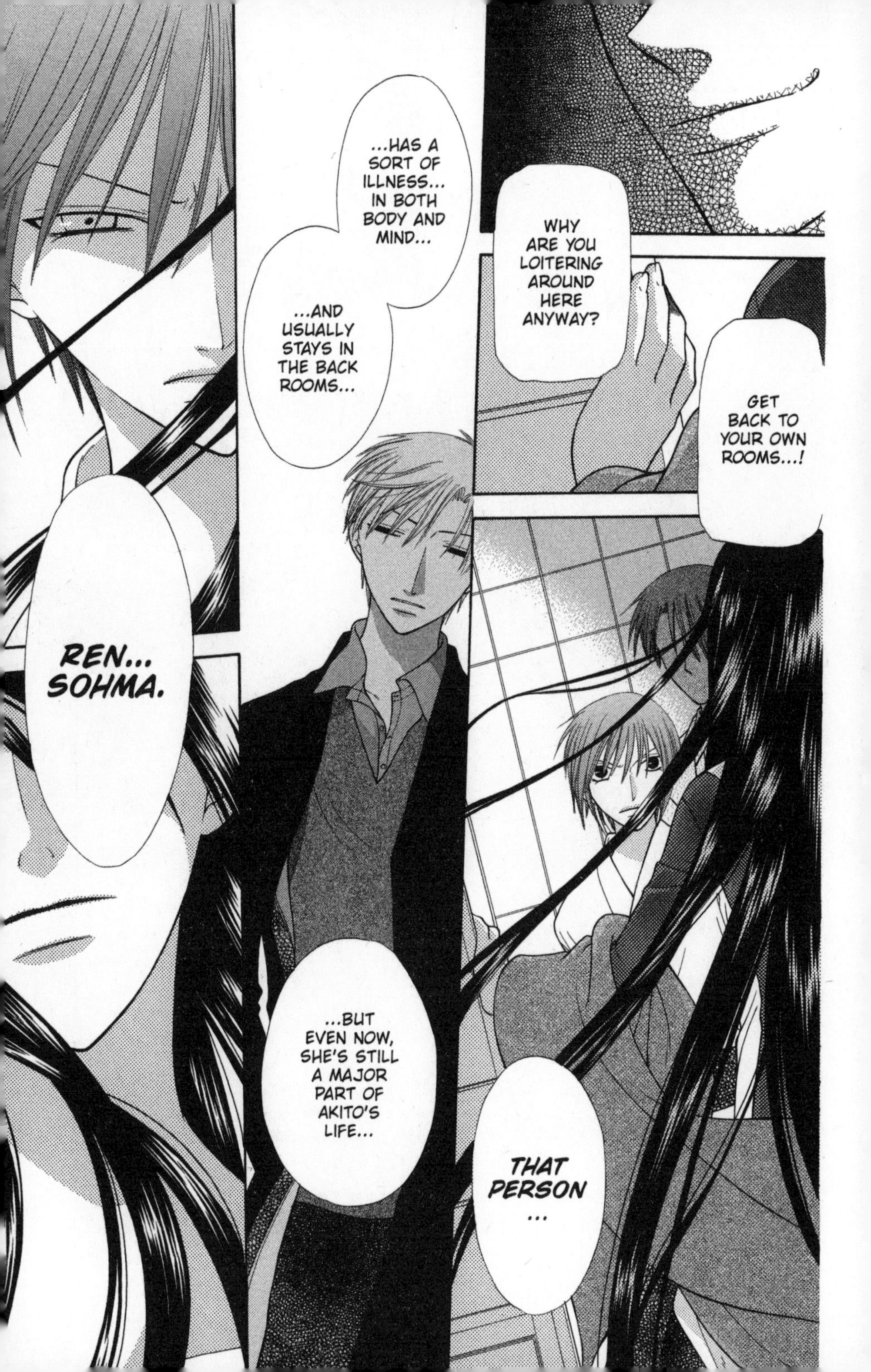
WHY ARE YOU LOITERING AROUND HERE ANYWAY?
GET BACK TO YOUR OWN ROOMS...!
THAT PERSON ...
...HAS A SORT OF ILLNESS... IN BOTH BODY AND MIND...
...AND USUALLY STAYS IN THE BACK ROOMS...
...BUT EVEN NOW, SHE'S STILL A MAJOR PART OF AKITO'S LIFE...
REN... SOHMA.

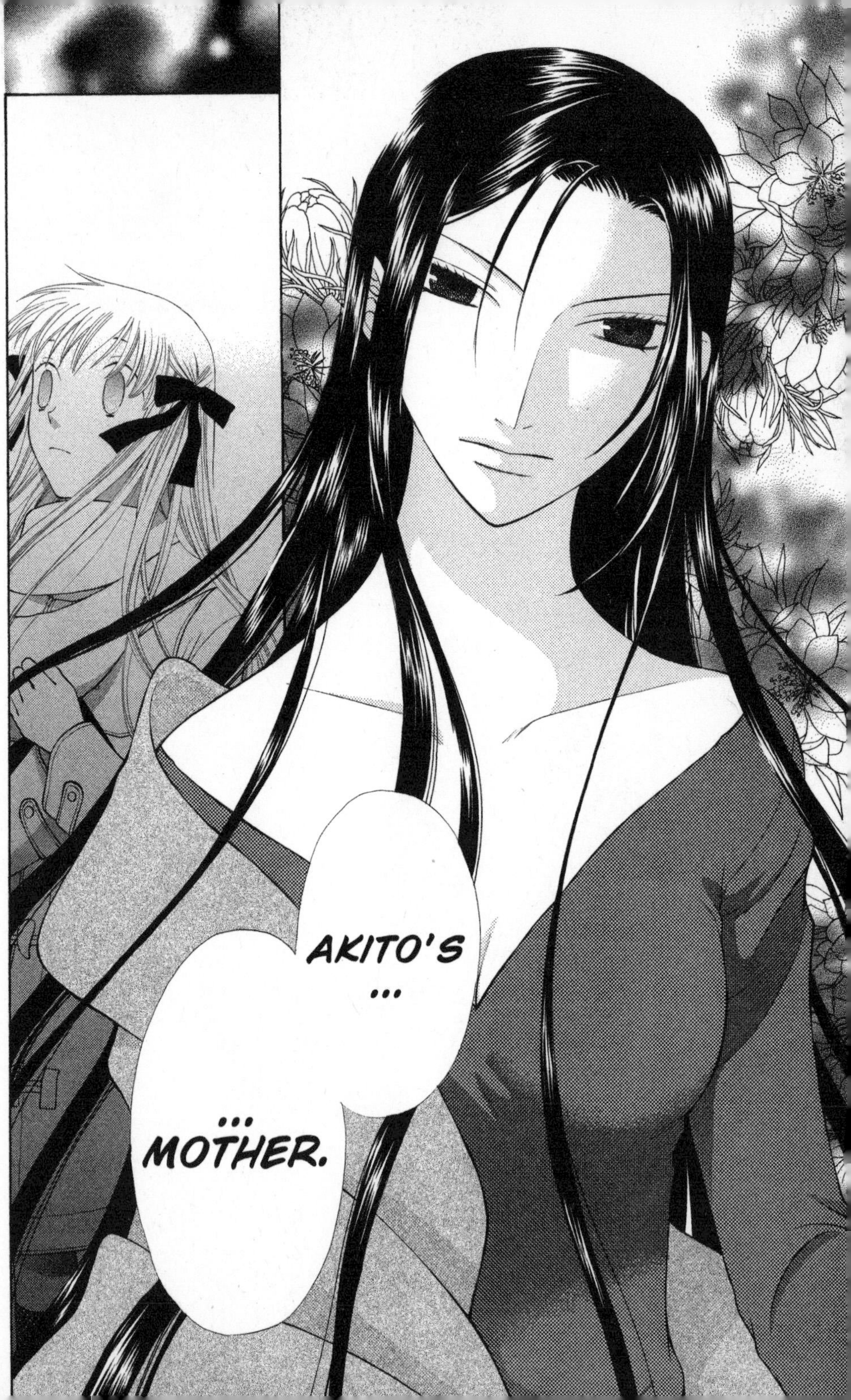
AKITO'S ...
... MOTHER.

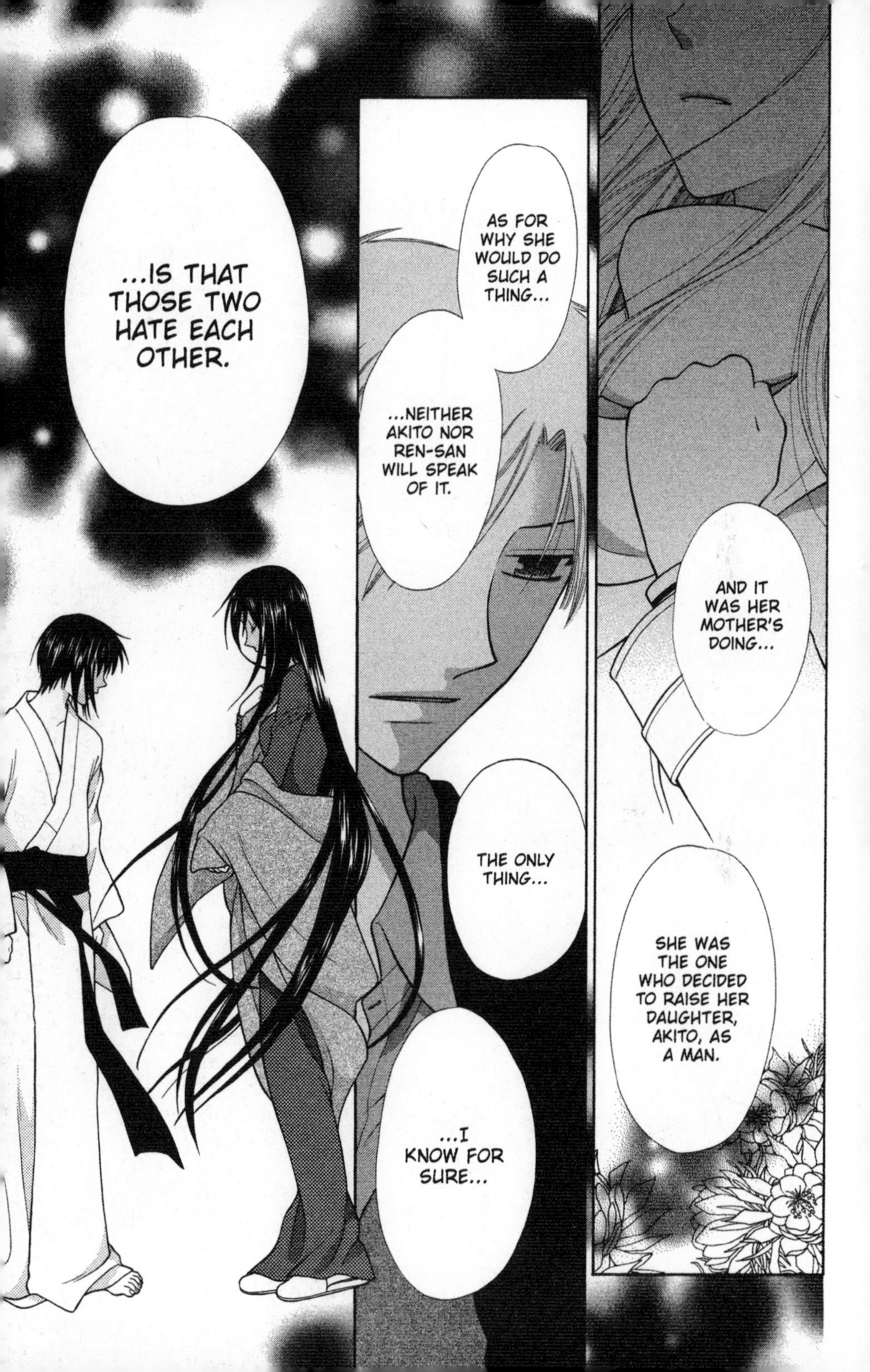
AND IT WAS HER MOTHER'S DOING...
SHE WAS THE ONE WHO DECIDED TO RAISE HER DAUGHTER, AKITO, AS A MAN.
AS FOR WHY SHE WOULD DO SUCH A THING...
...NEITHER AKITO NOR REN-SAN WILL SPEAK OF IT.
THE ONLY THING...
...I KNOW FOR SURE...
...IS THAT THOSE TWO HATE EACH OTHER.

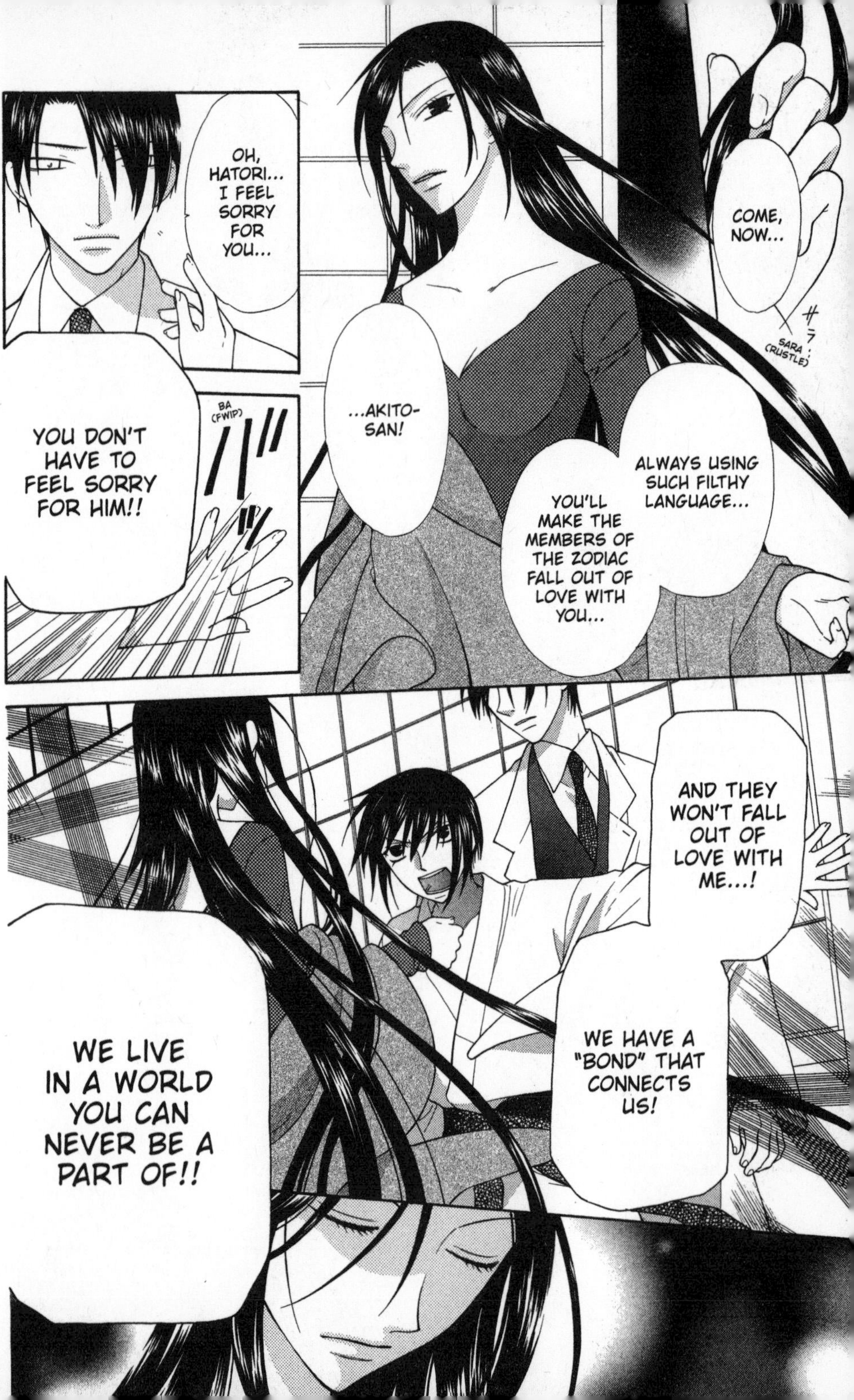

COME, NOW...
SARA (RUSTLE)
...AKITO-SAN!
ALWAYS USING SUCH FILTHY LANGUAGE...
YOU'LL MAKE THE MEMBERS OF THE ZODIAC FALL OUT OF LOVE WITH YOU...
OH, HATORI... I FEEL SORRY FOR YOU...
BA (FWIP)
YOU DON'T HAVE TO FEEL SORRY FOR HIM!!
AND THEY WON'T FALL OUT OF LOVE WITH ME...!
WE HAVE A "BOND" THAT CONNECTS US!
WE LIVE IN A WORLD YOU CAN NEVER BE A PART OF!!

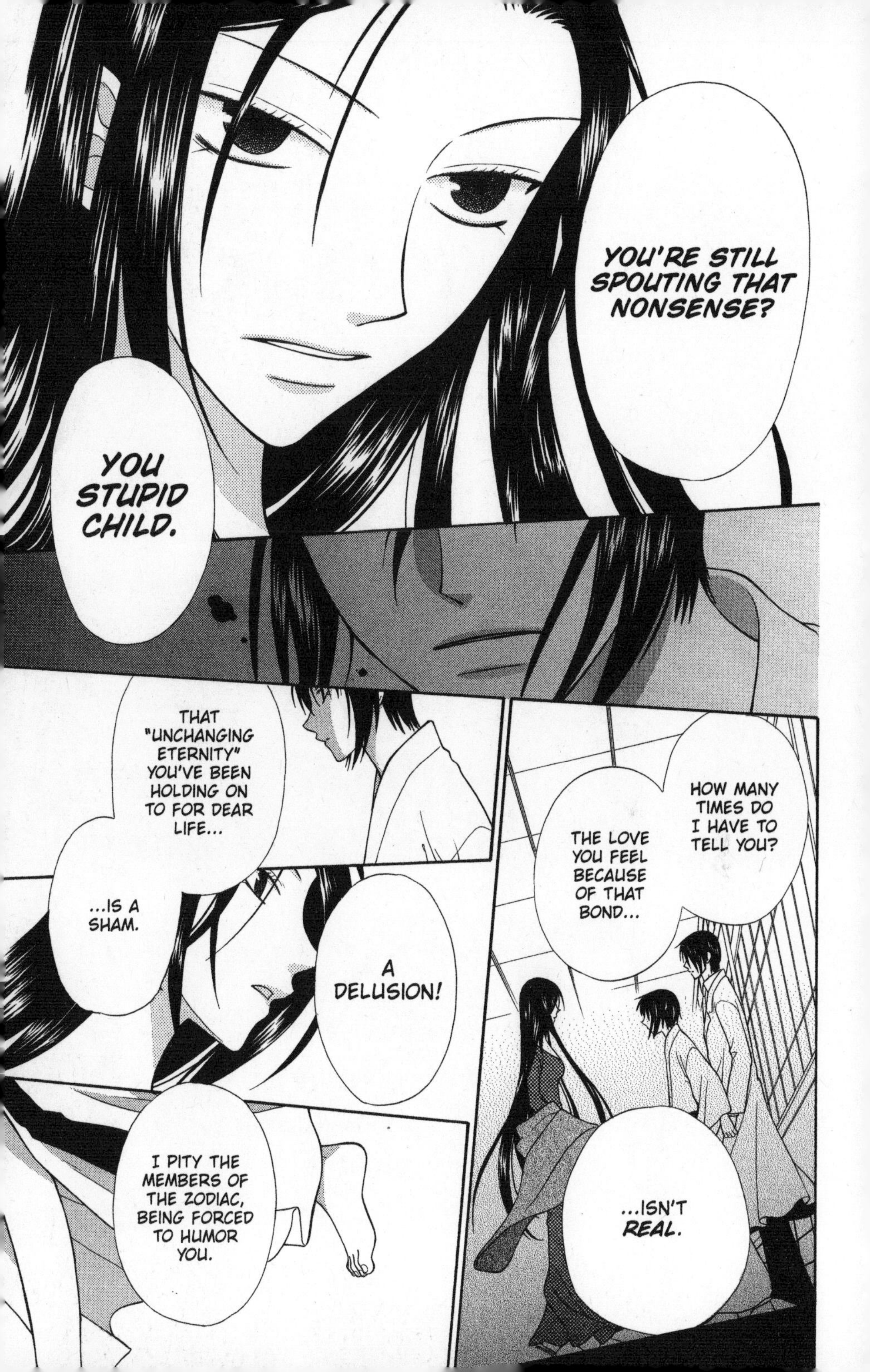
YOU'RE STILL SPOUTING THAT NONSENSE?
YOU STUPID CHILD.
HOW MANY TIMES DO I HAVE TO TELL YOU?
THE LOVE YOU FEEL BECAUSE OF THAT BOND...
...ISN'T REAL.
THAT "UNCHANGING ETERNITY" YOU'VE BEEN HOLDING ON TO FOR DEAR LIFE...
...IS A SHAM.
A DELUSION!
I PITY THE MEMBERS OF THE ZODIAC, BEING FORCED TO HUMOR YOU.

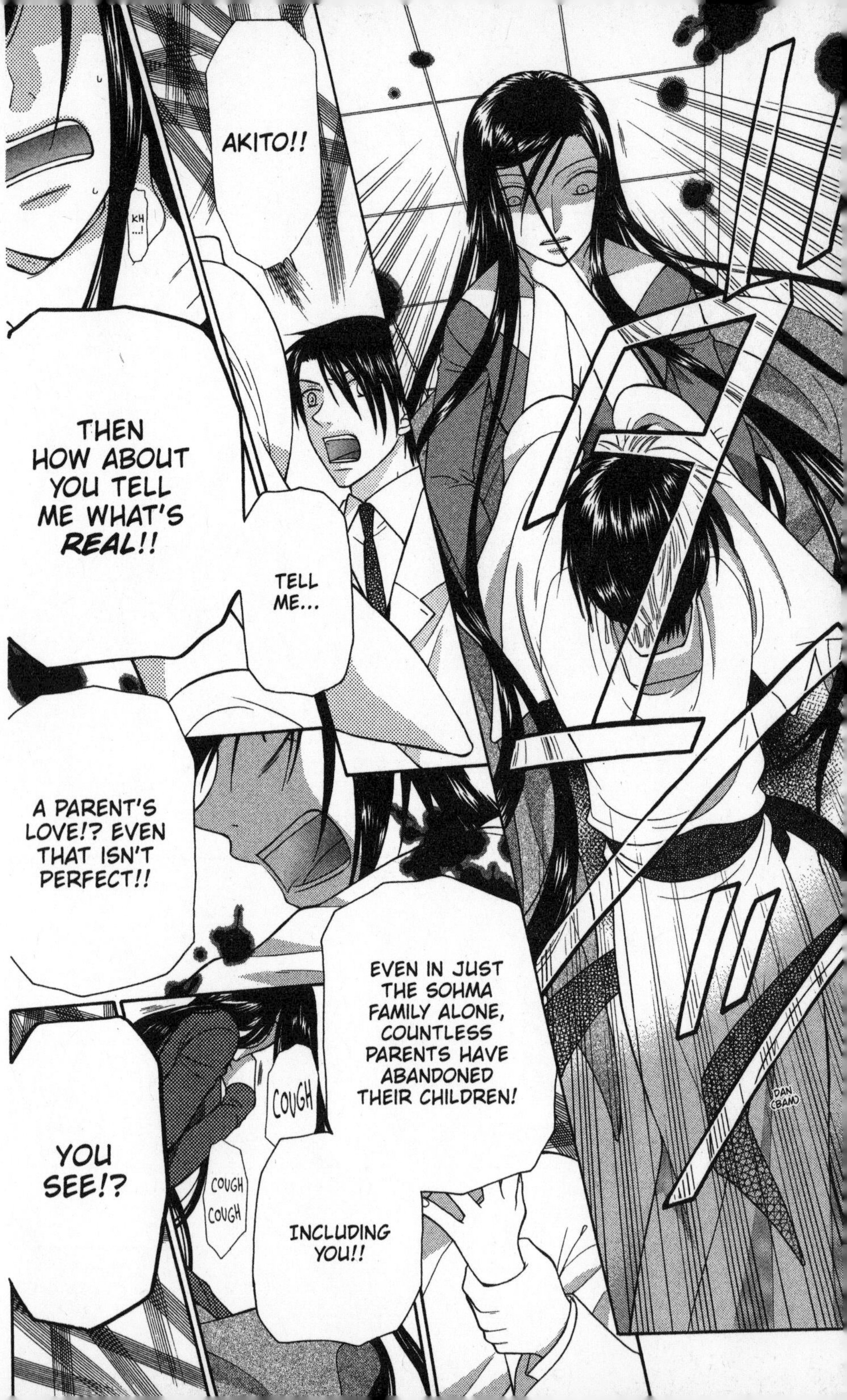
DAN (BAM)
AKITO!!
KH ...!
TELL ME...
THEN HOW ABOUT YOU TELL ME WHAT'S *REAL*!!
A PARENT'S LOVE!? EVEN THAT ISN'T PERFECT!!
EVEN IN JUST THE SOHMA FAMILY ALONE, COUNTLESS PARENTS HAVE ABANDONED THEIR CHILDREN!
COUGH
COUGH COUGH
YOU SEE!?
INCLUDING YOU!!

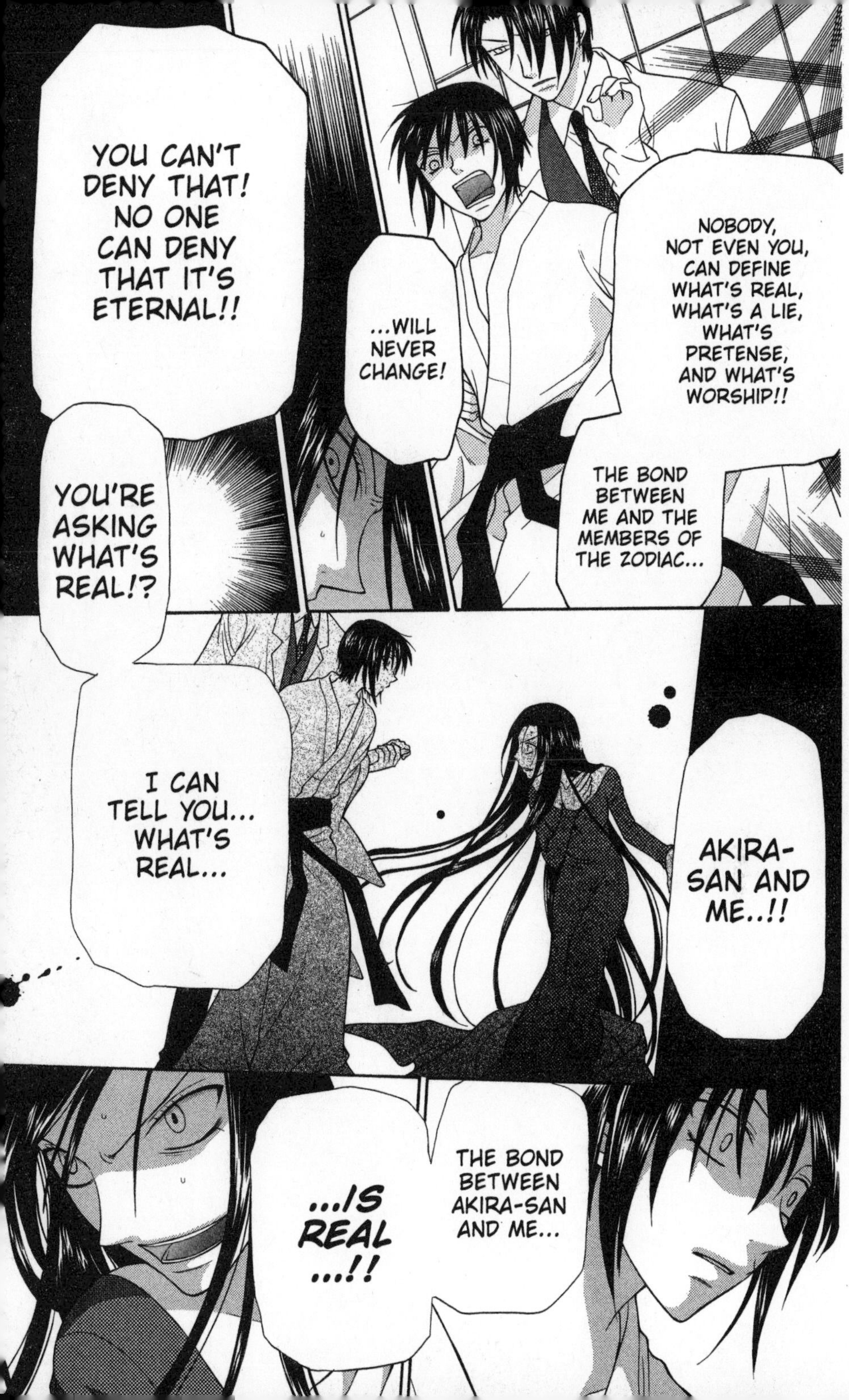
NOBODY, NOT EVEN YOU, CAN DEFINE WHAT'S REAL, WHAT'S A LIE, WHAT'S PRETENSE, AND WHAT'S WORSHIP!!
THE BOND BETWEEN ME AND THE MEMBERS OF THE ZODIAC...
...WILL NEVER CHANGE!
YOU CAN'T DENY THAT! NO ONE CAN DENY THAT IT'S ETERNAL!!
YOU'RE ASKING WHAT'S REAL!?
I CAN TELL YOU... WHAT'S REAL...
AKIRA-SAN AND ME..!!
THE BOND BETWEEN AKIRA-SAN AND ME...
...IS REAL ...!!

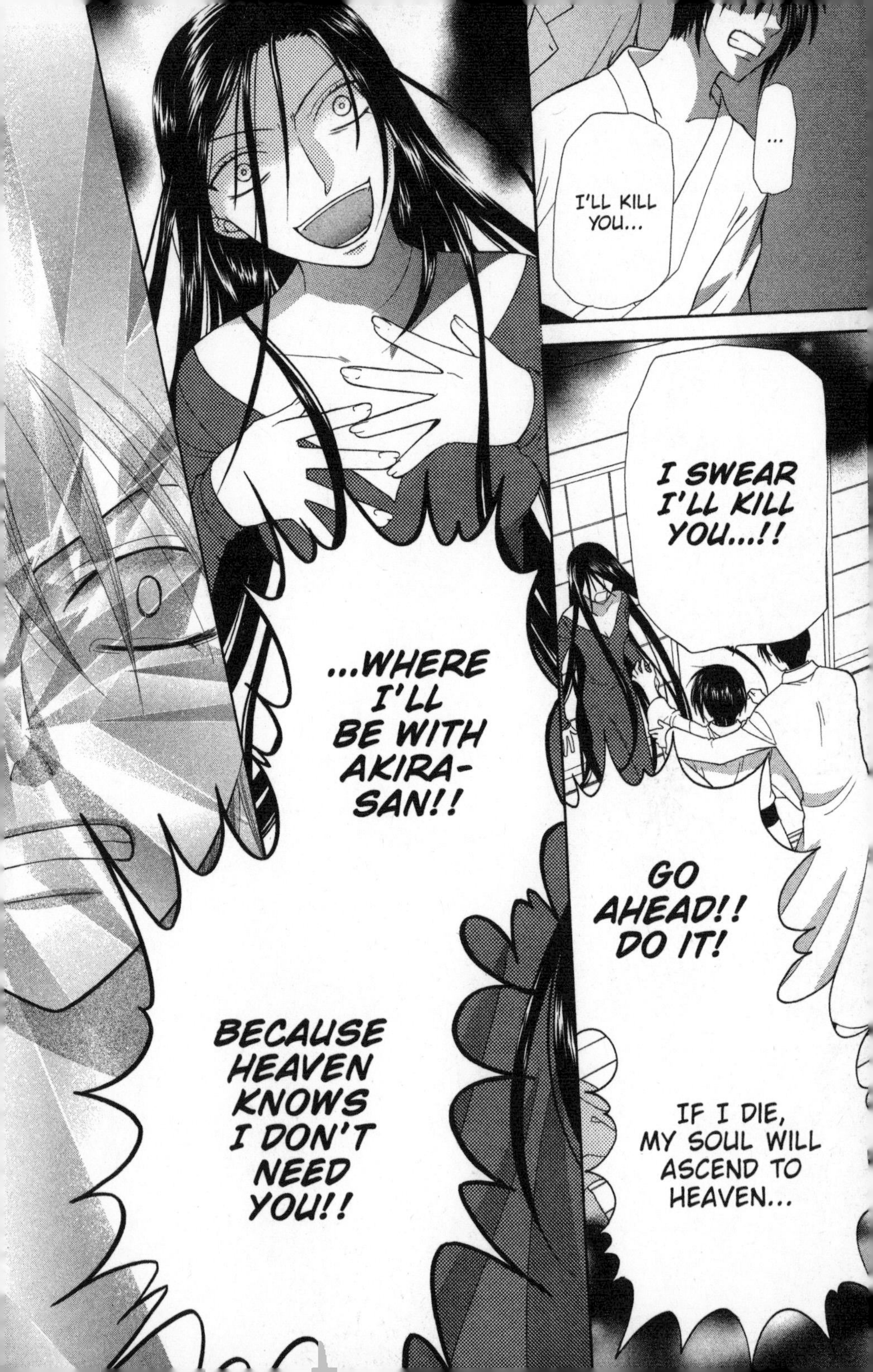
...
I'LL KILL YOU...
I SWEAR I'LL KILL YOU...!!
GO AHEAD!! DO IT!
IF I DIE, MY SOUL WILL ASCEND TO HEAVEN...
...WHERE I'LL BE WITH AKIRA-SAN!!
BECAUSE HEAVEN KNOWS I DON'T NEED YOU!!

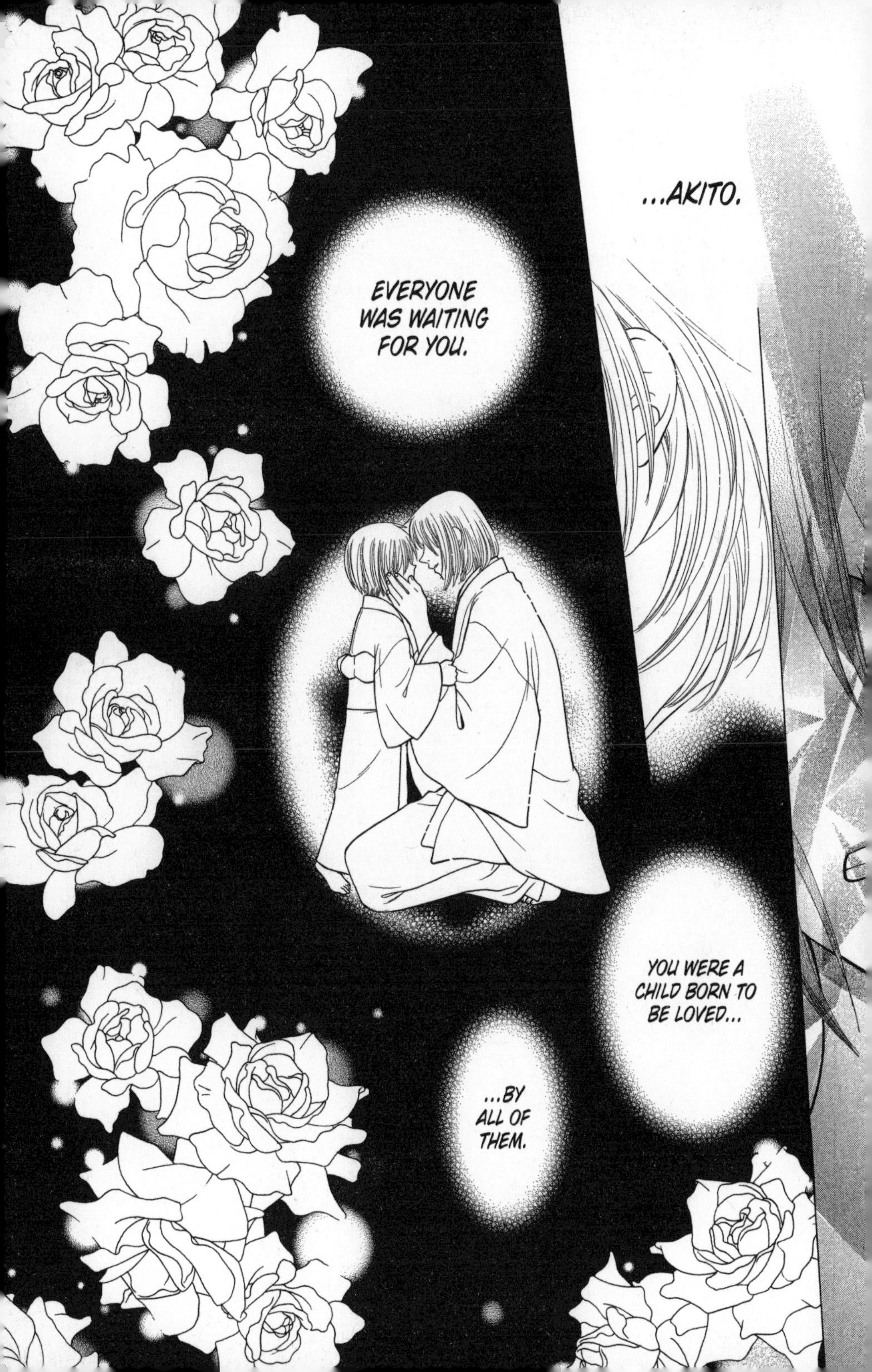
...AKITO.
EVERYONE WAS WAITING FOR YOU.
YOU WERE A CHILD BORN TO BE LOVED...
...BY ALL OF THEM.

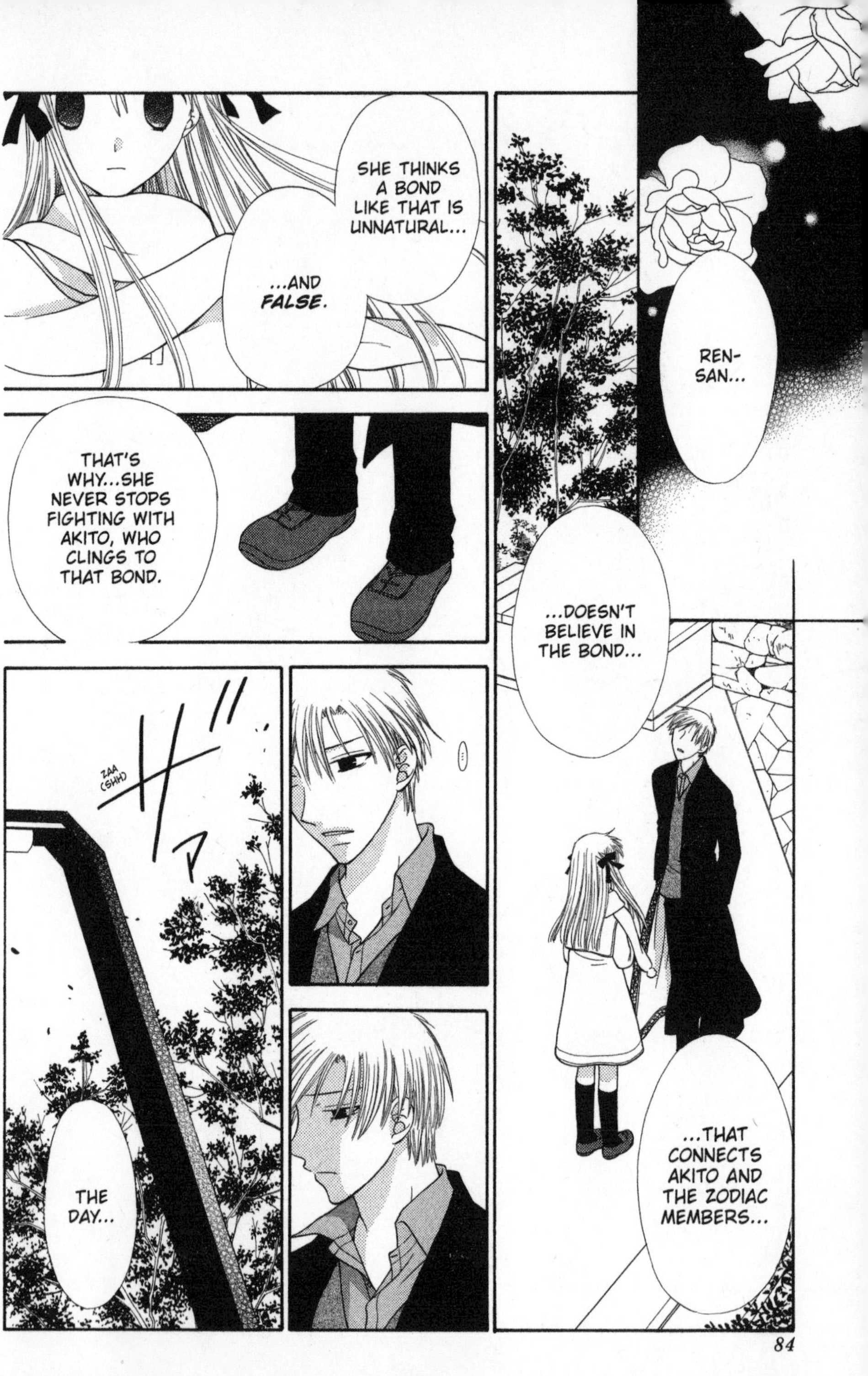
REN-SAN...
...DOESN'T BELIEVE IN THE BOND...
...THAT CONNECTS AKITO AND THE ZODIAC MEMBERS...
SHE THINKS A BOND LIKE THAT IS UNNATURAL...
...AND FALSE.
THAT'S WHY...SHE NEVER STOPS FIGHTING WITH AKITO, WHO CLINGS TO THAT BOND.
...
ZAA (SHH)
THE DAY...

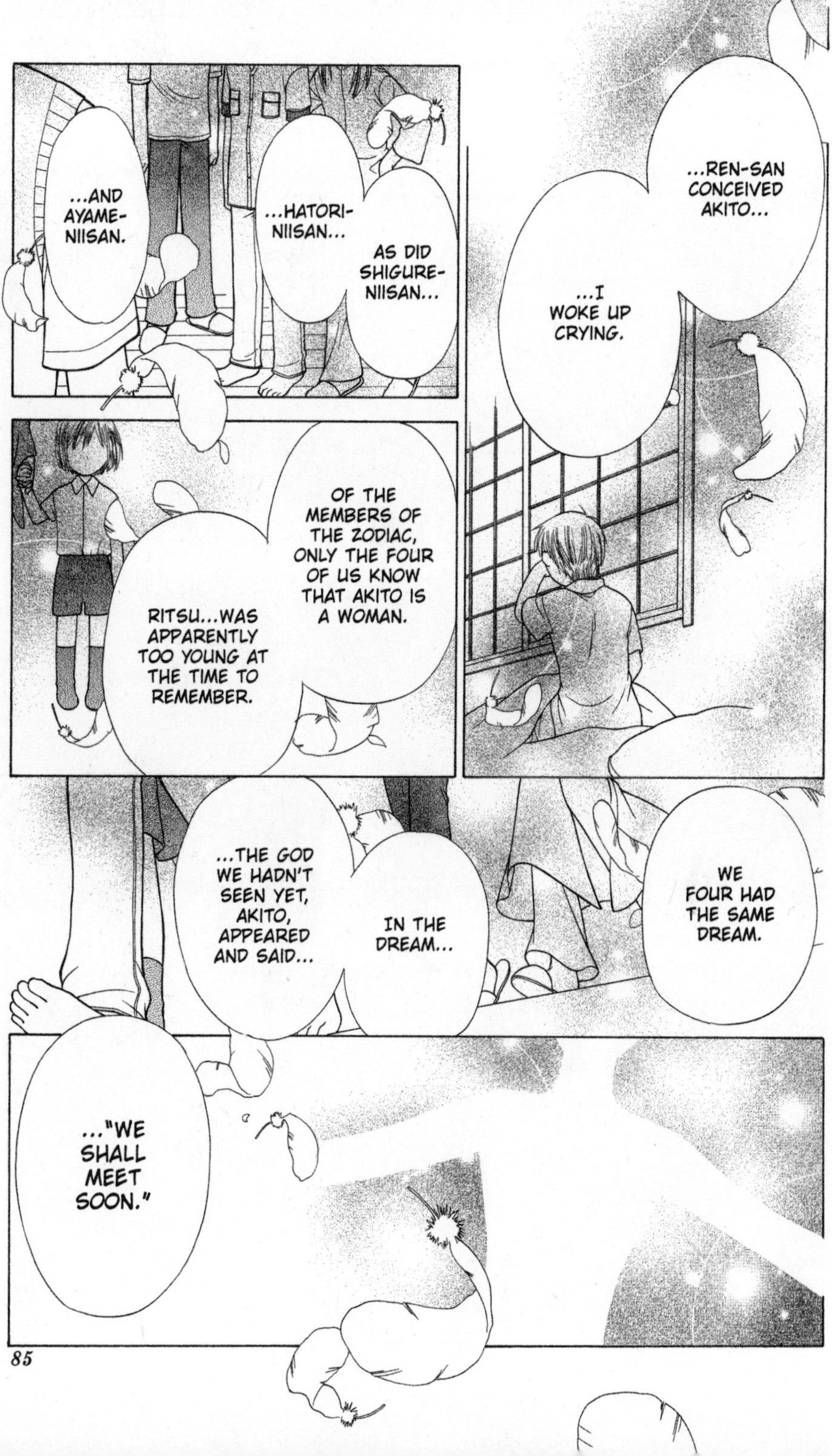
...REN-SAN CONCEIVED AKITO...
...I WOKE UP CRYING.
...HATORI-NIISAN...
AS DID SHIGURE-NIISAN...
...AND AYAME-NIISAN.
OF THE MEMBERS OF THE ZODIAC, ONLY THE FOUR OF US KNOW THAT AKITO IS A WOMAN.
RITSU...WAS APPARENTLY TOO YOUNG AT THE TIME TO REMEMBER.
WE FOUR HAD THE SAME DREAM.
IN THE DREAM...
...THE GOD WE HADN'T SEEN YET, AKITO, APPEARED AND SAID...
..."WE SHALL MEET SOON."

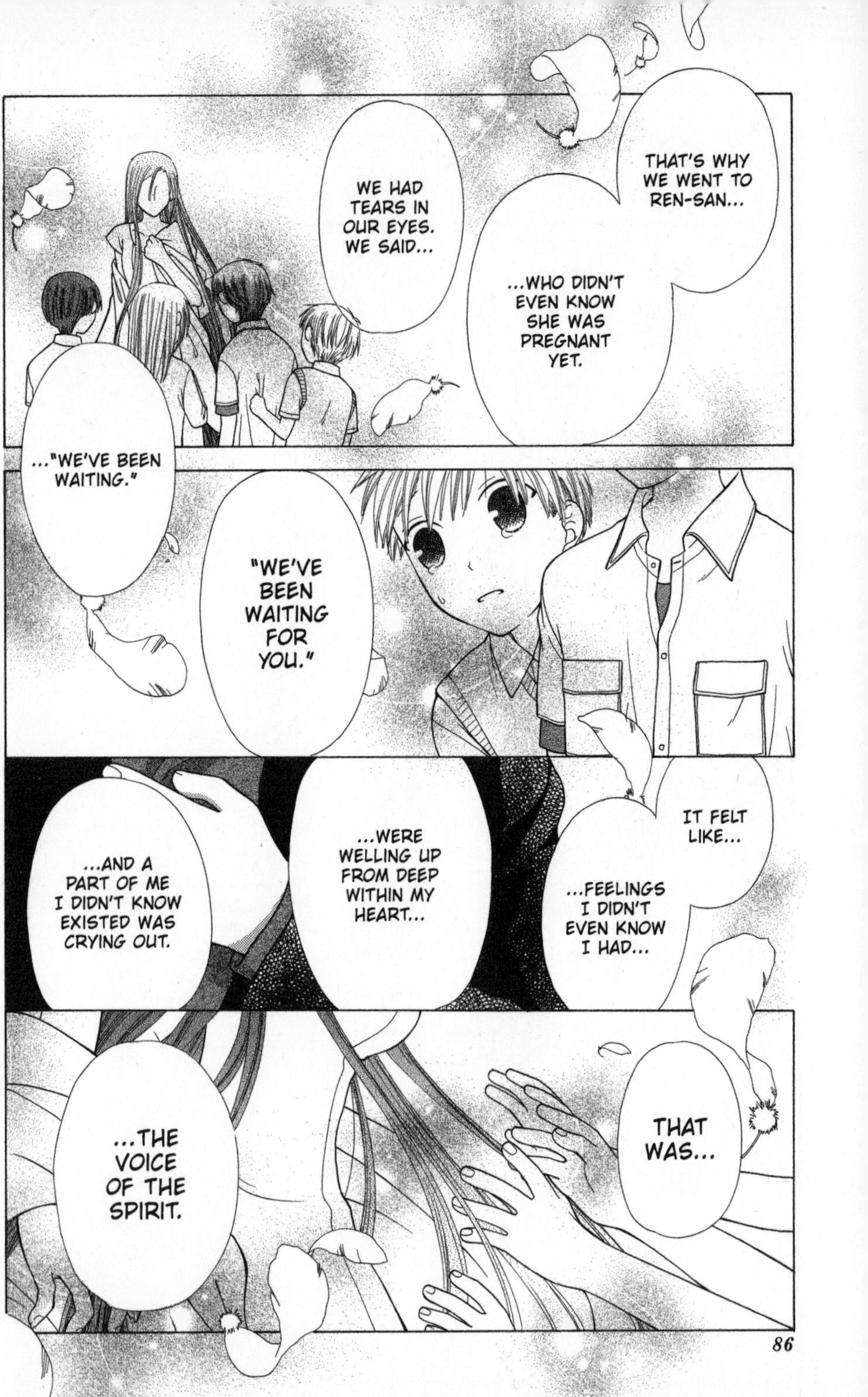
THAT'S WHY WE WENT TO REN-SAN...
...WHO DIDN'T EVEN KNOW SHE WAS PREGNANT YET.
WE HAD TEARS IN OUR EYES. WE SAID...
..."WE'VE BEEN WAITING."
"WE'VE BEEN WAITING FOR YOU."
IT FELT LIKE...
...FEELINGS I DIDN'T EVEN KNOW I HAD...
...WERE WELLING UP FROM DEEP WITHIN MY HEART...
...AND A PART OF ME I DIDN'T KNOW EXISTED WAS CRYING OUT.
THAT WAS...
...THE VOICE OF THE SPIRIT.

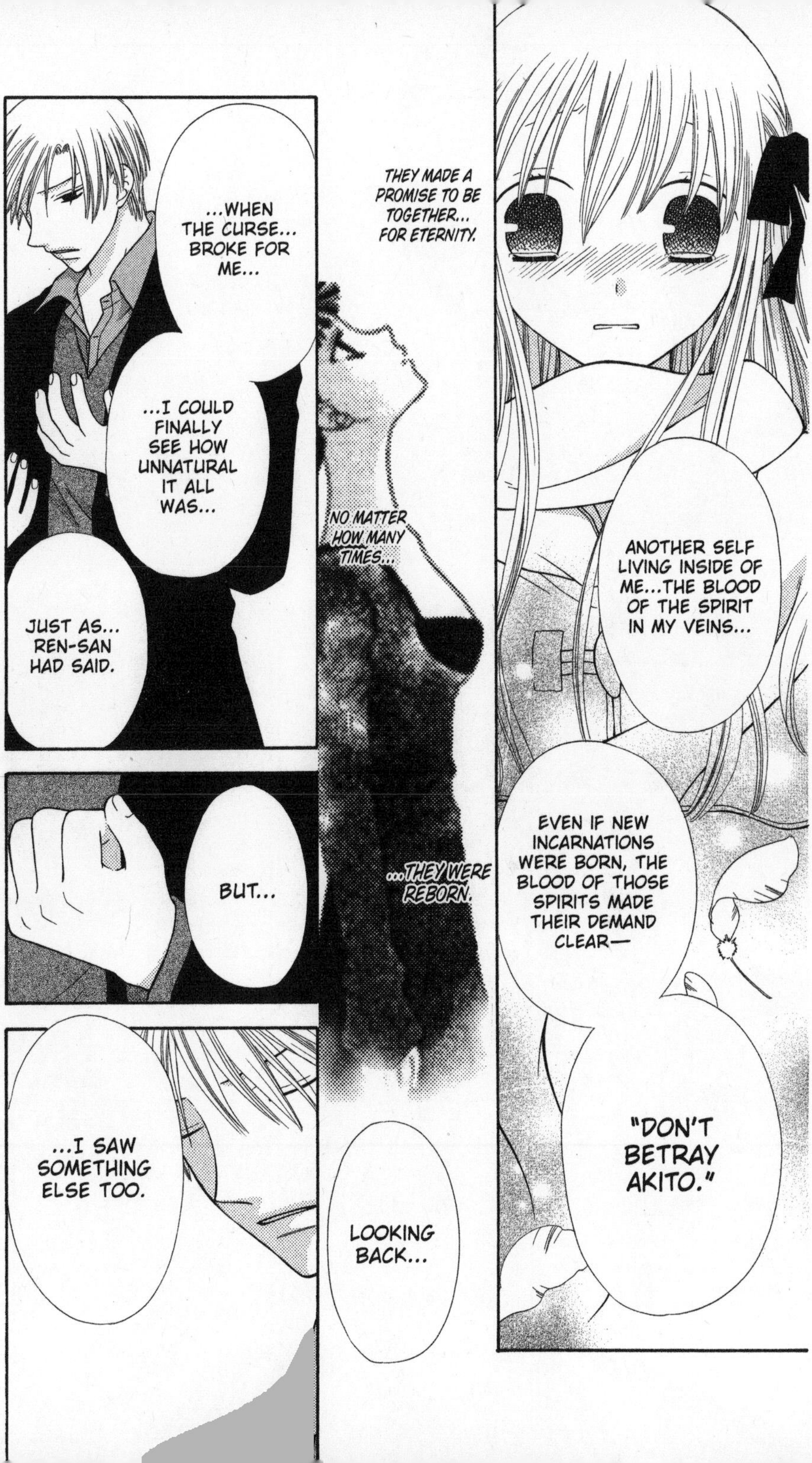
ANOTHER SELF LIVING INSIDE OF ME...THE BLOOD OF THE SPIRIT IN MY VEINS...
EVEN IF NEW INCARNATIONS WERE BORN, THE BLOOD OF THOSE SPIRITS MADE THEIR DEMAND CLEAR—
"DON'T BETRAY AKITO."
THEY MADE A PROMISE TO BE TOGETHER... FOR ETERNITY.
NO MATTER HOW MANY TIMES...
...THEY WERE REBORN.
...WHEN THE CURSE... BROKE FOR ME...
...I COULD FINALLY SEE HOW UNNATURAL IT ALL WAS...
JUST AS... REN-SAN HAD SAID.
BUT...
LOOKING BACK...
...I SAW SOMETHING ELSE TOO.

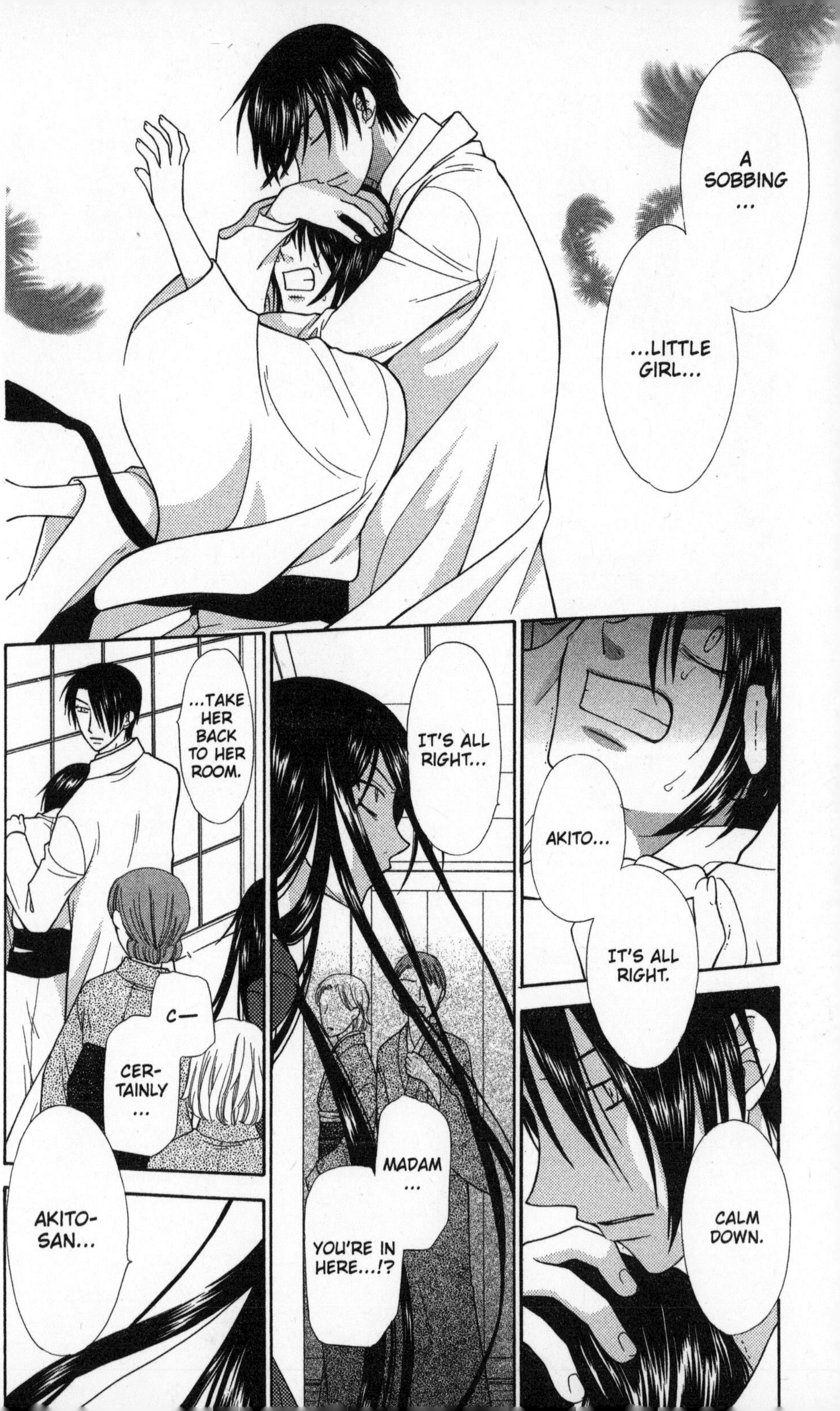
A SOBBING...
...LITTLE GIRL...
AKITO...
IT'S ALL RIGHT.
CALM DOWN.
IT'S ALL RIGHT...
MADAM...
YOU'RE IN HERE...!?
...TAKE HER BACK TO HER ROOM.
C—
CER-TAINLY...
AKITO-SAN...

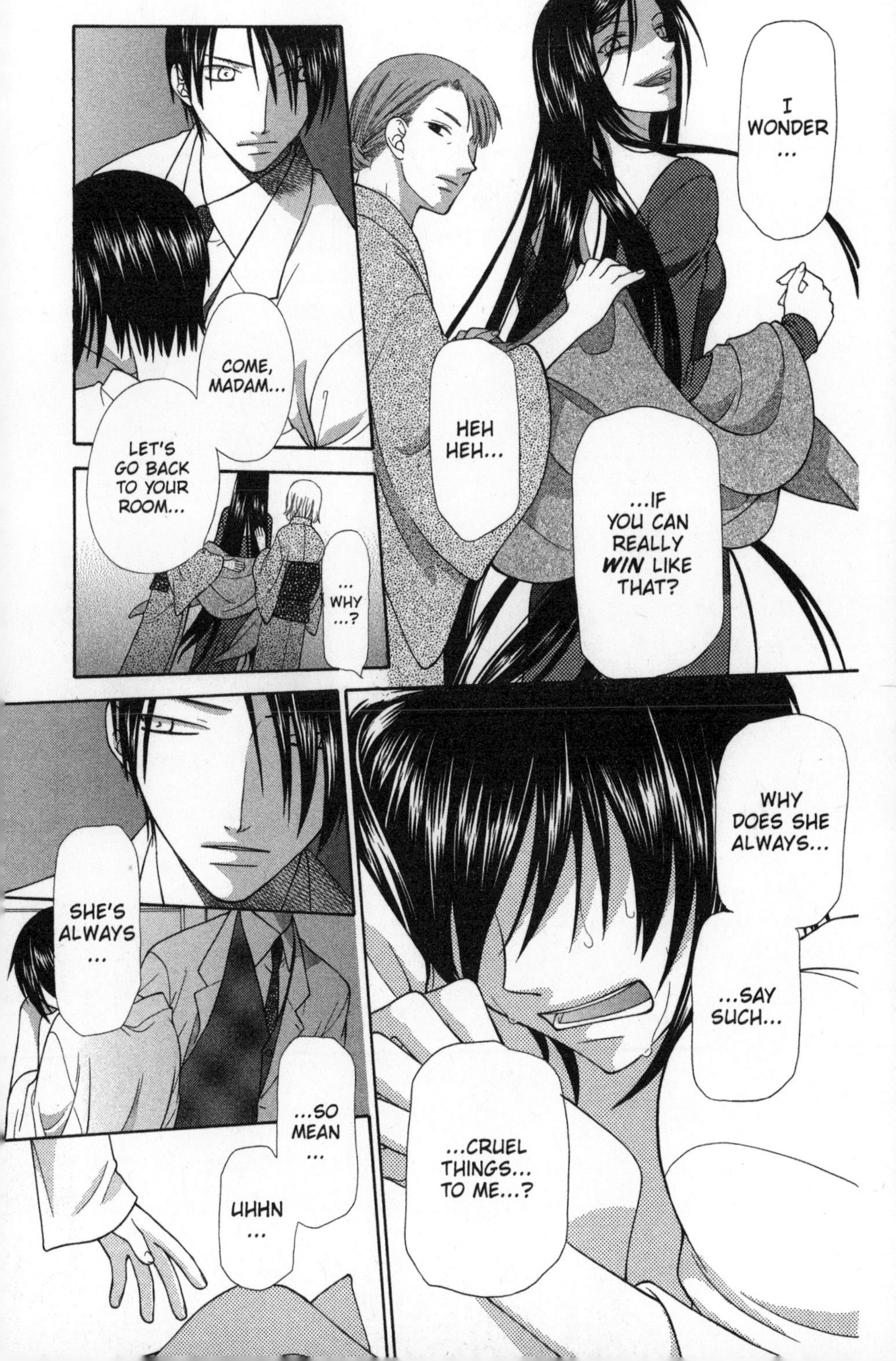

I WONDER...
HEH HEH...
...IF YOU CAN REALLY WIN LIKE THAT?
COME, MADAM...
LET'S GO BACK TO YOUR ROOM...
...WHY...?
WHY DOES SHE ALWAYS...
...SAY SUCH...
...CRUEL THINGS... TO ME...?
SHE'S ALWAYS...
...SO MEAN...
UHHN...

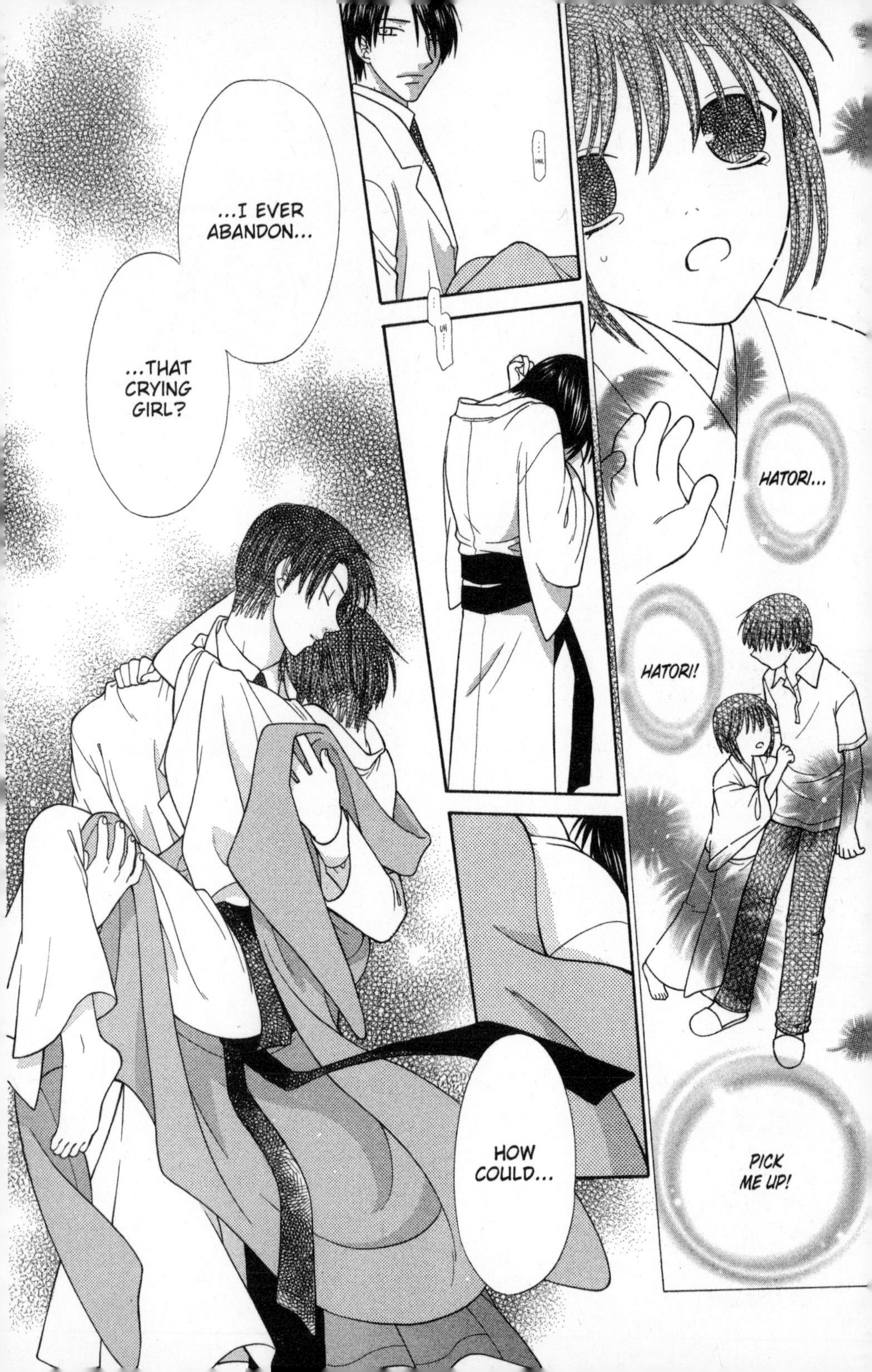
HATORI...
HATORI!
PICK ME UP!
...UMM.
...UH...
HOW COULD...
...I EVER ABANDON...
...THAT CRYING GIRL?

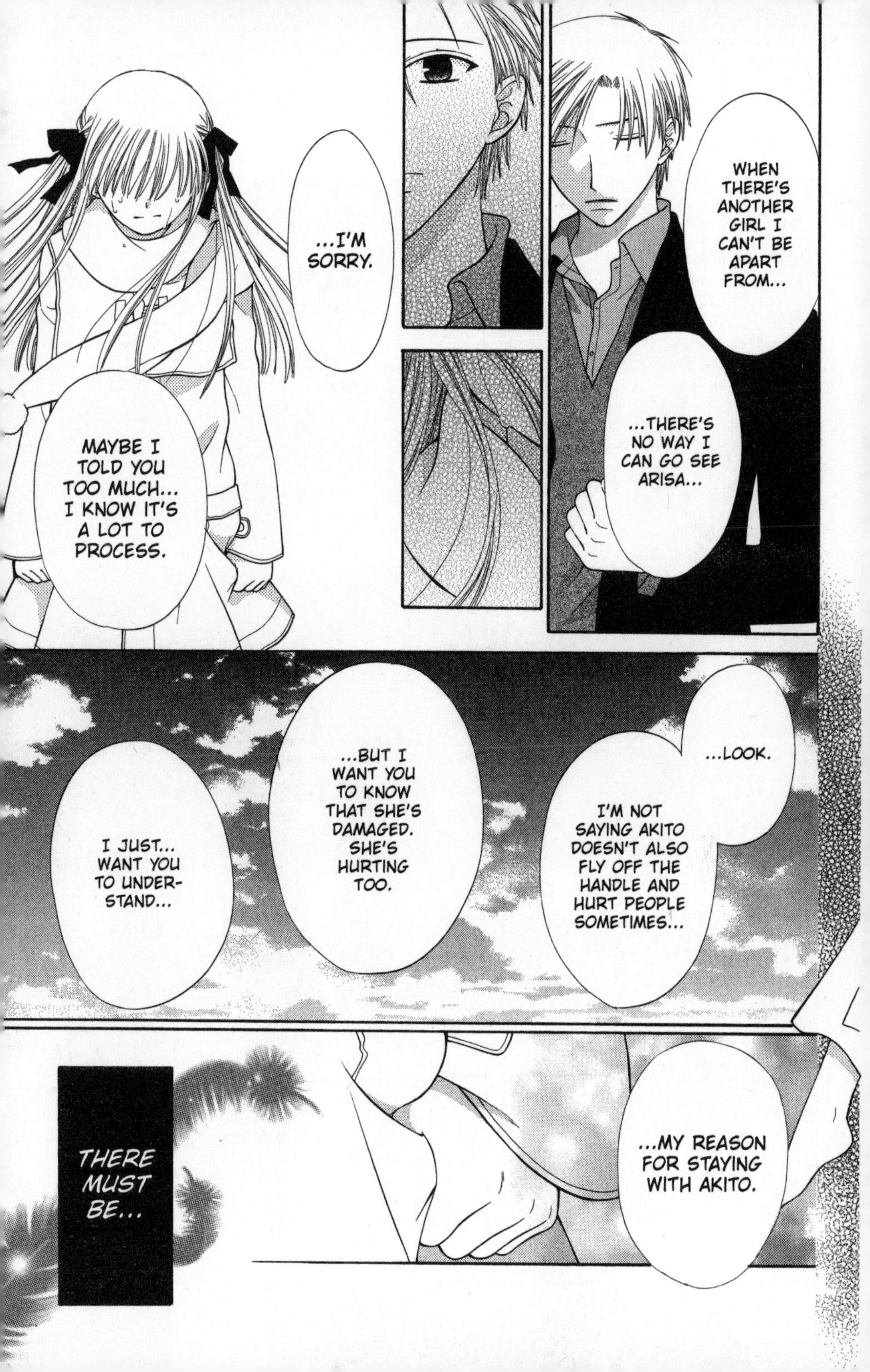
WHEN THERE'S ANOTHER GIRL I CAN'T BE APART FROM...
...THERE'S NO WAY I CAN GO SEE ARISA...
...I'M SORRY.
MAYBE I TOLD YOU TOO MUCH... I KNOW IT'S A LOT TO PROCESS.
...LOOK.
I'M NOT SAYING AKITO DOESN'T ALSO FLY OFF THE HANDLE AND HURT PEOPLE SOMETIMES...
...BUT I WANT YOU TO KNOW THAT SHE'S DAMAGED. SHE'S HURTING TOO.
I JUST... WANT YOU TO UNDER-STAND...
...MY REASON FOR STAYING WITH AKITO.
THERE MUST BE...

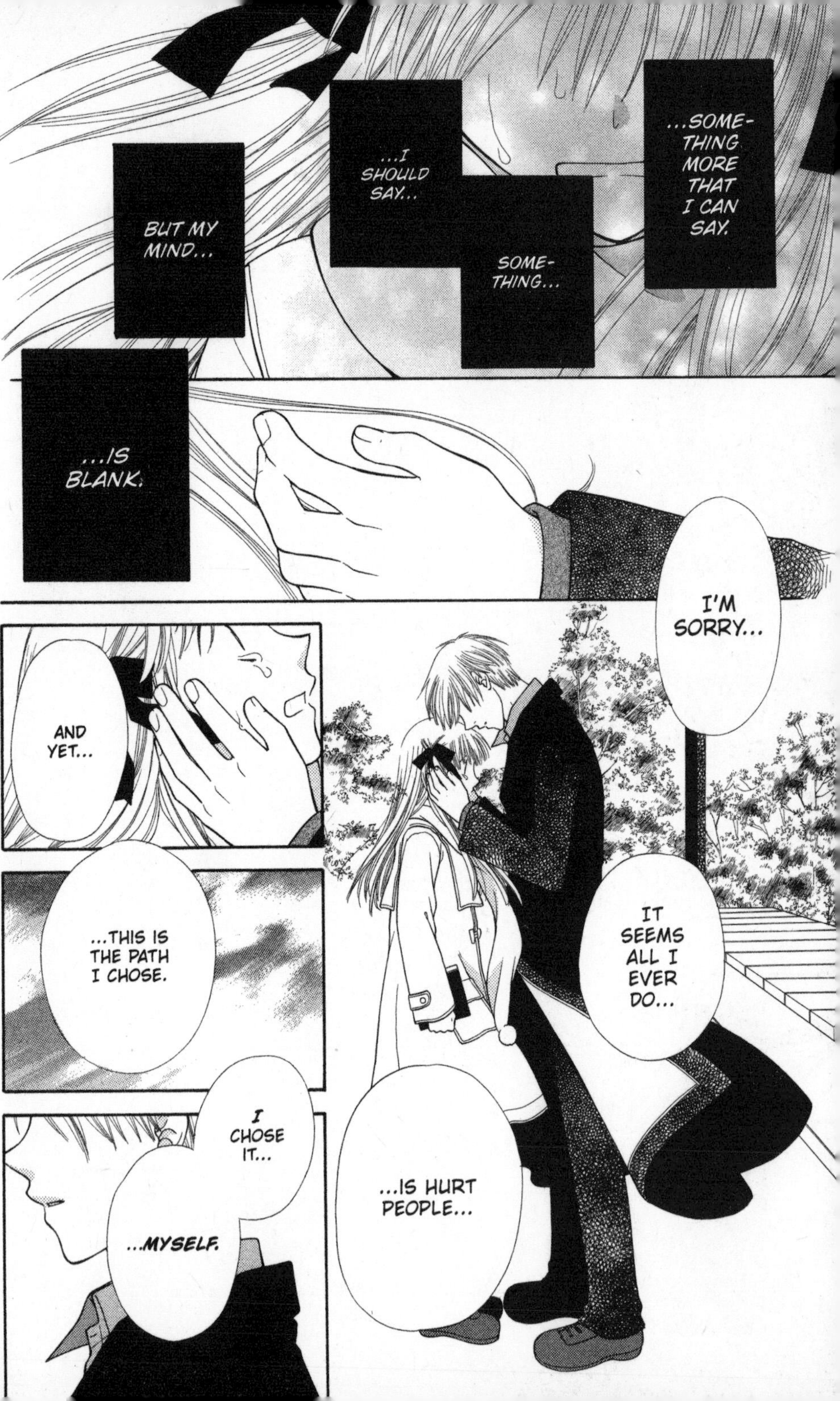
...I SHOULD SAY...
SOME-THING...
...SOME-THING MORE THAT I CAN SAY.
BUT MY MIND...
...IS BLANK.
I'M SORRY...
IT SEEMS ALL I EVER DO...
...IS HURT PEOPLE...
AND YET...
...THIS IS THE PATH I CHOSE.
I CHOSE IT...
...MYSELF.

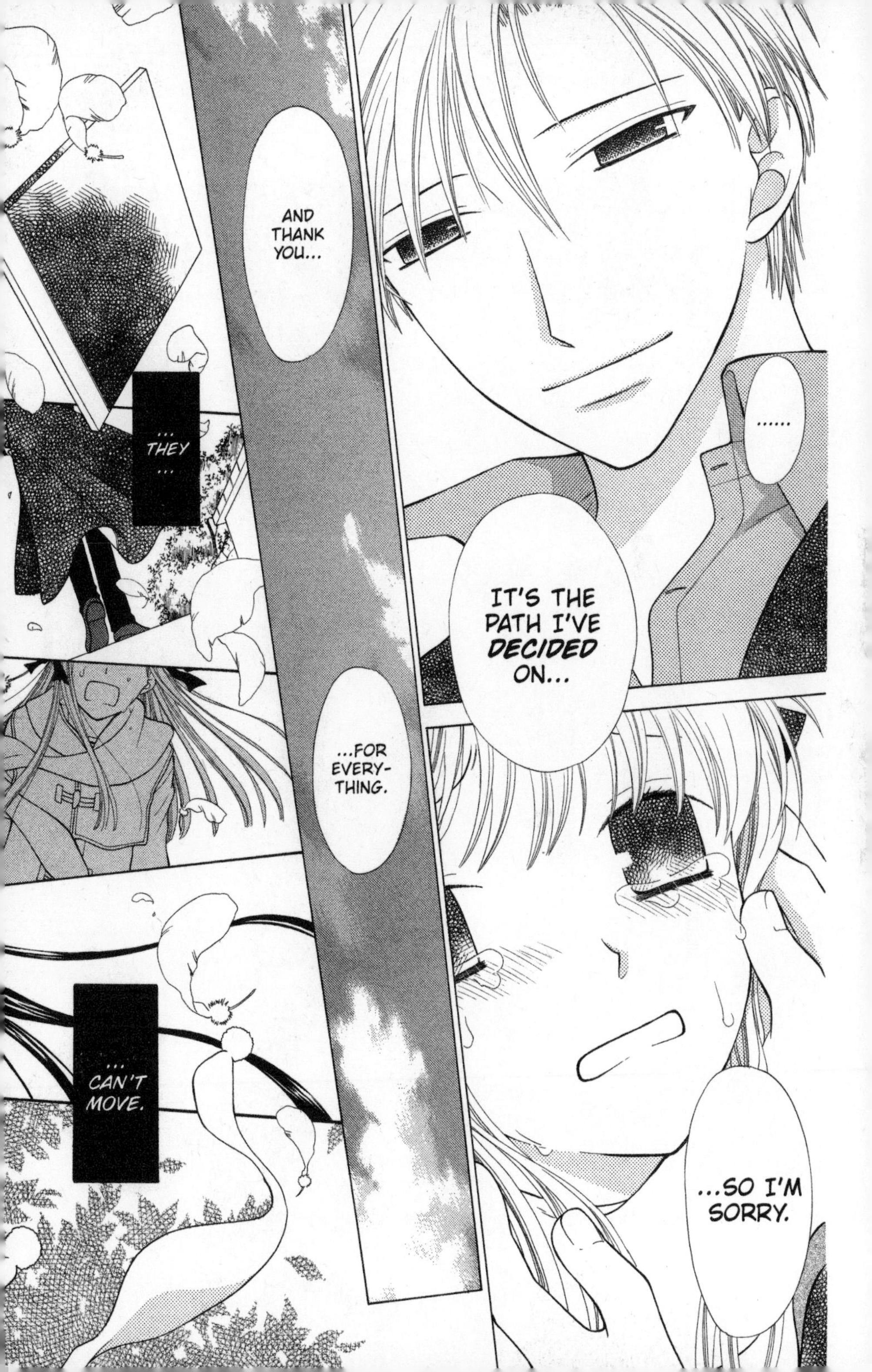
......
IT'S THE PATH I'VE DECIDED ON...
...SO I'M SORRY.
AND THANK YOU...
...FOR EVERYTHING.
...THEY...
...CAN'T MOVE.

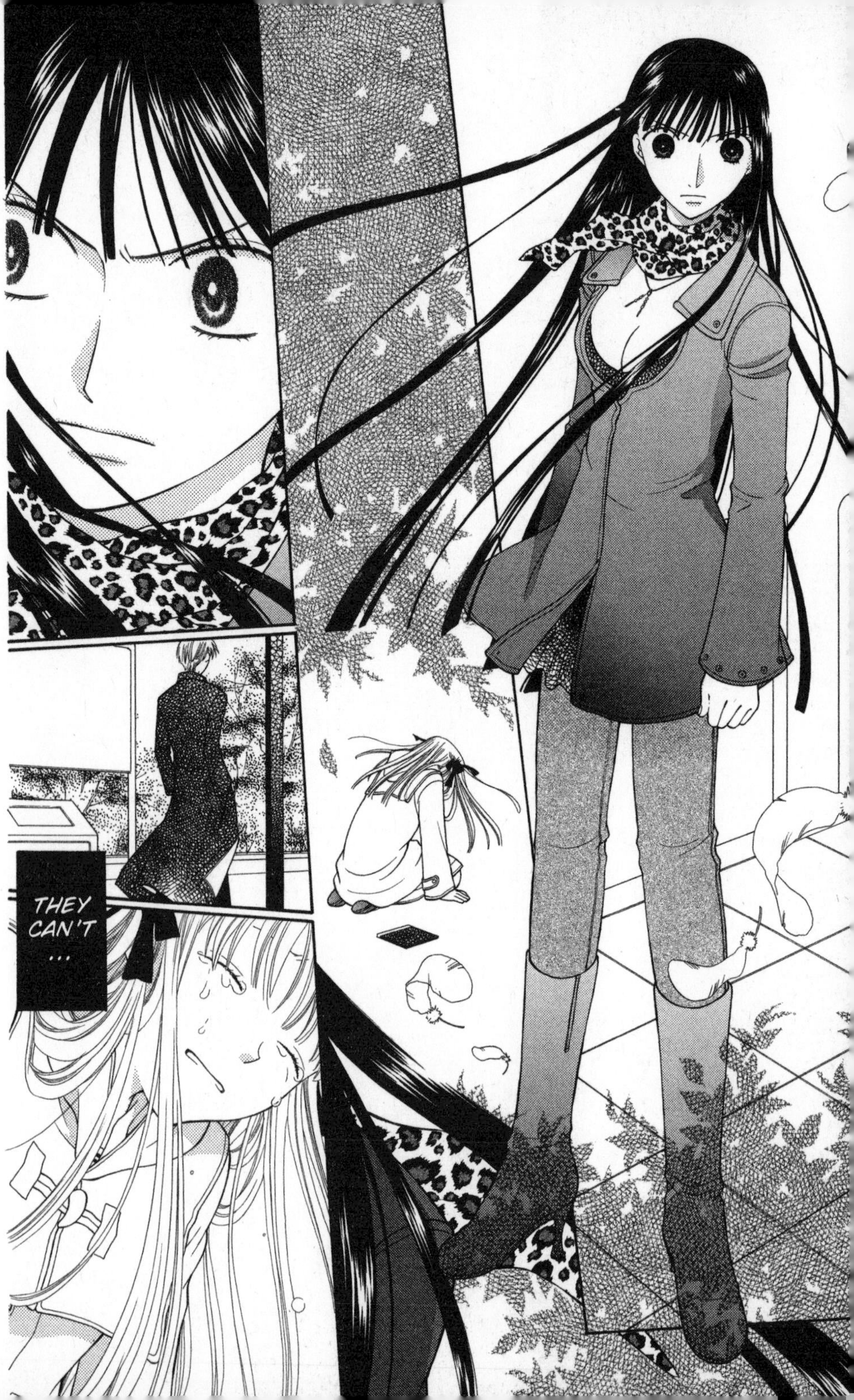
THEY CAN'T ...

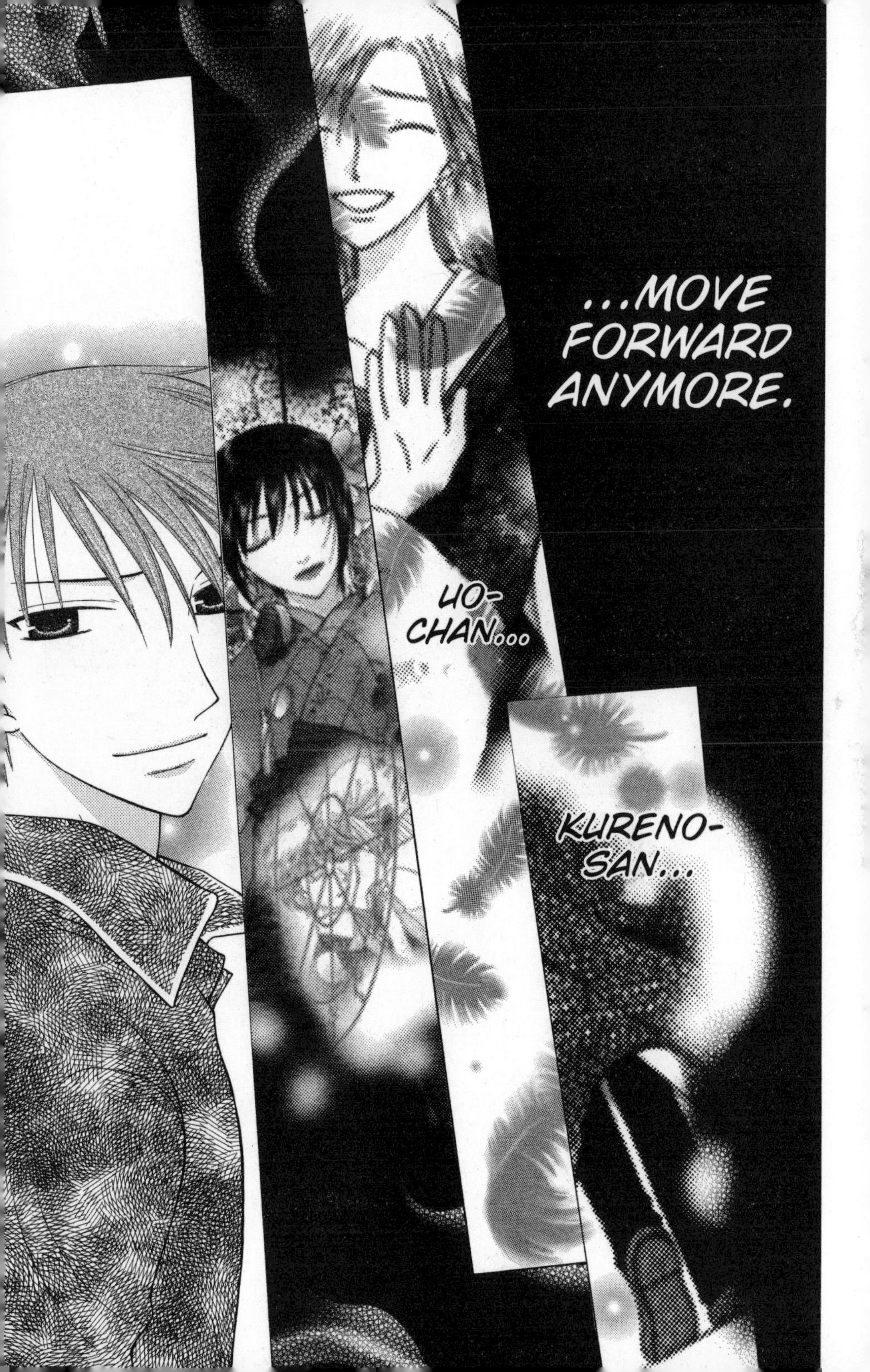
...MOVE FORWARD ANYMORE.
UO-CHAN...
KURENO-SAN...

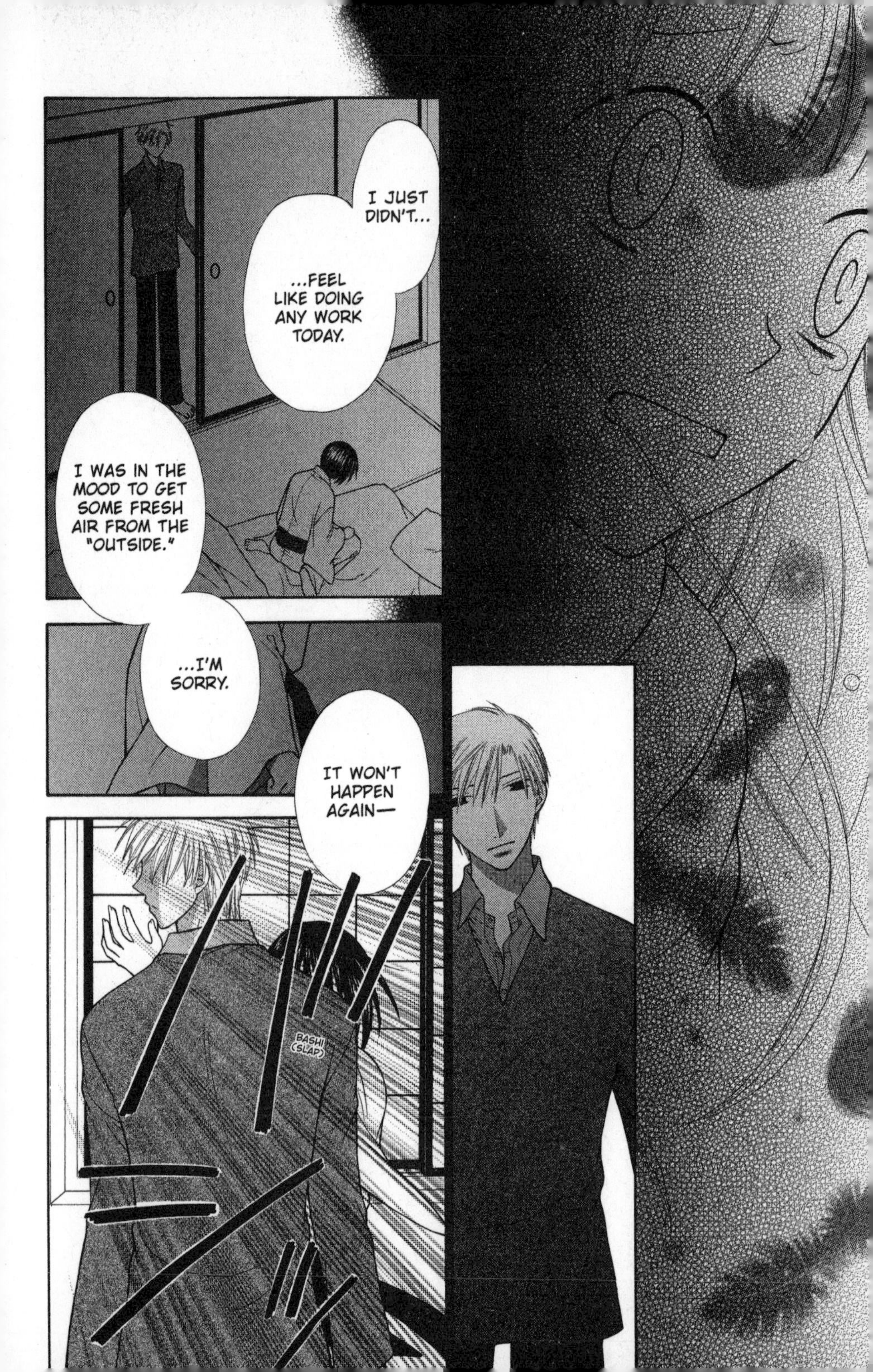

I JUST DIDN'T...
...FEEL LIKE DOING ANY WORK TODAY.
I WAS IN THE MOOD TO GET SOME FRESH AIR FROM THE "OUTSIDE."
...I'M SORRY.
IT WON'T HAPPEN AGAIN—
BASHI (SLAP)

SORROW...

...CONNECTS
US LIKE A
SPIRAL...

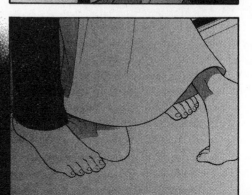

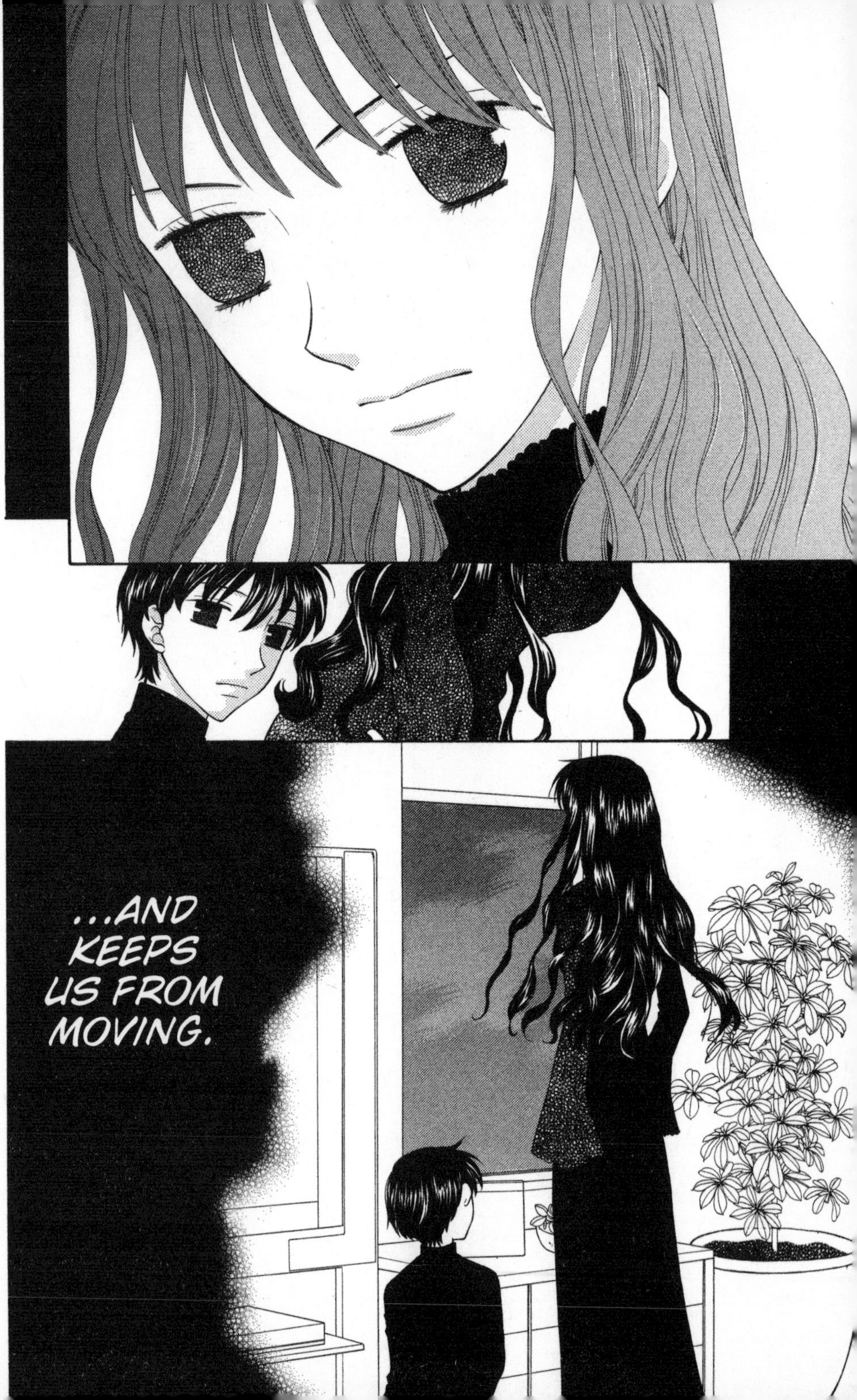
...AND KEEPS US FROM MOVING.

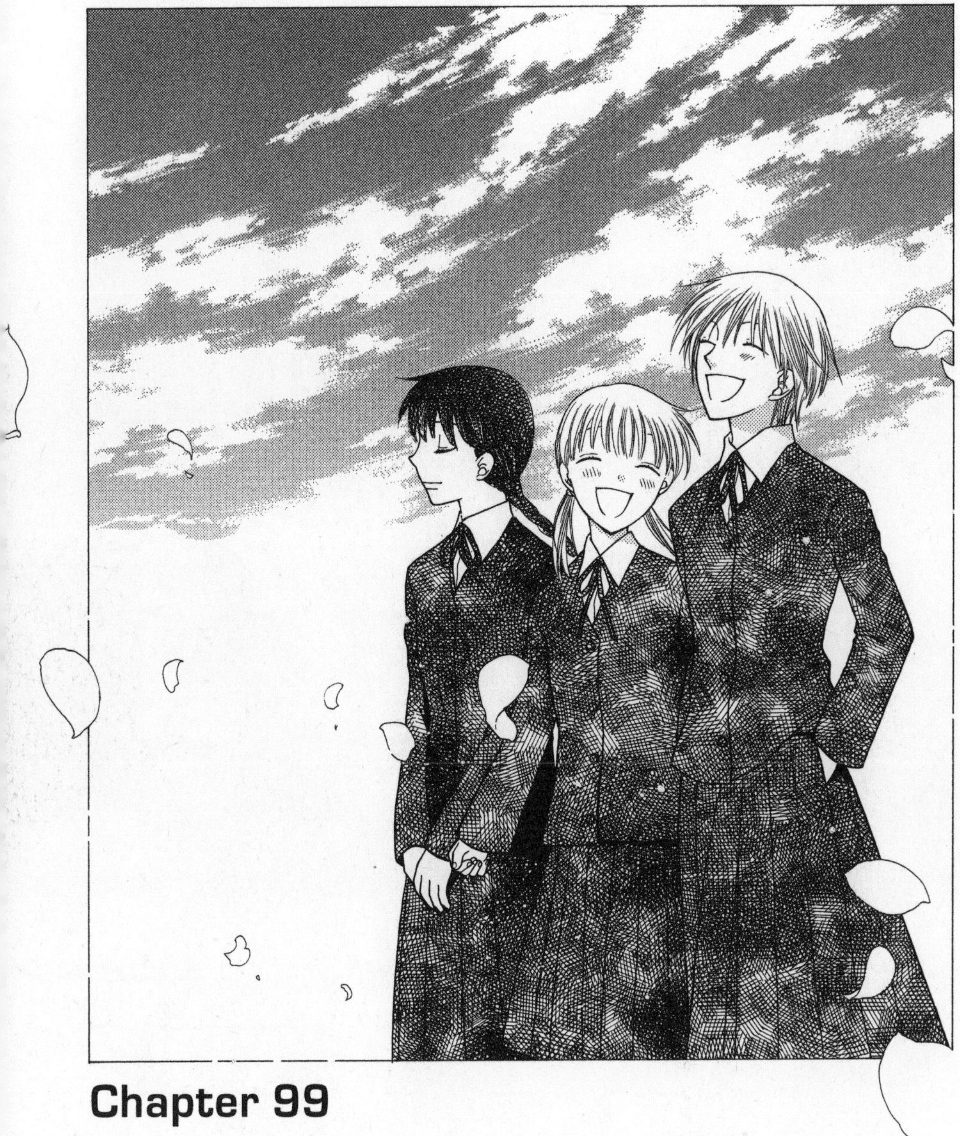

Chapter 99

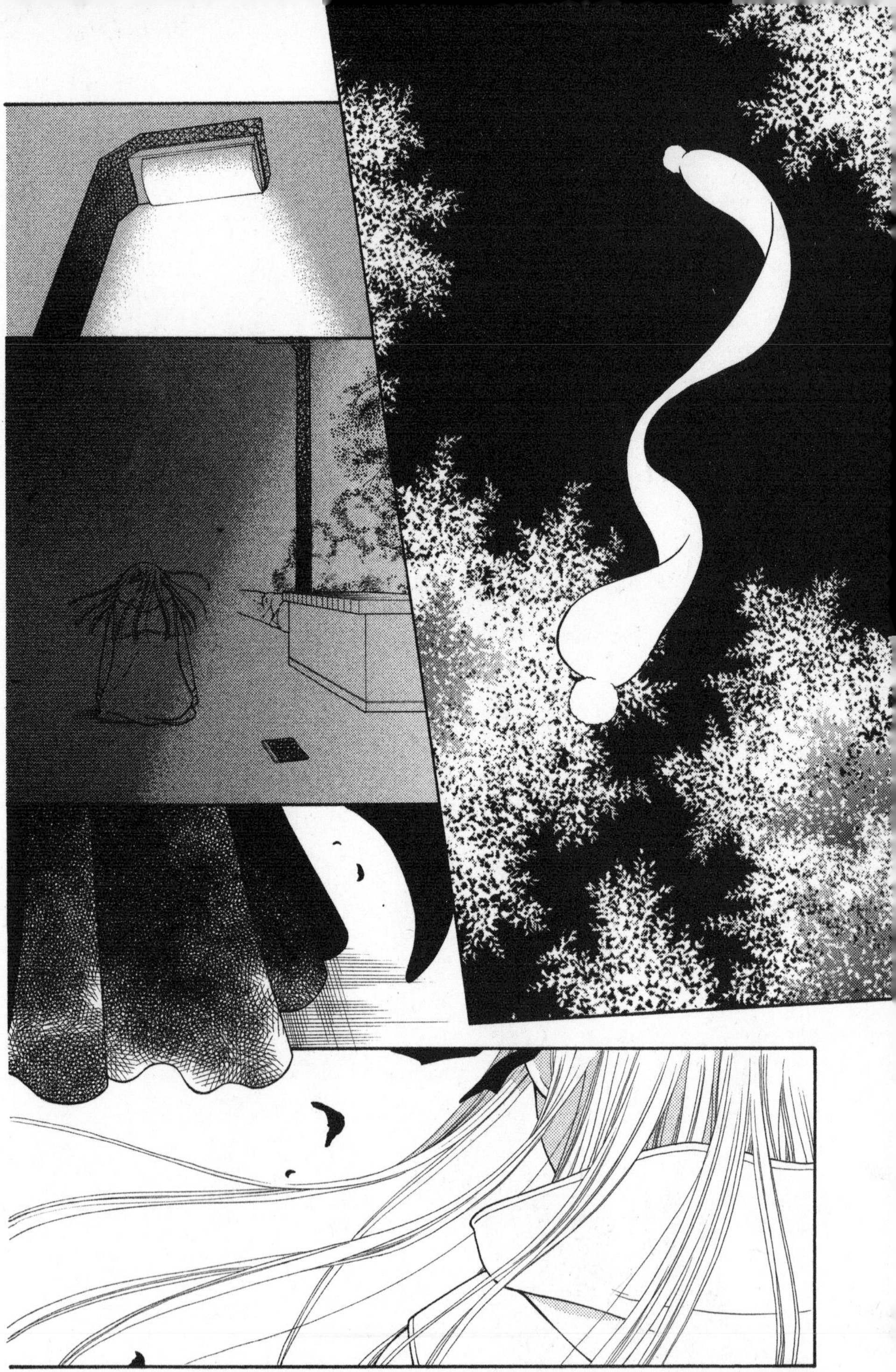

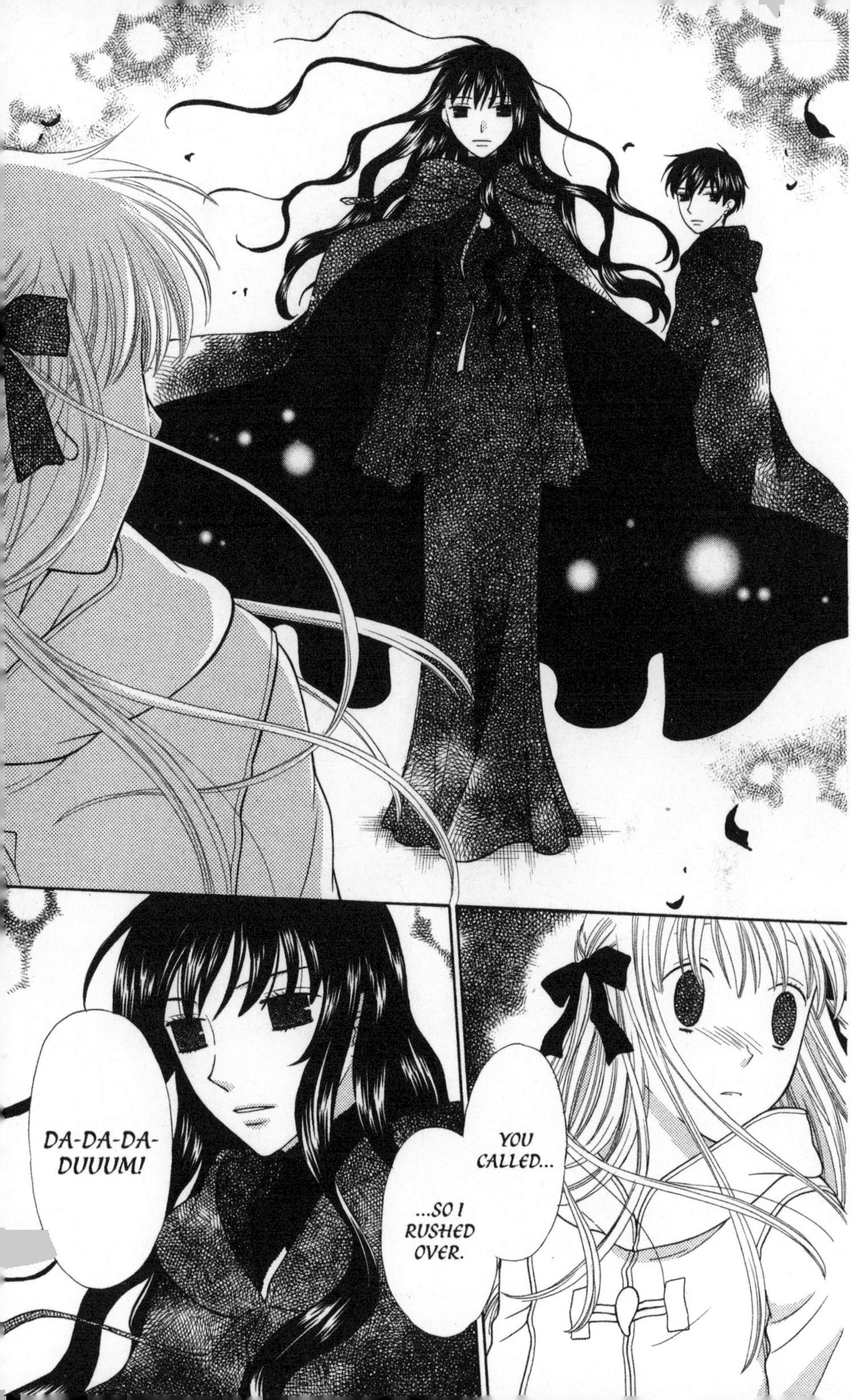
YOU CALLED...
...SO I RUSHED OVER.
DA-DA-DA-DUUUM!

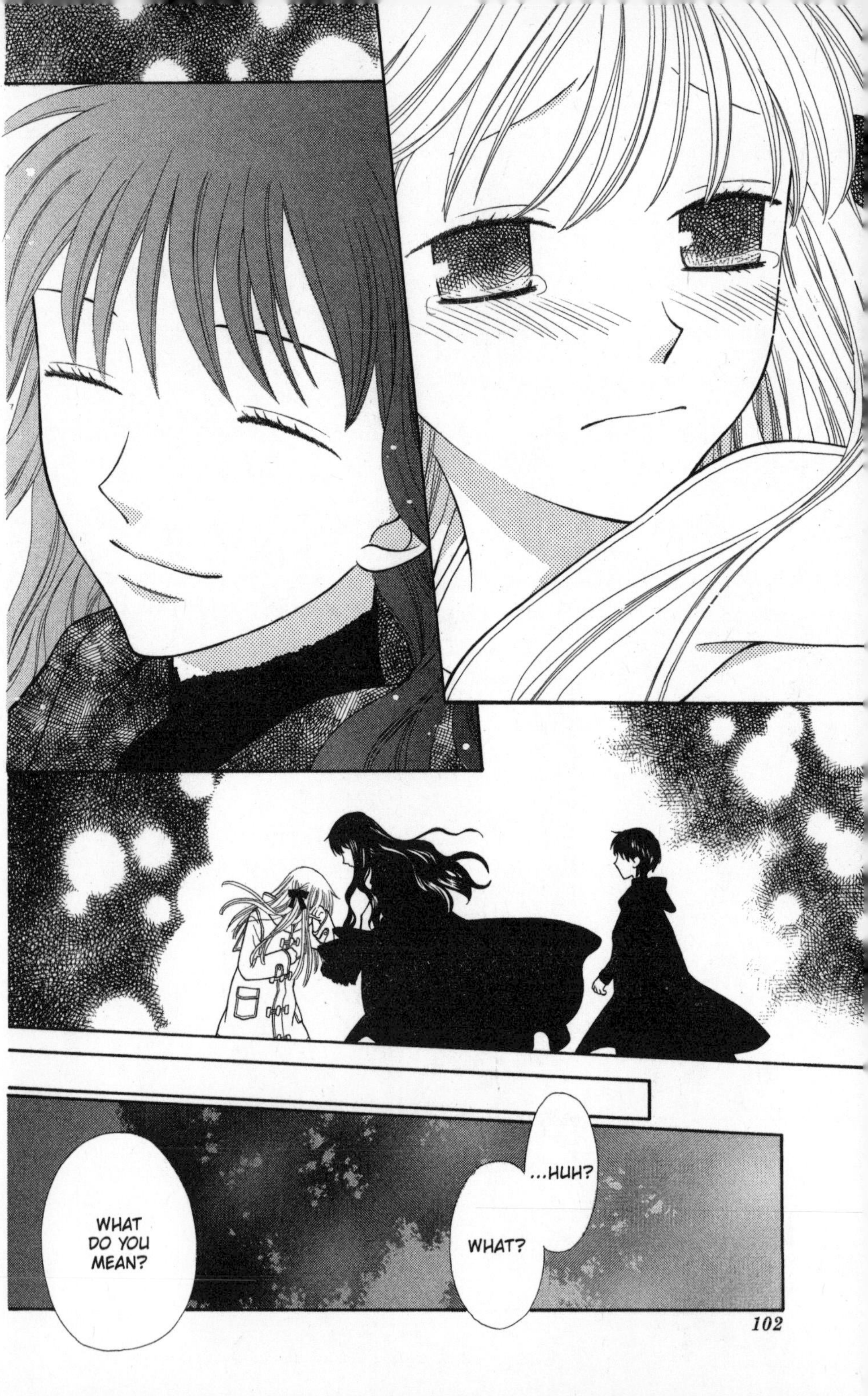
...HUH?
WHAT?
WHAT DO YOU MEAN?

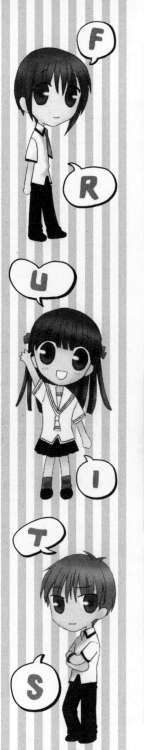

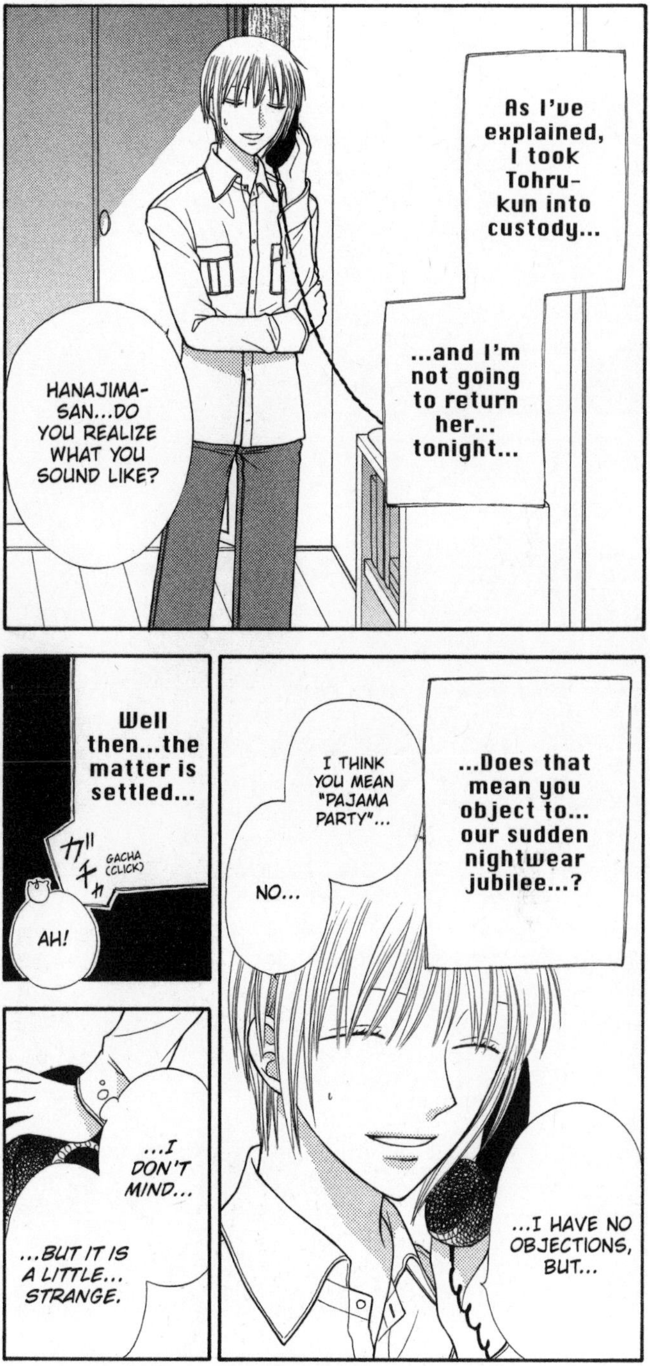
As I've explained, I took Tohru-kun into custody...
...and I'm not going to return her... tonight...
HANAJIMA-SAN...DO YOU REALIZE WHAT YOU SOUND LIKE?
...Does that mean you object to... our sudden nightwear jubilee...?
I THINK YOU MEAN "PAJAMA PARTY"...
NO...
...I HAVE NO OBJECTIONS, BUT...
Well then...the matter is settled...
ガチャ
GACHA (CLICK)
AH!
...I DON'T MIND...
...BUT IT IS A LITTLE... STRANGE.

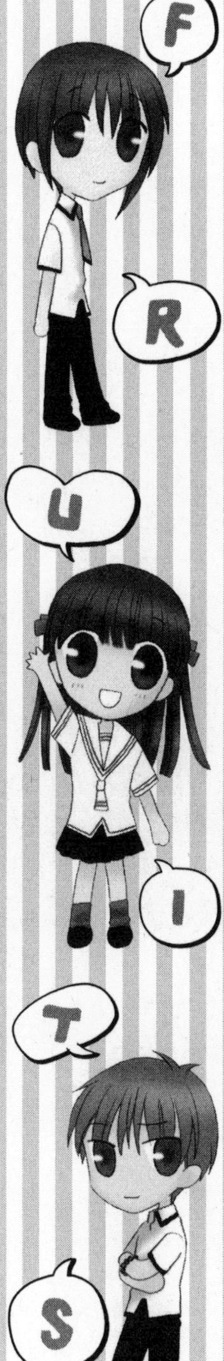
F
R
U
I
T
S

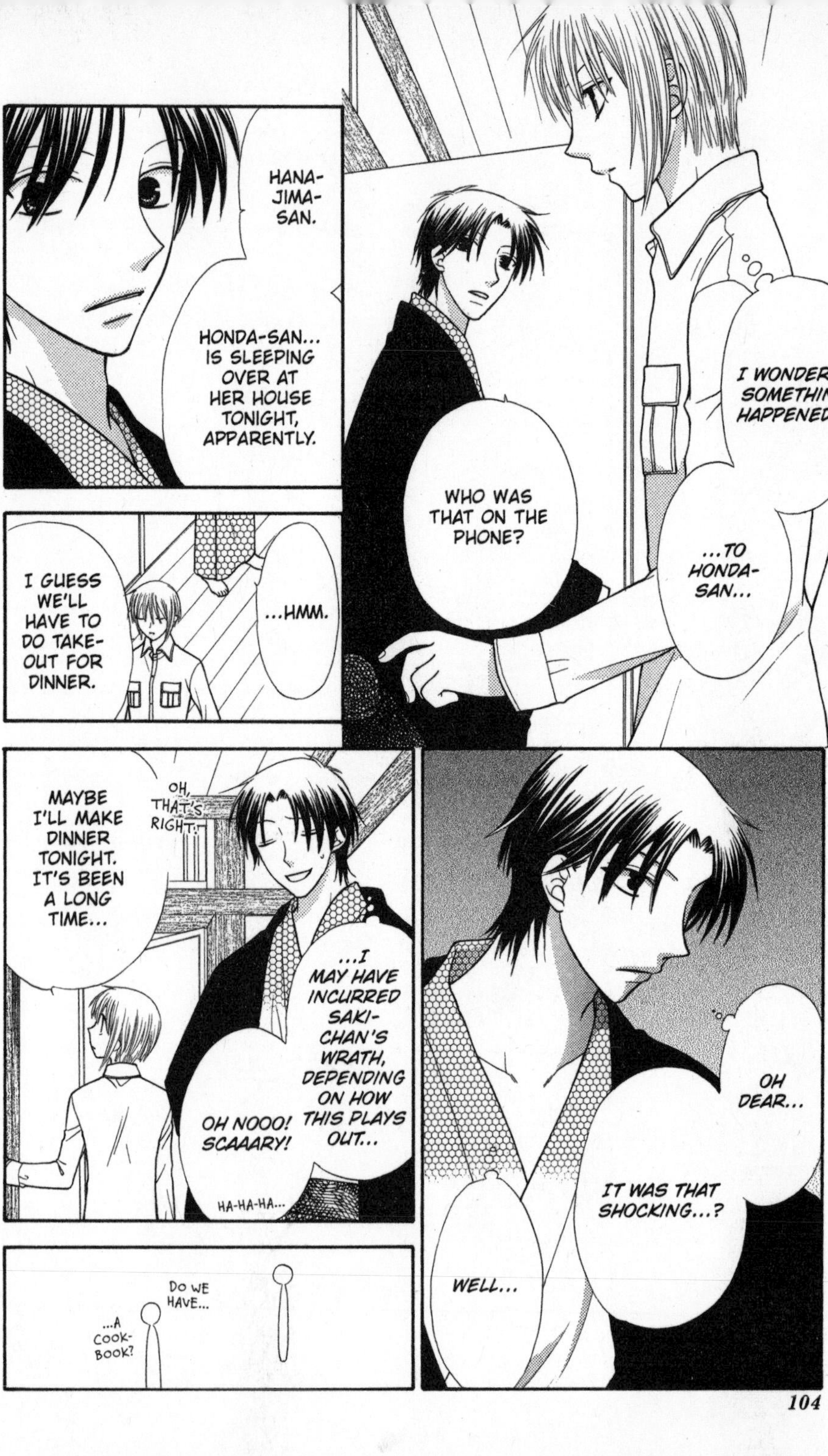
I WONDER IF SOMETHING HAPPENED...
...TO HONDA-SAN...
WHO WAS THAT ON THE PHONE?
HANA-JIMA-SAN.
HONDA-SAN... IS SLEEPING OVER AT HER HOUSE TONIGHT, APPARENTLY.
...HMM.
I GUESS WE'LL HAVE TO DO TAKE-OUT FOR DINNER.
OH DEAR...
IT WAS THAT SHOCKING...?
WELL...
OH, THAT'S RIGHT.
MAYBE I'LL MAKE DINNER TONIGHT. IT'S BEEN A LONG TIME...
...I MAY HAVE INCURRED SAKI-CHAN'S WRATH, DEPENDING ON HOW THIS PLAYS OUT...
OH NOOO! SCAAARY!
HA-HA-HA...
DO WE HAVE...
...A COOK-BOOK?

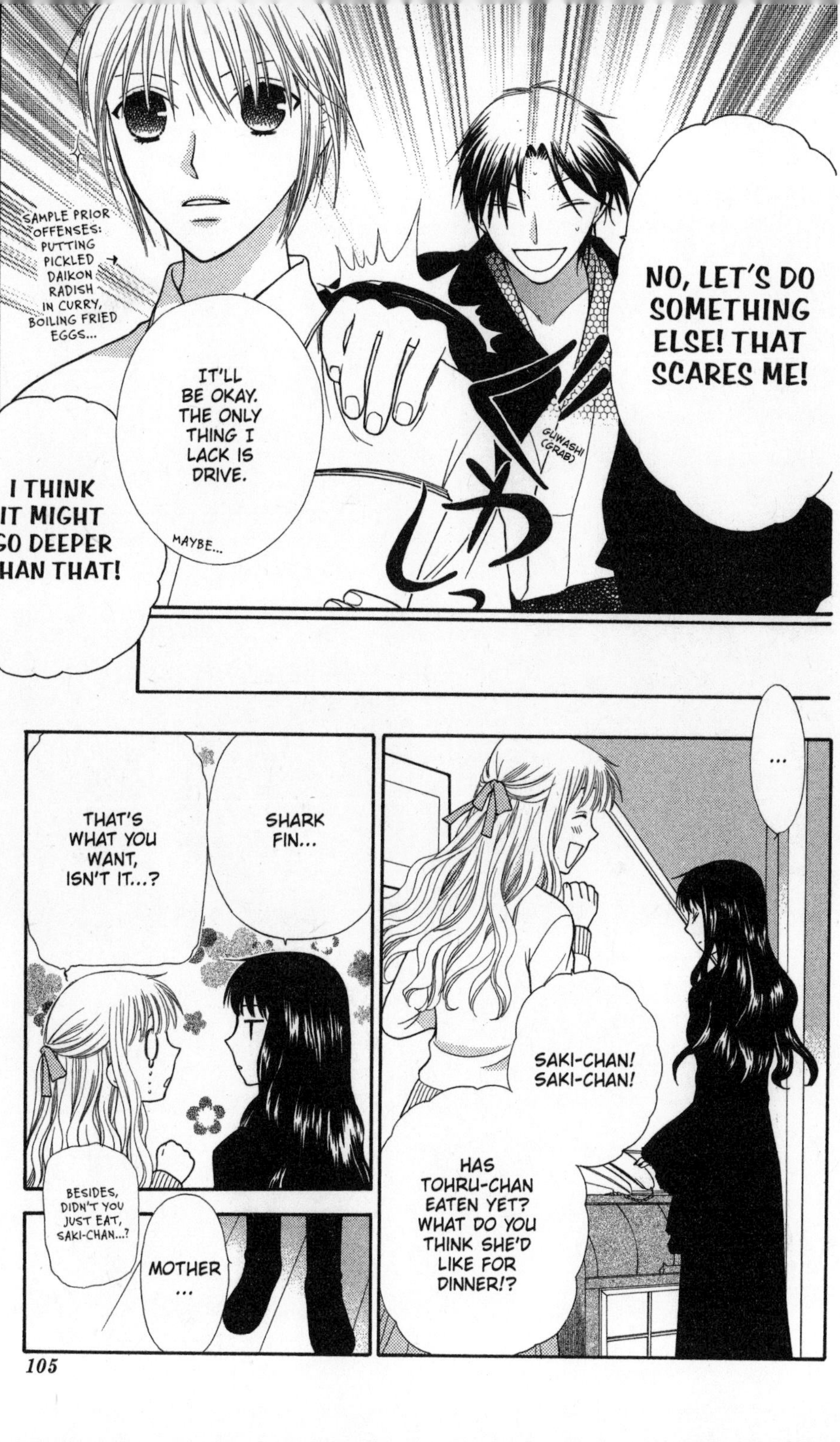
NO, LET'S DO SOMETHING ELSE! THAT SCARES ME!
GUWASHI (GRAB)
IT'LL BE OKAY. THE ONLY THING I LACK IS DRIVE.
MAYBE...
I THINK IT MIGHT GO DEEPER THAN THAT!
SAMPLE PRIOR OFFENSES: PUTTING PICKLED DAIKON RADISH IN CURRY, BOILING FRIED EGGS...
...
SAKI-CHAN! SAKI-CHAN!
HAS TOHRU-CHAN EATEN YET? WHAT DO YOU THINK SHE'D LIKE FOR DINNER!?
SHARK FIN...
THAT'S WHAT YOU WANT, ISN'T IT...?
MOTHER ...
BESIDES, DIDN'T YOU JUST EAT, SAKI-CHAN...?

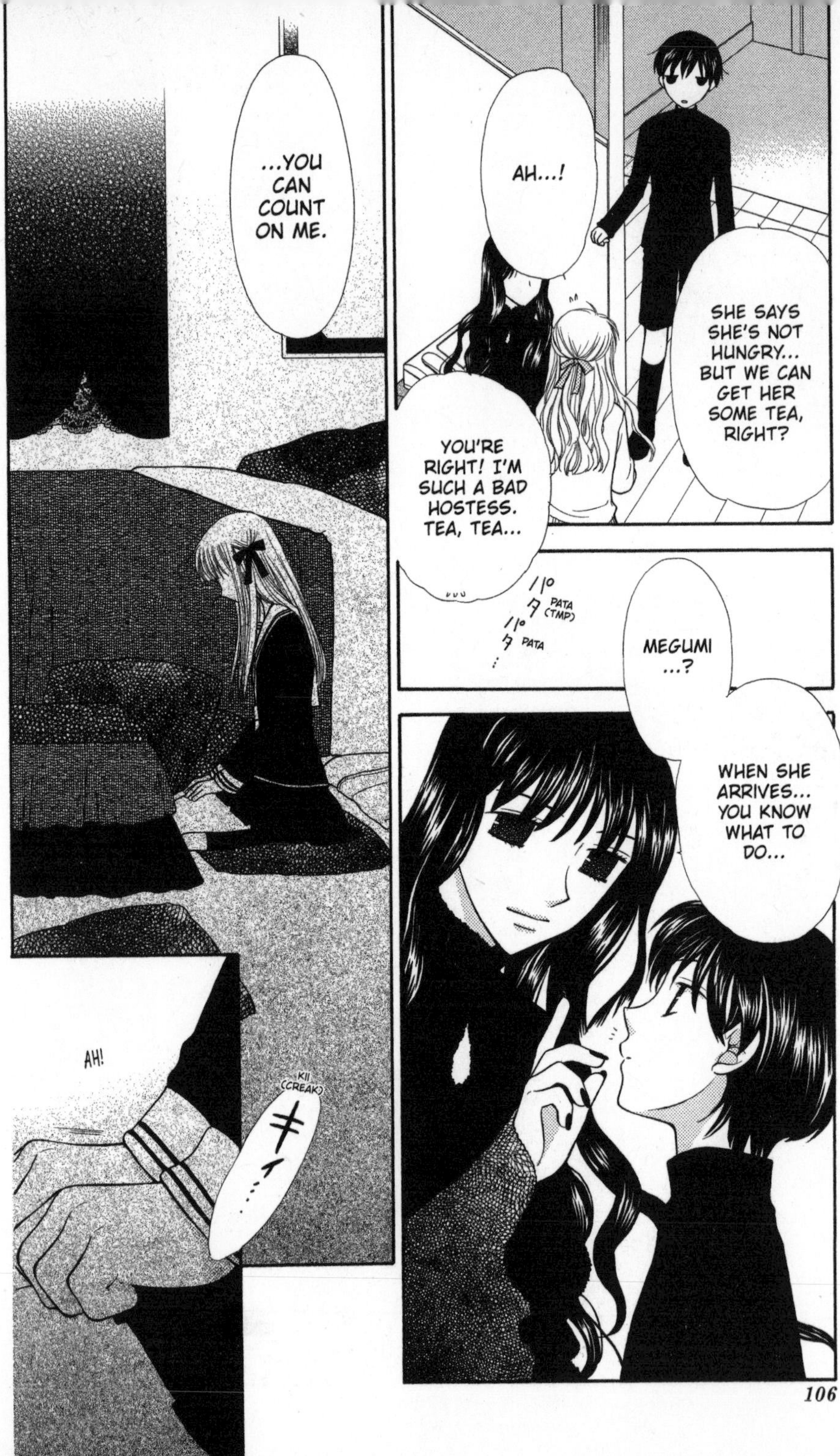
AH...!
SHE SAYS SHE'S NOT HUNGRY... BUT WE CAN GET HER SOME TEA, RIGHT?
YOU'RE RIGHT! I'M SUCH A BAD HOSTESS. TEA, TEA...
パタパタ
PATA (TMP) PATA
MEGUMI ...?
WHEN SHE ARRIVES... YOU KNOW WHAT TO DO...
...YOU CAN COUNT ON ME.
AH!
キイ...
KII (CREAK)

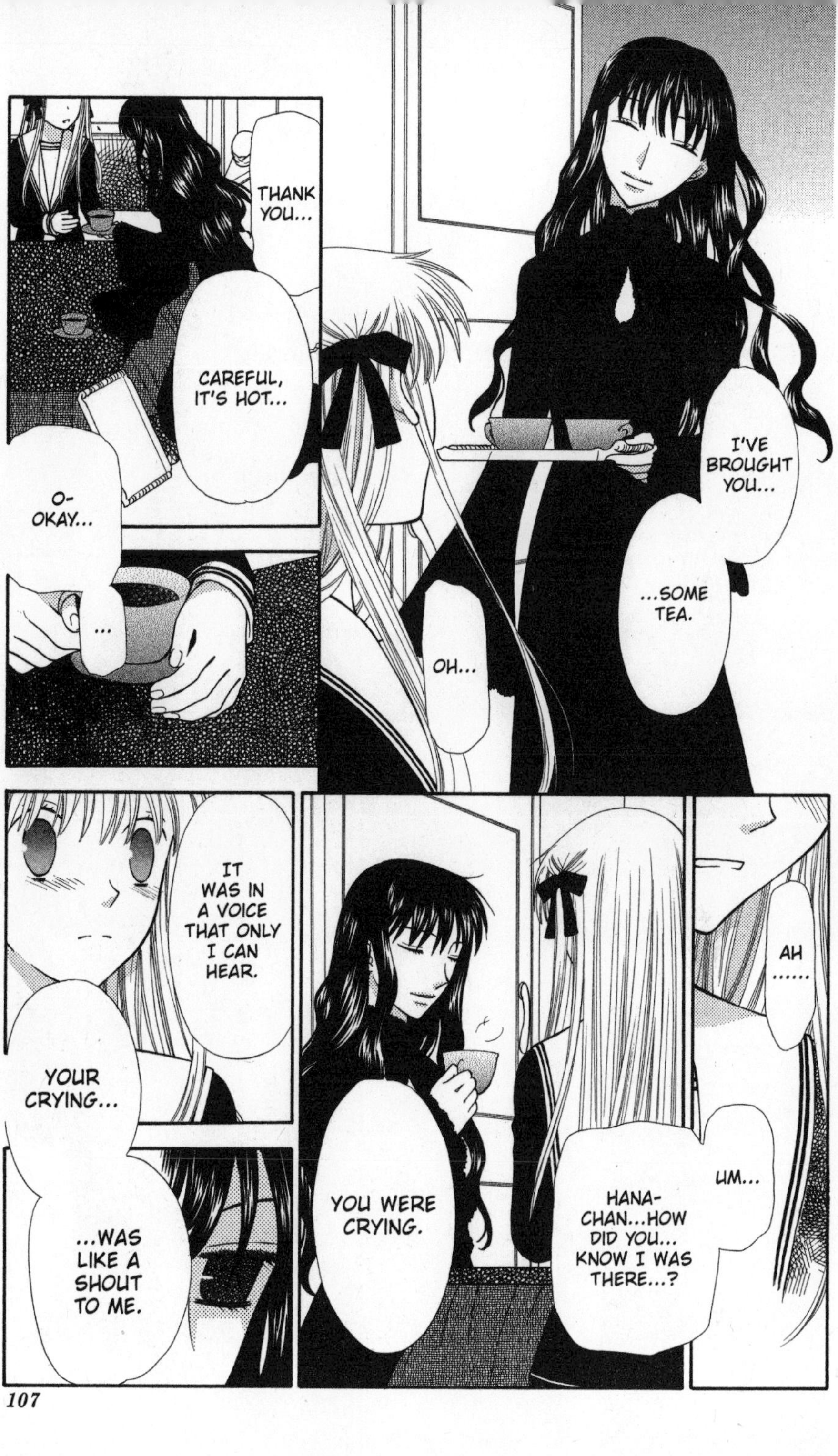
I'VE BROUGHT YOU...
...SOME TEA.
OH...
THANK YOU...
CAREFUL, IT'S HOT...
O-OKAY...
...
AH ......
UM...
HANA-CHAN...HOW DID YOU... KNOW I WAS THERE...?
YOU WERE CRYING.
IT WAS IN A VOICE THAT ONLY I CAN HEAR.
YOUR CRYING...
...WAS LIKE A SHOUT TO ME.

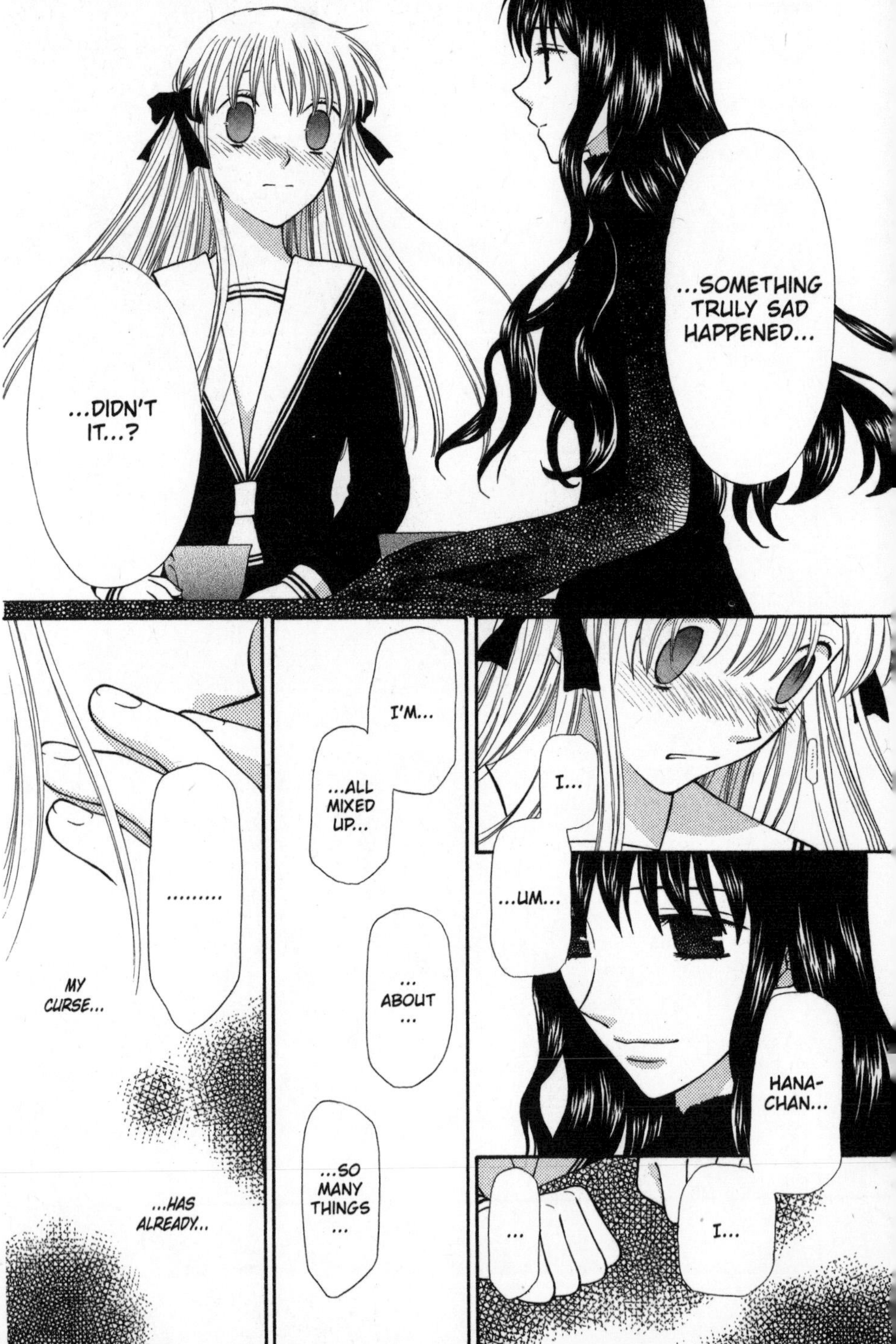
...SOMETHING TRULY SAD HAPPENED...
...DIDN'T IT...?
I...
...UM...
HANA-CHAN...
I...
...
I'M...
...ALL MIXED UP...
...ABOUT...
...SO MANY THINGS...
....
MY CURSE...
...HAS ALREADY...

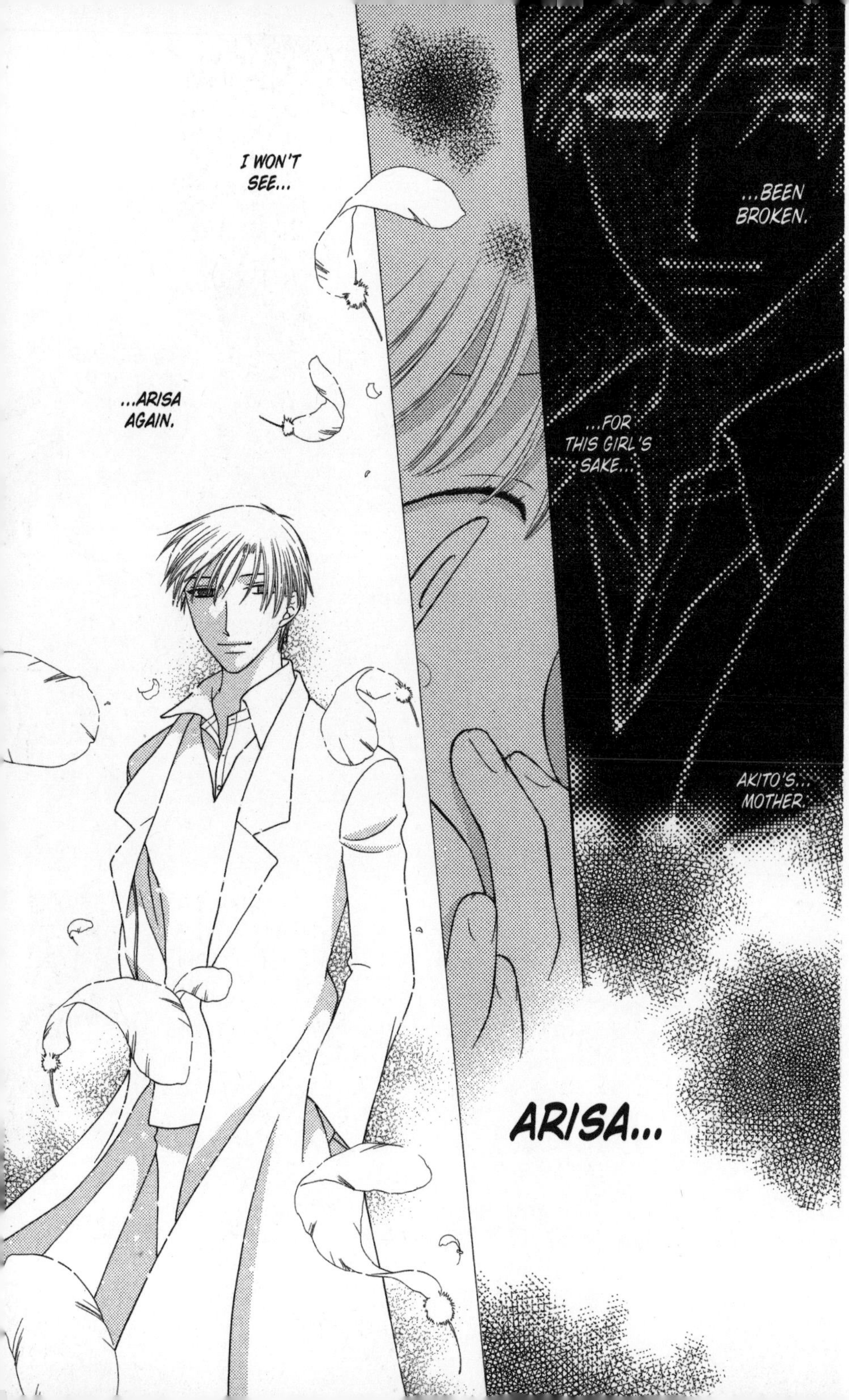
...BEEN BROKEN.
...FOR THIS GIRL'S SAKE...
AKITO'S... MOTHER.
ARISA...
I WON'T SEE...
...ARISA AGAIN.

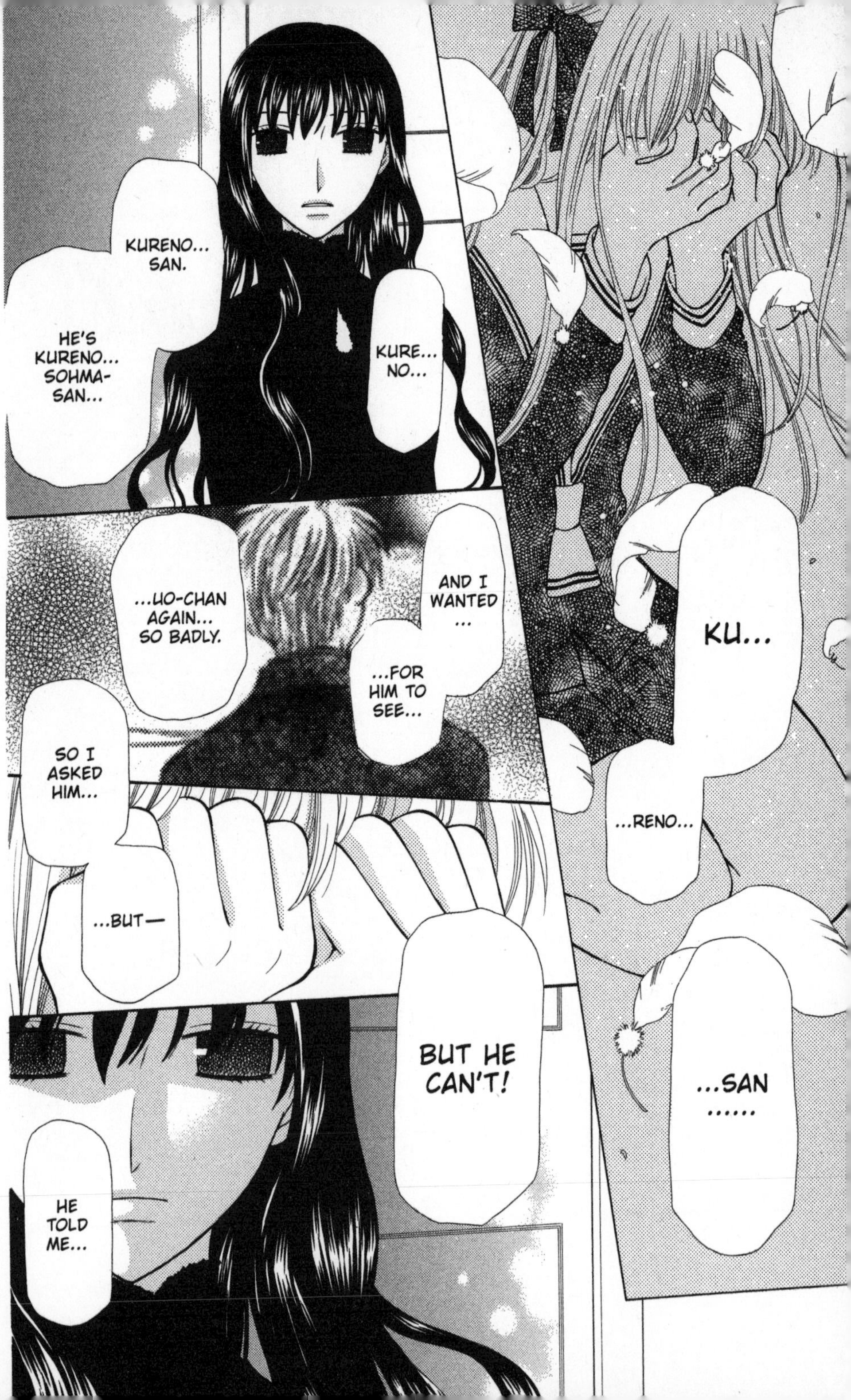
KU...
...RENO...
...SAN ......
KURE... NO...
KURENO... SAN.
HE'S KURENO... SOHMA-SAN...
AND I WANTED...
...FOR HIM TO SEE...
...UO-CHAN AGAIN... SO BADLY.
SO I ASKED HIM...
...BUT—
BUT HE CAN'T!
HE TOLD ME...

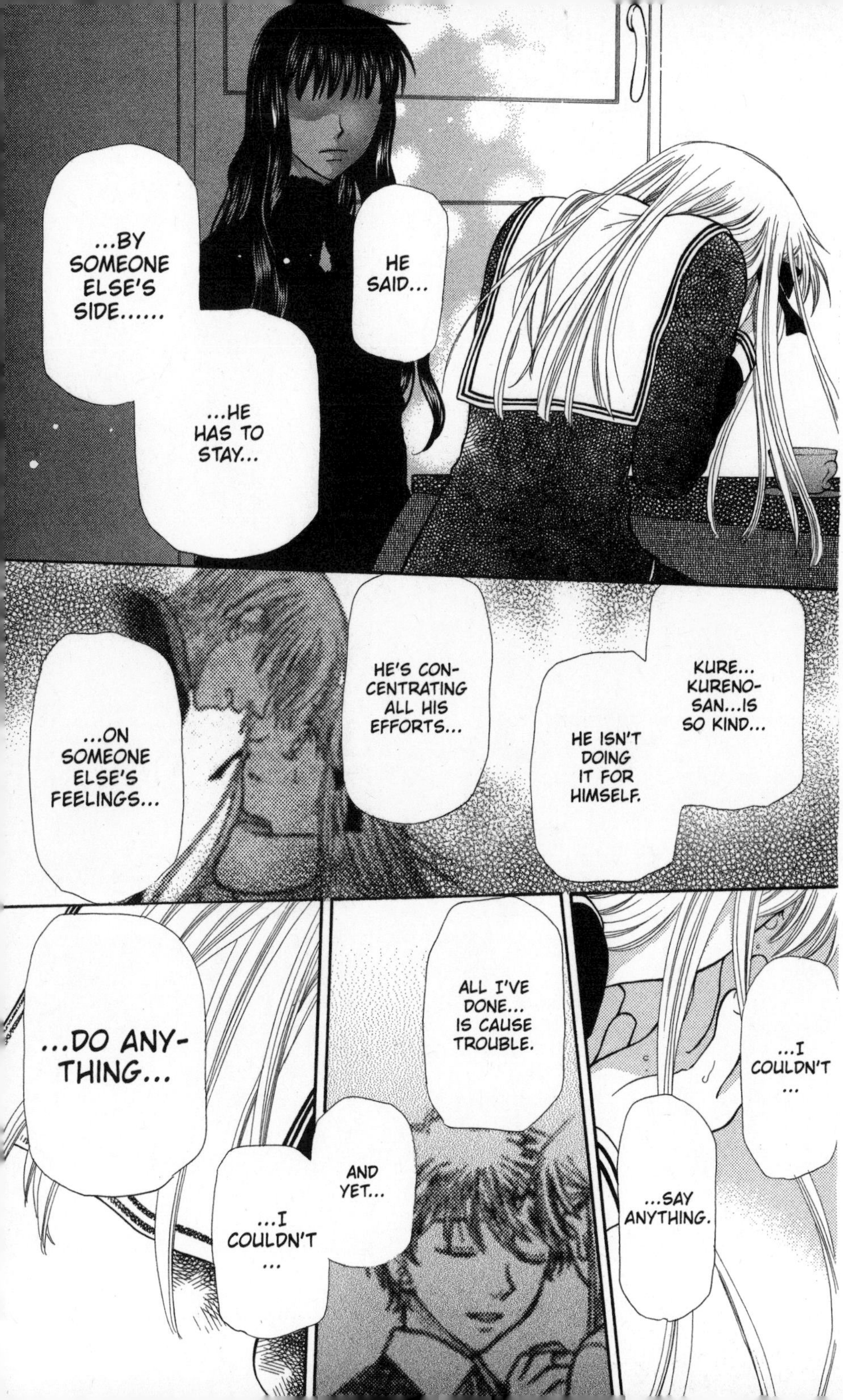
HE SAID...
...HE HAS TO STAY...
...BY SOMEONE ELSE'S SIDE......
KURE... KURENO-SAN...IS SO KIND...
HE ISN'T DOING IT FOR HIMSELF.
HE'S CONCENTRATING ALL HIS EFFORTS...
...ON SOMEONE ELSE'S FEELINGS...
...I COULDN'T ...
...SAY ANYTHING.
ALL I'VE DONE... IS CAUSE TROUBLE.
AND YET...
...I COULDN'T ...
...DO ANYTHING...

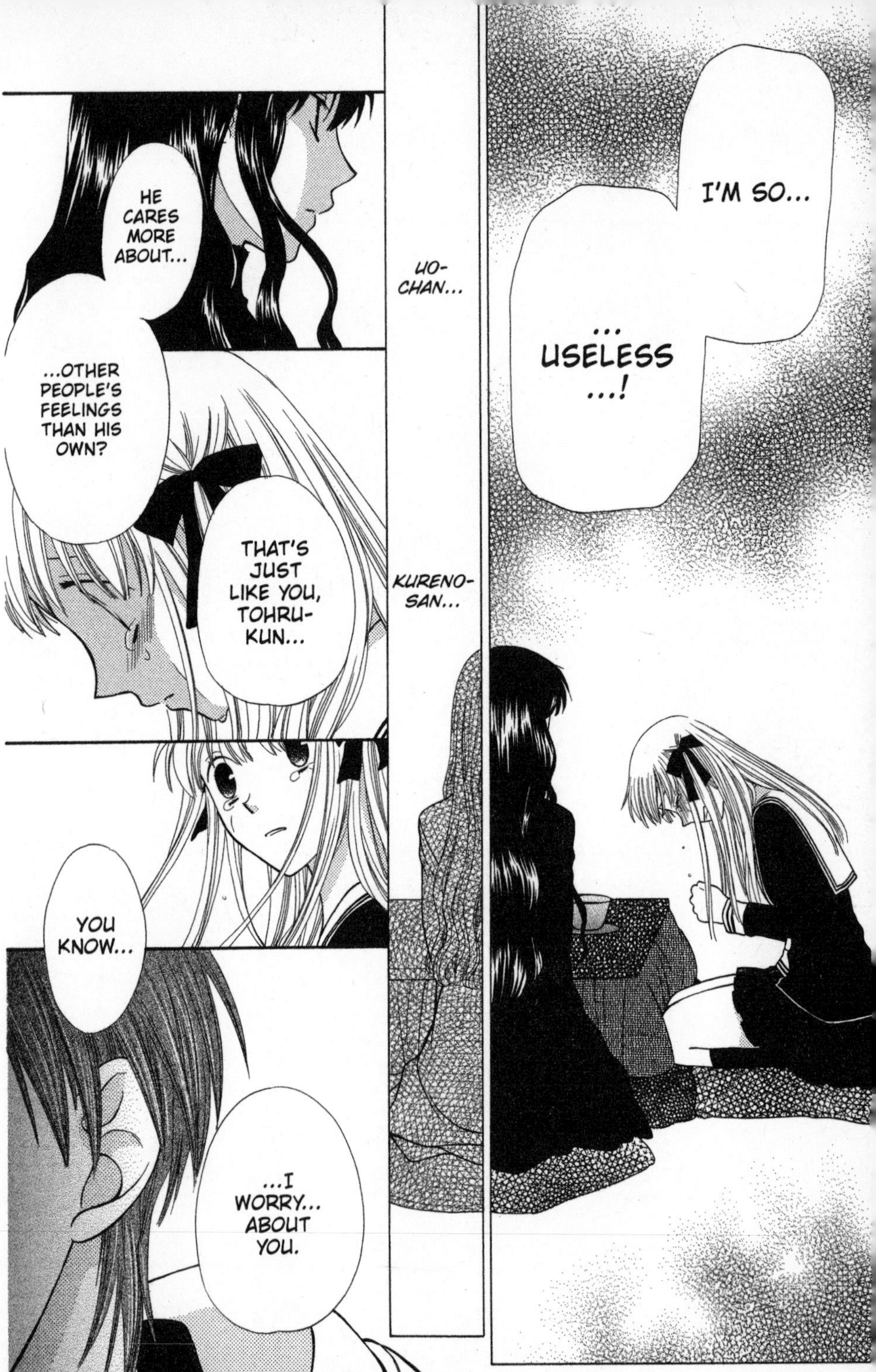
I'M SO...
...USELESS...!
UO-CHAN...
KURENO-SAN...
HE CARES MORE ABOUT...
...OTHER PEOPLE'S FEELINGS THAN HIS OWN?
THAT'S JUST LIKE YOU, TOHRU-KUN...
YOU KNOW...
...I WORRY... ABOUT YOU.

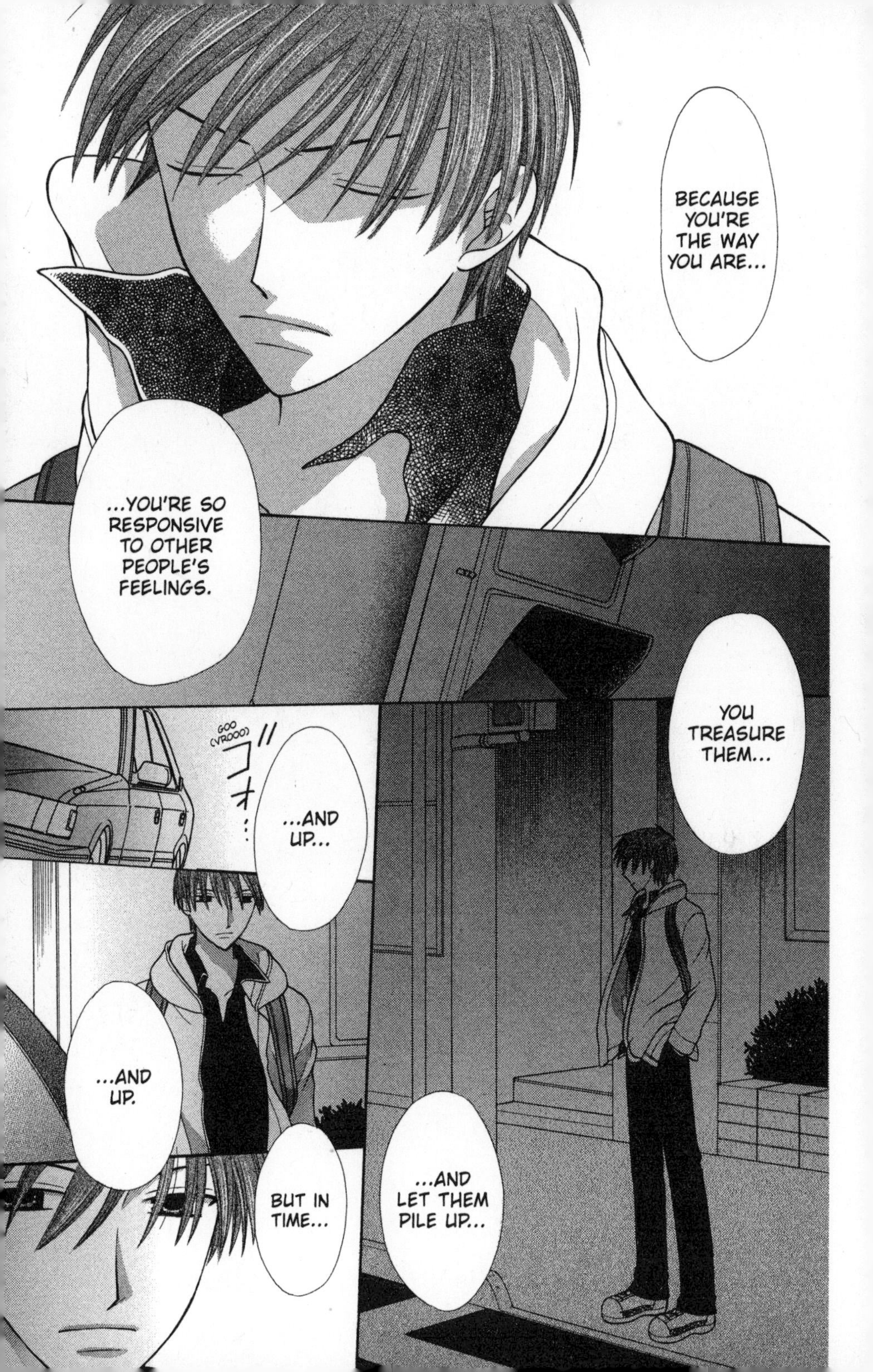
BECAUSE YOU'RE THE WAY YOU ARE...
...YOU'RE SO RESPONSIVE TO OTHER PEOPLE'S FEELINGS.
YOU TREASURE THEM...
...AND LET THEM PILE UP...
GOO (VROOO)
ゴォ…
...AND UP...
...AND UP.
BUT IN TIME...

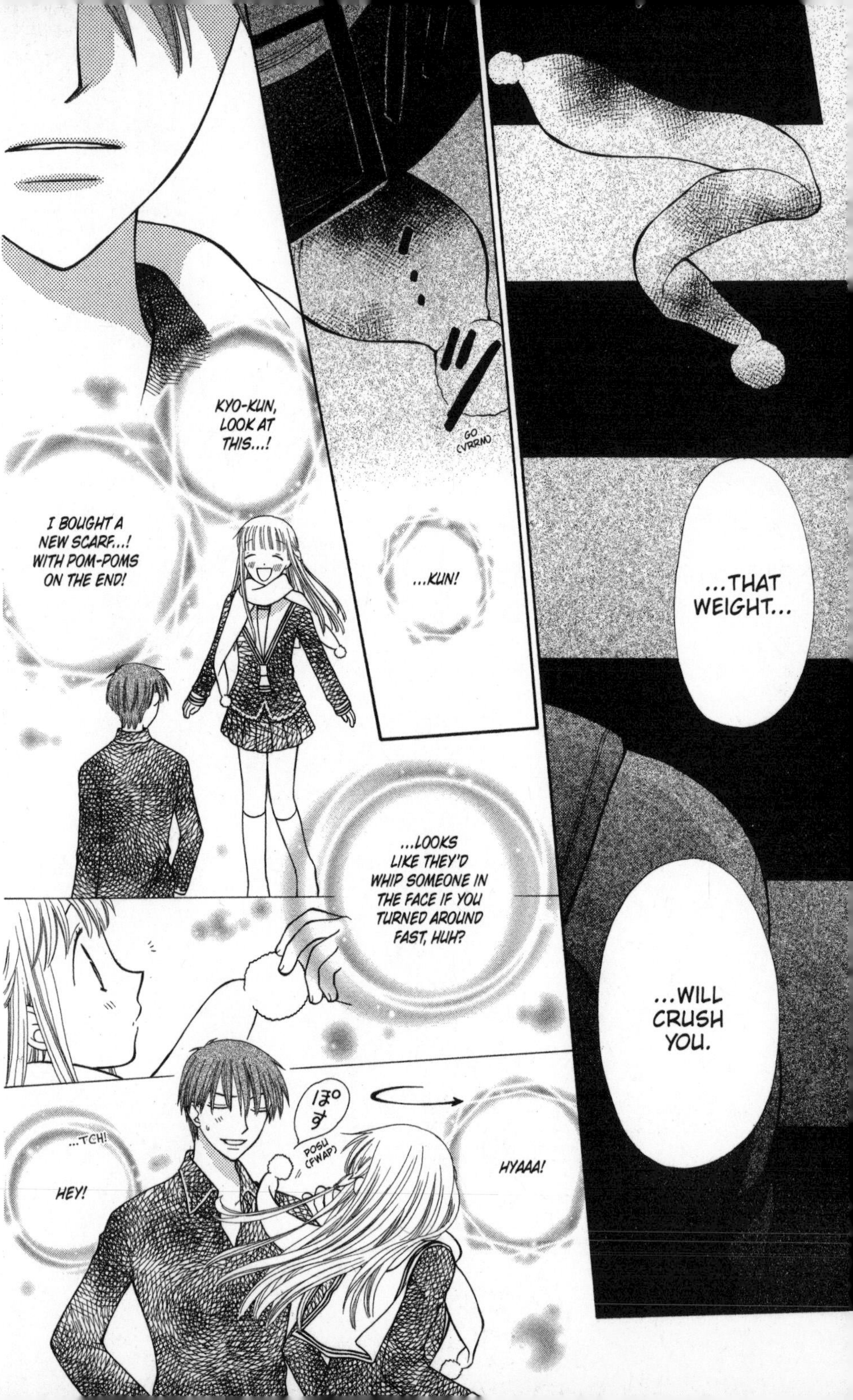

...THAT WEIGHT...
...WILL CRUSH YOU.
GO (VRRM)
...KUN!
KYO-KUN, LOOK AT THIS...!
I BOUGHT A NEW SCARF...! WITH POM-POMS ON THE END!
...LOOKS LIKE THEY'D WHIP SOMEONE IN THE FACE IF YOU TURNED AROUND FAST, HUH?
HYAAA!
ぽす
POSU (FWAP)
...TCH!
HEY!

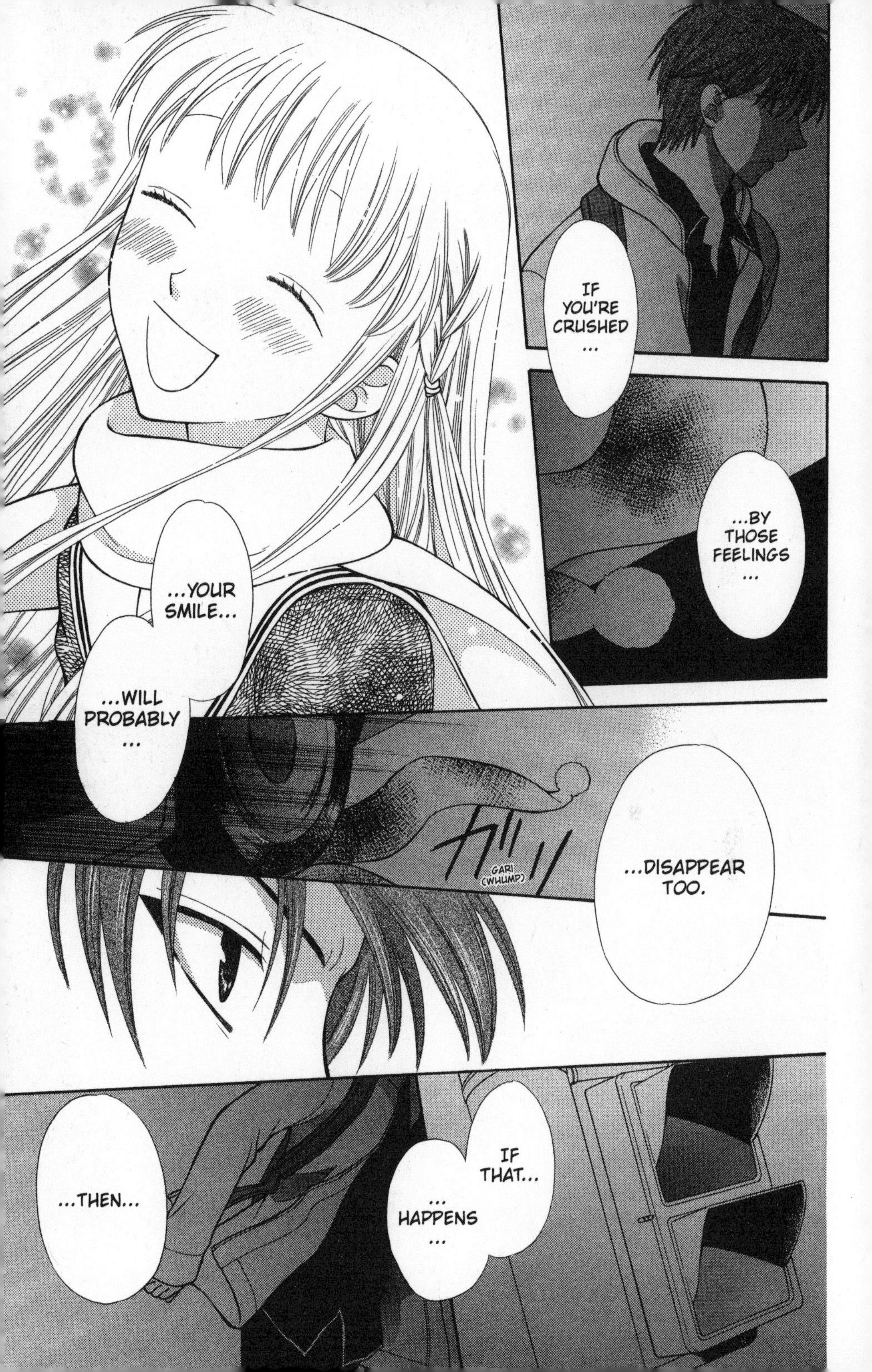
IF YOU'RE CRUSHED ...
...BY THOSE FEELINGS ...
...YOUR SMILE...
...WILL PROBABLY ...
ガリッ
GARI (WHUMP)
...DISAPPEAR TOO.
IF THAT... ... HAPPENS ...
...THEN...

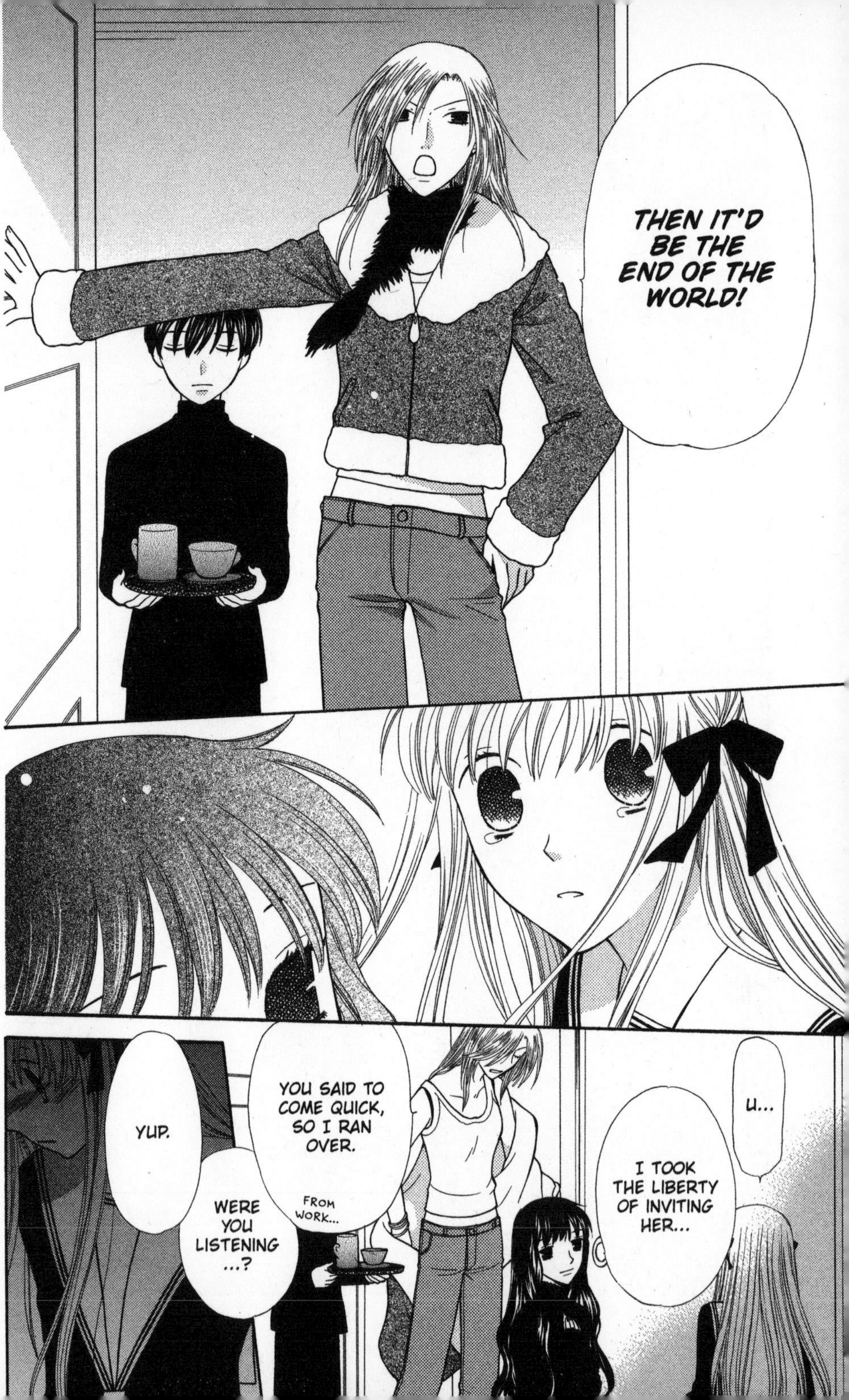
THEN IT'D BE THE END OF THE WORLD!
U...
I TOOK THE LIBERTY OF INVITING HER...
YOU SAID TO COME QUICK, SO I RAN OVER.
FROM WORK...
WERE YOU LISTENING ...?
YUP.

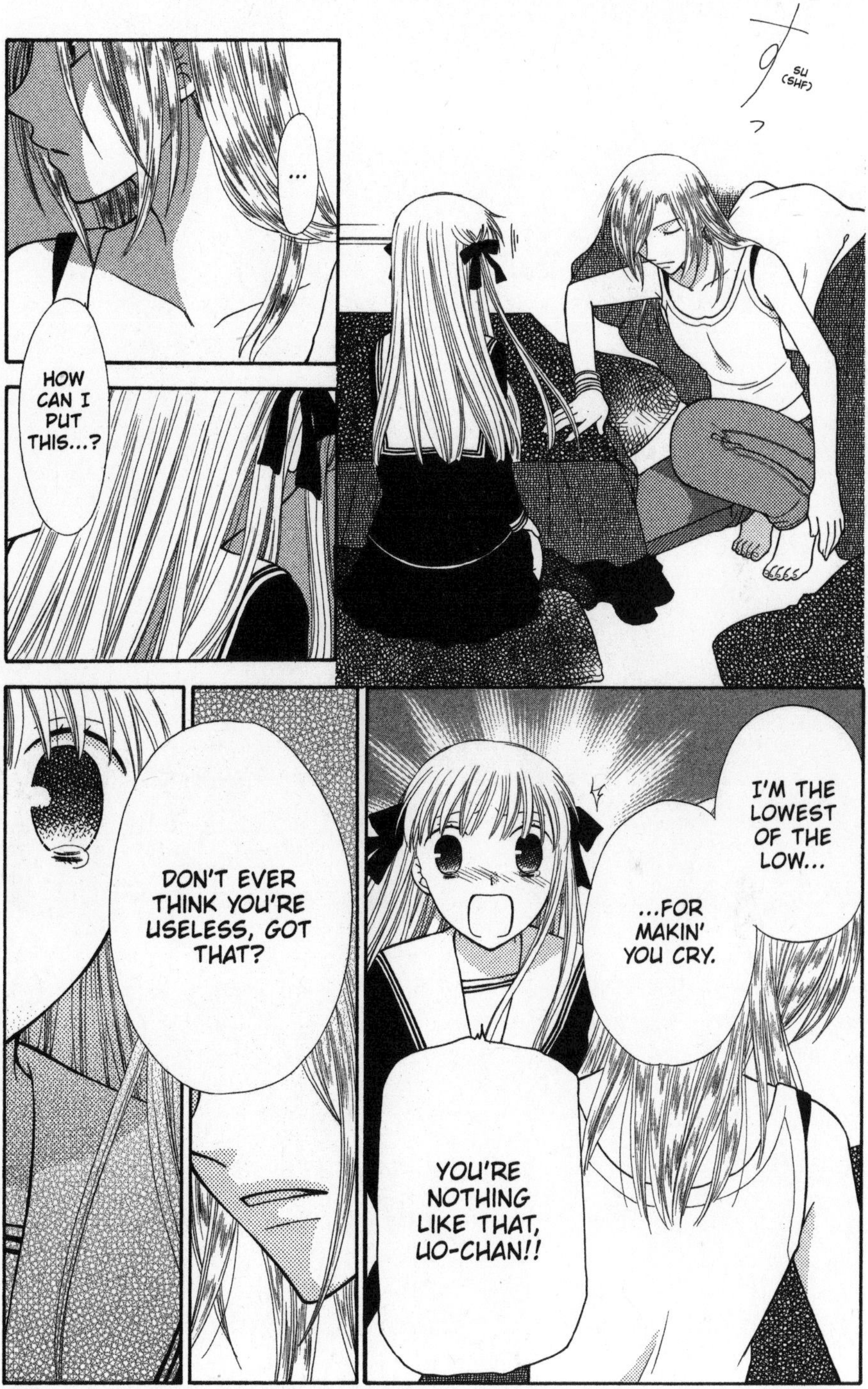
SU (SHF)
...
HOW CAN I PUT THIS...?
I'M THE LOWEST OF THE LOW...
...FOR MAKIN' YOU CRY.
YOU'RE NOTHING LIKE THAT, UO-CHAN!!
DON'T EVER THINK YOU'RE USELESS, GOT THAT?

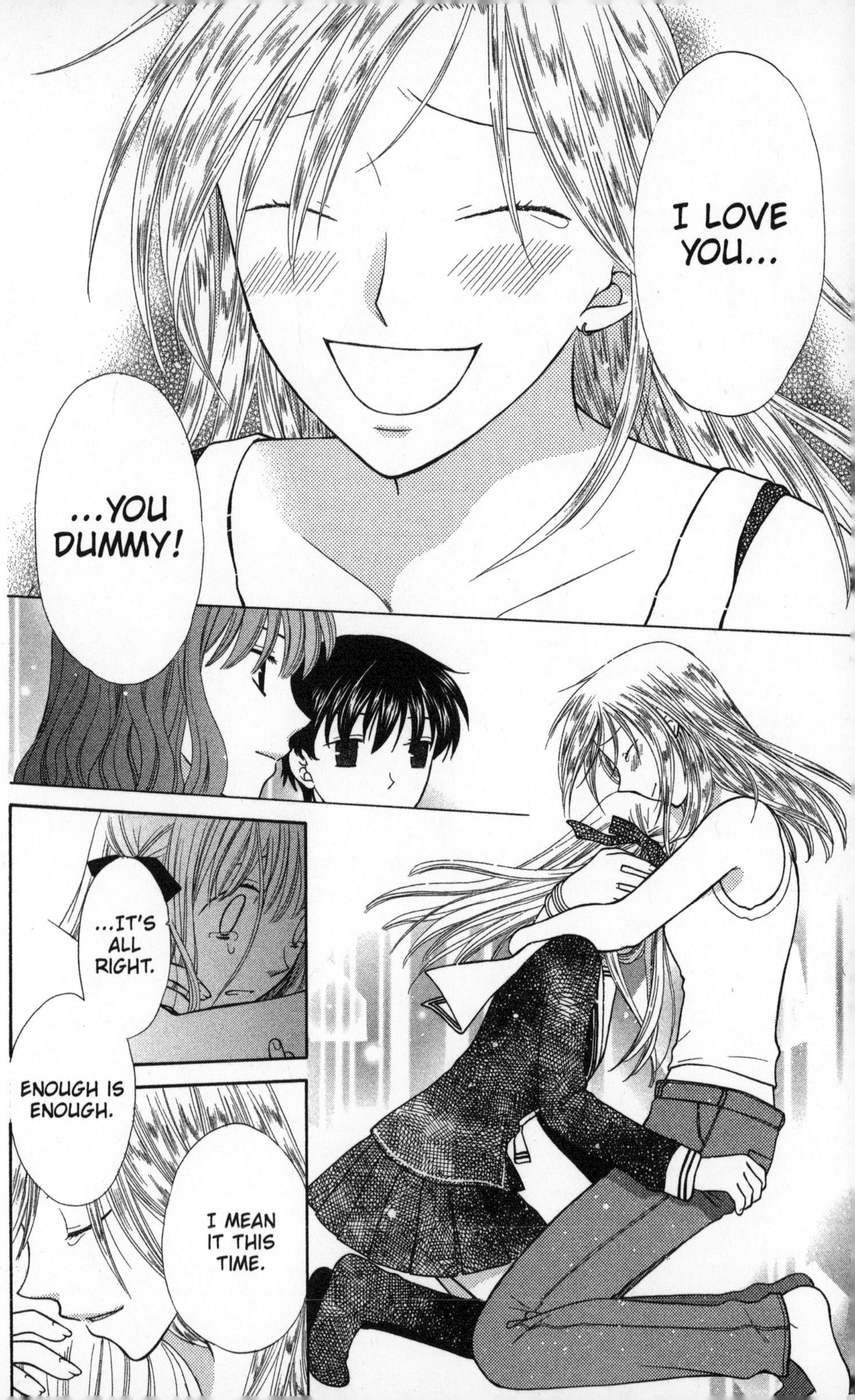
I LOVE YOU...
...YOU DUMMY!
...IT'S ALL RIGHT.
ENOUGH IS ENOUGH.
I MEAN IT THIS TIME.

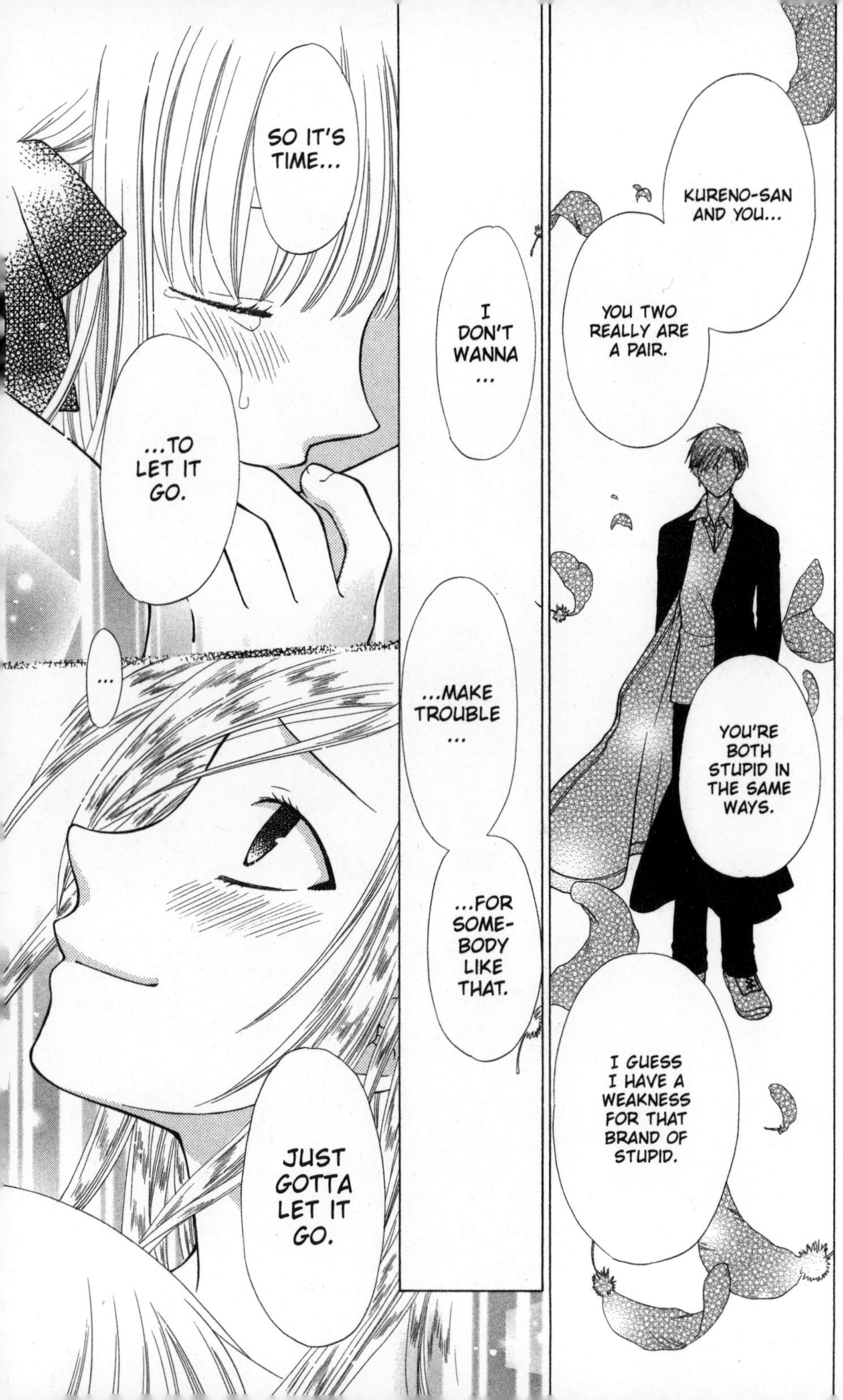
KURENO-SAN AND YOU...
YOU TWO REALLY ARE A PAIR.
YOU'RE BOTH STUPID IN THE SAME WAYS.
I GUESS I HAVE A WEAKNESS FOR THAT BRAND OF STUPID.
I DON'T WANNA ...
...MAKE TROUBLE ...
...FOR SOMEBODY LIKE THAT.
SO IT'S TIME...
...TO LET IT GO.
...
JUST GOTTA LET IT GO.

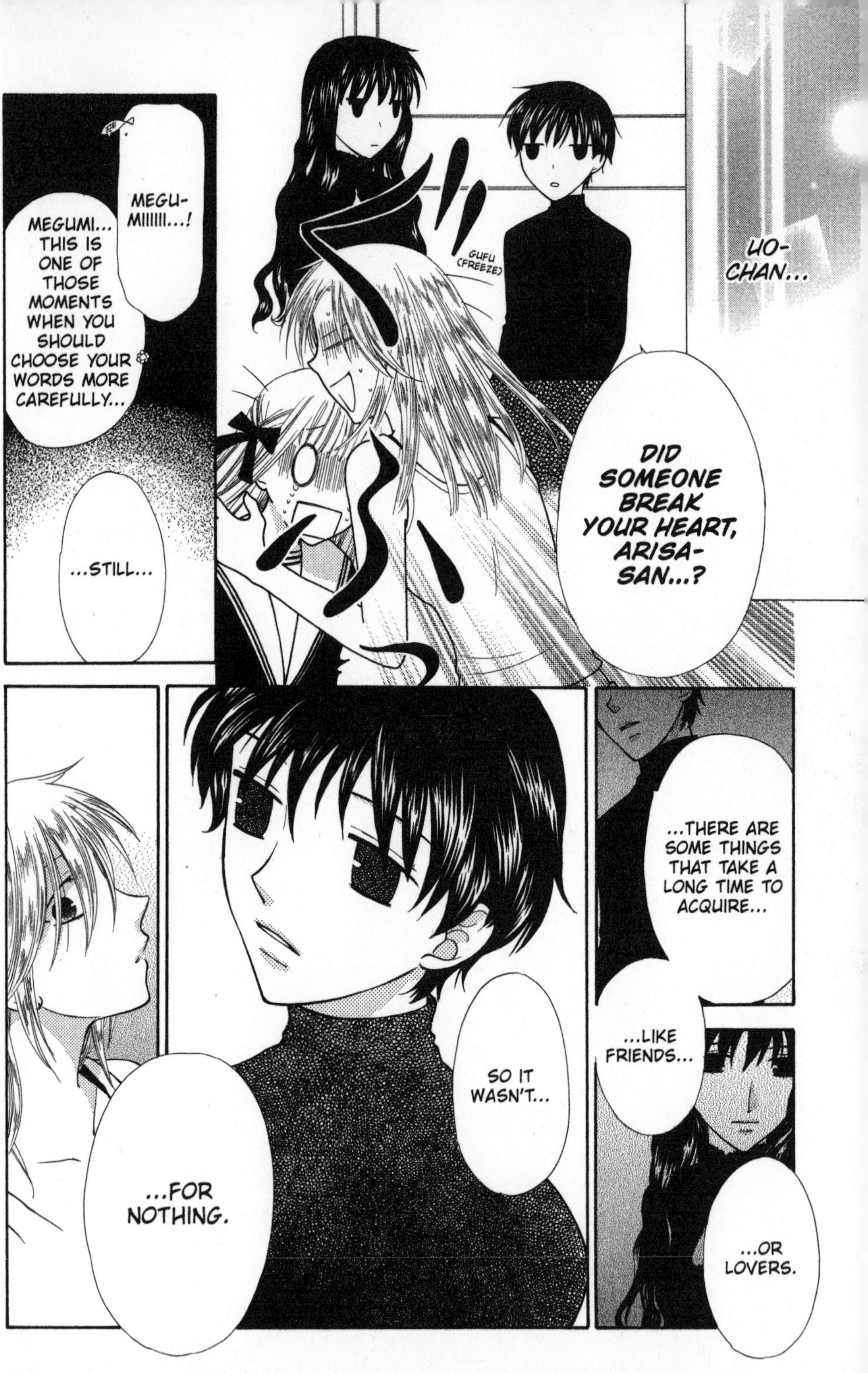
UO-CHAN...
DID SOMEONE BREAK YOUR HEART, ARISA-SAN...?
GUFU (FREEZE)
MEGU-MIIIIII...!
MEGUMI... THIS IS ONE OF THOSE MOMENTS WHEN YOU SHOULD CHOOSE YOUR WORDS MORE CAREFULLY...
...STILL...
...THERE ARE SOME THINGS THAT TAKE A LONG TIME TO ACQUIRE...
...LIKE FRIENDS...
...OR LOVERS.
SO IT WASN'T...
...FOR NOTHING.

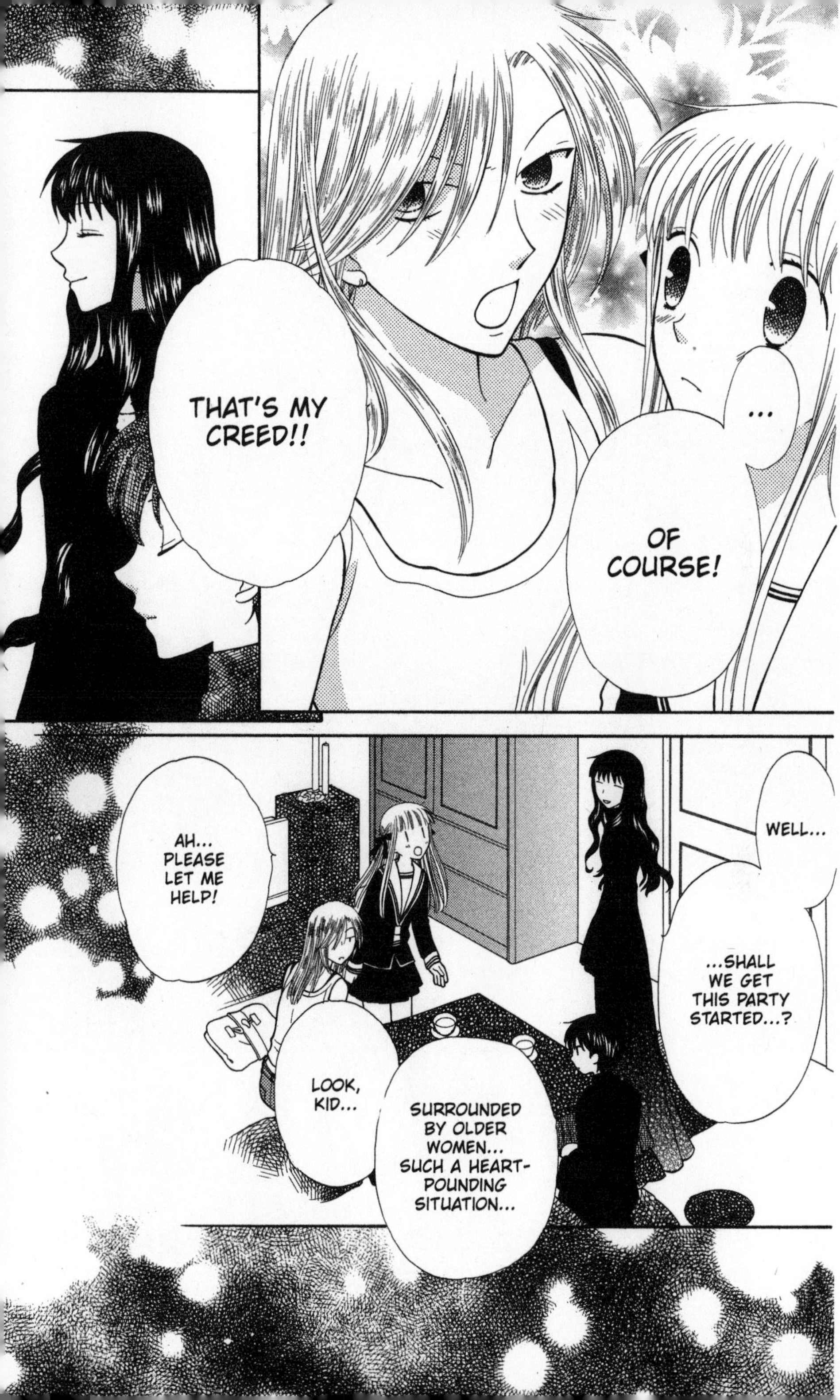
...
OF COURSE!
THAT'S MY CREED!!
WELL...
...SHALL WE GET THIS PARTY STARTED...?
AH... PLEASE LET ME HELP!
SURROUNDED BY OLDER WOMEN... SUCH A HEART-POUNDING SITUATION...
LOOK, KID...

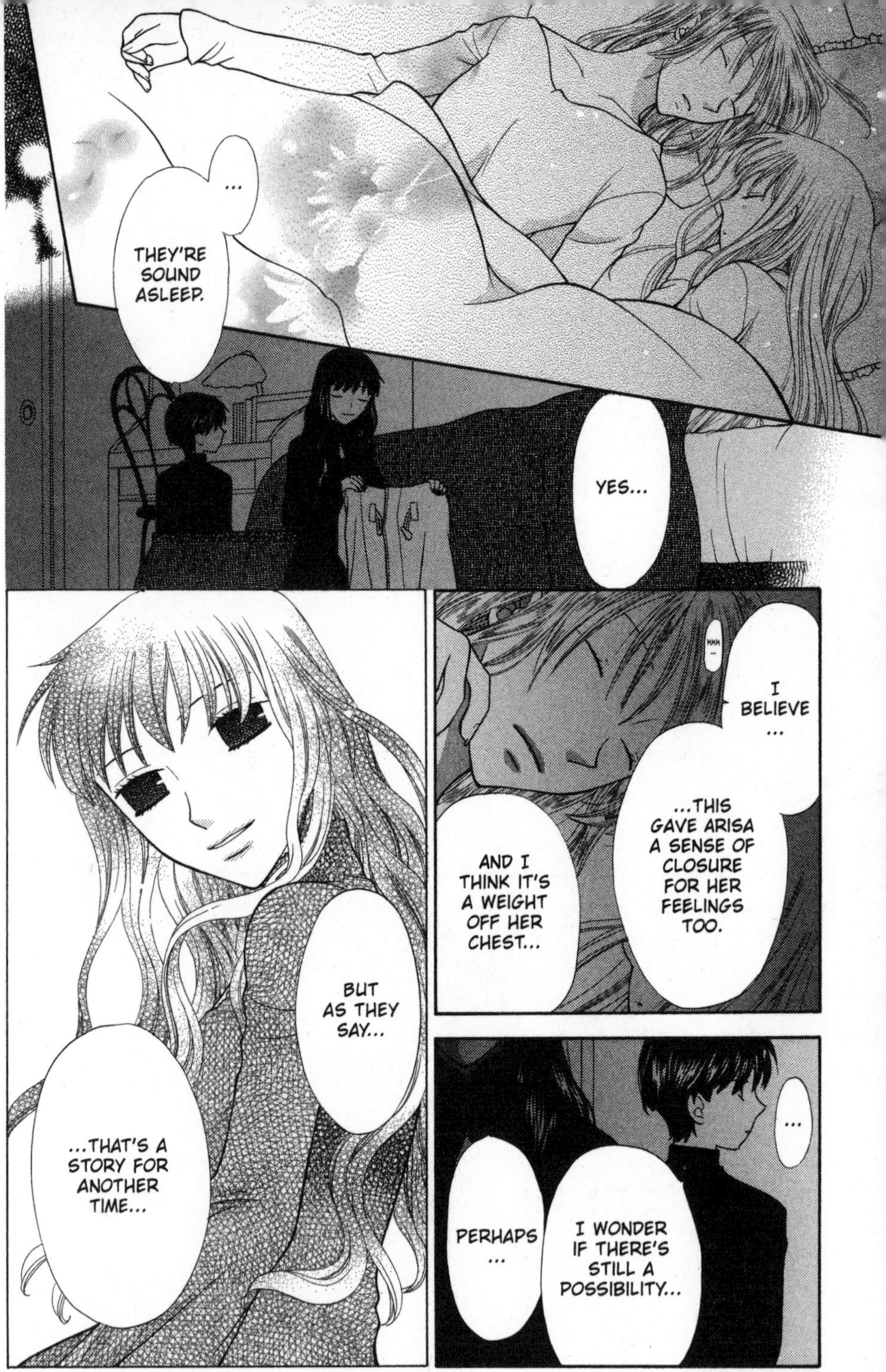
...
THEY'RE SOUND ASLEEP.
YES...
MMM...
I BELIEVE...
...THIS GAVE ARISA A SENSE OF CLOSURE FOR HER FEELINGS TOO.
AND I THINK IT'S A WEIGHT OFF HER CHEST...
...
I WONDER IF THERE'S STILL A POSSIBILITY...
PERHAPS...
BUT AS THEY SAY...
...THAT'S A STORY FOR ANOTHER TIME...

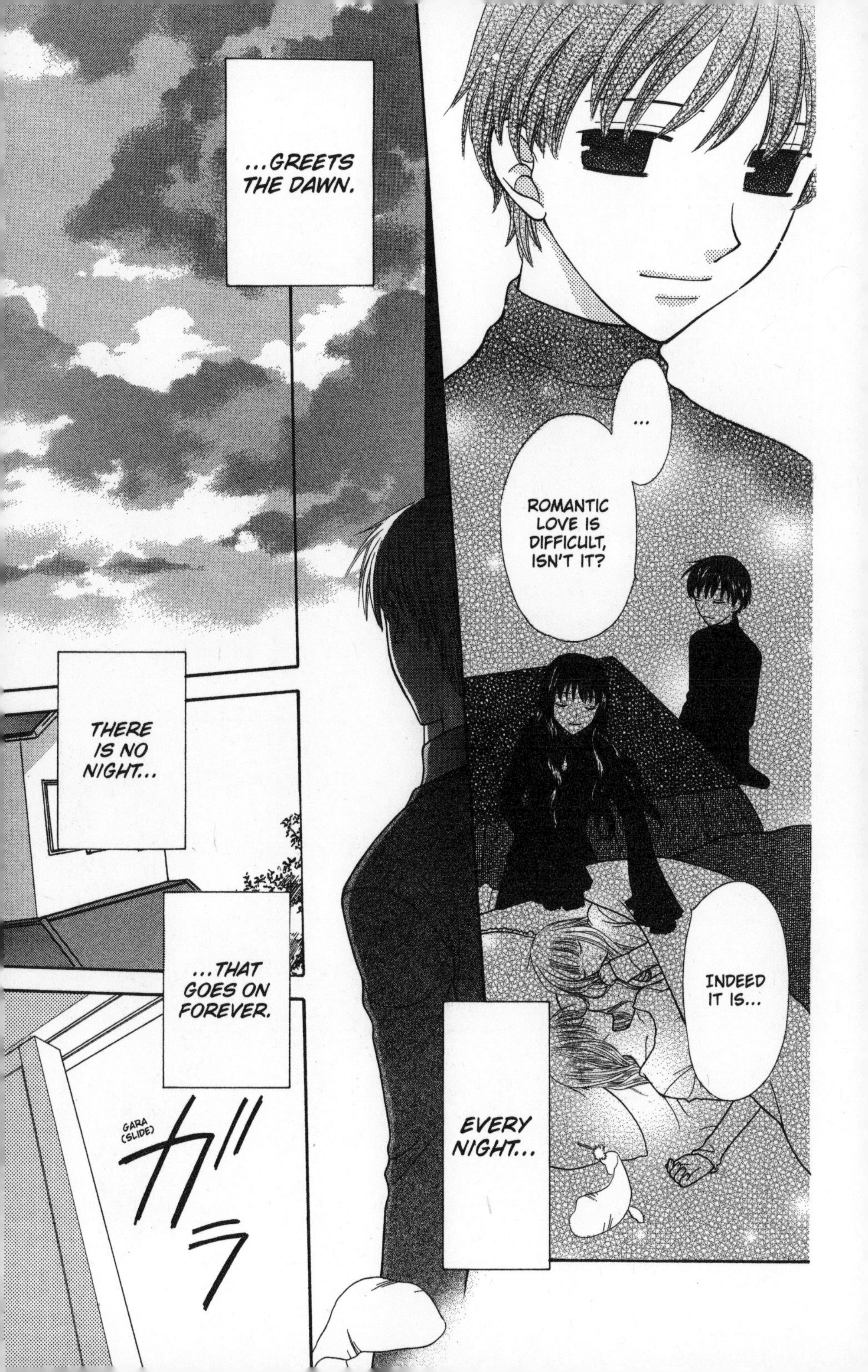
...
ROMANTIC LOVE IS DIFFICULT, ISN'T IT?
INDEED IT IS...
EVERY NIGHT...
...GREETS THE DAWN.
THERE IS NO NIGHT...
...THAT GOES ON FOREVER.
GARA (SLIDE)

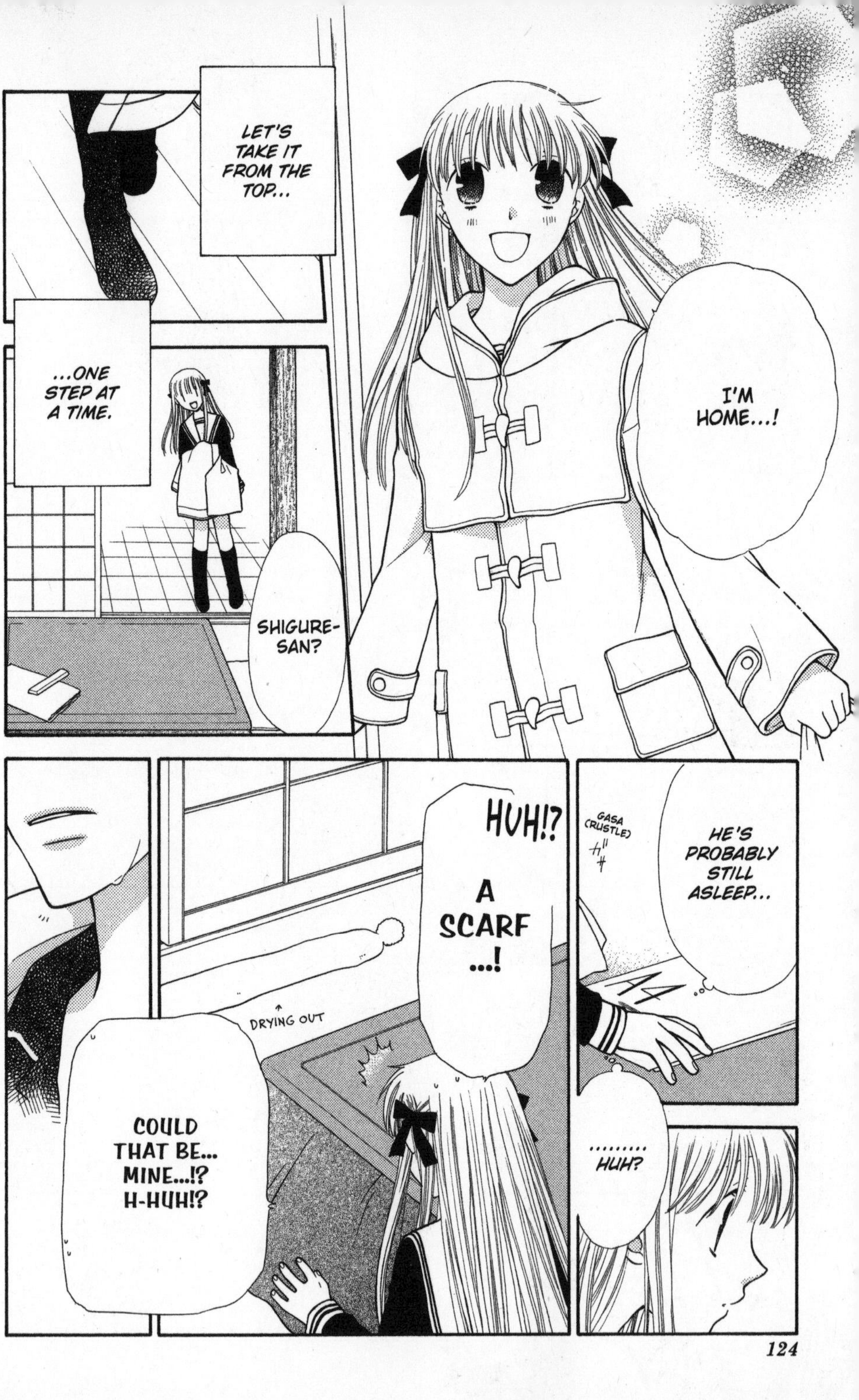
I'M HOME...!
LET'S TAKE IT FROM THE TOP...
...ONE STEP AT A TIME.
SHIGURE-SAN?
HE'S PROBABLY STILL ASLEEP...
GASA (RUSTLE)
.... HUH?
HUH!?
A SCARF ...!
DRYING OUT
COULD THAT BE... MINE...!? H-HUH!?

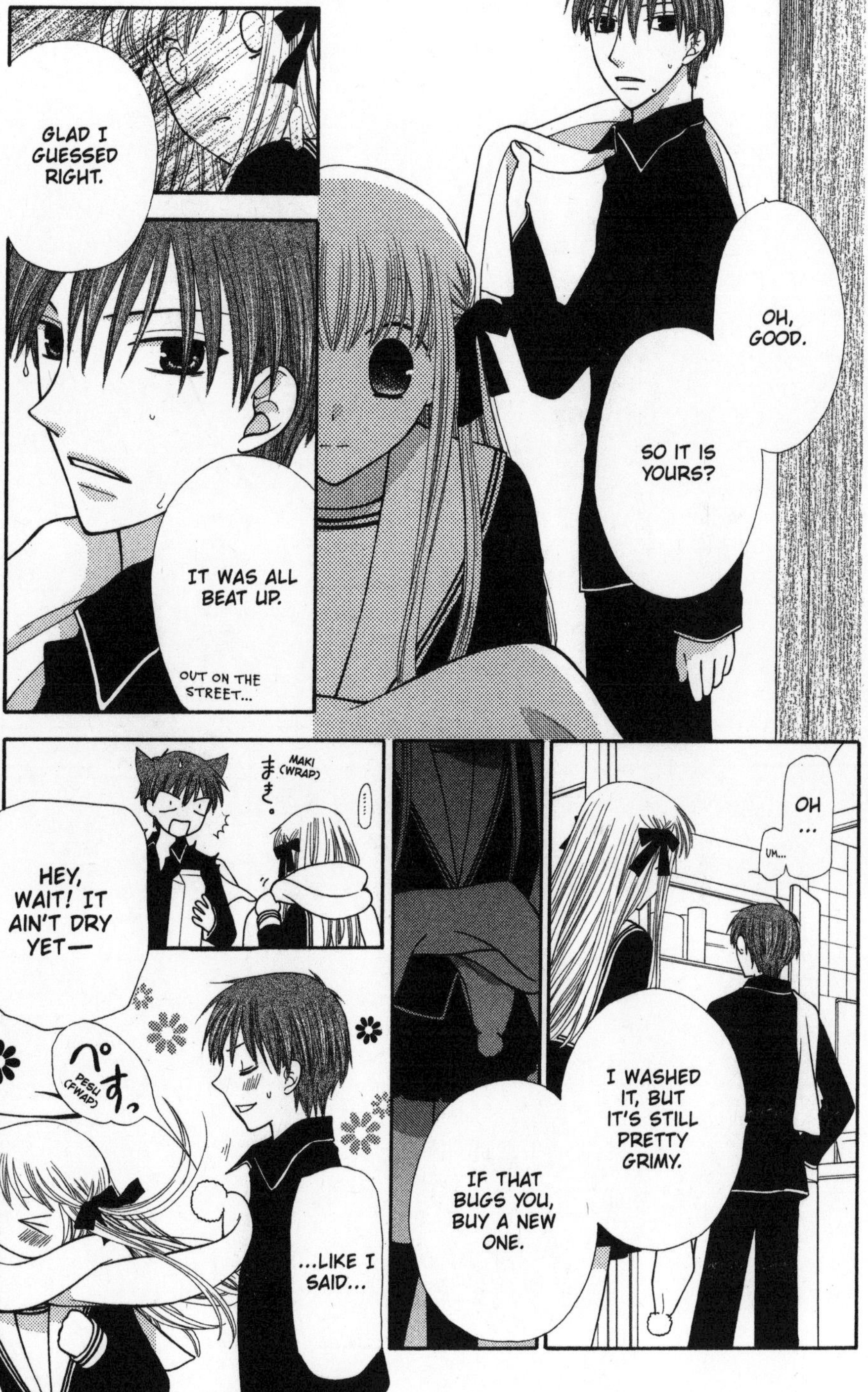

OH, GOOD.
SO IT IS YOURS?
GLAD I GUESSED RIGHT.
IT WAS ALL BEAT UP.
OUT ON THE STREET...
OH ...
UM...
I WASHED IT, BUT IT'S STILL PRETTY GRIMY.
IF THAT BUGS YOU, BUY A NEW ONE.
まき。
MAKI (WRAP)
......
HEY, WAIT! IT AIN'T DRY YET—
ぺすっ
PESU (FWAP)
...LIKE I SAID...

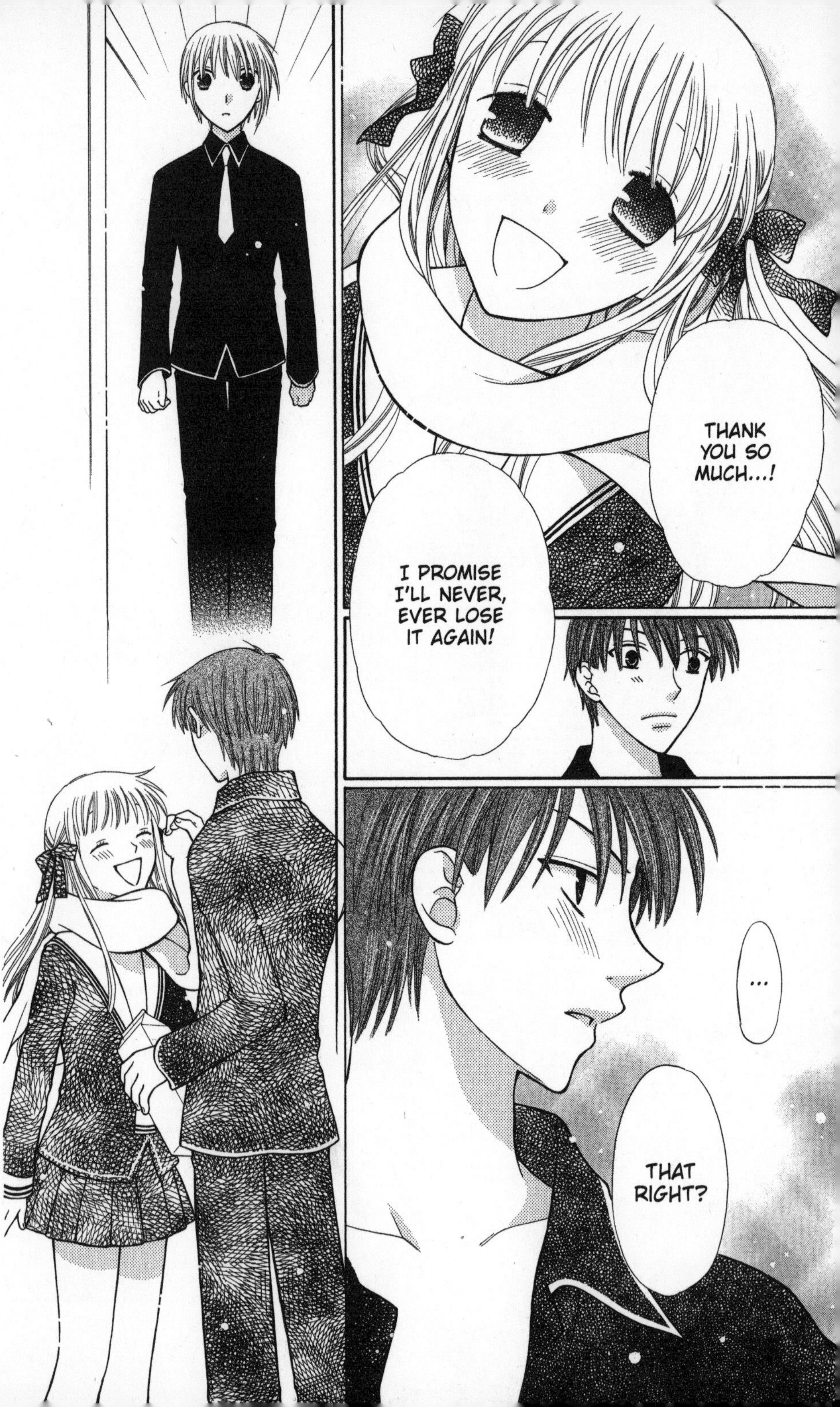
THANK YOU SO MUCH...!
I PROMISE I'LL NEVER, EVER LOSE IT AGAIN!
...
THAT RIGHT?

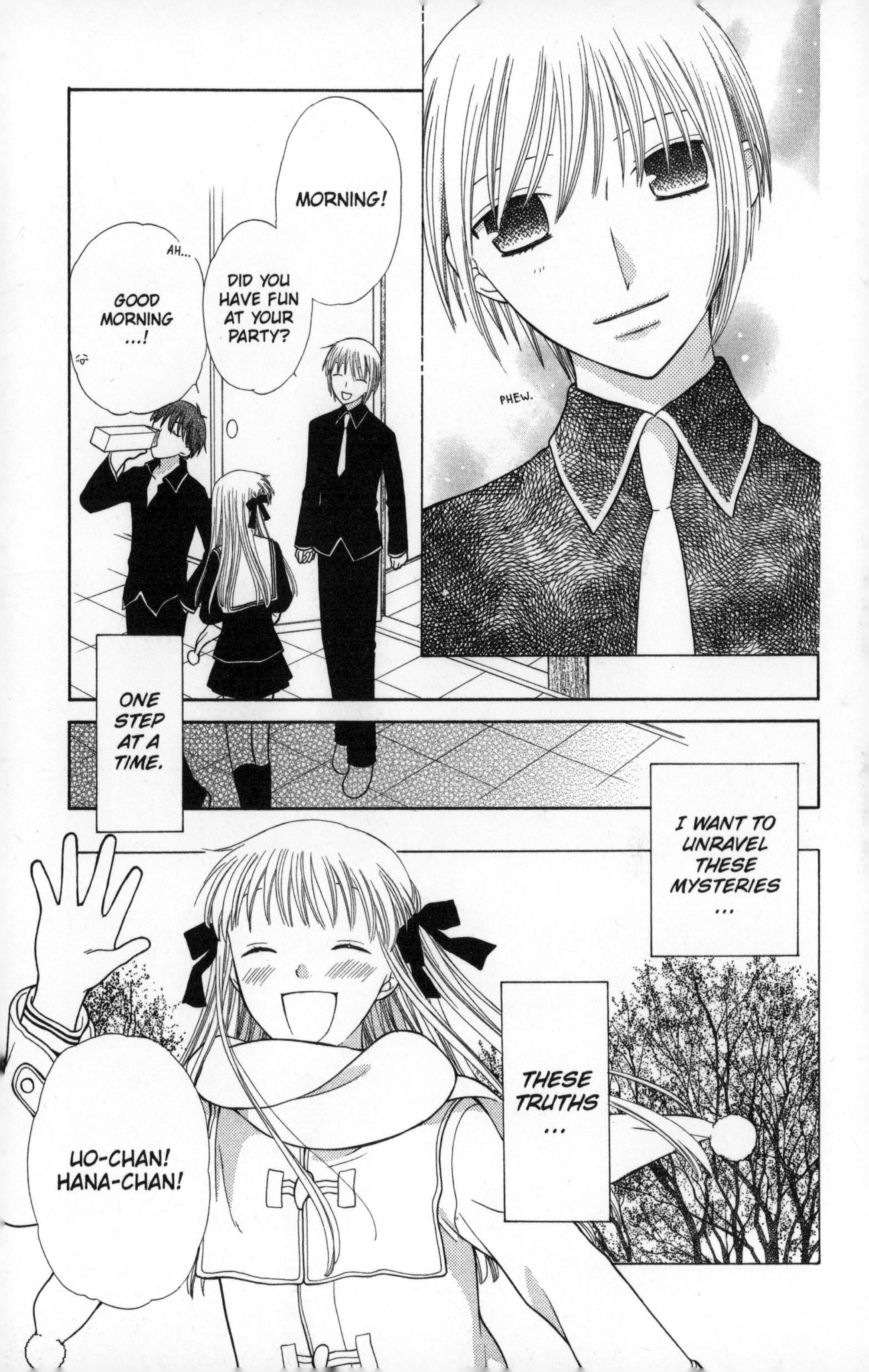
PHEW.
MORNING!
DID YOU HAVE FUN AT YOUR PARTY?
AH...
GOOD MORNING ...!
ONE STEP AT A TIME.
I WANT TO UNRAVEL THESE MYSTERIES ...
THESE TRUTHS ...
UO-CHAN! HANA-CHAN!

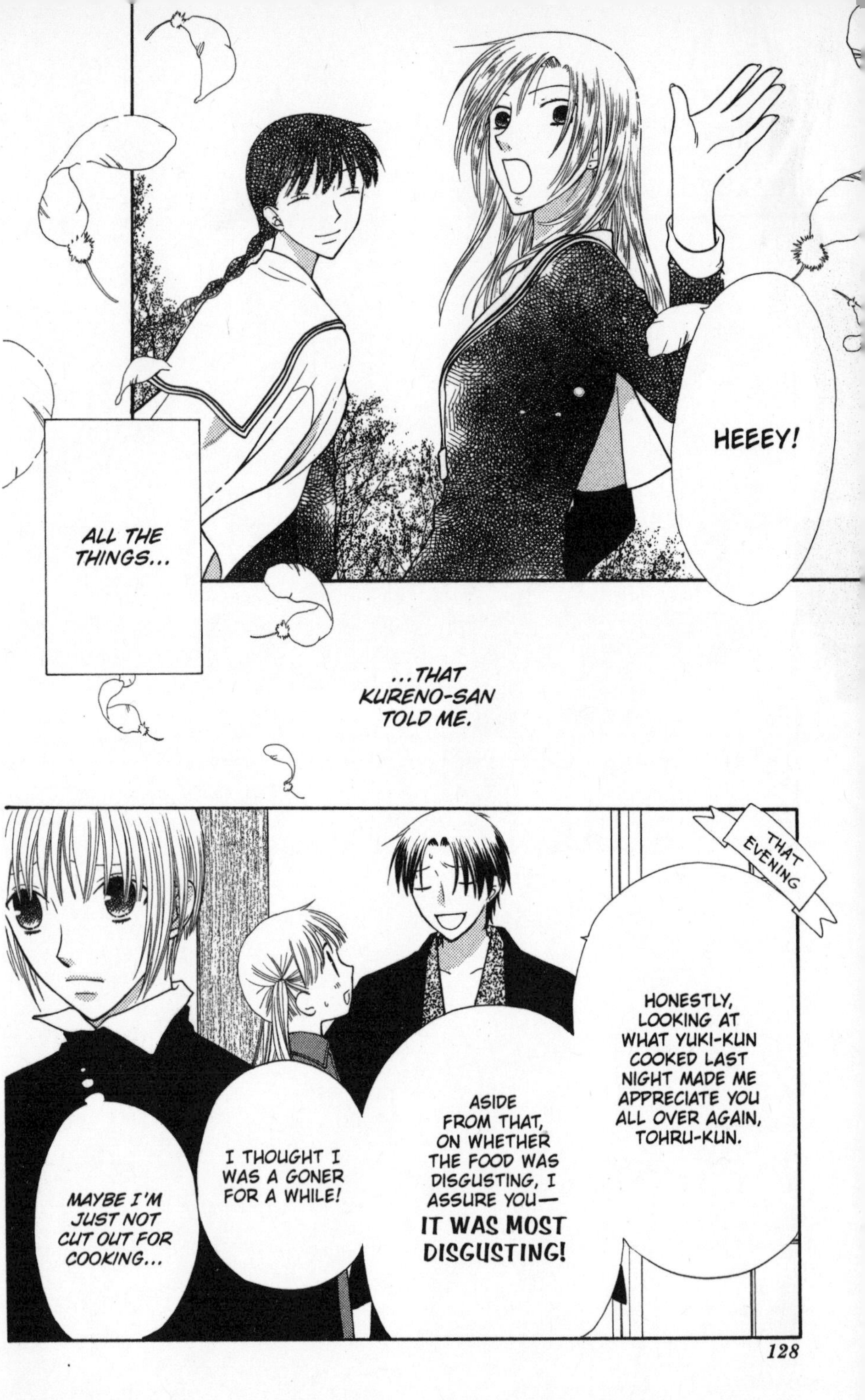
HEEEY!
ALL THE THINGS...
...THAT KURENO-SAN TOLD ME.
THAT EVENING
HONESTLY, LOOKING AT WHAT YUKI-KUN COOKED LAST NIGHT MADE ME APPRECIATE YOU ALL OVER AGAIN, TOHRU-KUN.
ASIDE FROM THAT, ON WHETHER THE FOOD WAS DISGUSTING, I ASSURE YOU— IT WAS MOST DISGUSTING!
I THOUGHT I WAS A GONER FOR A WHILE!
MAYBE I'M JUST NOT CUT OUT FOR COOKING...

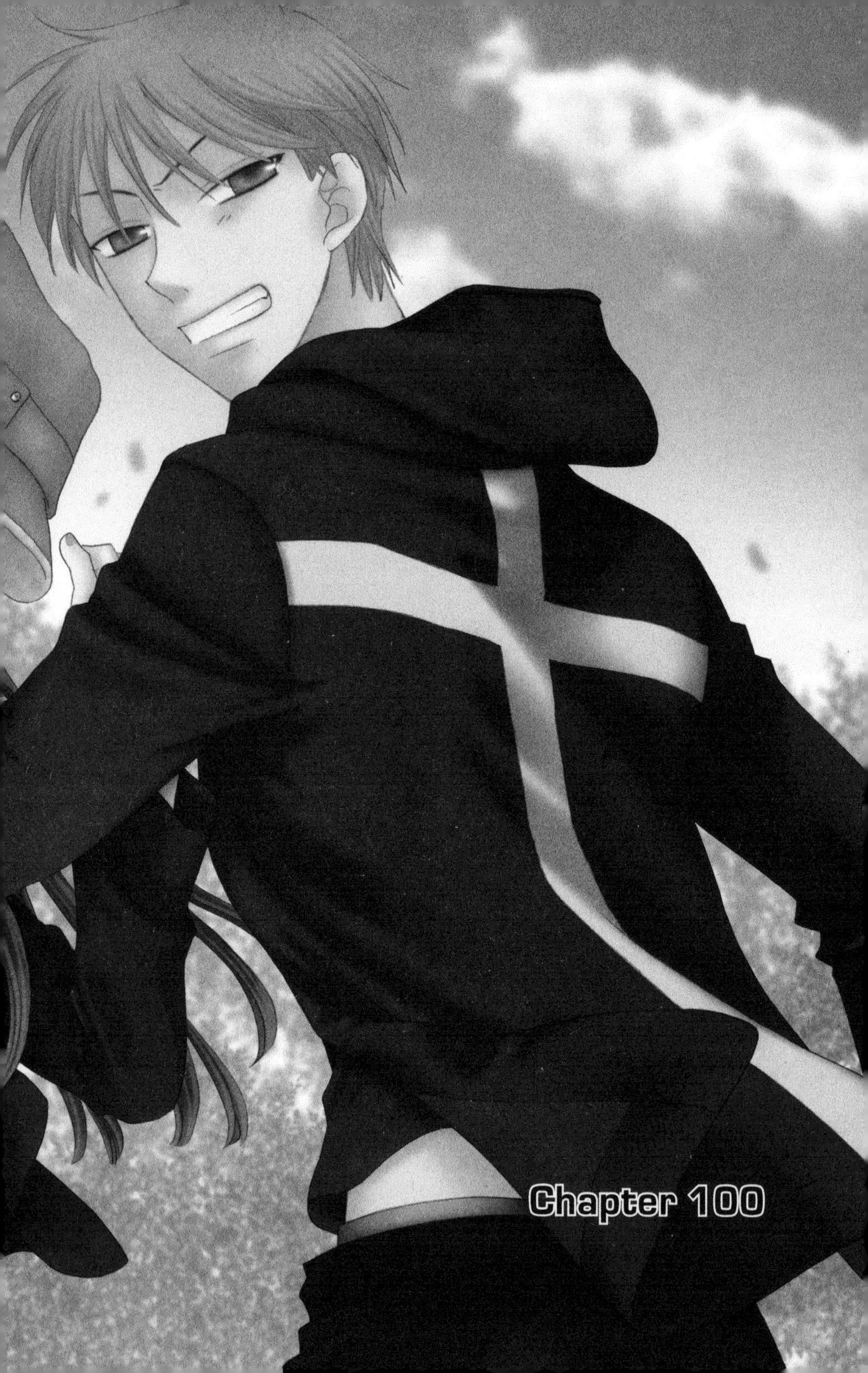
Chapter 100

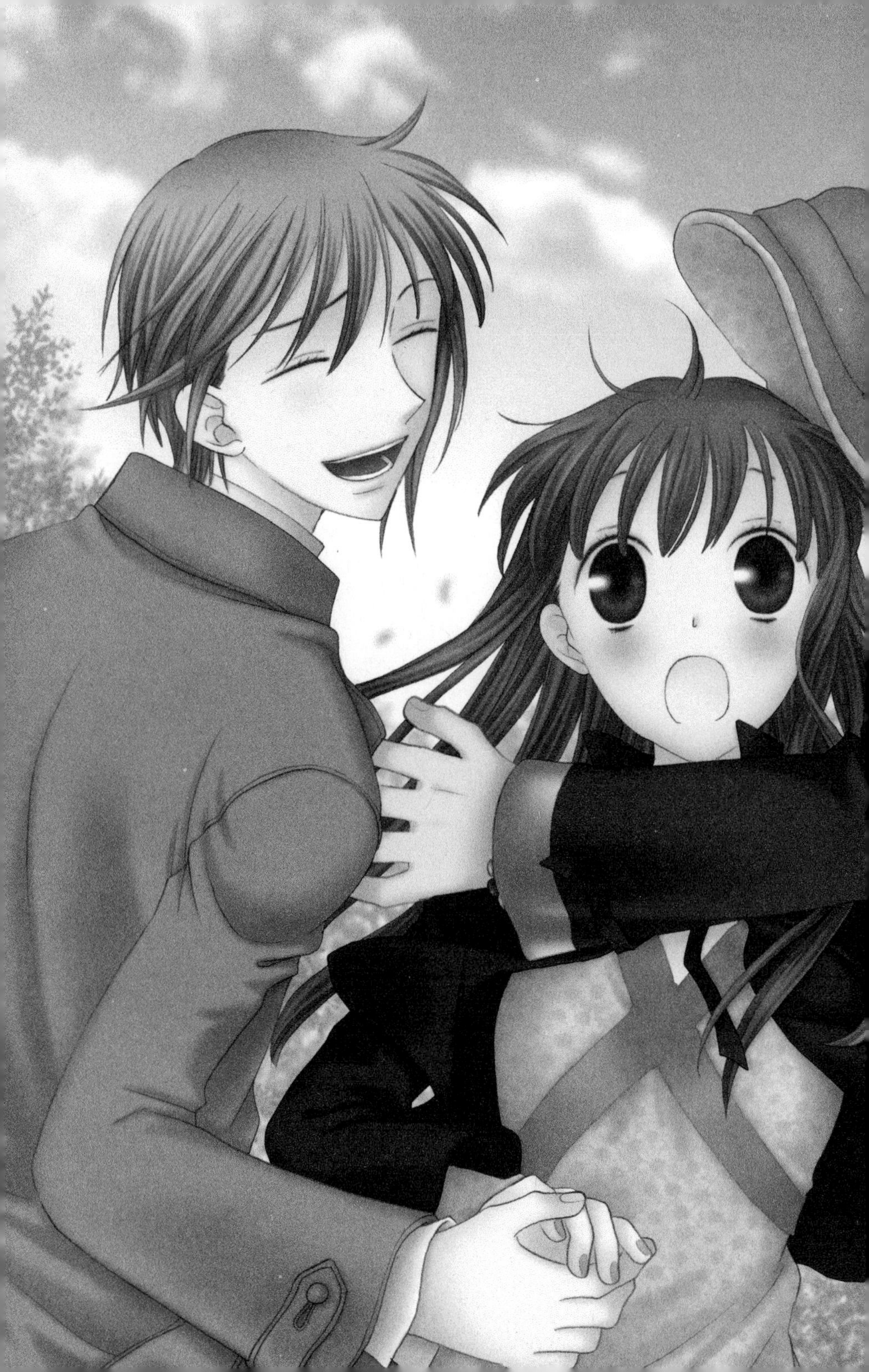

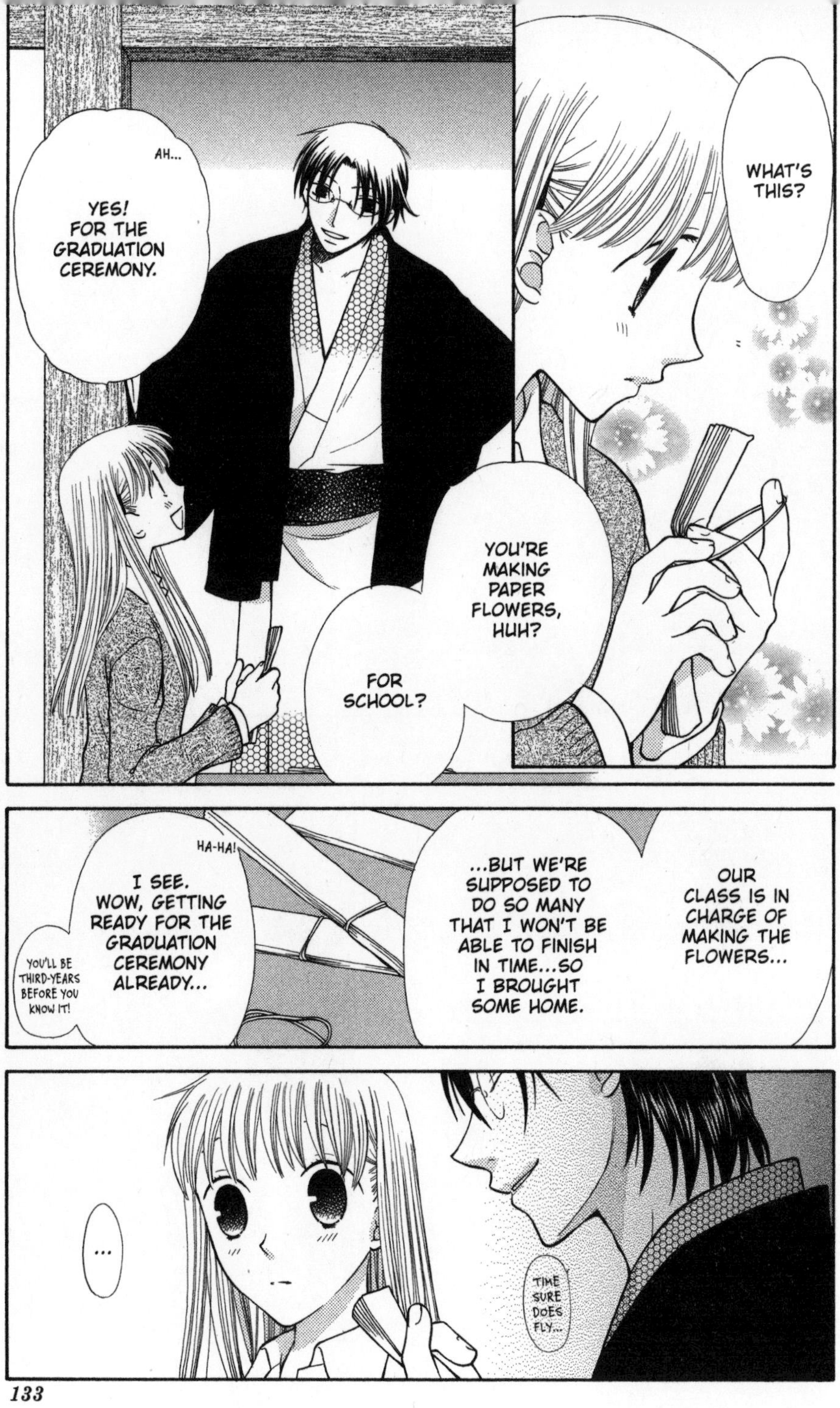
WHAT'S THIS?
YOU'RE MAKING PAPER FLOWERS, HUH?
FOR SCHOOL?
AH...
YES! FOR THE GRADUATION CEREMONY.
OUR CLASS IS IN CHARGE OF MAKING THE FLOWERS...
...BUT WE'RE SUPPOSED TO DO SO MANY THAT I WON'T BE ABLE TO FINISH IN TIME...SO I BROUGHT SOME HOME.
HA-HA!
I SEE. WOW, GETTING READY FOR THE GRADUATION CEREMONY ALREADY...
YOU'LL BE THIRD-YEARS BEFORE YOU KNOW IT!
TIME SURE DOES FLY...
...

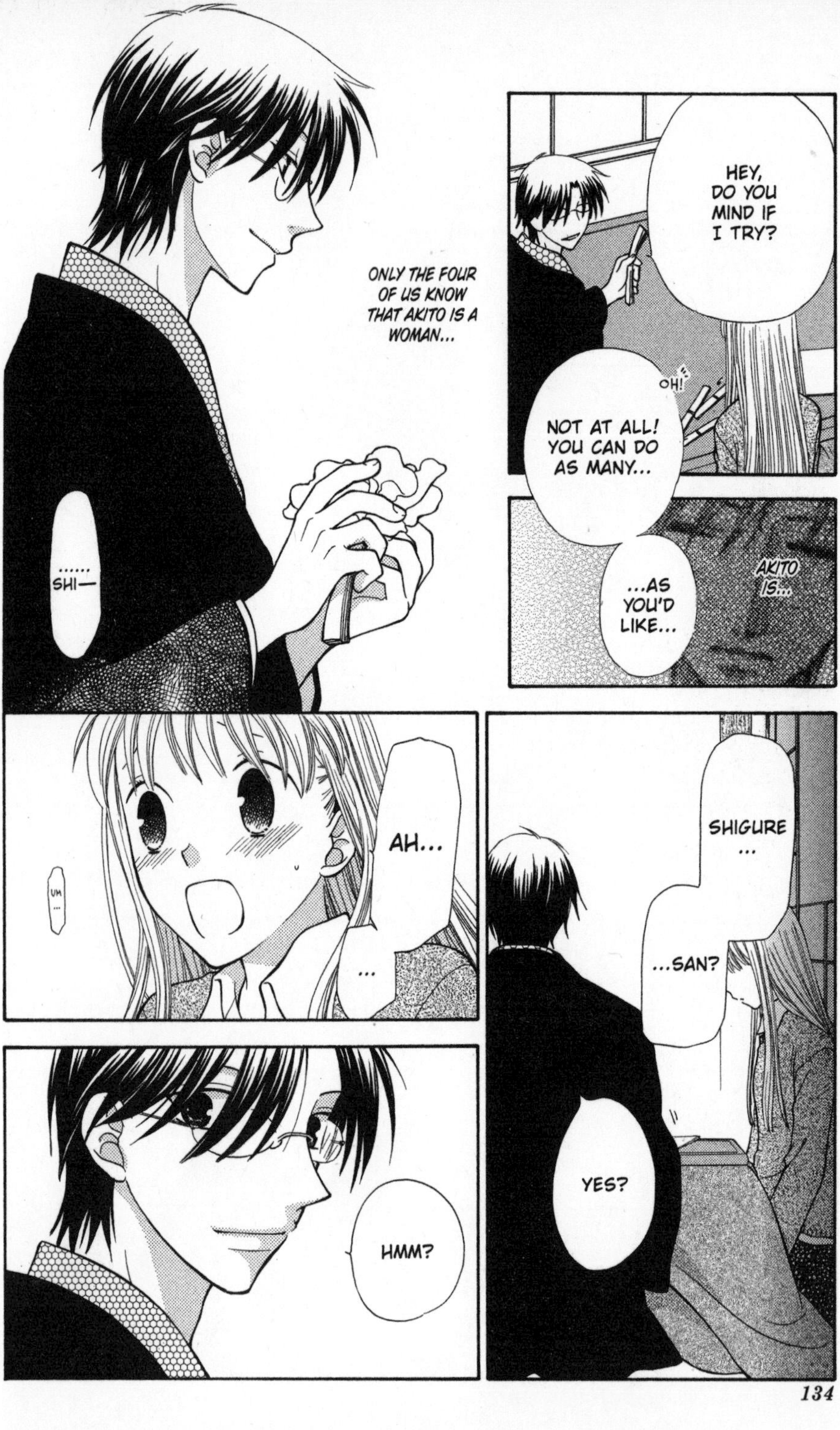
HEY, DO YOU MIND IF I TRY?
OH!
NOT AT ALL! YOU CAN DO AS MANY...
...AS YOU'D LIKE...
AKITO IS...
ONLY THE FOUR OF US KNOW THAT AKITO IS A WOMAN...
......SHI—
SHIGURE ...
...SAN?
YES?
AH...
...
UM ...
HMM?

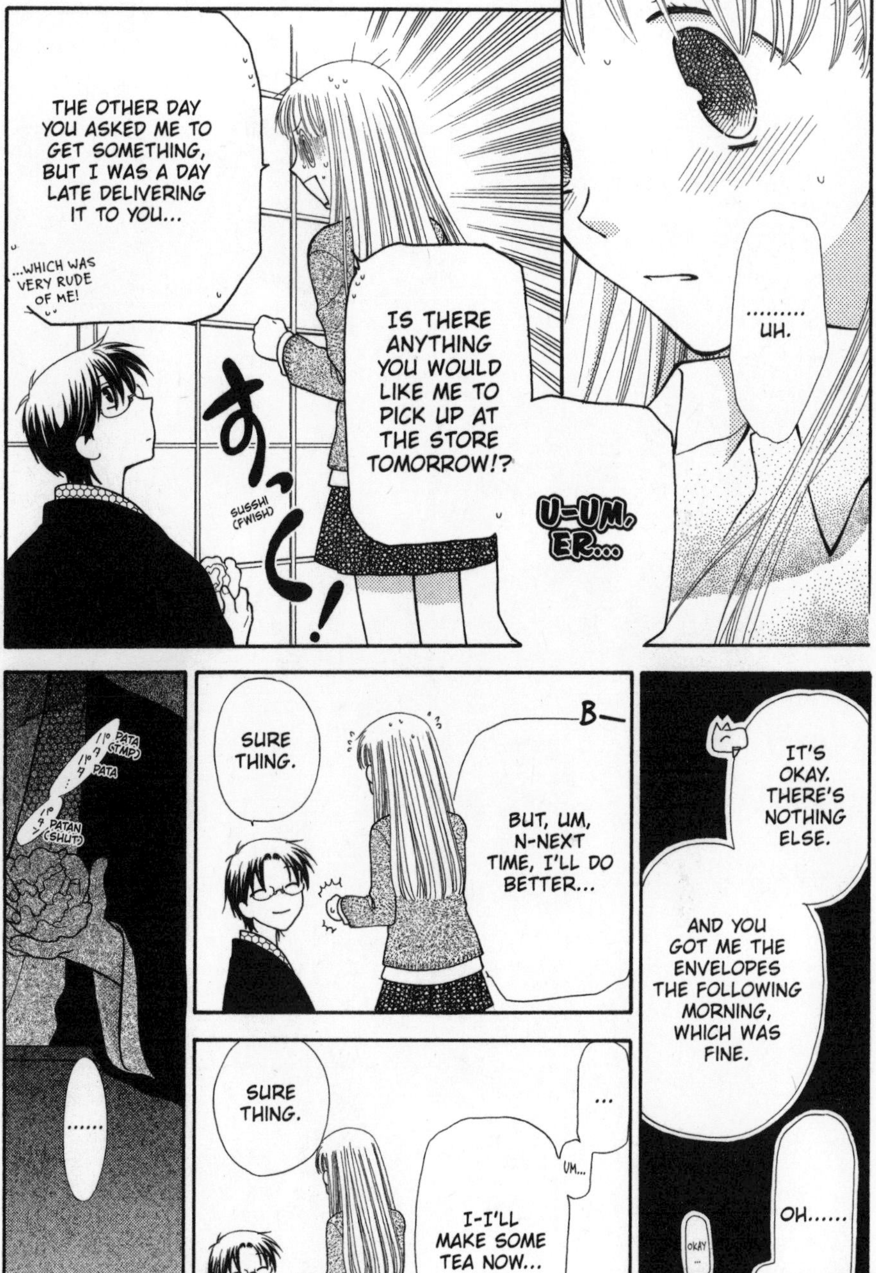
....
UH.
U-UM, ER...
THE OTHER DAY YOU ASKED ME TO GET SOMETHING, BUT I WAS A DAY LATE DELIVERING IT TO YOU...
...WHICH WAS VERY RUDE OF ME!
IS THERE ANYTHING YOU WOULD LIKE ME TO PICK UP AT THE STORE TOMORROW!?
SUSSHI (FWISH)
IT'S OKAY. THERE'S NOTHING ELSE.
AND YOU GOT ME THE ENVELOPES THE FOLLOWING MORNING, WHICH WAS FINE.
OH......
OKAY ...
...
B—
BUT, UM, N-NEXT TIME, I'LL DO BETTER...
SURE THING.
...
UM...
I-I'LL MAKE SOME TEA NOW...
SURE THING.
PATA (TMP)
PATA
PATAN (SHUT)
......

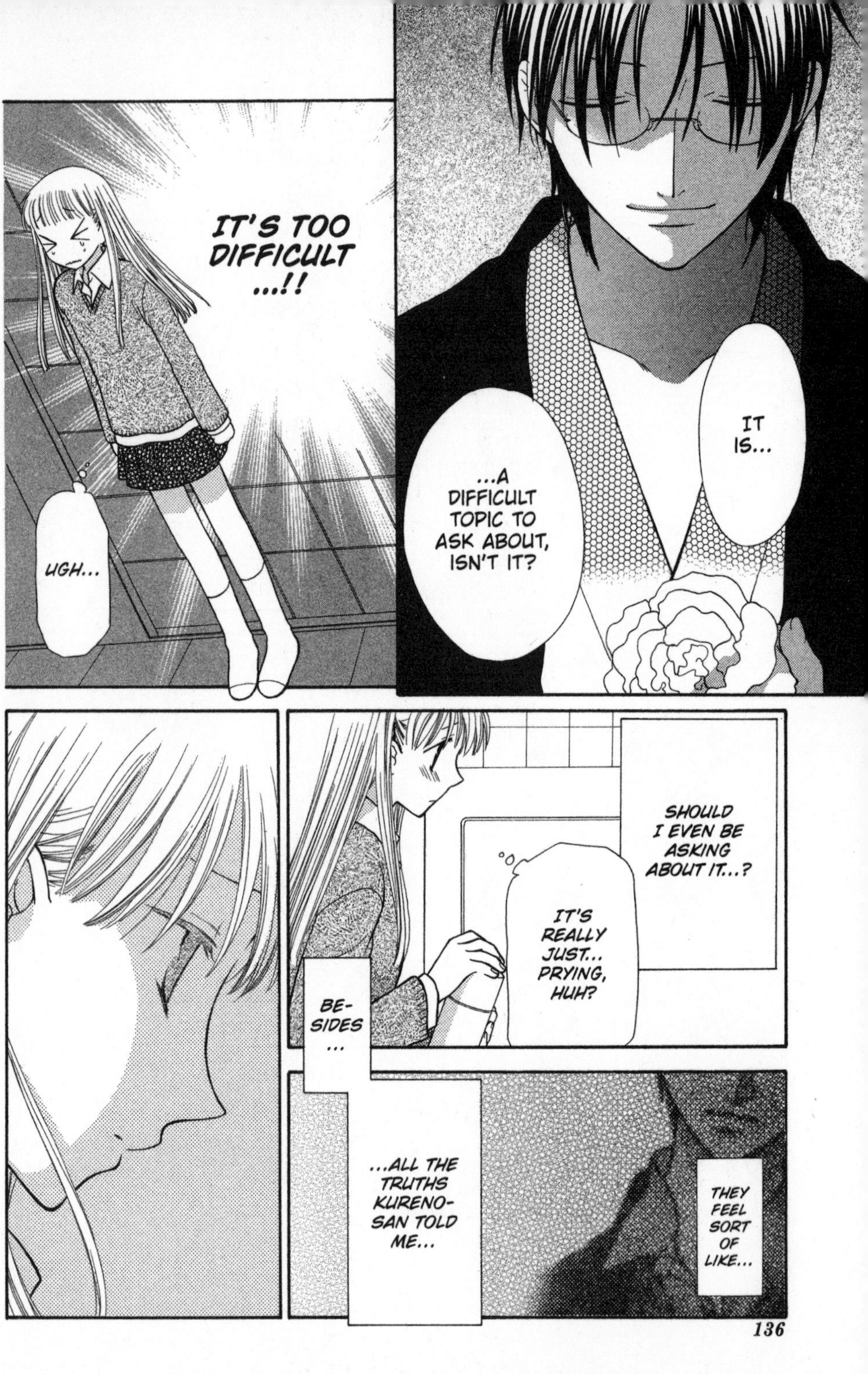
IT IS...
...A DIFFICULT TOPIC TO ASK ABOUT, ISN'T IT?
IT'S TOO DIFFICULT ...!!
UGH...
SHOULD I EVEN BE ASKING ABOUT IT...?
IT'S REALLY JUST... PRYING, HUH?
BE-SIDES...
...ALL THE TRUTHS KURENO-SAN TOLD ME...
THEY FEEL SORT OF LIKE...

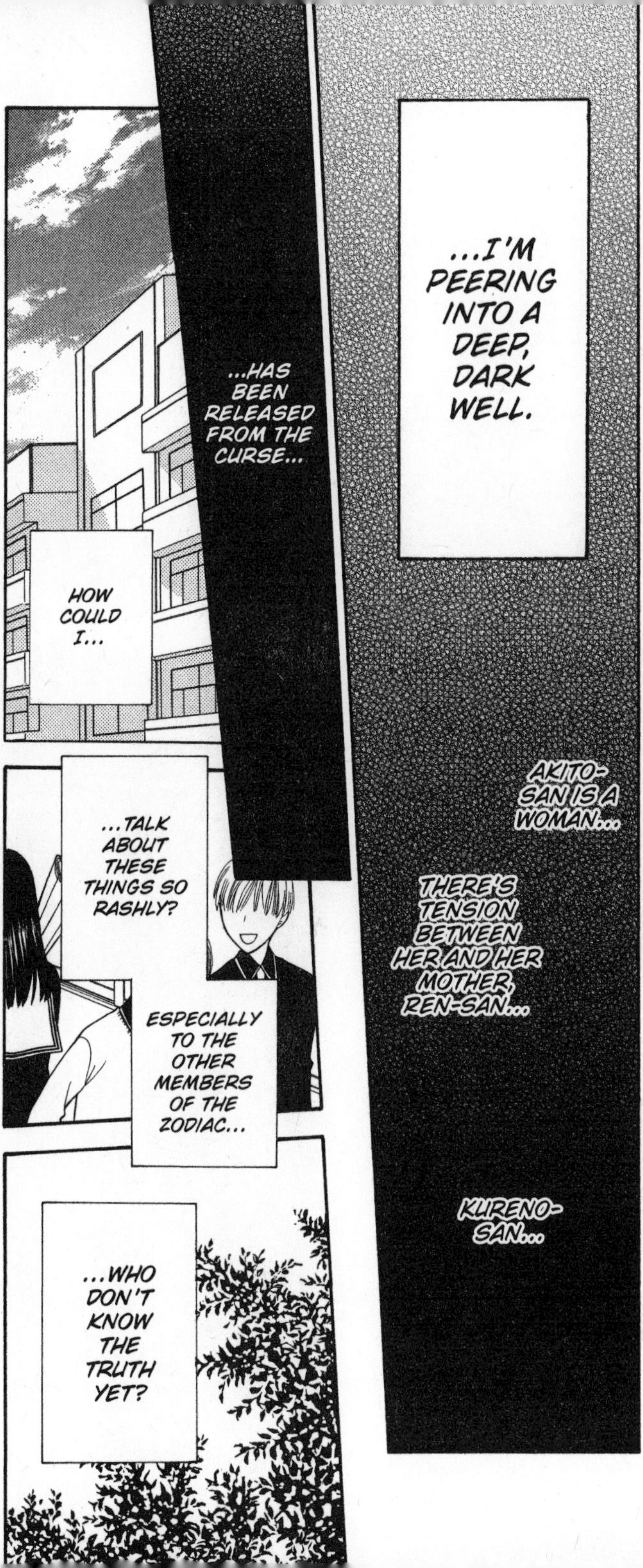
...I'M PEERING INTO A DEEP, DARK WELL.
AKITO-SAN IS A WOMAN...
THERE'S TENSION BETWEEN HER AND HER MOTHER, REN-SAN...
KURENO-SAN...
...HAS BEEN RELEASED FROM THE CURSE...
HOW COULD I...
...TALK ABOUT THESE THINGS SO RASHLY?
ESPECIALLY TO THE OTHER MEMBERS OF THE ZODIAC...
...WHO DON'T KNOW THE TRUTH YET?
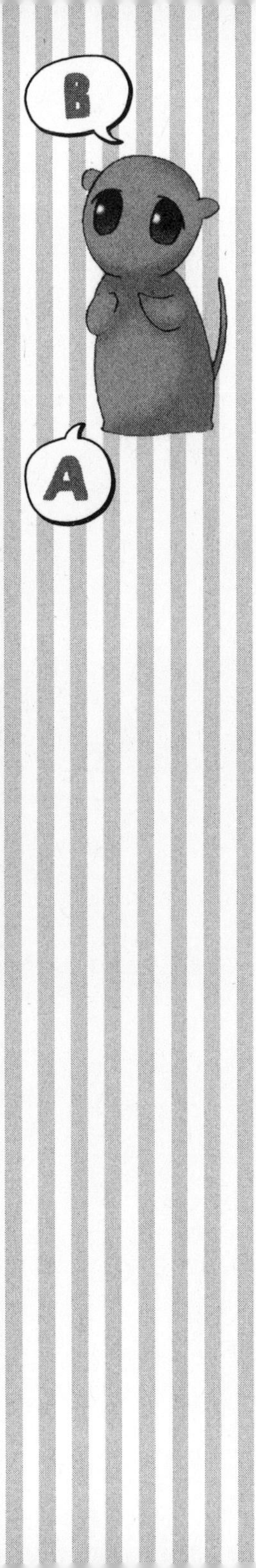
B
A

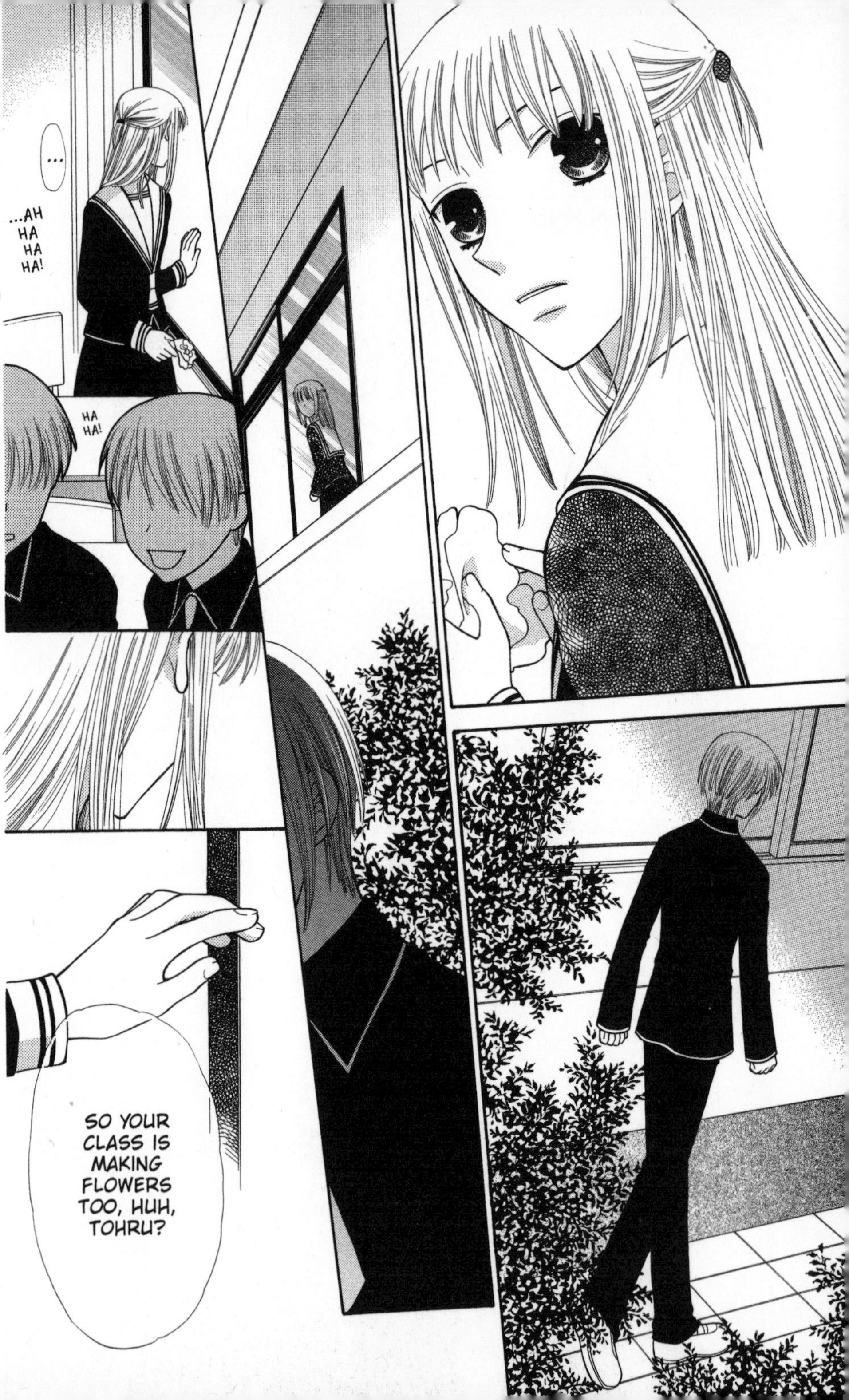
...
...AH HA HA HA!
HA HA!
SO YOUR CLASS IS MAKING FLOWERS TOO, HUH, TOHRU?

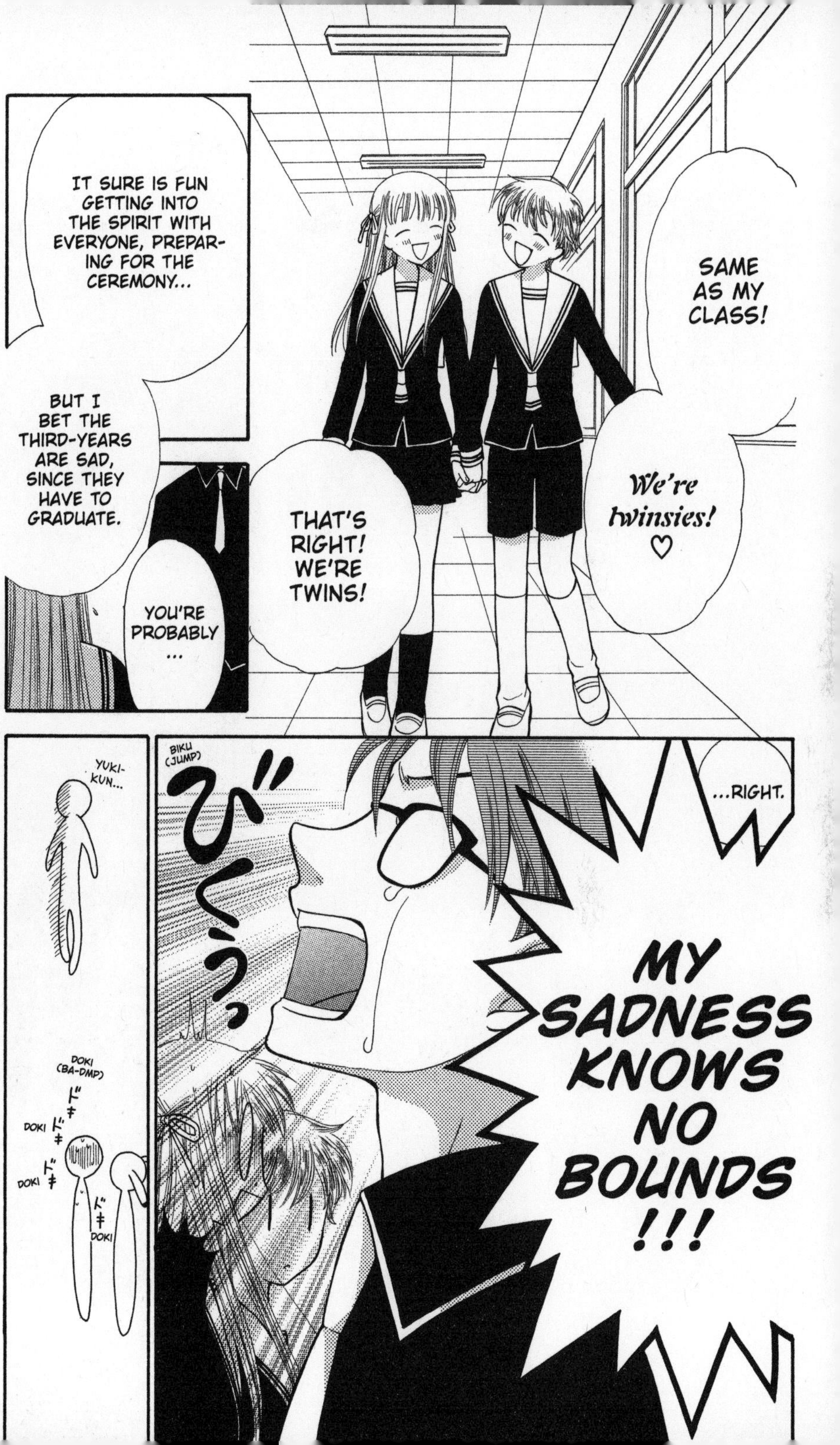
IT SURE IS FUN GETTING INTO THE SPIRIT WITH EVERYONE, PREPARING FOR THE CEREMONY...
SAME AS MY CLASS!
We're twinsies! ♡
THAT'S RIGHT! WE'RE TWINS!
BUT I BET THE THIRD-YEARS ARE SAD, SINCE THEY HAVE TO GRADUATE.
YOU'RE PROBABLY...
...RIGHT.
BIKU (JUMP)
びくっ
MY SADNESS KNOWS NO BOUNDS!!!
YUKI-KUN...
DOKI (BA-DMP)
ドキ
DOKI ドキ
DOKI ドキ
ドキ DOKI

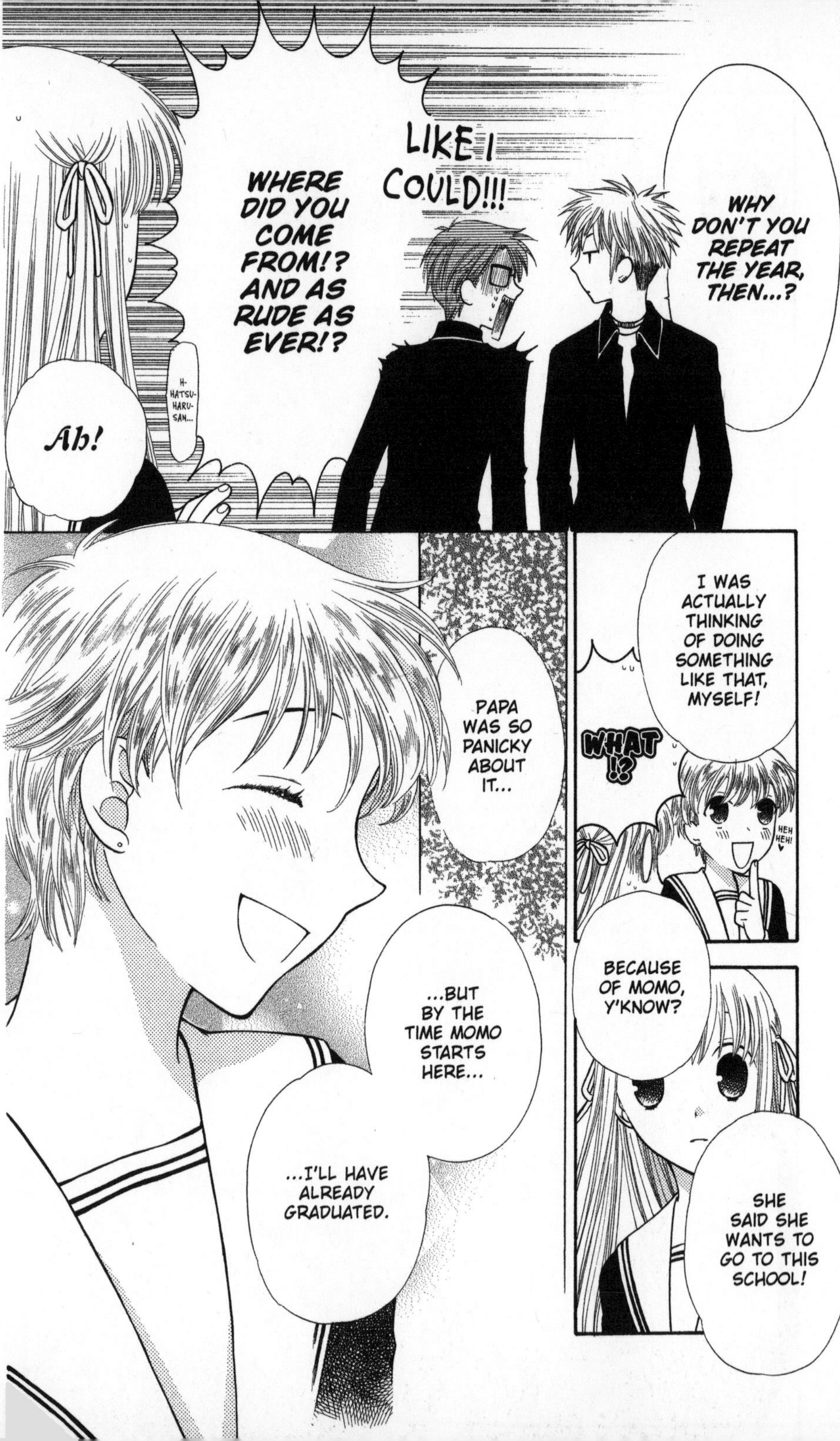
WHY DON'T YOU REPEAT THE YEAR, THEN...?
LIKE I COULD!!!
WHERE DID YOU COME FROM!? AND AS RUDE AS EVER!?
H-HATSU-HARU-SAN...
Ah!
I WAS ACTUALLY THINKING OF DOING SOMETHING LIKE THAT, MYSELF!
WHAT !?
HEH HEH!
BECAUSE OF MOMO, Y'KNOW?
SHE SAID SHE WANTS TO GO TO THIS SCHOOL!
PAPA WAS SO PANICKY ABOUT IT...
...BUT BY THE TIME MOMO STARTS HERE...
...I'LL HAVE ALREADY GRADUATED.

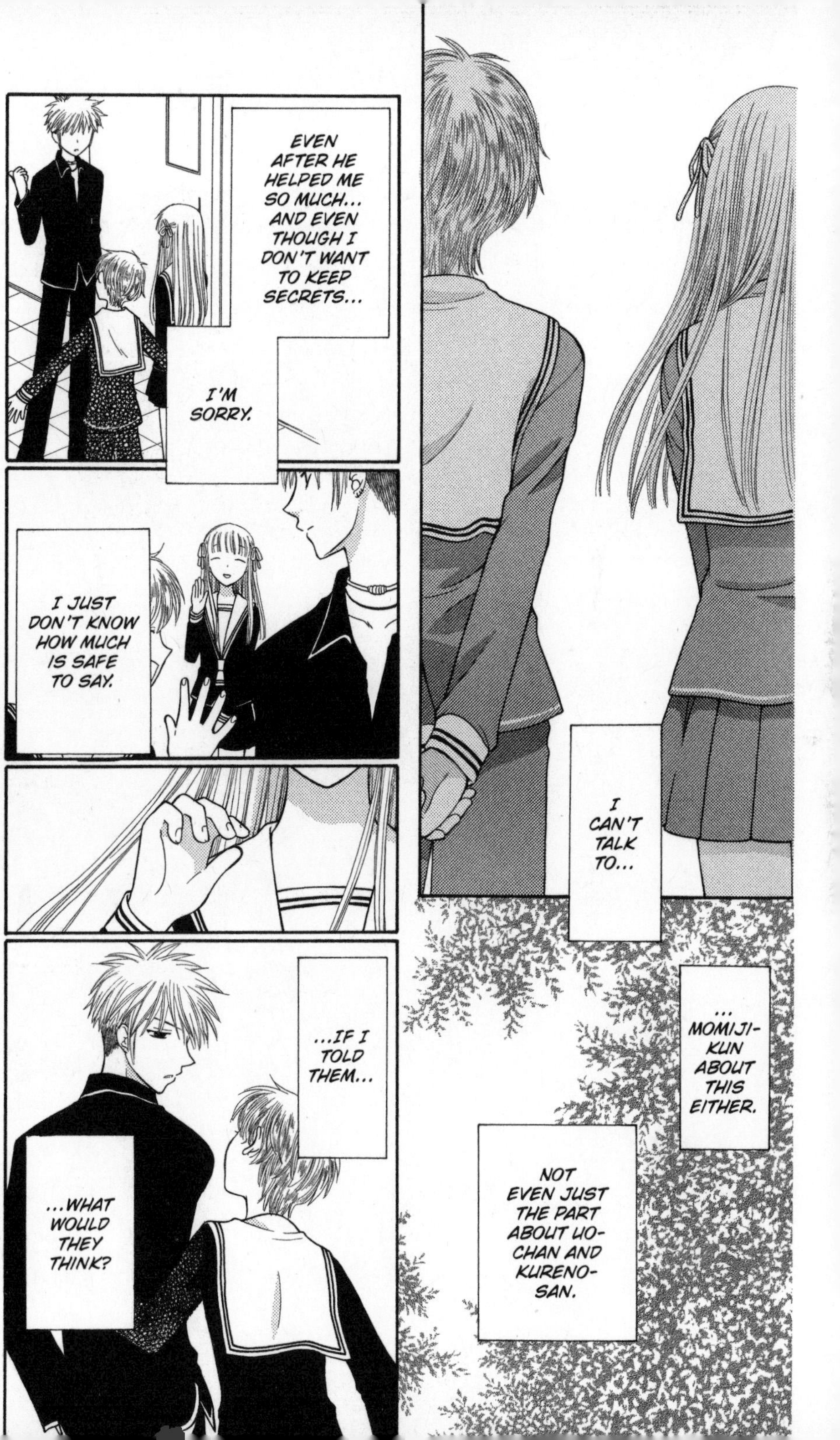
EVEN AFTER HE HELPED ME SO MUCH... AND EVEN THOUGH I DON'T WANT TO KEEP SECRETS...
I'M SORRY.
I JUST DON'T KNOW HOW MUCH IS SAFE TO SAY.
...IF I TOLD THEM...
...WHAT WOULD THEY THINK?
I CAN'T TALK TO...
...MOMIJI-KUN ABOUT THIS EITHER.
NOT EVEN JUST THE PART ABOUT UO-CHAN AND KURENO-SAN.

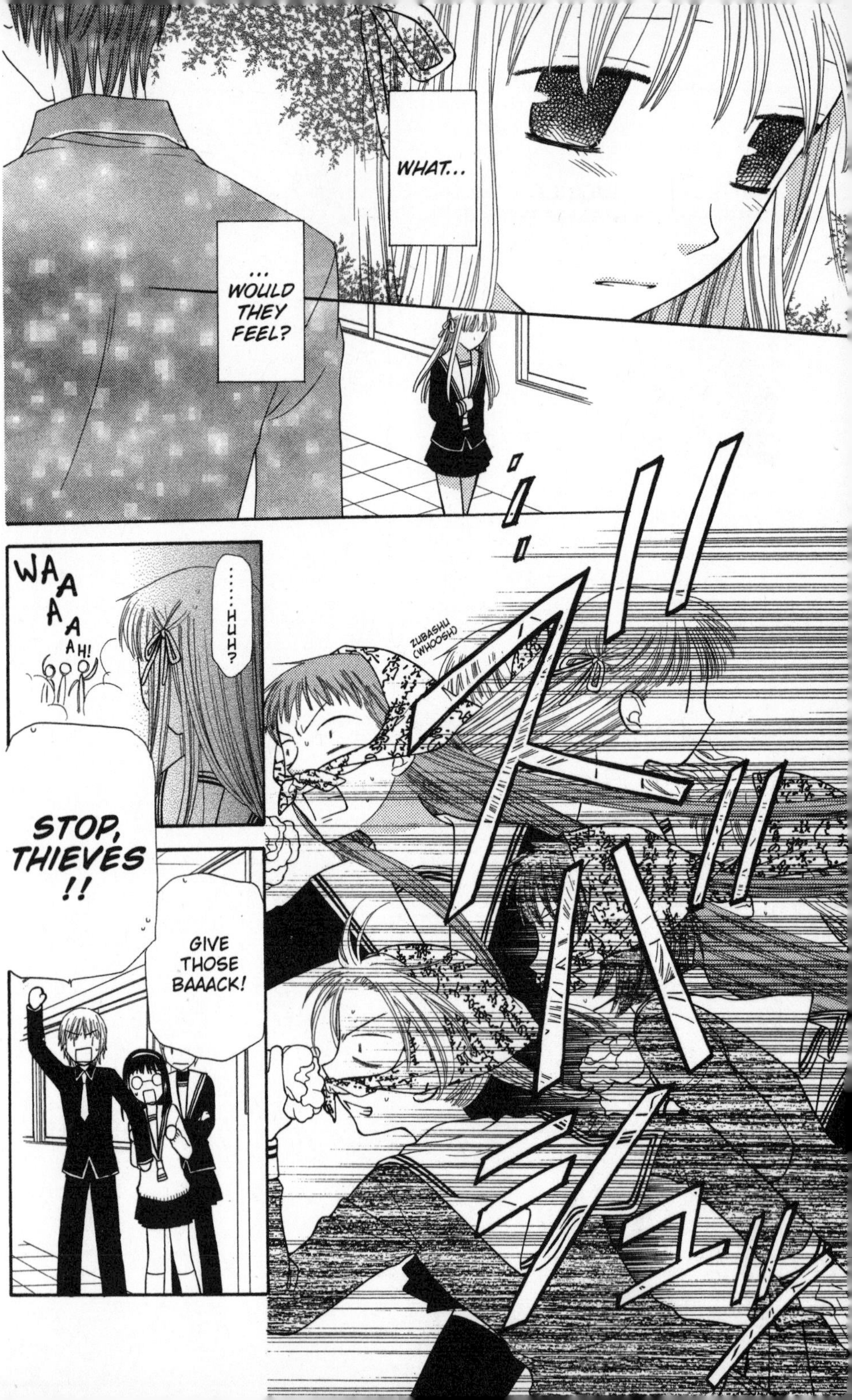
WHAT...
...WOULD THEY FEEL?
ZUBASHU (WHOOSH)
......HUH?
WAAAAAH!
STOP, THIEVES!!
GIVE THOSE BAAACK!

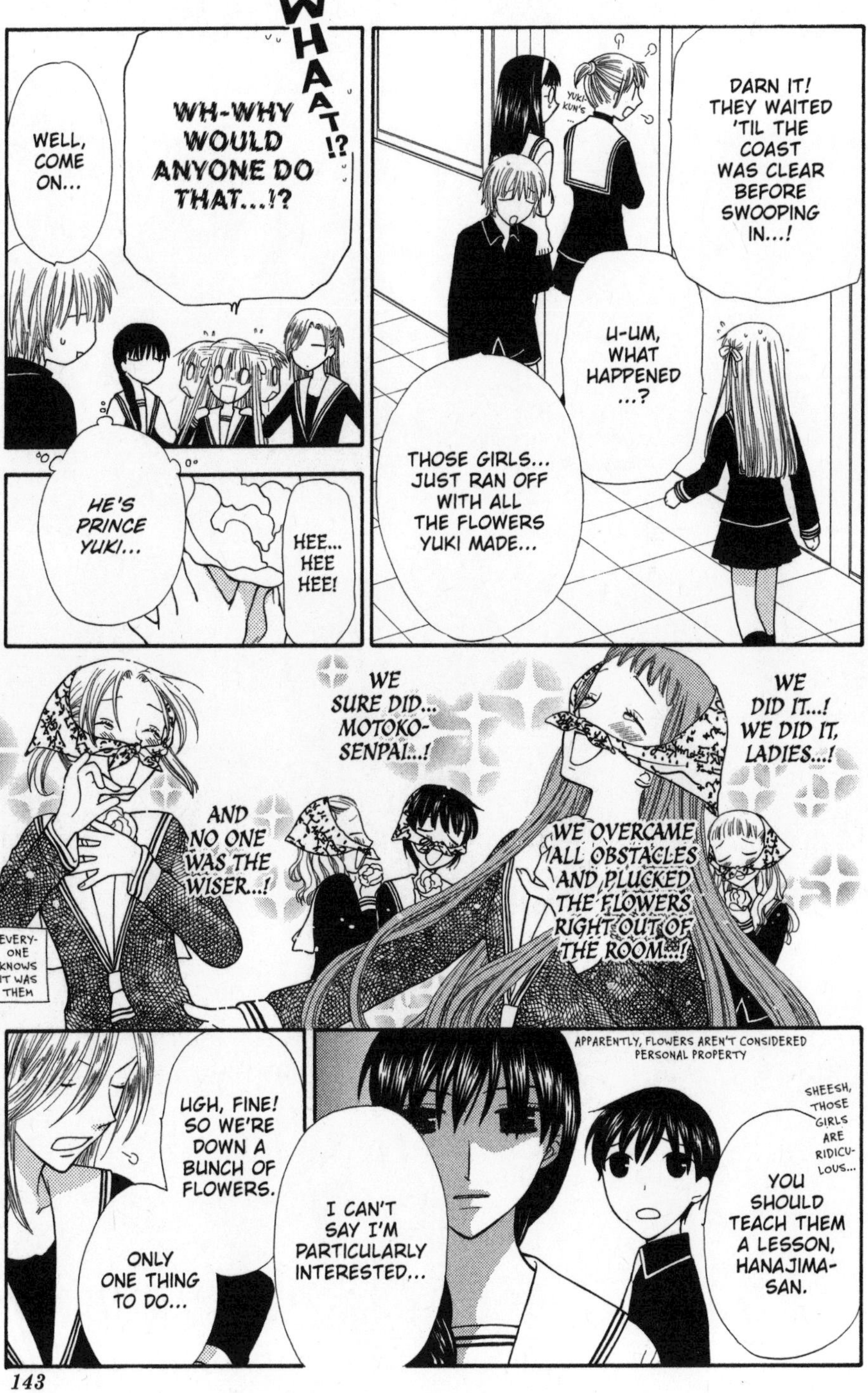

DARN IT! THEY WAITED 'TIL THE COAST WAS CLEAR BEFORE SWOOPING IN...!
YUKI-KUN'S...
U-UM, WHAT HAPPENED...?
THOSE GIRLS... JUST RAN OFF WITH ALL THE FLOWERS YUKI MADE...
WHAAT!?
WH-WHY WOULD ANYONE DO THAT...!?
WELL, COME ON...
HE'S PRINCE YUKI...
HEE... HEE HEE!
WE DID IT...! WE DID IT, LADIES...!
WE SURE DID... MOTOKO-SENPAI...!
WE OVERCAME ALL OBSTACLES AND PLUCKED THE FLOWERS RIGHT OUT OF THE ROOM...!
AND NO ONE WAS THE WISER...!
EVERYONE KNOWS IT WAS THEM
APPARENTLY, FLOWERS AREN'T CONSIDERED PERSONAL PROPERTY
SHEESH, THOSE GIRLS ARE RIDICULOUS...
YOU SHOULD TEACH THEM A LESSON, HANAJIMA-SAN.
I CAN'T SAY I'M PARTICULARLY INTERESTED...
UGH, FINE! SO WE'RE DOWN A BUNCH OF FLOWERS.
ONLY ONE THING TO DO...

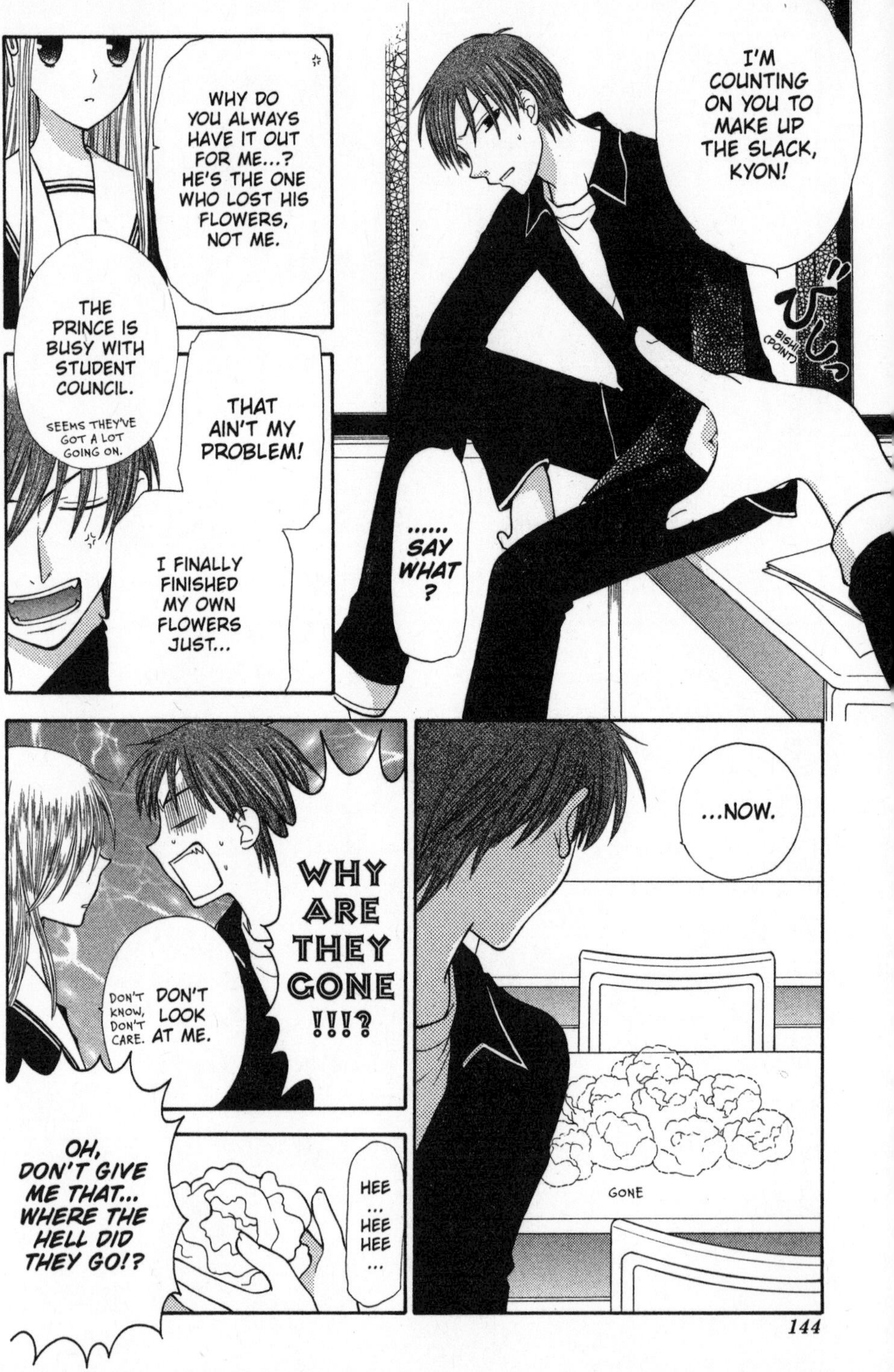

I'M COUNTING ON YOU TO MAKE UP THE SLACK, KYON!
BISHI (POINT)
...... SAY WHAT?
WHY DO YOU ALWAYS HAVE IT OUT FOR ME...? HE'S THE ONE WHO LOST HIS FLOWERS, NOT ME.
THE PRINCE IS BUSY WITH STUDENT COUNCIL.
SEEMS THEY'VE GOT A LOT GOING ON.
THAT AIN'T MY PROBLEM!
I FINALLY FINISHED MY OWN FLOWERS JUST...
...NOW.
GONE
WHY ARE THEY GONE !!!?
DON'T LOOK AT ME.
DON'T KNOW, DON'T CARE.
OH, DON'T GIVE ME THAT... WHERE THE HELL DID THEY GO!?
HEE ... HEE HEE ...

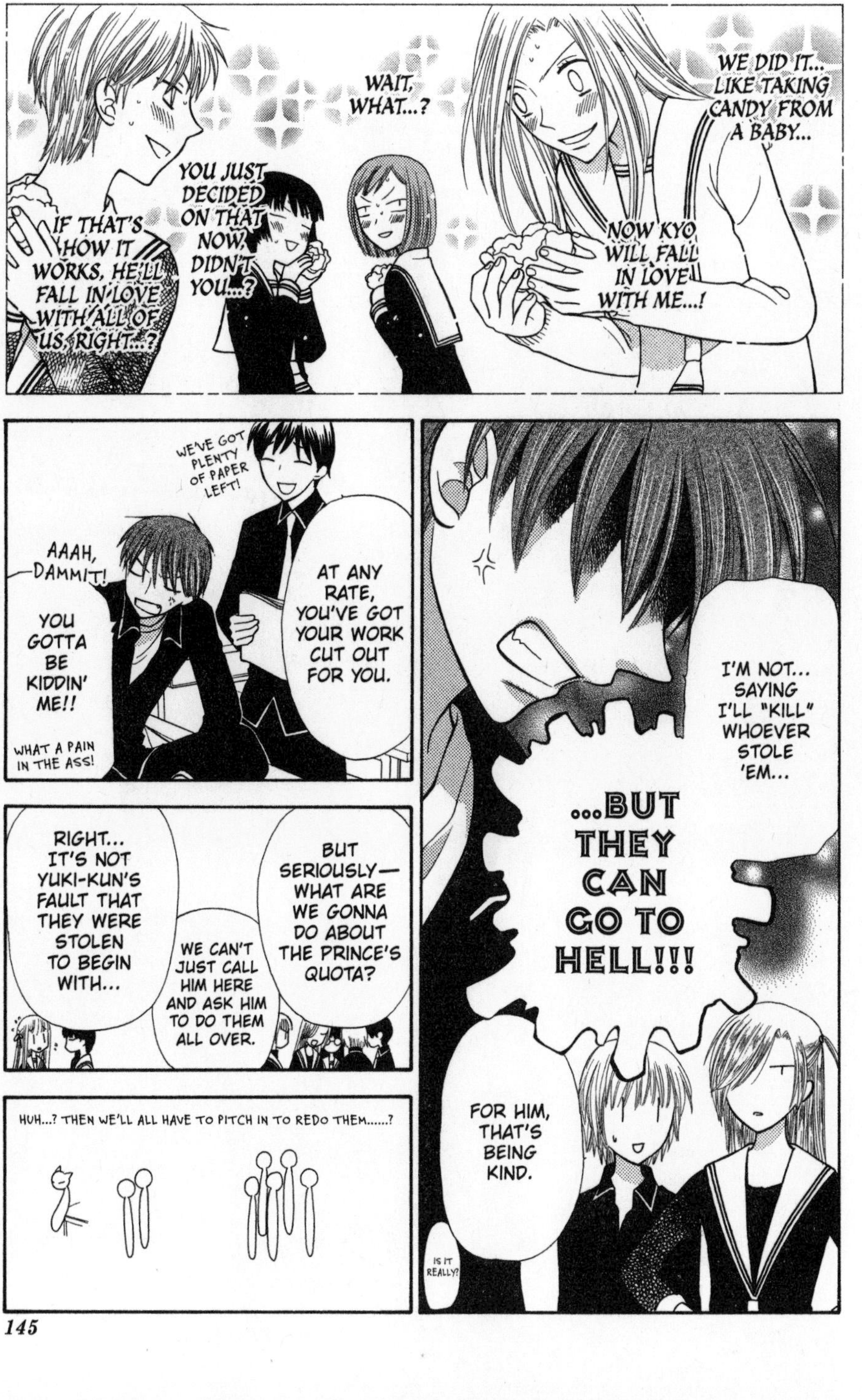
WE DID IT... LIKE TAKING CANDY FROM A BABY...
NOW KYO WILL FALL IN LOVE WITH ME...!
WAIT, WHAT...?
YOU JUST DECIDED ON THAT NOW, DIDN'T YOU...?
IF THAT'S HOW IT WORKS, HE'LL FALL IN LOVE WITH ALL OF US, RIGHT...?
I'M NOT... SAYING I'LL "KILL" WHOEVER STOLE 'EM...
...BUT THEY CAN GO TO HELL!!!
FOR HIM, THAT'S BEING KIND.
IS IT REALLY?
AT ANY RATE, YOU'VE GOT YOUR WORK CUT OUT FOR YOU.
WE'VE GOT PLENTY OF PAPER LEFT!
AAAH, DAMMIT!
YOU GOTTA BE KIDDIN' ME!!
WHAT A PAIN IN THE ASS!
BUT SERIOUSLY— WHAT ARE WE GONNA DO ABOUT THE PRINCE'S QUOTA?
WE CAN'T JUST CALL HIM HERE AND ASK HIM TO DO THEM ALL OVER.
RIGHT... IT'S NOT YUKI-KUN'S FAULT THAT THEY WERE STOLEN TO BEGIN WITH...
HUH...? THEN WE'LL ALL HAVE TO PITCH IN TO REDO THEM......?

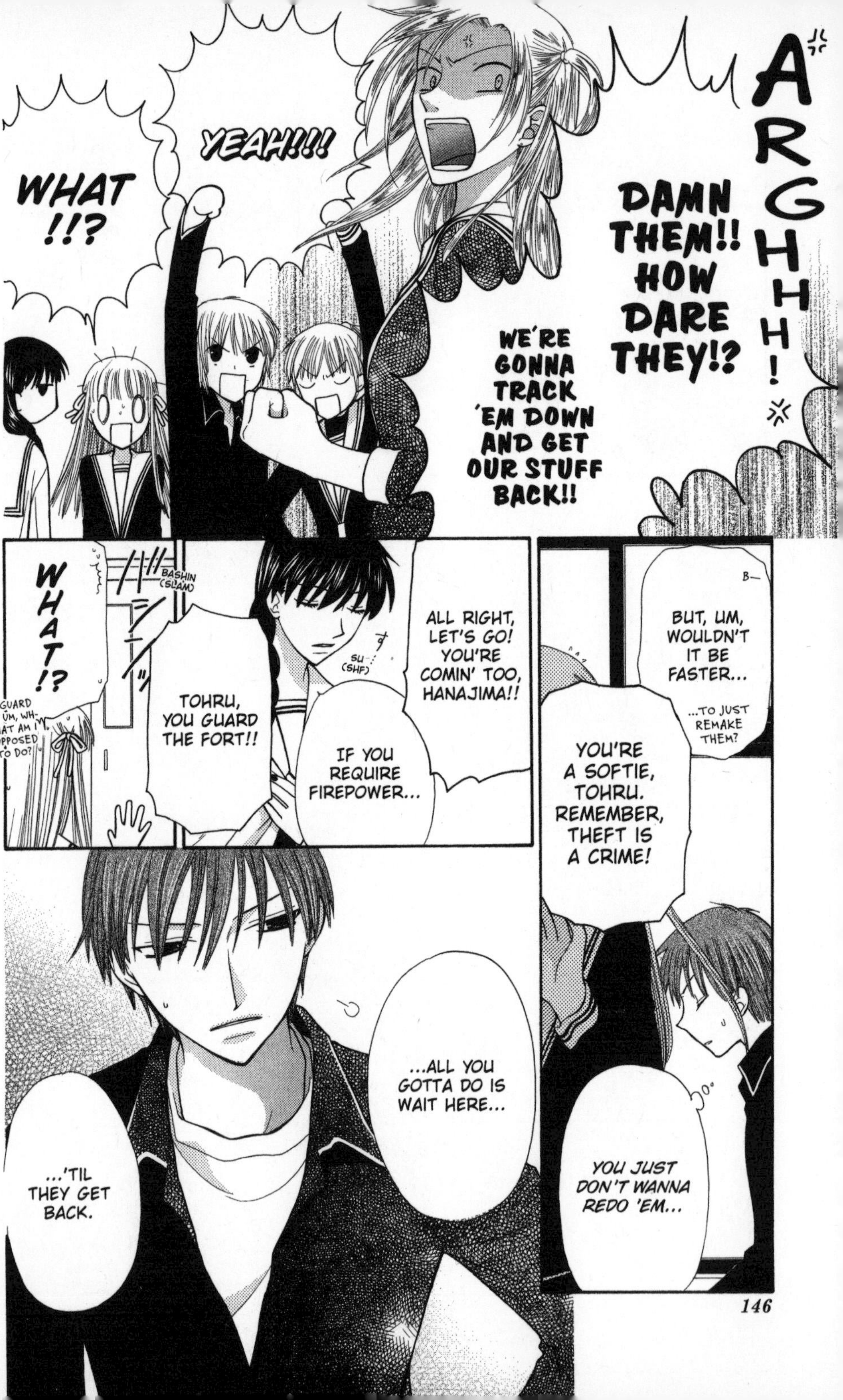
ARGHHH!
DAMN THEM!! HOW DARE THEY!?
WE'RE GONNA TRACK 'EM DOWN AND GET OUR STUFF BACK!!
YEAH!!!
WHAT!!?
B—
BUT, UM, WOULDN'T IT BE FASTER...
...TO JUST REMAKE THEM?
YOU'RE A SOFTIE, TOHRU. REMEMBER, THEFT IS A CRIME!
YOU JUST DON'T WANNA REDO 'EM...
ALL RIGHT, LET'S GO! YOU'RE COMIN' TOO, HANAJIMA!!
SU (SHF)
IF YOU REQUIRE FIREPOWER...
BASHIN (SLAM)
TOHRU, YOU GUARD THE FORT!!
WHAT!?
G-GUARD IT? UM, WH-WHAT AM I SUPPOSED TO DO?
...ALL YOU GOTTA DO IS WAIT HERE...
...'TIL THEY GET BACK.

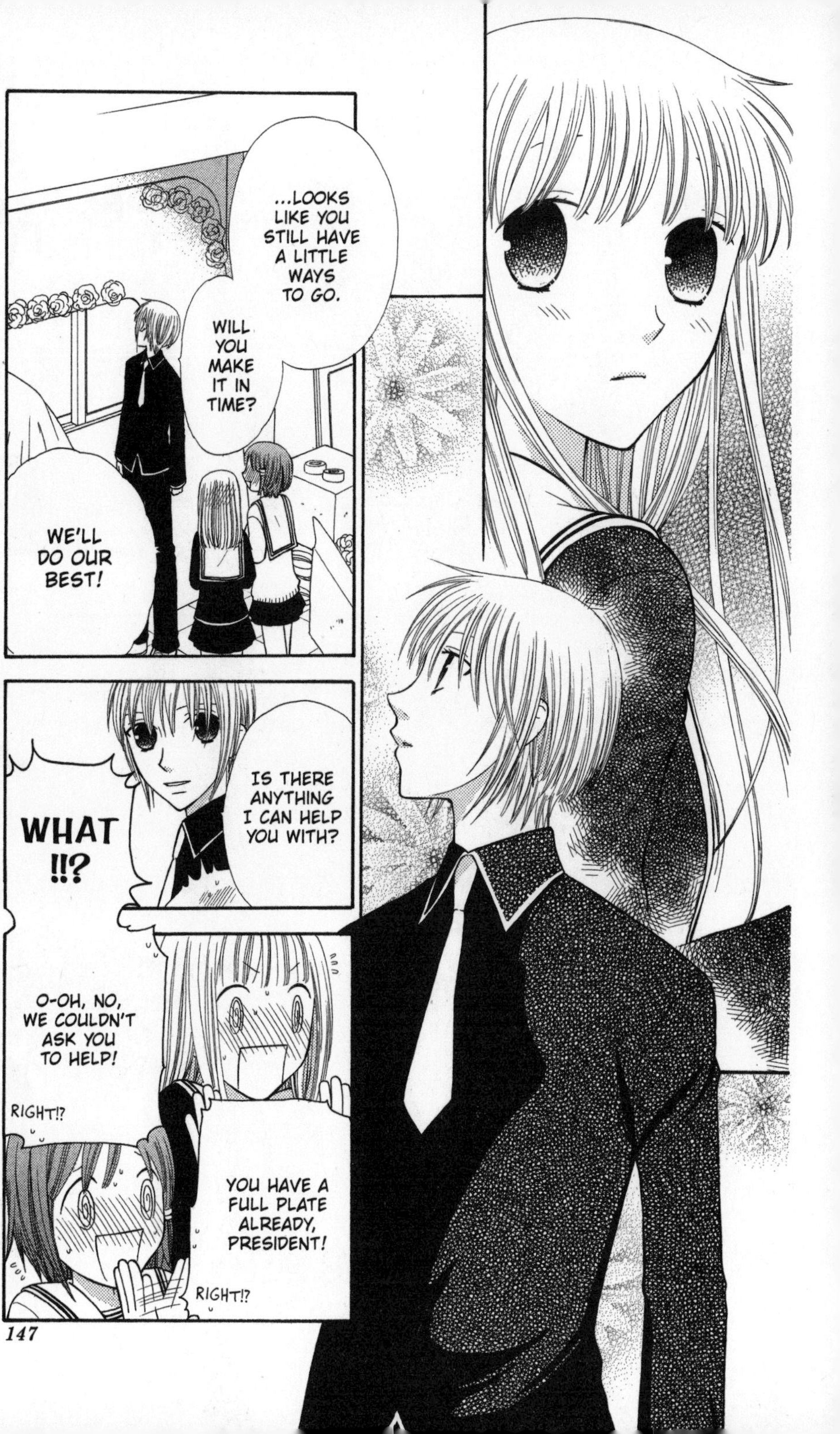
...LOOKS LIKE YOU STILL HAVE A LITTLE WAYS TO GO.
WILL YOU MAKE IT IN TIME?
WE'LL DO OUR BEST!
IS THERE ANYTHING I CAN HELP YOU WITH?
WHAT !!?
O-OH, NO, WE COULDN'T ASK YOU TO HELP!
RIGHT!?
YOU HAVE A FULL PLATE ALREADY, PRESIDENT!
RIGHT!?

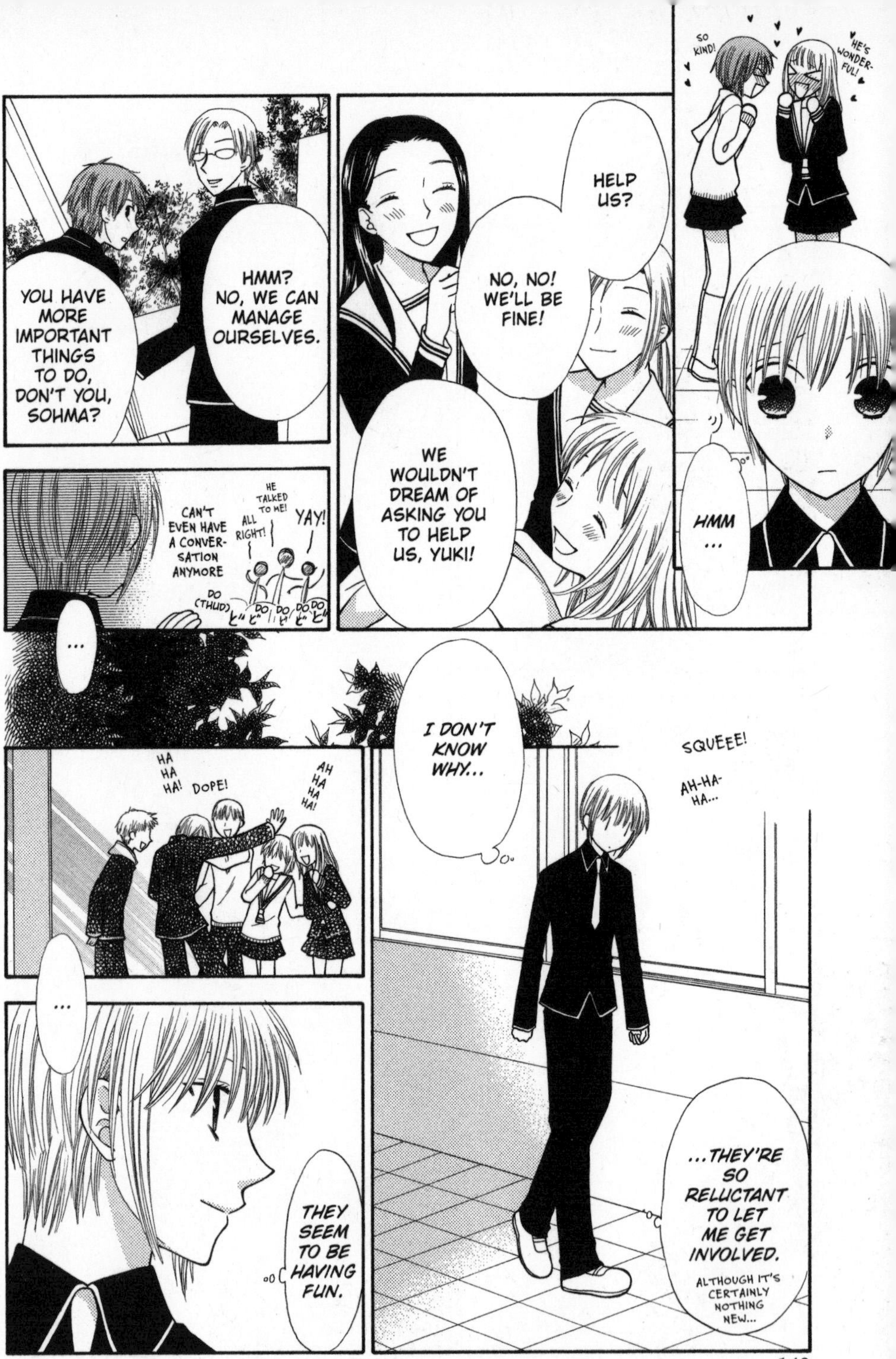
SO KIND!
HE'S WONDERFUL!
HMM...
HELP US?
NO, NO! WE'LL BE FINE!
WE WOULDN'T DREAM OF ASKING YOU TO HELP US, YUKI!
HMM? NO, WE CAN MANAGE OURSELVES.
YOU HAVE MORE IMPORTANT THINGS TO DO, DON'T YOU, SOHMA?
CAN'T EVEN HAVE A CONVERSATION ANYMORE
HE TALKED TO ME!
ALL RIGHT!
YAY!
DO (THUD) DO DO DO DO
...
I DON'T KNOW WHY...
SQUEEE!
AH-HA-HA...
...THEY'RE SO RELUCTANT TO LET ME GET INVOLVED.
ALTHOUGH IT'S CERTAINLY NOTHING NEW...
HA HA HA!
DOPE!
AH HA HA HA HA!
...
THEY SEEM TO BE HAVING FUN.

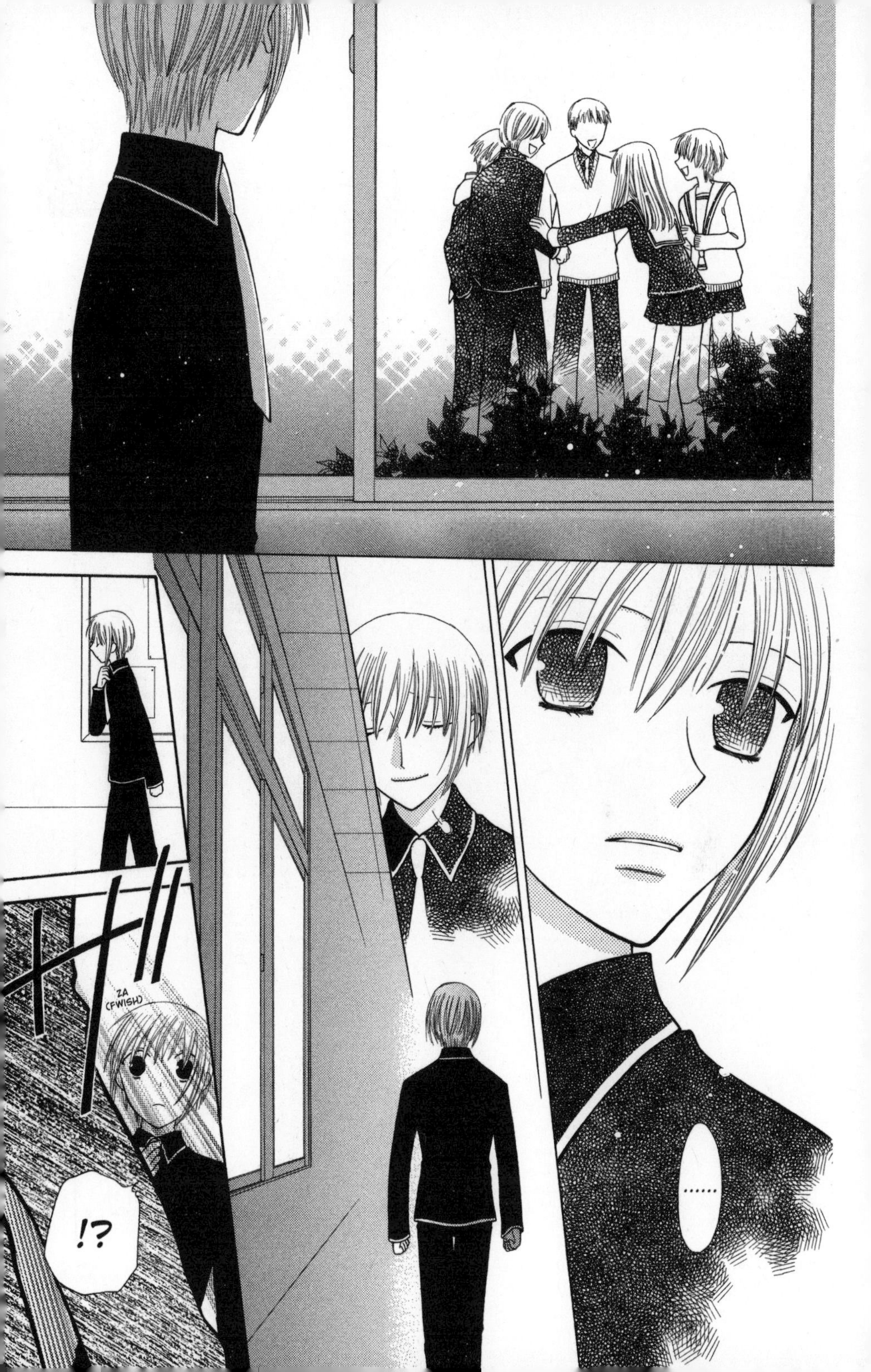
......
ZA (FWISH)
!?

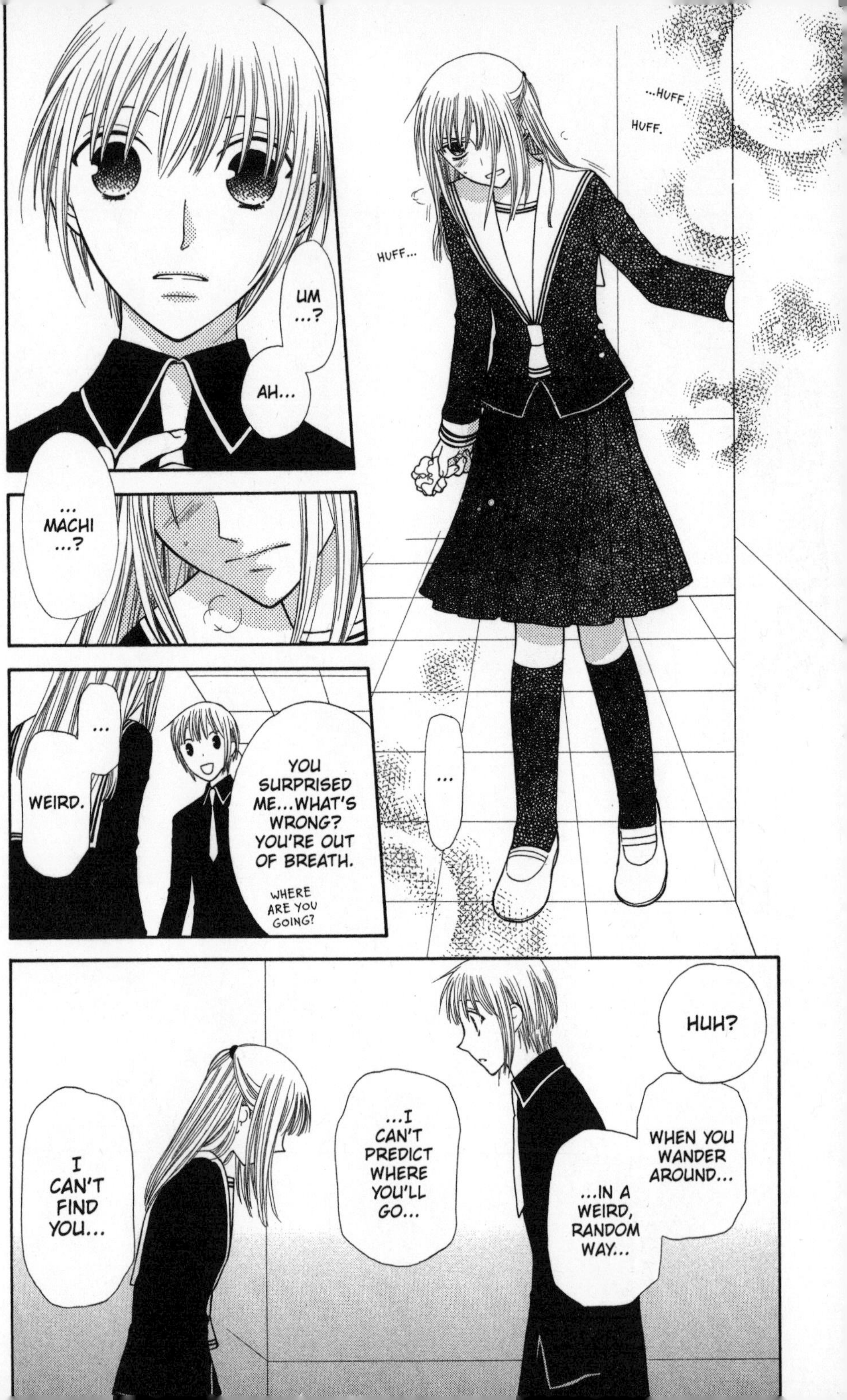
...HUFF.
HUFF.
HUFF...
...
UM ...?
AH...
... MACHI ...?
YOU SURPRISED ME...WHAT'S WRONG? YOU'RE OUT OF BREATH.
WHERE ARE YOU GOING?
... WEIRD.
HUH?
WHEN YOU WANDER AROUND...
...IN A WEIRD, RANDOM WAY...
...I CAN'T PREDICT WHERE YOU'LL GO...
I CAN'T FIND YOU...

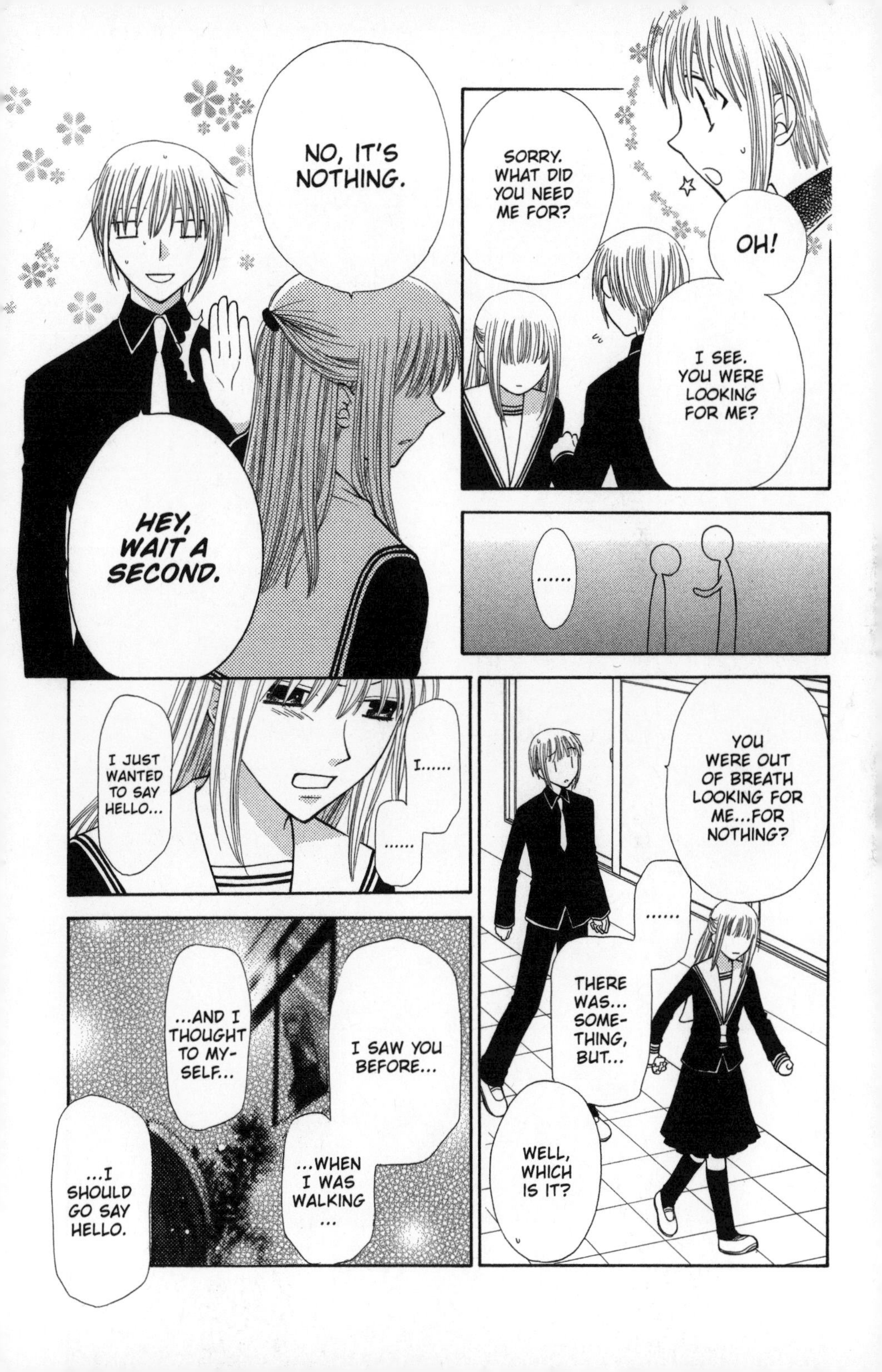
OH!
SORRY. WHAT DID YOU NEED ME FOR?
I SEE. YOU WERE LOOKING FOR ME?
......
NO, IT'S NOTHING.
HEY, WAIT A SECOND.
YOU WERE OUT OF BREATH LOOKING FOR ME...FOR NOTHING?
......
THERE WAS... SOME-THING, BUT...
WELL, WHICH IS IT?
I......
......
I JUST WANTED TO SAY HELLO...
I SAW YOU BEFORE...
...WHEN I WAS WALKING...
...AND I THOUGHT TO MY-SELF...
...I SHOULD GO SAY HELLO.

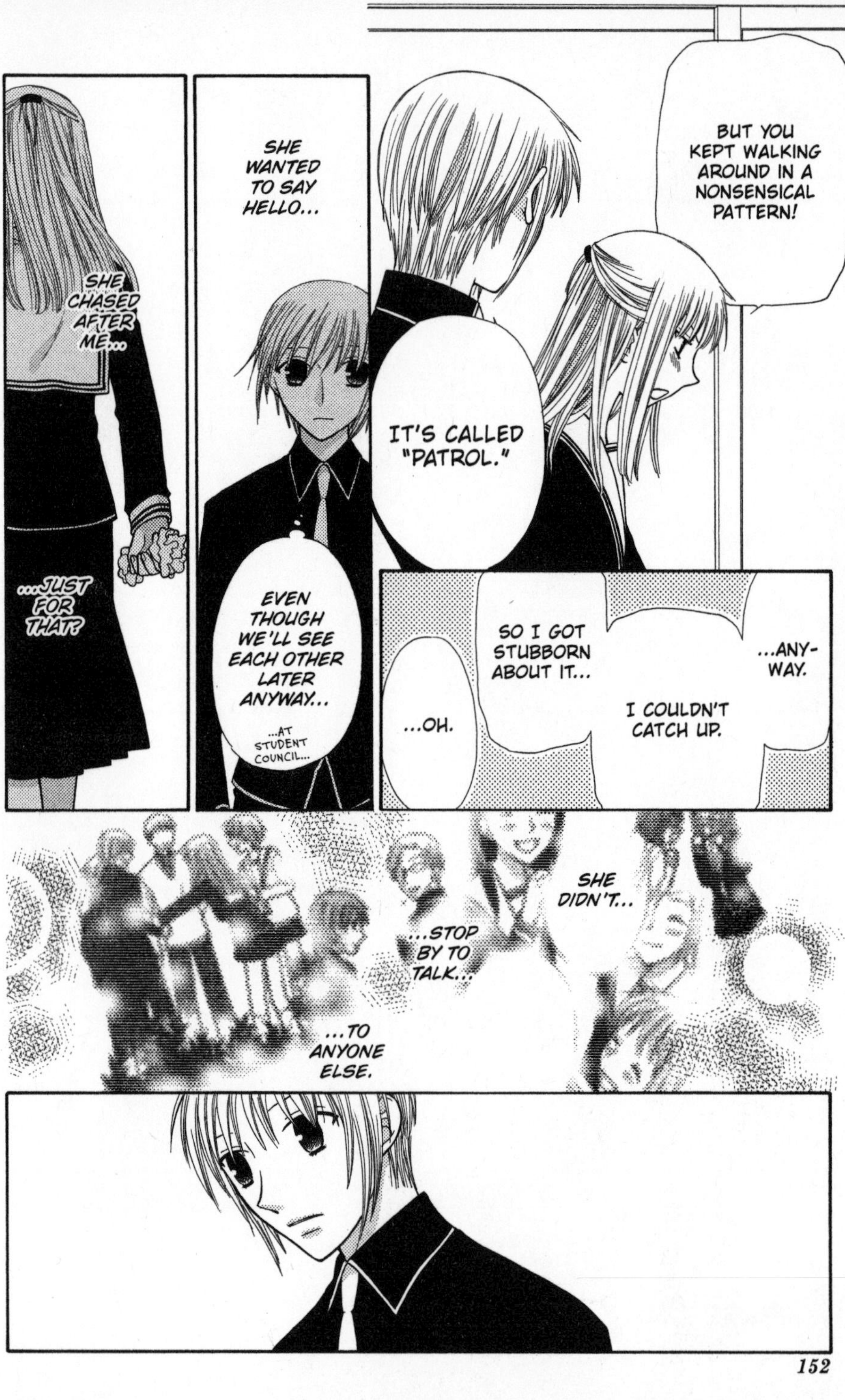
BUT YOU KEPT WALKING AROUND IN A NONSENSICAL PATTERN!
IT'S CALLED "PATROL."
SO I GOT STUBBORN ABOUT IT...
...ANY-WAY.
I COULDN'T CATCH UP.
...OH.
SHE WANTED TO SAY HELLO...
EVEN THOUGH WE'LL SEE EACH OTHER LATER ANYWAY...
...AT STUDENT COUNCIL...
SHE CHASED AFTER ME...
...JUST FOR THAT?
SHE DIDN'T...
...STOP BY TO TALK...
...TO ANYONE ELSE.

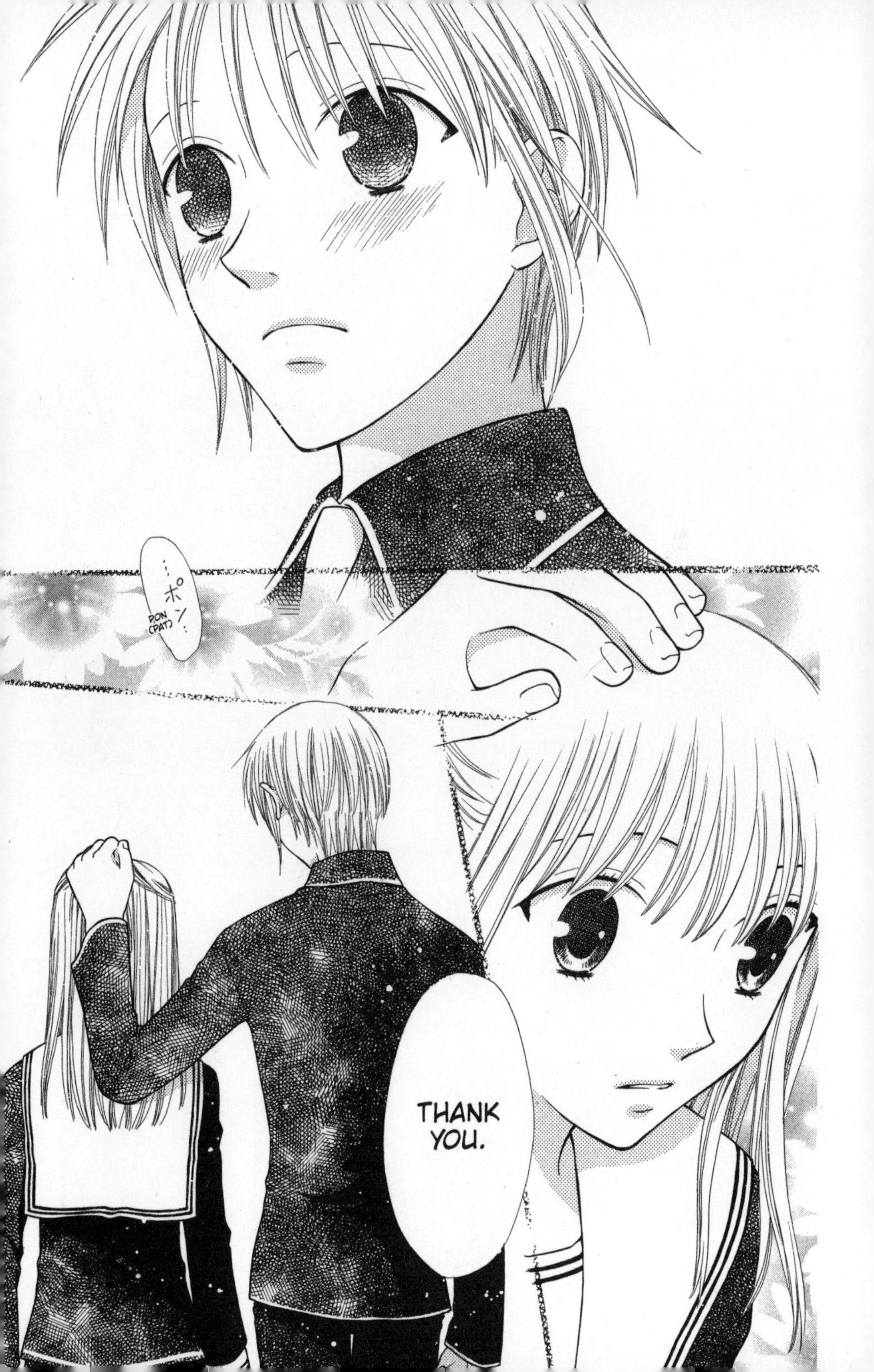

…ポン…
PON (PAT)
THANK YOU.

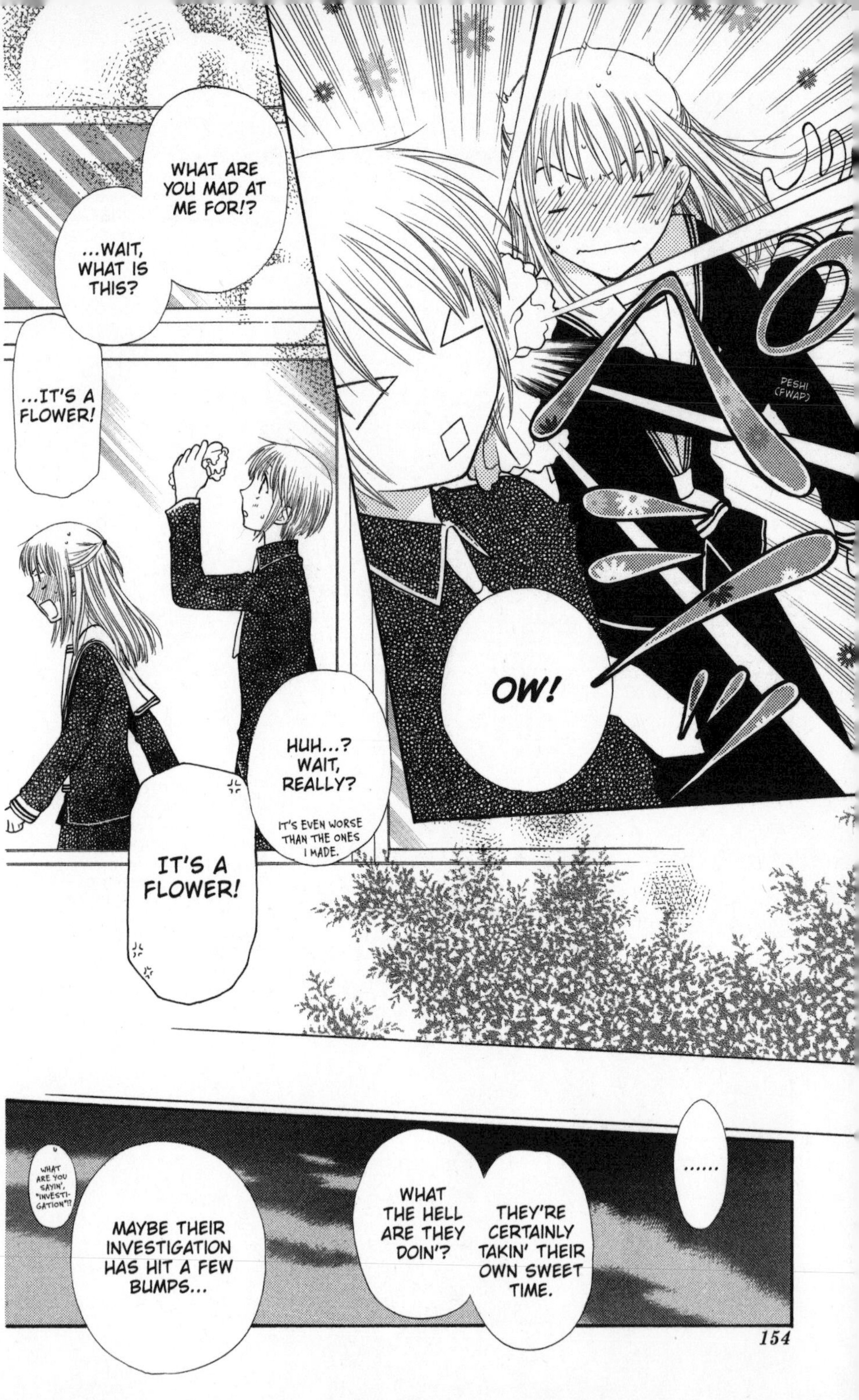
PESHI (FWAP)
OW!
WHAT ARE YOU MAD AT ME FOR!?
...WAIT, WHAT IS THIS?
...IT'S A FLOWER!
HUH...? WAIT, REALLY?
IT'S EVEN WORSE THAN THE ONES I MADE.
IT'S A FLOWER!
......
THEY'RE CERTAINLY TAKIN' THEIR OWN SWEET TIME.
WHAT THE HELL ARE THEY DOIN'?
MAYBE THEIR INVESTIGATION HAS HIT A FEW BUMPS...
WHAT ARE YOU SAYIN', "INVESTI-GATION"!?

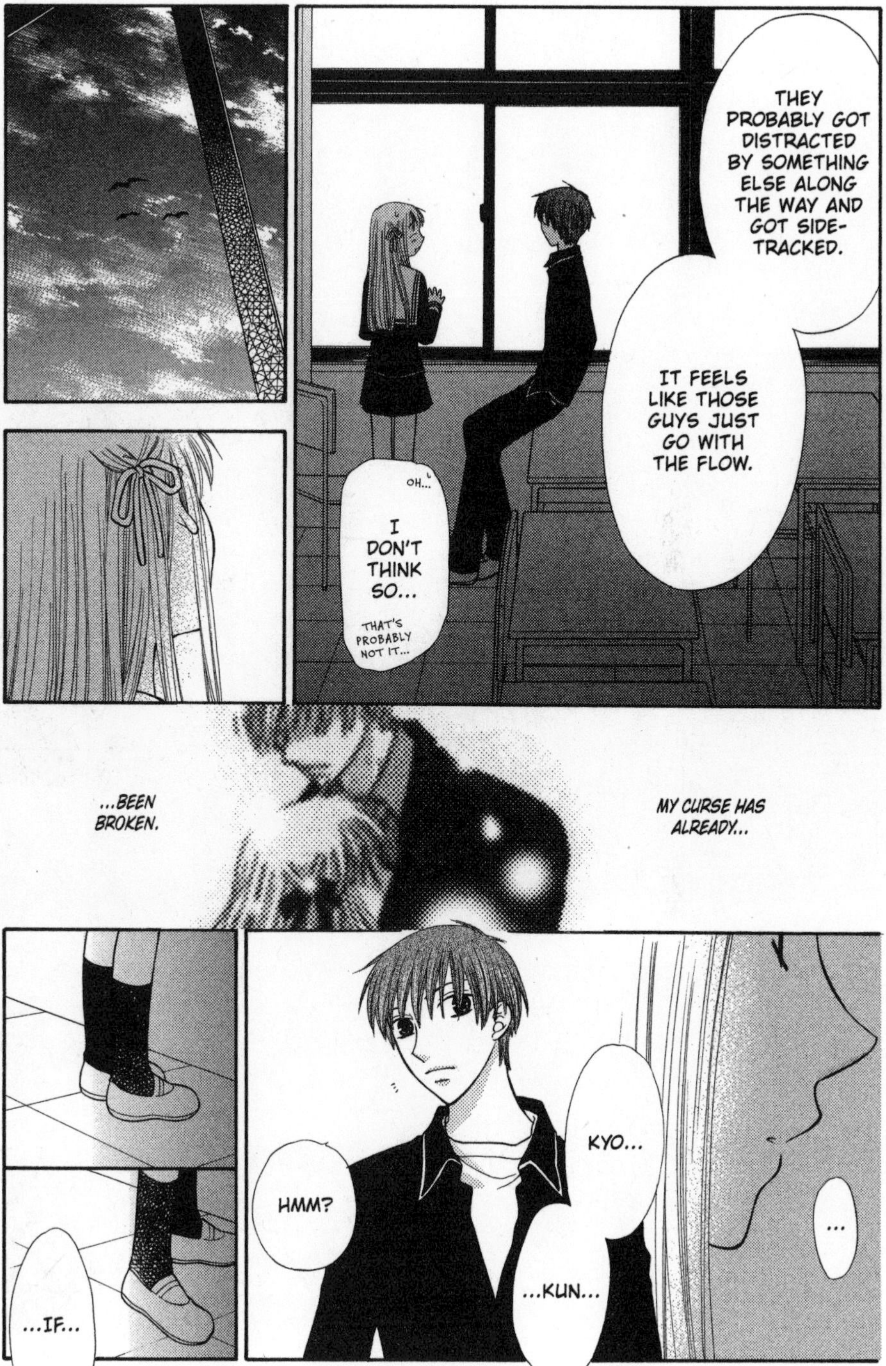
THEY PROBABLY GOT DISTRACTED BY SOMETHING ELSE ALONG THE WAY AND GOT SIDE-TRACKED.
IT FEELS LIKE THOSE GUYS JUST GO WITH THE FLOW.
OH...
I DON'T THINK SO...
THAT'S PROBABLY NOT IT...
MY CURSE HAS ALREADY...
...BEEN BROKEN.
...
KYO...
...KUN...
HMM?
...IF...

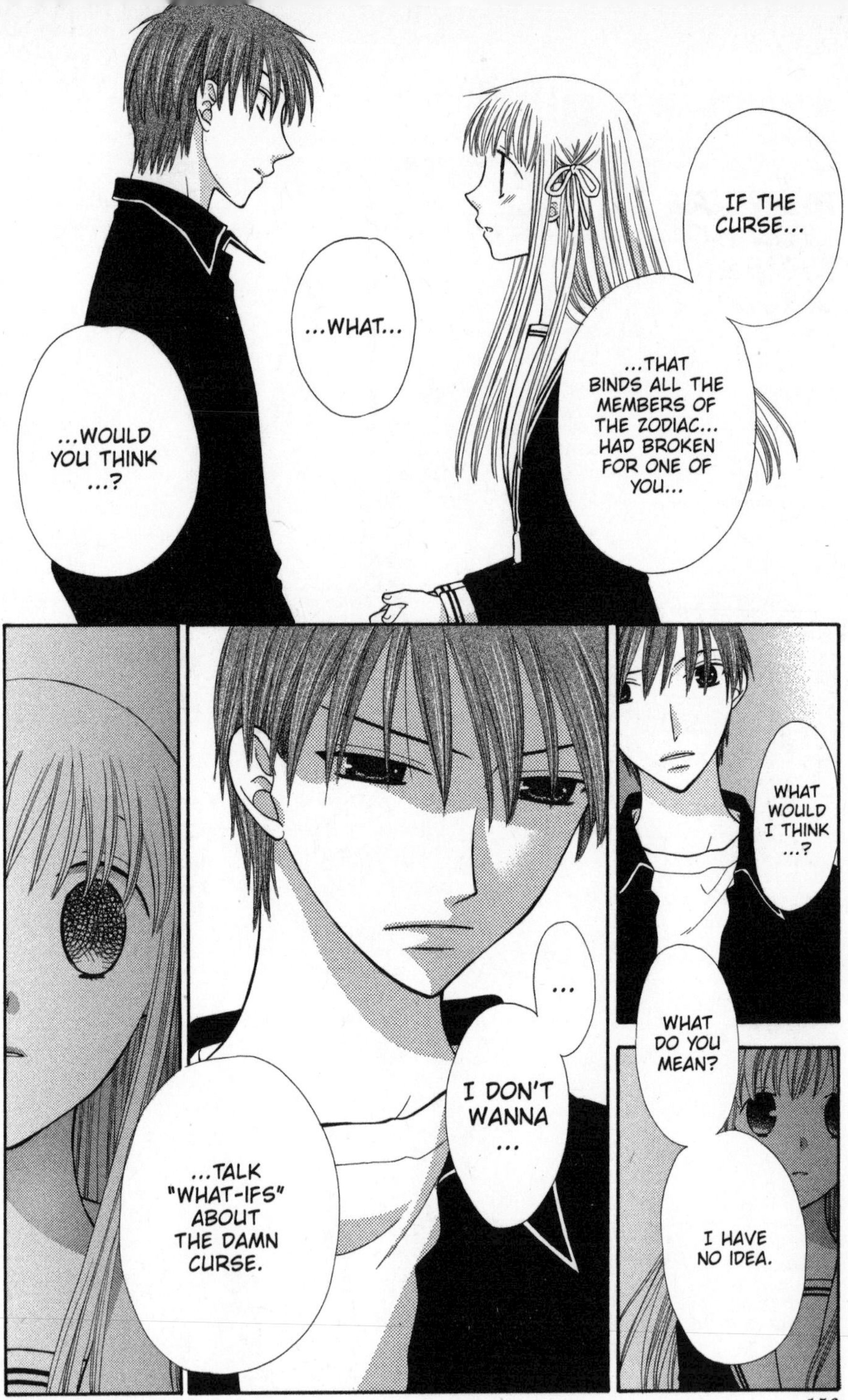
IF THE CURSE...
...THAT BINDS ALL THE MEMBERS OF THE ZODIAC... HAD BROKEN FOR ONE OF YOU...
...WHAT...
...WOULD YOU THINK ...?
WHAT WOULD I THINK ...?
WHAT DO YOU MEAN?
I HAVE NO IDEA.
...
I DON'T WANNA ...
...TALK "WHAT-IFS" ABOUT THE DAMN CURSE.

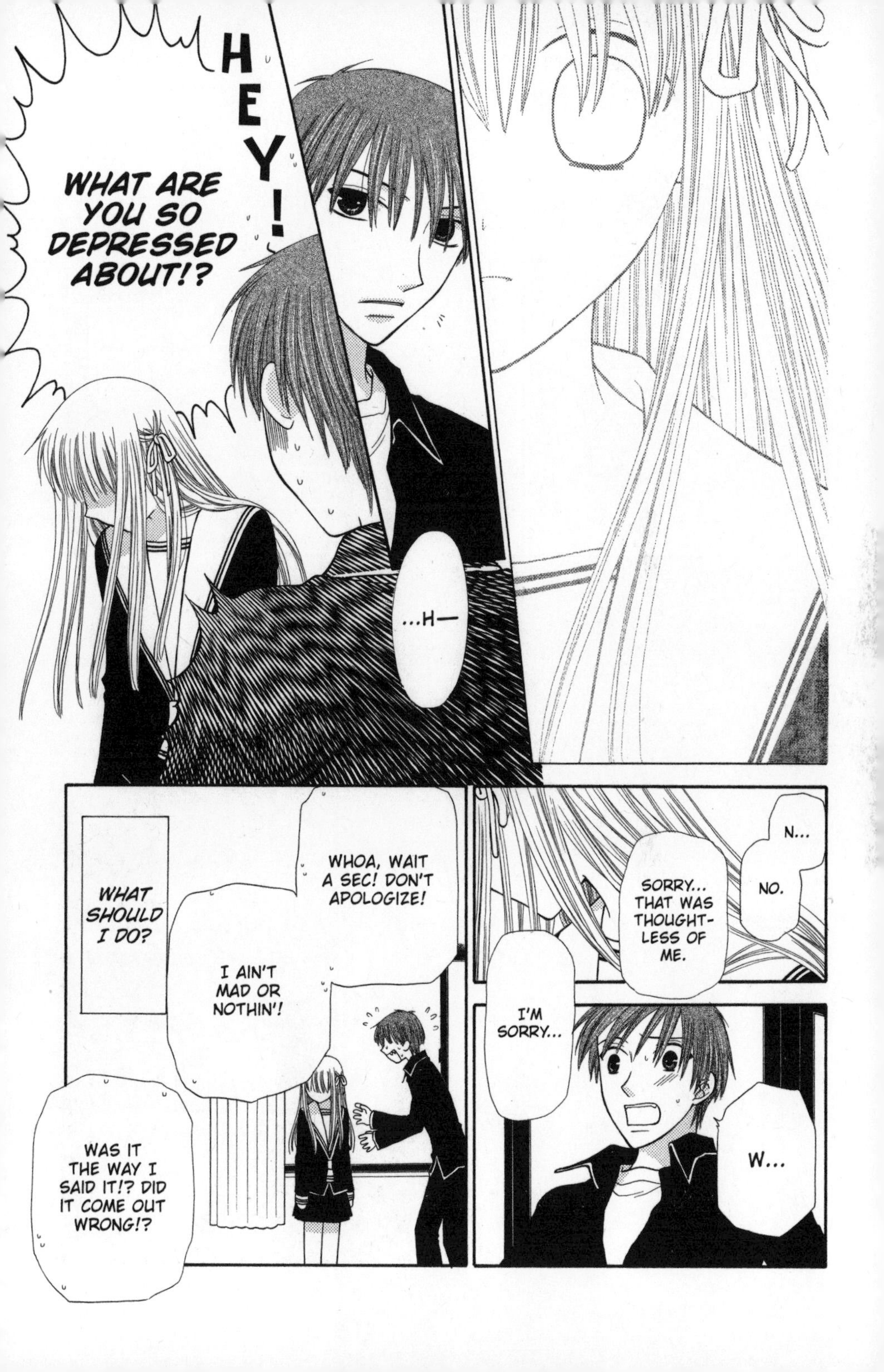

...H—
HEY!
WHAT ARE YOU SO DEPRESSED ABOUT!?
N...
NO.
SORRY... THAT WAS THOUGHT-LESS OF ME.
I'M SORRY...
W...
WHOA, WAIT A SEC! DON'T APOLOGIZE!
I AIN'T MAD OR NOTHIN'!
WHAT SHOULD I DO?
WAS IT THE WAY I SAID IT!? DID IT COME OUT WRONG!?

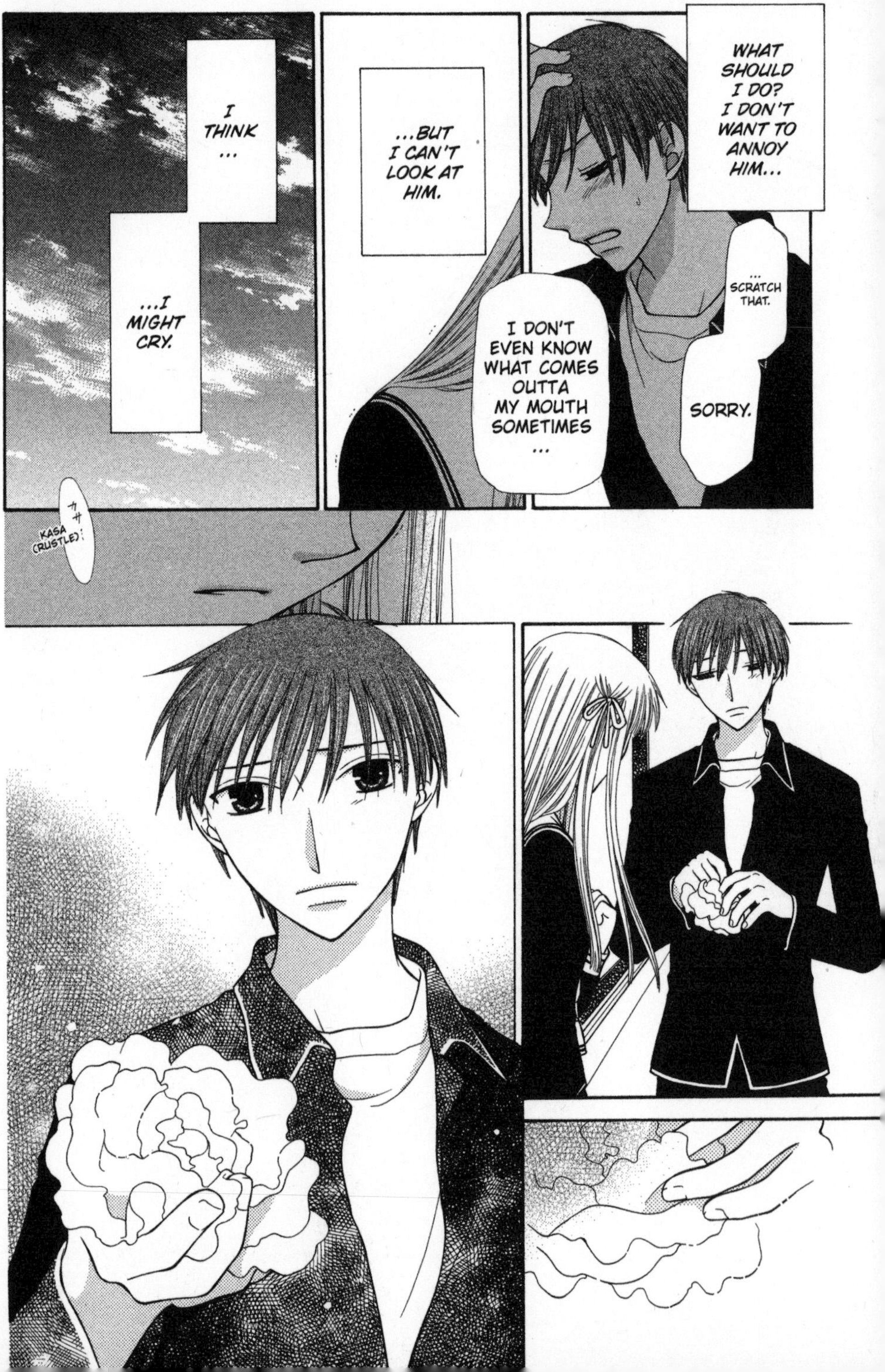
WHAT SHOULD I DO? I DON'T WANT TO ANNOY HIM...
...SCRATCH THAT.
SORRY.
I DON'T EVEN KNOW WHAT COMES OUTTA MY MOUTH SOMETIMES...
...BUT I CAN'T LOOK AT HIM.
I THINK...
...I MIGHT CRY.
KASA (RUSTLE)

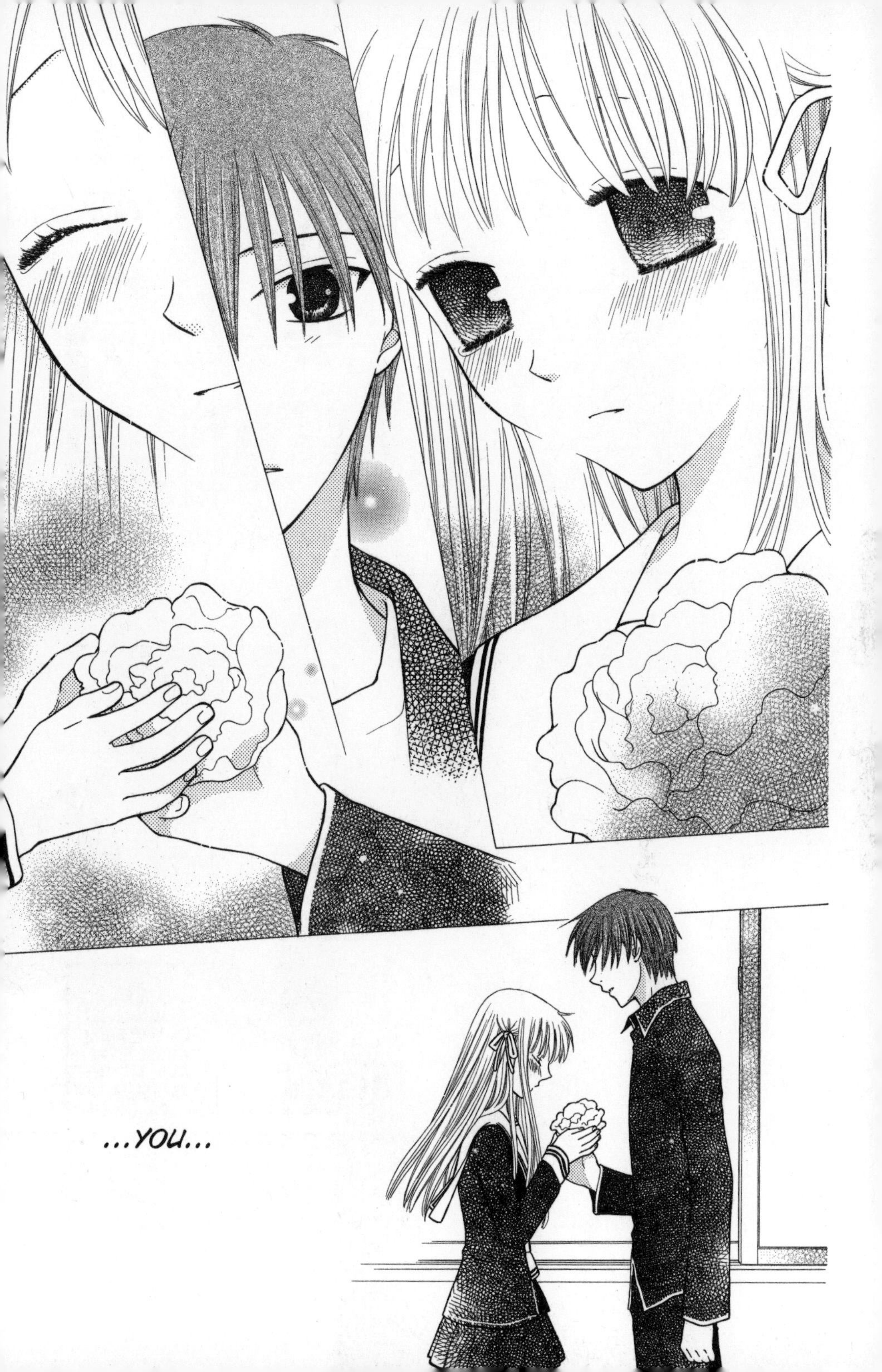
...YOU...

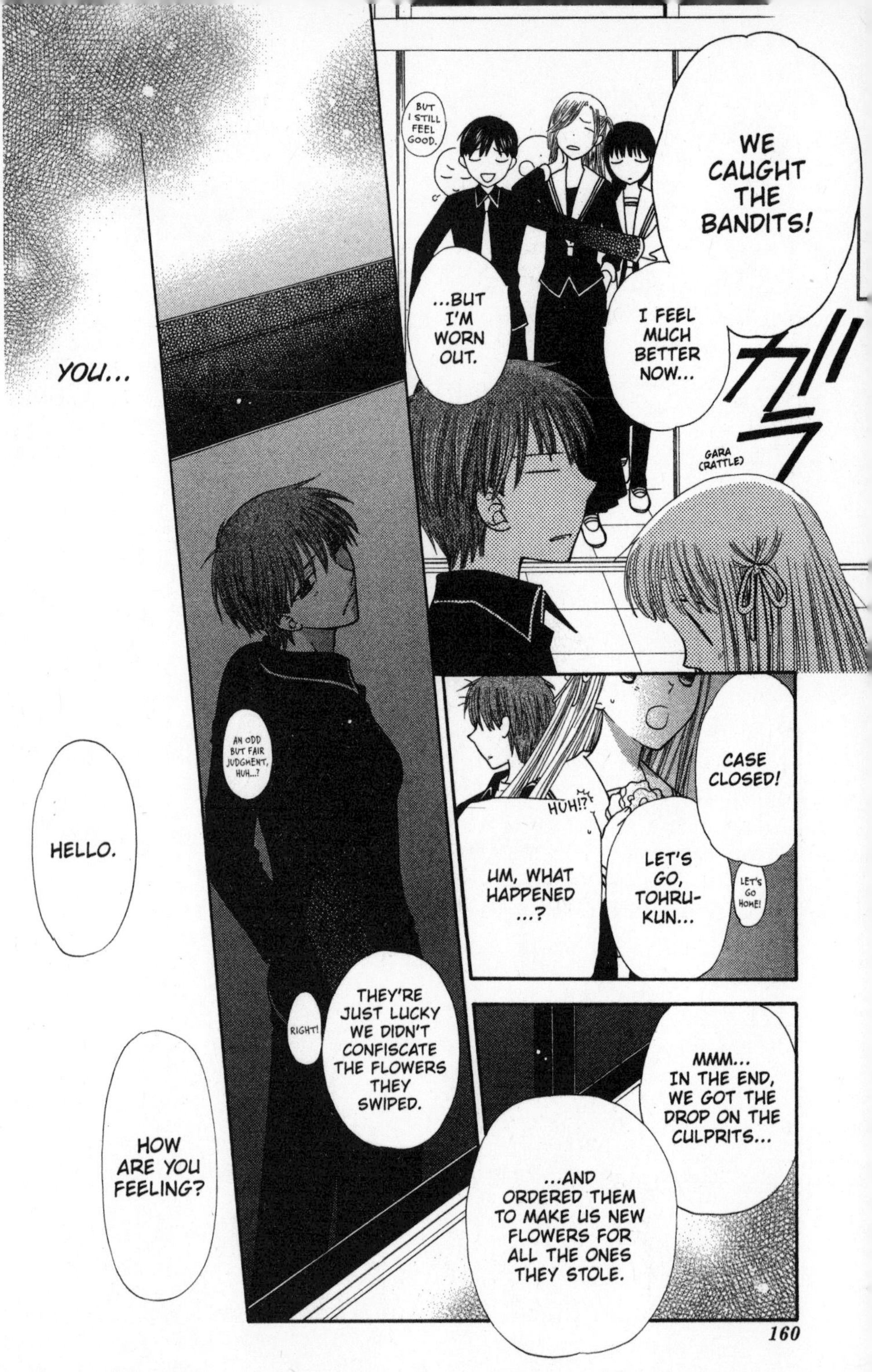
WE CAUGHT THE BANDITS!
I FEEL MUCH BETTER NOW...
...BUT I'M WORN OUT.
BUT I STILL FEEL GOOD.
GARA (RATTLE)
CASE CLOSED!
LET'S GO HOME!
LET'S GO, TOHRU-KUN...
HUH!?
UM, WHAT HAPPENED ...?
MMM... IN THE END, WE GOT THE DROP ON THE CULPRITS...
...AND ORDERED THEM TO MAKE US NEW FLOWERS FOR ALL THE ONES THEY STOLE.
THEY'RE JUST LUCKY WE DIDN'T CONFISCATE THE FLOWERS THEY SWIPED.
RIGHT!
AN ODD BUT FAIR JUDGMENT, HUH...?
YOU...
HELLO.
HOW ARE YOU FEELING?

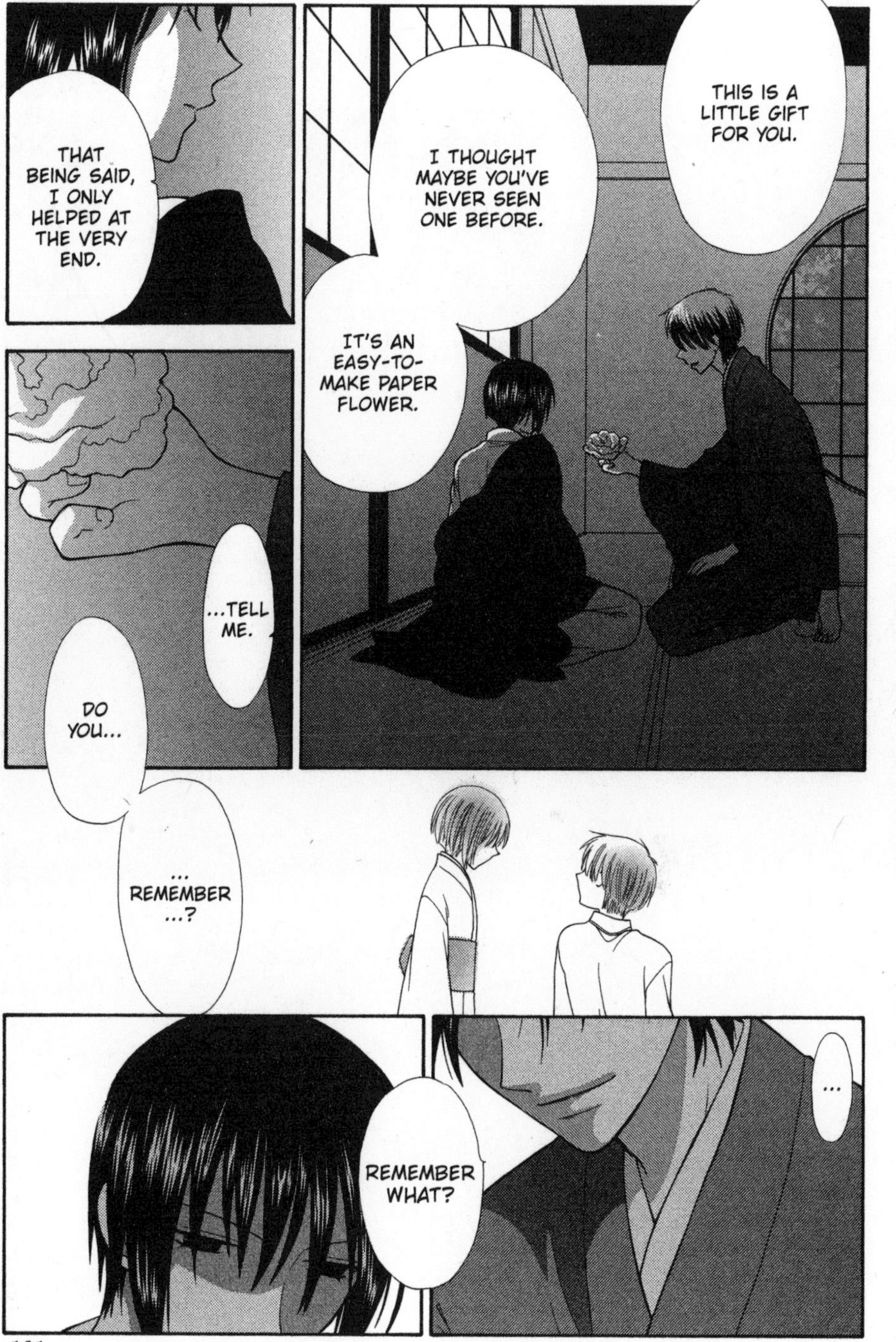
THIS IS A LITTLE GIFT FOR YOU.
I THOUGHT MAYBE YOU'VE NEVER SEEN ONE BEFORE.
IT'S AN EASY-TO-MAKE PAPER FLOWER.
THAT BEING SAID, I ONLY HELPED AT THE VERY END.
...TELL ME.
DO YOU...
...REMEMBER...?
...
REMEMBER WHAT?

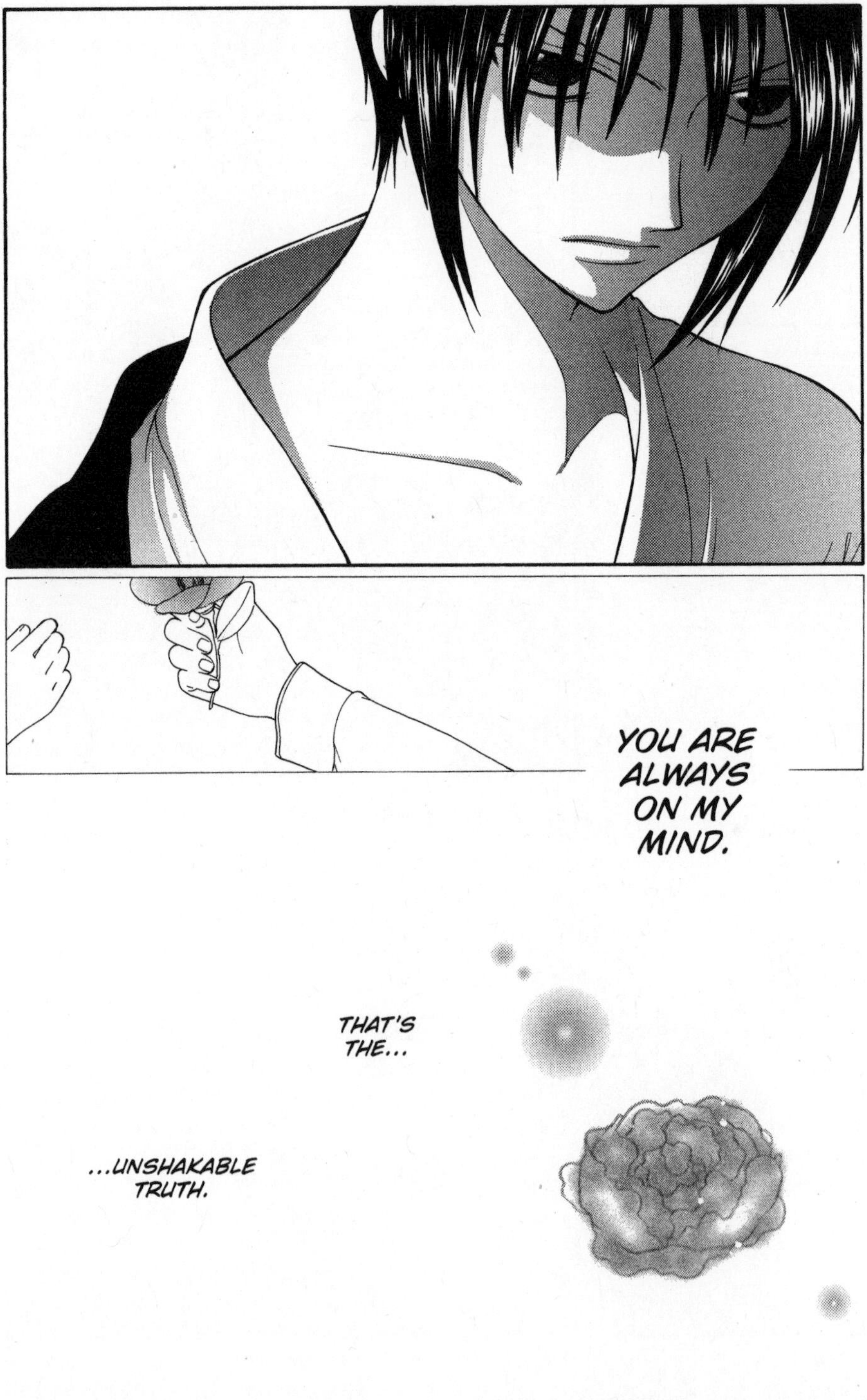
YOU ARE ALWAYS ON MY MIND.
THAT'S THE...
...UNSHAKABLE TRUTH.

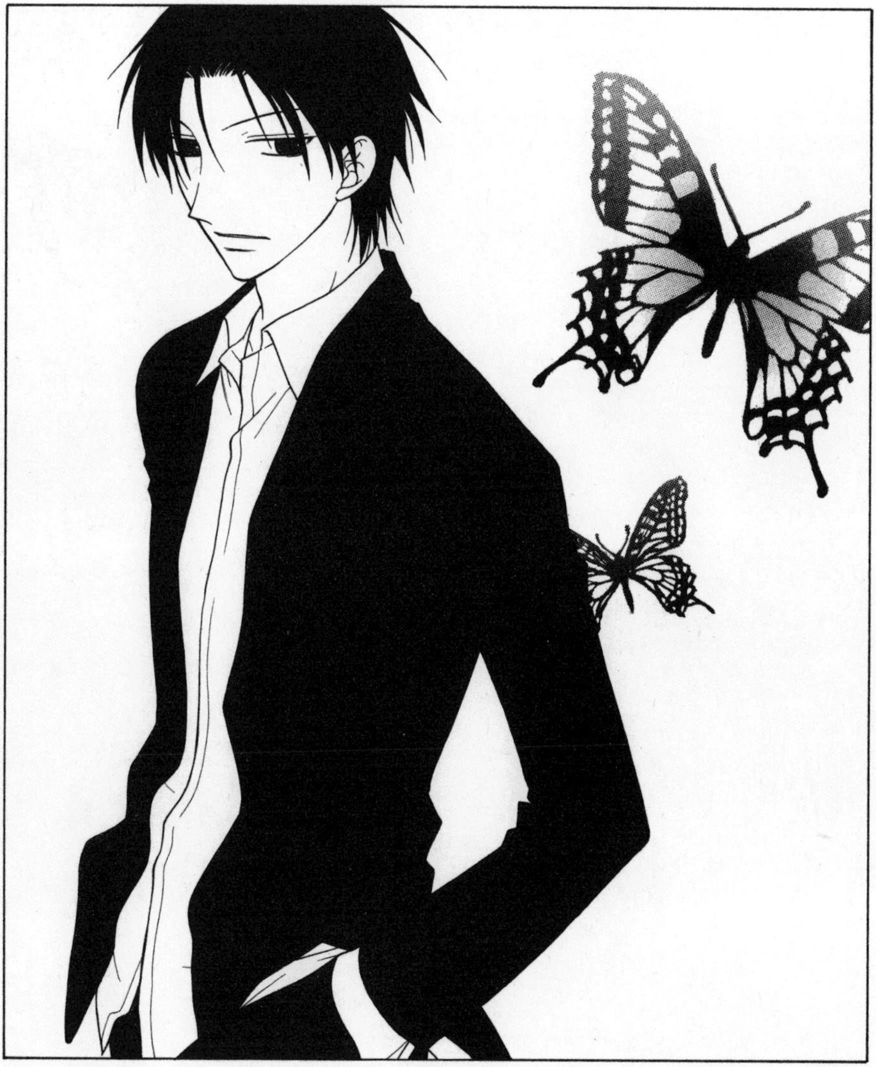

Chapter 101

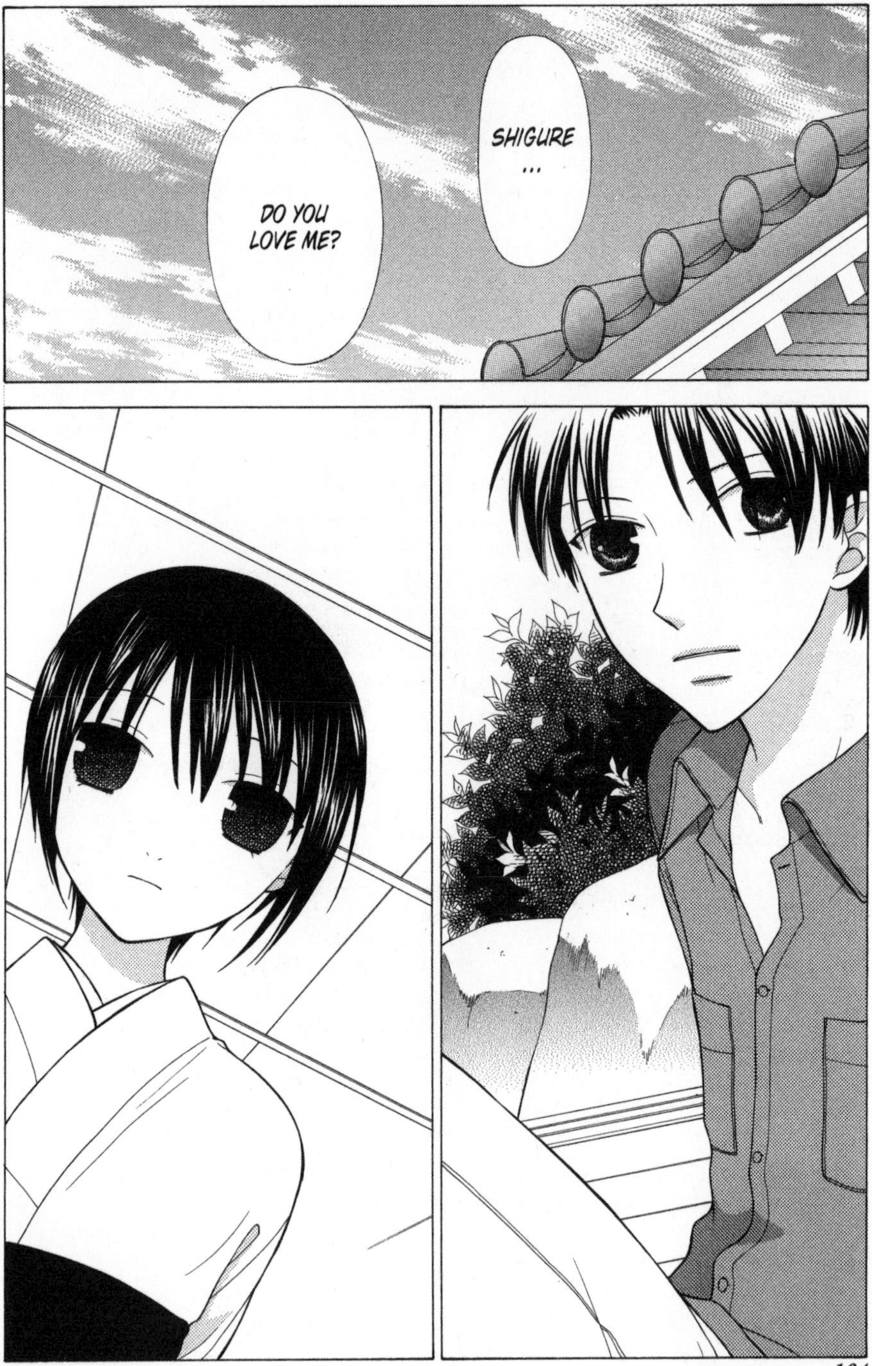
SHIGURE ...
DO YOU LOVE ME?

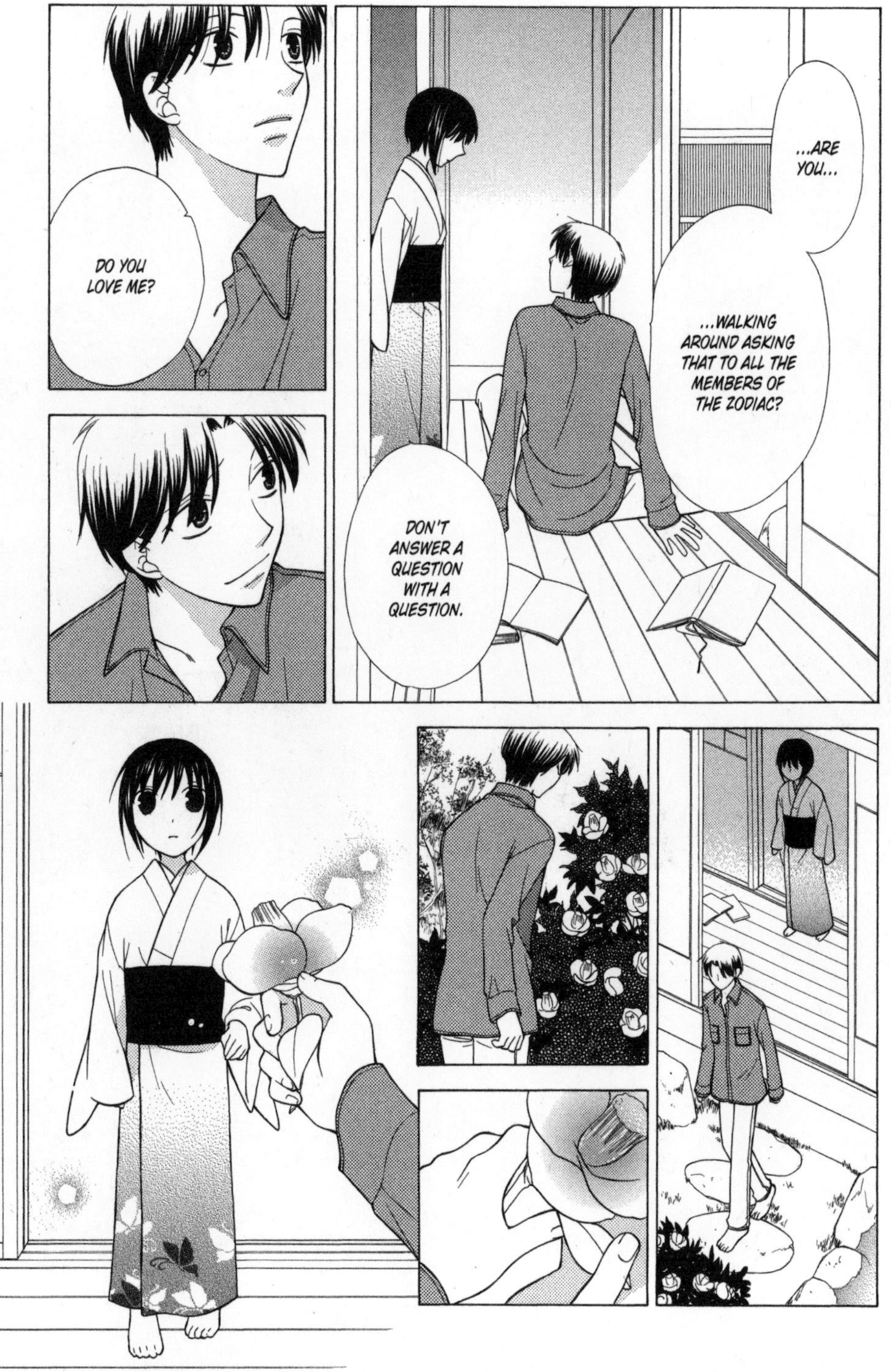
...ARE YOU...
...WALKING AROUND ASKING THAT TO ALL THE MEMBERS OF THE ZODIAC?
DON'T ANSWER A QUESTION WITH A QUESTION.
DO YOU LOVE ME?

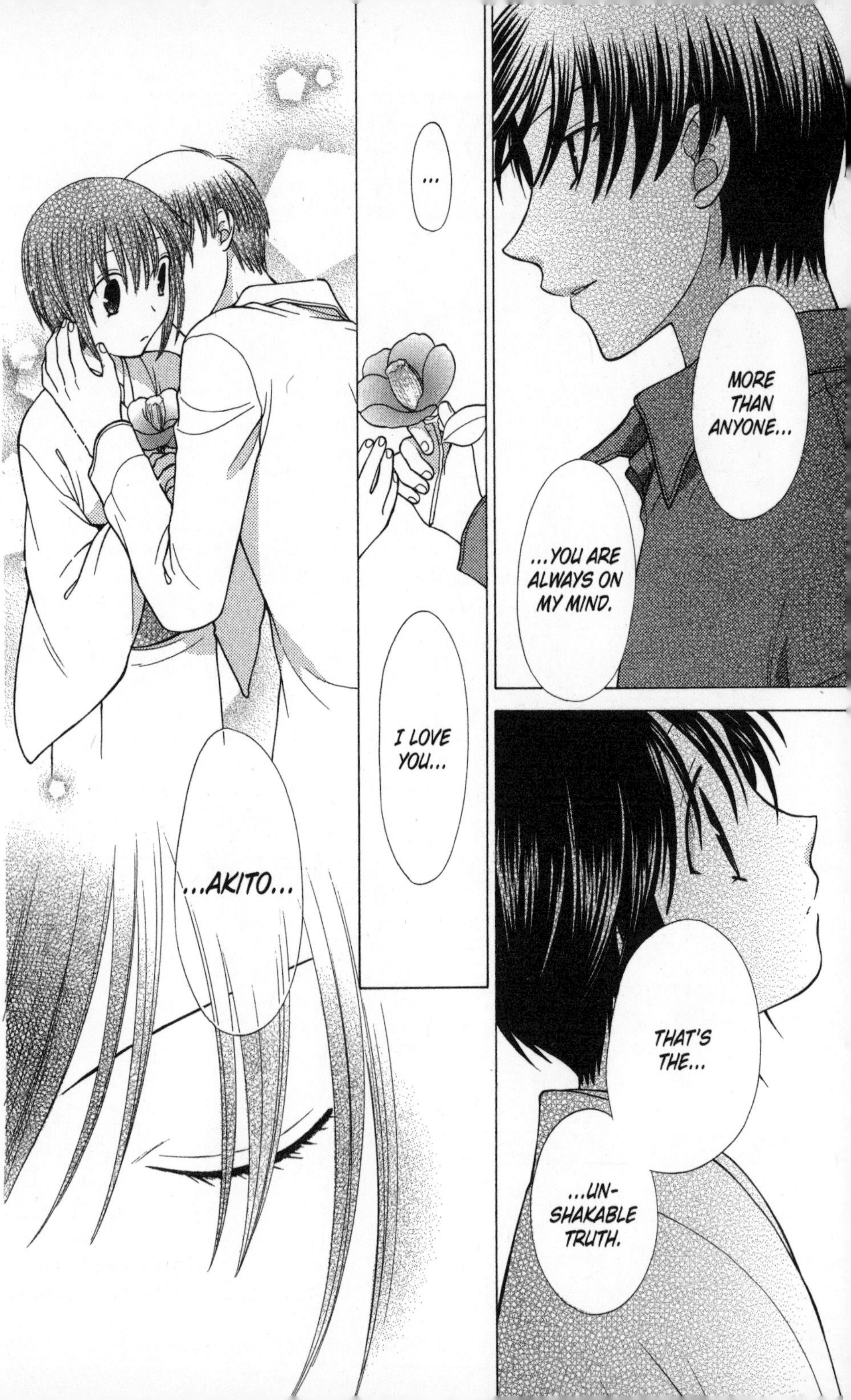
MORE THAN ANYONE...
...YOU ARE ALWAYS ON MY MIND.
THAT'S THE...
...UN-SHAKABLE TRUTH.
...
I LOVE YOU...
...AKITO...

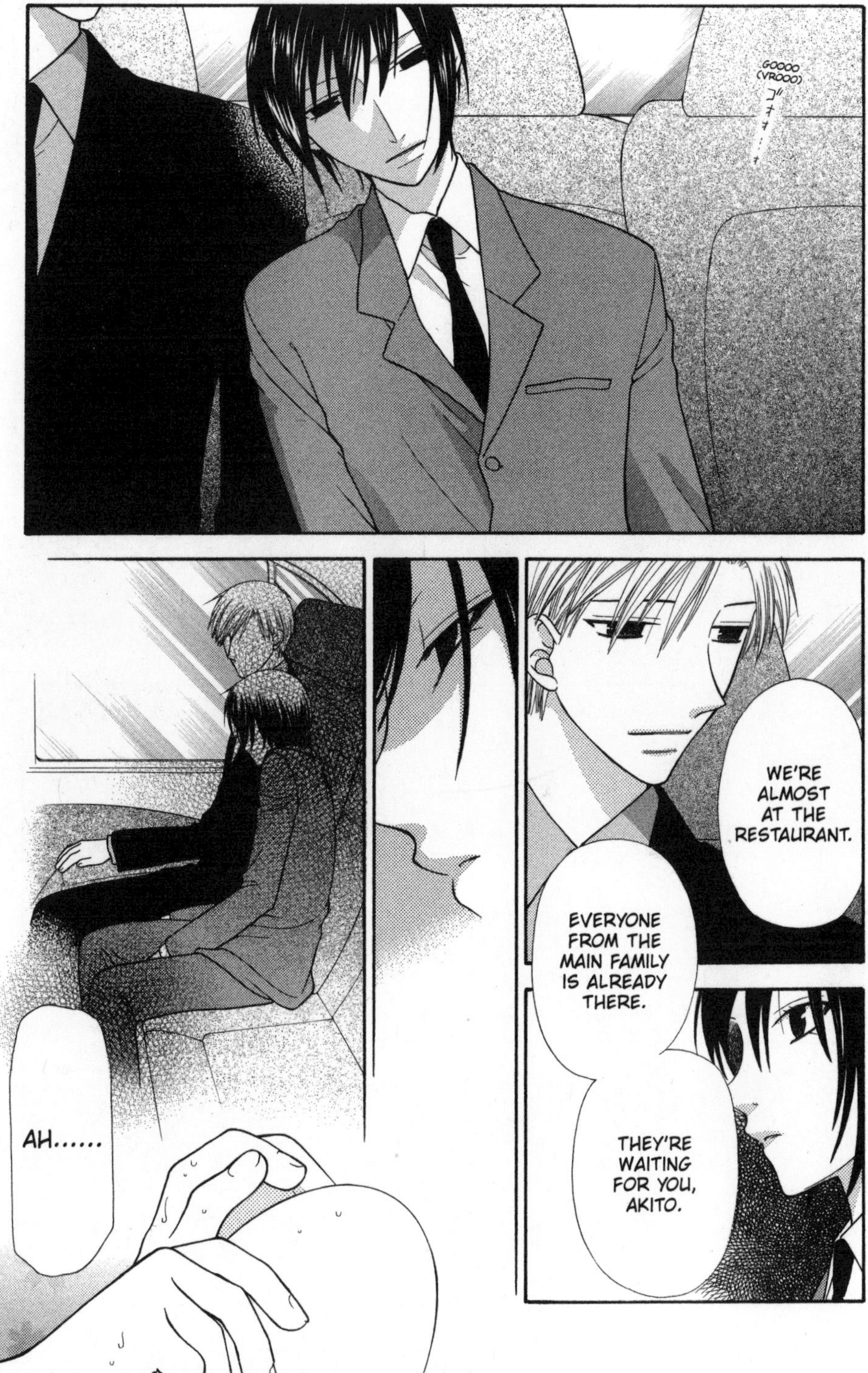
GOOOO (VROOO)
WE'RE ALMOST AT THE RESTAURANT.
EVERYONE FROM THE MAIN FAMILY IS ALREADY THERE.
THEY'RE WAITING FOR YOU, AKITO.
AH......

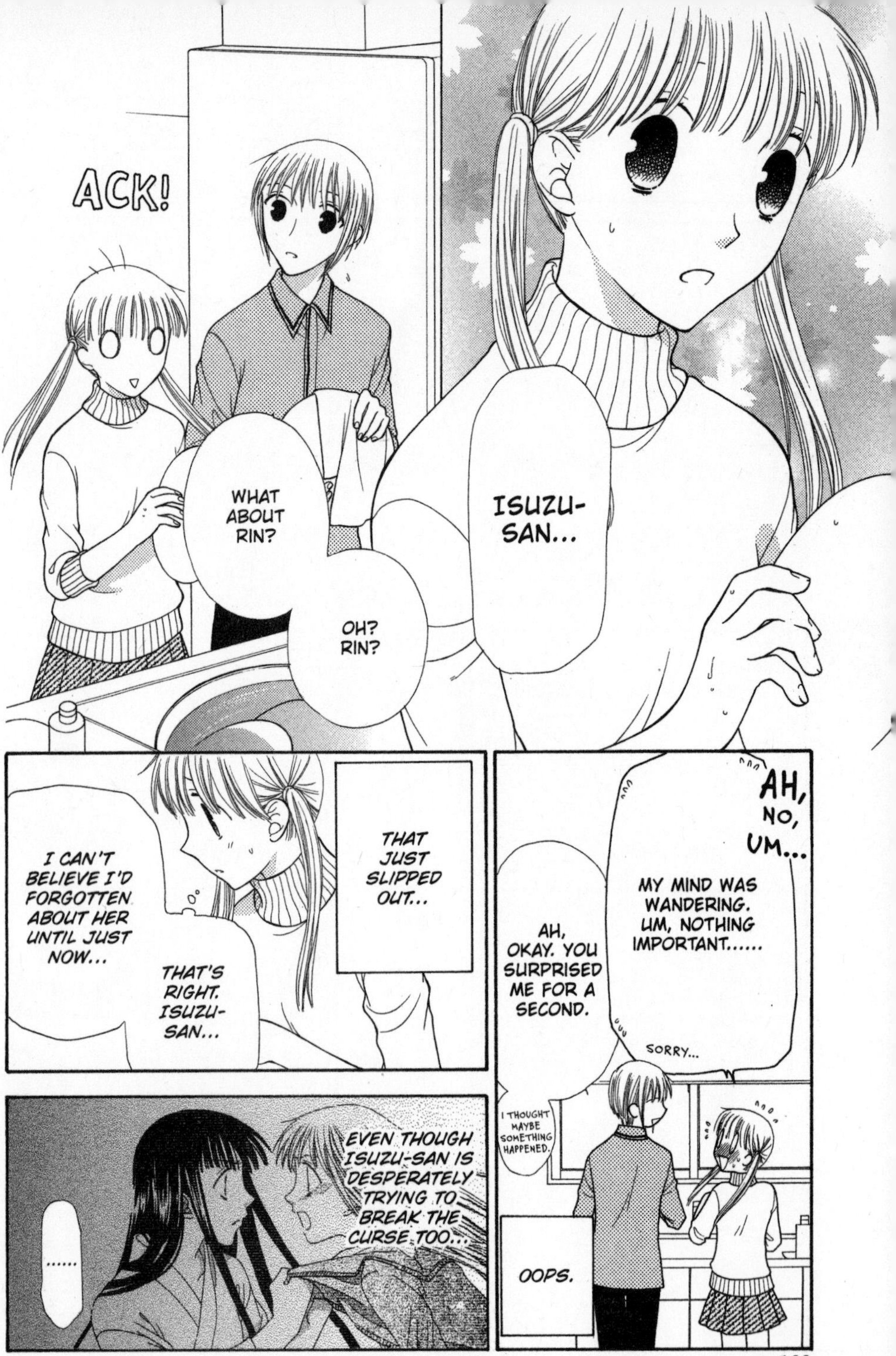
ISUZU-SAN...
ACK!
WHAT ABOUT RIN?
OH? RIN?
AH, NO, UM...
MY MIND WAS WANDERING. UM, NOTHING IMPORTANT......
AH, OKAY. YOU SURPRISED ME FOR A SECOND.
SORRY...
I THOUGHT MAYBE SOMETHING HAPPENED.
OOPS.
THAT JUST SLIPPED OUT...
I CAN'T BELIEVE I'D FORGOTTEN ABOUT HER UNTIL JUST NOW...
THAT'S RIGHT. ISUZU-SAN...
EVEN THOUGH ISUZU-SAN IS DESPERATELY TRYING TO BREAK THE CURSE TOO...
......

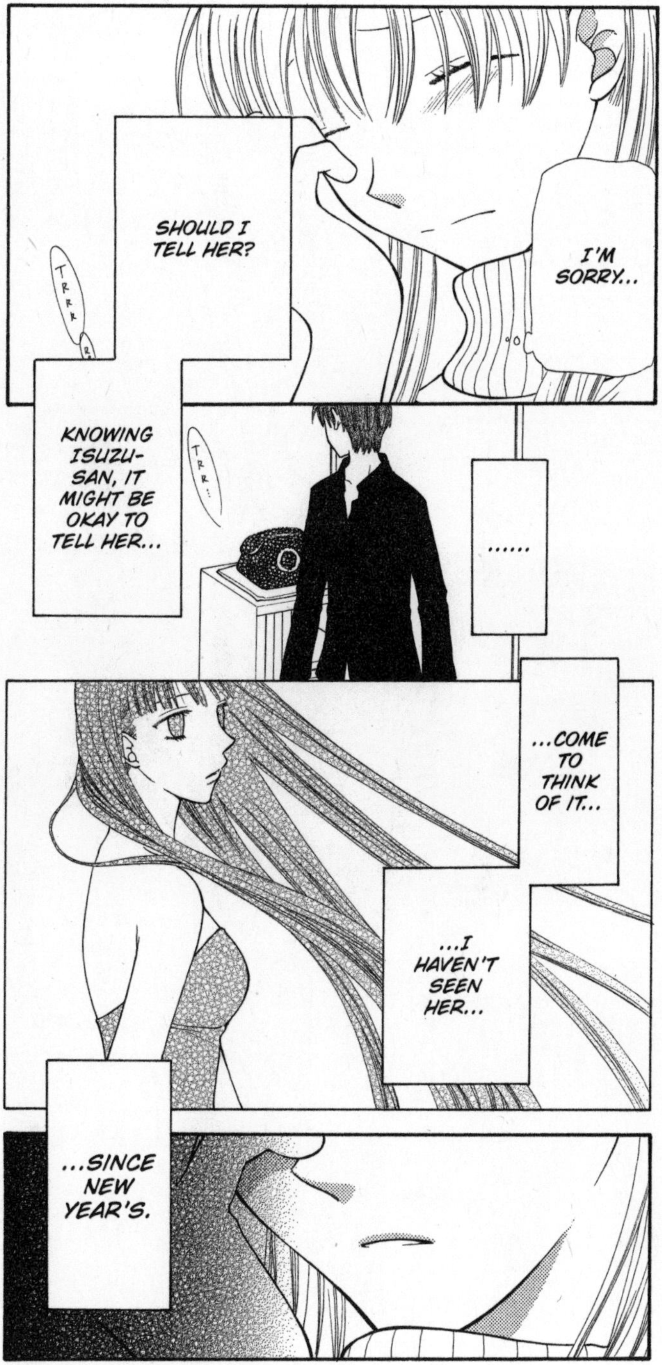
I'M SORRY...
SHOULD I TELL HER?
TRRR
R
......
KNOWING ISUZU-SAN, IT MIGHT BE OKAY TO TELL HER...
TRR...
...COME TO THINK OF IT...
...I HAVEN'T SEEN HER...
...SINCE NEW YEAR'S.
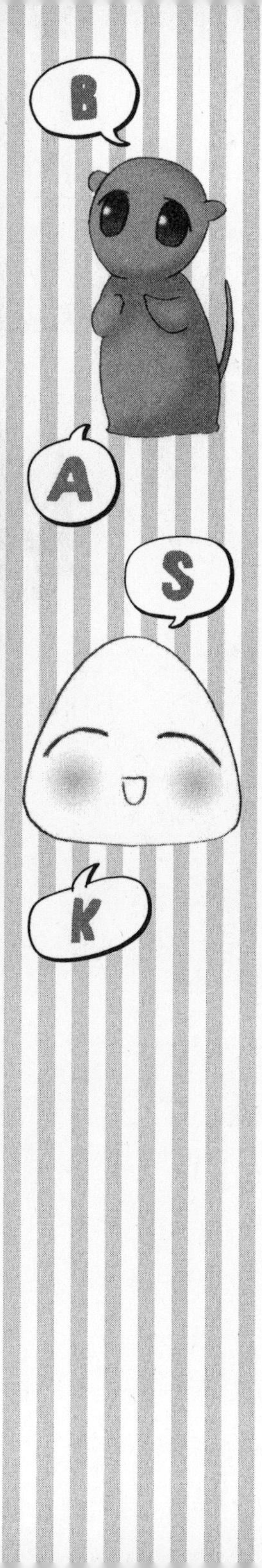
B
A
S
K

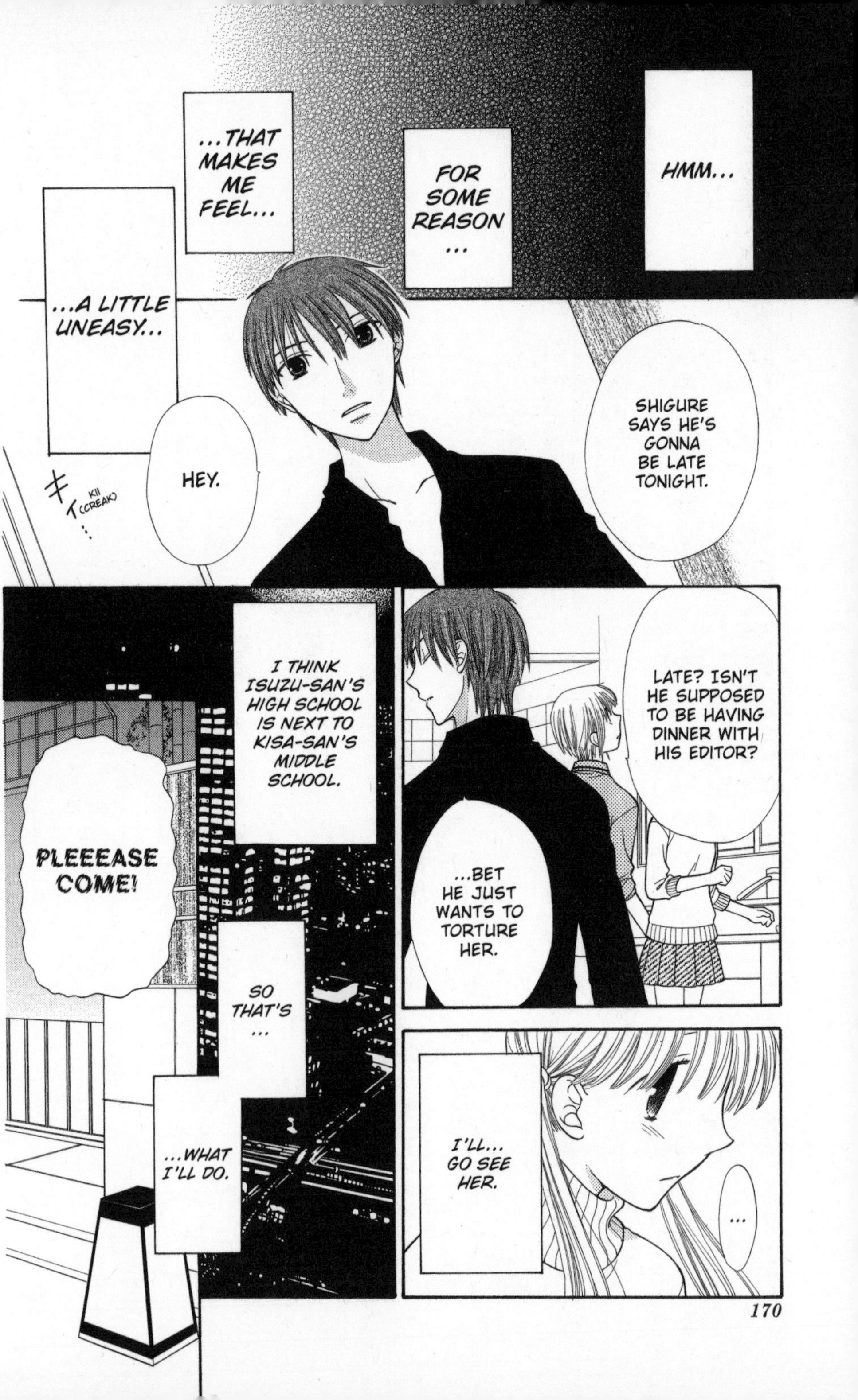
HMM...
FOR SOME REASON ...
...THAT MAKES ME FEEL...
...A LITTLE UNEASY...
KII (CREAK)
HEY.
SHIGURE SAYS HE'S GONNA BE LATE TONIGHT.
LATE? ISN'T HE SUPPOSED TO BE HAVING DINNER WITH HIS EDITOR?
...BET HE JUST WANTS TO TORTURE HER.
...
I'LL... GO SEE HER.
I THINK ISUZU-SAN'S HIGH SCHOOL IS NEXT TO KISA-SAN'S MIDDLE SCHOOL.
PLEEEASE COME!
SO THAT'S ...
...WHAT I'LL DO.

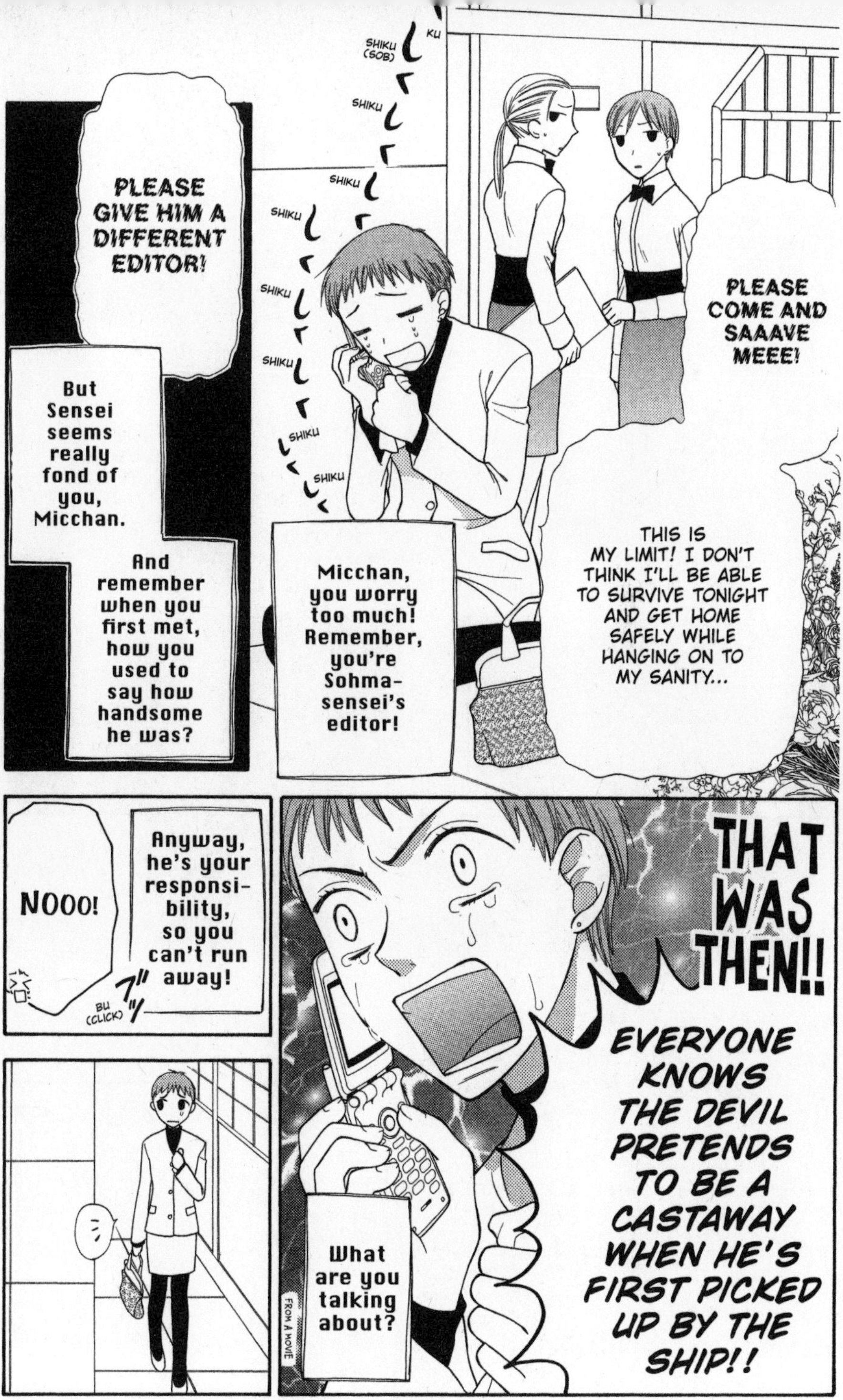
KU
SHIKU (SOB)
SHIKU
SHIKU
SHIKU
SHIKU
SHIKU
SHIKU
SHIKU
PLEASE COME AND SAAAVE MEEE!
THIS IS MY LIMIT! I DON'T THINK I'LL BE ABLE TO SURVIVE TONIGHT AND GET HOME SAFELY WHILE HANGING ON TO MY SANITY...
Micchan, you worry too much! Remember, you're Sohma-sensei's editor!
PLEASE GIVE HIM A DIFFERENT EDITOR!
But Sensei seems really fond of you, Micchan.
And remember when you first met, how you used to say how handsome he was?
THAT WAS THEN!!
EVERYONE KNOWS THE DEVIL PRETENDS TO BE A CASTAWAY WHEN HE'S FIRST PICKED UP BY THE SHIP!!
What are you talking about?
FROM A MOVIE
Anyway, he's your responsibility, so you can't run away!
NOOO!
BU (CLICK)

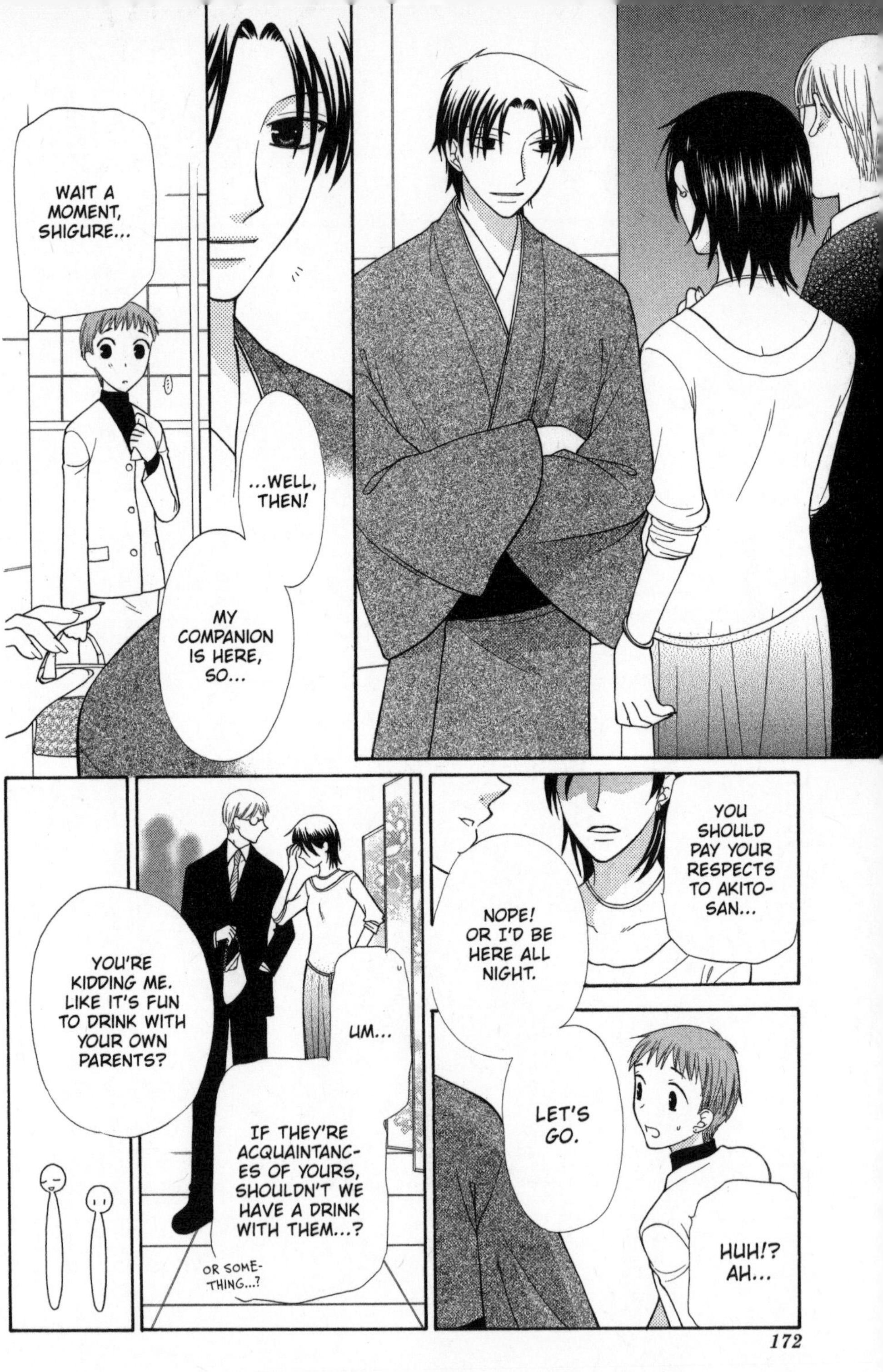
...WELL, THEN!
MY COMPANION IS HERE, SO...
WAIT A MOMENT, SHIGURE...
YOU SHOULD PAY YOUR RESPECTS TO AKITO-SAN...
NOPE! OR I'D BE HERE ALL NIGHT.
LET'S GO.
HUH!? AH...
UM...
IF THEY'RE ACQUAINTANCES OF YOURS, SHOULDN'T WE HAVE A DRINK WITH THEM...?
OR SOMETHING...?
YOU'RE KIDDING ME. LIKE IT'S FUN TO DRINK WITH YOUR OWN PARENTS?

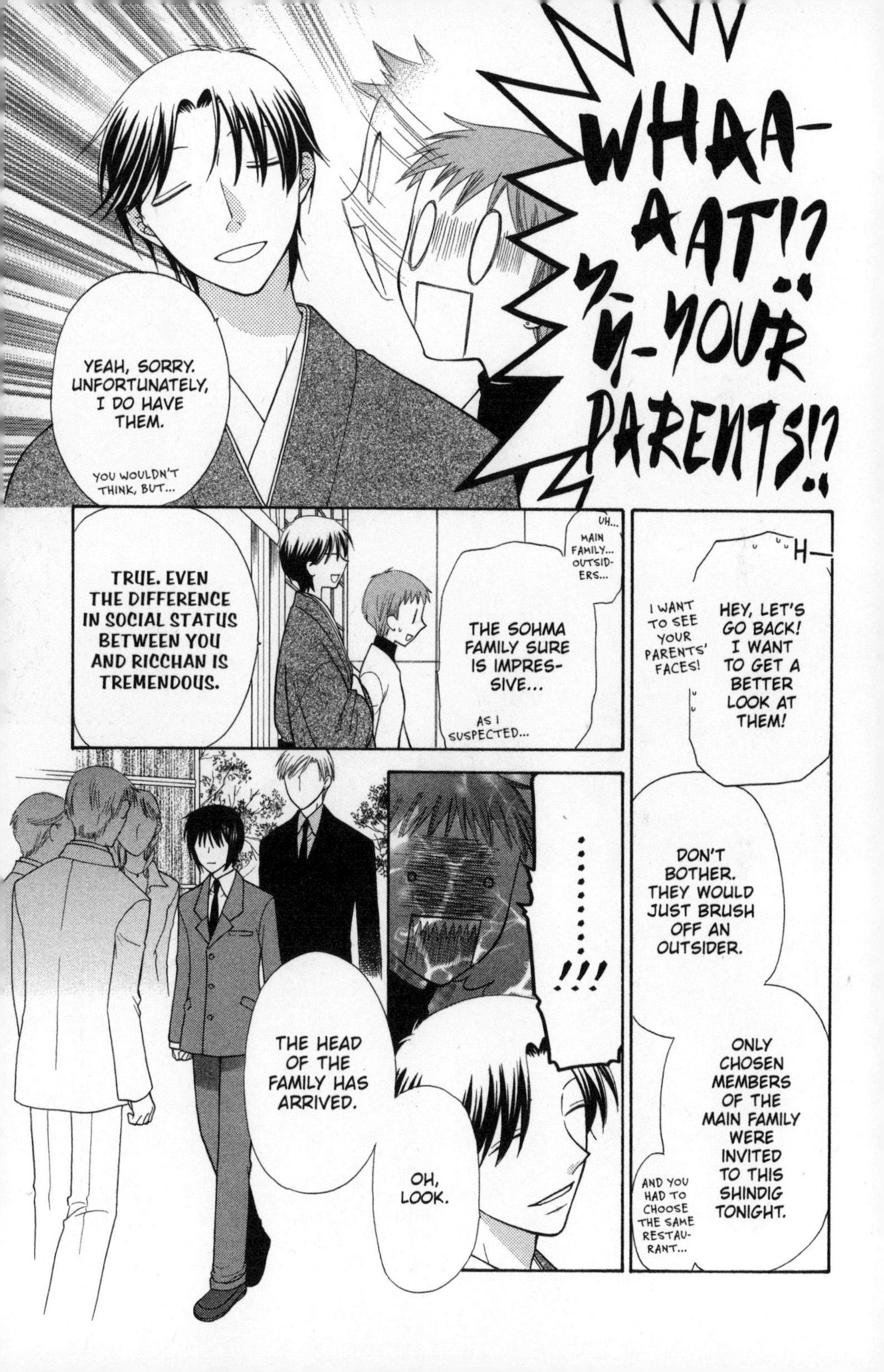
WHAA-AAT!? Y-YOUR PARENTS!?
YEAH, SORRY. UNFORTUNATELY, I DO HAVE THEM.
YOU WOULDN'T THINK, BUT...
H—
HEY, LET'S GO BACK! I WANT TO GET A BETTER LOOK AT THEM!
I WANT TO SEE YOUR PARENTS' FACES!
DON'T BOTHER. THEY WOULD JUST BRUSH OFF AN OUTSIDER.
ONLY CHOSEN MEMBERS OF THE MAIN FAMILY WERE INVITED TO THIS SHINDIG TONIGHT.
AND YOU HAD TO CHOOSE THE SAME RESTAURANT...
UH... MAIN FAMILY... OUTSIDERS...
THE SOHMA FAMILY SURE IS IMPRESSIVE...
AS I SUSPECTED...
TRUE. EVEN THE DIFFERENCE IN SOCIAL STATUS BETWEEN YOU AND RICCHAN IS TREMENDOUS.
......!!!
OH, LOOK.
THE HEAD OF THE FAMILY HAS ARRIVED.

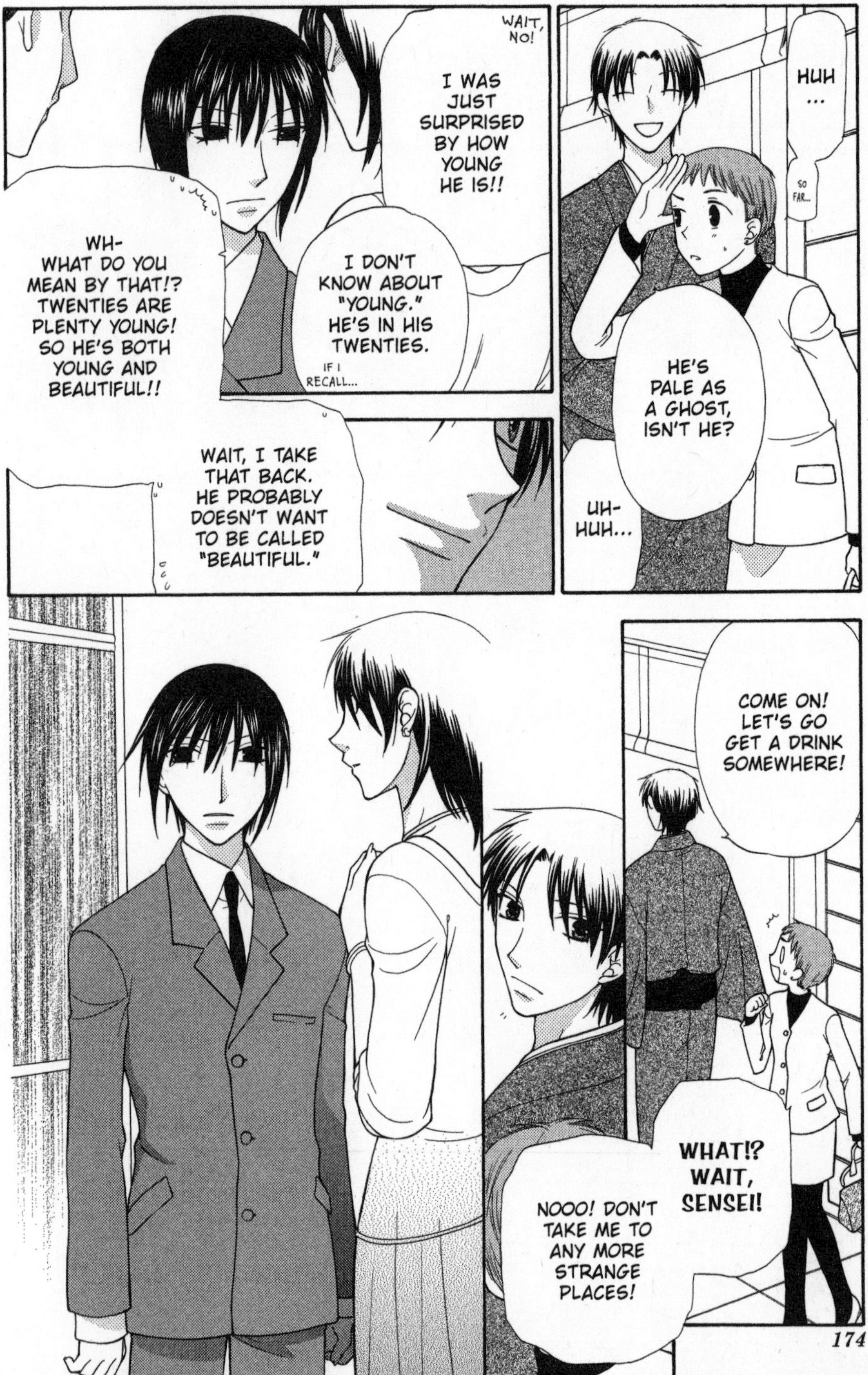
HUH ...
SO FAR...
HE'S PALE AS A GHOST, ISN'T HE?
UH-HUH...
WAIT, NO!
I WAS JUST SURPRISED BY HOW YOUNG HE IS!!
I DON'T KNOW ABOUT "YOUNG." HE'S IN HIS TWENTIES.
IF I RECALL...
WH- WHAT DO YOU MEAN BY THAT!? TWENTIES ARE PLENTY YOUNG! SO HE'S BOTH YOUNG AND BEAUTIFUL!!
WAIT, I TAKE THAT BACK. HE PROBABLY DOESN'T WANT TO BE CALLED "BEAUTIFUL."
COME ON! LET'S GO GET A DRINK SOMEWHERE!
WHAT!? WAIT, SENSEI!
NOOO! DON'T TAKE ME TO ANY MORE STRANGE PLACES!

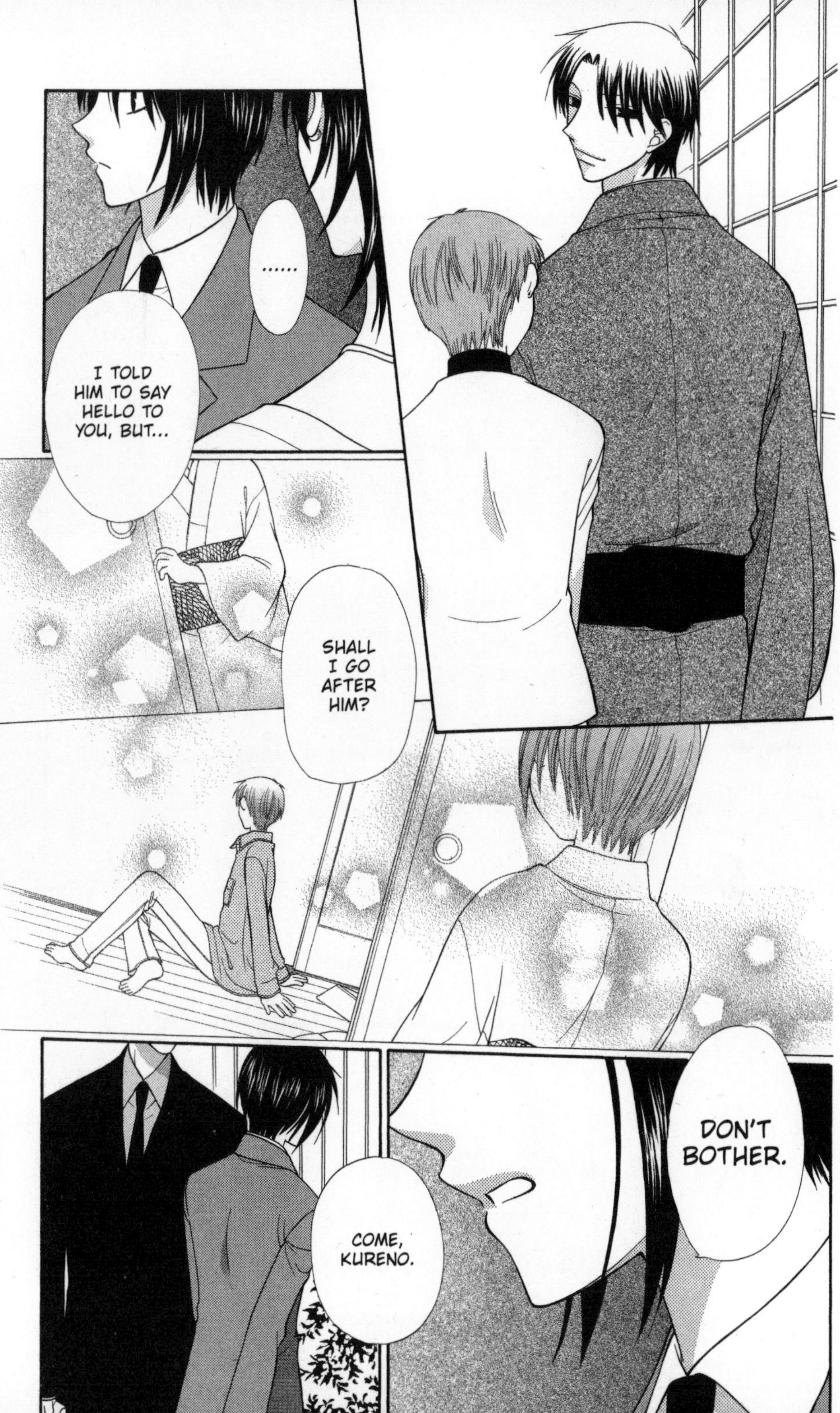
......
I TOLD HIM TO SAY HELLO TO YOU, BUT...
SHALL I GO AFTER HIM?
DON'T BOTHER.
COME, KURENO.

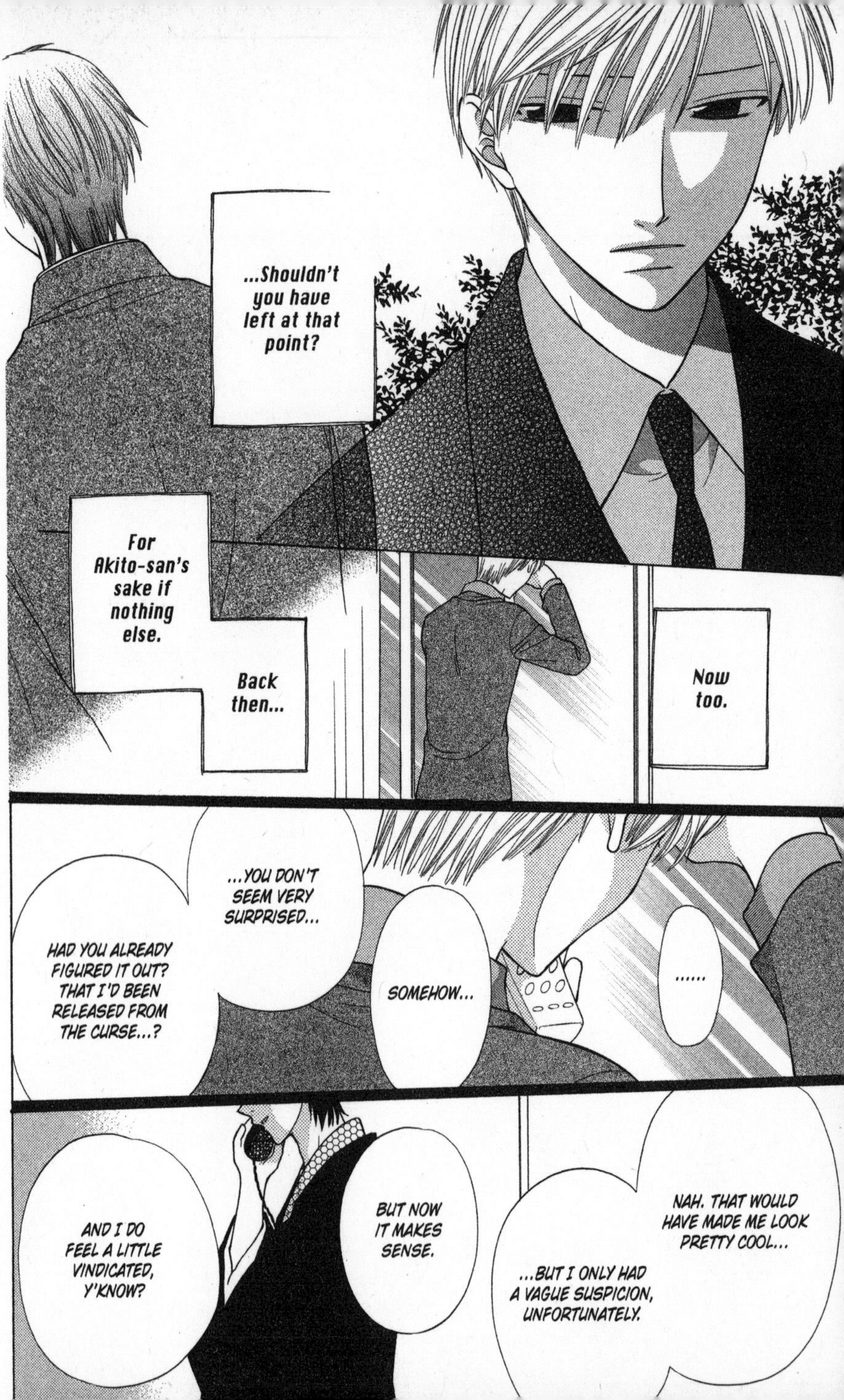
...Shouldn't you have left at that point?
For Akito-san's sake if nothing else.
Back then...
Now too.
......
SOMEHOW...
...YOU DON'T SEEM VERY SURPRISED...
HAD YOU ALREADY FIGURED IT OUT? THAT I'D BEEN RELEASED FROM THE CURSE...?
NAH. THAT WOULD HAVE MADE ME LOOK PRETTY COOL...
...BUT I ONLY HAD A VAGUE SUSPICION, UNFORTUNATELY.
BUT NOW IT MAKES SENSE.
AND I DO FEEL A LITTLE VINDICATED, Y'KNOW?

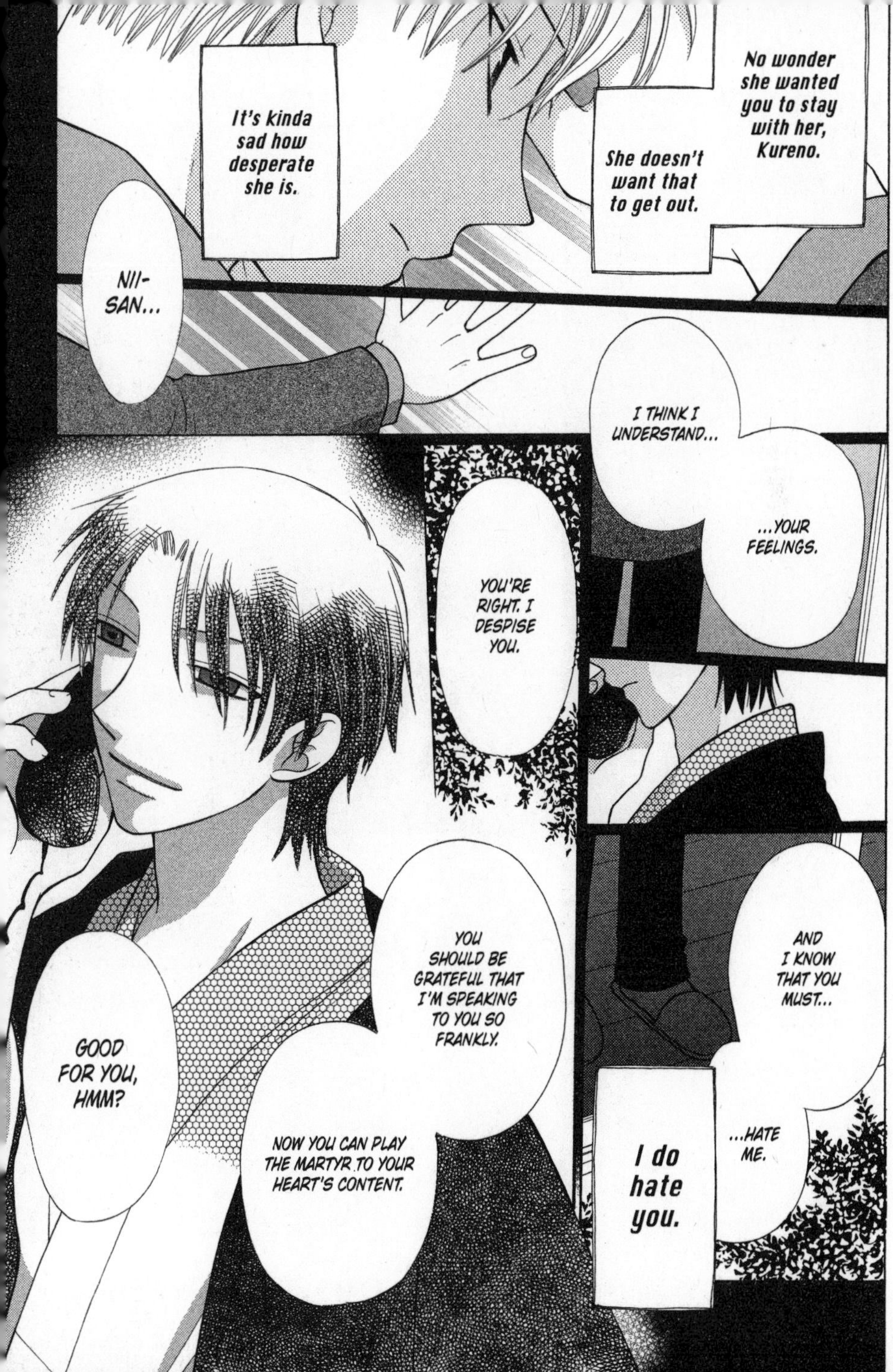
No wonder she wanted you to stay with her, Kureno.
She doesn't want that to get out.
It's kinda sad how desperate she is.
NII-SAN...
I THINK I UNDERSTAND...
...YOUR FEELINGS.
AND I KNOW THAT YOU MUST...
...HATE ME.
I do hate you.
YOU'RE RIGHT. I DESPISE YOU.
YOU SHOULD BE GRATEFUL THAT I'M SPEAKING TO YOU SO FRANKLY.
NOW YOU CAN PLAY THE MARTYR TO YOUR HEART'S CONTENT.
GOOD FOR YOU, HMM?

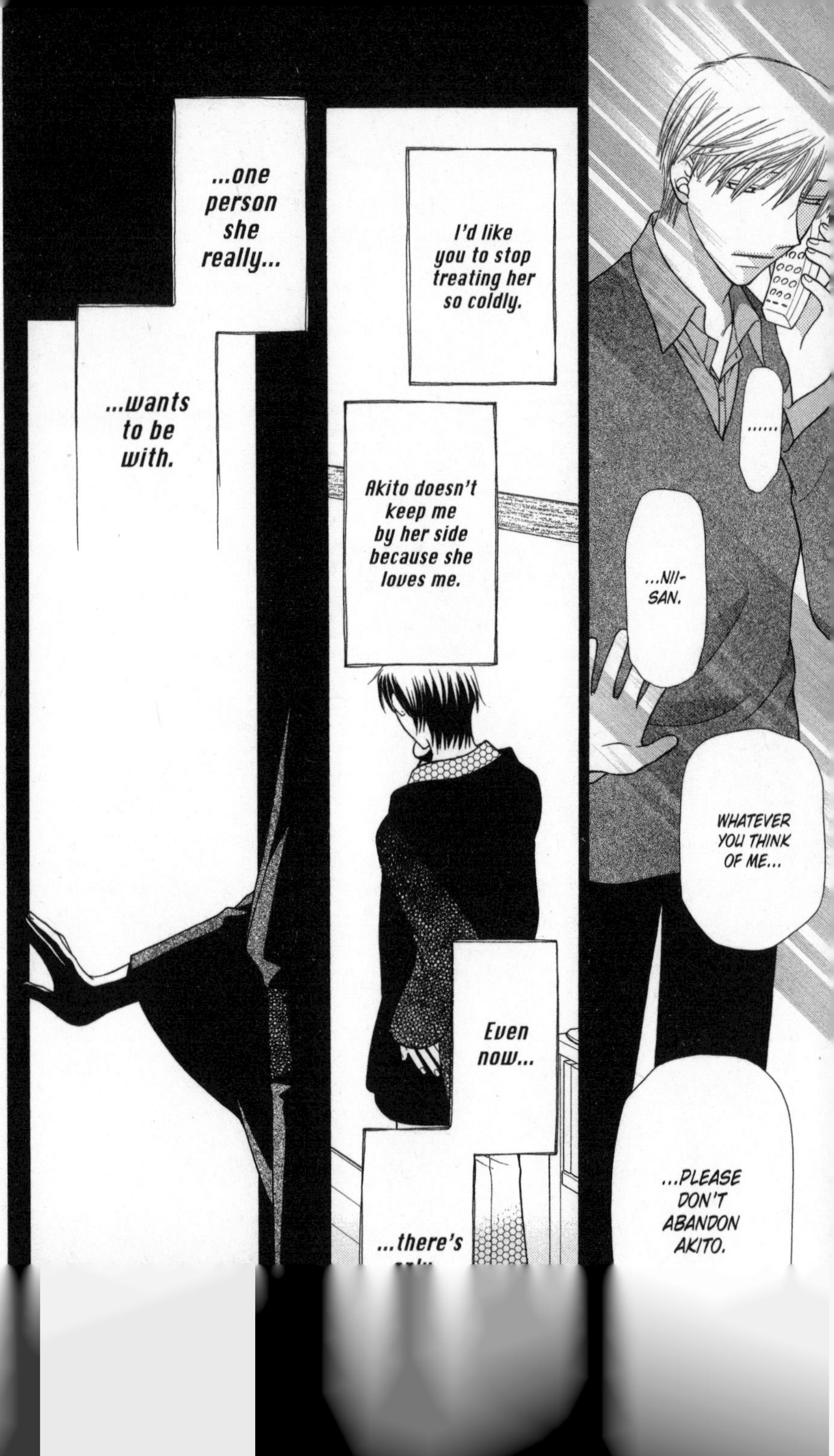
......
...NII-SAN.
WHATEVER YOU THINK OF ME...
...PLEASE DON'T ABANDON AKITO.
I'd like you to stop treating her so coldly.
Akito doesn't keep me by her side because she loves me.
Even now...
...there's
...one person she really...
...wants to be with.

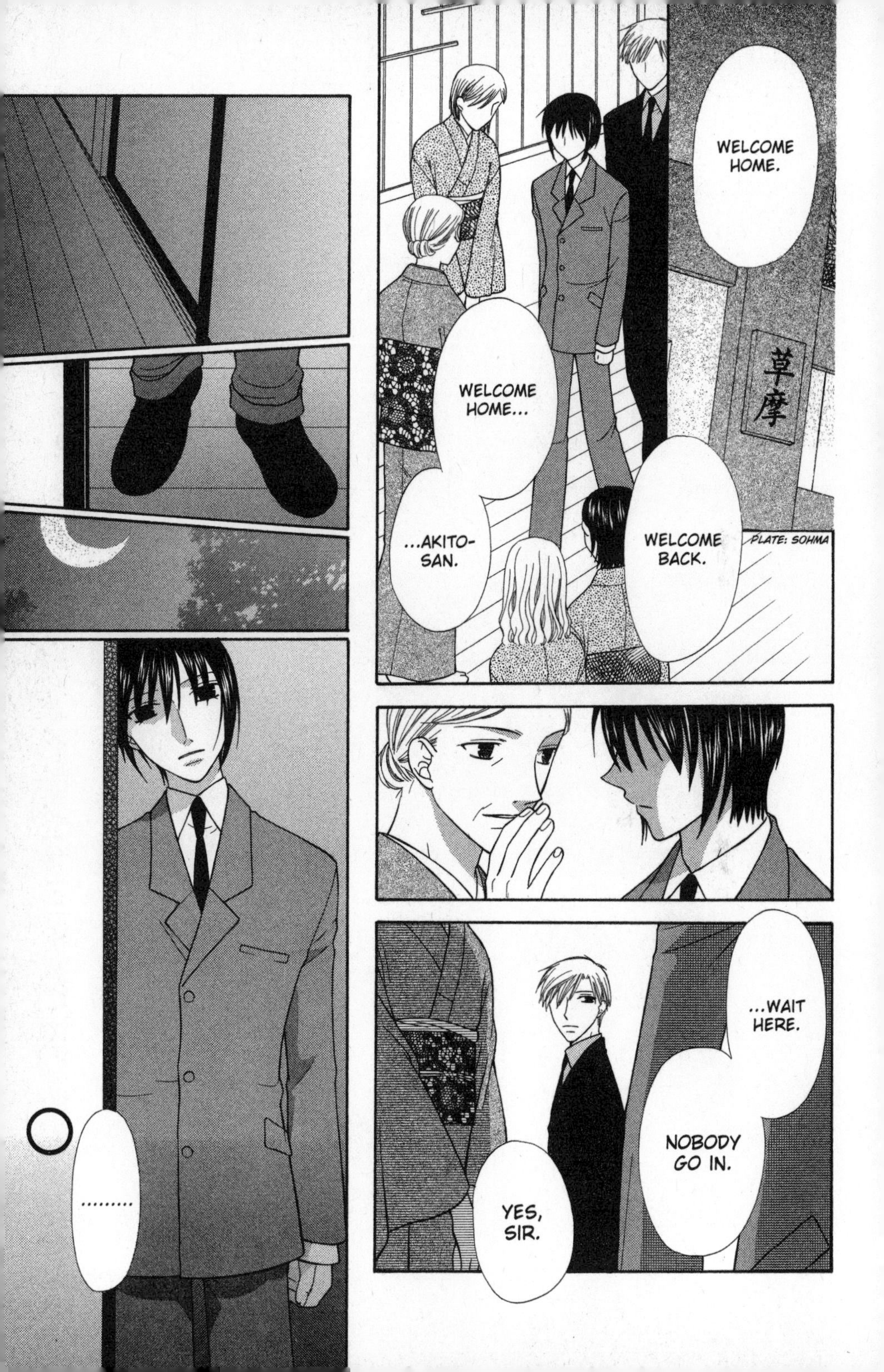
WELCOME HOME.
WELCOME HOME...
...AKITO-SAN.
WELCOME BACK.
PLATE: SOHMA
草摩
...WAIT HERE.
NOBODY GO IN.
YES, SIR.
....

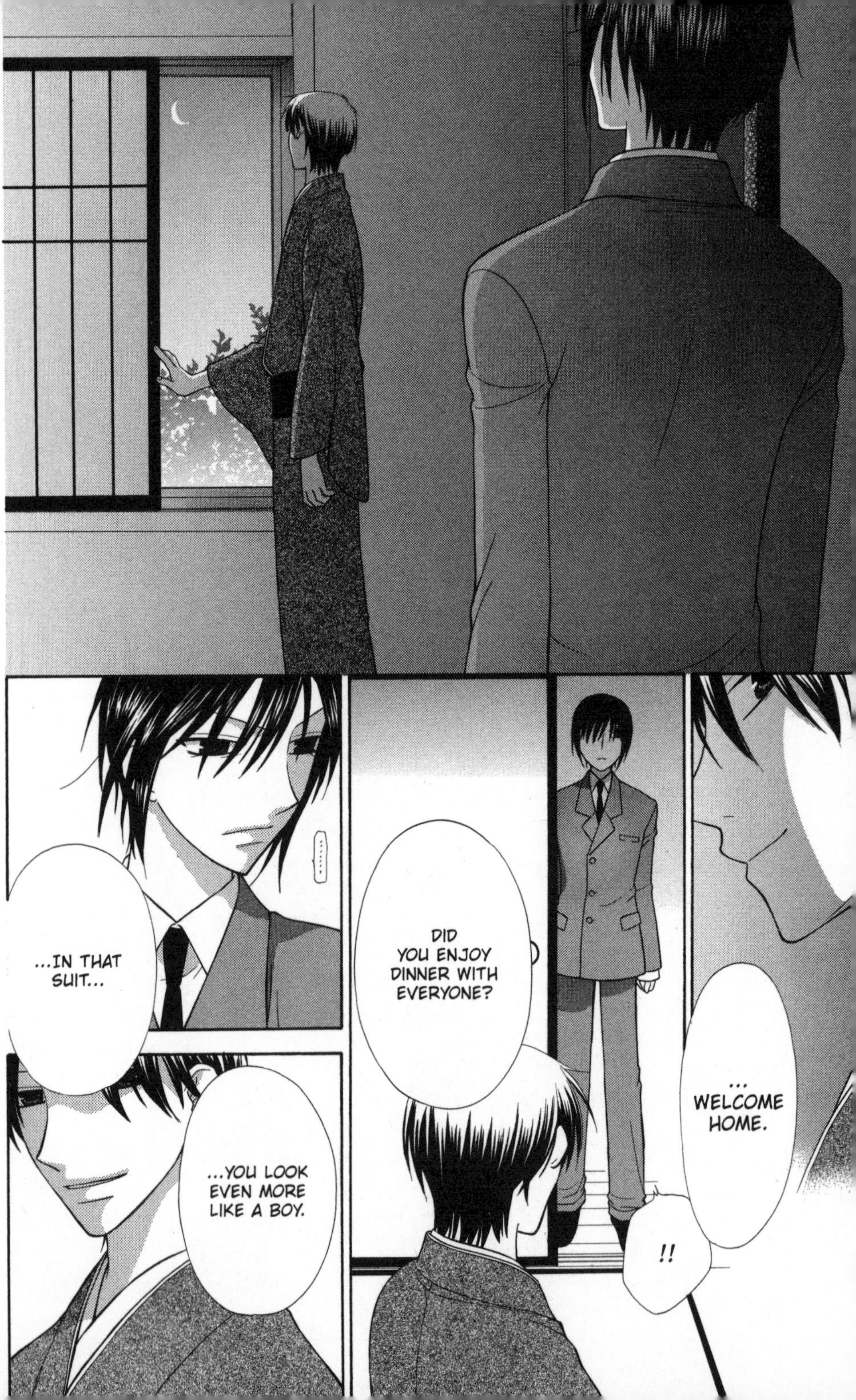
...
WELCOME HOME.
!!
DID YOU ENJOY DINNER WITH EVERYONE?
......
...IN THAT SUIT...
...YOU LOOK EVEN MORE LIKE A BOY.

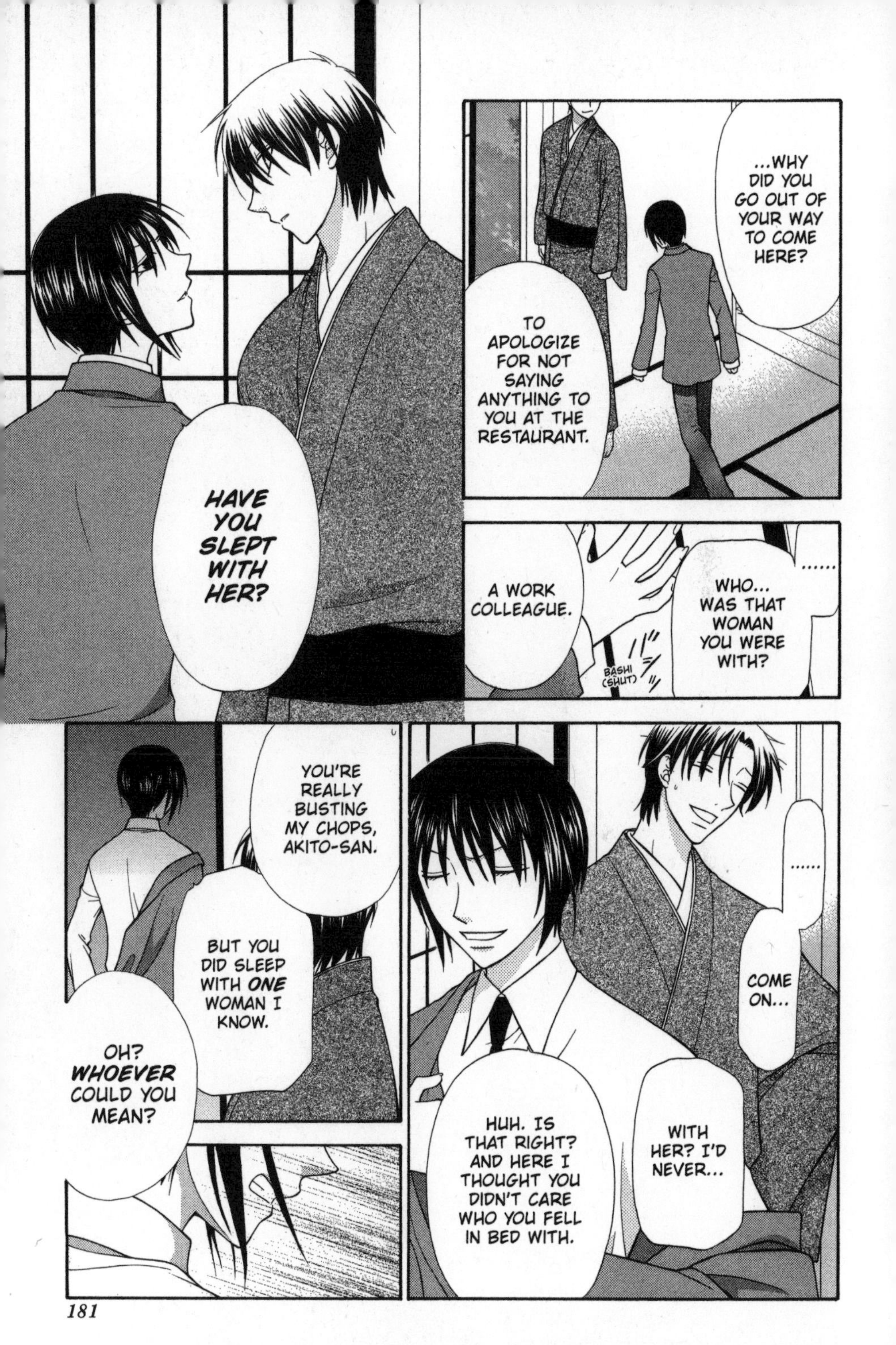
...WHY DID YOU GO OUT OF YOUR WAY TO COME HERE?
TO APOLOGIZE FOR NOT SAYING ANYTHING TO YOU AT THE RESTAURANT.
......
WHO... WAS THAT WOMAN YOU WERE WITH?
BASHI (SHUT)
A WORK COLLEAGUE.
HAVE YOU SLEPT WITH HER?
......
COME ON...
WITH HER? I'D NEVER...
HUH. IS THAT RIGHT? AND HERE I THOUGHT YOU DIDN'T CARE WHO YOU FELL IN BED WITH.
YOU'RE REALLY BUSTING MY CHOPS, AKITO-SAN.
BUT YOU DID SLEEP WITH *ONE* WOMAN I KNOW.
OH? *WHOEVER* COULD YOU MEAN?

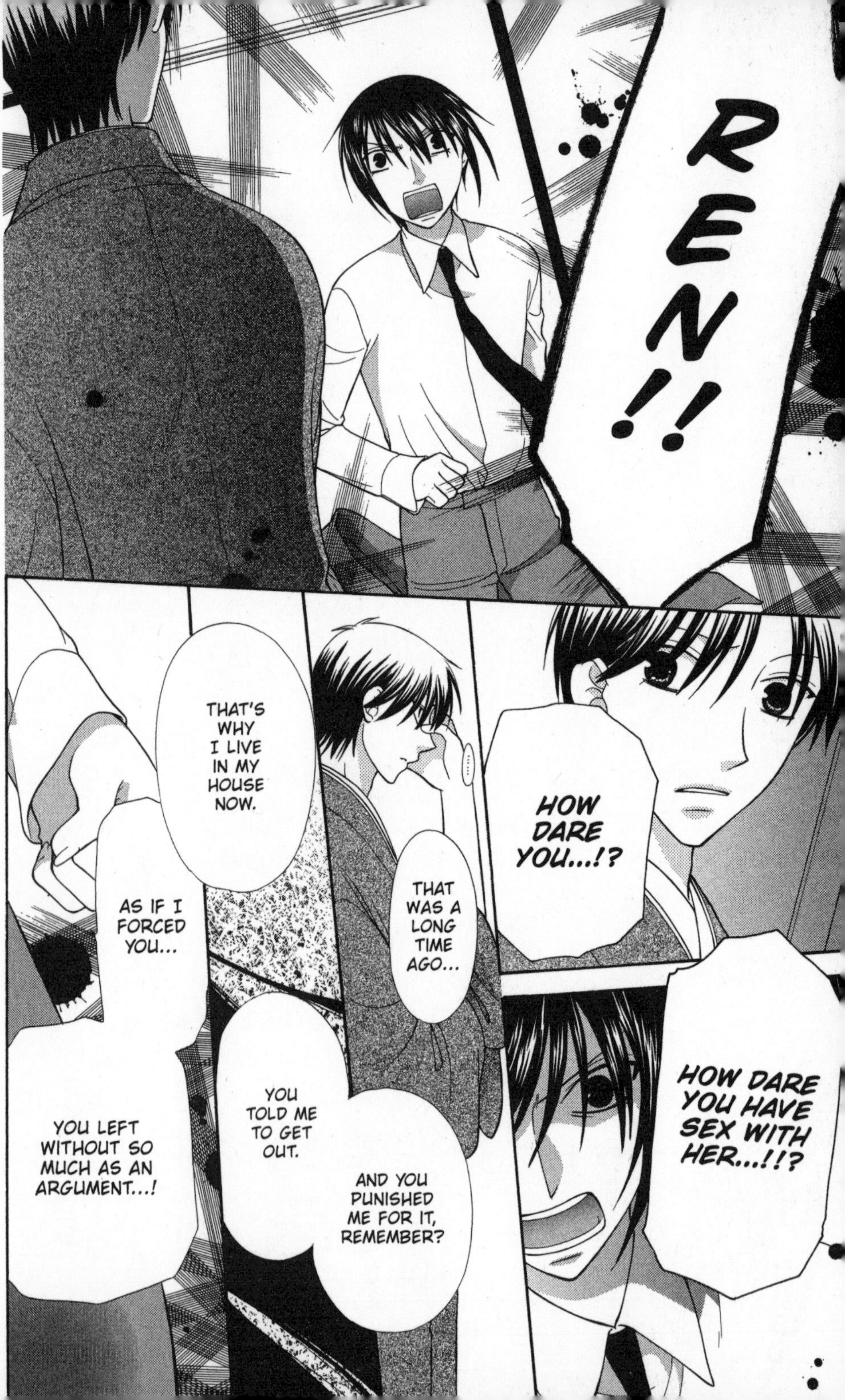
REN!!
HOW DARE YOU...!?
HOW DARE YOU HAVE SEX WITH HER...!!?
...
THAT'S WHY I LIVE IN MY HOUSE NOW.
THAT WAS A LONG TIME AGO...
AS IF I FORCED YOU...
YOU TOLD ME TO GET OUT.
AND YOU PUNISHED ME FOR IT, REMEMBER?
YOU LEFT WITHOUT SO MUCH AS AN ARGUMENT...!

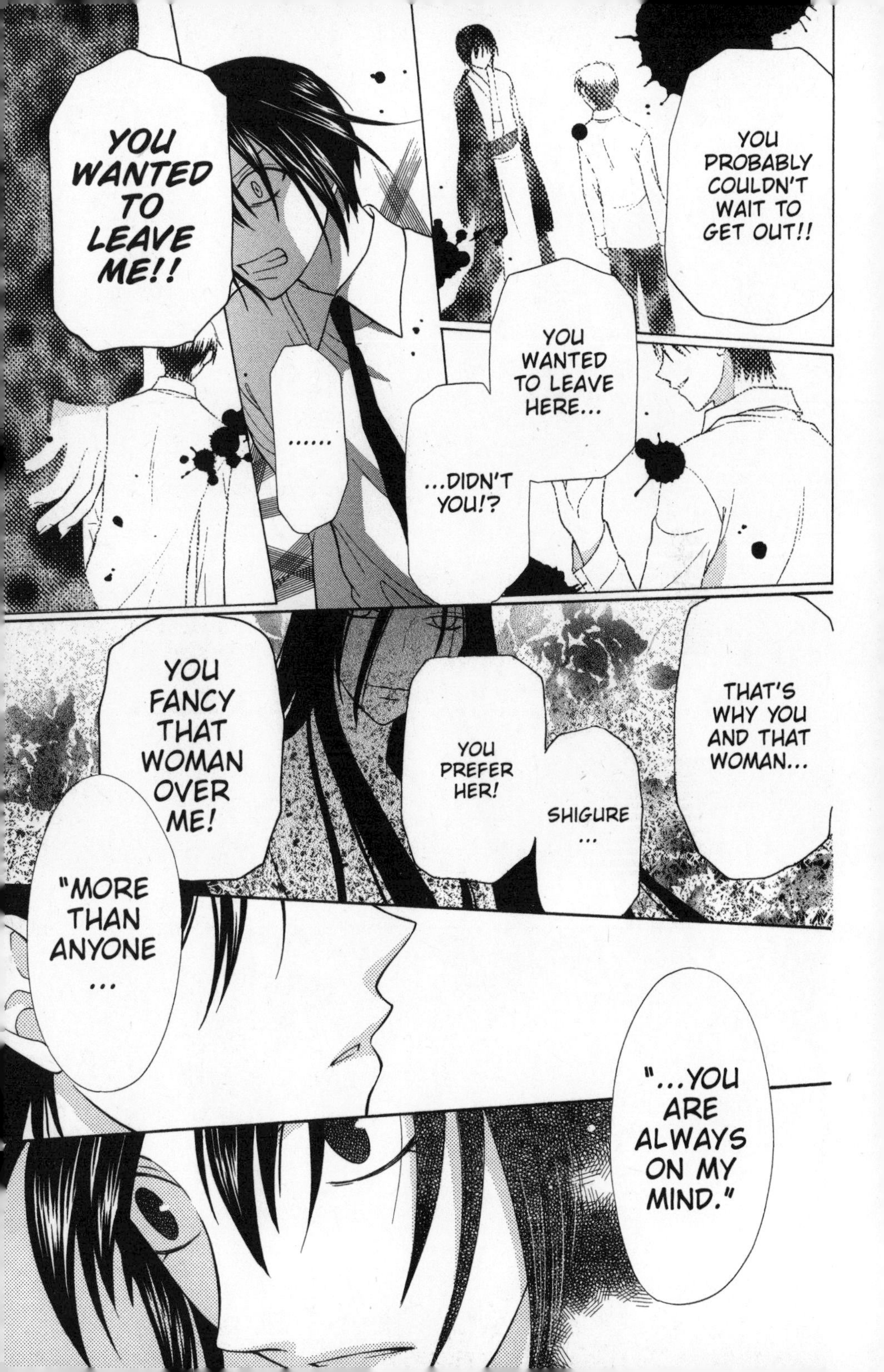
YOU PROBABLY COULDN'T WAIT TO GET OUT!!
YOU WANTED TO LEAVE HERE...
...DIDN'T YOU!?
YOU WANTED TO LEAVE ME!!
......
THAT'S WHY YOU AND THAT WOMAN...
SHIGURE...
YOU PREFER HER!
YOU FANCY THAT WOMAN OVER ME!
"MORE THAN ANYONE...
"...YOU ARE ALWAYS ON MY MIND."

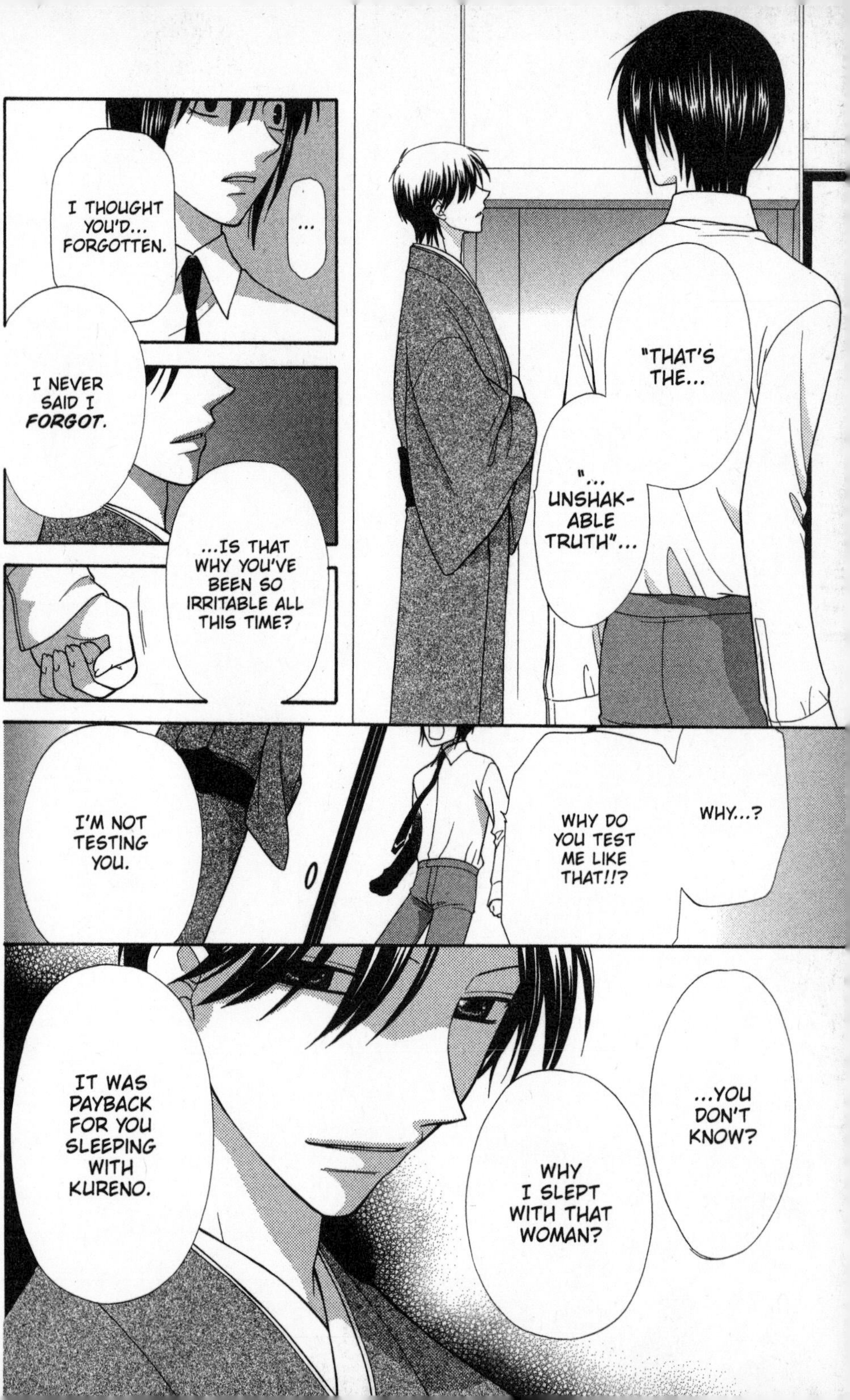
"THAT'S THE...
"...UNSHAKABLE TRUTH"...
...
I THOUGHT YOU'D... FORGOTTEN.
I NEVER SAID I *FORGOT*.
...IS THAT WHY YOU'VE BEEN SO IRRITABLE ALL THIS TIME?
WHY...?
WHY DO YOU TEST ME LIKE THAT!!?
I'M NOT TESTING YOU.
...YOU DON'T KNOW?
WHY I SLEPT WITH THAT WOMAN?
IT WAS PAYBACK FOR YOU SLEEPING WITH KURENO.

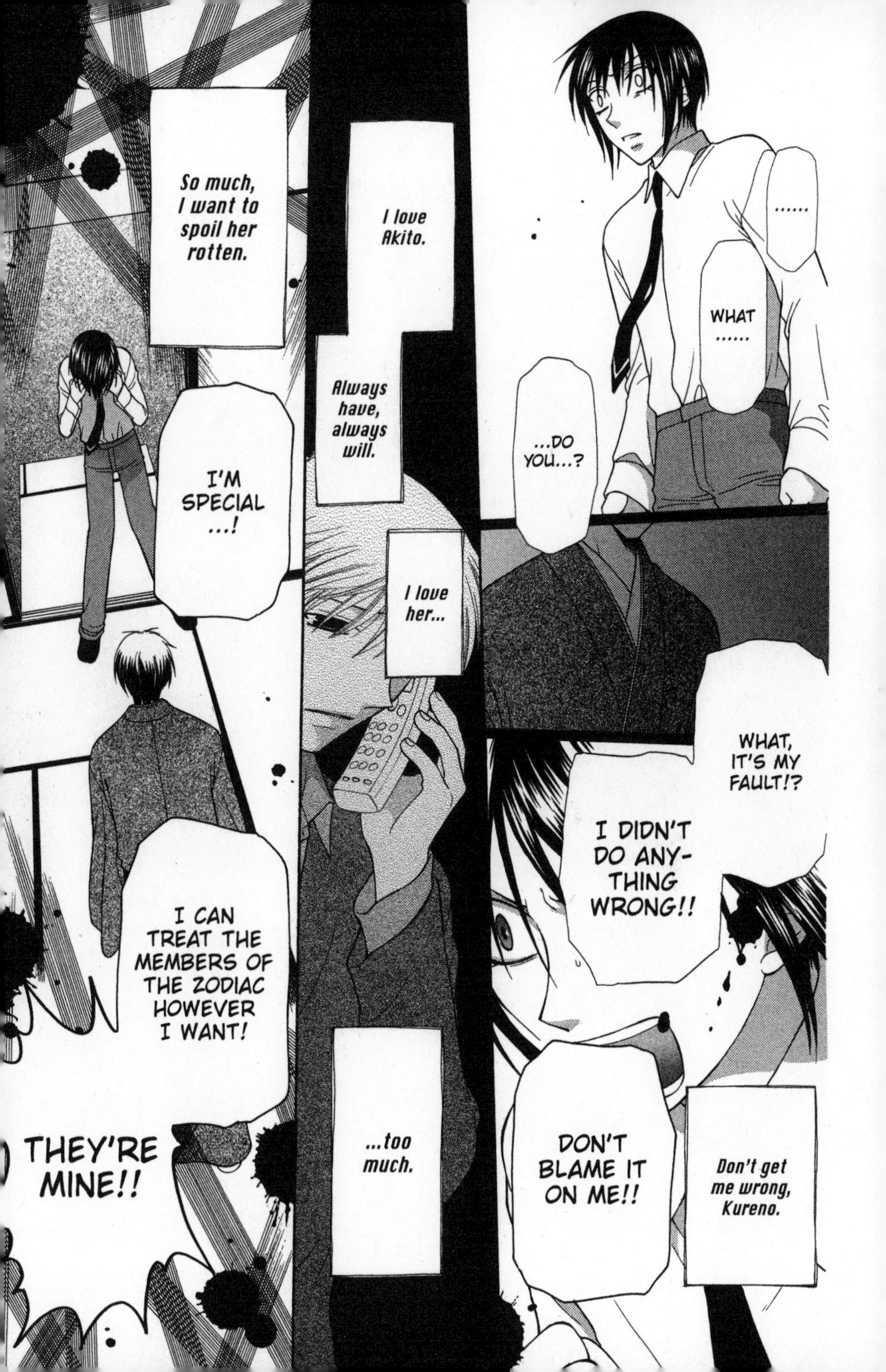
......
WHAT ......
...DO YOU...?
WHAT, IT'S MY FAULT!?
I DIDN'T DO ANY-THING WRONG!!
Don't get me wrong, Kureno.
DON'T BLAME IT ON ME!!
I love Akito.
Always have, always will.
I love her...
...too much.
So much, I want to spoil her rotten.
I'M SPECIAL ...!
I CAN TREAT THE MEMBERS OF THE ZODIAC HOWEVER I WANT!
THEY'RE MINE!!

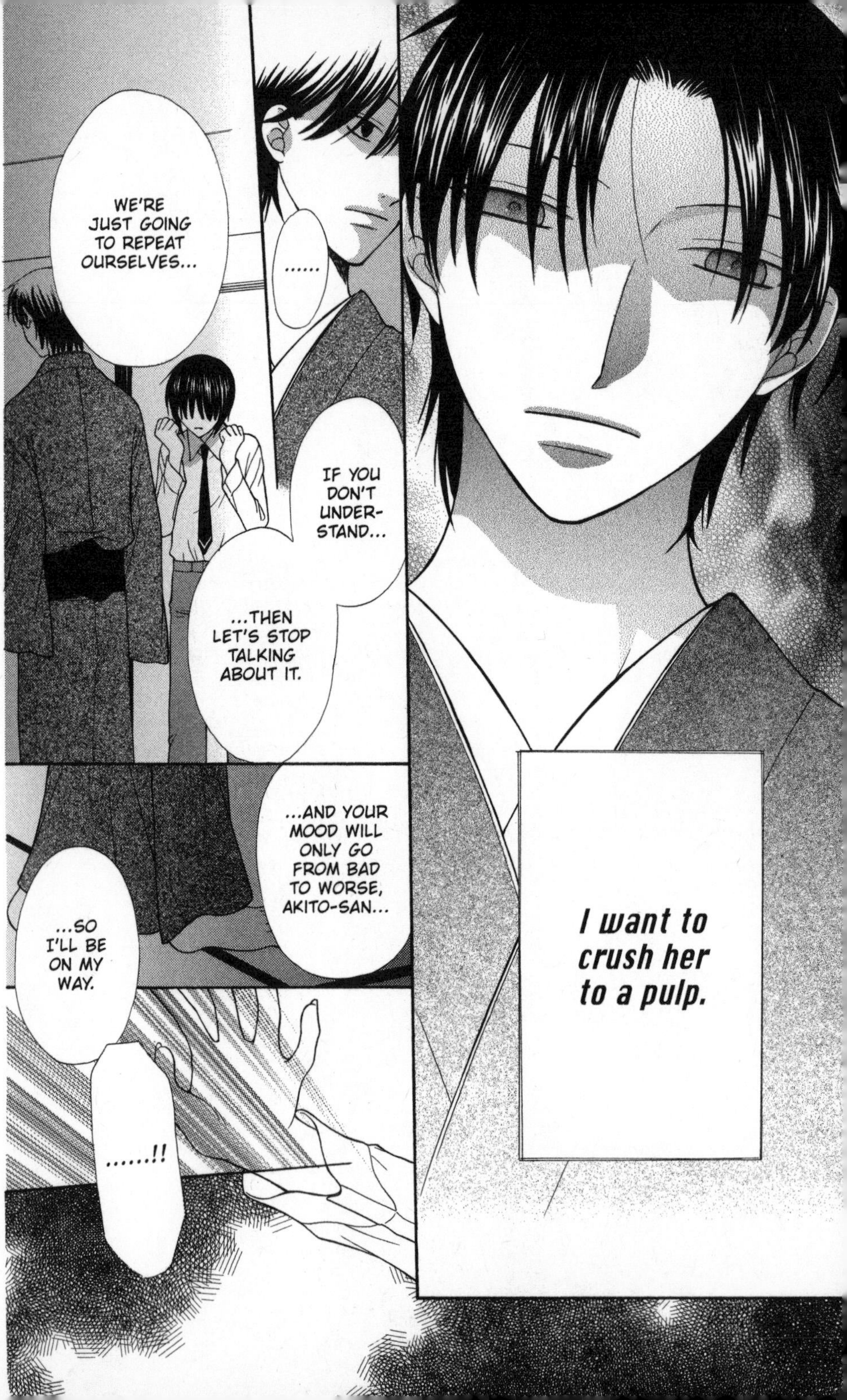
I want to crush her to a pulp.
......
WE'RE JUST GOING TO REPEAT OURSELVES...
IF YOU DON'T UNDER-STAND...
...THEN LET'S STOP TALKING ABOUT IT.
...AND YOUR MOOD WILL ONLY GO FROM BAD TO WORSE, AKITO-SAN...
...SO I'LL BE ON MY WAY.
......!!

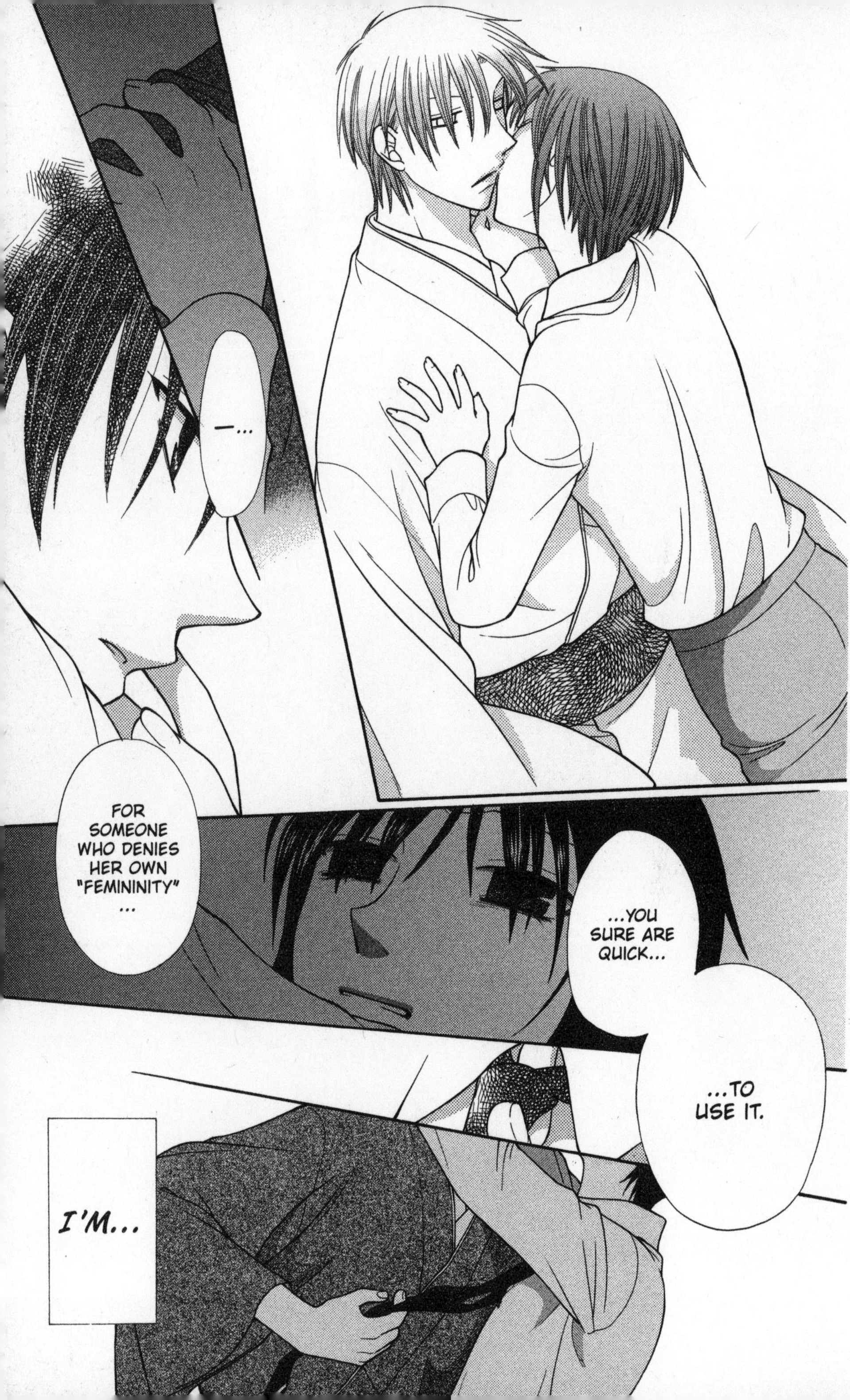
—...
FOR SOMEONE WHO DENIES HER OWN "FEMININITY" ...
...YOU SURE ARE QUICK...
...TO USE IT.
I'M...

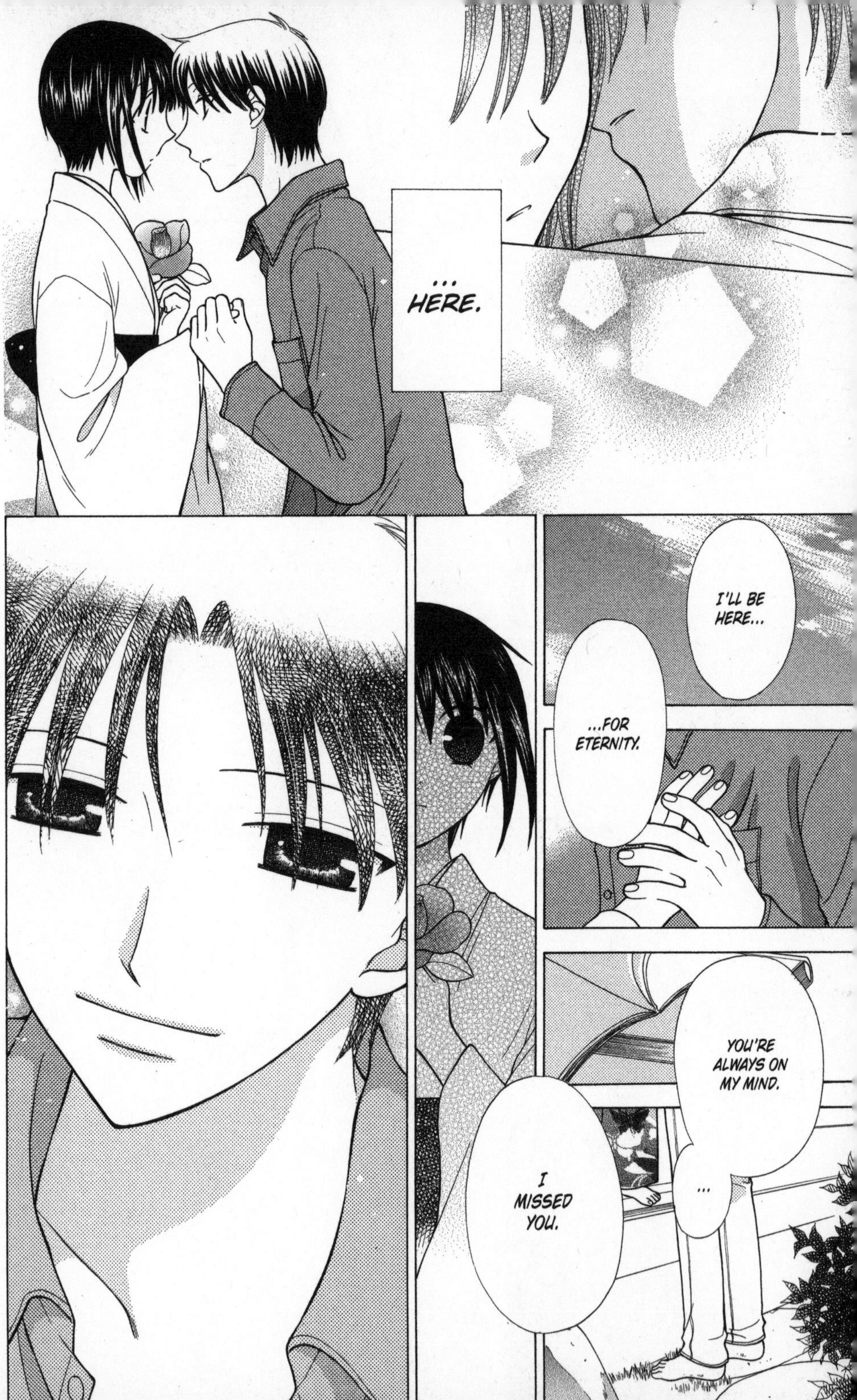
...HERE.
I'LL BE HERE...
...FOR ETERNITY.
YOU'RE ALWAYS ON MY MIND.
...
I MISSED YOU.

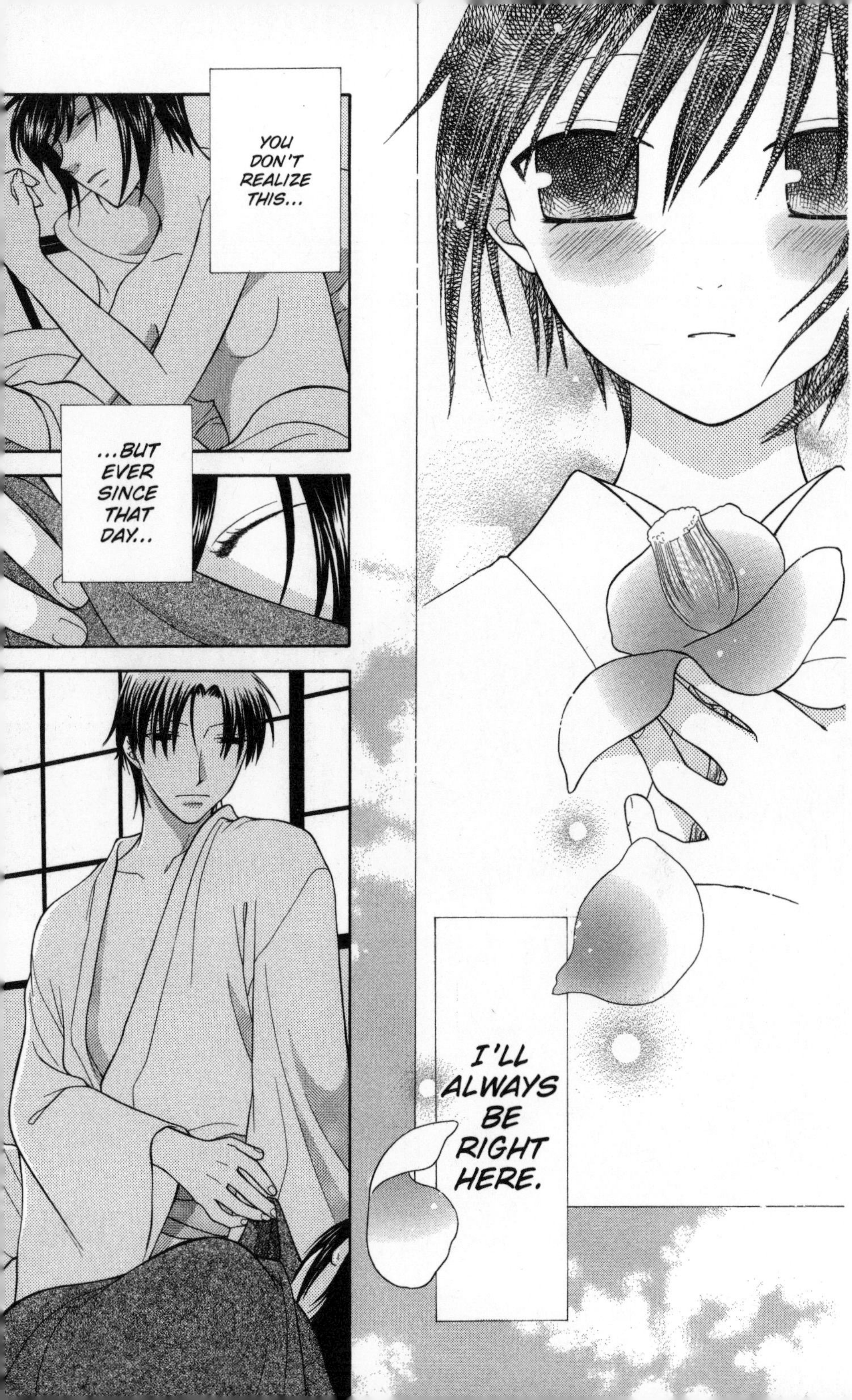
I'LL ALWAYS BE RIGHT HERE.
YOU DON'T REALIZE THIS...
...BUT EVER SINCE THAT DAY...

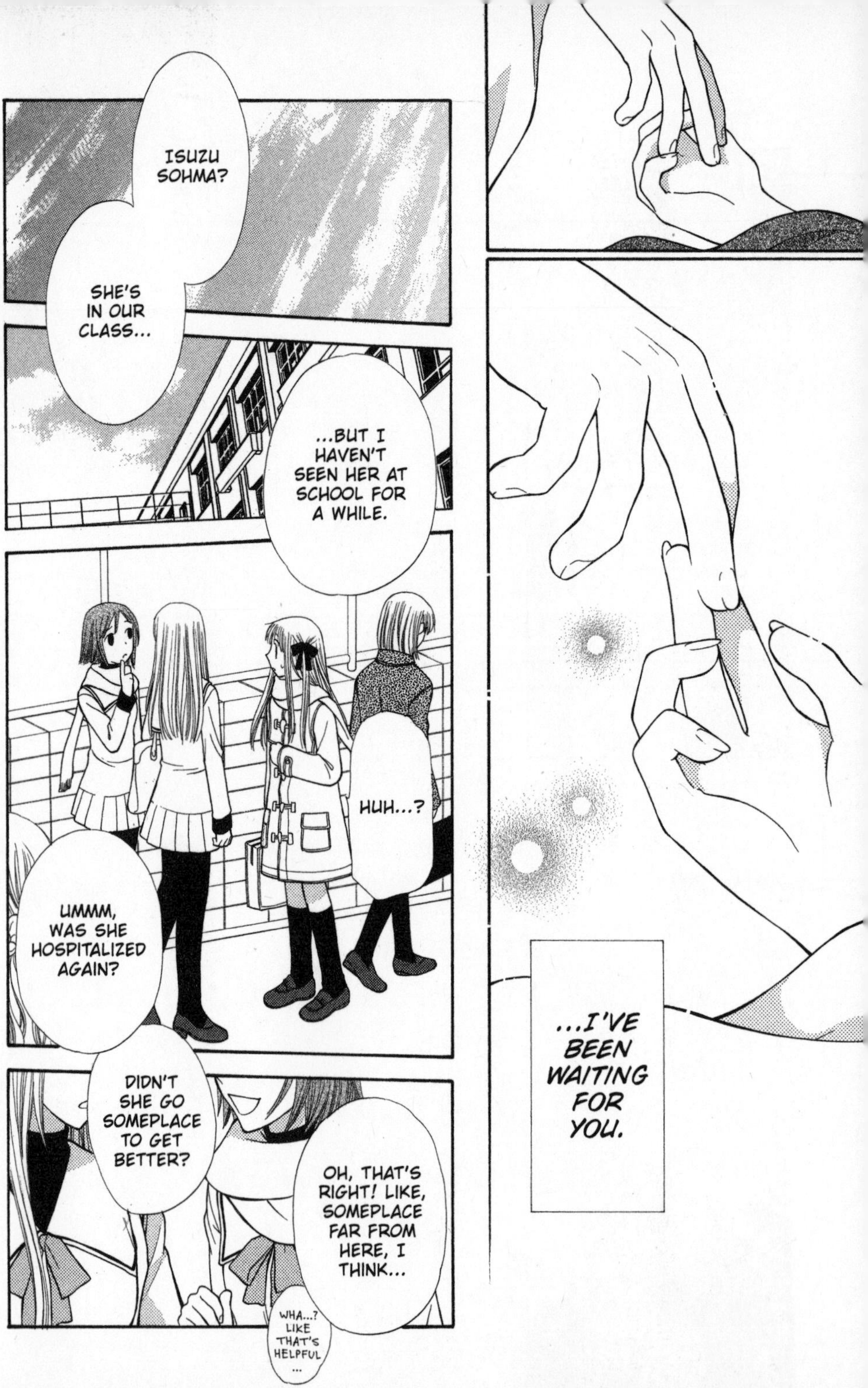
...I'VE BEEN WAITING FOR YOU.
ISUZU SOHMA?
SHE'S IN OUR CLASS...
...BUT I HAVEN'T SEEN HER AT SCHOOL FOR A WHILE.
HUH...?
UMMM, WAS SHE HOSPITALIZED AGAIN?
DIDN'T SHE GO SOMEPLACE TO GET BETTER?
OH, THAT'S RIGHT! LIKE, SOMEPLACE FAR FROM HERE, I THINK...
WHA...? LIKE THAT'S HELPFUL ...

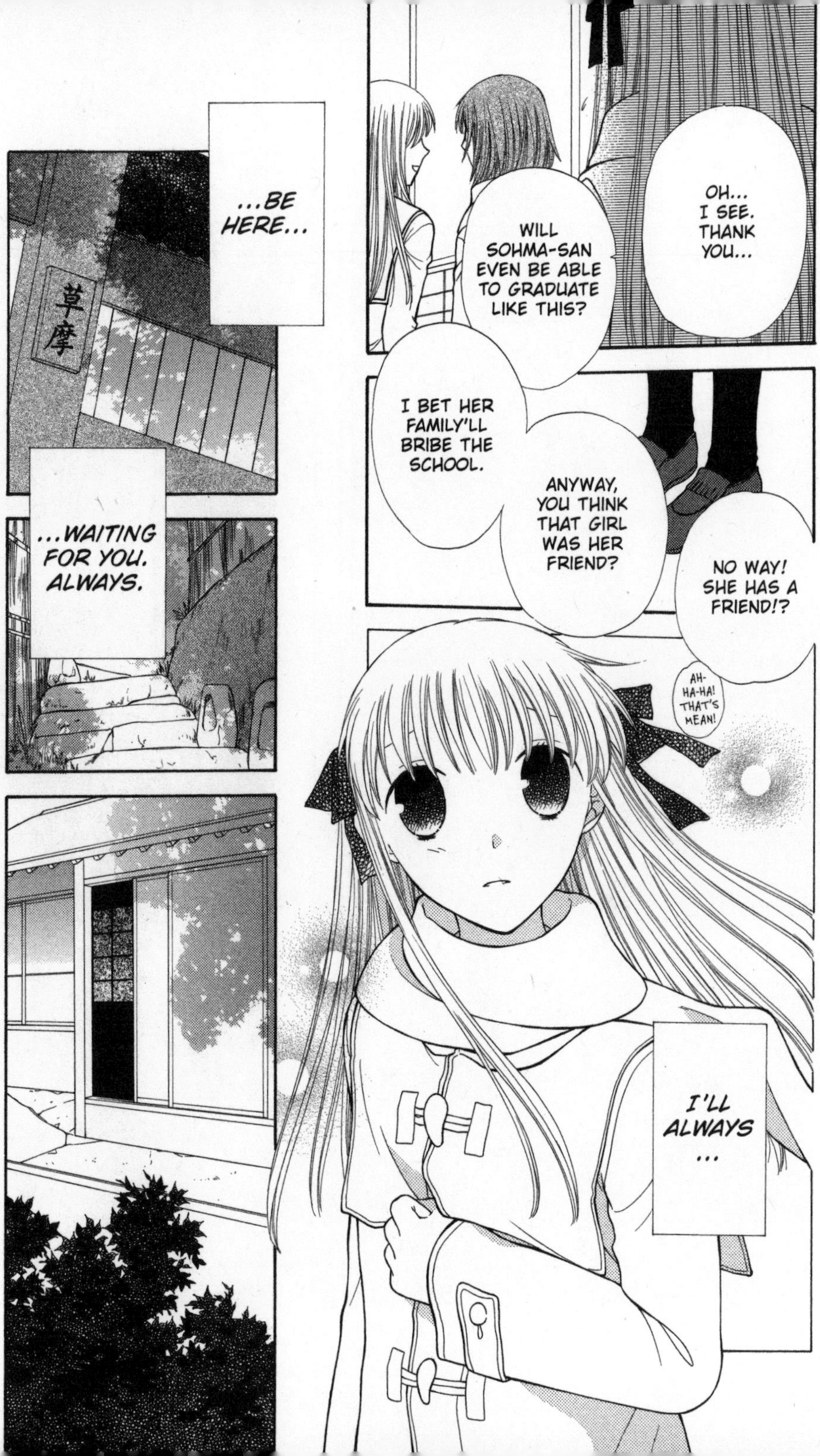
OH... I SEE. THANK YOU...
WILL SOHMA-SAN EVEN BE ABLE TO GRADUATE LIKE THIS?
I BET HER FAMILY'LL BRIBE THE SCHOOL.
ANYWAY, YOU THINK THAT GIRL WAS HER FRIEND?
NO WAY! SHE HAS A FRIEND!?
AH-HA-HA! THAT'S MEAN!
I'LL ALWAYS ...
...BE HERE...
草摩
...WAITING FOR YOU. ALWAYS.

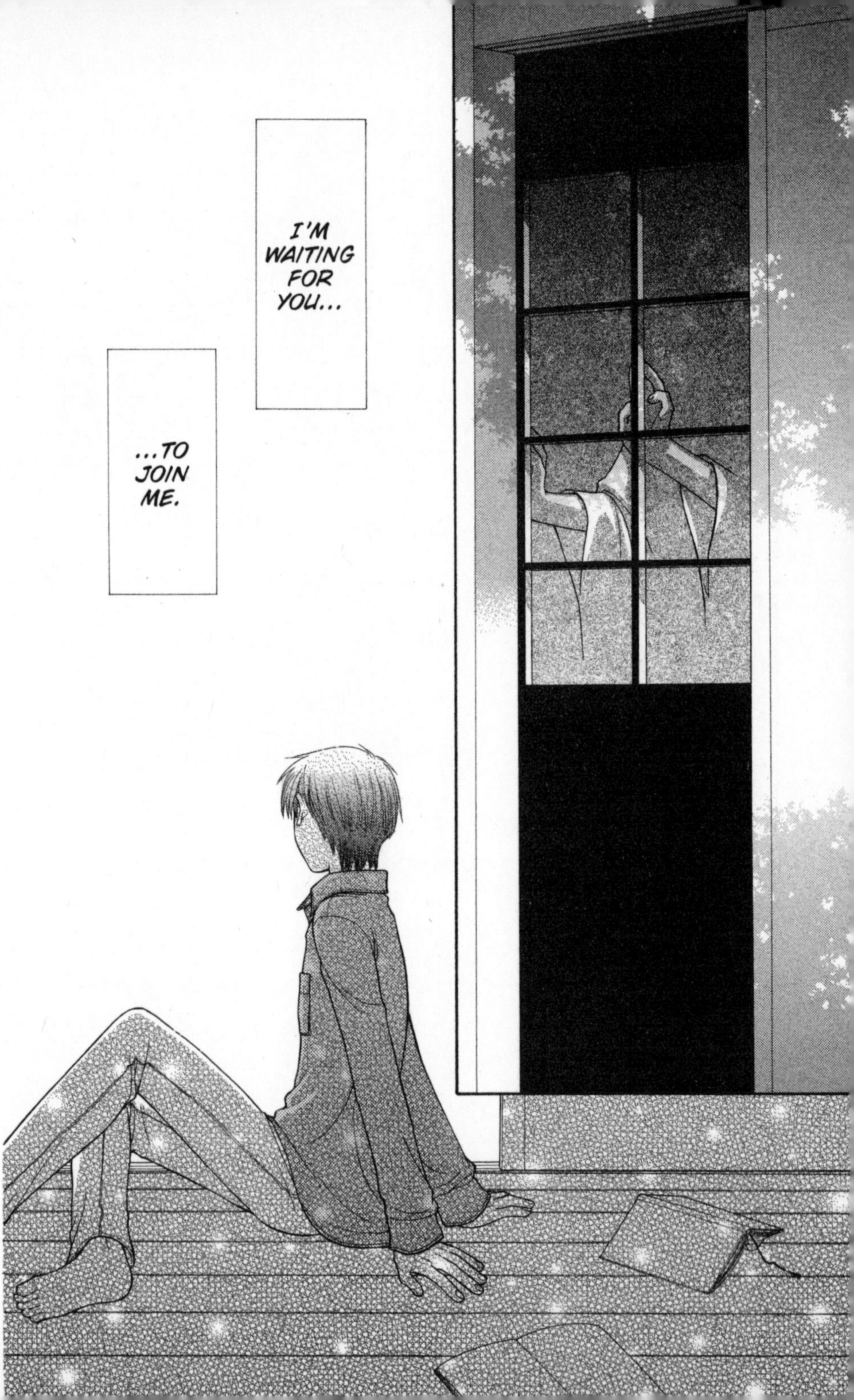
I'M WAITING FOR YOU...
...TO JOIN ME.

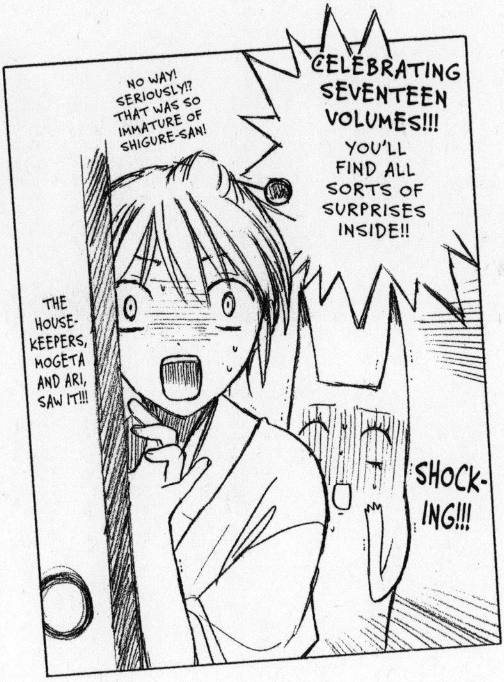
CELEBRATING SEVENTEEN VOLUMES!!!
YOU'LL FIND ALL SORTS OF SURPRISES INSIDE!!
NO WAY! SERIOUSLY!? THAT WAS SO IMMATURE OF SHIGURE-SAN!
THE HOUSE-KEEPERS, MOGETA AND ARI, SAW IT!!!
SHOCK-ING!!!

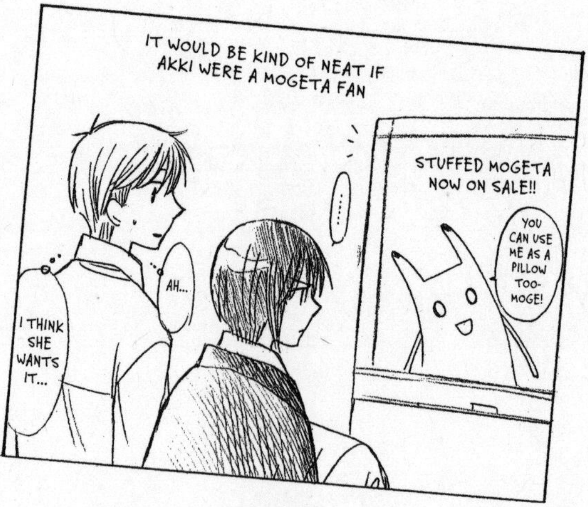
IT WOULD BE KIND OF NEAT IF AKKI WERE A MOGETA FAN
STUFFED MOGETA NOW ON SALE!!
YOU CAN USE ME AS A PILLOW TOO-MOGE!
......
AH...
I THINK SHE WANTS IT...

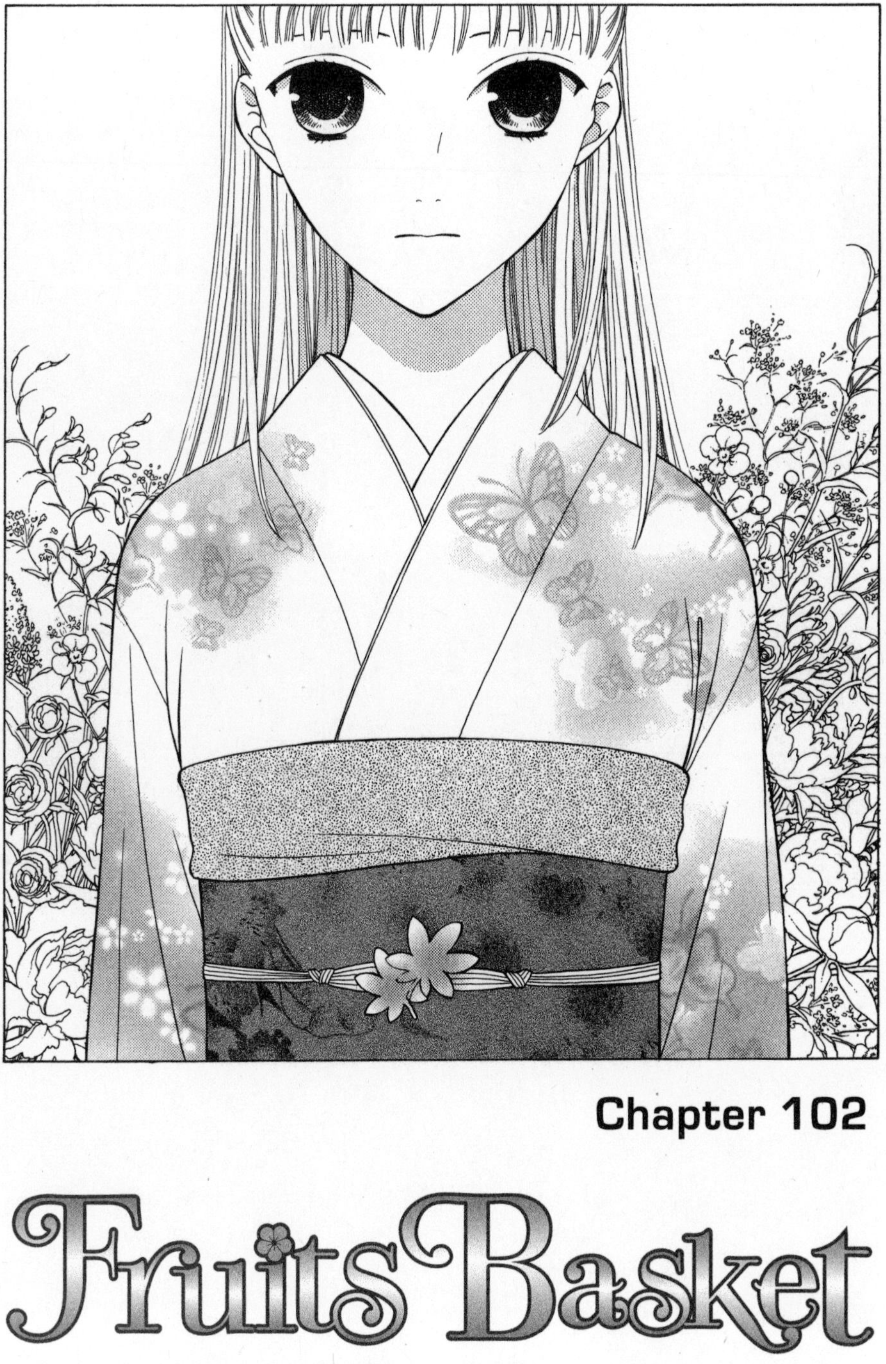

Chapter 102

Fruits Basket

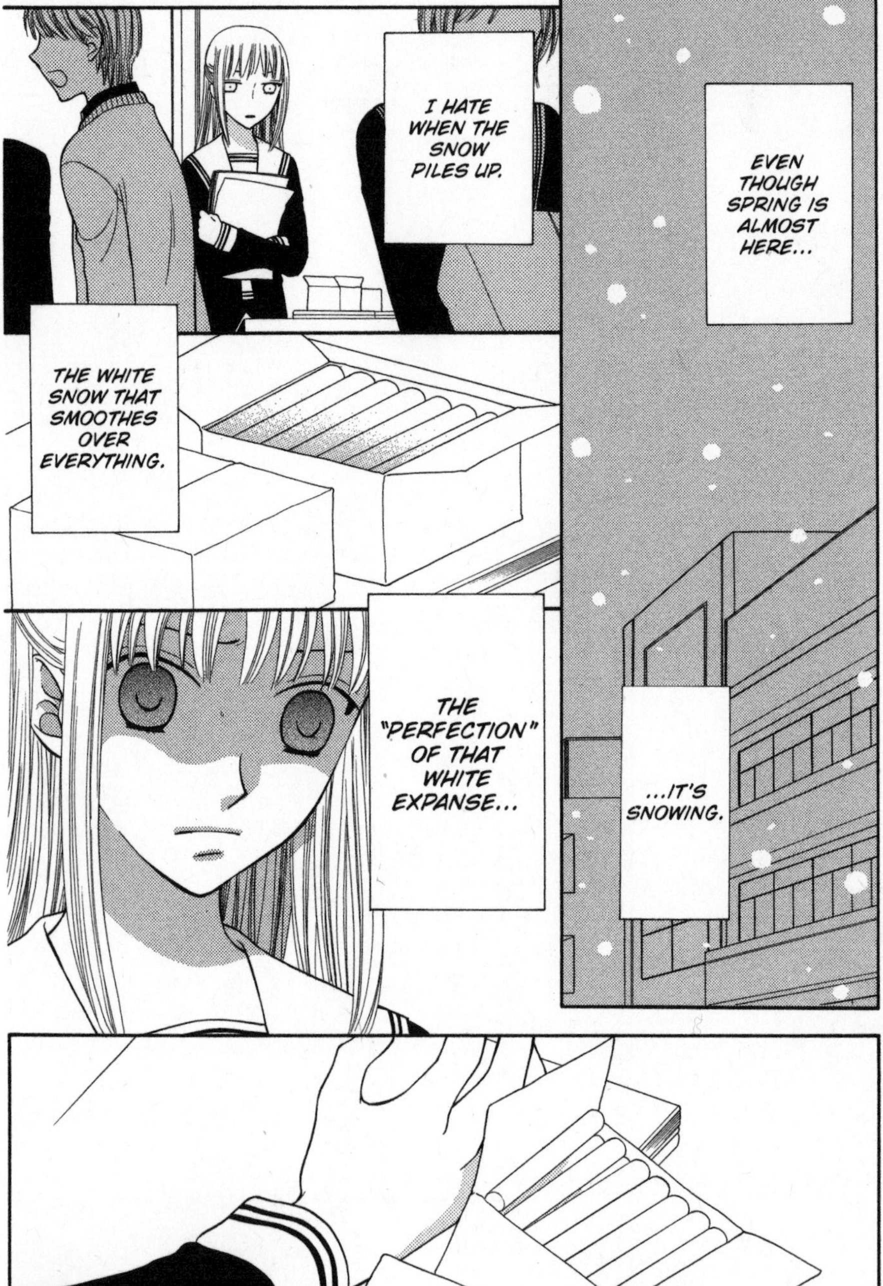
EVEN THOUGH SPRING IS ALMOST HERE...
...IT'S SNOWING.
I HATE WHEN THE SNOW PILES UP.
THE WHITE SNOW THAT SMOOTHES OVER EVERYTHING.
THE "PERFECTION" OF THAT WHITE EXPANSE...

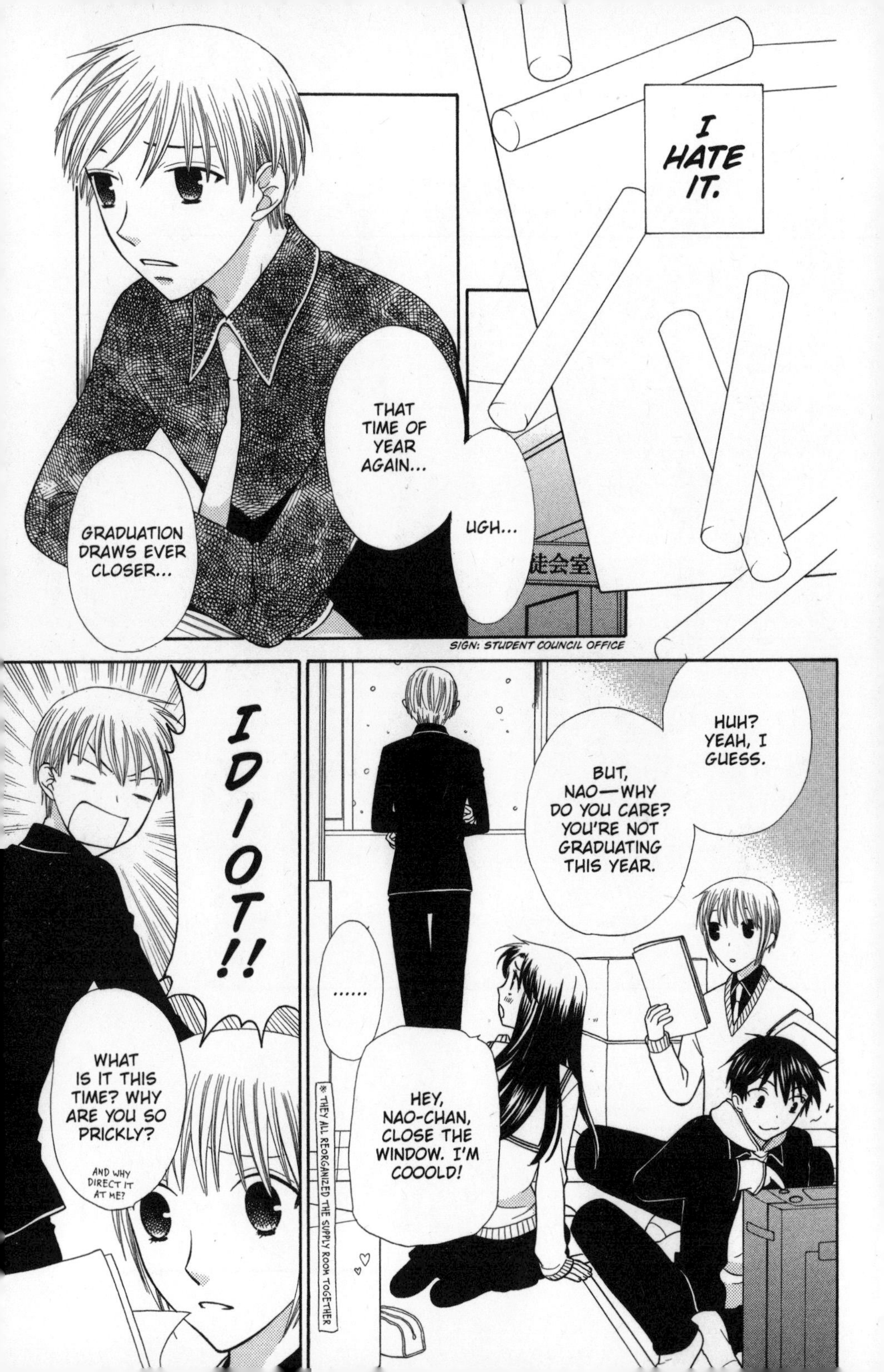
I HATE IT.
THAT TIME OF YEAR AGAIN...
UGH...
GRADUATION DRAWS EVER CLOSER...
徒会室
SIGN: STUDENT COUNCIL OFFICE
HUH? YEAH, I GUESS.
BUT, NAO—WHY DO YOU CARE? YOU'RE NOT GRADUATING THIS YEAR.
......
HEY, NAO-CHAN, CLOSE THE WINDOW. I'M COOOLD!
※ THEY ALL REORGANIZED THE SUPPLY ROOM TOGETHER
IDIOT!!
WHAT IS IT THIS TIME? WHY ARE YOU SO PRICKLY?
AND WHY DIRECT IT AT ME?

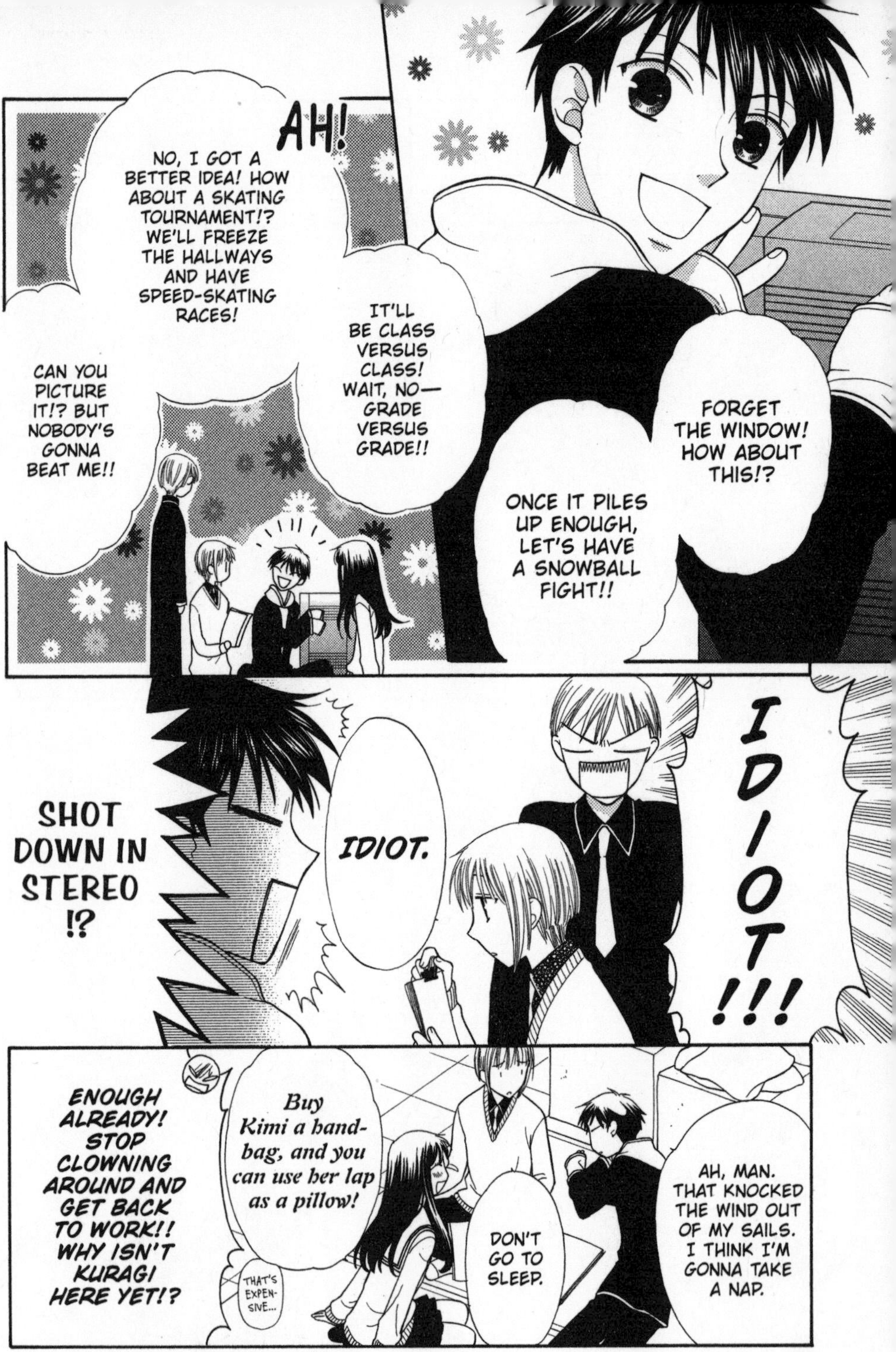
FORGET THE WINDOW! HOW ABOUT THIS!?
ONCE IT PILES UP ENOUGH, LET'S HAVE A SNOWBALL FIGHT!!
AH!
NO, I GOT A BETTER IDEA! HOW ABOUT A SKATING TOURNAMENT!? WE'LL FREEZE THE HALLWAYS AND HAVE SPEED-SKATING RACES!
IT'LL BE CLASS VERSUS CLASS! WAIT, NO—GRADE VERSUS GRADE!!
CAN YOU PICTURE IT!? BUT NOBODY'S GONNA BEAT ME!!
IDIOT!!!
IDIOT.
SHOT DOWN IN STEREO!?
AH, MAN. THAT KNOCKED THE WIND OUT OF MY SAILS. I THINK I'M GONNA TAKE A NAP.
DON'T GO TO SLEEP.
Buy Kimi a handbag, and you can use her lap as a pillow!
THAT'S EXPENSIVE...
ENOUGH ALREADY! STOP CLOWNING AROUND AND GET BACK TO WORK!! WHY ISN'T KURAGI HERE YET!?

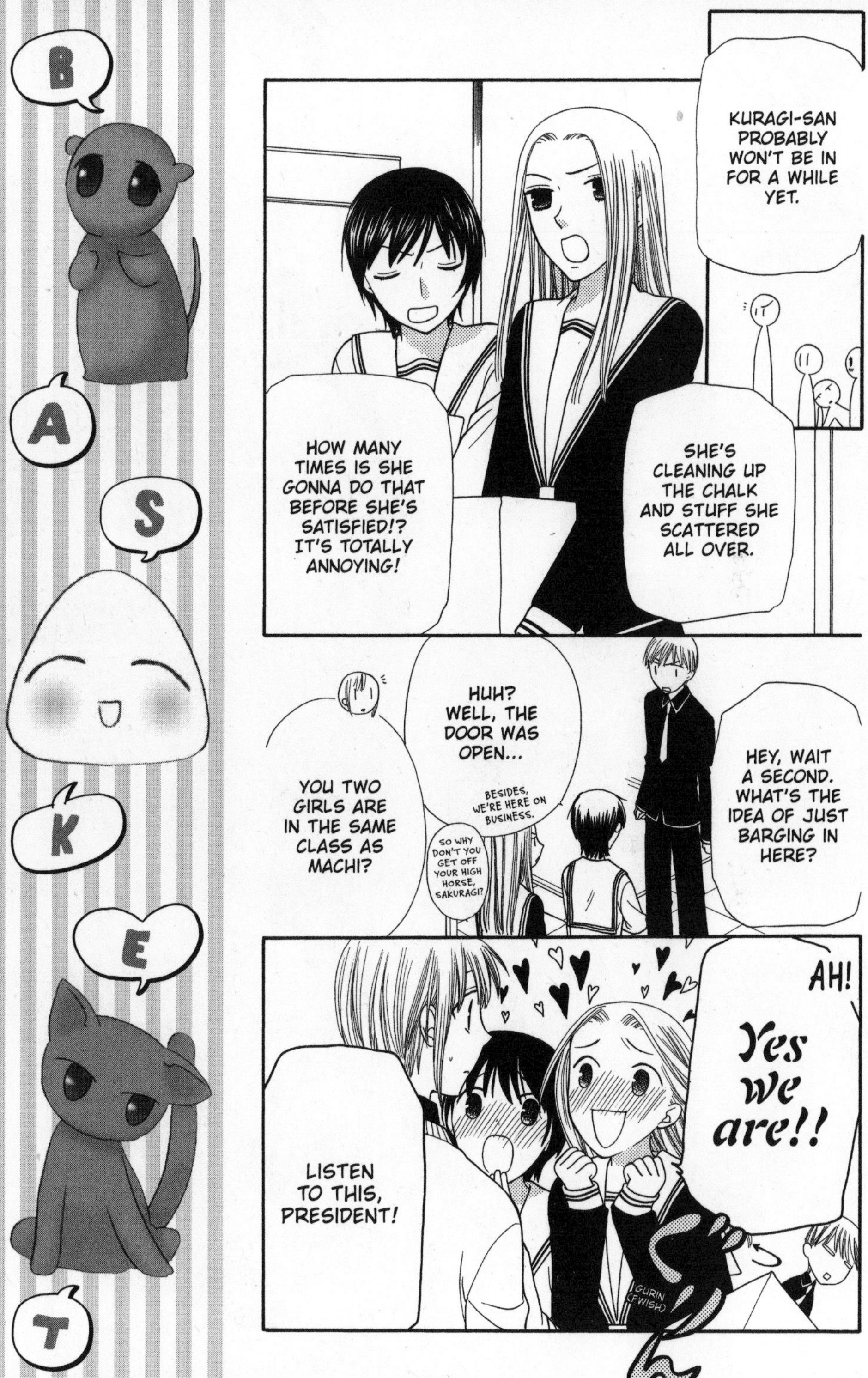
KURAGI-SAN PROBABLY WON'T BE IN FOR A WHILE YET.
SHE'S CLEANING UP THE CHALK AND STUFF SHE SCATTERED ALL OVER.
HOW MANY TIMES IS SHE GONNA DO THAT BEFORE SHE'S SATISFIED!? IT'S TOTALLY ANNOYING!
HEY, WAIT A SECOND. WHAT'S THE IDEA OF JUST BARGING IN HERE?
HUH? WELL, THE DOOR WAS OPEN...
BESIDES, WE'RE HERE ON BUSINESS.
SO WHY DON'T YOU GET OFF YOUR HIGH HORSE, SAKURAGI?
YOU TWO GIRLS ARE IN THE SAME CLASS AS MACHI?
AH!
Yes we are!!
LISTEN TO THIS, PRESIDENT!
GURIN (FWISH)
B
A
S
K
E
T

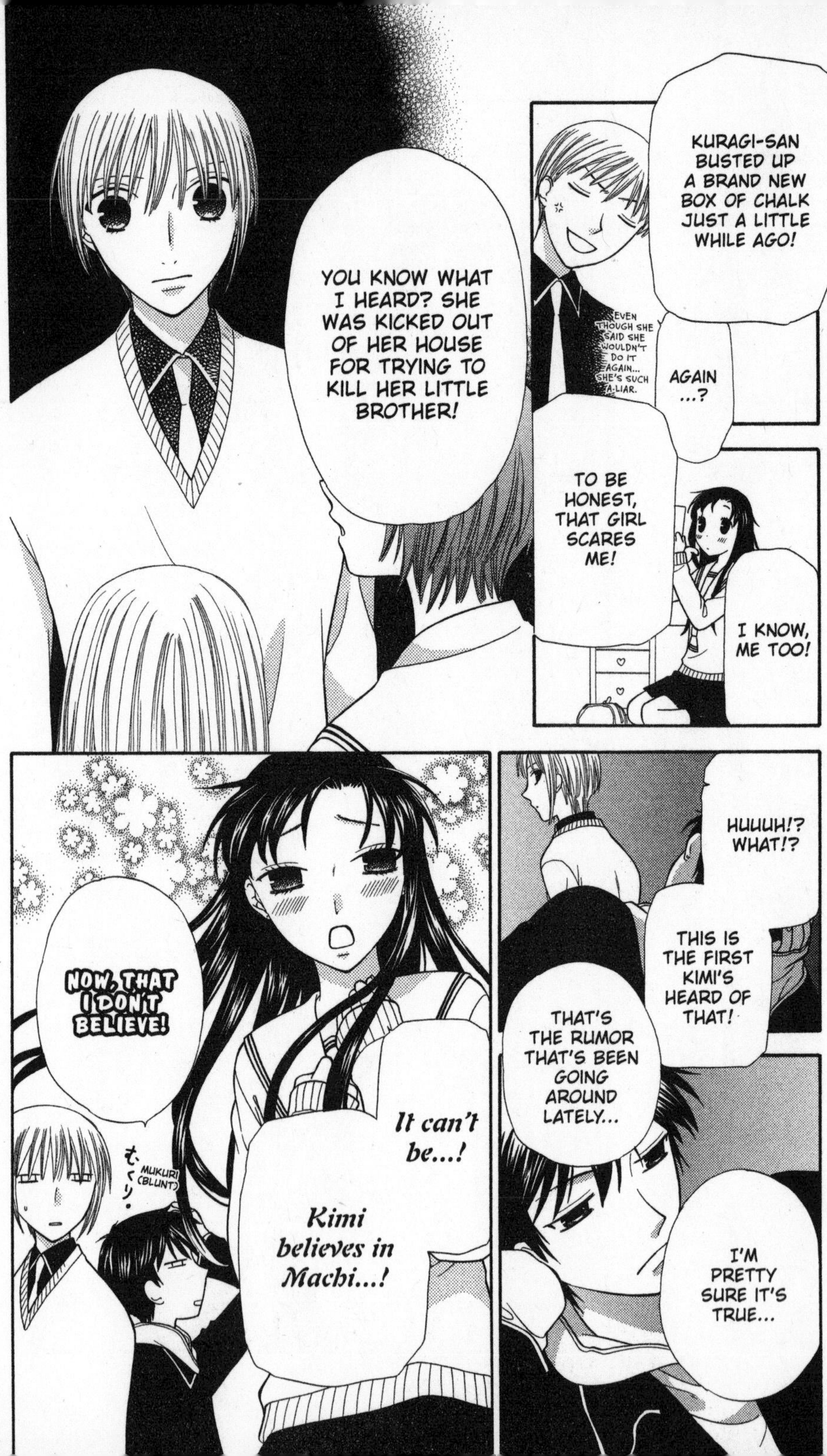
KURAGI-SAN BUSTED UP A BRAND NEW BOX OF CHALK JUST A LITTLE WHILE AGO!
EVEN THOUGH SHE SAID SHE WOULDN'T DO IT AGAIN... SHE'S SUCH A LIAR.
AGAIN ...?
TO BE HONEST, THAT GIRL SCARES ME!
I KNOW, ME TOO!
YOU KNOW WHAT I HEARD? SHE WAS KICKED OUT OF HER HOUSE FOR TRYING TO KILL HER LITTLE BROTHER!
HUUUH!? WHAT!?
THIS IS THE FIRST KIMI'S HEARD OF THAT!
THAT'S THE RUMOR THAT'S BEEN GOING AROUND LATELY...
I'M PRETTY SURE IT'S TRUE...
NOW, THAT I DON'T BELIEVE!
It can't be...!
Kimi believes in Machi...!
むくり。
MUKURI (BLUNT)

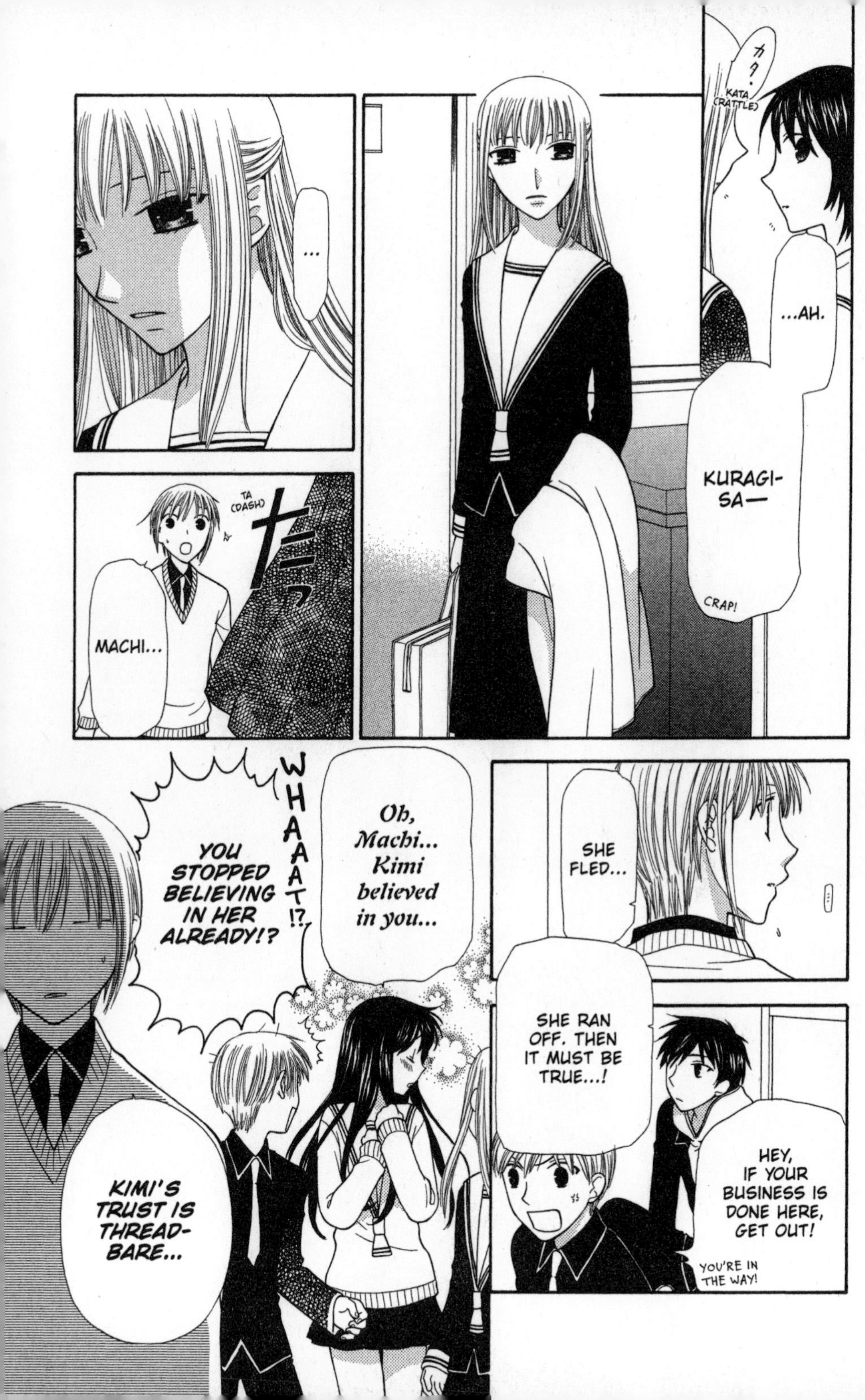
カタ
KATA (RATTLE)
...AH.
KURAGI-SA—
CRAP!
...
TA (DASH)
MACHI...
SHE FLED...
SHE RAN OFF. THEN IT MUST BE TRUE...!
HEY, IF YOUR BUSINESS IS DONE HERE, GET OUT!
YOU'RE IN THE WAY!
Oh, Machi... Kimi believed in you...
WHAAAAT!?
YOU STOPPED BELIEVING IN HER ALREADY!?
KIMI'S TRUST IS THREAD-BARE...

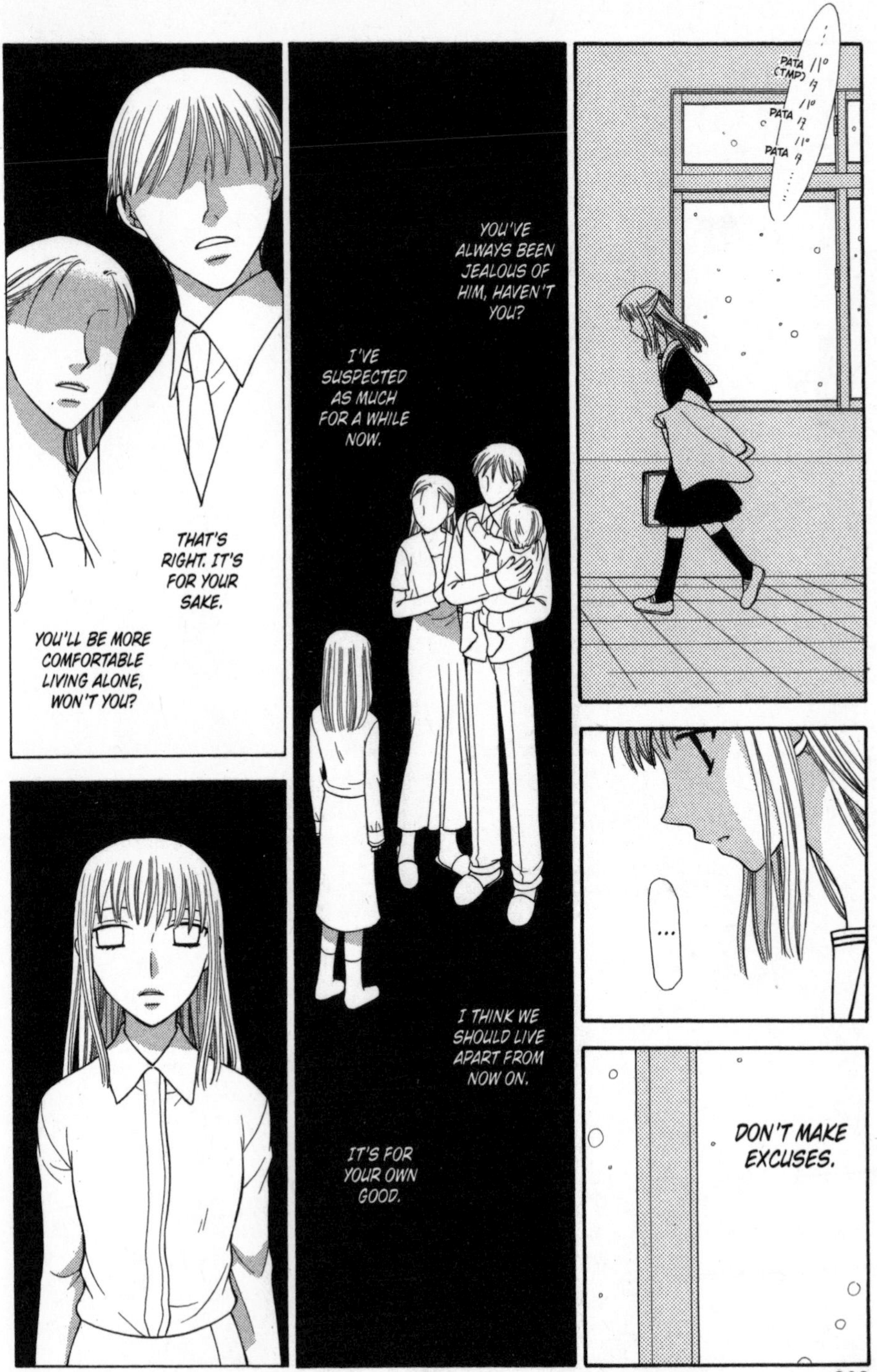
PATA (TMP)
PATA
PATA
...
DON'T MAKE EXCUSES.
YOU'VE ALWAYS BEEN JEALOUS OF HIM, HAVEN'T YOU?
I'VE SUSPECTED AS MUCH FOR A WHILE NOW.
I THINK WE SHOULD LIVE APART FROM NOW ON.
IT'S FOR YOUR OWN GOOD.
THAT'S RIGHT. IT'S FOR YOUR SAKE.
YOU'LL BE MORE COMFORTABLE LIVING ALONE, WON'T YOU?

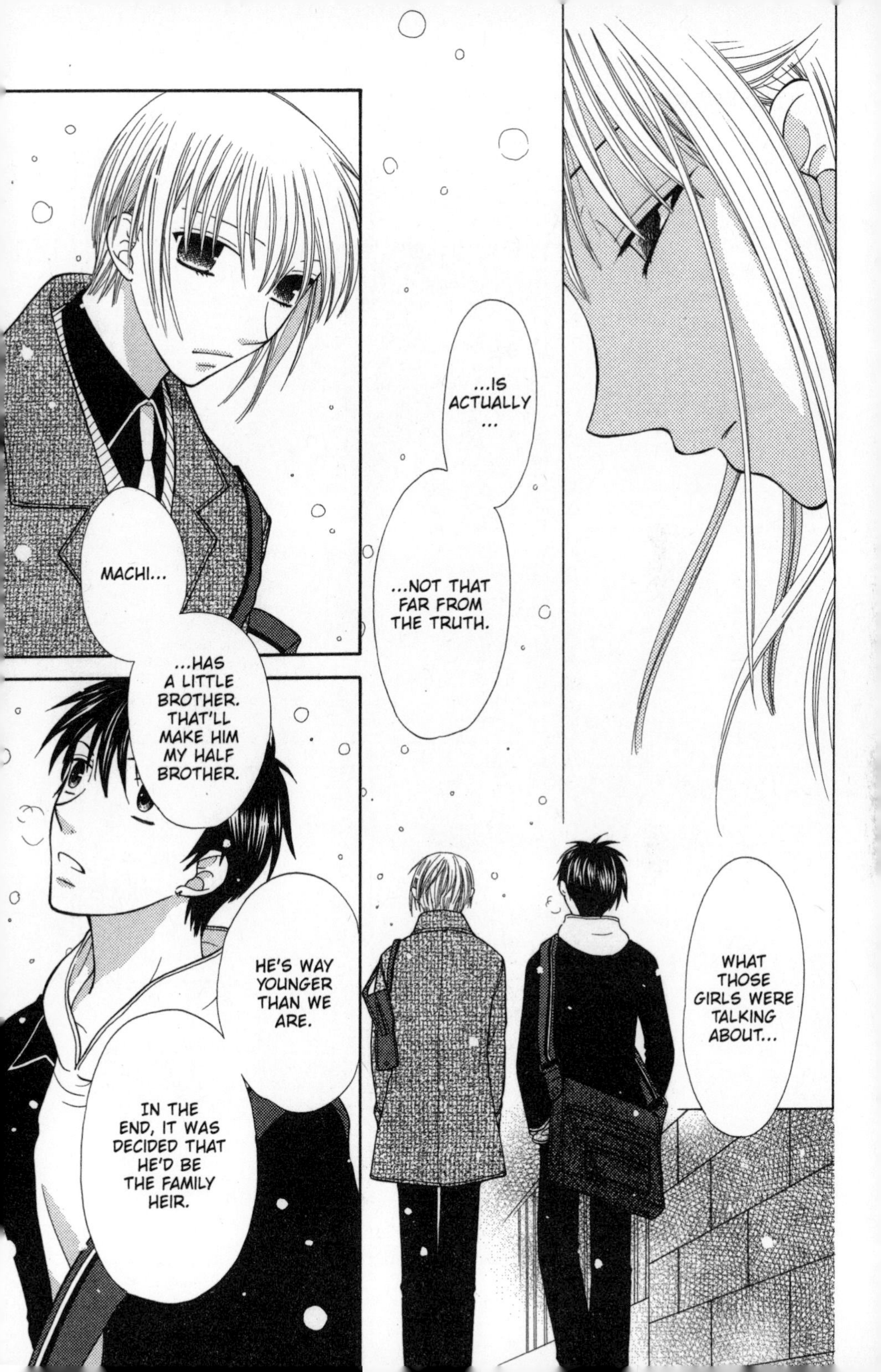
WHAT THOSE GIRLS WERE TALKING ABOUT...
...IS ACTUALLY ...
...NOT THAT FAR FROM THE TRUTH.
MACHI...
...HAS A LITTLE BROTHER. THAT'LL MAKE HIM MY HALF BROTHER.
HE'S WAY YOUNGER THAN WE ARE.
IN THE END, IT WAS DECIDED THAT HE'D BE THE FAMILY HEIR.

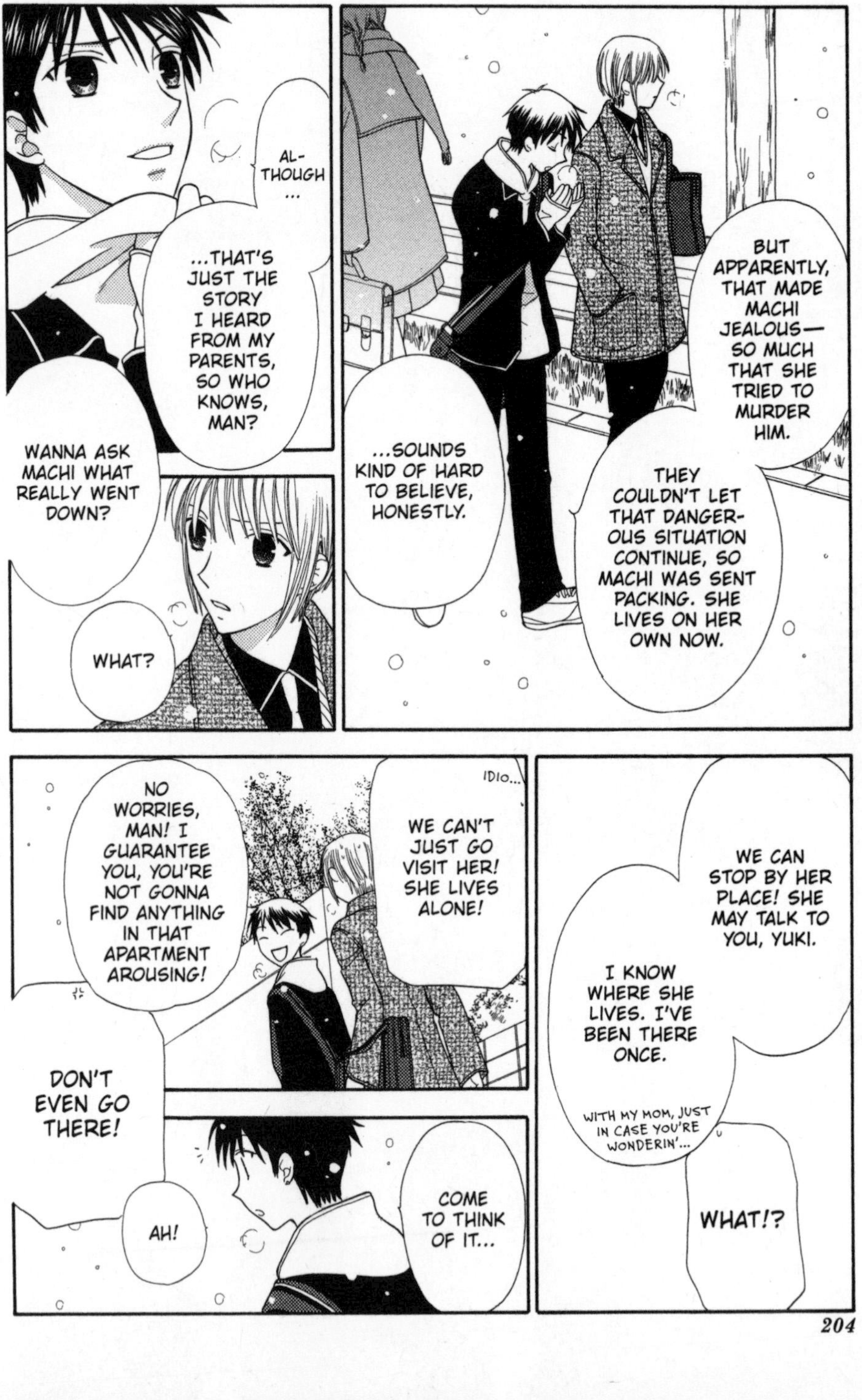
BUT APPARENTLY, THAT MADE MACHI JEALOUS—SO MUCH THAT SHE TRIED TO MURDER HIM.
THEY COULDN'T LET THAT DANGER-OUS SITUATION CONTINUE, SO MACHI WAS SENT PACKING. SHE LIVES ON HER OWN NOW.
...SOUNDS KIND OF HARD TO BELIEVE, HONESTLY.
AL-THOUGH ...
...THAT'S JUST THE STORY I HEARD FROM MY PARENTS, SO WHO KNOWS, MAN?
WANNA ASK MACHI WHAT REALLY WENT DOWN?
WHAT?
WE CAN STOP BY HER PLACE! SHE MAY TALK TO YOU, YUKI.
I KNOW WHERE SHE LIVES. I'VE BEEN THERE ONCE.
WITH MY MOM, JUST IN CASE YOU'RE WONDERIN'...
WHAT!?
IDIO...
WE CAN'T JUST GO VISIT HER! SHE LIVES ALONE!
NO WORRIES, MAN! I GUARANTEE YOU, YOU'RE NOT GONNA FIND ANYTHING IN THAT APARTMENT AROUSING!
DON'T EVEN GO THERE!
COME TO THINK OF IT...
AH!

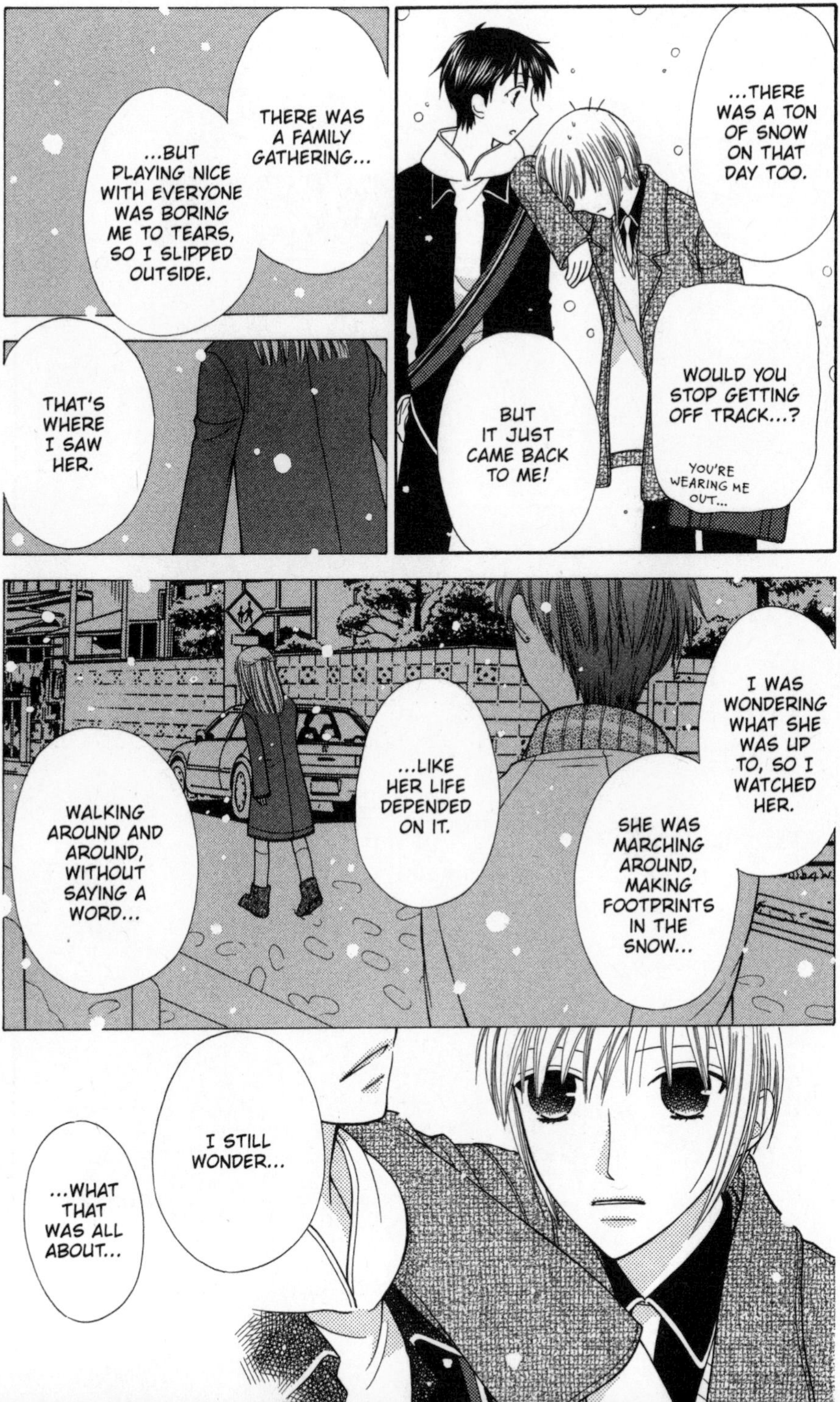
...THERE WAS A TON OF SNOW ON THAT DAY TOO.
WOULD YOU STOP GETTING OFF TRACK...?
YOU'RE WEARING ME OUT...
BUT IT JUST CAME BACK TO ME!
THERE WAS A FAMILY GATHERING...
...BUT PLAYING NICE WITH EVERYONE WAS BORING ME TO TEARS, SO I SLIPPED OUTSIDE.
THAT'S WHERE I SAW HER.
I WAS WONDERING WHAT SHE WAS UP TO, SO I WATCHED HER.
SHE WAS MARCHING AROUND, MAKING FOOTPRINTS IN THE SNOW...
...LIKE HER LIFE DEPENDED ON IT.
WALKING AROUND AND AROUND, WITHOUT SAYING A WORD...
I STILL WONDER...
...WHAT THAT WAS ALL ABOUT...

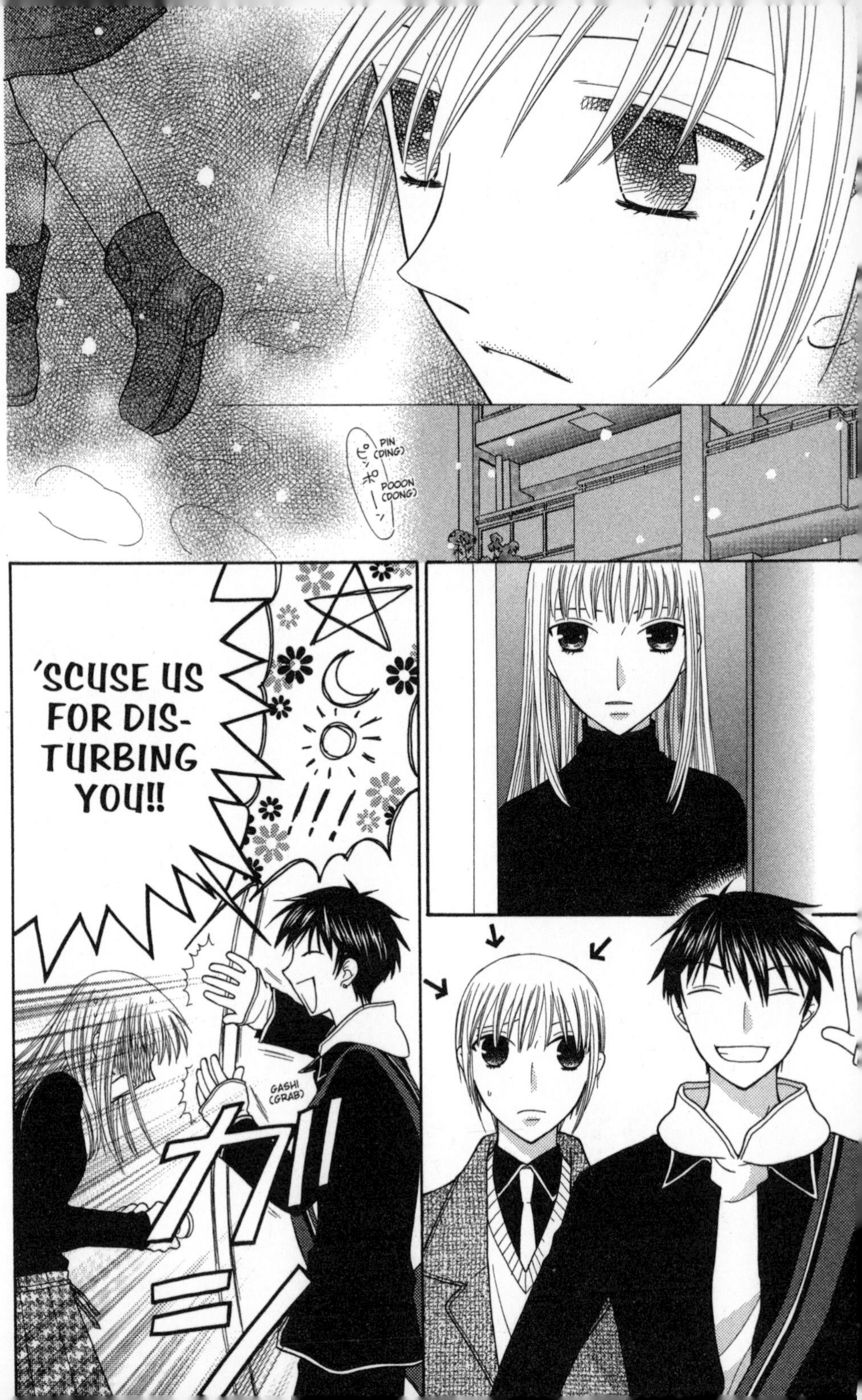
PIN (DING)
POOON (DONG)
'SCUSE US FOR DIS-TURBING YOU!!
GASHI (GRAB)

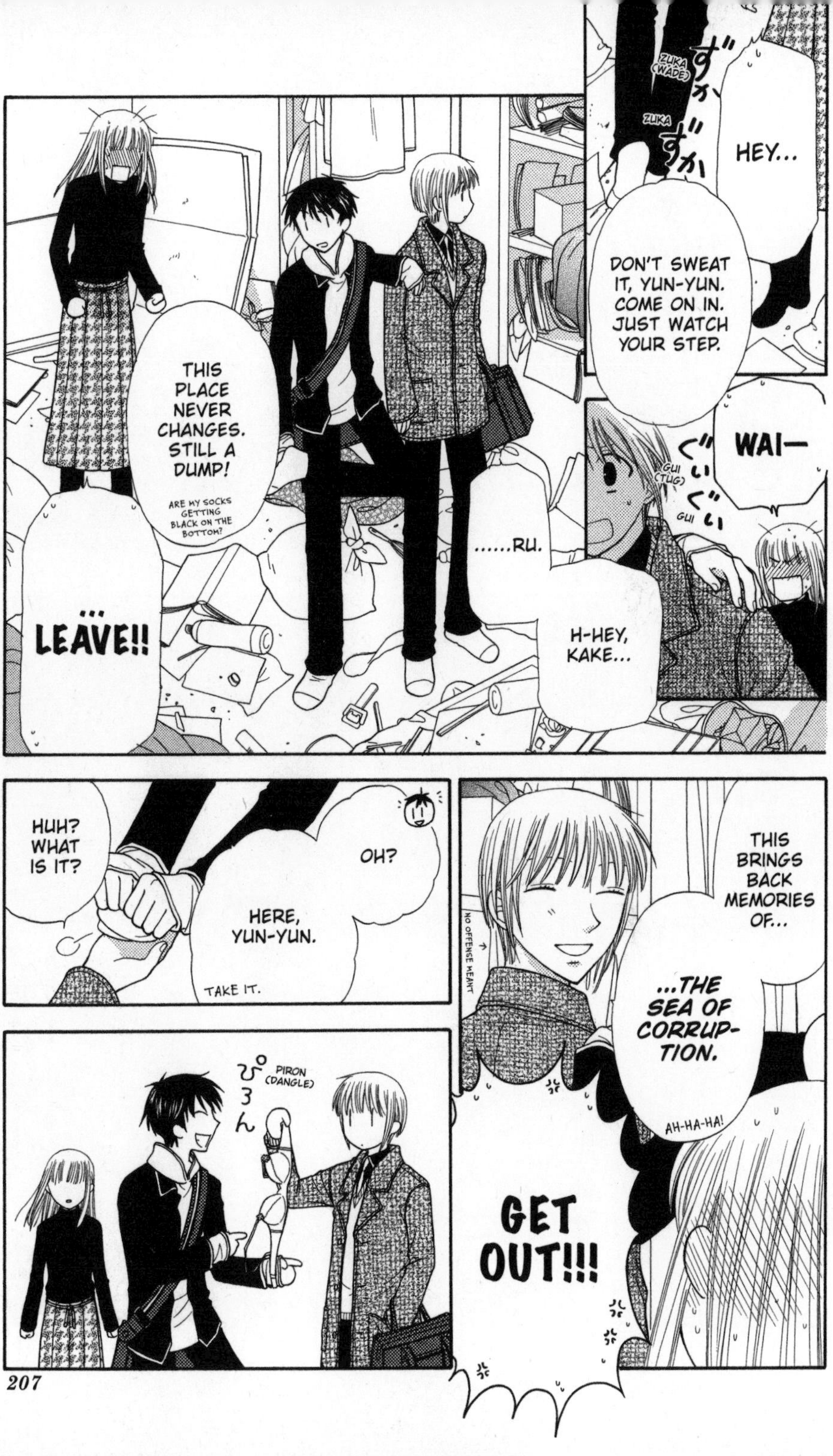

ZUKA (WADE)
ZUKA
HEY...
DON'T SWEAT IT, YUN-YUN. COME ON IN. JUST WATCH YOUR STEP.
WAI—
GUI (TUG)
GUI
H-HEY, KAKE...
THIS PLACE NEVER CHANGES. STILL A DUMP!
ARE MY SOCKS GETTING BLACK ON THE BOTTOM?
......RU.
...LEAVE!!
THIS BRINGS BACK MEMORIES OF...
...THE SEA OF CORRUPTION.
NO OFFENSE MEANT
AH-HA-HA!
GET OUT!!!
OH?
HERE, YUN-YUN.
TAKE IT.
HUH? WHAT IS IT?
PIRON (DANGLE)

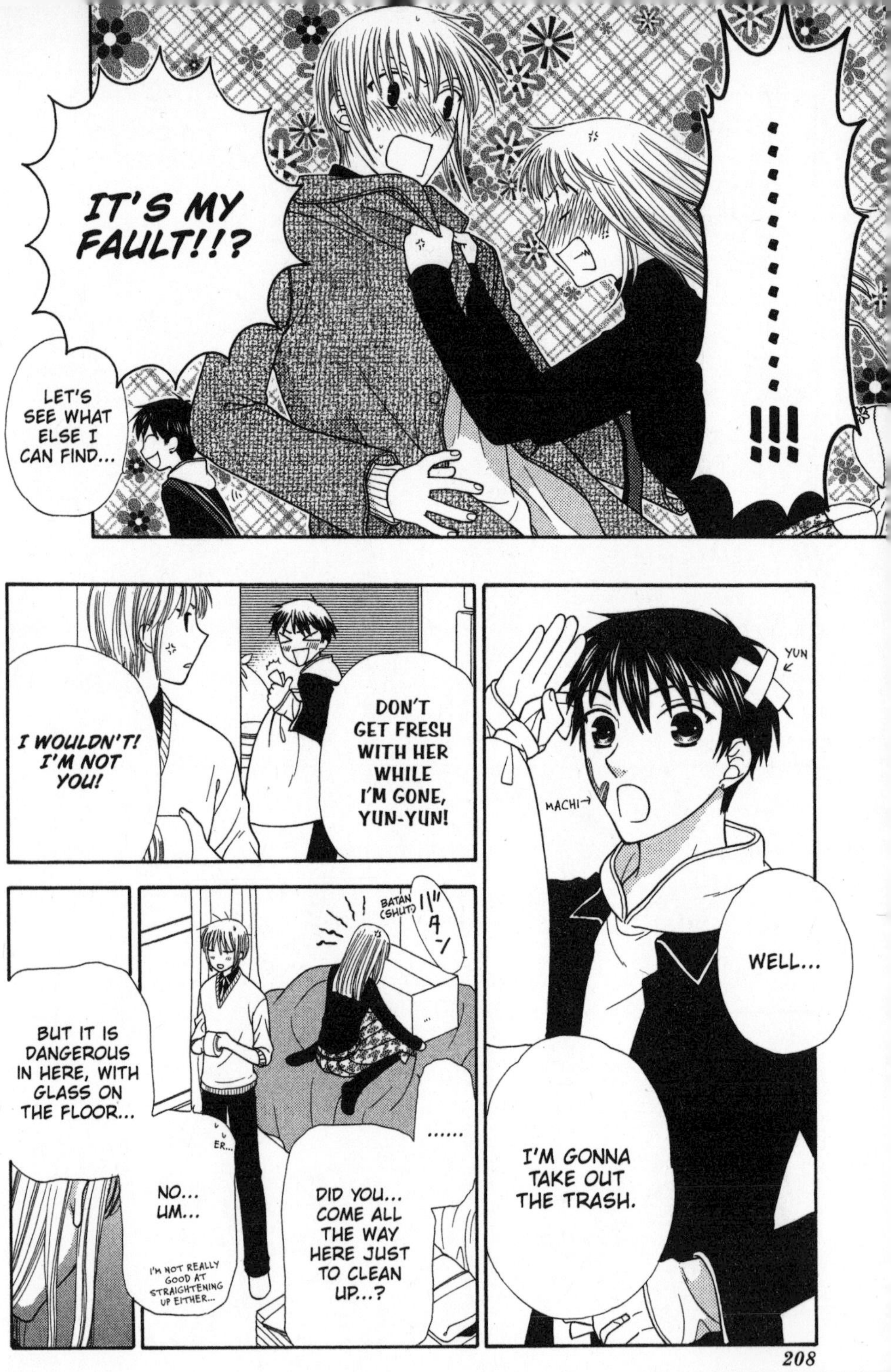
..........!!!
IT'S MY FAULT!!?
LET'S SEE WHAT ELSE I CAN FIND...
YUN
MACHI→
WELL...
I'M GONNA TAKE OUT THE TRASH.
DON'T GET FRESH WITH HER WHILE I'M GONE, YUN-YUN!
I WOULDN'T! I'M NOT YOU!
BATAN (SHUT)
......
DID YOU... COME ALL THE WAY HERE JUST TO CLEAN UP...?
BUT IT IS DANGEROUS IN HERE, WITH GLASS ON THE FLOOR...
ER...
NO... UM...
I'M NOT REALLY GOOD AT STRAIGHTENING UP EITHER...

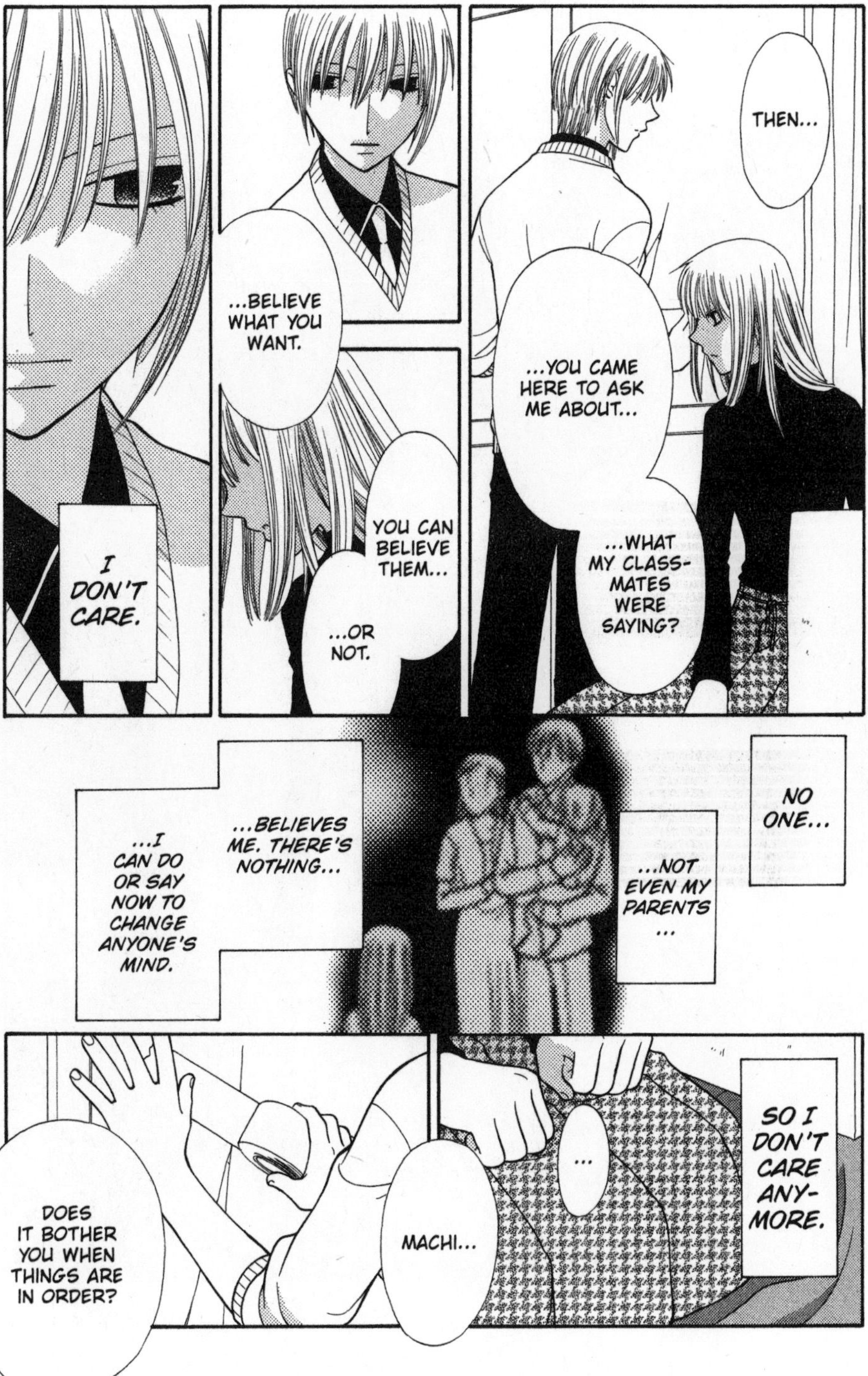
THEN...
...YOU CAME HERE TO ASK ME ABOUT...
...WHAT MY CLASS-MATES WERE SAYING?
...BELIEVE WHAT YOU WANT.
YOU CAN BELIEVE THEM...
...OR NOT.
I DON'T CARE.
NO ONE...
...NOT EVEN MY PARENTS...
...BELIEVES ME. THERE'S NOTHING...
...I CAN DO OR SAY NOW TO CHANGE ANYONE'S MIND.
SO I DON'T CARE ANY-MORE.
...
MACHI...
DOES IT BOTHER YOU WHEN THINGS ARE IN ORDER?

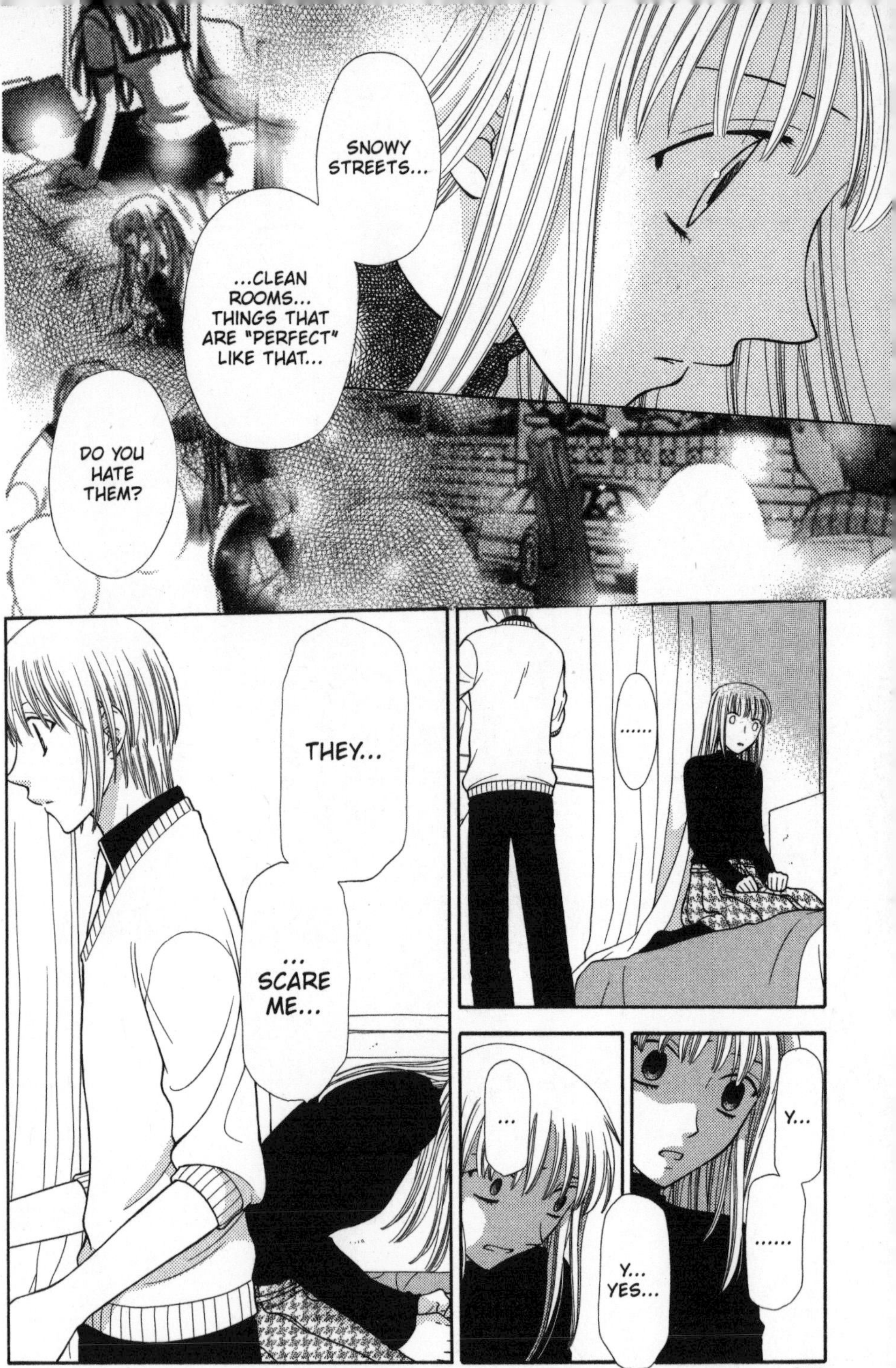
SNOWY STREETS...
...CLEAN ROOMS... THINGS THAT ARE "PERFECT" LIKE THAT...
DO YOU HATE THEM?
......
Y...
......
...
Y... YES...
THEY...
...SCARE ME...

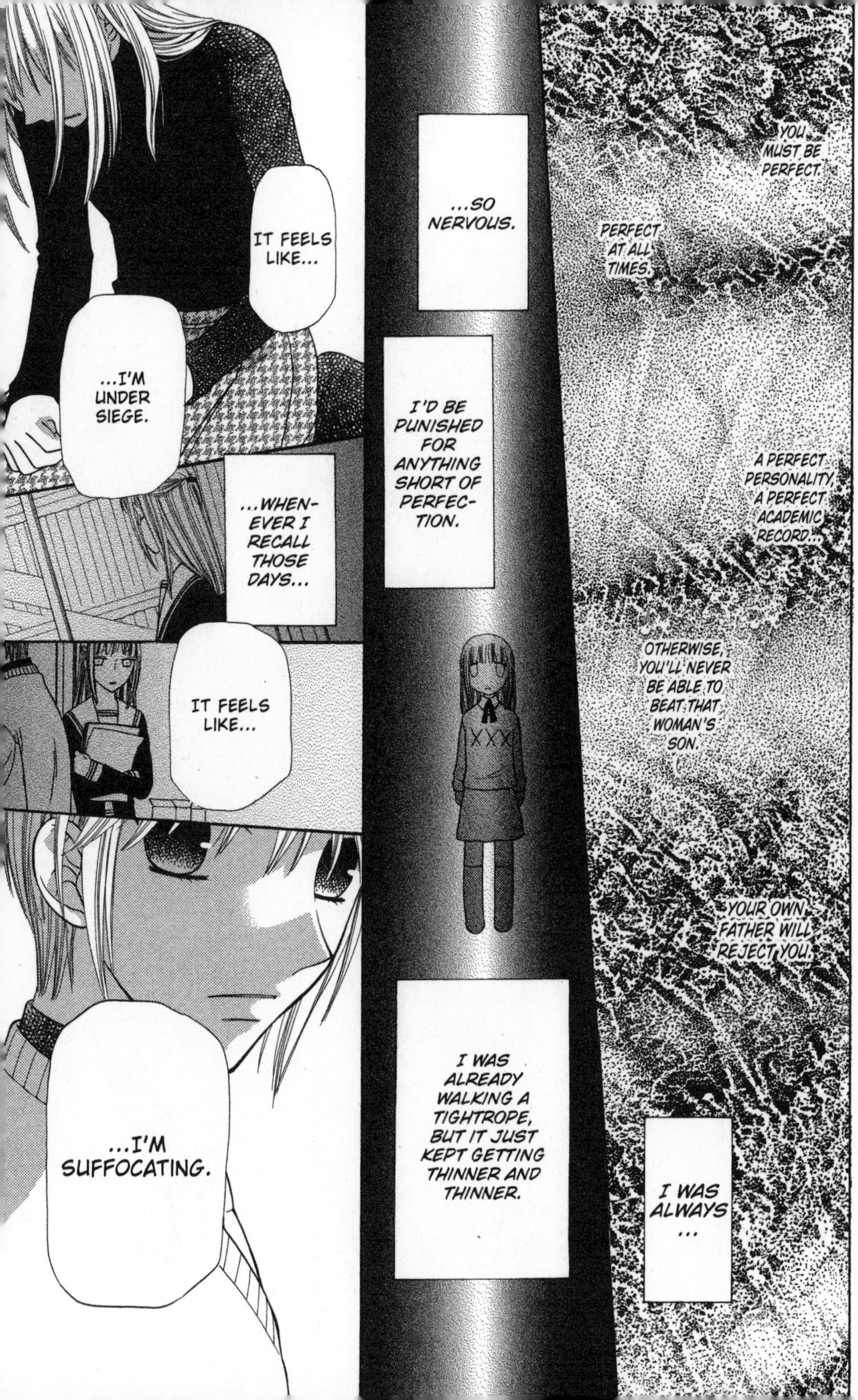
YOU MUST BE PERFECT.
PERFECT AT ALL TIMES.
A PERFECT PERSONALITY, A PERFECT ACADEMIC RECORD...
OTHERWISE, YOU'LL NEVER BE ABLE TO BEAT THAT WOMAN'S SON.
YOUR OWN FATHER WILL REJECT YOU.
I WAS ALWAYS ...
...SO NERVOUS.
I'D BE PUNISHED FOR ANYTHING SHORT OF PERFECTION.
I WAS ALREADY WALKING A TIGHTROPE, BUT IT JUST KEPT GETTING THINNER AND THINNER.
IT FEELS LIKE...
...I'M UNDER SIEGE.
...WHENEVER I RECALL THOSE DAYS...
IT FEELS LIKE...
...I'M SUFFOCATING.

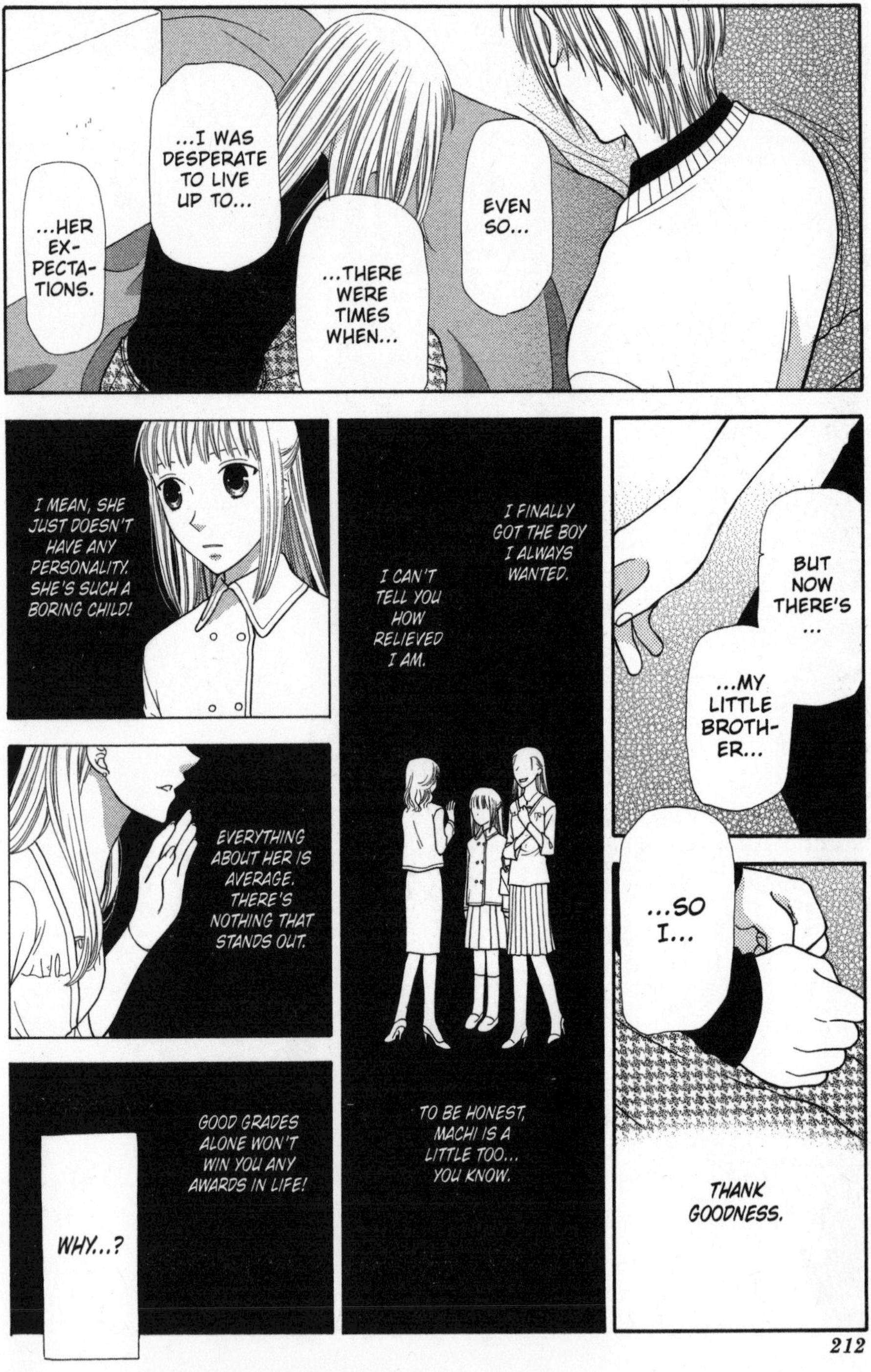
EVEN SO...
...THERE WERE TIMES WHEN...
...I WAS DESPERATE TO LIVE UP TO...
...HER EX-PECTA-TIONS.
BUT NOW THERE'S...
...MY LITTLE BROTH-ER...
...SO I...
THANK GOODNESS.
I FINALLY GOT THE BOY I ALWAYS WANTED.
I CAN'T TELL YOU HOW RELIEVED I AM.
TO BE HONEST, MACHI IS A LITTLE TOO... YOU KNOW.
I MEAN, SHE JUST DOESN'T HAVE ANY PERSONALITY. SHE'S SUCH A BORING CHILD!
EVERYTHING ABOUT HER IS AVERAGE. THERE'S NOTHING THAT STANDS OUT.
GOOD GRADES ALONE WON'T WIN YOU ANY AWARDS IN LIFE!
WHY...?

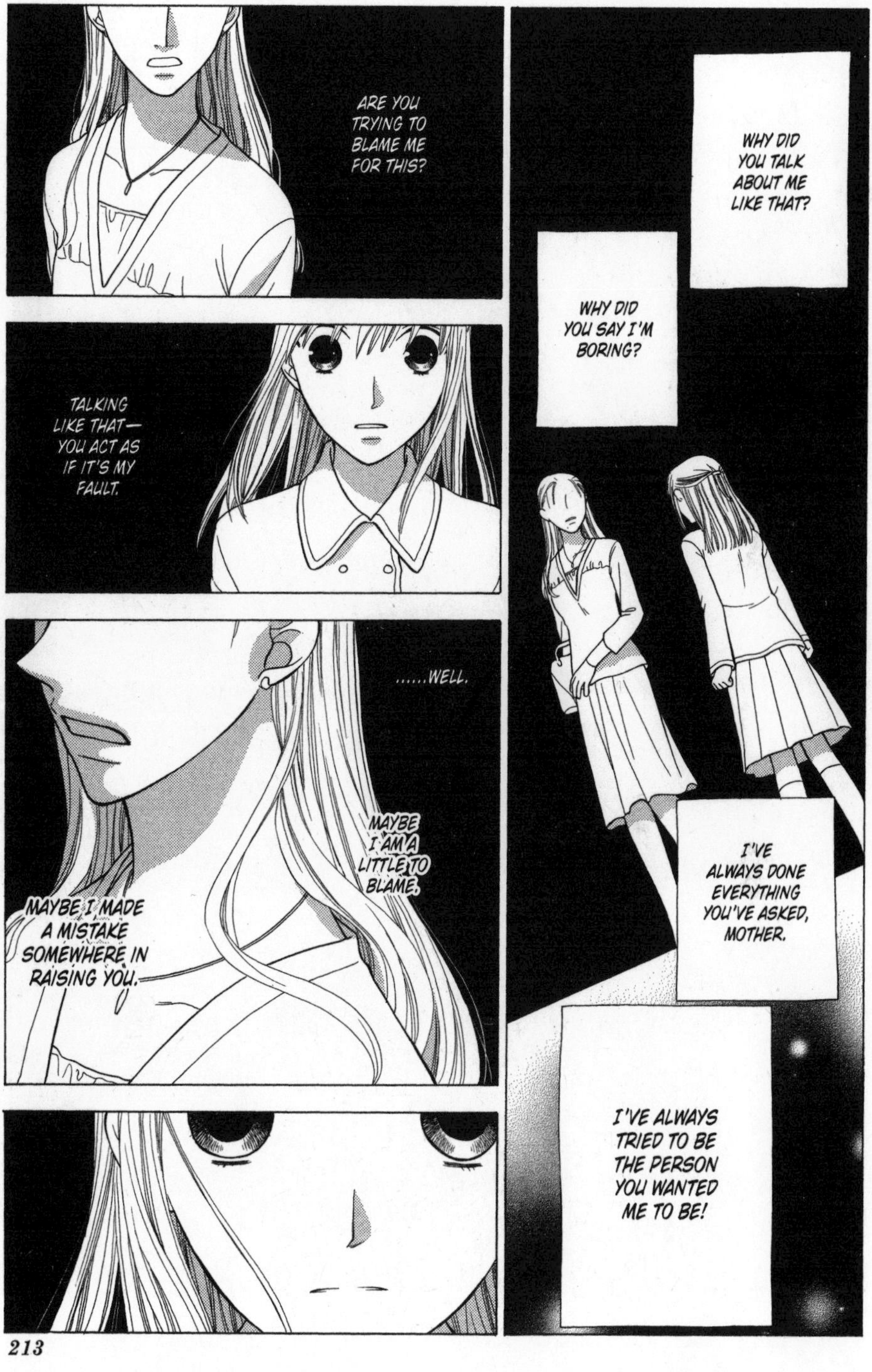
WHY DID YOU TALK ABOUT ME LIKE THAT?
WHY DID YOU SAY I'M BORING?
I'VE ALWAYS DONE EVERYTHING YOU'VE ASKED, MOTHER.
I'VE ALWAYS TRIED TO BE THE PERSON YOU WANTED ME TO BE!
ARE YOU TRYING TO BLAME ME FOR THIS?
TALKING LIKE THAT— YOU ACT AS IF IT'S MY FAULT.
......WELL.
MAYBE I AM A LITTLE TO BLAME.
MAYBE I MADE A MISTAKE SOMEWHERE IN RAISING YOU.

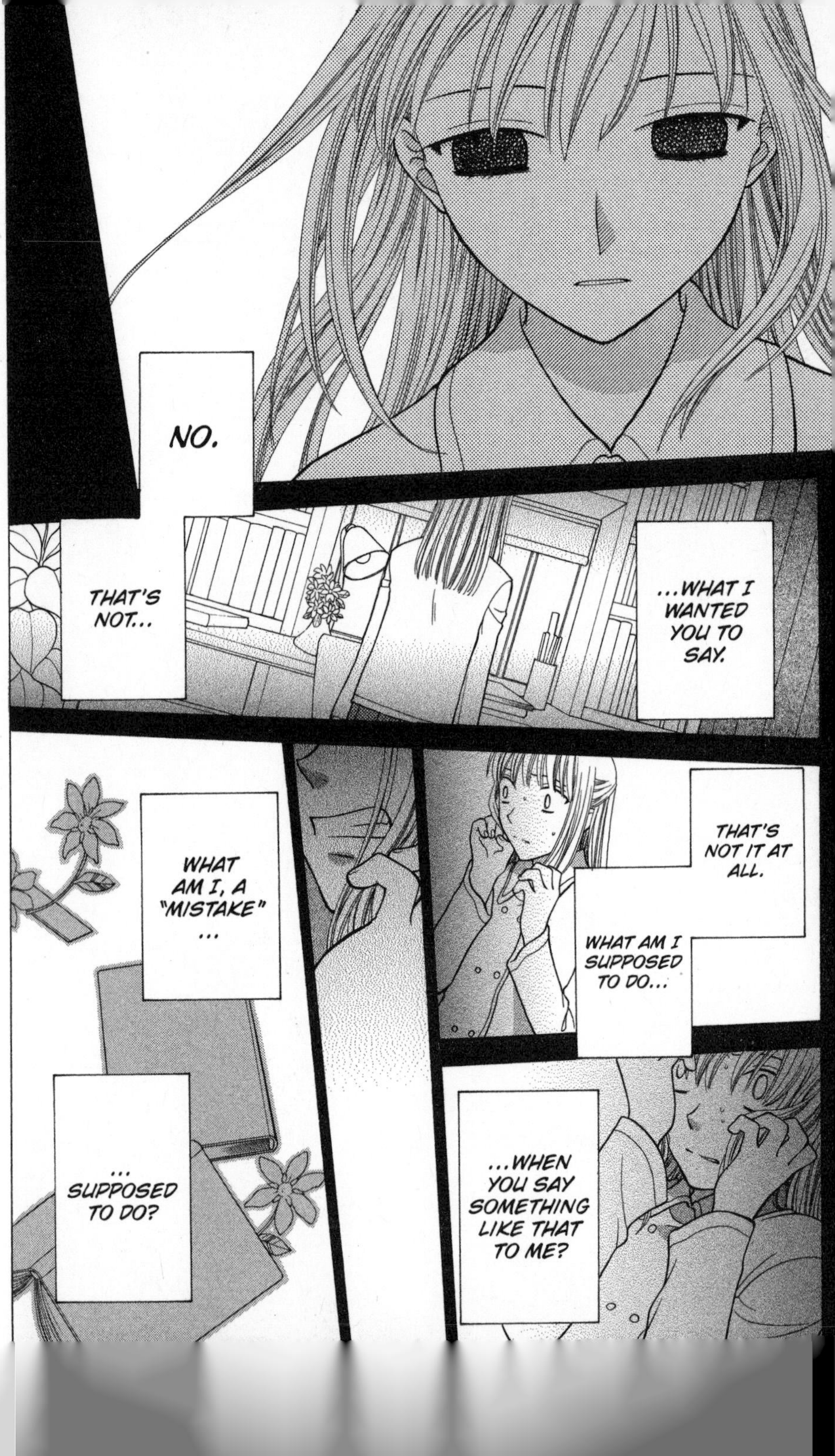
NO.
THAT'S NOT...
...WHAT I WANTED YOU TO SAY.
THAT'S NOT IT AT ALL.
WHAT AM I SUPPOSED TO DO...
...WHEN YOU SAY SOMETHING LIKE THAT TO ME?
WHAT AM I, A "MISTAKE" ...
... SUPPOSED TO DO?

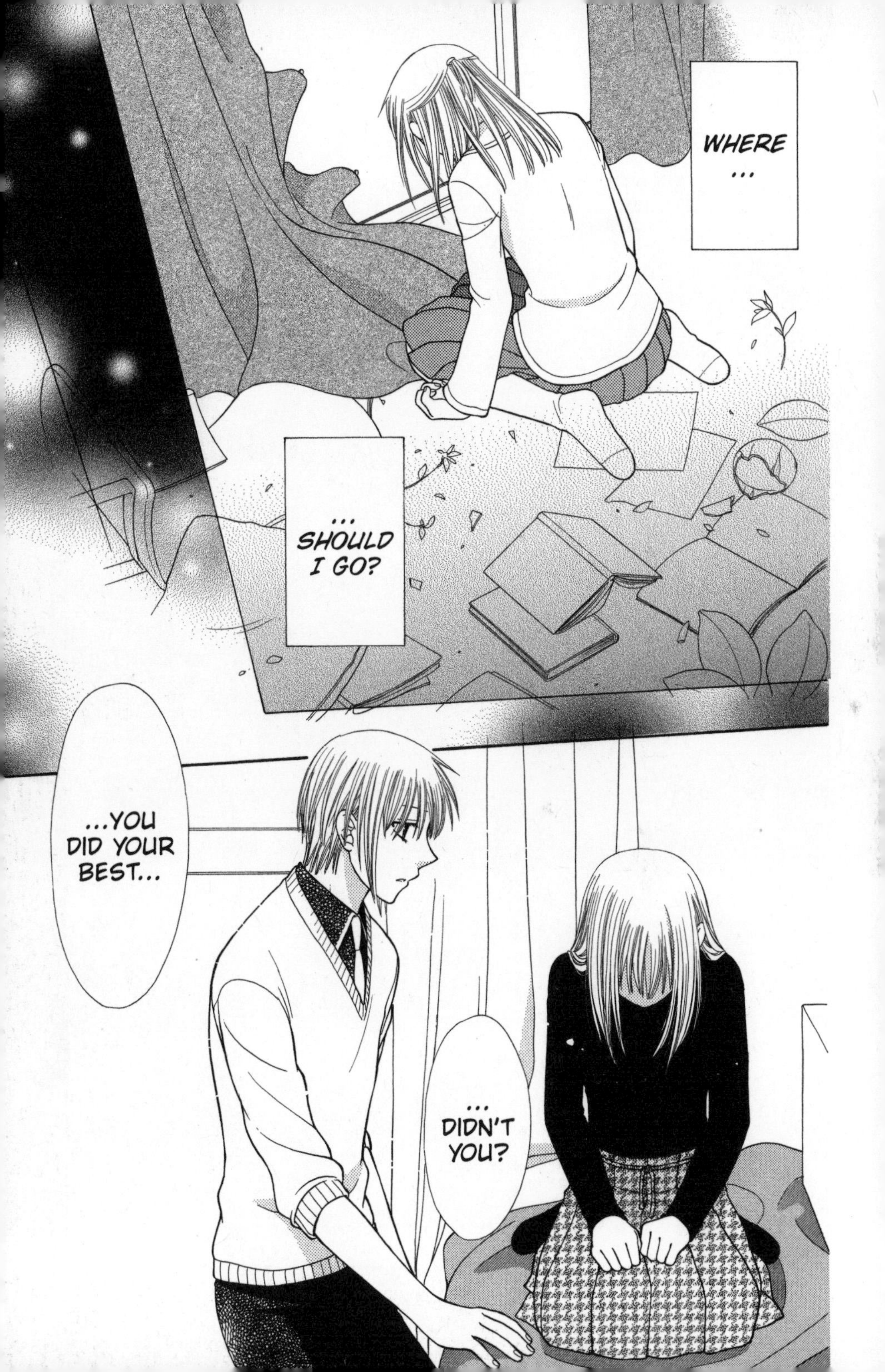
WHERE …
… SHOULD I GO?
…YOU DID YOUR BEST…
… DIDN'T YOU?

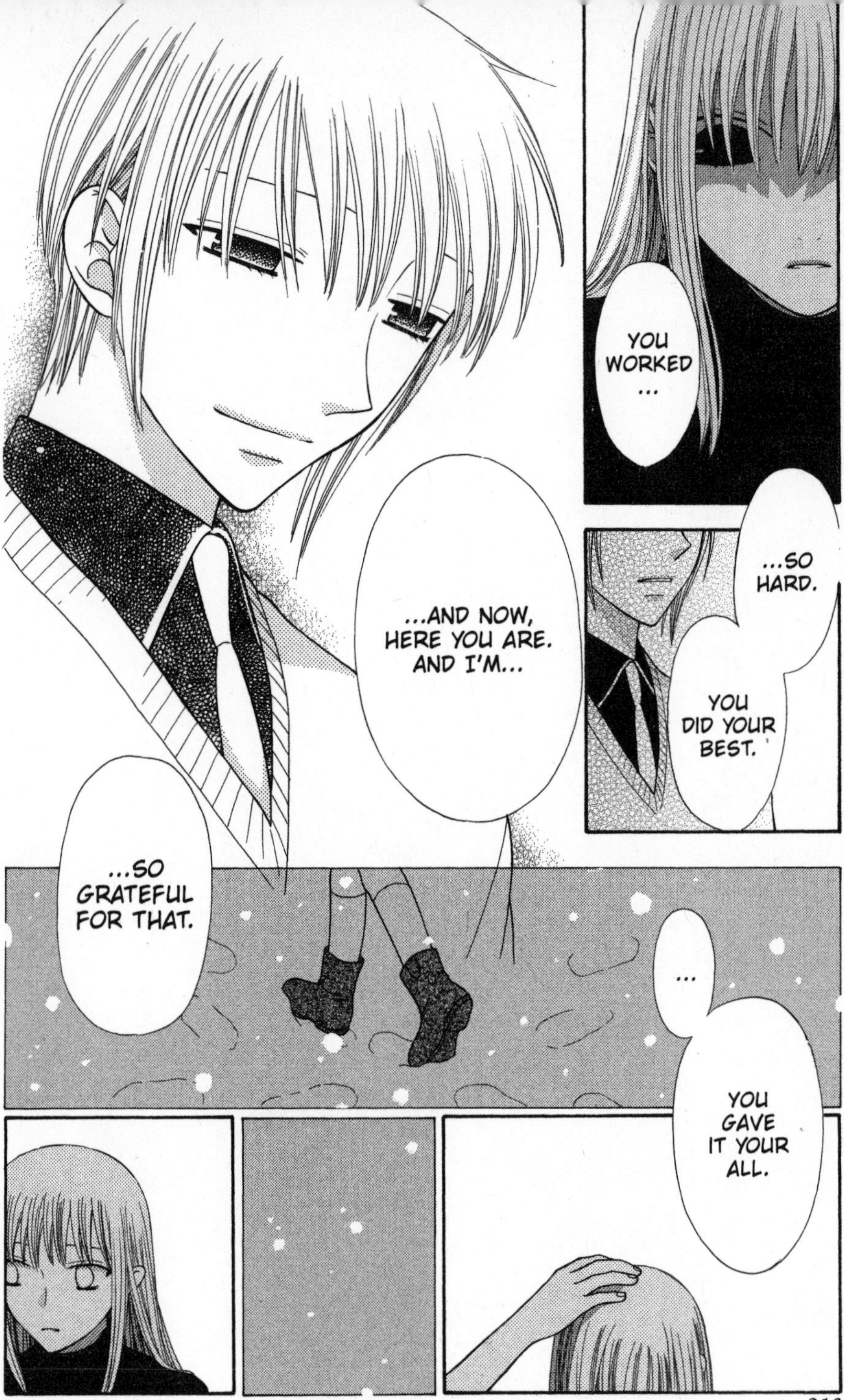
YOU WORKED ...
...SO HARD.
YOU DID YOUR BEST.
...AND NOW, HERE YOU ARE. AND I'M...
...SO GRATEFUL FOR THAT.
...
YOU GAVE IT YOUR ALL.

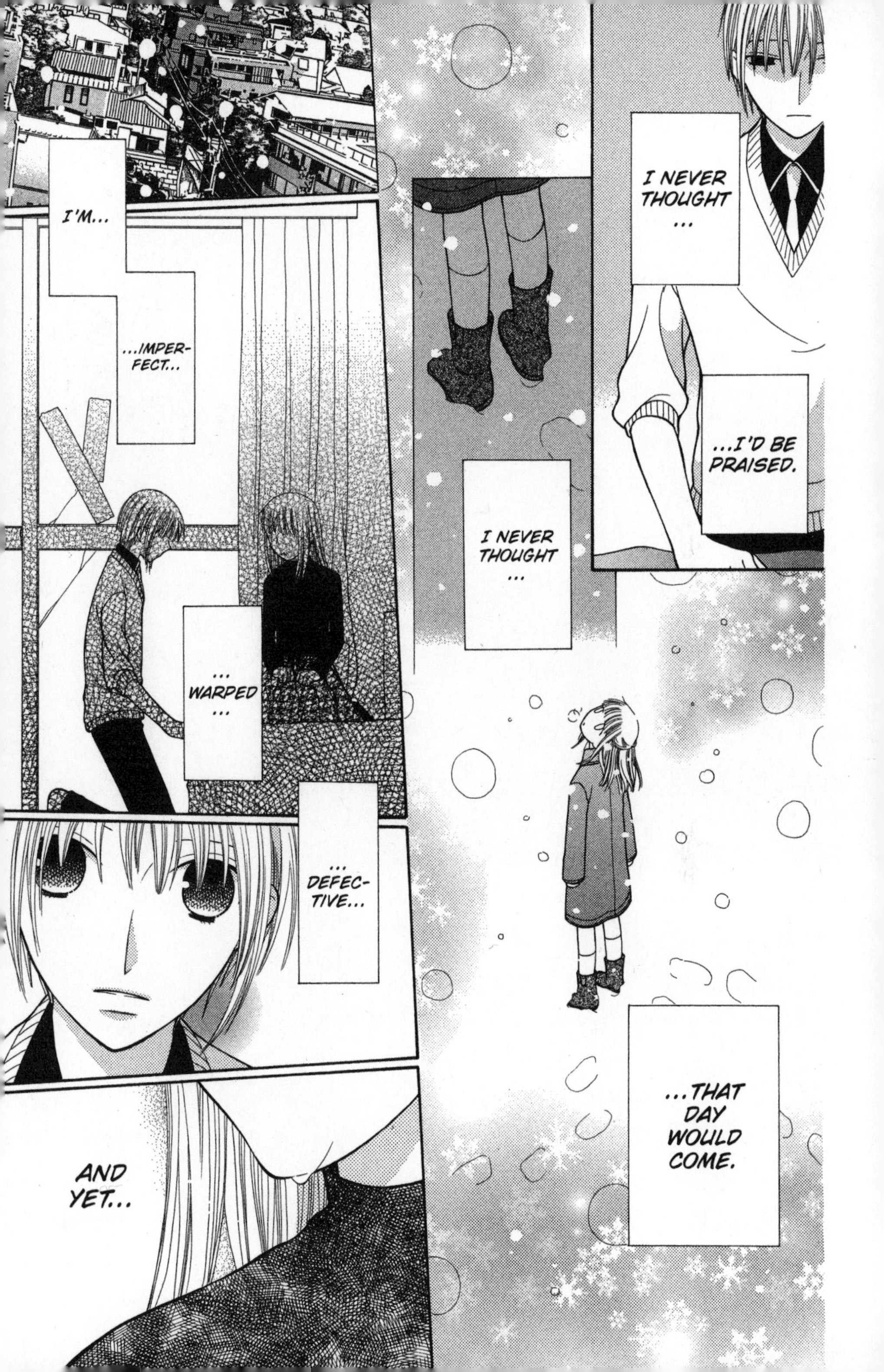
I NEVER THOUGHT ...
...I'D BE PRAISED.
I NEVER THOUGHT ...
...THAT DAY WOULD COME.
I'M...
...IMPERFECT...
... WARPED ...
... DEFECTIVE...
AND YET...

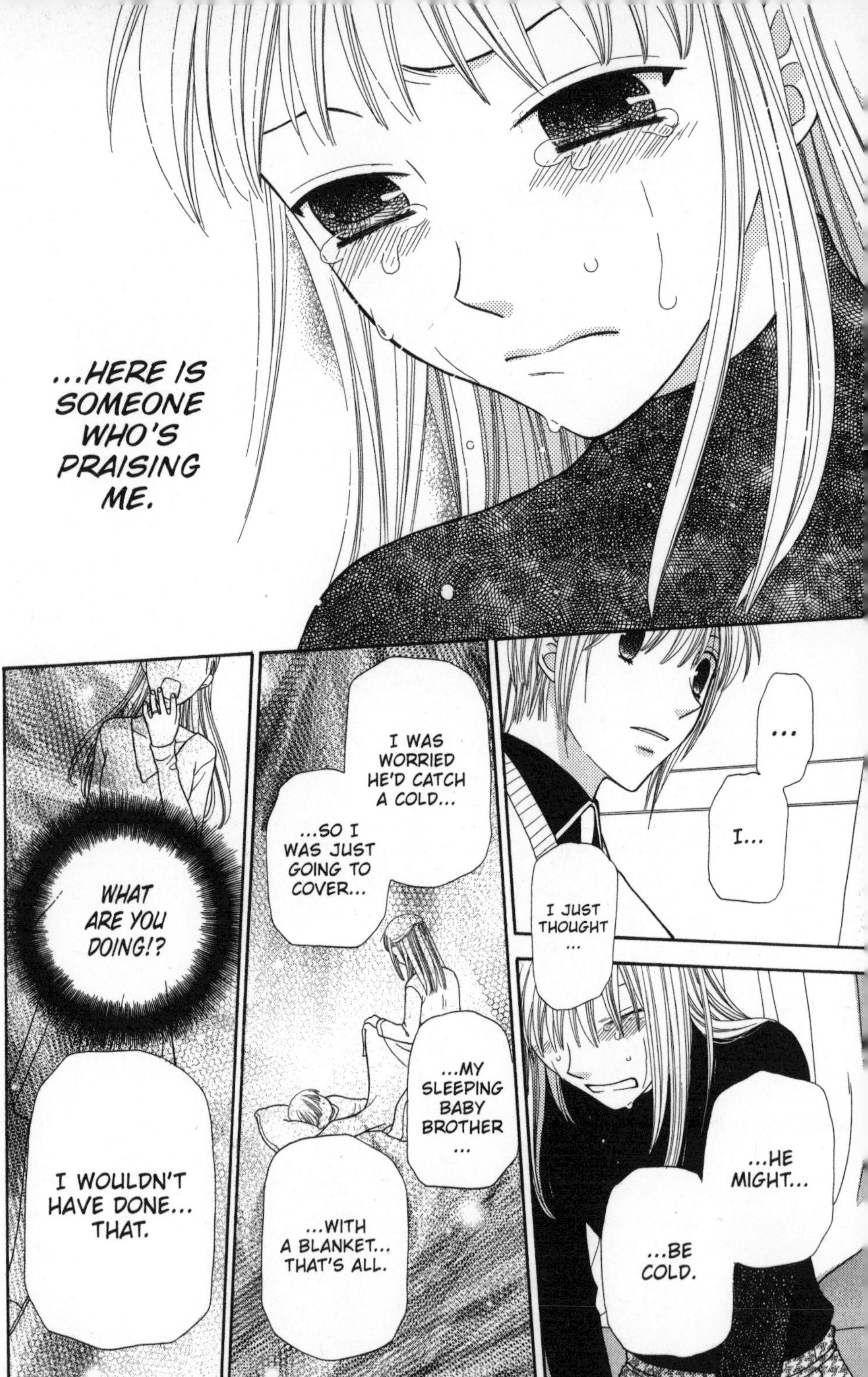
...HERE IS SOMEONE WHO'S PRAISING ME.
...
I...
I JUST THOUGHT...
...HE MIGHT...
...BE COLD.
I WAS WORRIED HE'D CATCH A COLD...
...SO I WAS JUST GOING TO COVER...
...MY SLEEPING BABY BROTHER...
...WITH A BLANKET... THAT'S ALL.
WHAT ARE YOU DOING!?
I WOULDN'T HAVE DONE... THAT.

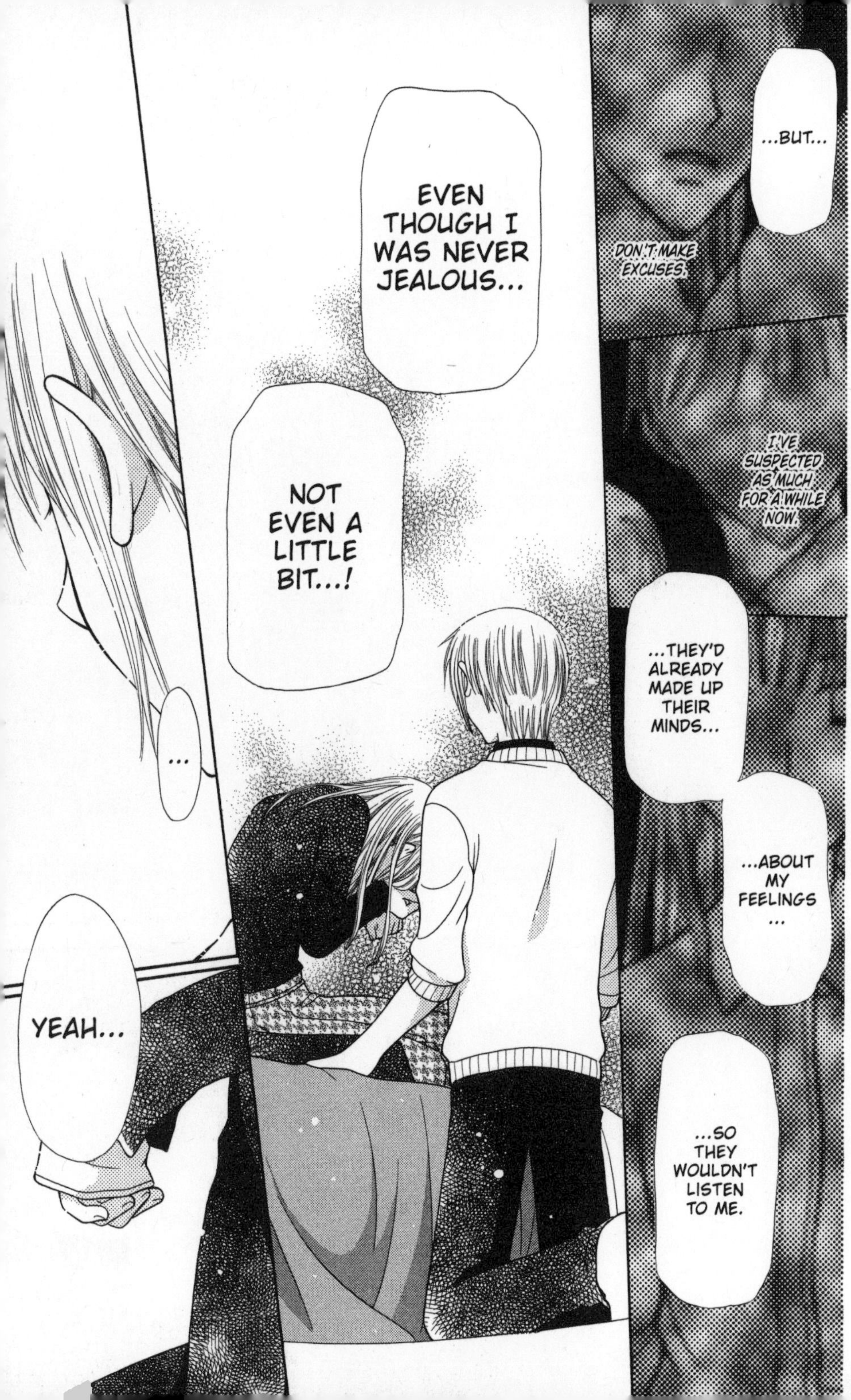
...BUT...
DON'T MAKE EXCUSES.
I'VE SUSPECTED AS MUCH FOR A WHILE NOW.
...THEY'D ALREADY MADE UP THEIR MINDS...
...ABOUT MY FEELINGS...
...SO THEY WOULDN'T LISTEN TO ME.
EVEN THOUGH I WAS NEVER JEALOUS...
NOT EVEN A LITTLE BIT...!
...
YEAH...

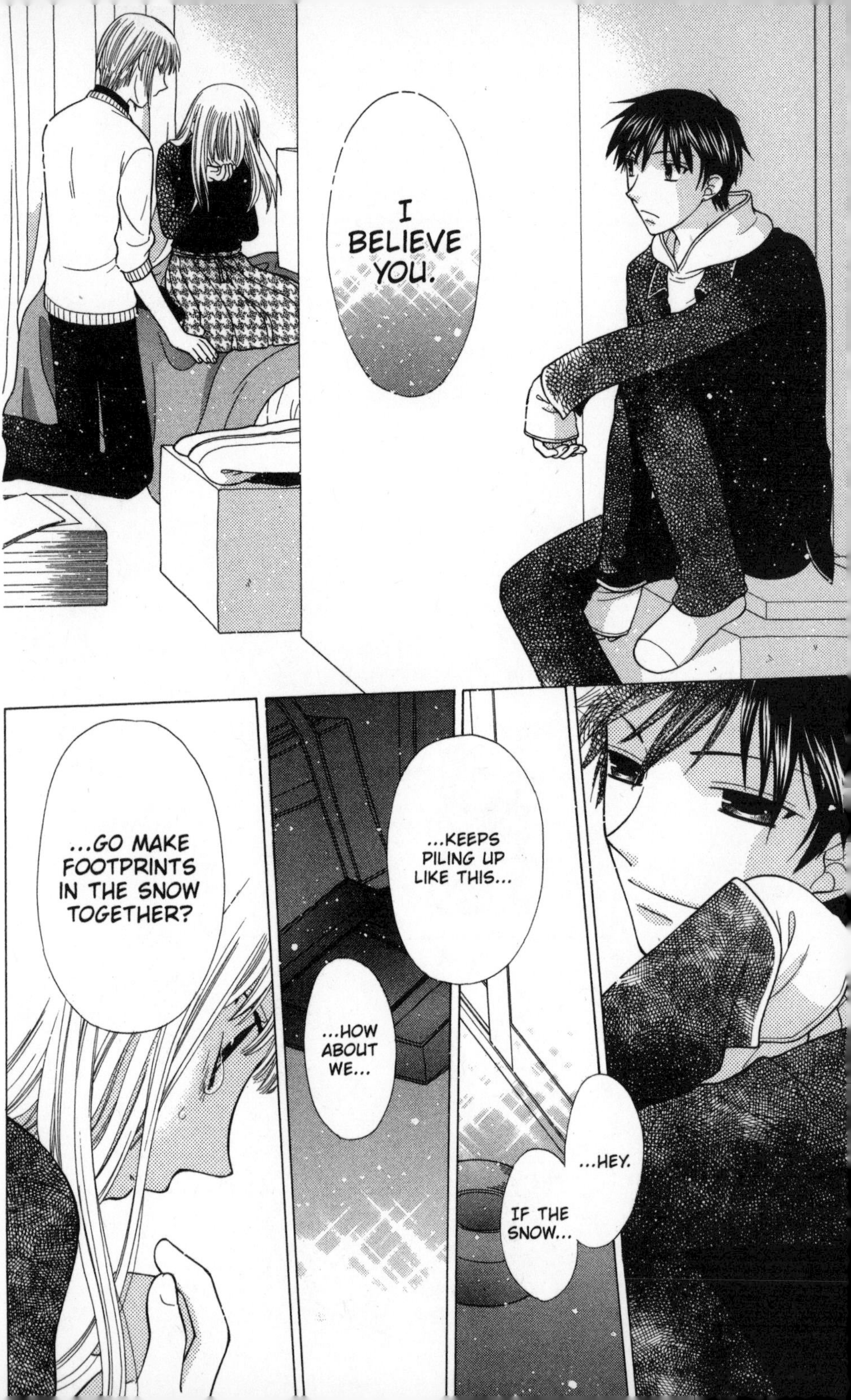
I BELIEVE YOU.
...HEY.
IF THE SNOW...
...KEEPS PILING UP LIKE THIS...
...HOW ABOUT WE...
...GO MAKE FOOTPRINTS IN THE SNOW TOGETHER?

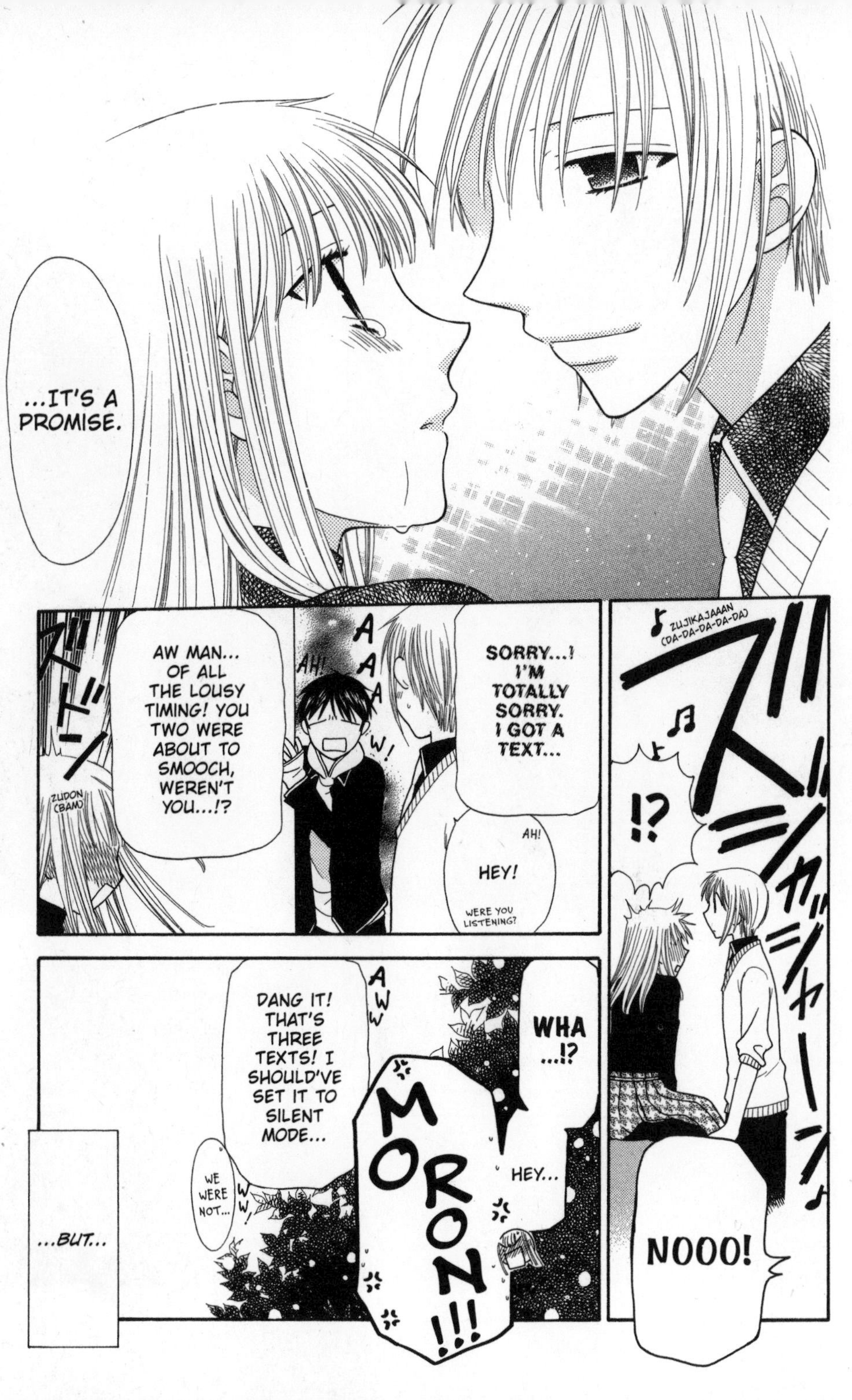
...IT'S A PROMISE.
ZUJIKAJAAAN (DA-DA-DA-DA-DA)
!?
NOOO!
SORRY...! I'M TOTALLY SORRY. I GOT A TEXT...
AAAAW!
AH!
AH!
HEY!
WERE YOU LISTENING?
AW MAN... OF ALL THE LOUSY TIMING! YOU TWO WERE ABOUT TO SMOOCH, WEREN'T YOU...!?
ZUDON (BAM)
WHA ...!?
HEY...
MORON!!!
AWW
DANG IT! THAT'S THREE TEXTS! I SHOULD'VE SET IT TO SILENT MODE...
WWW!
WE WERE NOT...
...BUT...

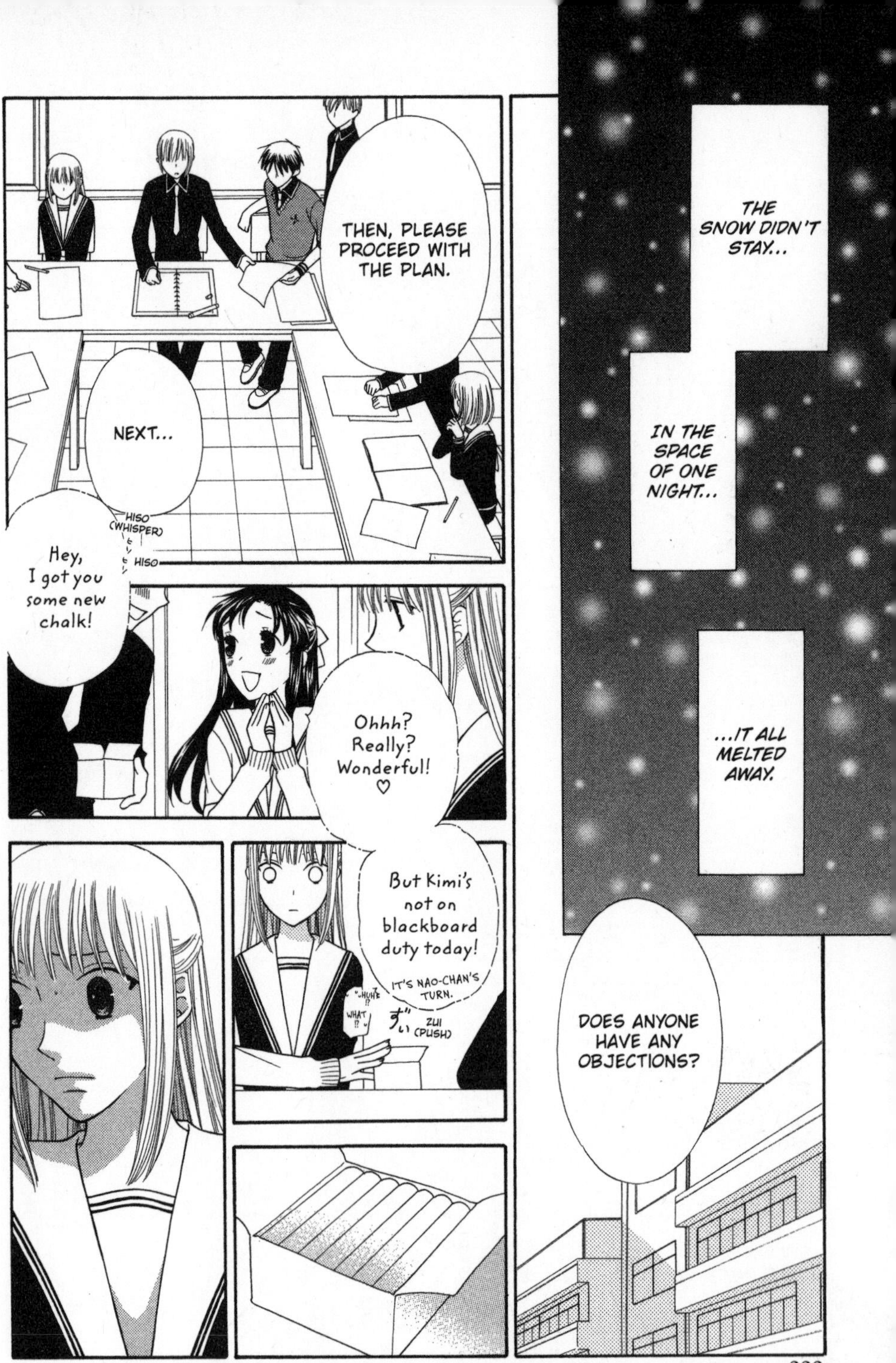
THE SNOW DIDN'T STAY...
IN THE SPACE OF ONE NIGHT...
...IT ALL MELTED AWAY.
DOES ANYONE HAVE ANY OBJECTIONS?
THEN, PLEASE PROCEED WITH THE PLAN.
NEXT...
HISO (WHISPER)
HISO
Hey, I got you some new chalk!
Ohhh? Really? Wonderful! ♡
But Kimi's not on blackboard duty today!
IT'S NAO-CHAN'S TURN.
"HUH?!"
"WHAT?!"
ZUI (PUSH)

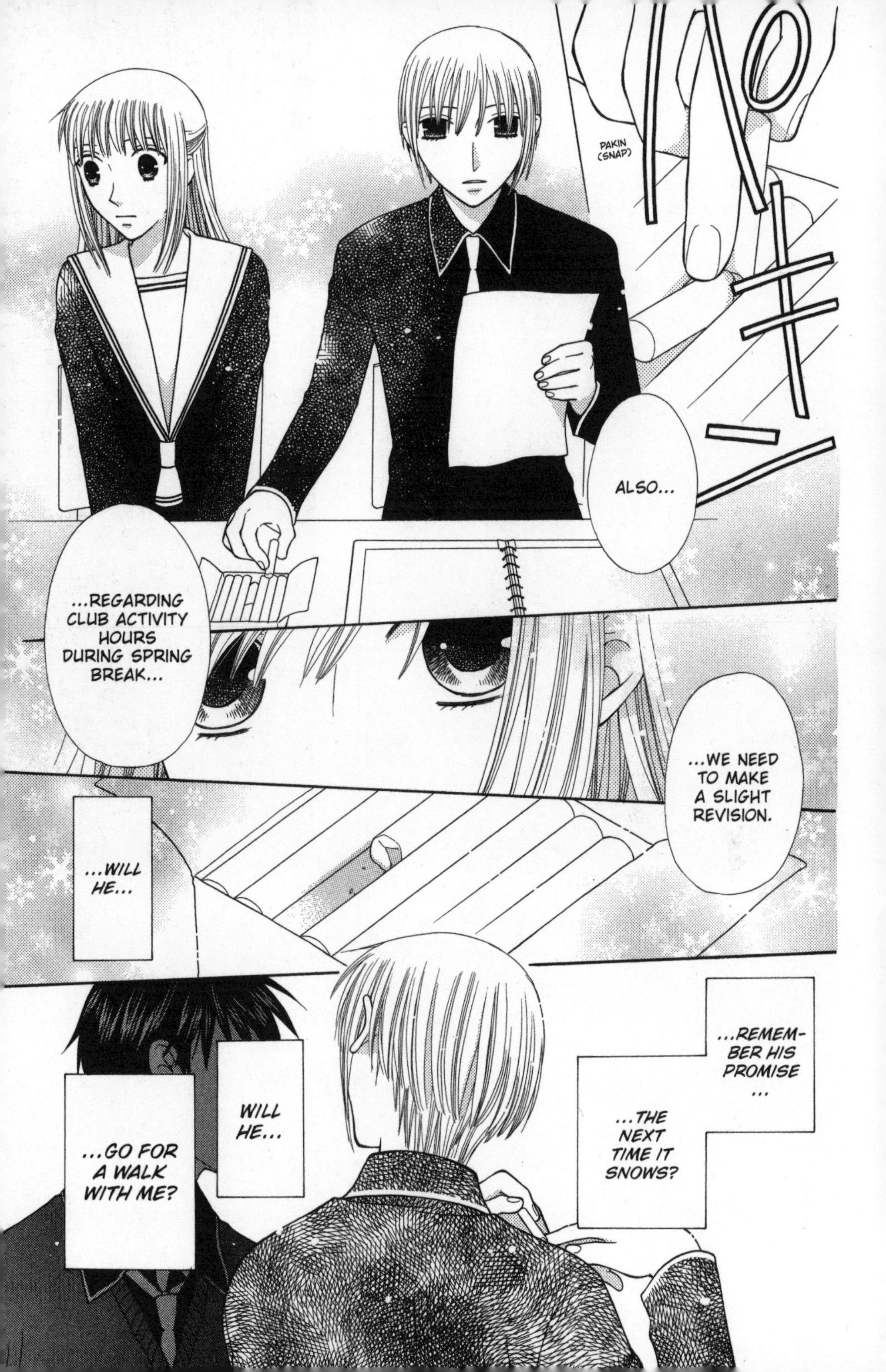
PAKIN (SNAP)
ALSO...
...REGARDING CLUB ACTIVITY HOURS DURING SPRING BREAK...
...WE NEED TO MAKE A SLIGHT REVISION.
...WILL HE...
...REMEMBER HIS PROMISE...
...THE NEXT TIME IT SNOWS?
WILL HE...
...GO FOR A WALK WITH ME?

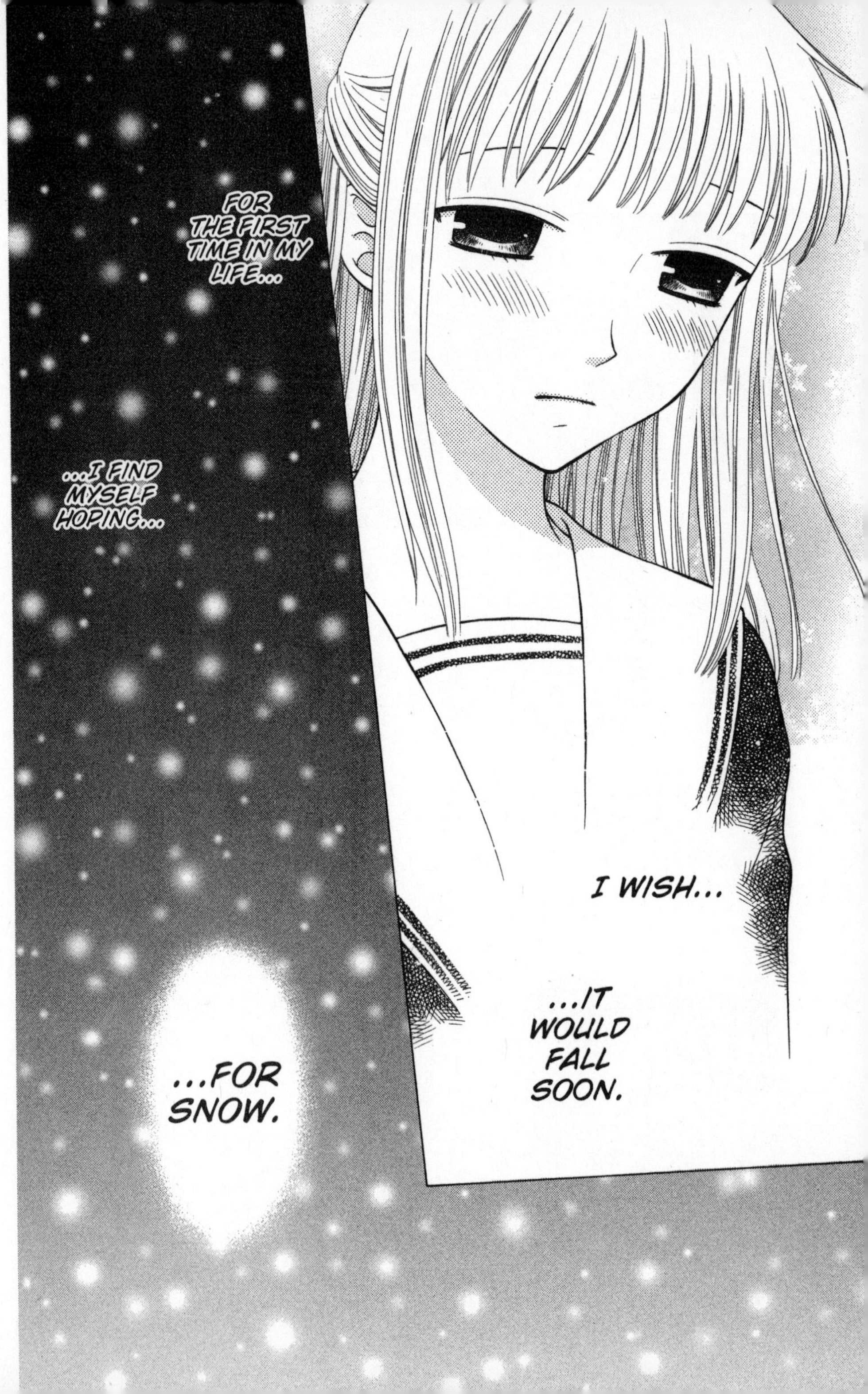
I WISH...
...IT WOULD FALL SOON.
FOR THE FIRST TIME IN MY LIFE...
...I FIND MYSELF HOPING...
...FOR SNOW.

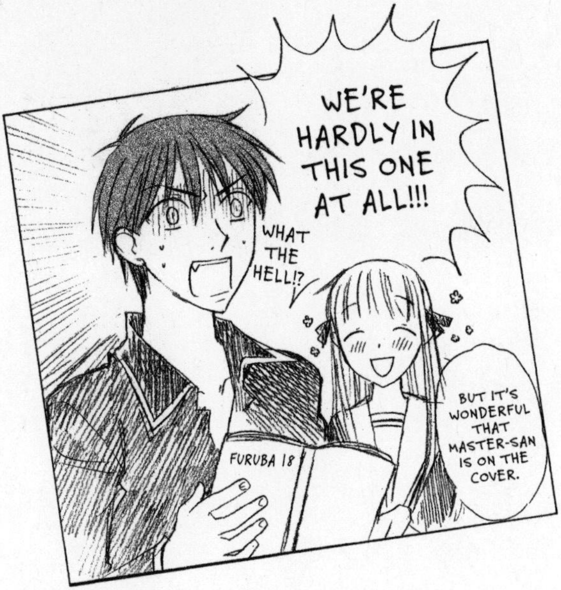
WE'RE HARDLY IN THIS ONE AT ALL!!!
WHAT THE HELL!?
FURUBA 18
BUT IT'S WONDERFUL THAT MASTER-SAN IS ON THE COVER.

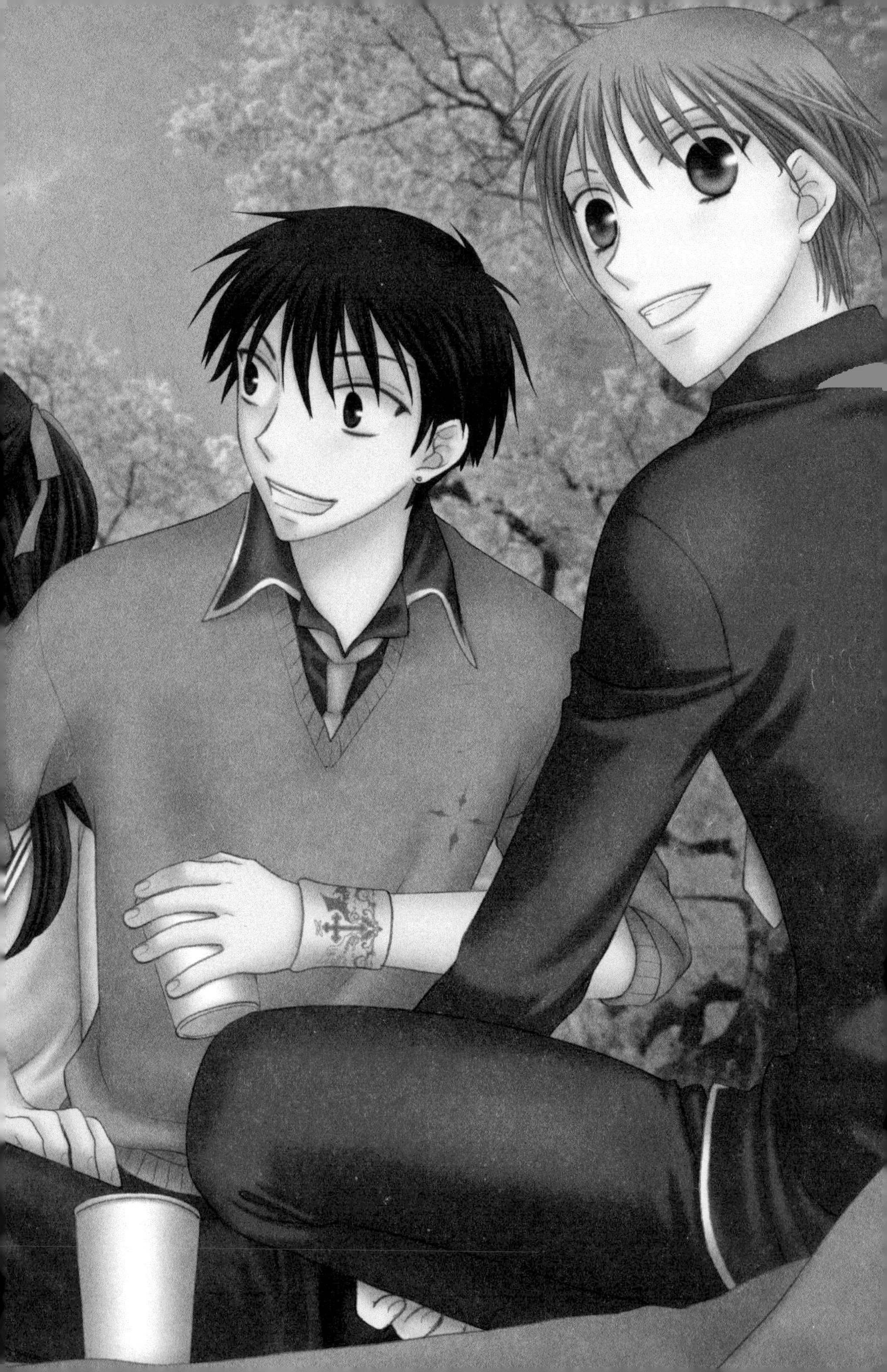

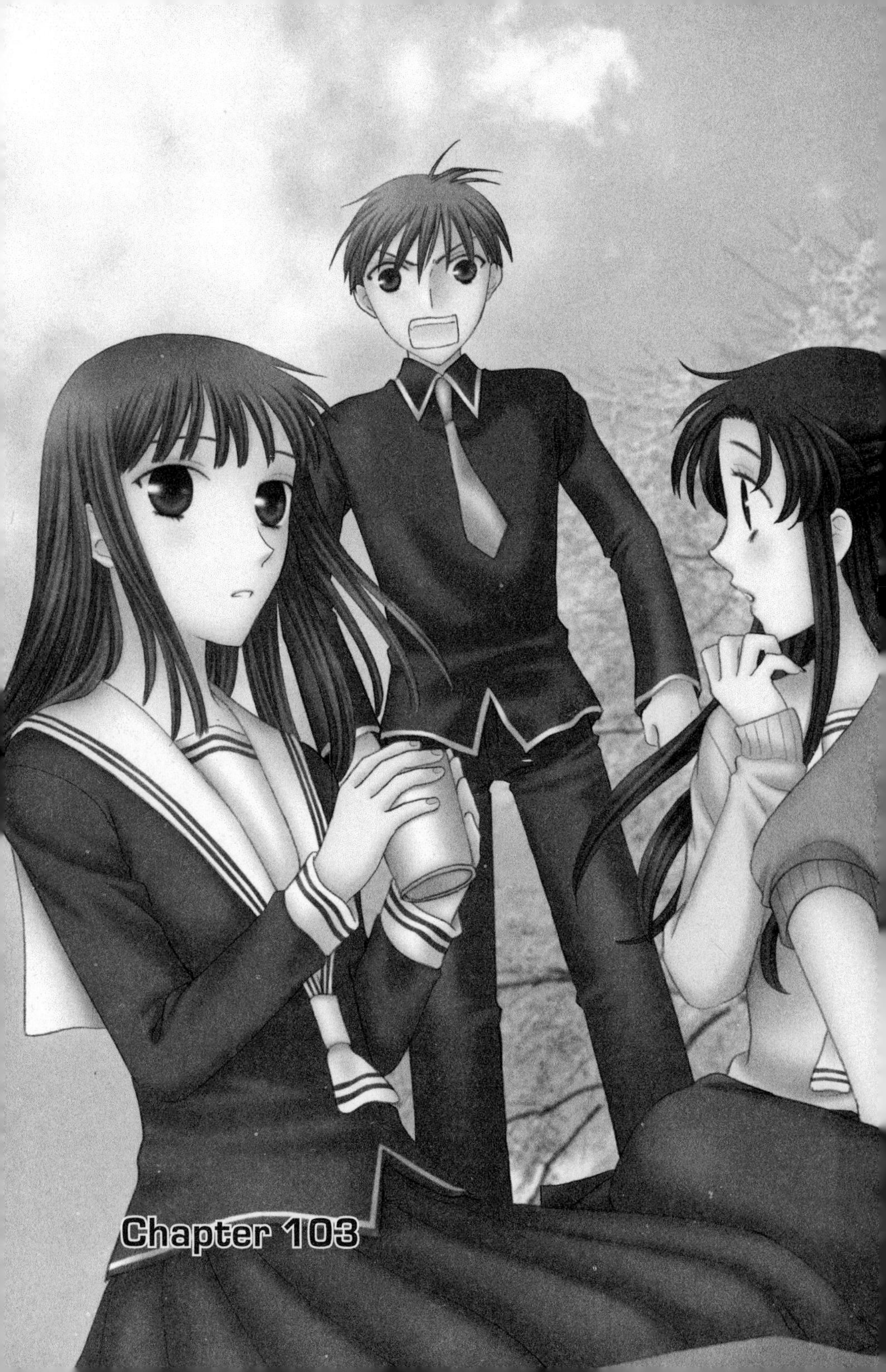
Chapter 103

I'D BEEN THINKING ABOUT IT FOR A LONG TIME.

...I'M SORRY.

...MOST WANT TO GET ACROSS TO YOU...?

WITH OUR FAREWELL ON THE HORIZON...

TO YOU...

...WHOM I LOVE?

... WHAT DID I...

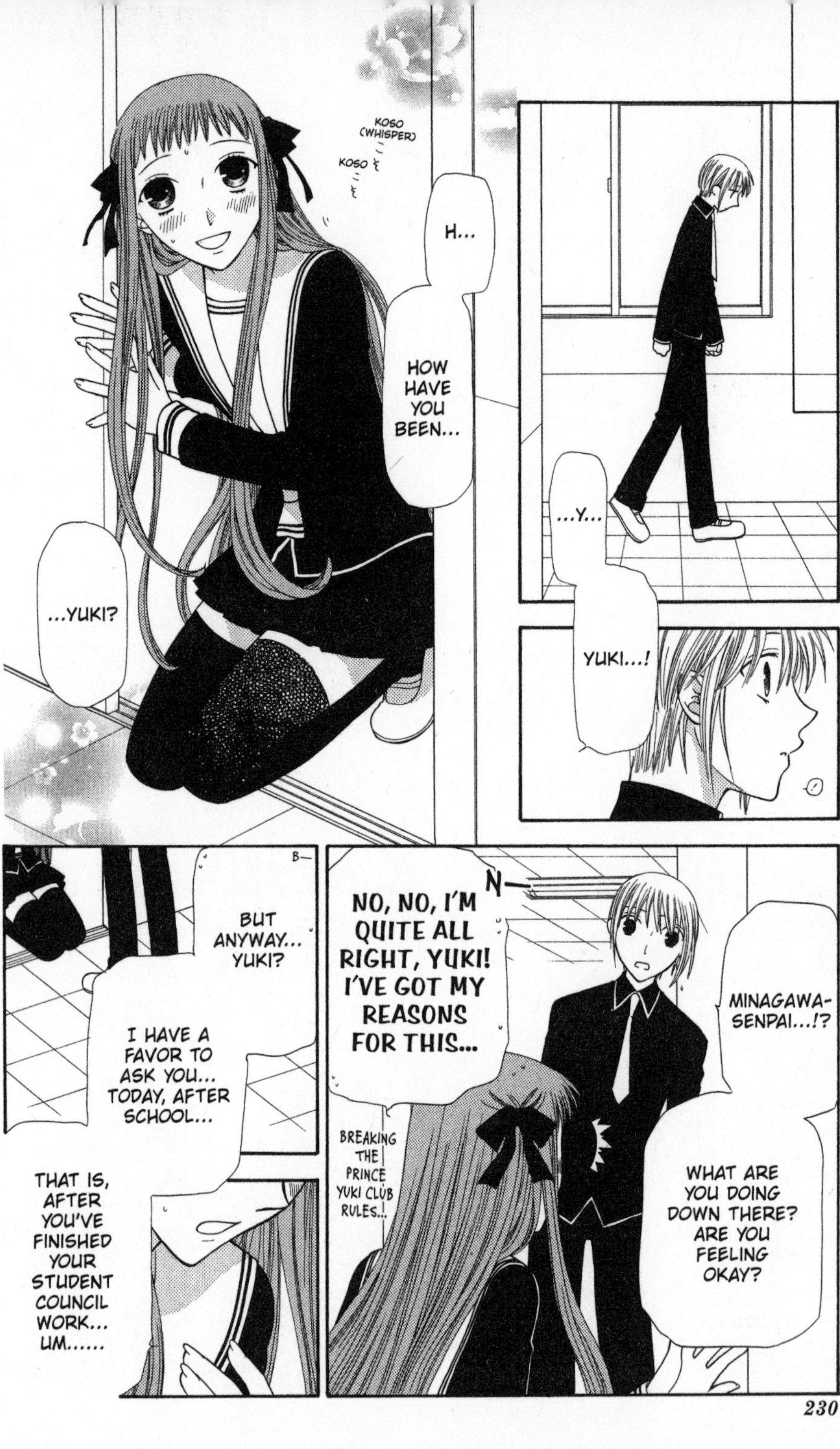
...Y...
YUKI...!
KOSO (WHISPER)
KOSO
H...
HOW HAVE YOU BEEN...
...YUKI?
MINAGAWA-SENPAI...!?
WHAT ARE YOU DOING DOWN THERE? ARE YOU FEELING OKAY?
N—
NO, NO, I'M QUITE ALL RIGHT, YUKI! I'VE GOT MY REASONS FOR THIS...
BREAKING THE PRINCE YUKI CLUB RULES..!
B—
BUT ANYWAY... YUKI?
I HAVE A FAVOR TO ASK YOU... TODAY, AFTER SCHOOL...
THAT IS, AFTER YOU'VE FINISHED YOUR STUDENT COUNCIL WORK... UM......

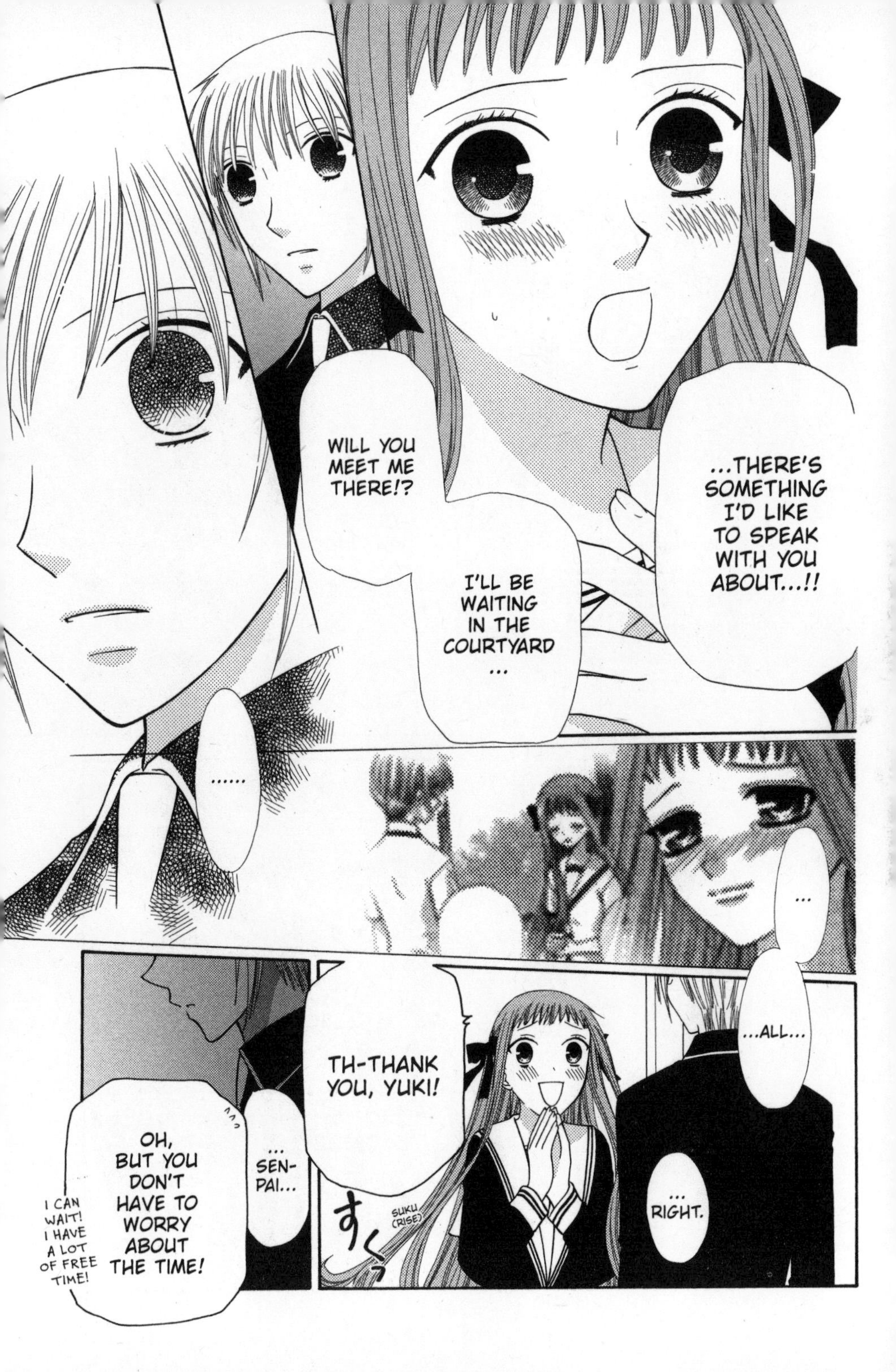

...THERE'S SOMETHING I'D LIKE TO SPEAK WITH YOU ABOUT...!!
I'LL BE WAITING IN THE COURTYARD...
WILL YOU MEET ME THERE!?
......
...
...ALL...
...RIGHT.
TH-THANK YOU, YUKI!
すくっ
SUKU (RISE)
...SEN-PAI...
OH, BUT YOU DON'T HAVE TO WORRY ABOUT THE TIME!
I CAN WAIT! I HAVE A LOT OF FREE TIME!

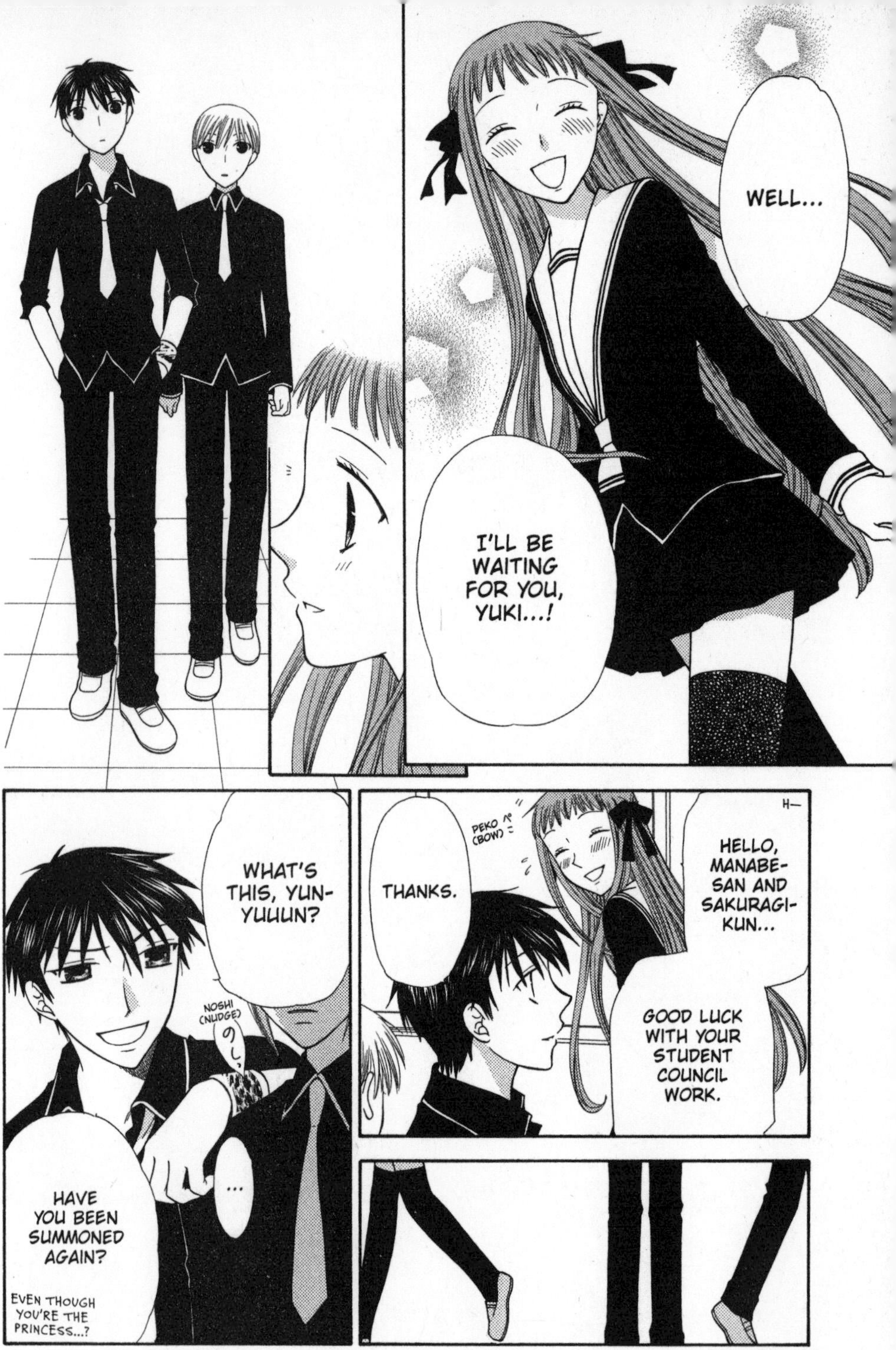
WELL...
I'LL BE WAITING FOR YOU, YUKI...!
H—
HELLO, MANABE-SAN AND SAKURAGI-KUN...
PEKO (BOW)
GOOD LUCK WITH YOUR STUDENT COUNCIL WORK.
THANKS.
WHAT'S THIS, YUN-YUUUN?
NOSHI (NUDGE)
...
HAVE YOU BEEN SUMMONED AGAIN?
EVEN THOUGH YOU'RE THE PRINCESS...?

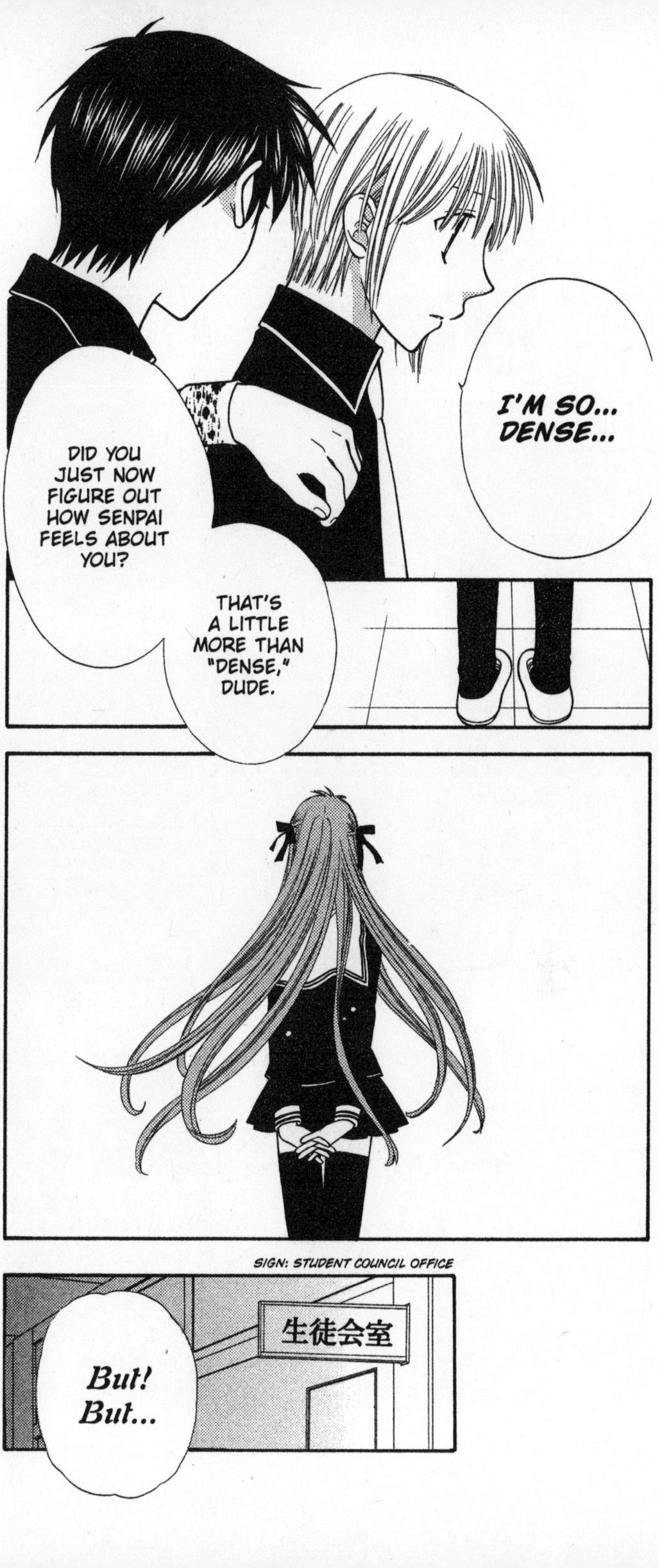
I'M SO... DENSE...
DID YOU JUST NOW FIGURE OUT HOW SENPAI FEELS ABOUT YOU?
THAT'S A LITTLE MORE THAN "DENSE," DUDE.
SIGN: STUDENT COUNCIL OFFICE
生徒会室
But! But...

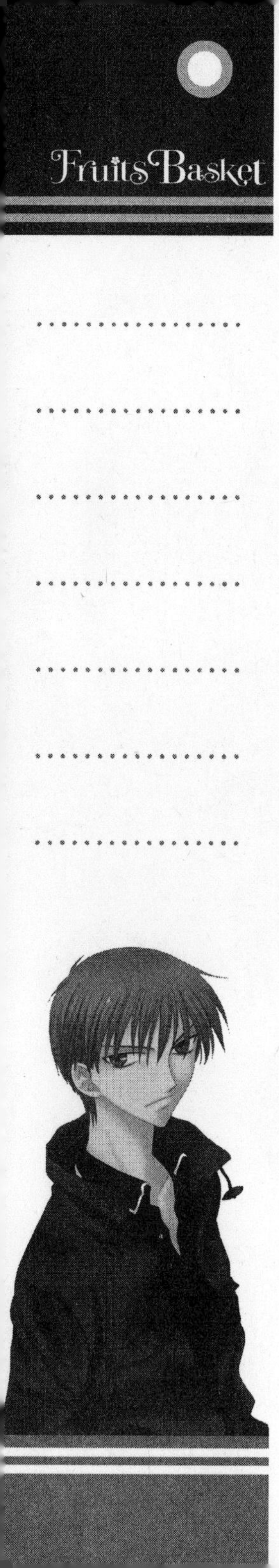
Fruits Basket

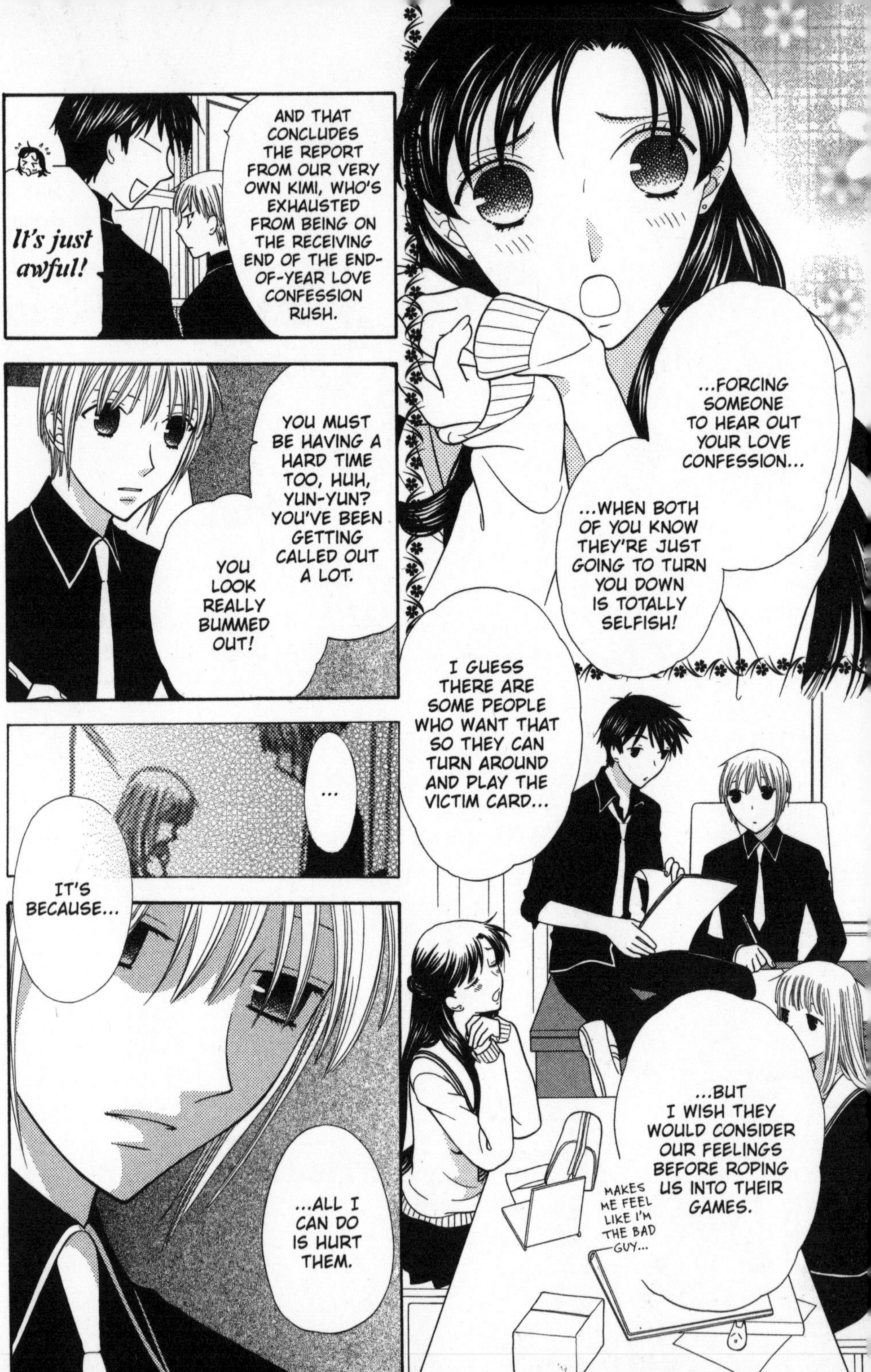
...FORCING SOMEONE TO HEAR OUT YOUR LOVE CONFESSION...
...WHEN BOTH OF YOU KNOW THEY'RE JUST GOING TO TURN YOU DOWN IS TOTALLY SELFISH!
I GUESS THERE ARE SOME PEOPLE WHO WANT THAT SO THEY CAN TURN AROUND AND PLAY THE VICTIM CARD...
...BUT I WISH THEY WOULD CONSIDER OUR FEELINGS BEFORE ROPING US INTO THEIR GAMES.
MAKES ME FEEL LIKE I'M THE BAD GUY...
AND THAT CONCLUDES THE REPORT FROM OUR VERY OWN KIMI, WHO'S EXHAUSTED FROM BEING ON THE RECEIVING END OF THE END-OF-YEAR LOVE CONFESSION RUSH.
It's just awful!
YOU MUST BE HAVING A HARD TIME TOO, HUH, YUN-YUN? YOU'VE BEEN GETTING CALLED OUT A LOT.
YOU LOOK REALLY BUMMED OUT!
...
IT'S BECAUSE...
...ALL I CAN DO IS HURT THEM.

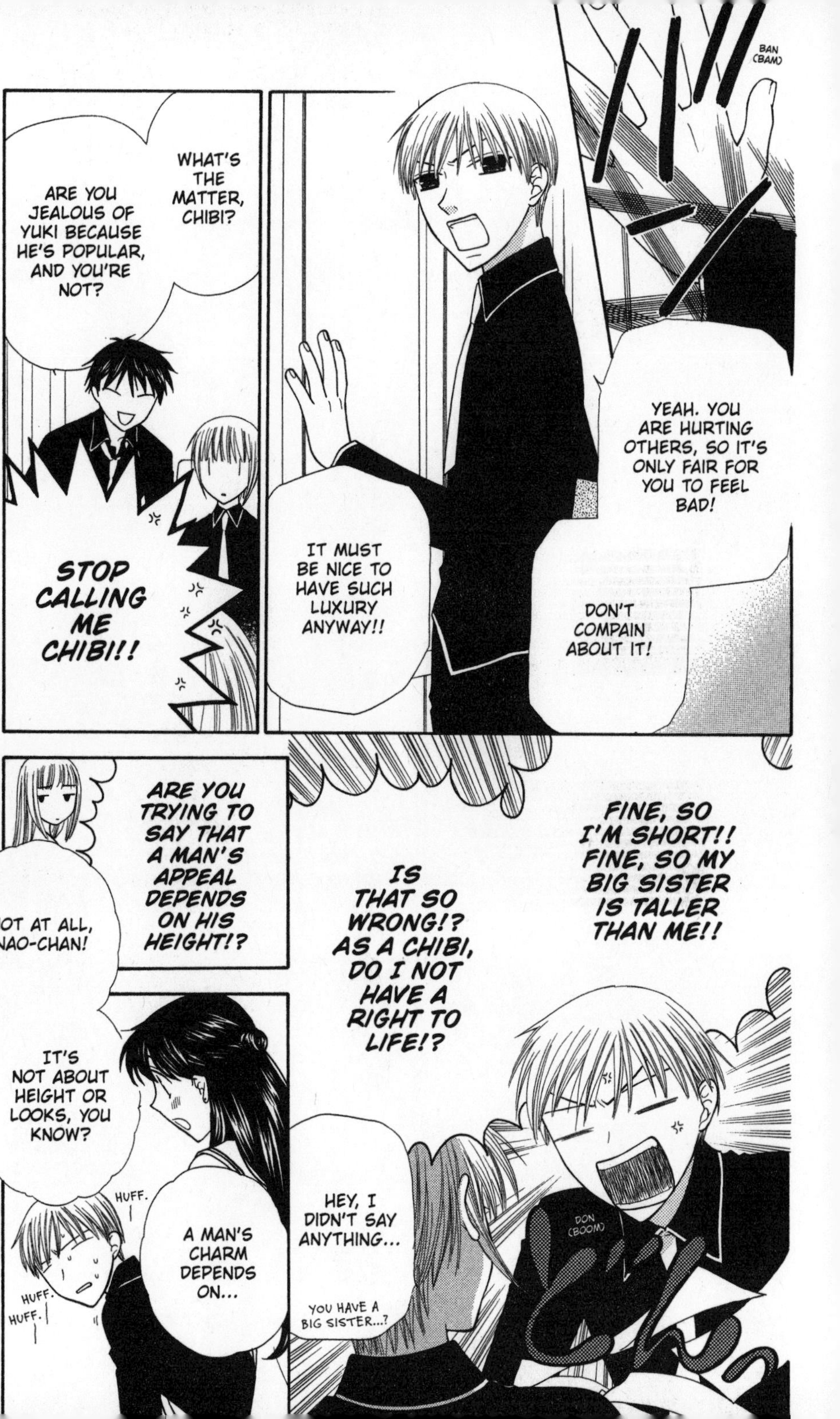
BAN (BAM)
YEAH. YOU ARE HURTING OTHERS, SO IT'S ONLY FAIR FOR YOU TO FEEL BAD!
DON'T COMPAIN ABOUT IT!
IT MUST BE NICE TO HAVE SUCH LUXURY ANYWAY!!
WHAT'S THE MATTER, CHIBI?
ARE YOU JEALOUS OF YUKI BECAUSE HE'S POPULAR, AND YOU'RE NOT?
STOP CALLING ME CHIBI!!
FINE, SO I'M SHORT!! FINE, SO MY BIG SISTER IS TALLER THAN ME!!
IS THAT SO WRONG!? AS A CHIBI, DO I NOT HAVE A RIGHT TO LIFE!?
DON (BOOM)
HEY, I DIDN'T SAY ANYTHING...
YOU HAVE A BIG SISTER...?
ARE YOU TRYING TO SAY THAT A MAN'S APPEAL DEPENDS ON HIS HEIGHT!?
NOT AT ALL, NAO-CHAN!
IT'S NOT ABOUT HEIGHT OR LOOKS, YOU KNOW?
HUFF.
A MAN'S CHARM DEPENDS ON...
HUFF. HUFF.

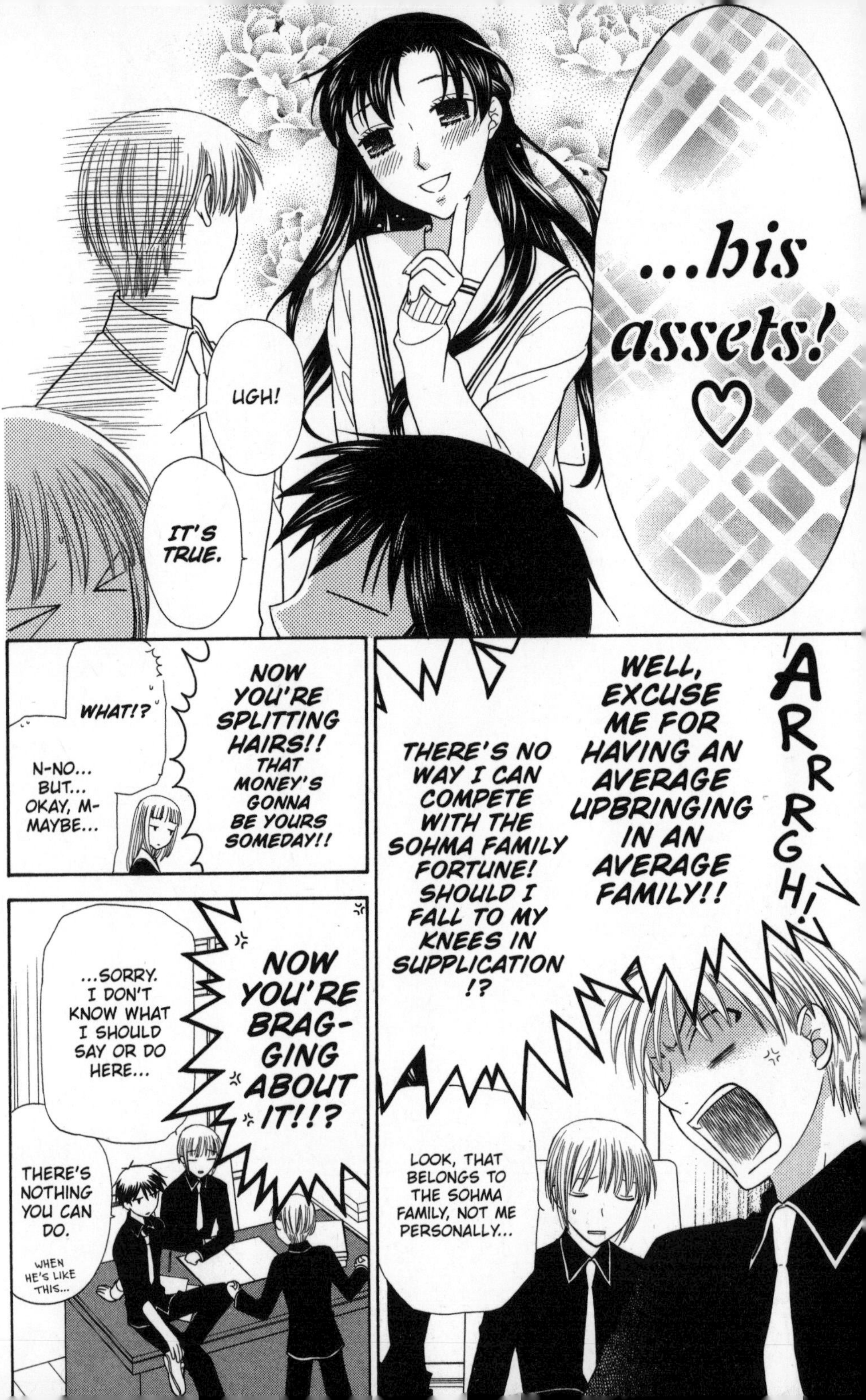
...his assets! ♡
UGH!
IT'S TRUE.
ARRRGH!
WELL, EXCUSE ME FOR HAVING AN AVERAGE UPBRINGING IN AN AVERAGE FAMILY!!
THERE'S NO WAY I CAN COMPETE WITH THE SOHMA FAMILY FORTUNE! SHOULD I FALL TO MY KNEES IN SUPPLICATION!?
LOOK, THAT BELONGS TO THE SOHMA FAMILY, NOT ME PERSONALLY...
NOW YOU'RE SPLITTING HAIRS!! THAT MONEY'S GONNA BE YOURS SOMEDAY!!
WHAT!?
N-NO... BUT... OKAY, M-MAYBE...
NOW YOU'RE BRAG-GING ABOUT IT!!?
...SORRY. I DON'T KNOW WHAT I SHOULD SAY OR DO HERE...
THERE'S NOTHING YOU CAN DO.
WHEN HE'S LIKE THIS...

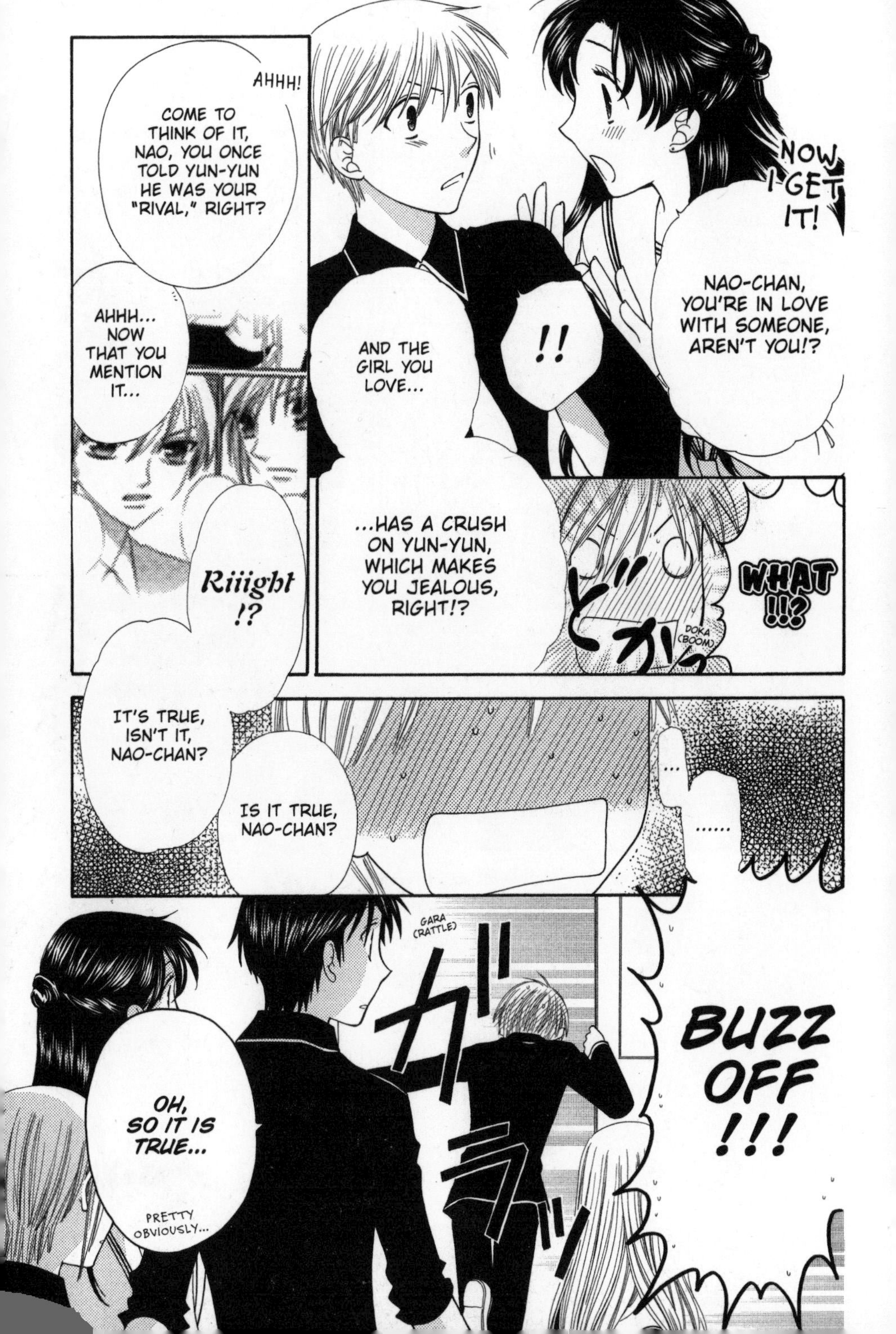
NOW, I GET IT!
NAO-CHAN, YOU'RE IN LOVE WITH SOMEONE, AREN'T YOU!?
!!
AND THE GIRL YOU LOVE...
...HAS A CRUSH ON YUN-YUN, WHICH MAKES YOU JEALOUS, RIGHT!?
WHAT !!?
DOKA (BOOM)
AHHH!
COME TO THINK OF IT, NAO, YOU ONCE TOLD YUN-YUN HE WAS YOUR "RIVAL," RIGHT?
AHHH... NOW THAT YOU MENTION IT...
Riiight !?
...
......
IS IT TRUE, NAO-CHAN?
IT'S TRUE, ISN'T IT, NAO-CHAN?
BUZZ OFF !!!
GARA (RATTLE)
OH, SO IT IS TRUE...
PRETTY OBVIOUSLY...

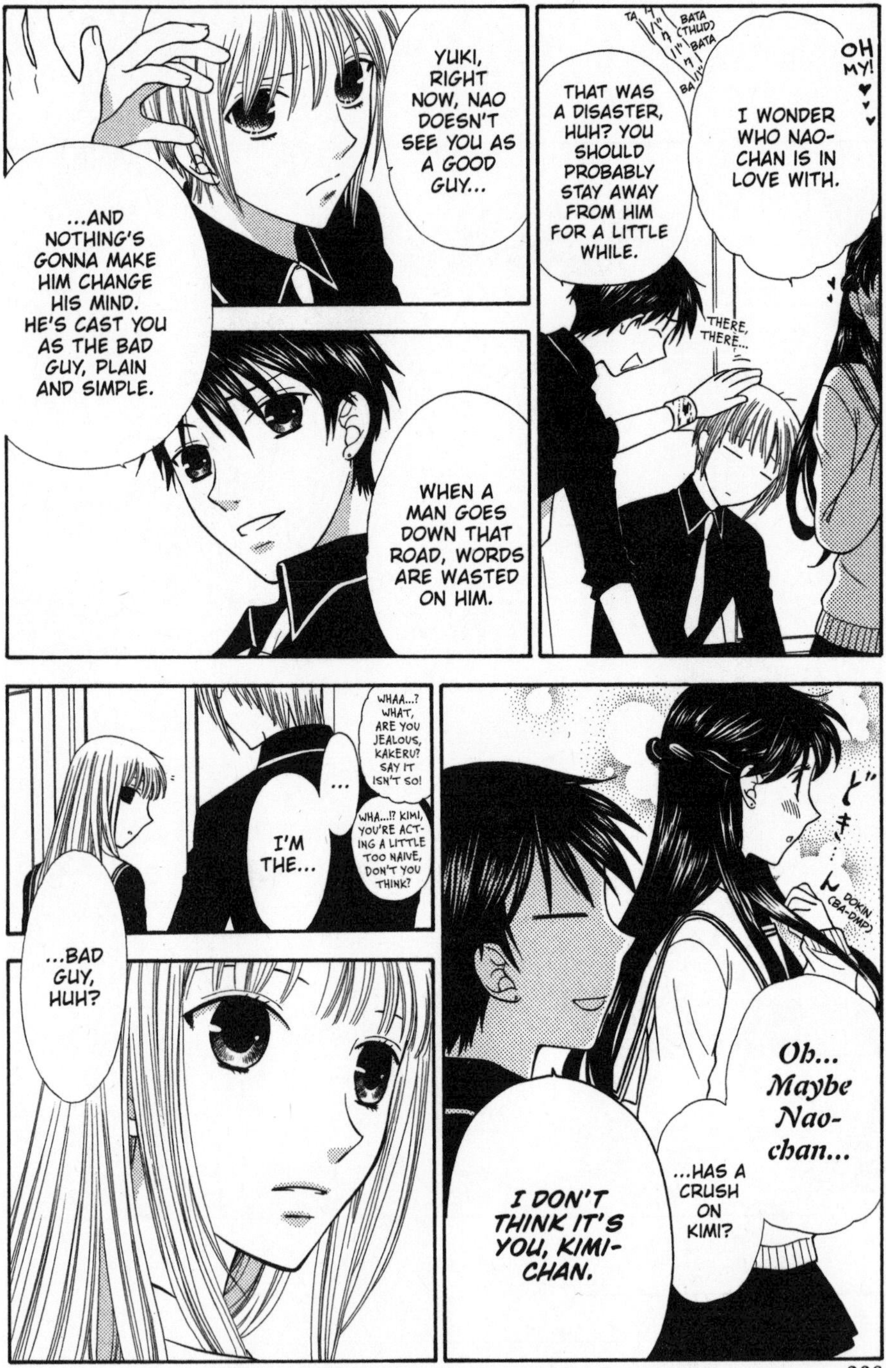
OH MY!
I WONDER WHO NAO-CHAN IS IN LOVE WITH.
TA
BATA (THUD)
BATA
BA
THAT WAS A DISASTER, HUH? YOU SHOULD PROBABLY STAY AWAY FROM HIM FOR A LITTLE WHILE.
THERE, THERE...
YUKI, RIGHT NOW, NAO DOESN'T SEE YOU AS A GOOD GUY...
...AND NOTHING'S GONNA MAKE HIM CHANGE HIS MIND. HE'S CAST YOU AS THE BAD GUY, PLAIN AND SIMPLE.
WHEN A MAN GOES DOWN THAT ROAD, WORDS ARE WASTED ON HIM.
DOKIN (BA-DMP)
Oh... Maybe Nao-chan...
...HAS A CRUSH ON KIMI?
I DON'T THINK IT'S YOU, KIMI-CHAN.
WHAA...? WHAT, ARE YOU JEALOUS, KAKERU? SAY IT ISN'T SO!
...
WHA...!? KIMI, YOU'RE ACTING A LITTLE TOO NAIVE, DON'T YOU THINK?
I'M THE...
...BAD GUY, HUH?

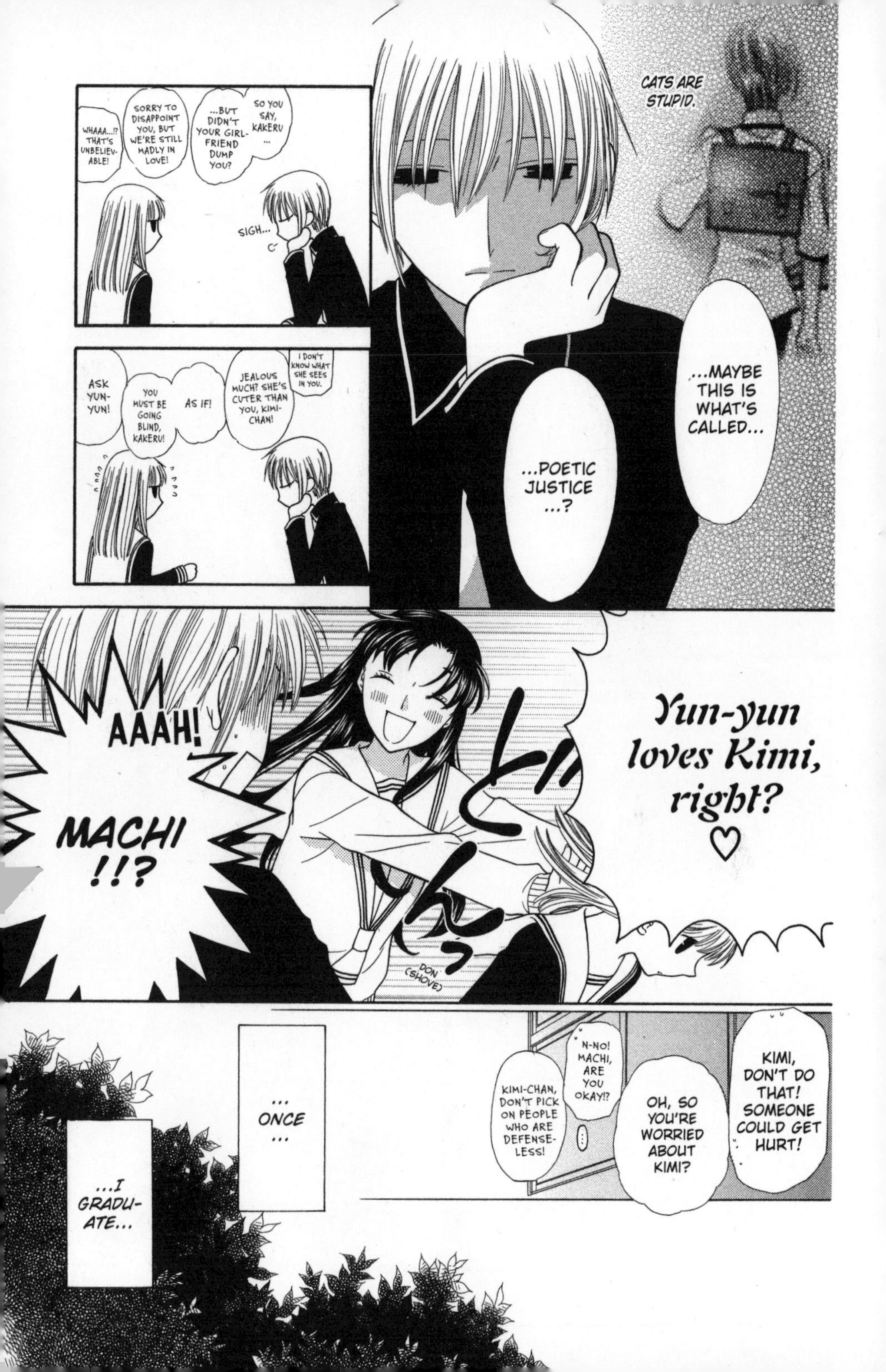
CATS ARE STUPID.
...MAYBE THIS IS WHAT'S CALLED...
...POETIC JUSTICE ...?
SO YOU SAY, KAKERU ...
...BUT DIDN'T YOUR GIRL-FRIEND DUMP YOU?
SORRY TO DISAPPOINT YOU, BUT WE'RE STILL MADLY IN LOVE!
WHAAA...!? THAT'S UNBELIEV-ABLE!
SIGH...
I DON'T KNOW WHAT SHE SEES IN YOU.
JEALOUS MUCH? SHE'S CUTER THAN YOU, KIMI-CHAN!
AS IF!
YOU MUST BE GOING BLIND, KAKERU!
ASK YUN-YUN!
Yun-yun loves Kimi, right? ♡
DON (SHOVE)
AAAH!
MACHI !!?
KIMI, DON'T DO THAT! SOMEONE COULD GET HURT!
OH, SO YOU'RE WORRIED ABOUT KIMI?
N-NO! MACHI, ARE YOU OKAY!?
...
KIMI-CHAN, DON'T PICK ON PEOPLE WHO ARE DEFENSE-LESS!
... ONCE ...
...I GRADU-ATE...

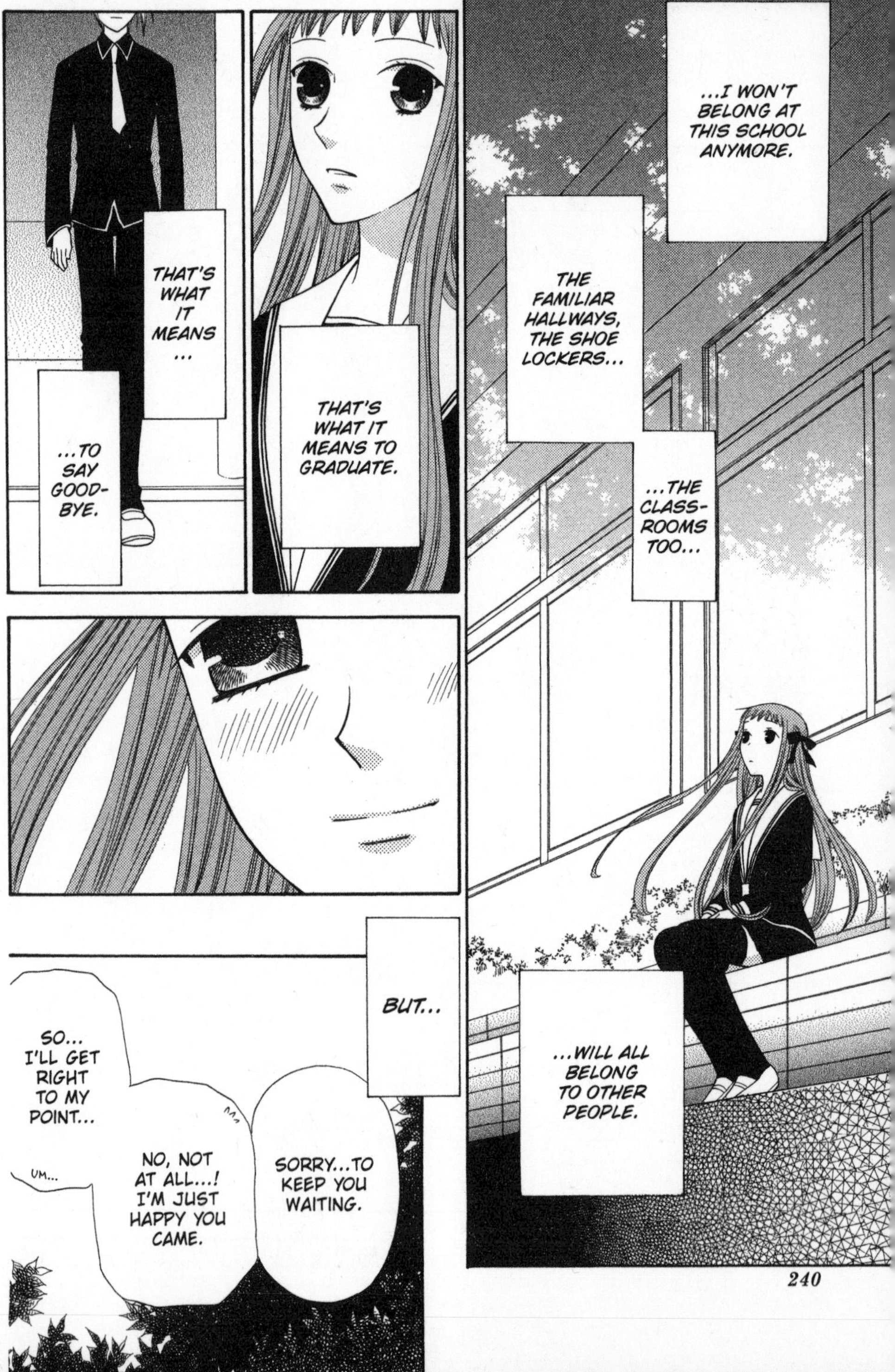
...I WON'T BELONG AT THIS SCHOOL ANYMORE.
THE FAMILIAR HALLWAYS, THE SHOE LOCKERS...
...THE CLASSROOMS TOO...
...WILL ALL BELONG TO OTHER PEOPLE.
THAT'S WHAT IT MEANS TO GRADUATE.
THAT'S WHAT IT MEANS...
...TO SAY GOOD-BYE.
BUT...
SORRY...TO KEEP YOU WAITING.
NO, NOT AT ALL...! I'M JUST HAPPY YOU CAME.
UM...
SO... I'LL GET RIGHT TO MY POINT...

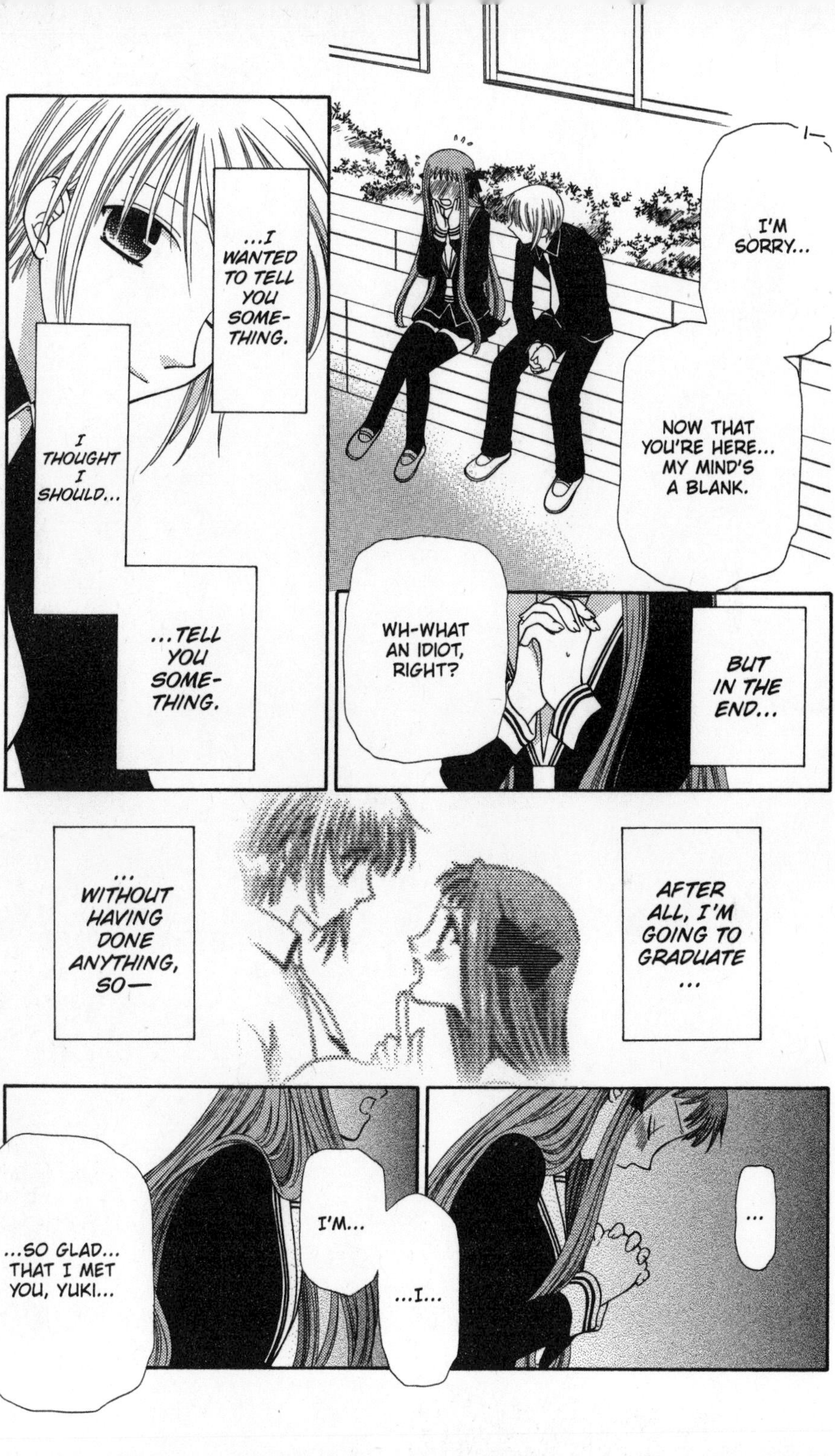
I'M SORRY...
NOW THAT YOU'RE HERE... MY MIND'S A BLANK.
BUT IN THE END...
WH-WHAT AN IDIOT, RIGHT?
...I WANTED TO TELL YOU SOME-THING.
I THOUGHT I SHOULD...
...TELL YOU SOME-THING.
AFTER ALL, I'M GOING TO GRADUATE ...
... WITHOUT HAVING DONE ANYTHING, SO—
...
I'M...
...I...
...SO GLAD... THAT I MET YOU, YUKI...

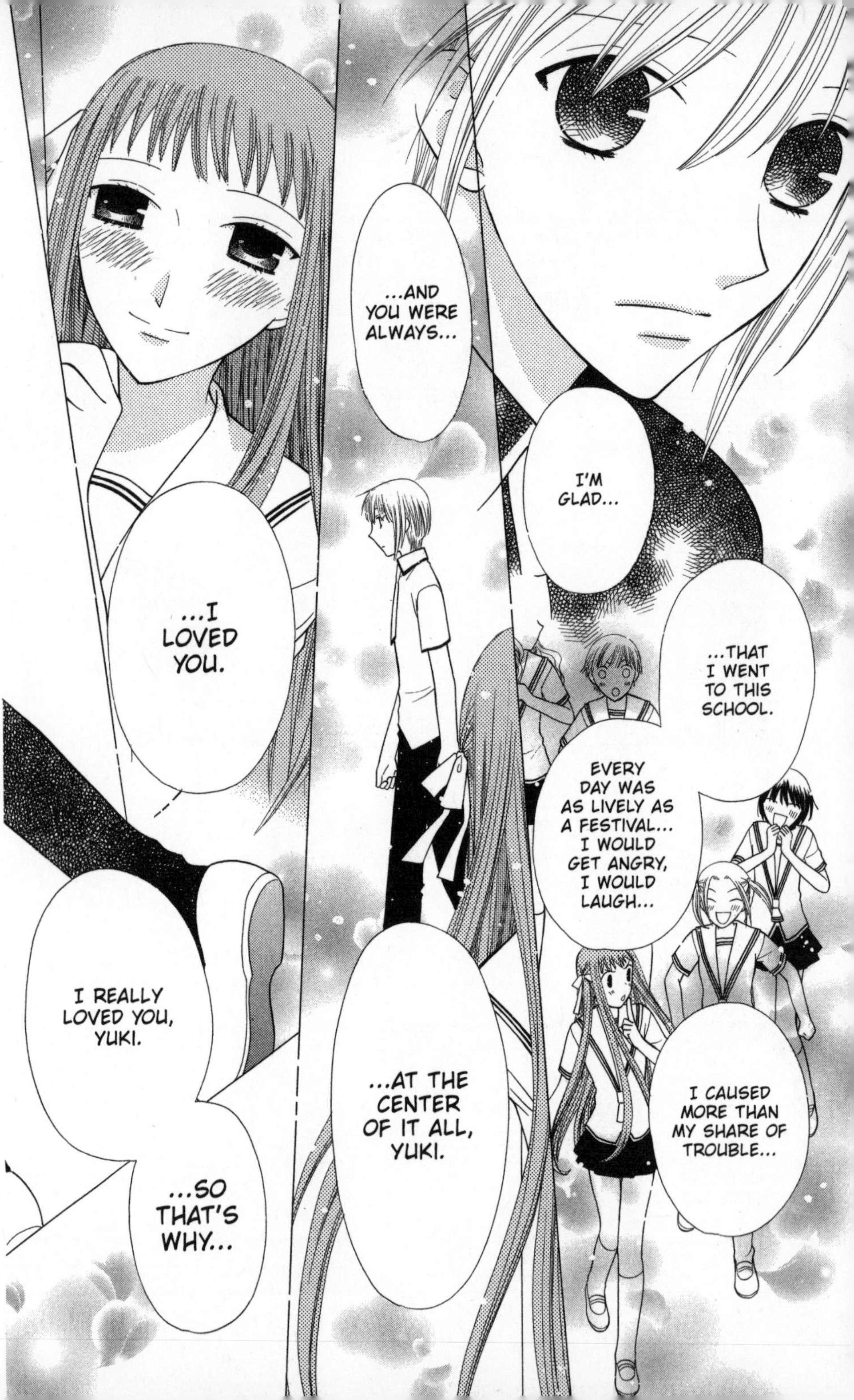
I'M GLAD...
...THAT I WENT TO THIS SCHOOL.
EVERY DAY WAS AS LIVELY AS A FESTIVAL... I WOULD GET ANGRY, I WOULD LAUGH...
I CAUSED MORE THAN MY SHARE OF TROUBLE...
...AND YOU WERE ALWAYS...
...AT THE CENTER OF IT ALL, YUKI.
...I LOVED YOU.
I REALLY LOVED YOU, YUKI.
...SO THAT'S WHY...

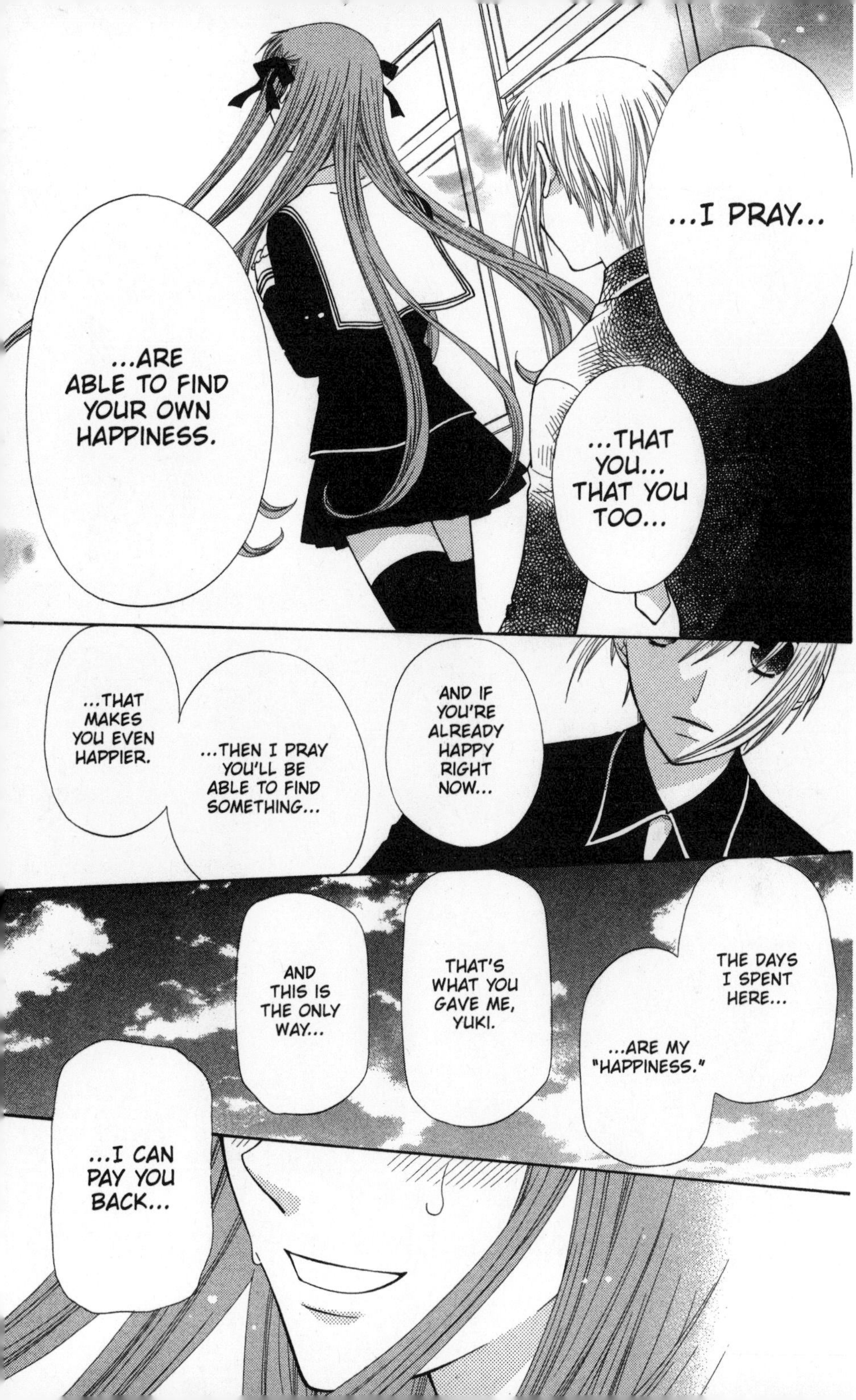
...I PRAY...
...THAT YOU... THAT YOU TOO...
...ARE ABLE TO FIND YOUR OWN HAPPINESS.
AND IF YOU'RE ALREADY HAPPY RIGHT NOW...
...THEN I PRAY YOU'LL BE ABLE TO FIND SOMETHING...
...THAT MAKES YOU EVEN HAPPIER.
THE DAYS I SPENT HERE...
...ARE MY "HAPPINESS."
THAT'S WHAT YOU GAVE ME, YUKI.
AND THIS IS THE ONLY WAY...
...I CAN PAY YOU BACK...

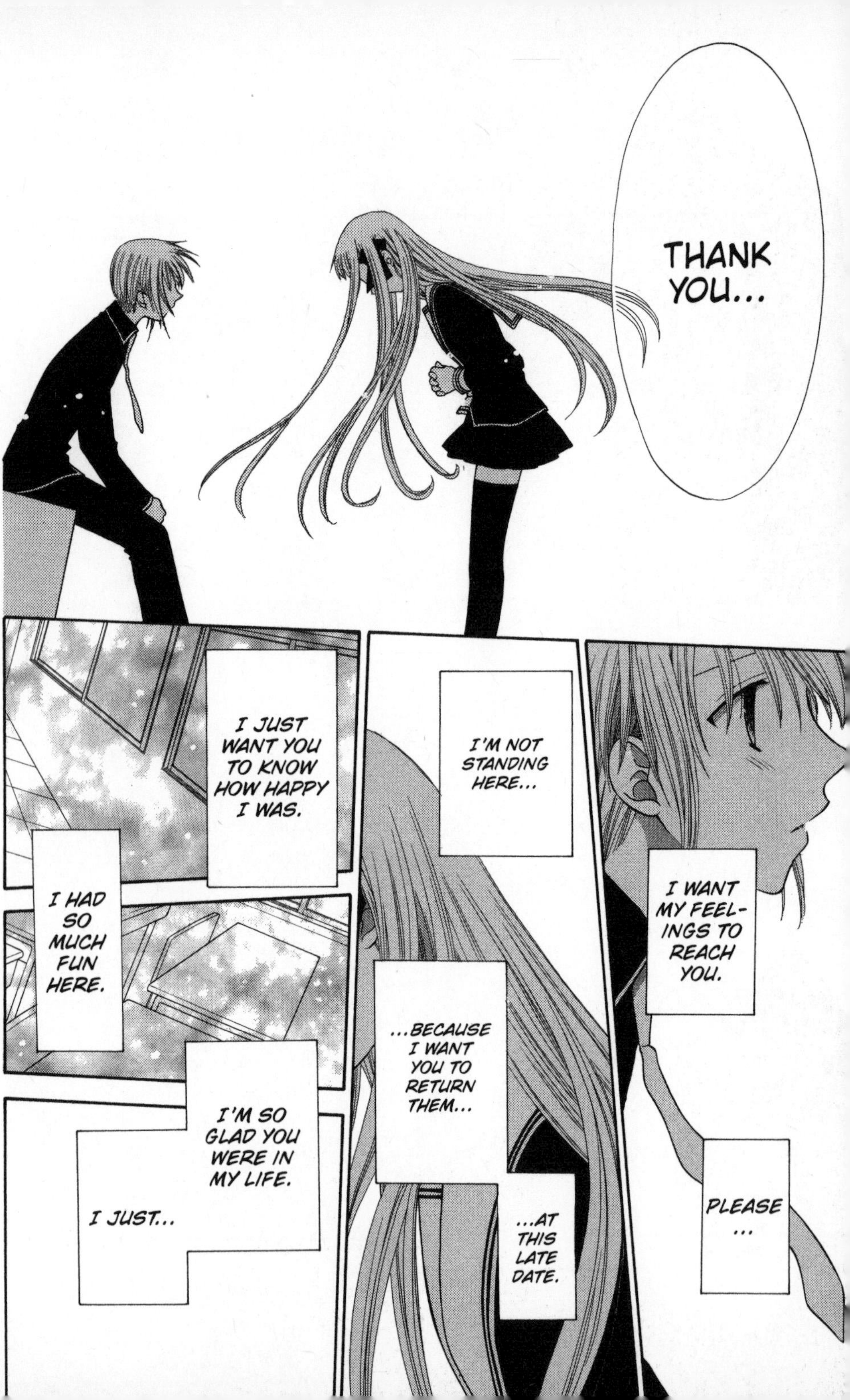
THANK YOU...
I WANT MY FEEL-INGS TO REACH YOU.
PLEASE ...
I'M NOT STANDING HERE...
...BECAUSE I WANT YOU TO RETURN THEM...
...AT THIS LATE DATE.
I JUST WANT YOU TO KNOW HOW HAPPY I WAS.
I HAD SO MUCH FUN HERE.
I'M SO GLAD YOU WERE IN MY LIFE.
I JUST...

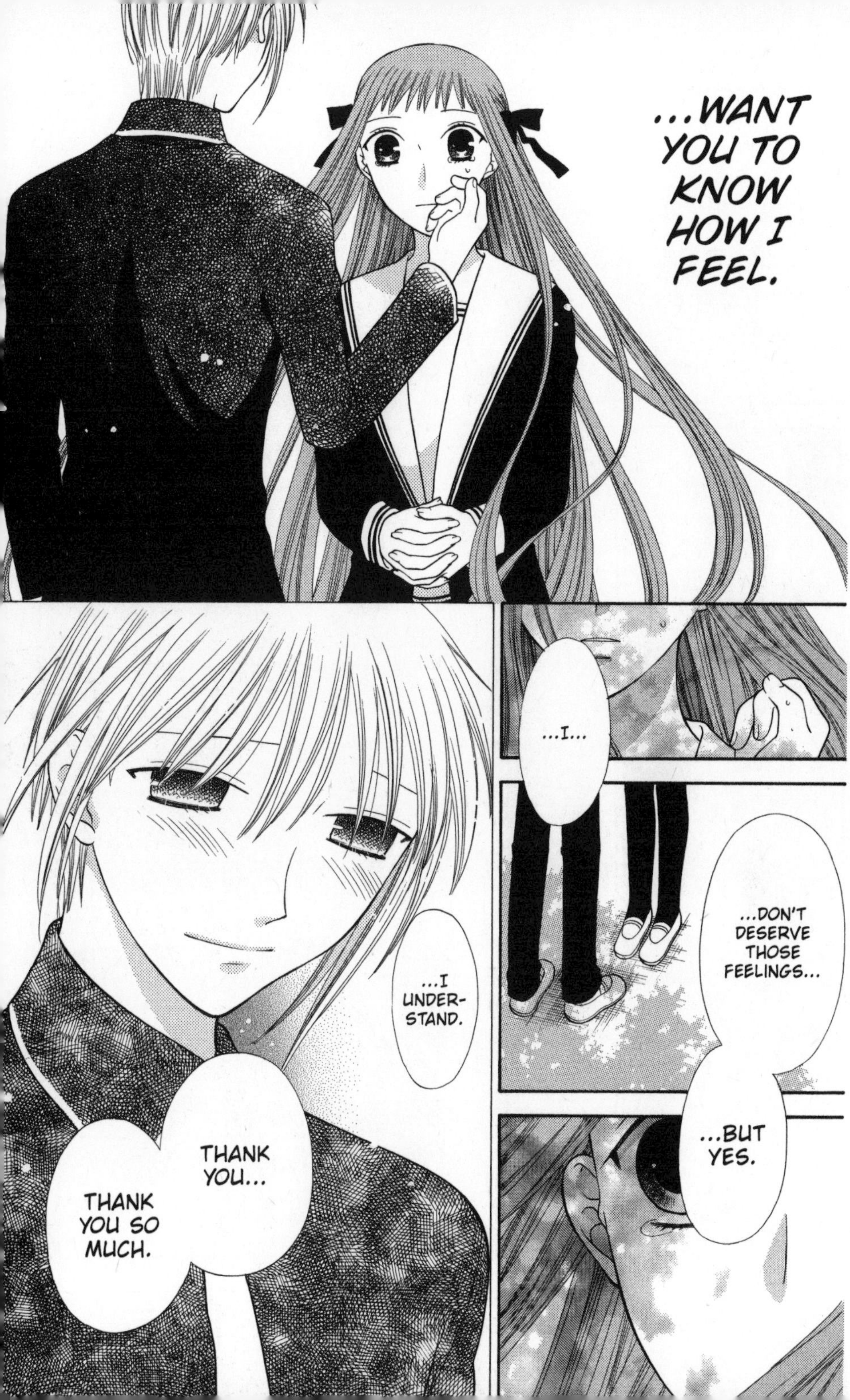
...WANT YOU TO KNOW HOW I FEEL.
...I...
...DON'T DESERVE THOSE FEELINGS...
...BUT YES.
...I UNDER-STAND.
THANK YOU...
THANK YOU SO MUCH.

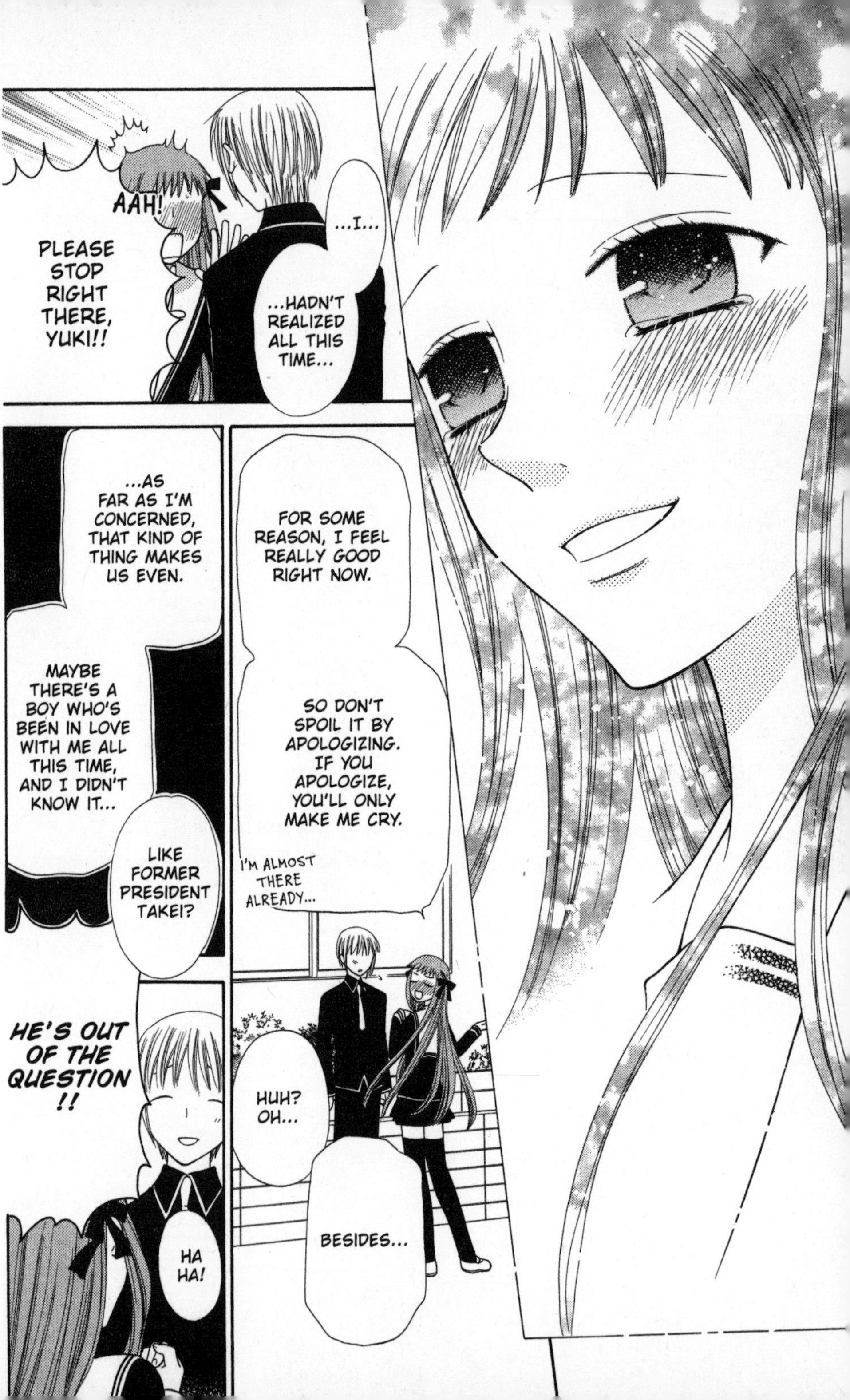
...I...
...HADN'T REALIZED ALL THIS TIME...
AAH!
PLEASE STOP RIGHT THERE, YUKI!!
FOR SOME REASON, I FEEL REALLY GOOD RIGHT NOW.
SO DON'T SPOIL IT BY APOLOGIZING. IF YOU APOLOGIZE, YOU'LL ONLY MAKE ME CRY.
I'M ALMOST THERE ALREADY...
...AS FAR AS I'M CONCERNED, THAT KIND OF THING MAKES US EVEN.
MAYBE THERE'S A BOY WHO'S BEEN IN LOVE WITH ME ALL THIS TIME, AND I DIDN'T KNOW IT...
LIKE FORMER PRESIDENT TAKEI?
HE'S OUT OF THE QUESTION!!
HA HA!
HUH? OH...
BESIDES...

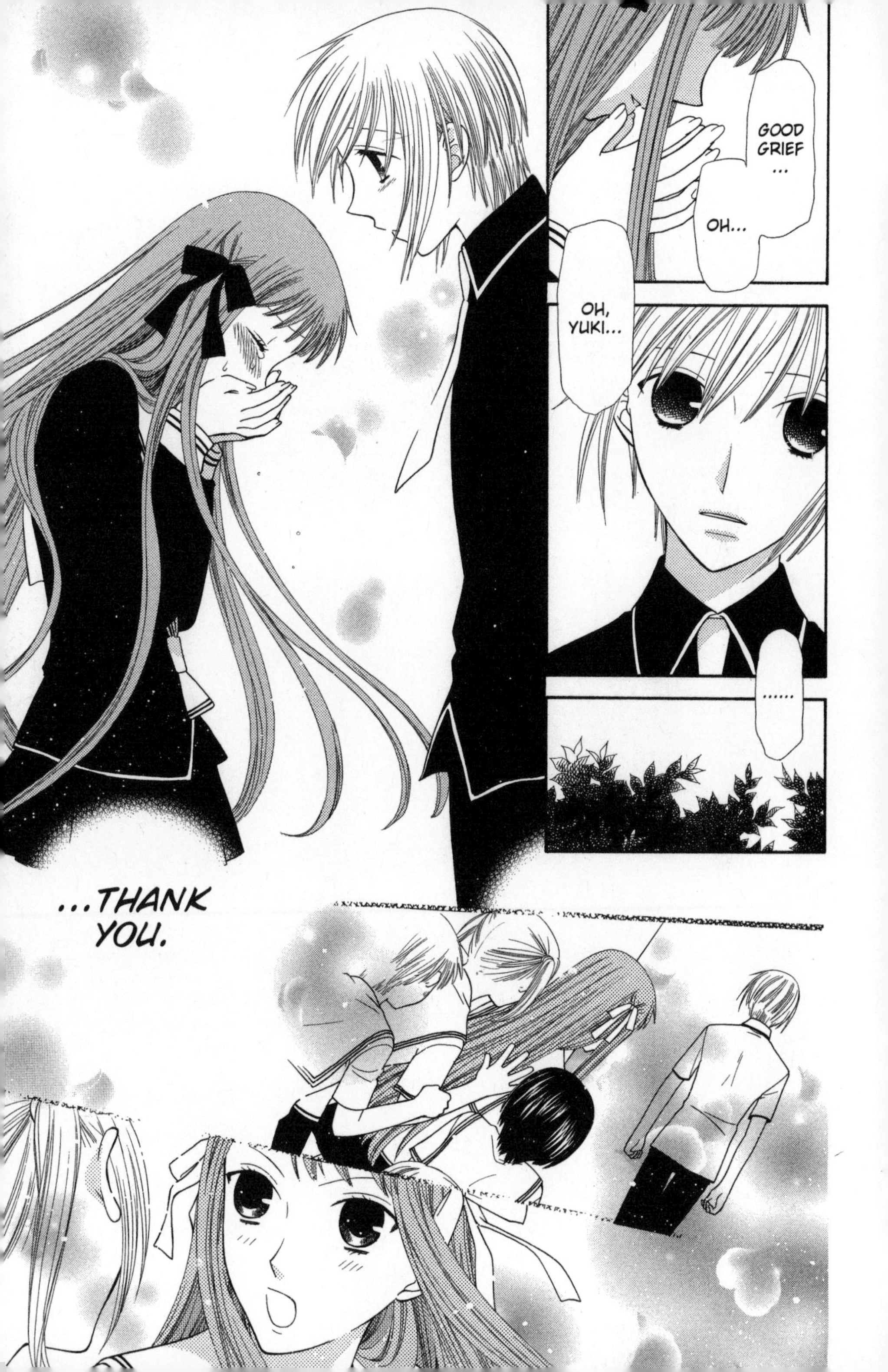
GOOD GRIEF ...
OH...
OH, YUKI...
......
...THANK YOU.

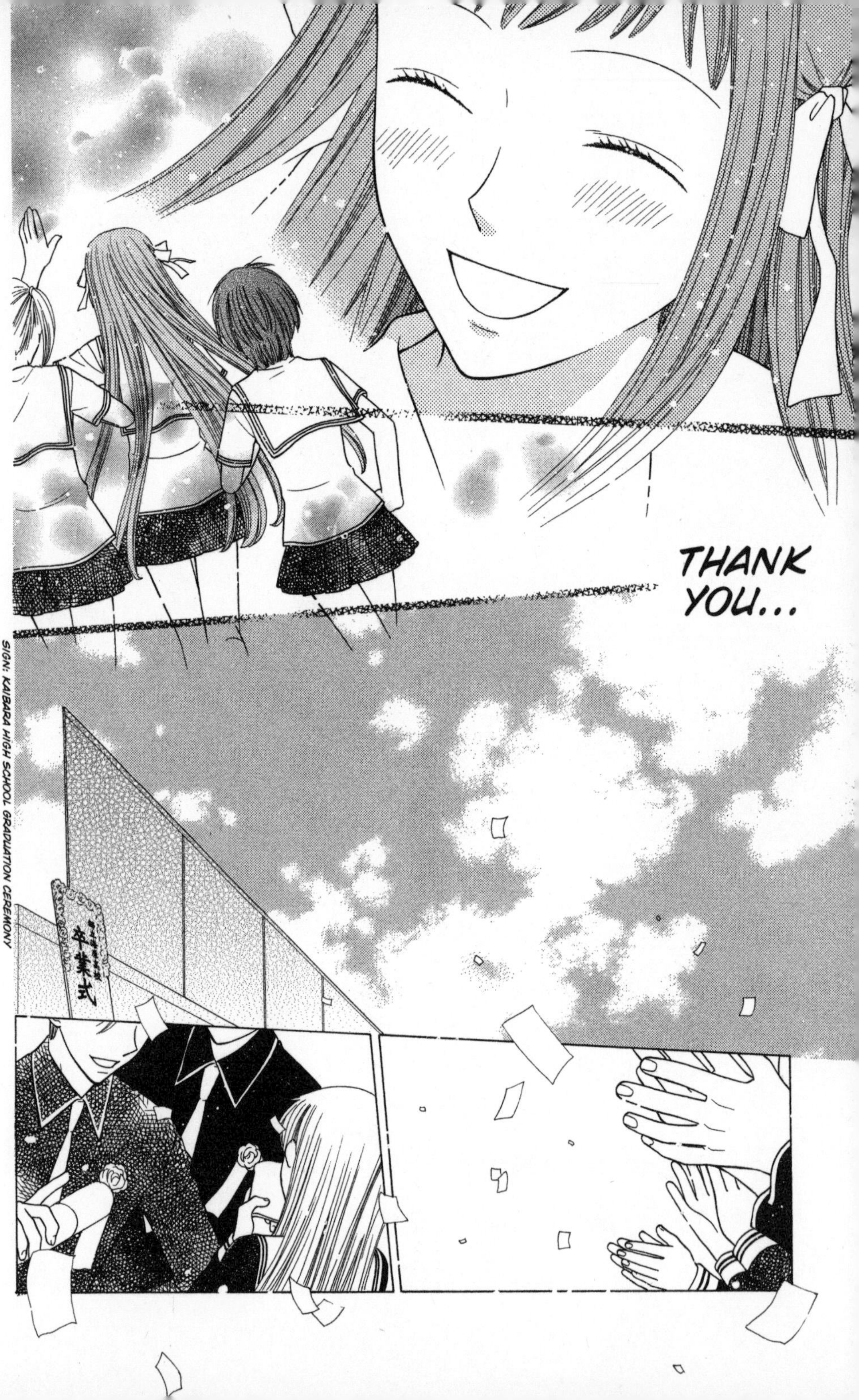
THANK YOU...
SIGN: KAIBARA HIGH SCHOOL GRADUATION CEREMONY
卒業式

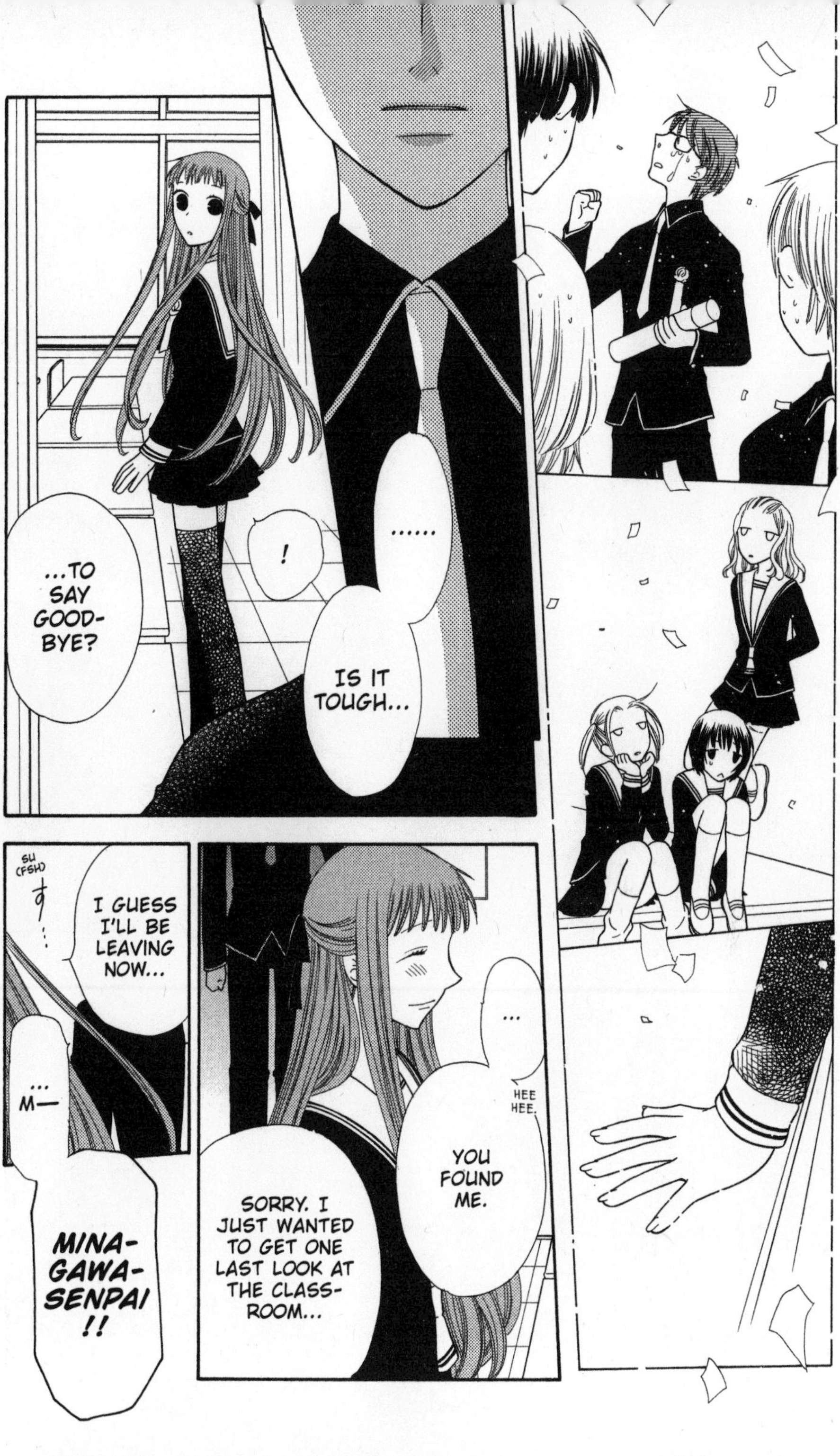

......
!
IS IT TOUGH...
...TO SAY GOOD-BYE?
...
HEE HEE.
YOU FOUND ME.
SORRY. I JUST WANTED TO GET ONE LAST LOOK AT THE CLASSROOM...
SU (FSH) す
I GUESS I'LL BE LEAVING NOW...
... M—
MINAGAWA-SENPAI!!

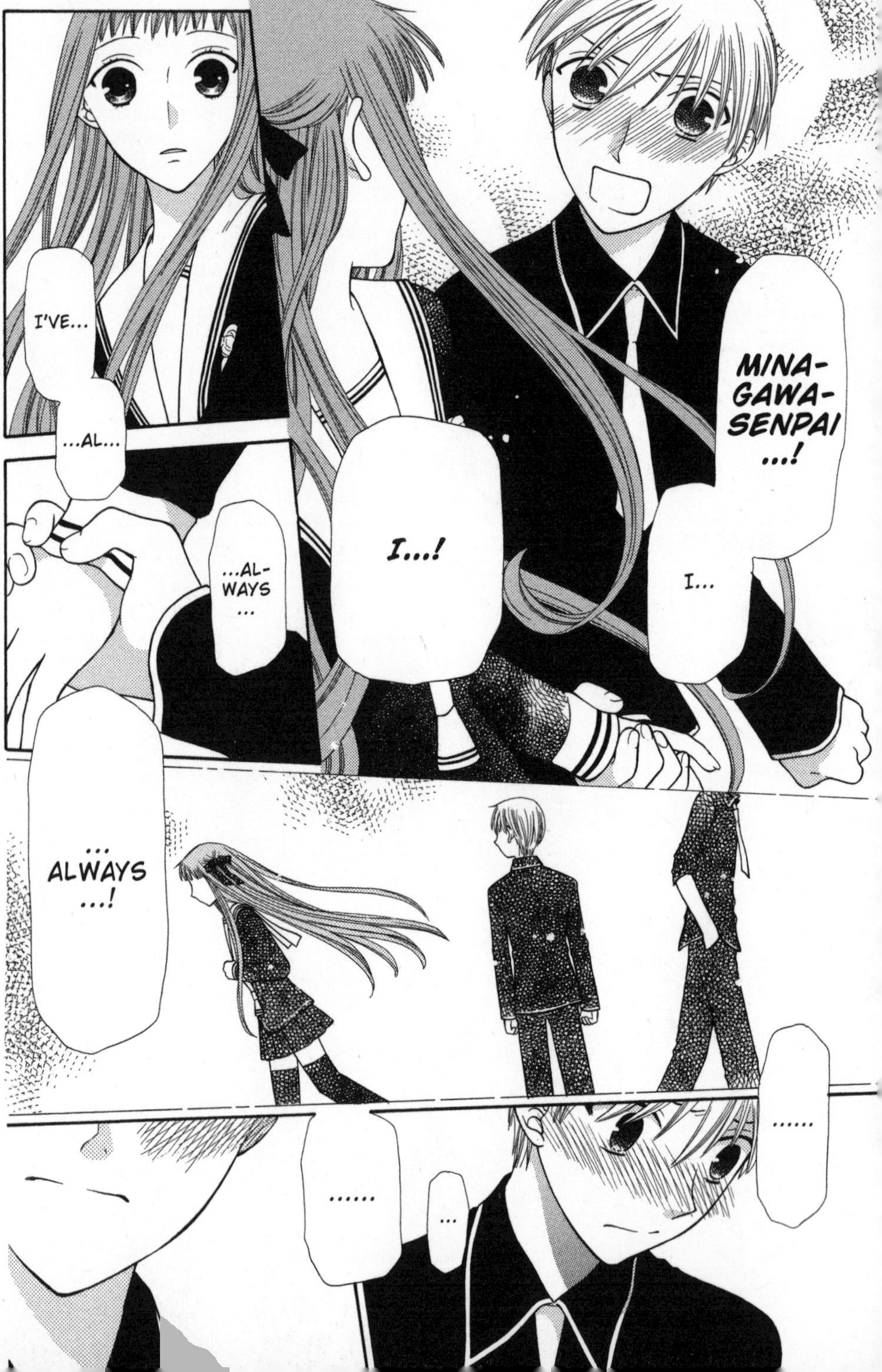
MINA-GAWA-SENPAI...!
I...
I...!
I'VE...
...AL...
...AL-WAYS...
...ALWAYS...!
......
......
...

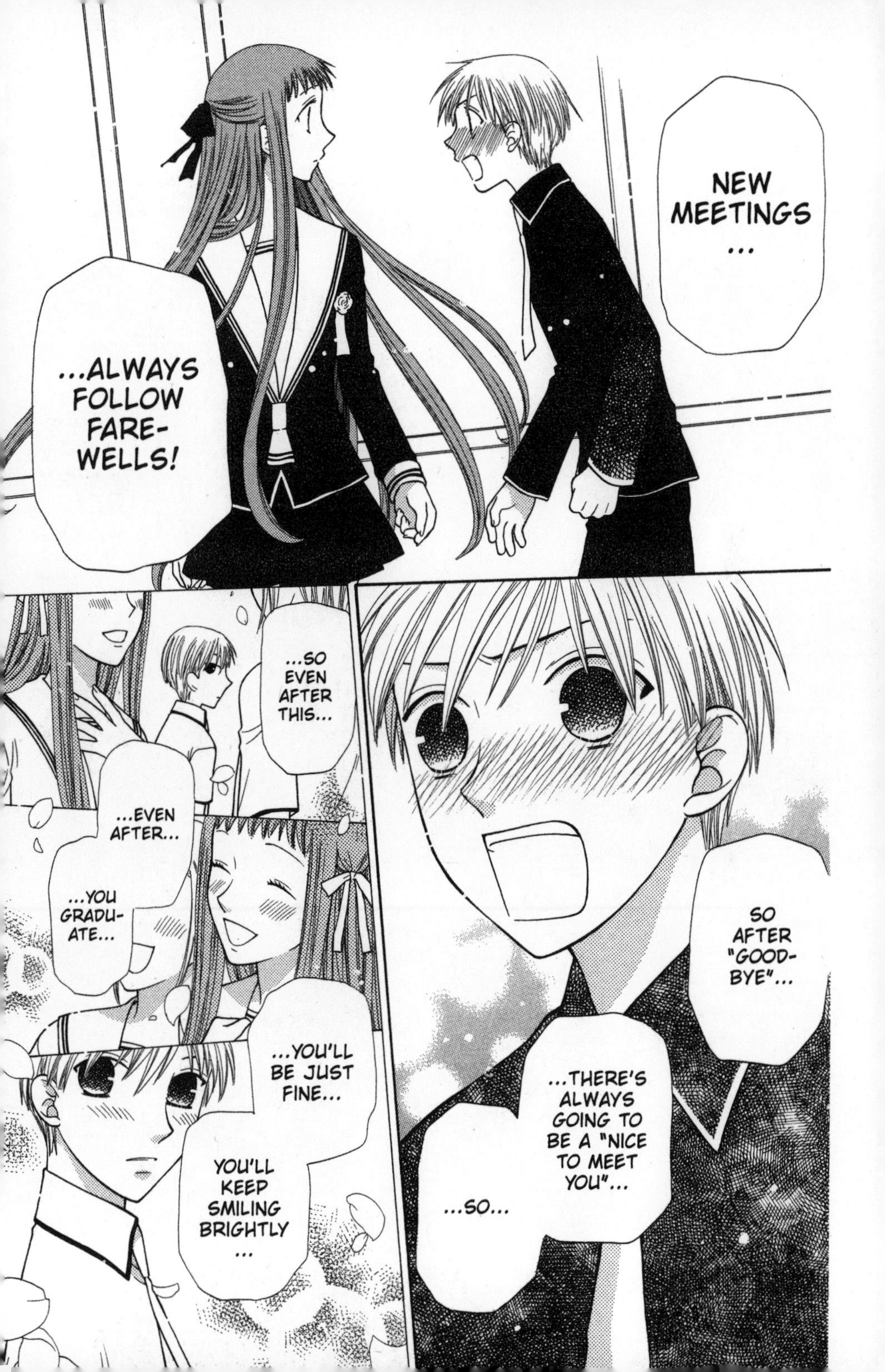
NEW MEETINGS ...
...ALWAYS FOLLOW FARE-WELLS!
SO AFTER "GOOD-BYE"...
...THERE'S ALWAYS GOING TO BE A "NICE TO MEET YOU"...
...SO...
...SO EVEN AFTER THIS...
...EVEN AFTER...
...YOU GRADU-ATE...
...YOU'LL BE JUST FINE...
YOU'LL KEEP SMILING BRIGHTLY ...

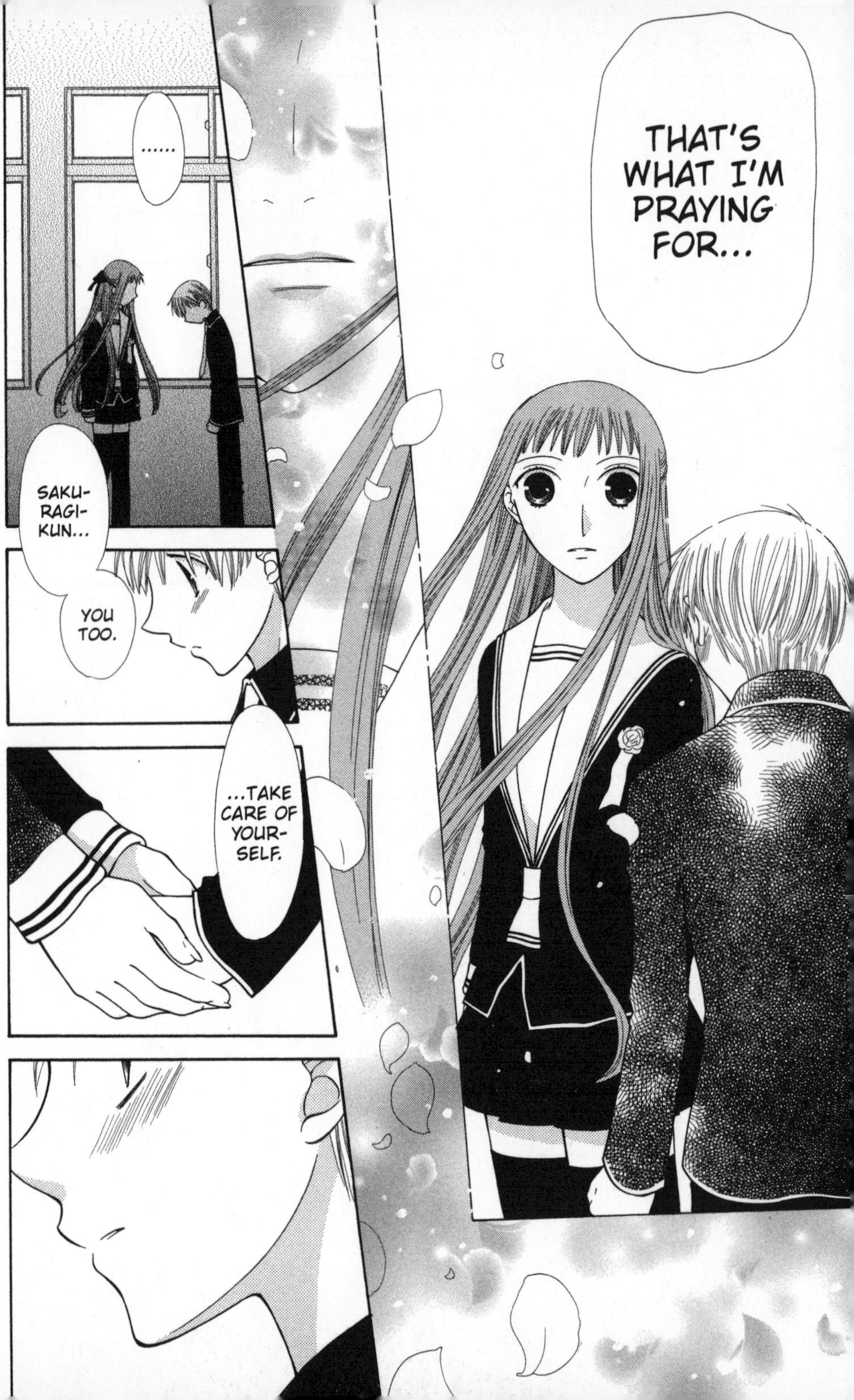
THAT'S WHAT I'M PRAYING FOR...
......
SAKURAGI-KUN...
YOU TOO.
...TAKE CARE OF YOURSELF.

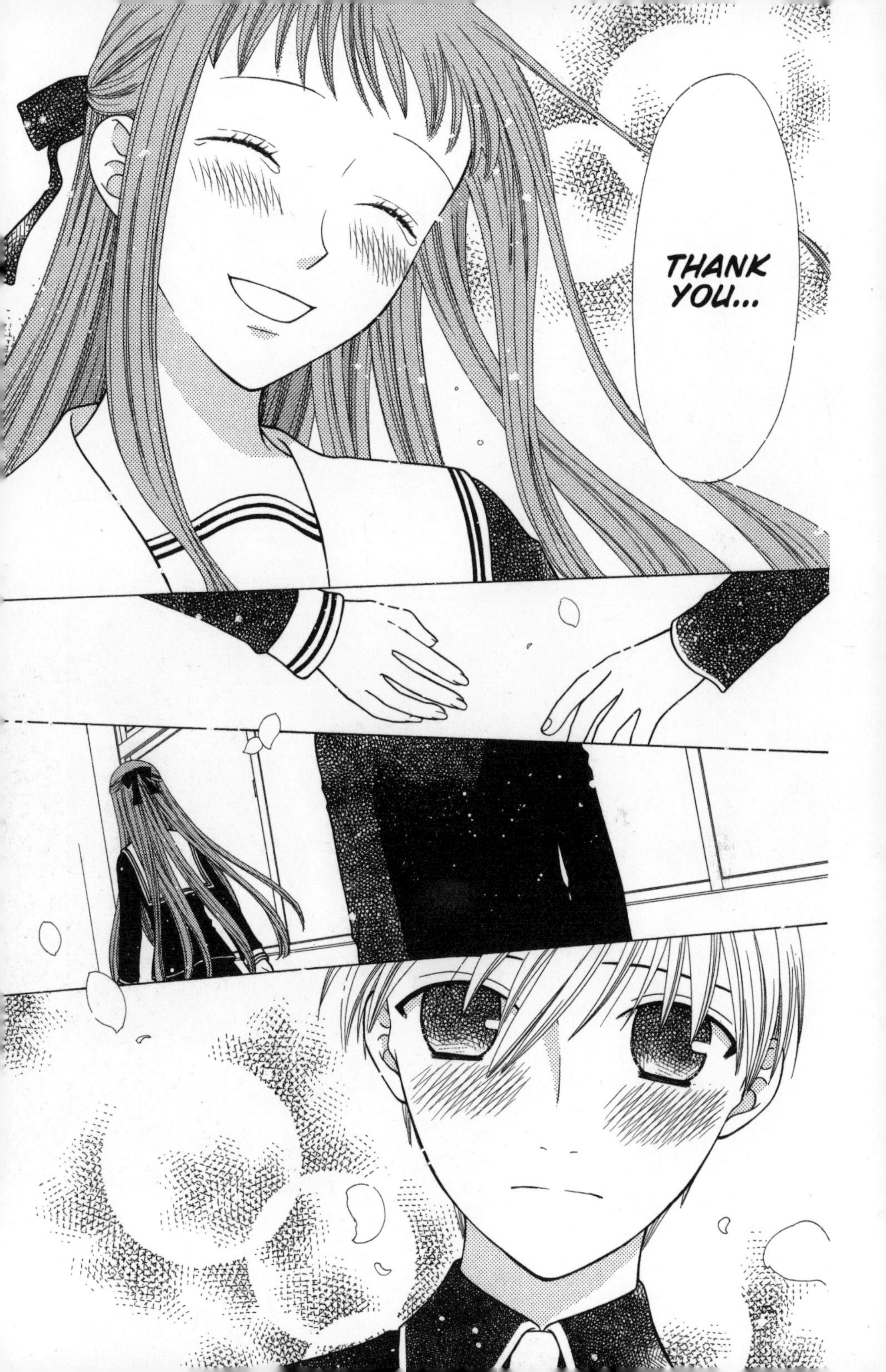
THANK YOU...

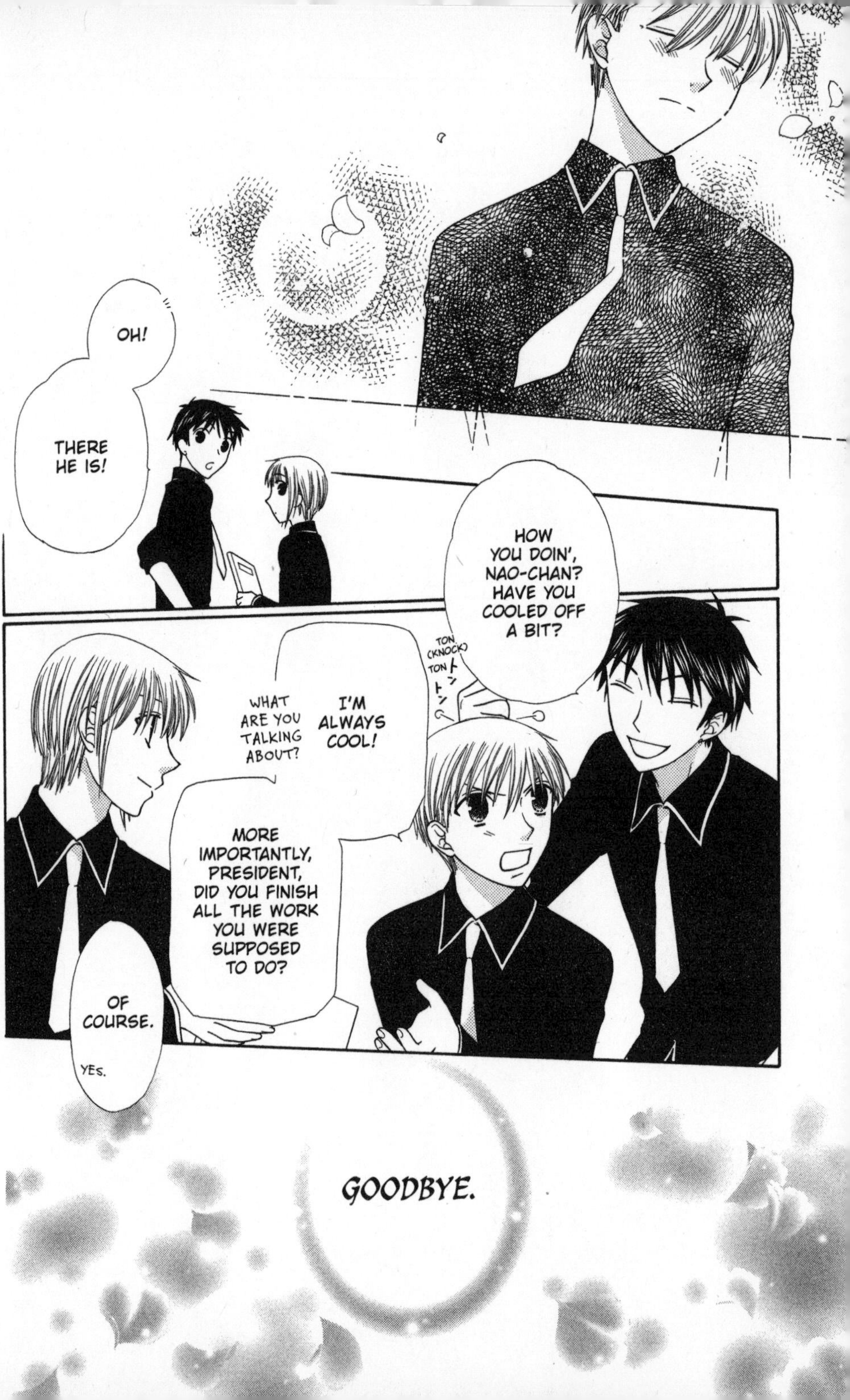
OH!
THERE HE IS!
HOW YOU DOIN', NAO-CHAN? HAVE YOU COOLED OFF A BIT?
TON (KNOCK) TON トン トン
I'M ALWAYS COOL!
WHAT ARE YOU TALKING ABOUT?
MORE IMPORTANTLY, PRESIDENT, DID YOU FINISH ALL THE WORK YOU WERE SUPPOSED TO DO?
OF COURSE.
YES.
GOODBYE.

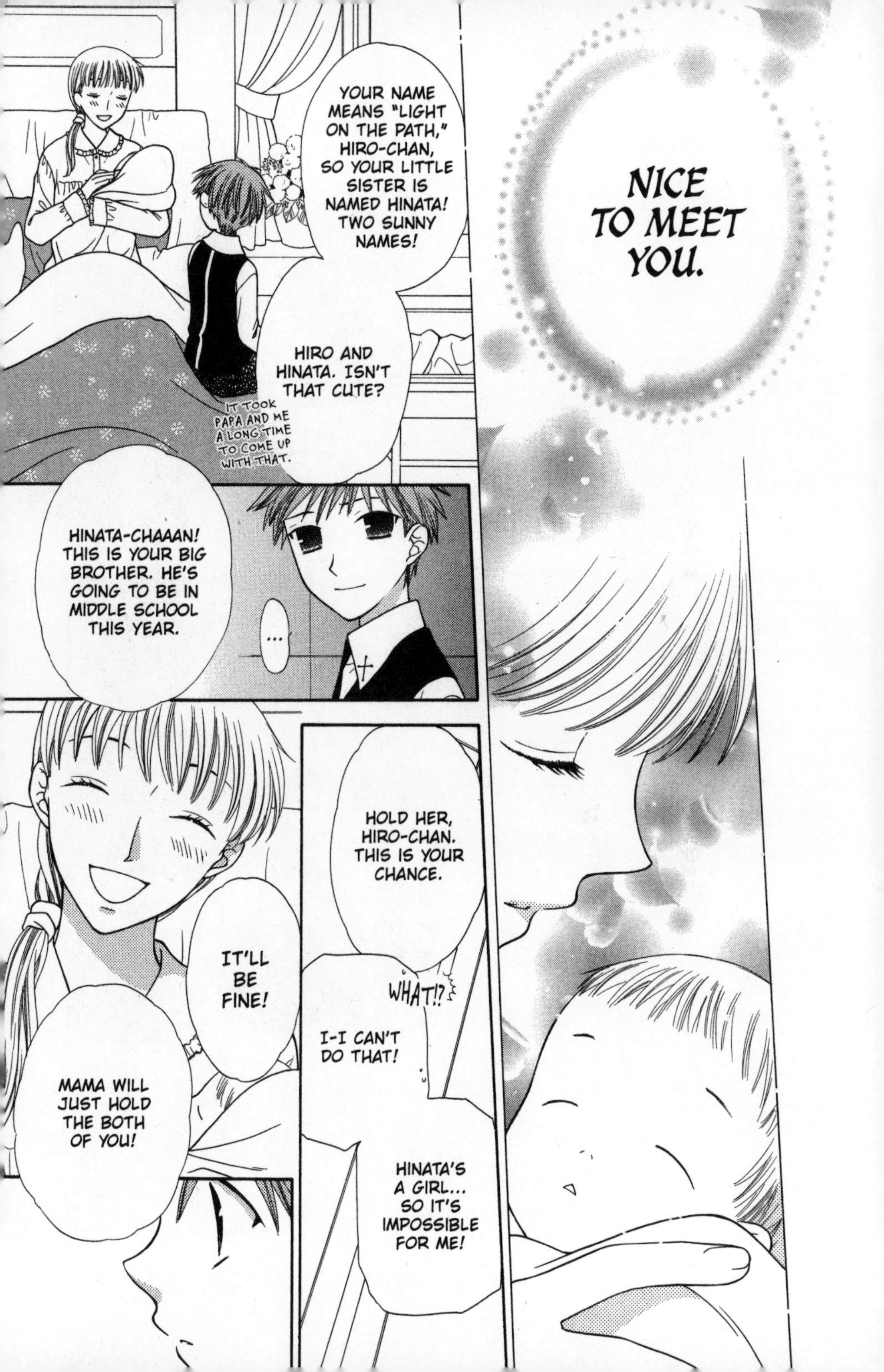
NICE TO MEET YOU.
YOUR NAME MEANS "LIGHT ON THE PATH," HIRO-CHAN, SO YOUR LITTLE SISTER IS NAMED HINATA! TWO SUNNY NAMES!
HIRO AND HINATA. ISN'T THAT CUTE?
IT TOOK PAPA AND ME A LONG TIME TO COME UP WITH THAT.
HINATA-CHAAAN! THIS IS YOUR BIG BROTHER. HE'S GOING TO BE IN MIDDLE SCHOOL THIS YEAR.
...
HOLD HER, HIRO-CHAN. THIS IS YOUR CHANCE.
WHAT!?
I-I CAN'T DO THAT!
HINATA'S A GIRL... SO IT'S IMPOSSIBLE FOR ME!
IT'LL BE FINE!
MAMA WILL JUST HOLD THE BOTH OF YOU!

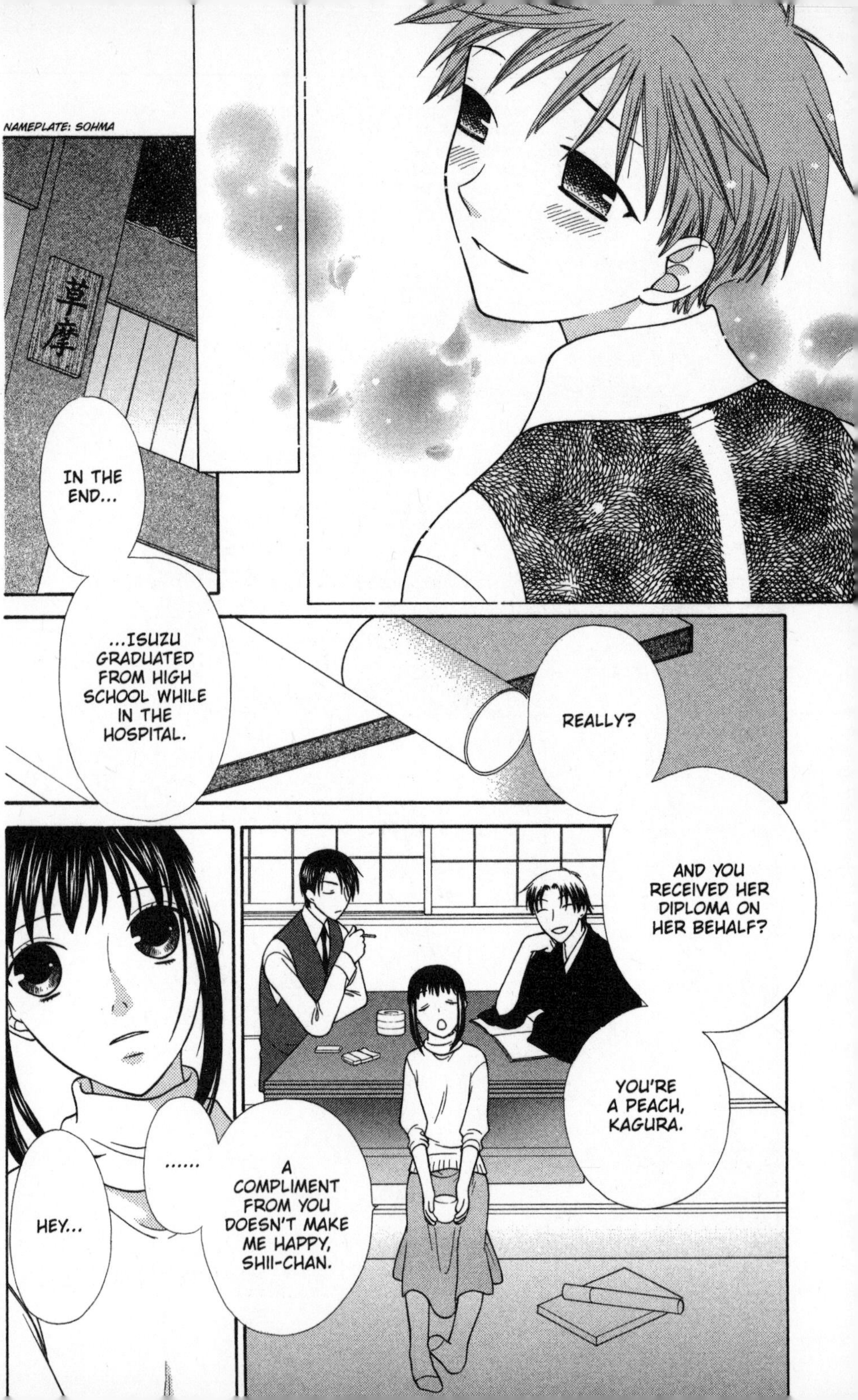
NAMEPLATE: SOHMA
IN THE END...
...ISUZU GRADUATED FROM HIGH SCHOOL WHILE IN THE HOSPITAL.
REALLY?
AND YOU RECEIVED HER DIPLOMA ON HER BEHALF?
YOU'RE A PEACH, KAGURA.
A COMPLIMENT FROM YOU DOESN'T MAKE ME HAPPY, SHII-CHAN.
......
HEY...

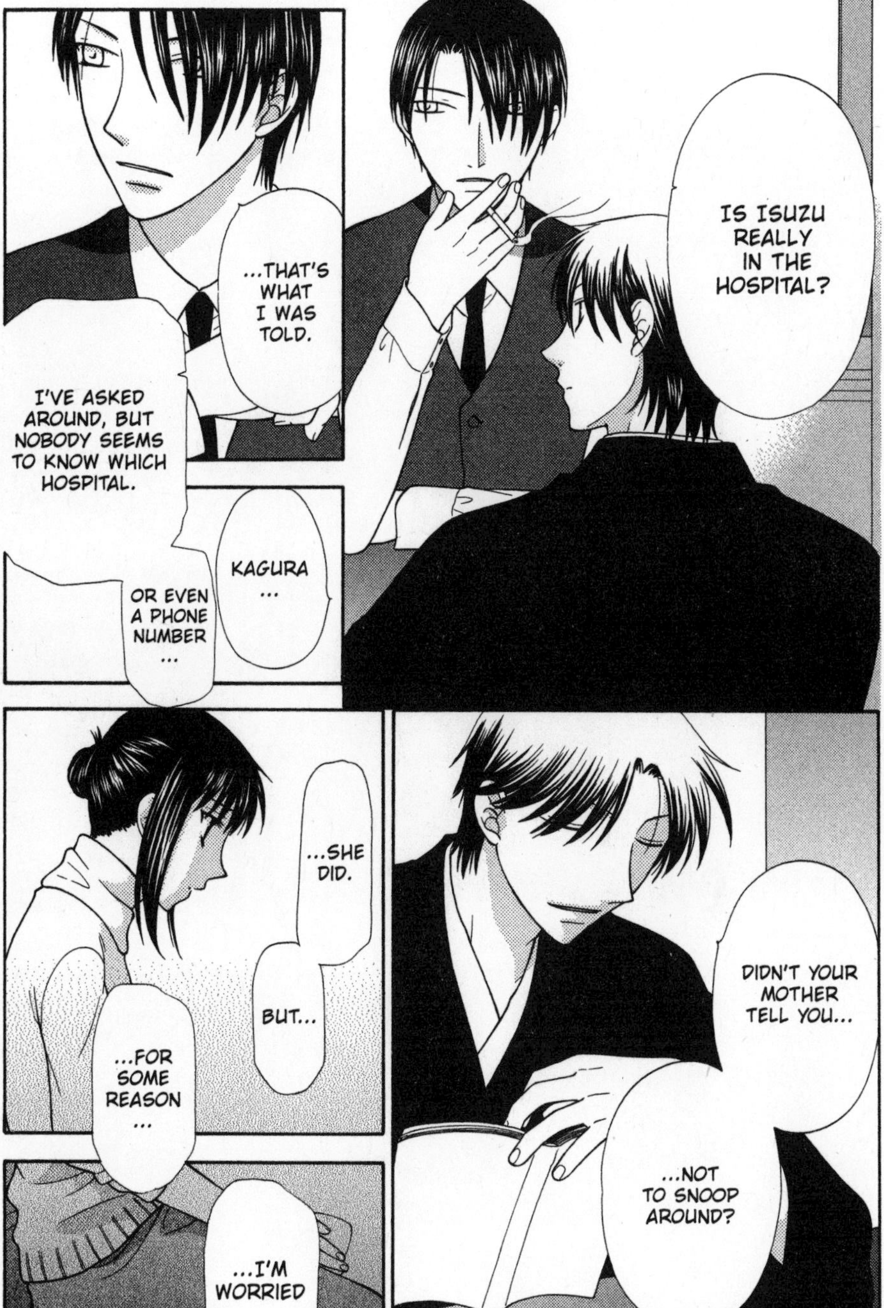

IS ISUZU REALLY IN THE HOSPITAL?
...THAT'S WHAT I WAS TOLD.
I'VE ASKED AROUND, BUT NOBODY SEEMS TO KNOW WHICH HOSPITAL.
KAGURA...
OR EVEN A PHONE NUMBER...
DIDN'T YOUR MOTHER TELL YOU...
...NOT TO SNOOP AROUND?
...SHE DID.
BUT...
...FOR SOME REASON...
...I'M WORRIED...

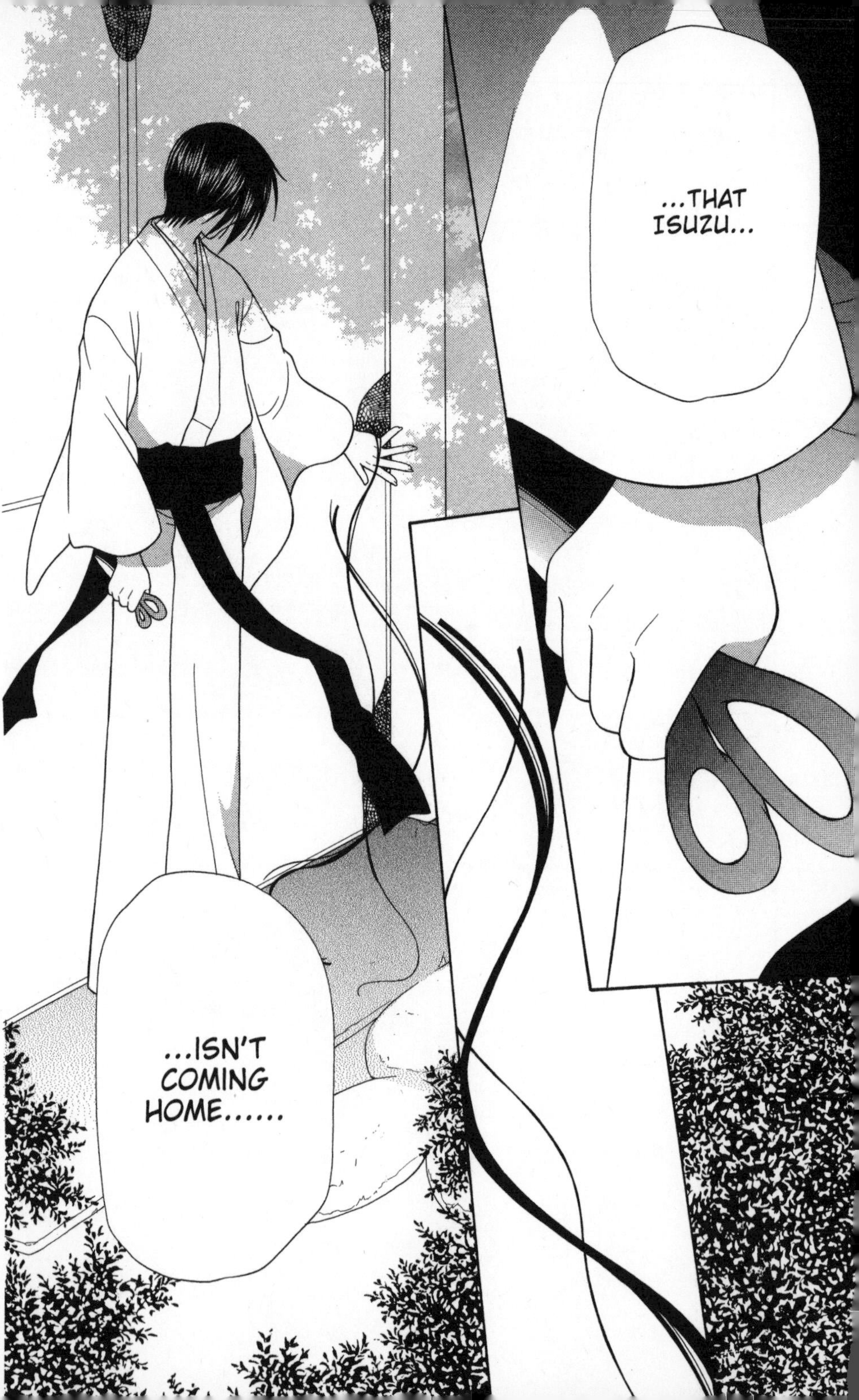
...THAT ISUZU...
...ISN'T COMING HOME......

COLLECTOR'S EDITION

Fruits Basket

COLLECTOR'S EDITION

Fruits Basket

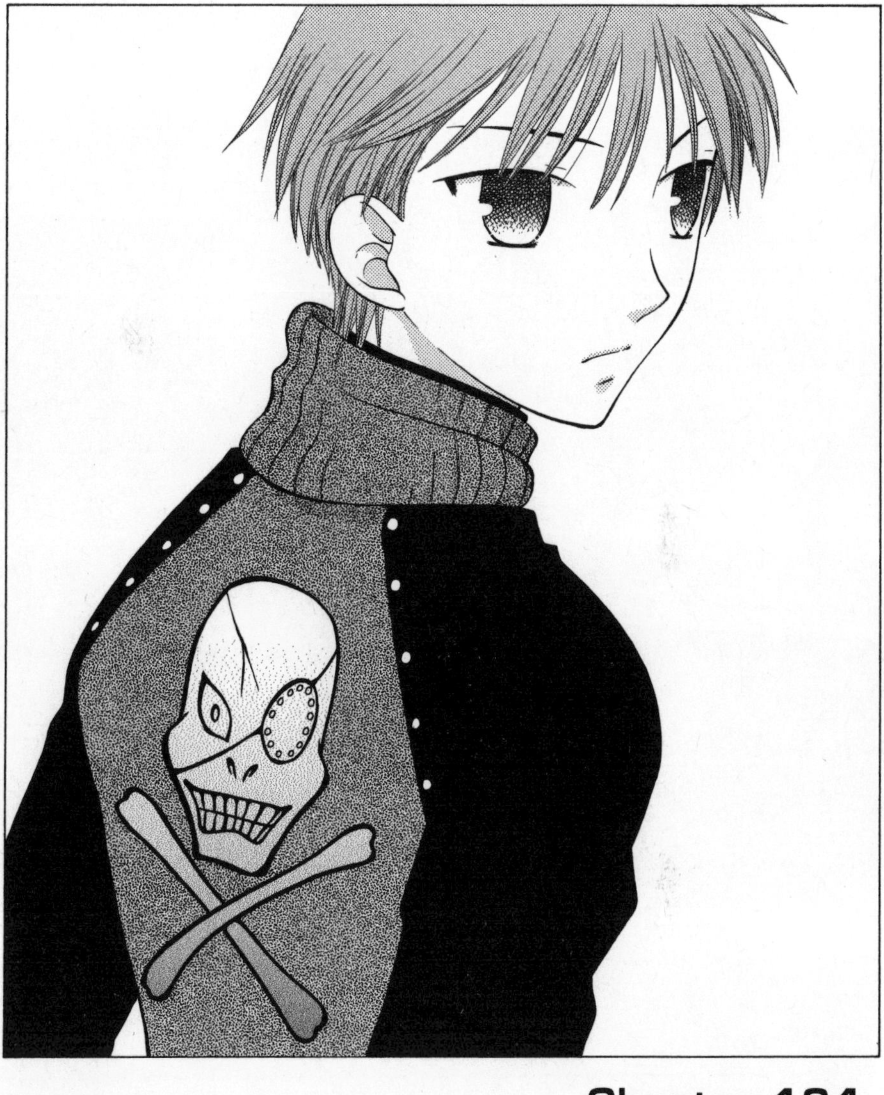

Chapter 104

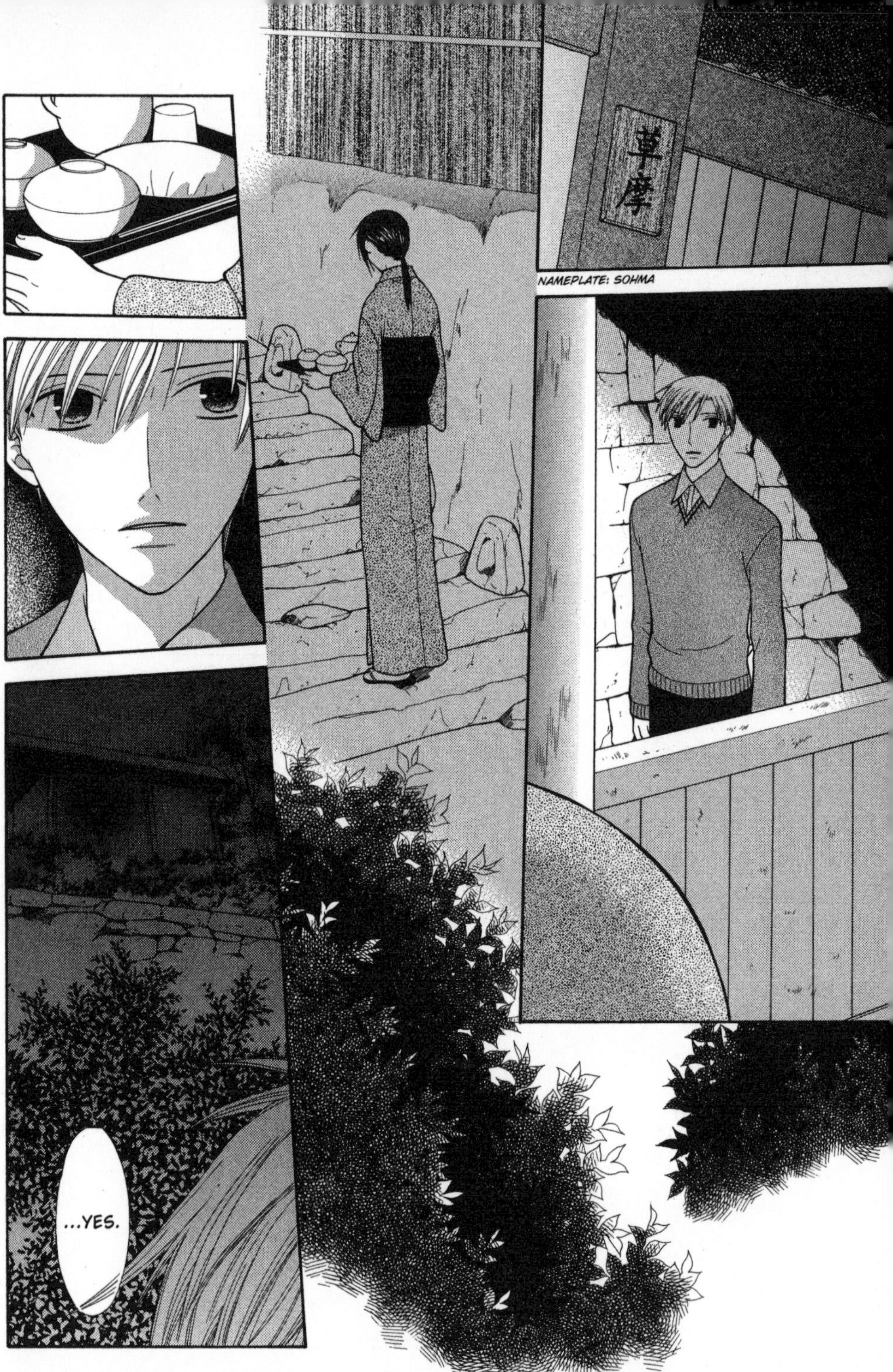
草摩
NAMEPLATE: SOHMA
...YES.

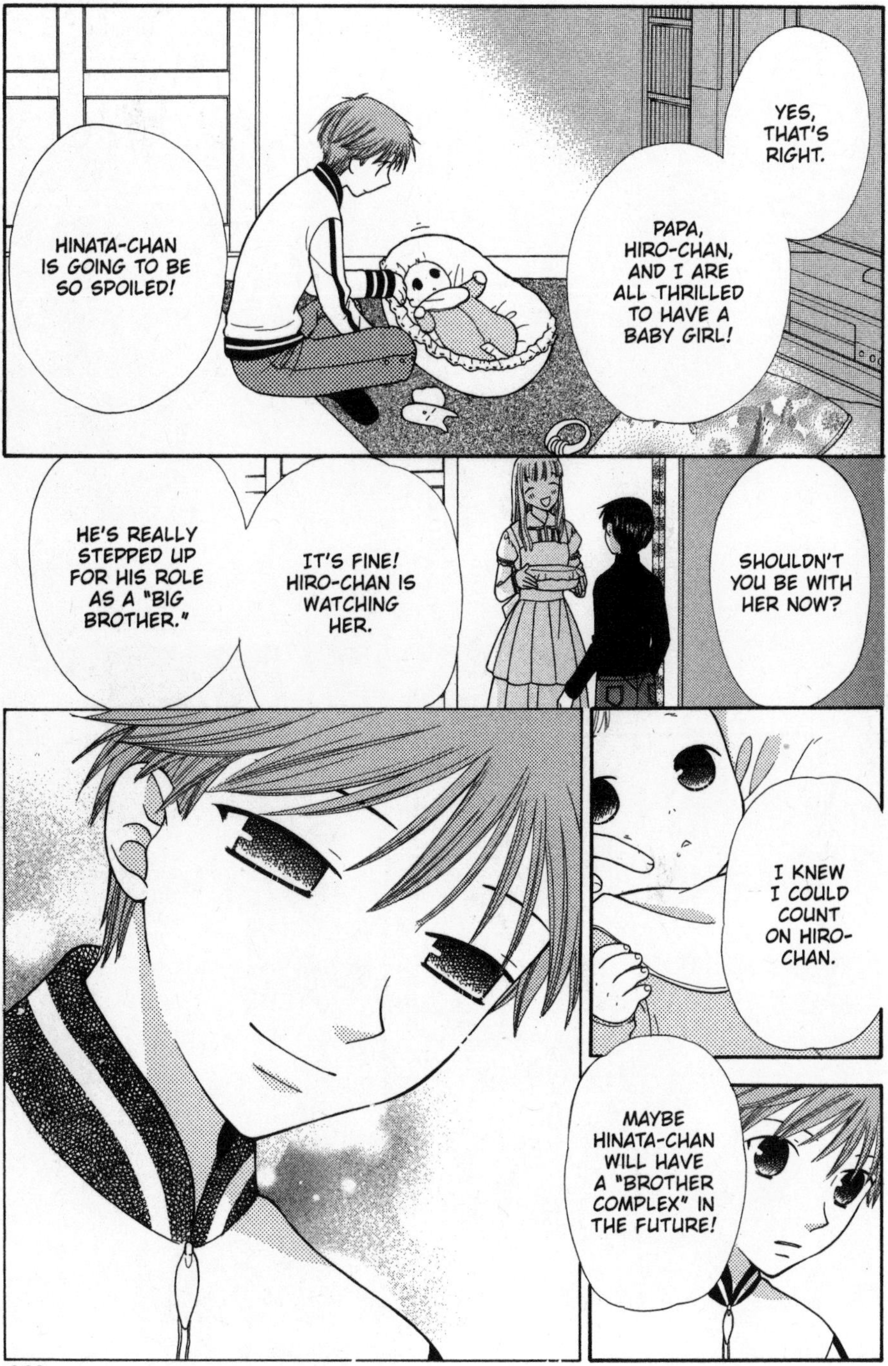
YES, THAT'S RIGHT.
PAPA, HIRO-CHAN, AND I ARE ALL THRILLED TO HAVE A BABY GIRL!
HINATA-CHAN IS GOING TO BE SO SPOILED!
SHOULDN'T YOU BE WITH HER NOW?
IT'S FINE! HIRO-CHAN IS WATCHING HER.
HE'S REALLY STEPPED UP FOR HIS ROLE AS A "BIG BROTHER."
I KNEW I COULD COUNT ON HIRO-CHAN.
MAYBE HINATA-CHAN WILL HAVE A "BROTHER COMPLEX" IN THE FUTURE!

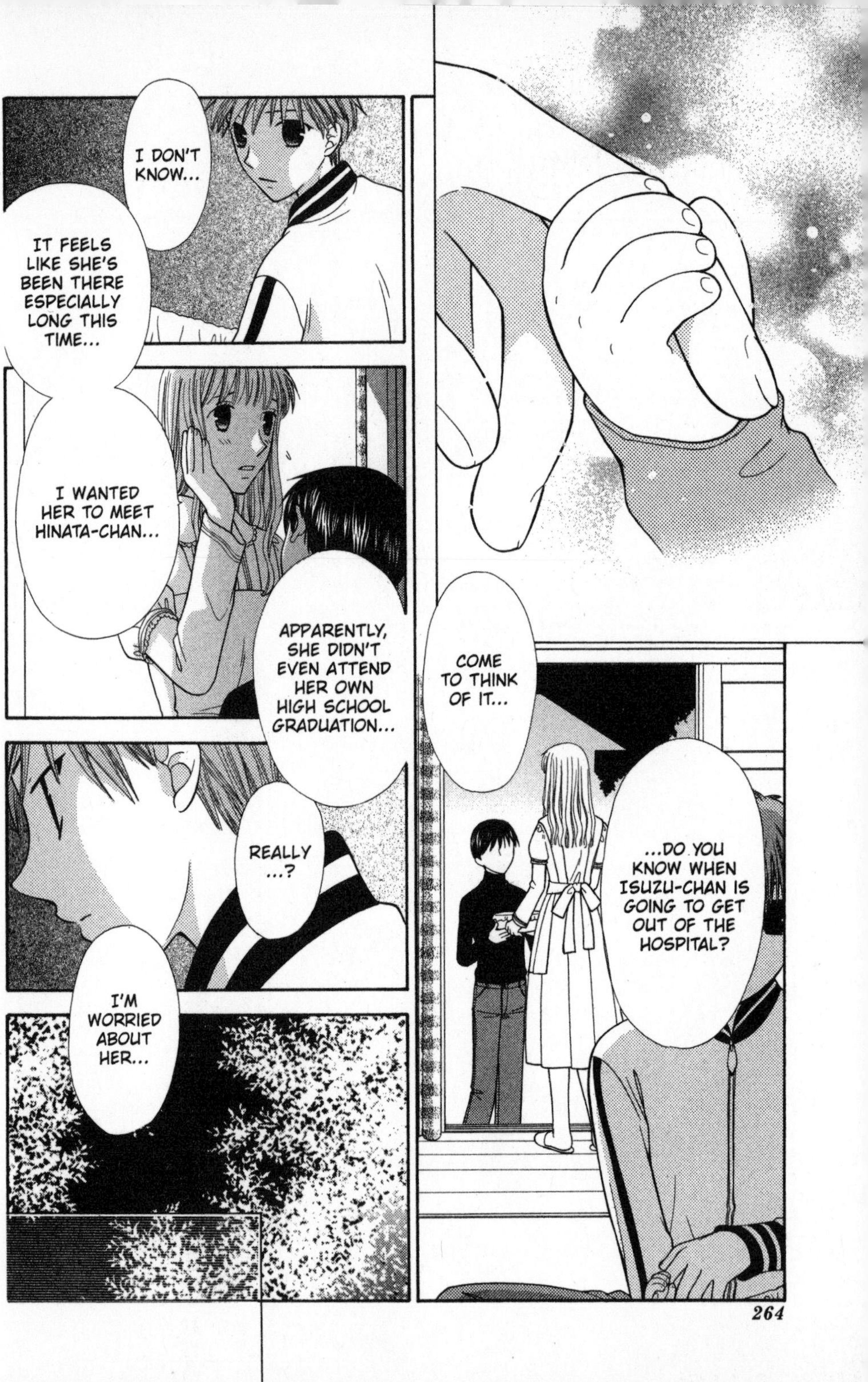
COME TO THINK OF IT...
...DO YOU KNOW WHEN ISUZU-CHAN IS GOING TO GET OUT OF THE HOSPITAL?
I DON'T KNOW...
IT FEELS LIKE SHE'S BEEN THERE ESPECIALLY LONG THIS TIME...
I WANTED HER TO MEET HINATA-CHAN...
APPARENTLY, SHE DIDN'T EVEN ATTEND HER OWN HIGH SCHOOL GRADUATION...
REALLY ...?
I'M WORRIED ABOUT HER...

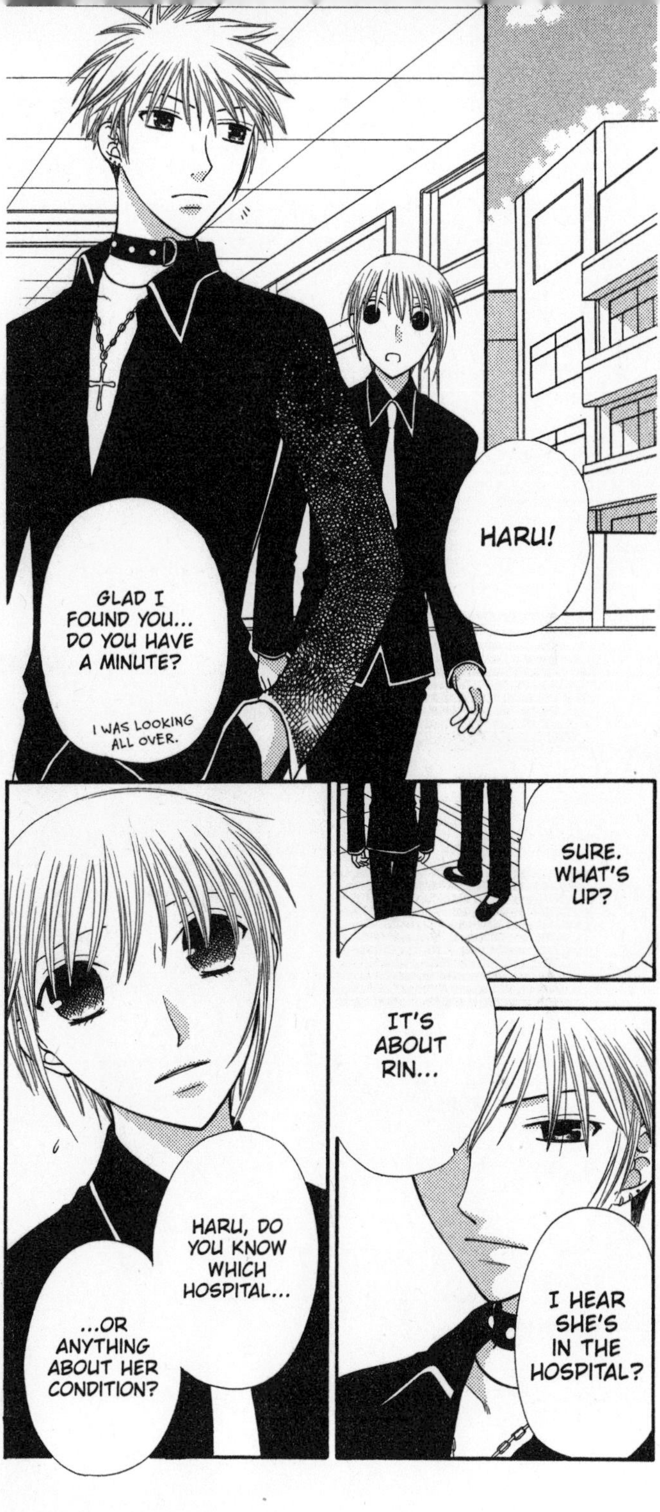
HARU!
GLAD I FOUND YOU... DO YOU HAVE A MINUTE?
I WAS LOOKING ALL OVER.
SURE. WHAT'S UP?
IT'S ABOUT RIN...
I HEAR SHE'S IN THE HOSPITAL?
HARU, DO YOU KNOW WHICH HOSPITAL...
...OR ANYTHING ABOUT HER CONDITION?

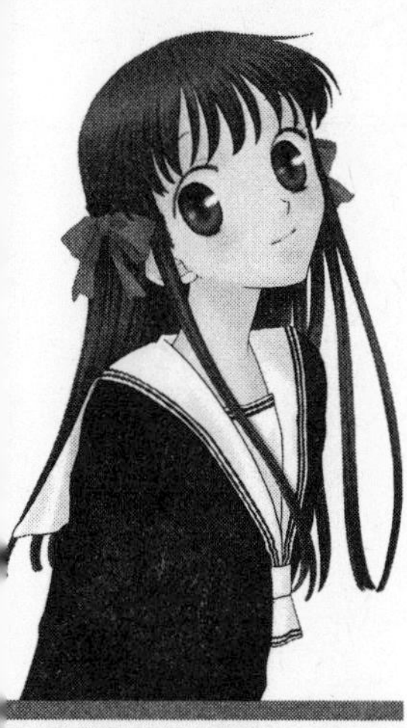

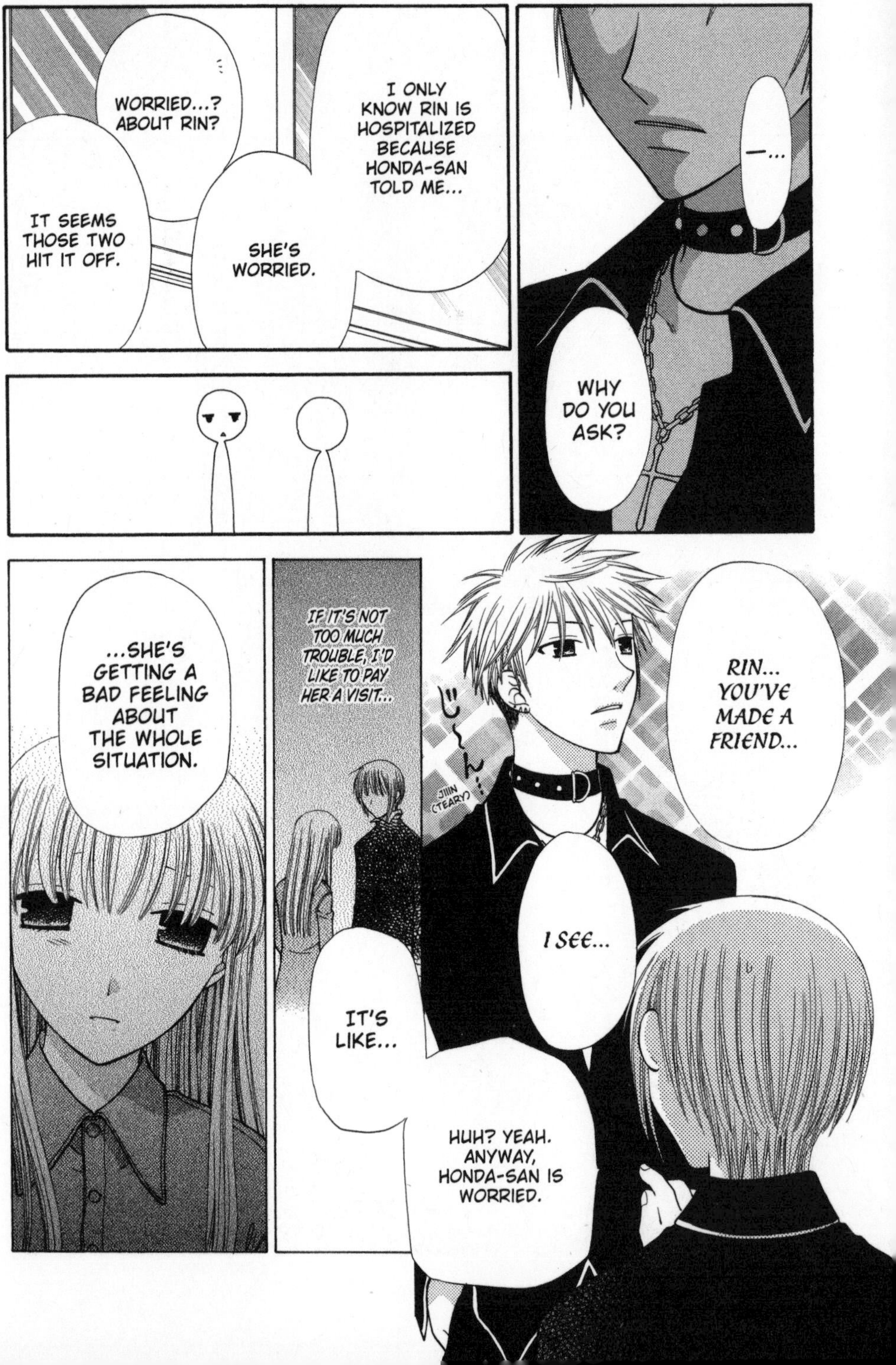
—...
WHY DO YOU ASK?
I ONLY KNOW RIN IS HOSPITALIZED BECAUSE HONDA-SAN TOLD ME...
WORRIED...? ABOUT RIN?
SHE'S WORRIED.
IT SEEMS THOSE TWO HIT IT OFF.
RIN... YOU'VE MADE A FRIEND...
JIIIN (TEARY)
I SEE...
IT'S LIKE...
HUH? YEAH. ANYWAY, HONDA-SAN IS WORRIED.
IF IT'S NOT TOO MUCH TROUBLE, I'D LIKE TO PAY HER A VISIT...
...SHE'S GETTING A BAD FEELING ABOUT THE WHOLE SITUATION.

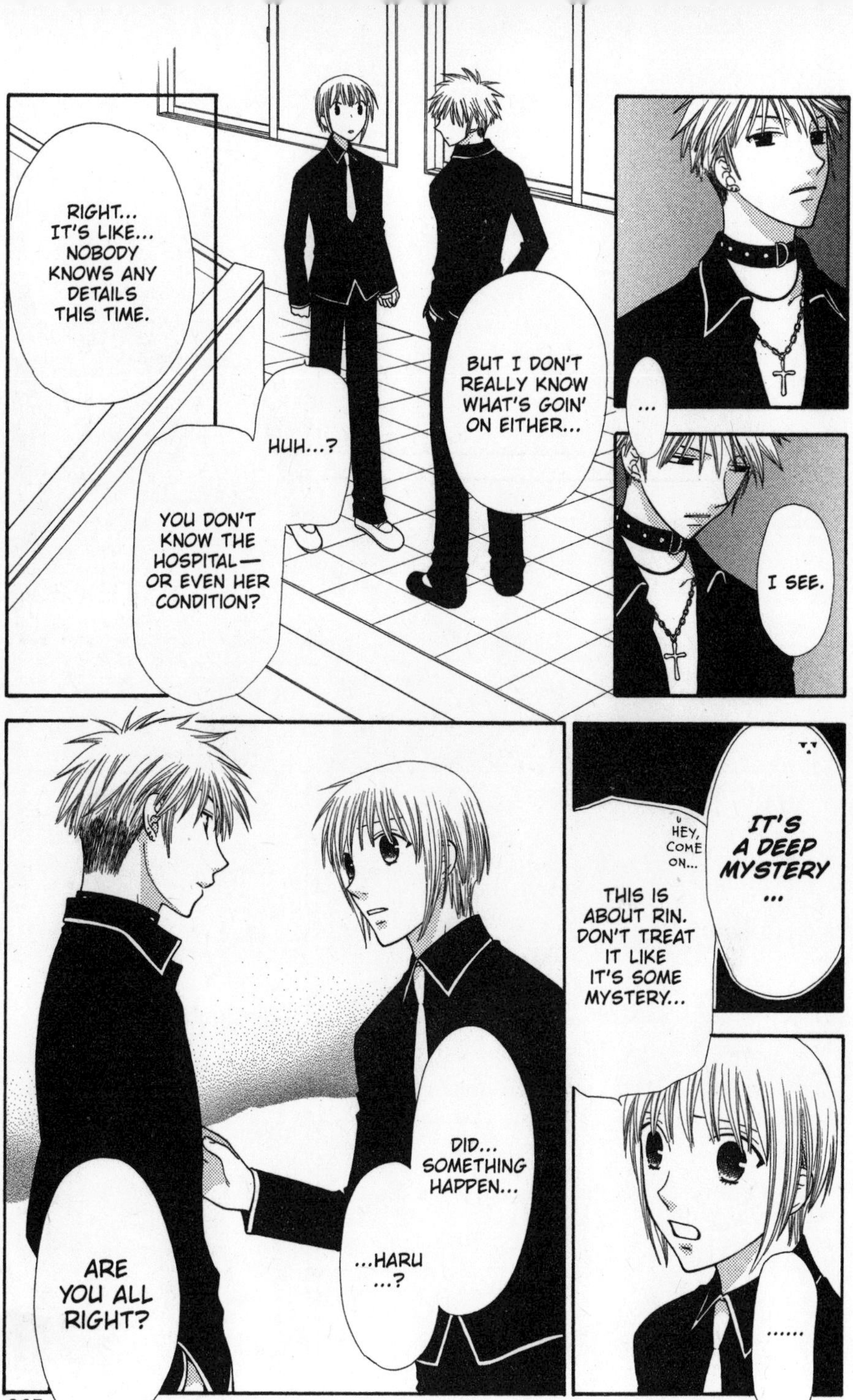
...
I SEE.
RIGHT... IT'S LIKE... NOBODY KNOWS ANY DETAILS THIS TIME.
BUT I DON'T REALLY KNOW WHAT'S GOIN' ON EITHER...
HUH...?
YOU DON'T KNOW THE HOSPITAL— OR EVEN HER CONDITION?
IT'S A DEEP MYSTERY ...
HEY, COME ON...
THIS IS ABOUT RIN. DON'T TREAT IT LIKE IT'S SOME MYSTERY...
......
DID... SOMETHING HAPPEN...
...HARU ...?
ARE YOU ALL RIGHT?

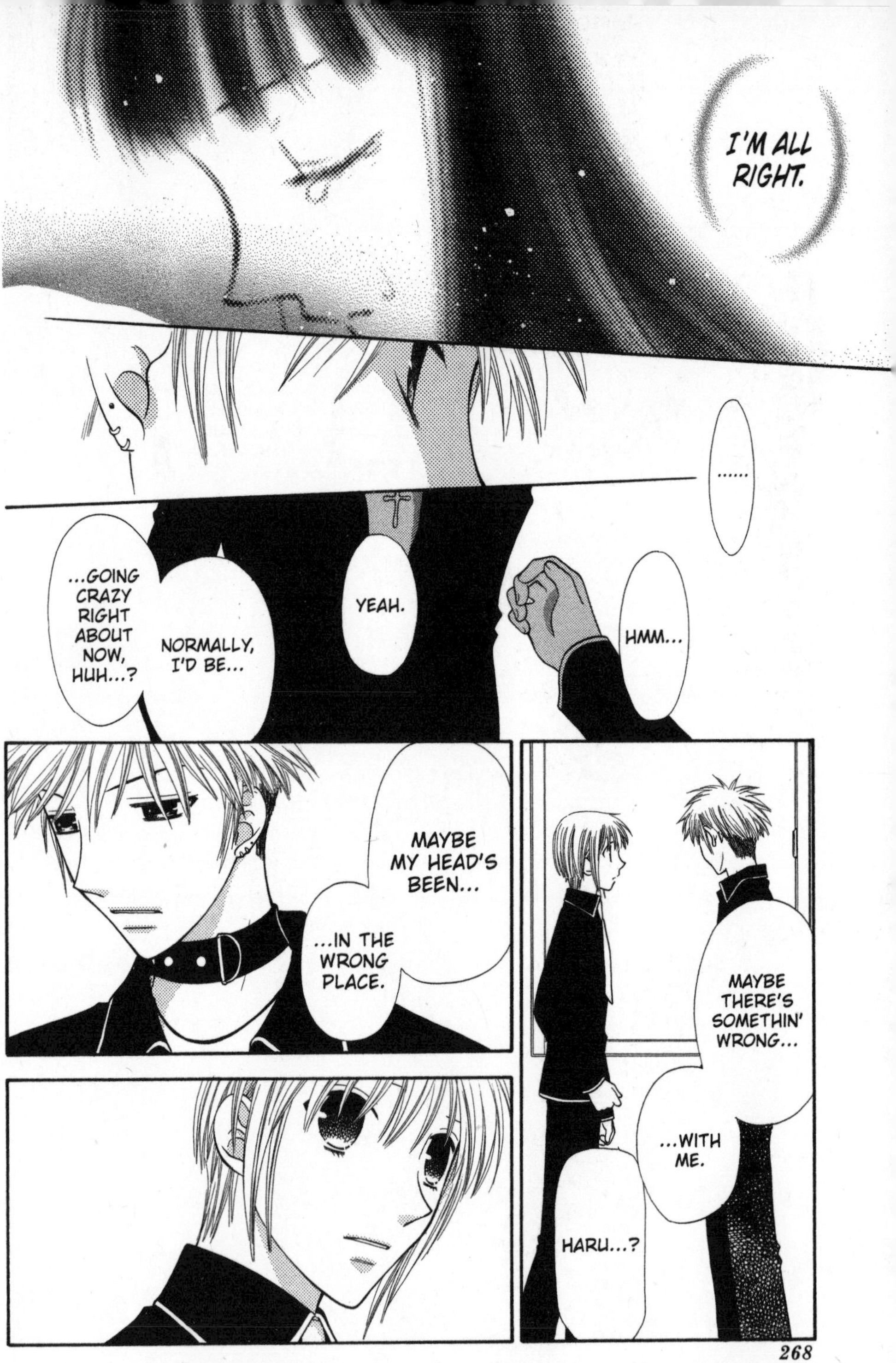
I'M ALL RIGHT.
......
HMM...
YEAH.
NORMALLY, I'D BE...
...GOING CRAZY RIGHT ABOUT NOW, HUH...?
MAYBE THERE'S SOMETHIN' WRONG...
...WITH ME.
HARU...?
MAYBE MY HEAD'S BEEN...
...IN THE WRONG PLACE.

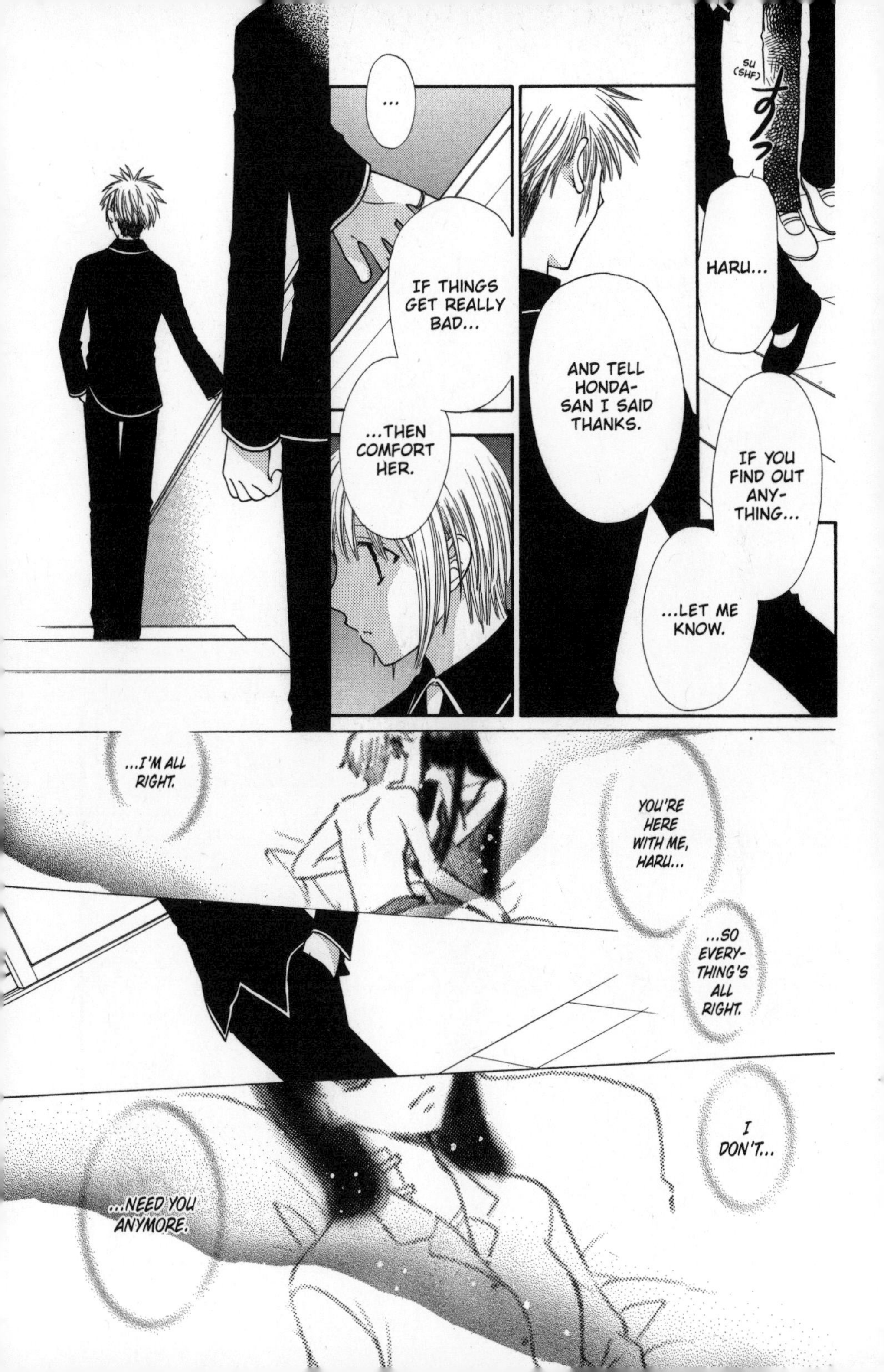
SU (SHF)
すっ
HARU...
IF YOU FIND OUT ANYTHING...
...LET ME KNOW.
AND TELL HONDA-SAN I SAID THANKS.
...
IF THINGS GET REALLY BAD...
...THEN COMFORT HER.
...I'M ALL RIGHT.
YOU'RE HERE WITH ME, HARU...
...SO EVERYTHING'S ALL RIGHT.
I DON'T...
...NEED YOU ANYMORE.

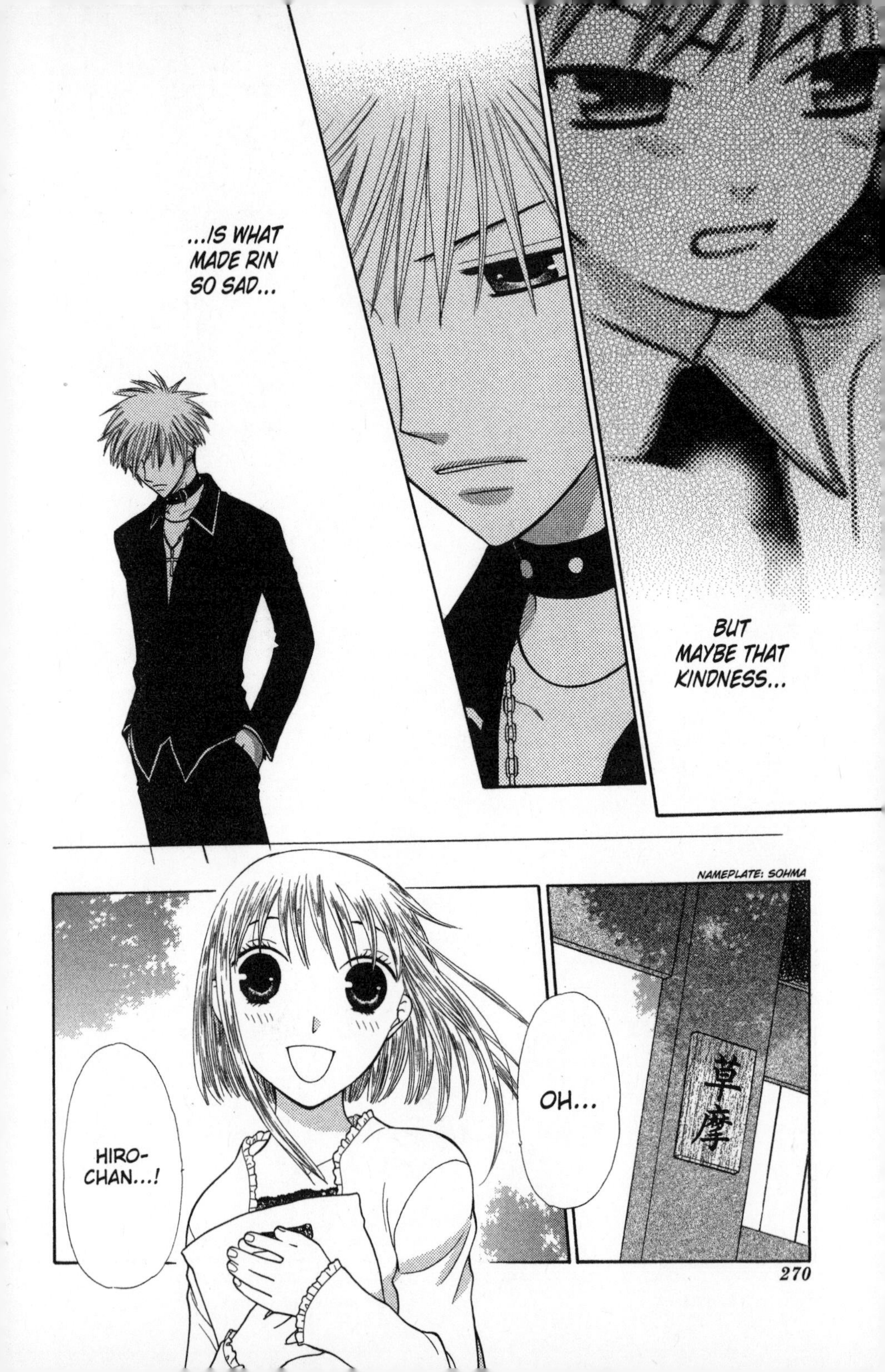
BUT MAYBE THAT KINDNESS...
...IS WHAT MADE RIN SO SAD...
NAMEPLATE: SOHMA
草摩
OH...
HIRO-CHAN...!

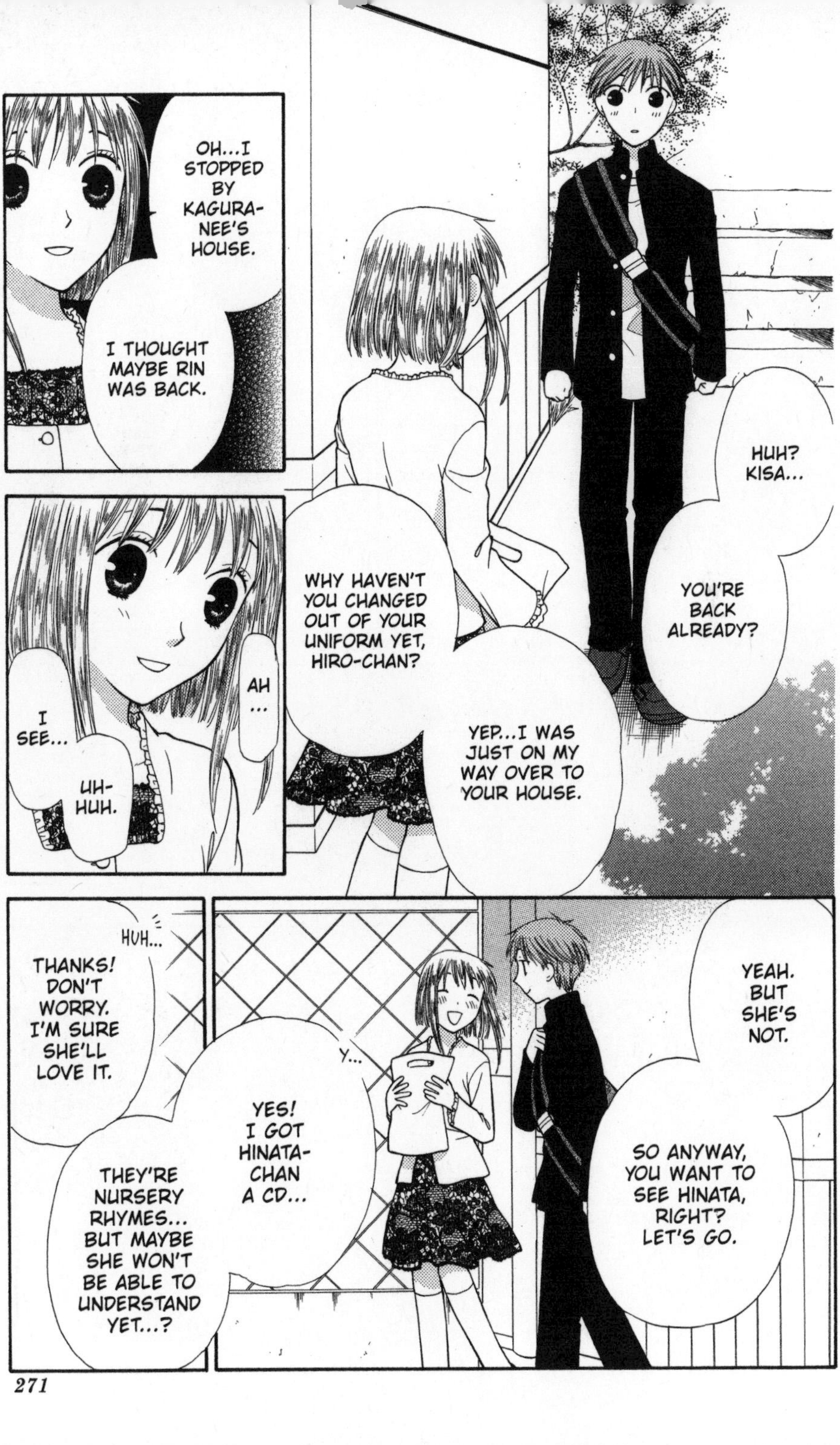
HUH? KISA...
YOU'RE BACK ALREADY?
WHY HAVEN'T YOU CHANGED OUT OF YOUR UNIFORM YET, HIRO-CHAN?
YEP...I WAS JUST ON MY WAY OVER TO YOUR HOUSE.
OH...I STOPPED BY KAGURA-NEE'S HOUSE.
I THOUGHT MAYBE RIN WAS BACK.
AH...
I SEE...
UH-HUH.
YEAH. BUT SHE'S NOT.
SO ANYWAY, YOU WANT TO SEE HINATA, RIGHT? LET'S GO.
Y...
YES! I GOT HINATA-CHAN A CD...
THEY'RE NURSERY RHYMES... BUT MAYBE SHE WON'T BE ABLE TO UNDERSTAND YET...?
HUH...
THANKS! DON'T WORRY. I'M SURE SHE'LL LOVE IT.

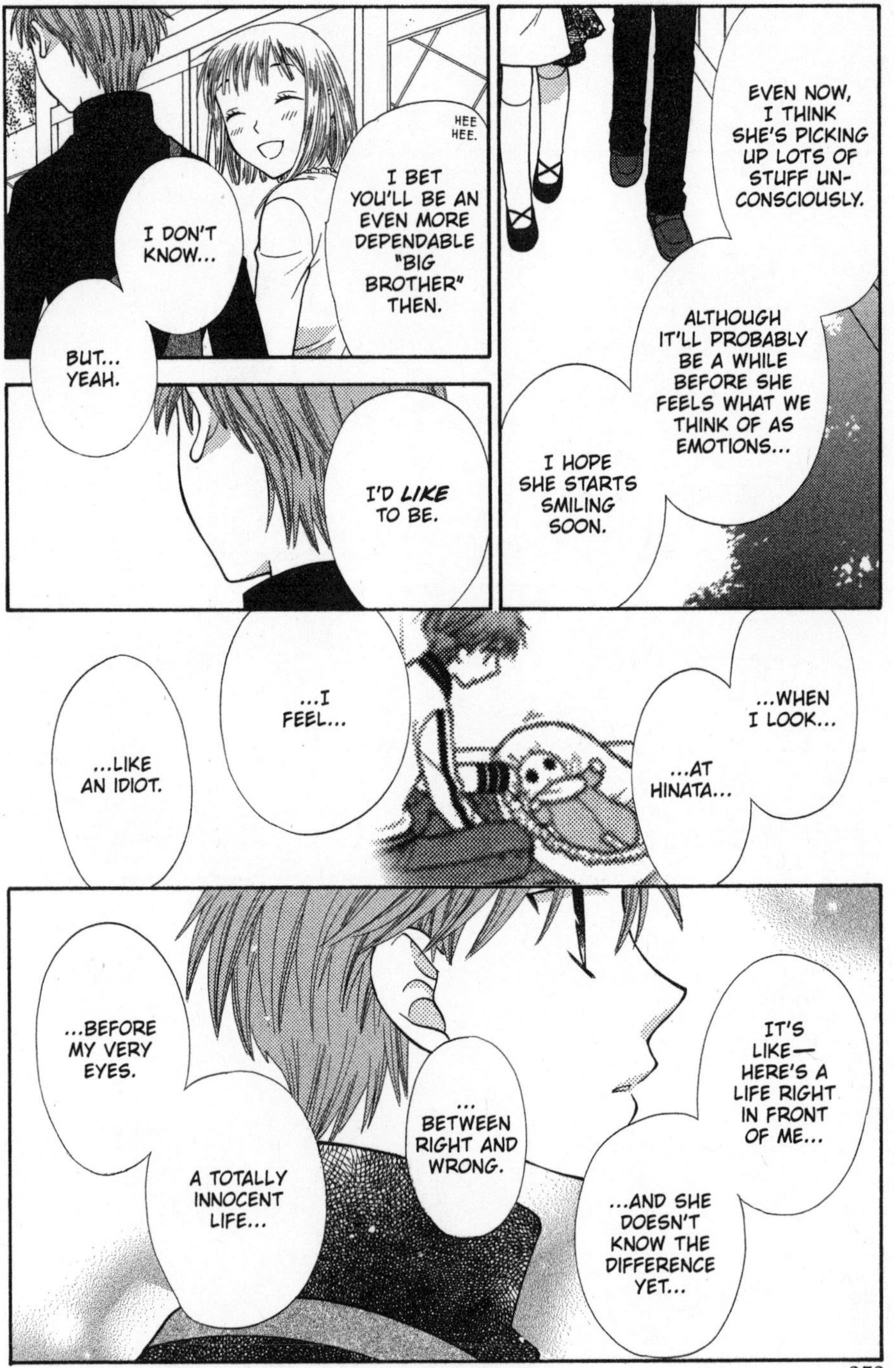
EVEN NOW, I THINK SHE'S PICKING UP LOTS OF STUFF UN-CONSCIOUSLY.
ALTHOUGH IT'LL PROBABLY BE A WHILE BEFORE SHE FEELS WHAT WE THINK OF AS EMOTIONS...
I HOPE SHE STARTS SMILING SOON.
HEE HEE.
I BET YOU'LL BE AN EVEN MORE DEPENDABLE "BIG BROTHER" THEN.
I DON'T KNOW...
BUT... YEAH.
I'D *LIKE* TO BE.
...WHEN I LOOK...
...AT HINATA...
...I FEEL...
...LIKE AN IDIOT.
IT'S LIKE— HERE'S A LIFE RIGHT IN FRONT OF ME...
...AND SHE DOESN'T KNOW THE DIFFERENCE YET...
... BETWEEN RIGHT AND WRONG.
A TOTALLY INNOCENT LIFE...
...BEFORE MY VERY EYES.

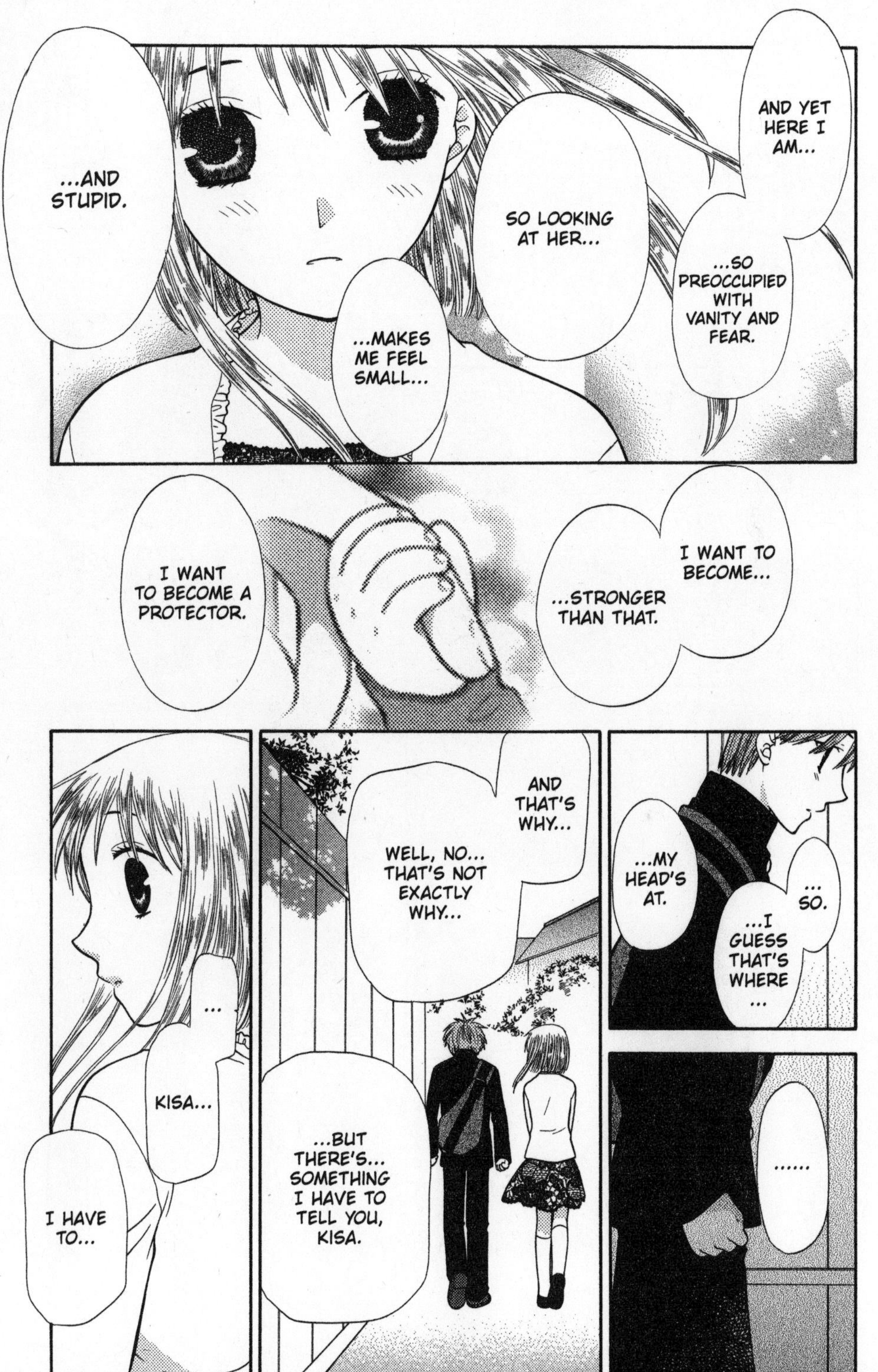
AND YET HERE I AM...
...SO PREOCCUPIED WITH VANITY AND FEAR.
SO LOOKING AT HER...
...MAKES ME FEEL SMALL...
...AND STUPID.
I WANT TO BECOME...
...STRONGER THAN THAT.
I WANT TO BECOME A PROTECTOR.
... SO.
...I GUESS THAT'S WHERE ...
...MY HEAD'S AT.
......
AND THAT'S WHY...
WELL, NO... THAT'S NOT EXACTLY WHY...
...BUT THERE'S... SOMETHING I HAVE TO TELL YOU, KISA.
...
KISA...
I HAVE TO...

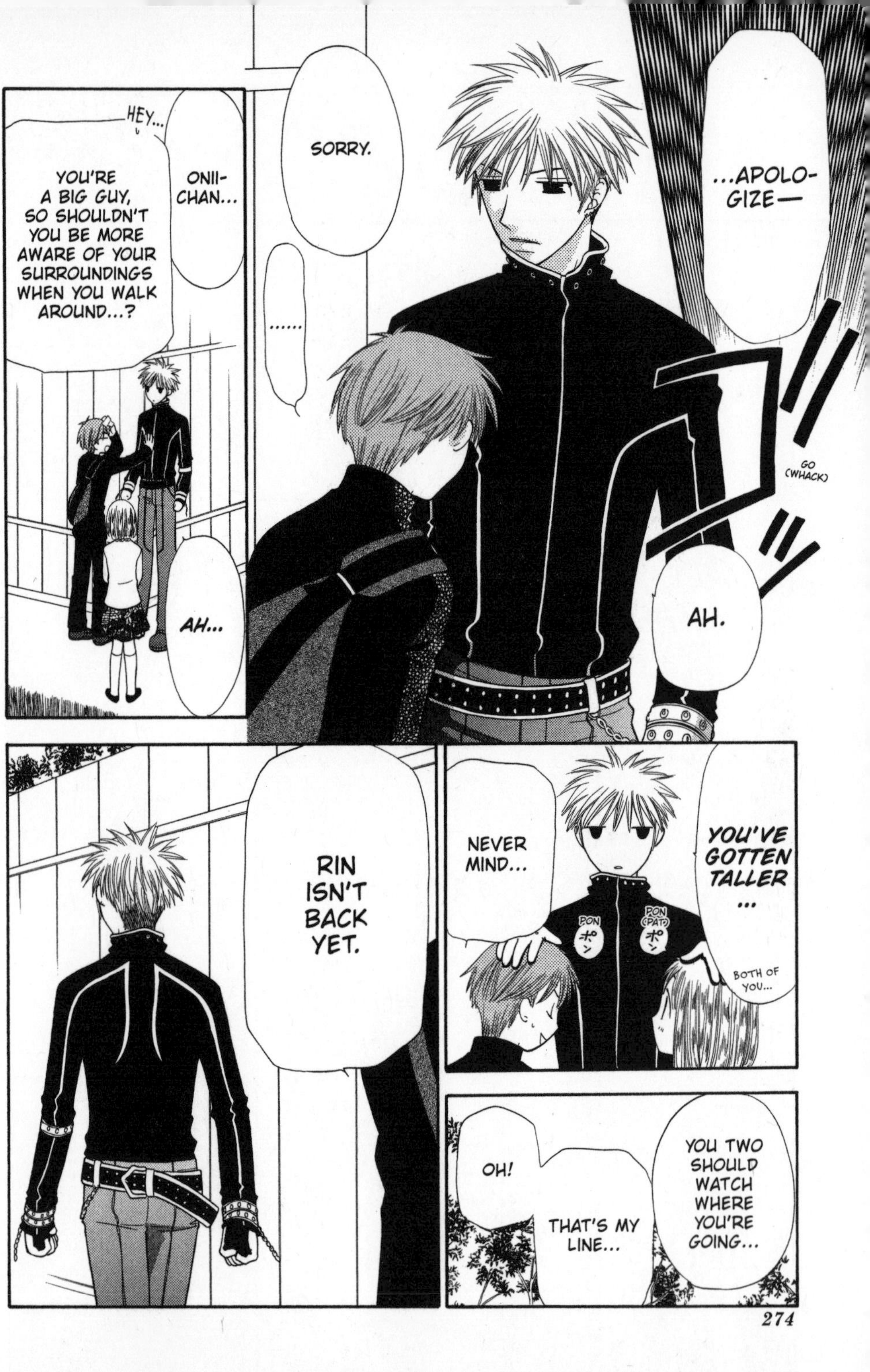
...APOLO-GIZE—
GO (WHACK)
AH.
SORRY.
......
ONII-CHAN...
HEY...
YOU'RE A BIG GUY, SO SHOULDN'T YOU BE MORE AWARE OF YOUR SURROUNDINGS WHEN YOU WALK AROUND...?
AH...
YOU'VE GOTTEN TALLER ...
PON (PAT)
PON
BOTH OF YOU...
NEVER MIND...
YOU TWO SHOULD WATCH WHERE YOU'RE GOING...
OH!
THAT'S MY LINE...
RIN ISN'T BACK YET.

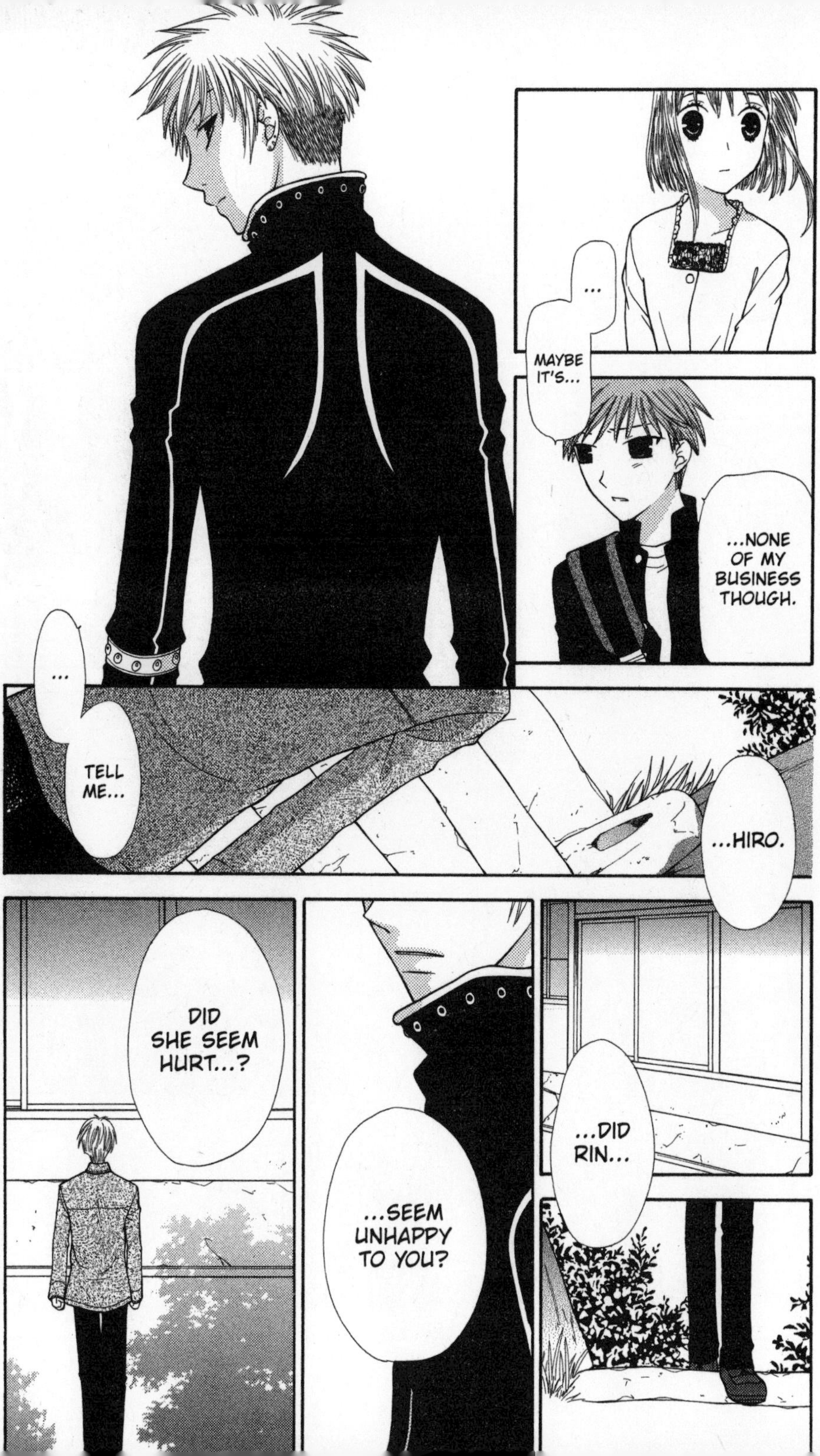
...
MAYBE IT'S...
...NONE OF MY BUSINESS THOUGH.
...
TELL ME...
...HIRO.
...DID RIN...
...SEEM UNHAPPY TO YOU?
DID SHE SEEM HURT...?

ARE YOU TALKING ABOUT WHAT I SAID BACK THEN!?

F-FORGET THAT...

THAT WAS JUST...

...ME TAKING MY OWN GUILT OUT ON YOU.

HUH...?

......
WAIT.

...I DO KNOW...

...THAT SHE WAS SUFFERING.

...

...BUT...

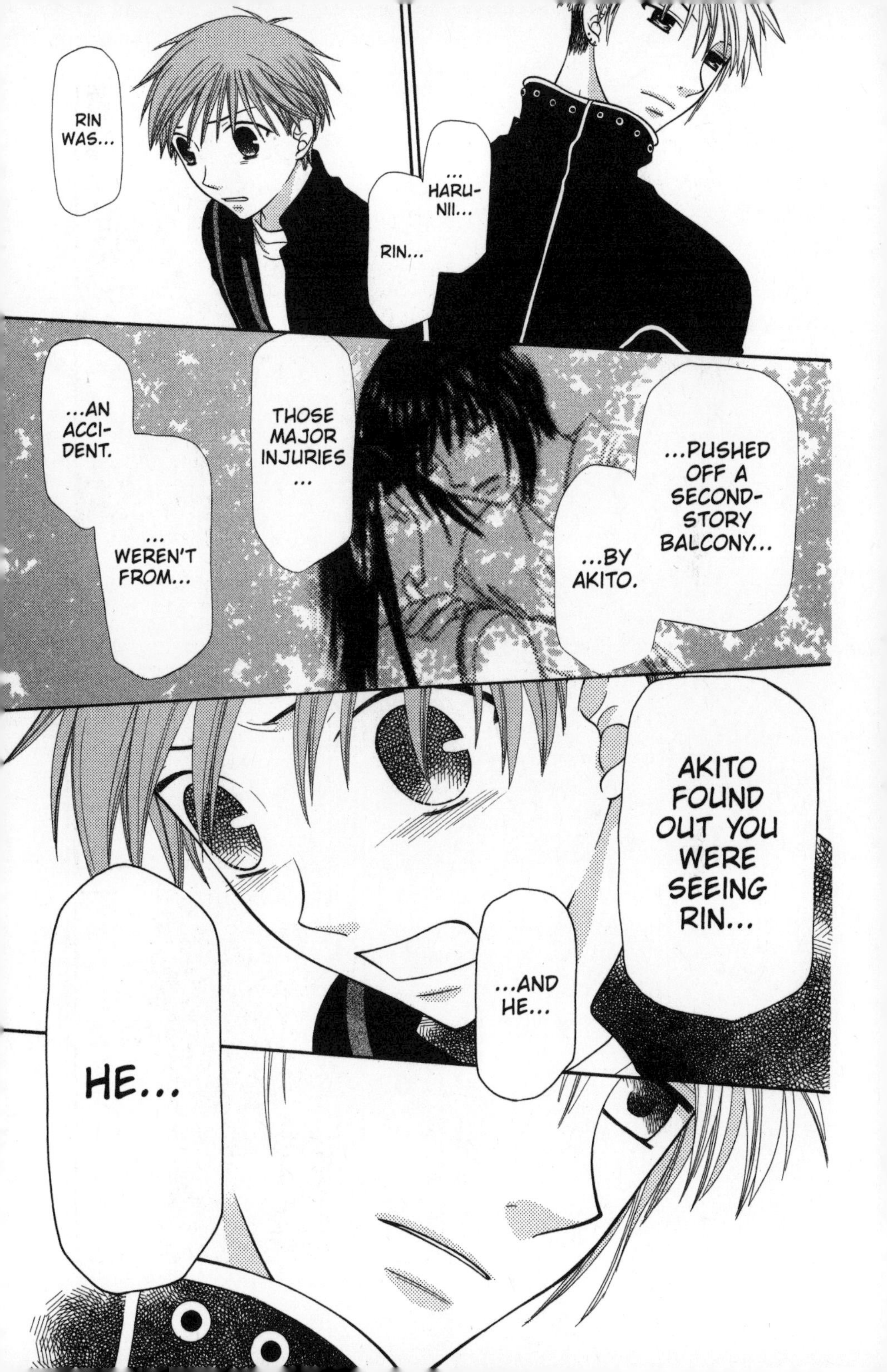

... HARU-NII...
RIN...
RIN WAS...
...PUSHED OFF A SECOND-STORY BALCONY...
...BY AKITO.
THOSE MAJOR INJURIES ...
... WEREN'T FROM...
...AN ACCI-DENT.
AKITO FOUND OUT YOU WERE SEEING RIN...
...AND HE...
HE...

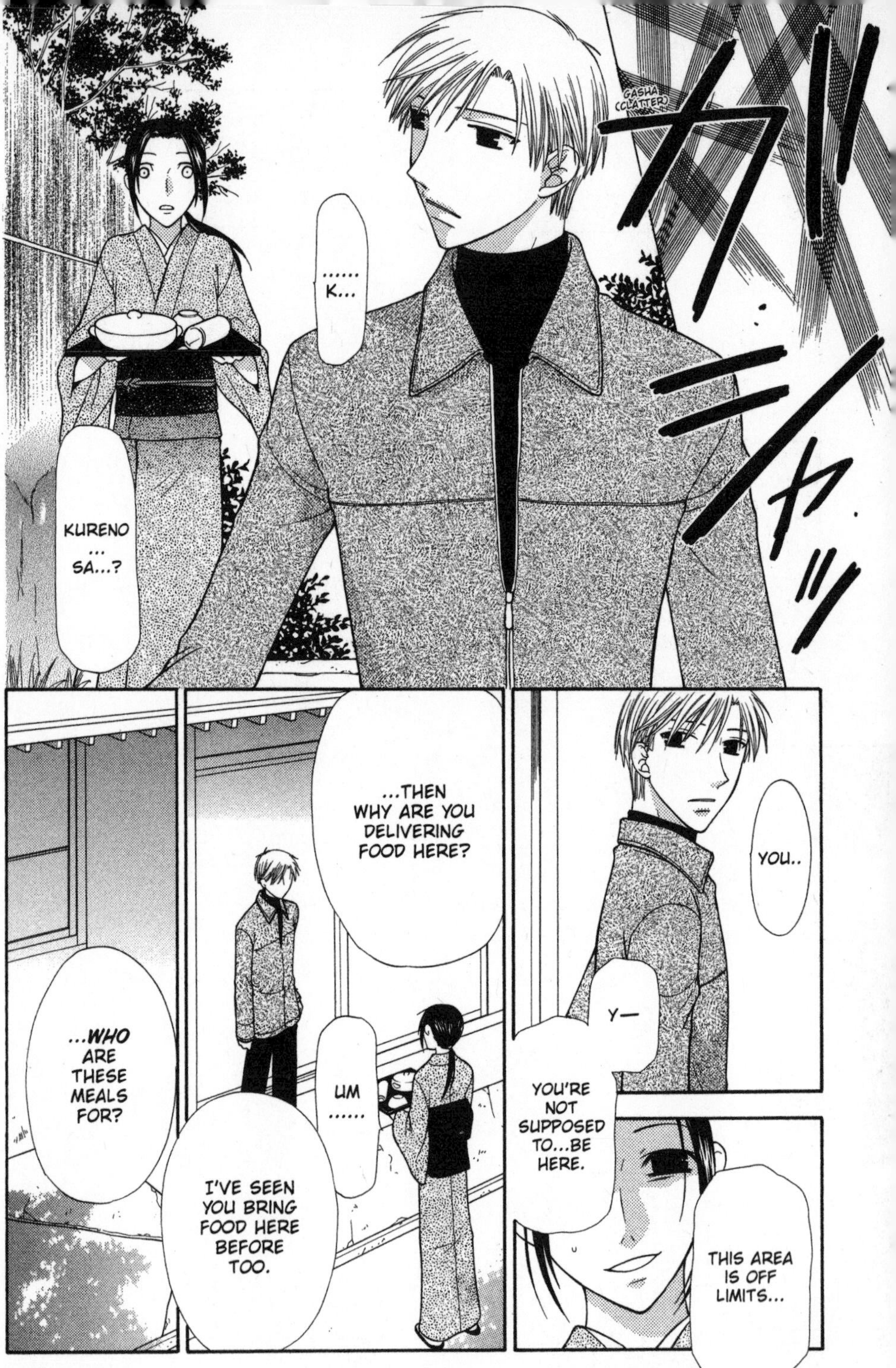
ガシャッ
GASHA (CLATTER)
......K...
KURENO ... SA...?
YOU..
Y—
YOU'RE NOT SUPPOSED TO...BE HERE.
THIS AREA IS OFF LIMITS...
...THEN WHY ARE YOU DELIVERING FOOD HERE?
UM ......
I'VE SEEN YOU BRING FOOD HERE BEFORE TOO.
...WHO ARE THESE MEALS FOR?

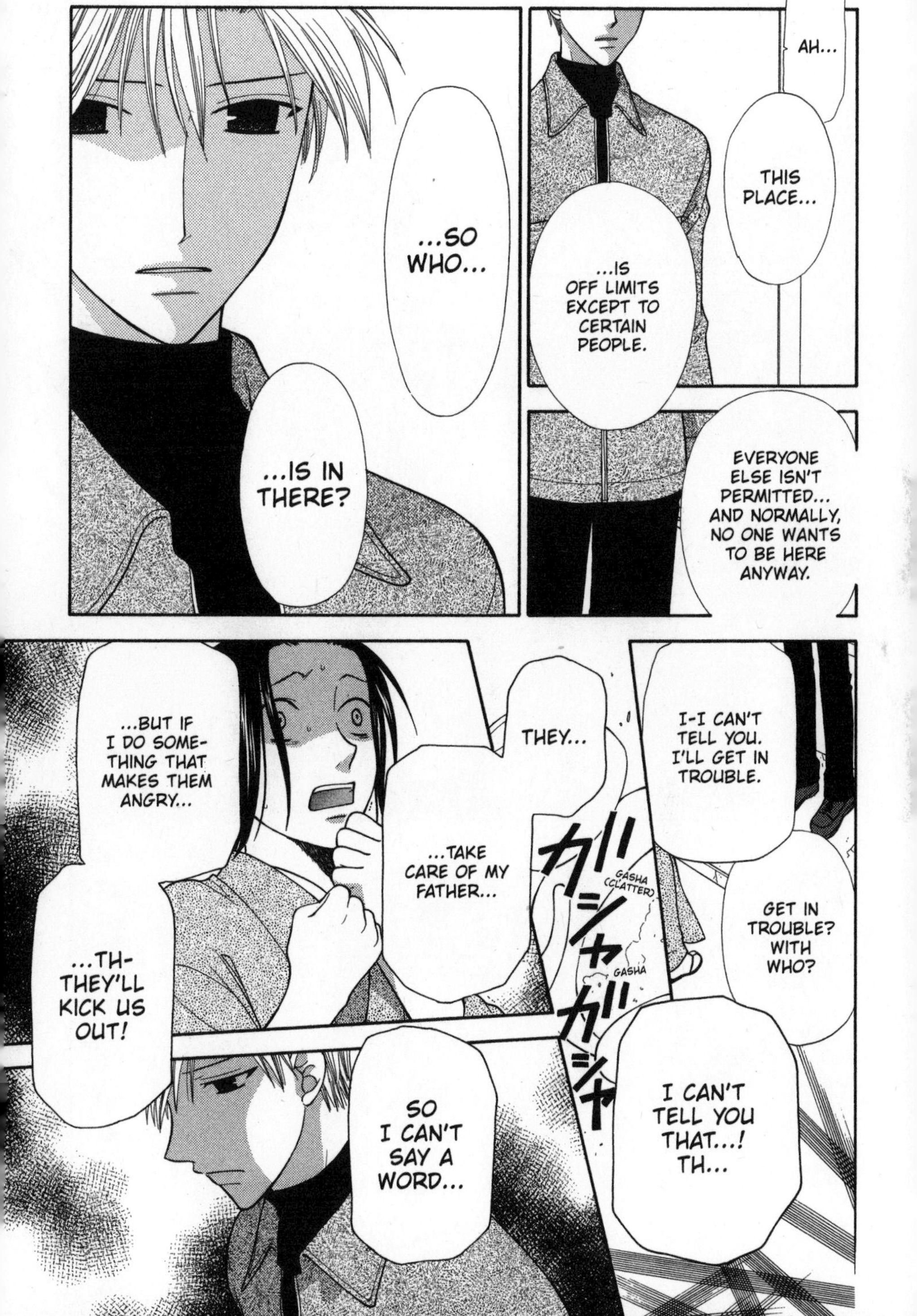
AH...
THIS PLACE...
...IS OFF LIMITS EXCEPT TO CERTAIN PEOPLE.
EVERYONE ELSE ISN'T PERMITTED... AND NORMALLY, NO ONE WANTS TO BE HERE ANYWAY.
...SO WHO...
...IS IN THERE?
I-I CAN'T TELL YOU. I'LL GET IN TROUBLE.
GET IN TROUBLE? WITH WHO?
GASHA (CLATTER)
GASHA
I CAN'T TELL YOU THAT...! TH...
THEY...
...TAKE CARE OF MY FATHER...
...BUT IF I DO SOME-THING THAT MAKES THEM ANGRY...
...TH-THEY'LL KICK US OUT!
SO I CAN'T SAY A WORD...

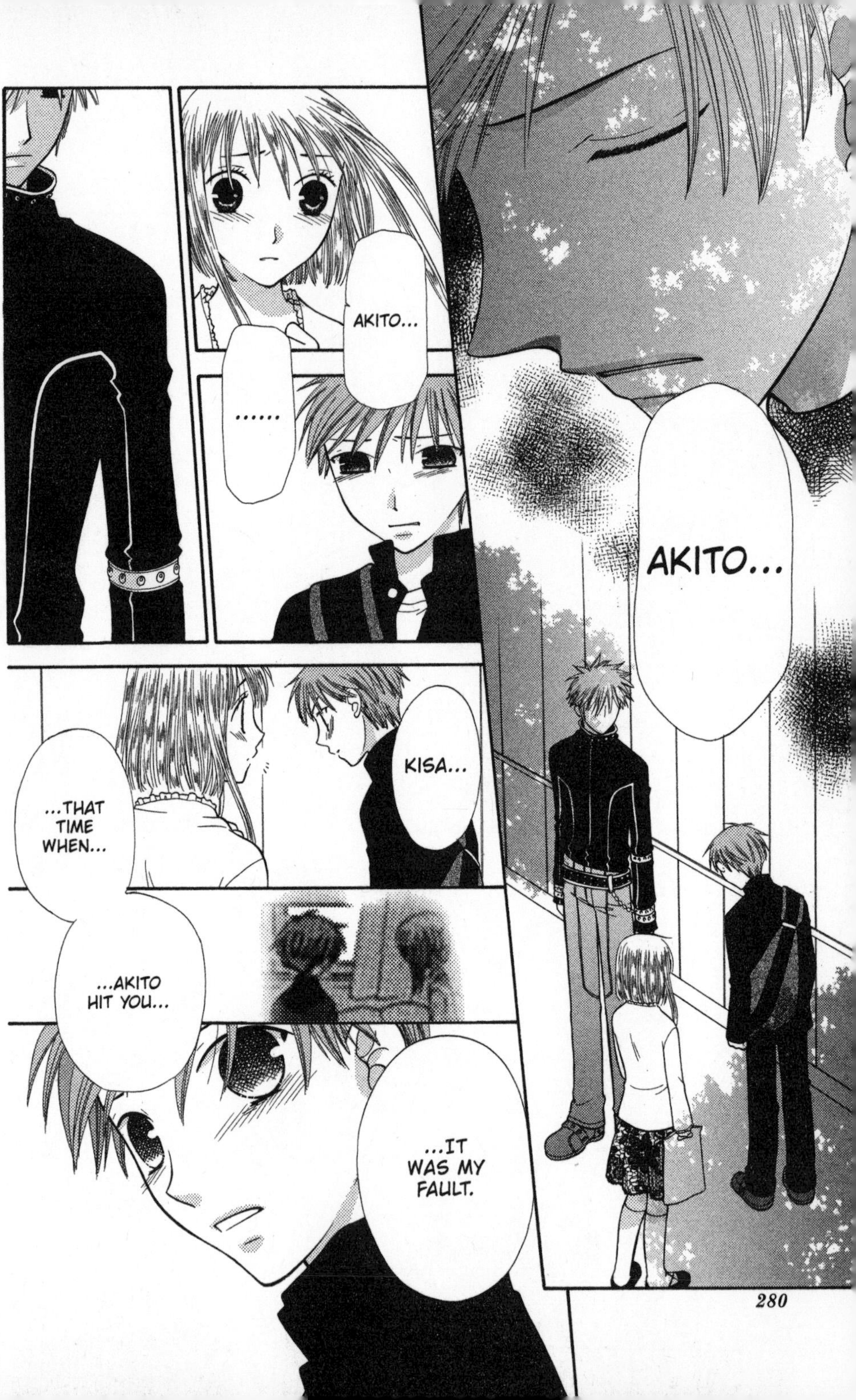
AKITO...
AKITO...
......
KISA...
...THAT TIME WHEN...
...AKITO HIT YOU...
...IT WAS MY FAULT.

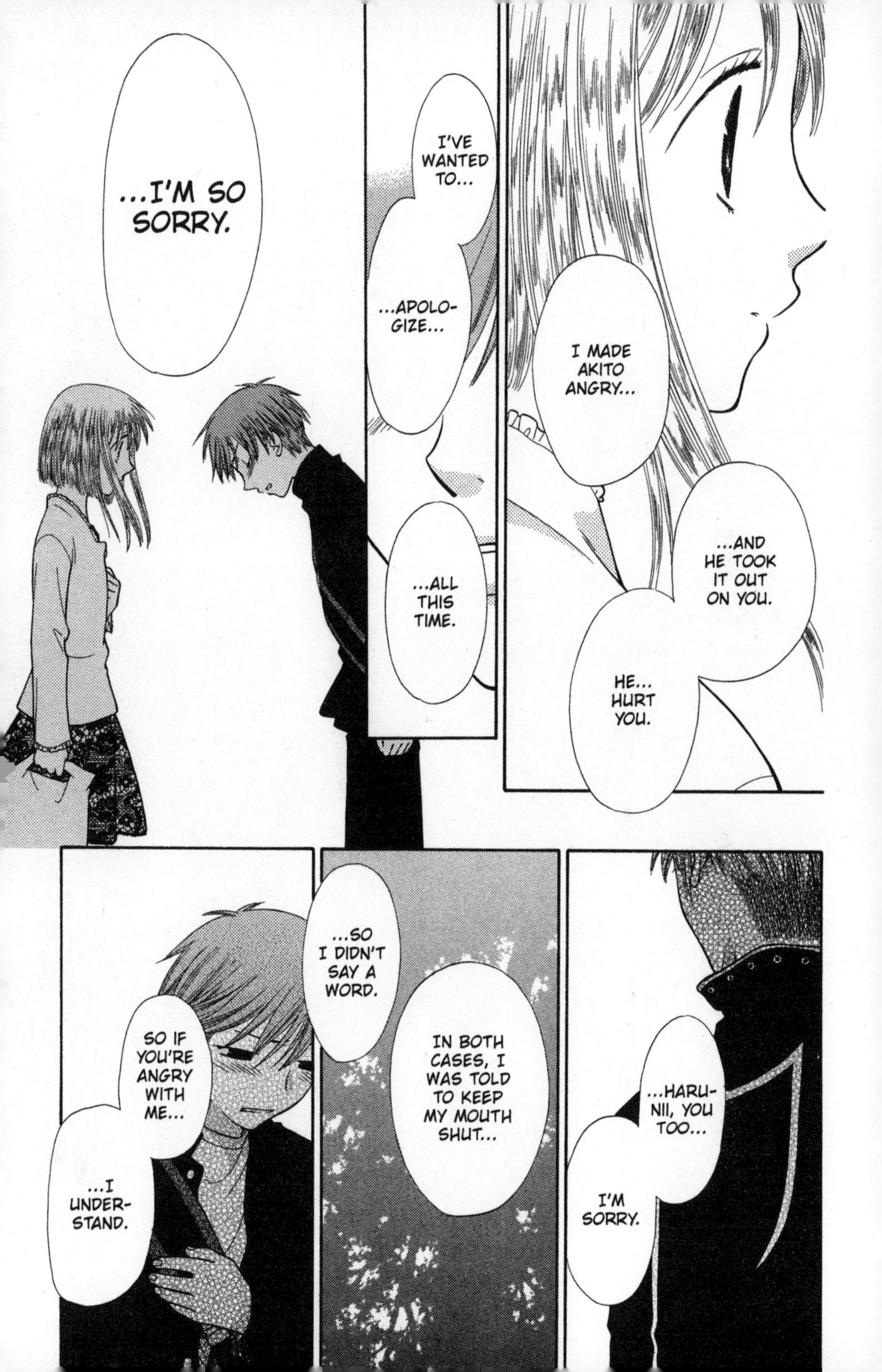
I MADE AKITO ANGRY...
...AND HE TOOK IT OUT ON YOU.
HE... HURT YOU.
I'VE WANTED TO...
...APOLOGIZE...
...ALL THIS TIME.
...I'M SO SORRY.
...HARU-NII, YOU TOO...
I'M SORRY.
IN BOTH CASES, I WAS TOLD TO KEEP MY MOUTH SHUT...
...SO I DIDN'T SAY A WORD.
SO IF YOU'RE ANGRY WITH ME...
...I UNDERSTAND.

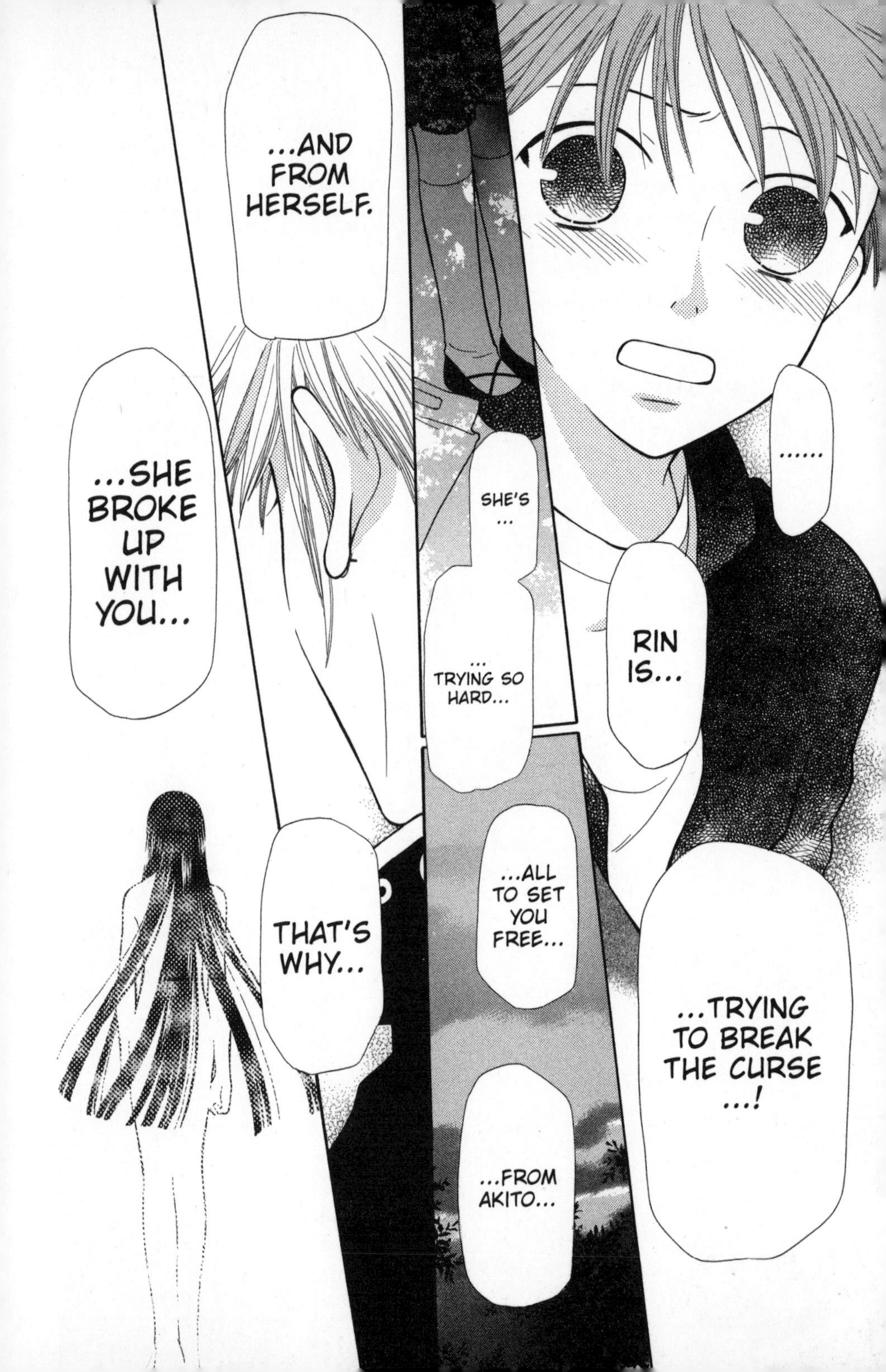
......
RIN IS...
...TRYING TO BREAK THE CURSE ...!
SHE'S ...
... TRYING SO HARD...
...ALL TO SET YOU FREE...
...FROM AKITO...
...AND FROM HERSELF.
THAT'S WHY...
...SHE BROKE UP WITH YOU...

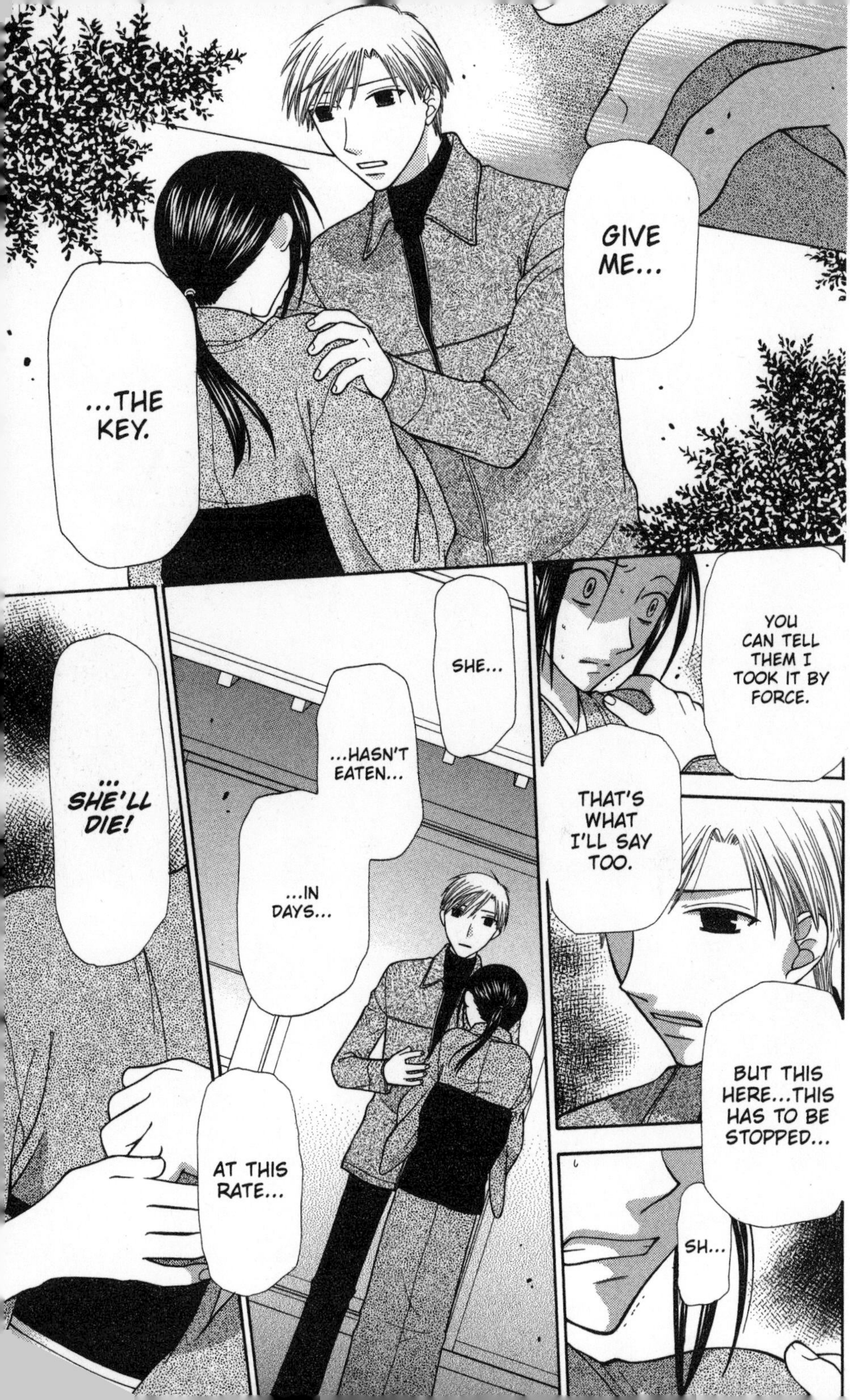
GIVE ME...
...THE KEY.
YOU CAN TELL THEM I TOOK IT BY FORCE.
THAT'S WHAT I'LL SAY TOO.
BUT THIS HERE...THIS HAS TO BE STOPPED...
SH...
SHE...
...HASN'T EATEN...
...IN DAYS...
AT THIS RATE...
...SHE'LL DIE!

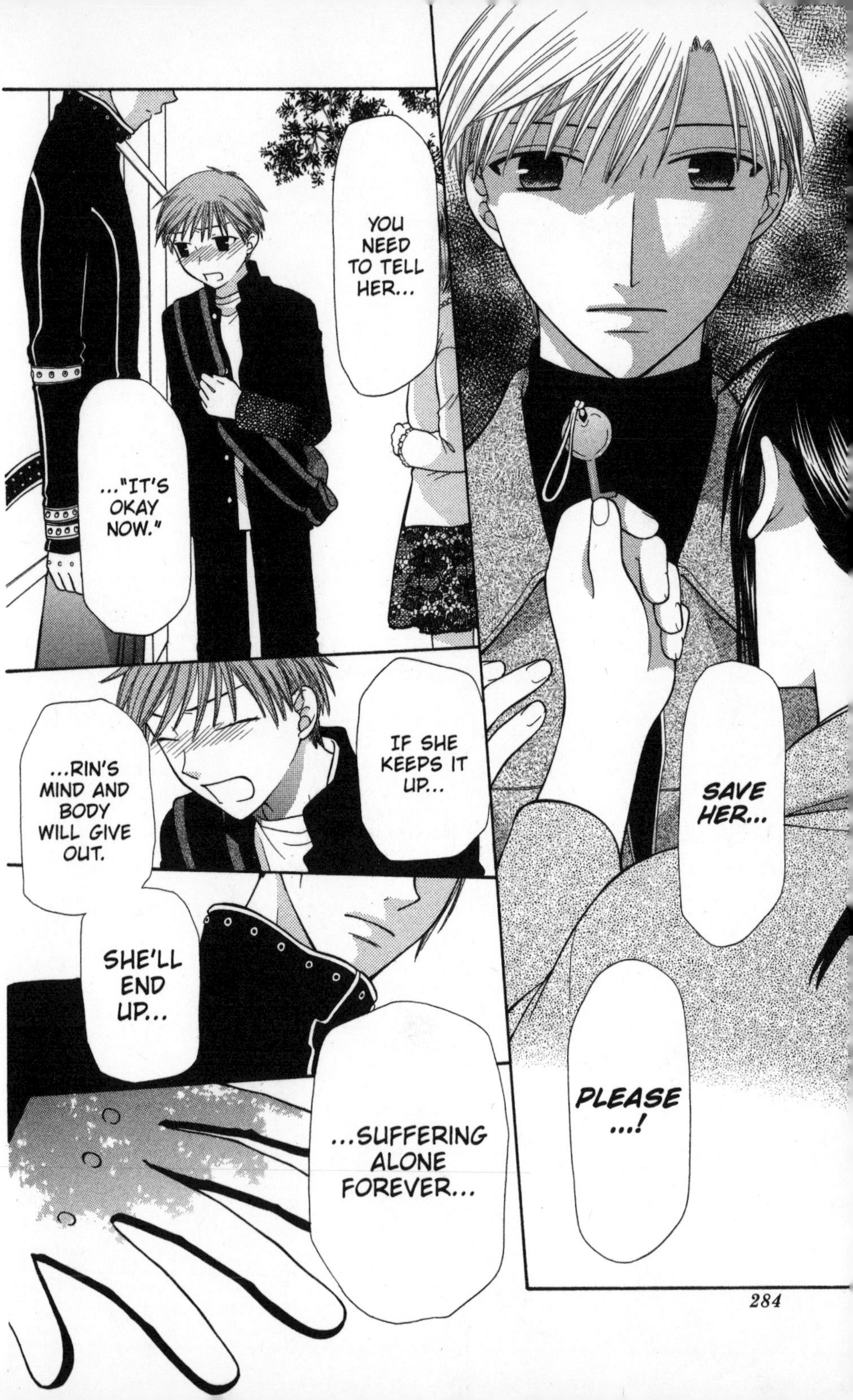
SAVE HER...
PLEASE ...!
YOU NEED TO TELL HER...
..."IT'S OKAY NOW."
IF SHE KEEPS IT UP...
...RIN'S MIND AND BODY WILL GIVE OUT.
SHE'LL END UP...
...SUFFERING ALONE FOREVER...

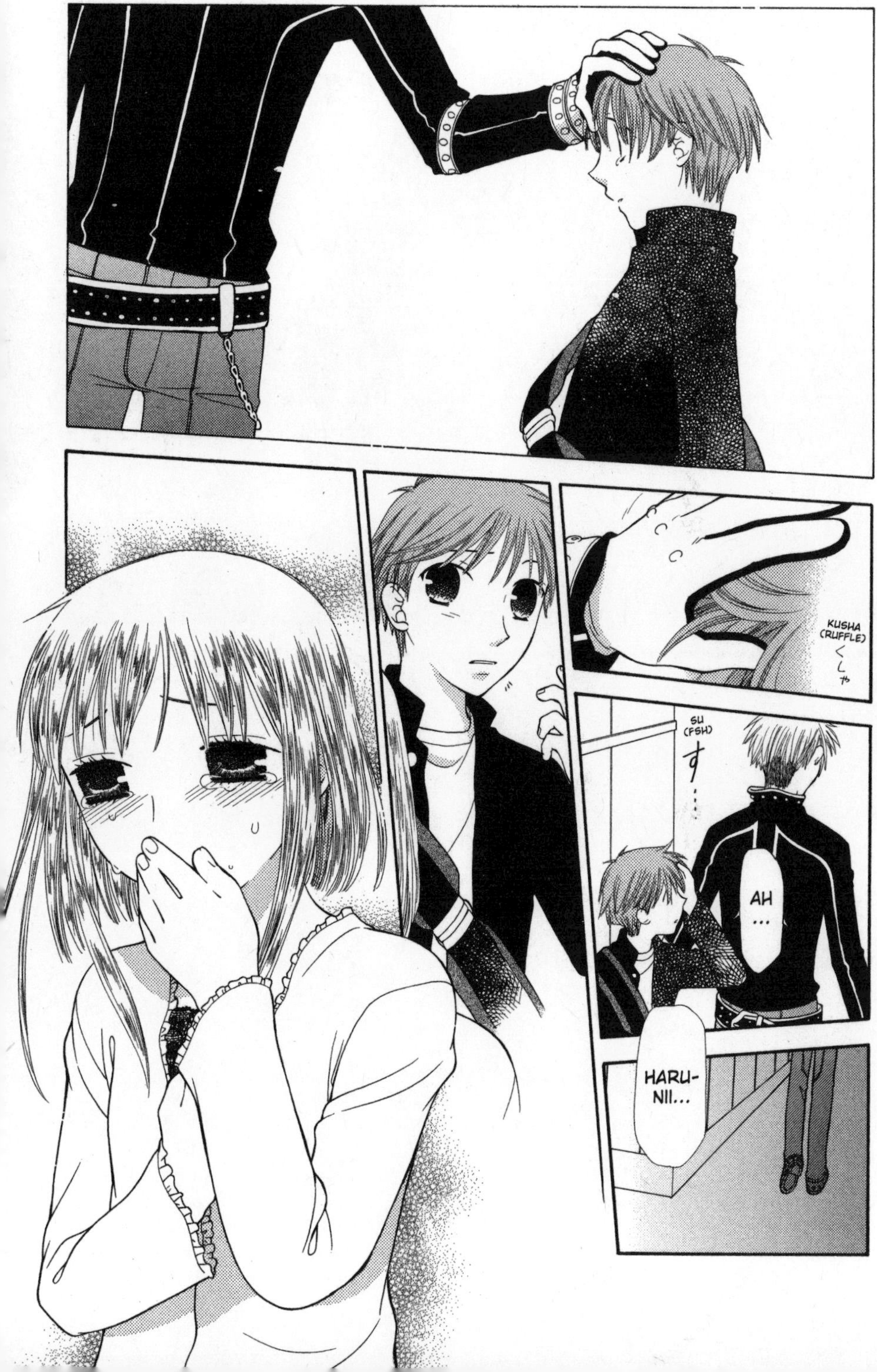
KUSHA (RUFFLE)
くしゃ
SU (FSH)
す…
AH ...
HARU-NII...

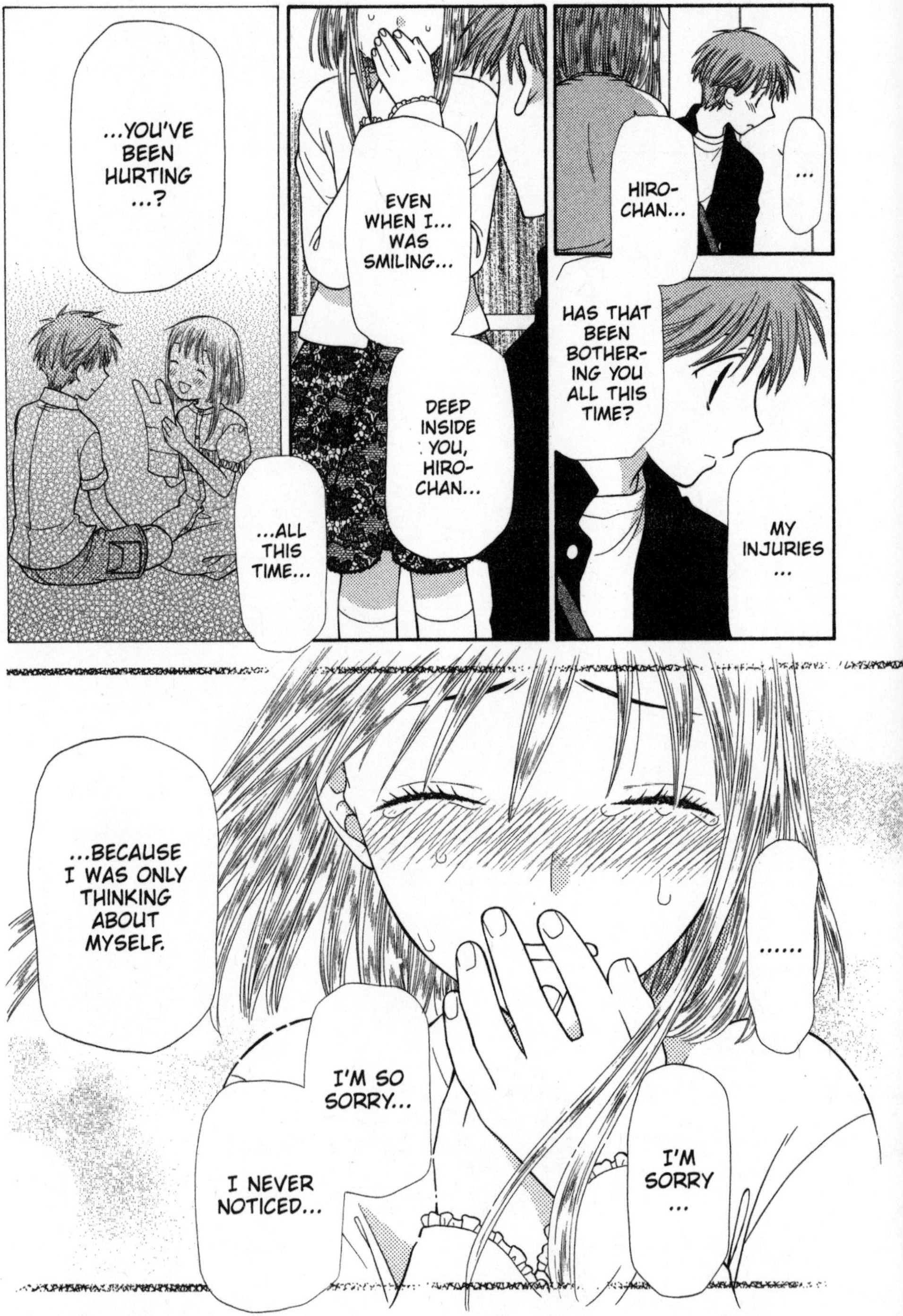
...
HIRO-CHAN...
MY INJURIES...
HAS THAT BEEN BOTHERING YOU ALL THIS TIME?
EVEN WHEN I... WAS SMILING...
DEEP INSIDE YOU, HIRO-CHAN...
...ALL THIS TIME...
...YOU'VE BEEN HURTING...?
......
I'M SORRY...
I'M SO SORRY...
I NEVER NOTICED...
...BECAUSE I WAS ONLY THINKING ABOUT MYSELF.

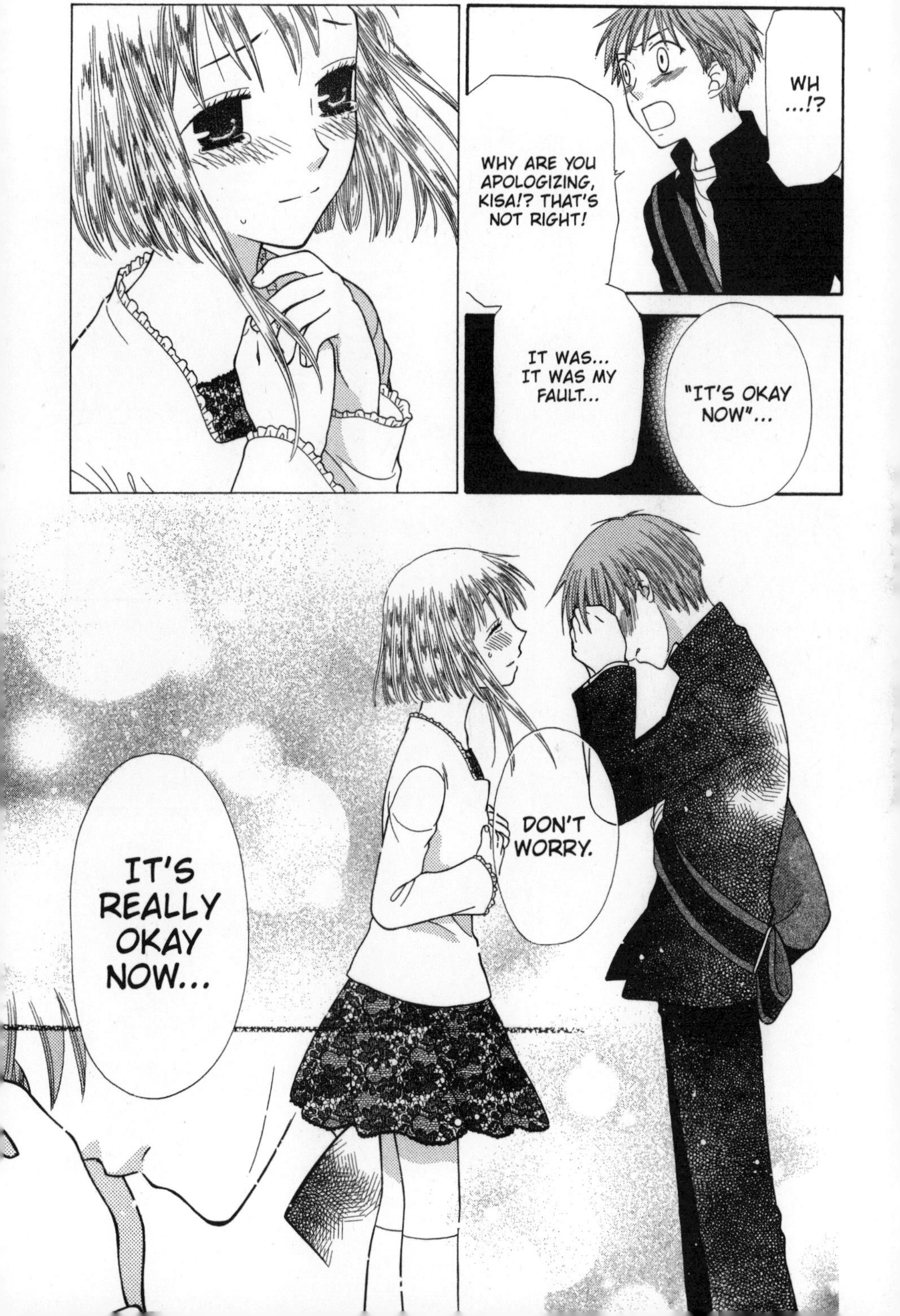
WH ...!?
WHY ARE YOU APOLOGIZING, KISA!? THAT'S NOT RIGHT!
IT WAS... IT WAS MY FAULT...
"IT'S OKAY NOW"...
DON'T WORRY.
IT'S REALLY OKAY NOW...

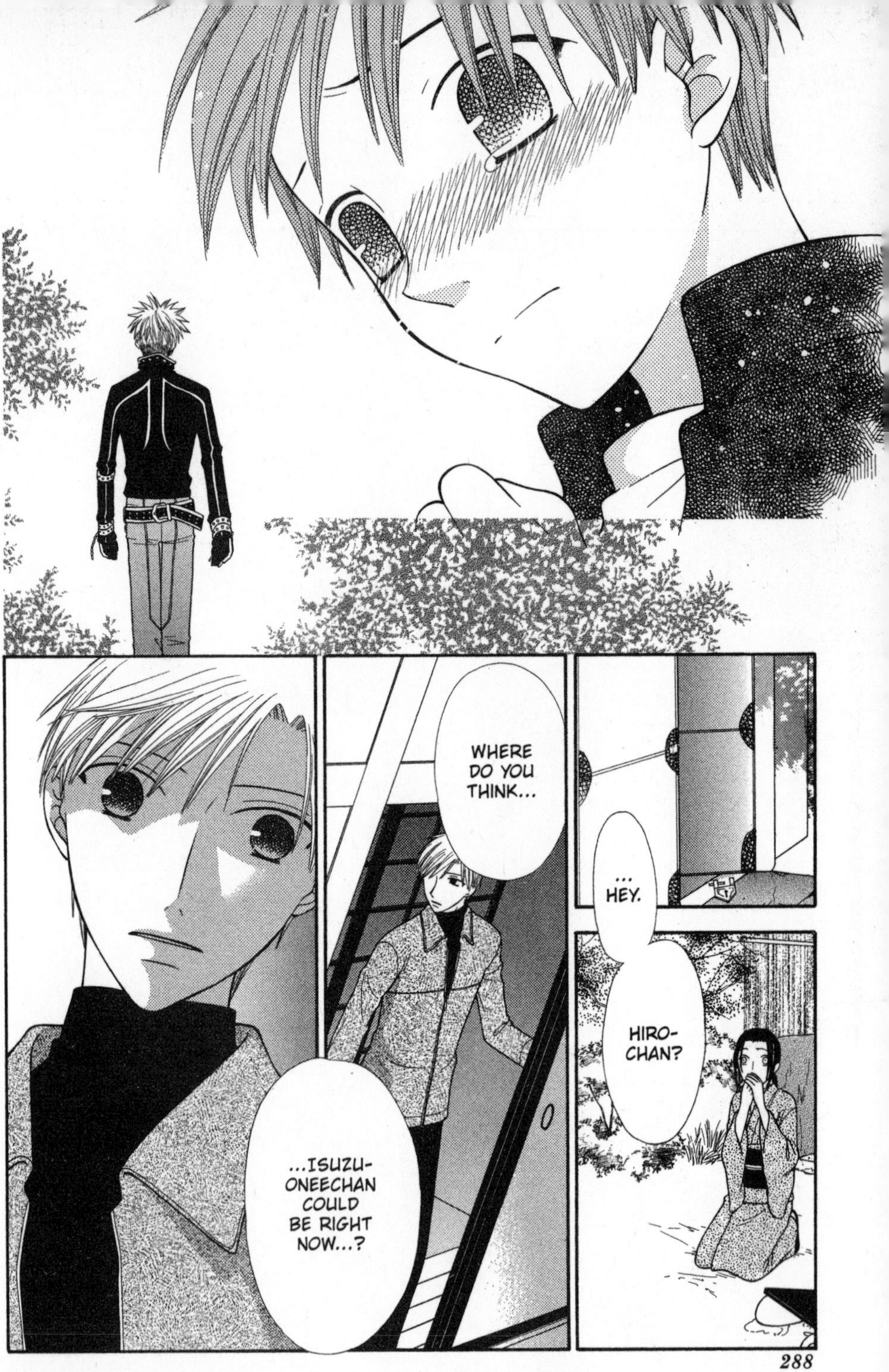
...HEY.
HIRO-CHAN?
WHERE DO YOU THINK...
...ISUZU-ONEECHAN COULD BE RIGHT NOW...?

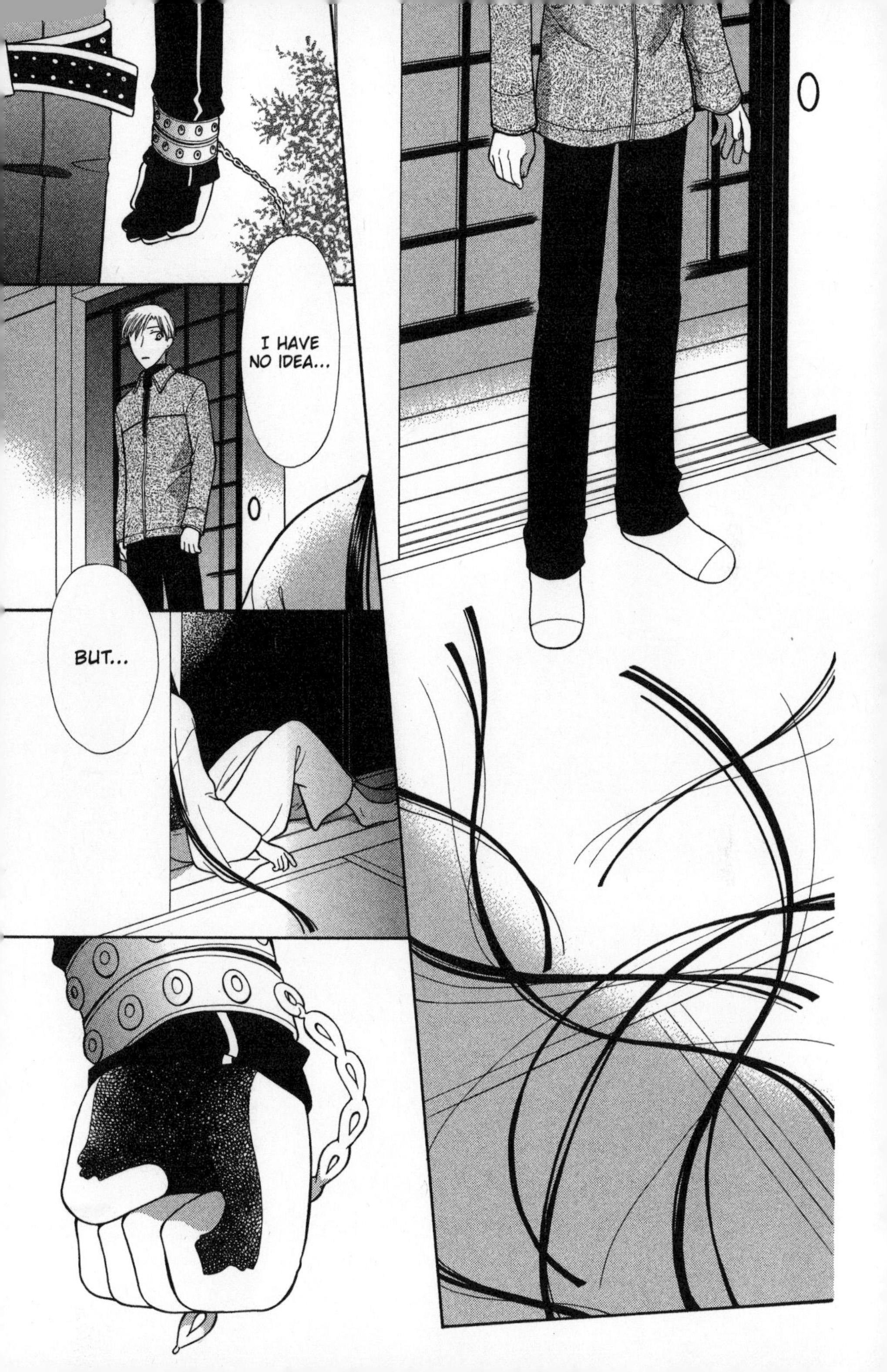
I HAVE NO IDEA...
BUT...

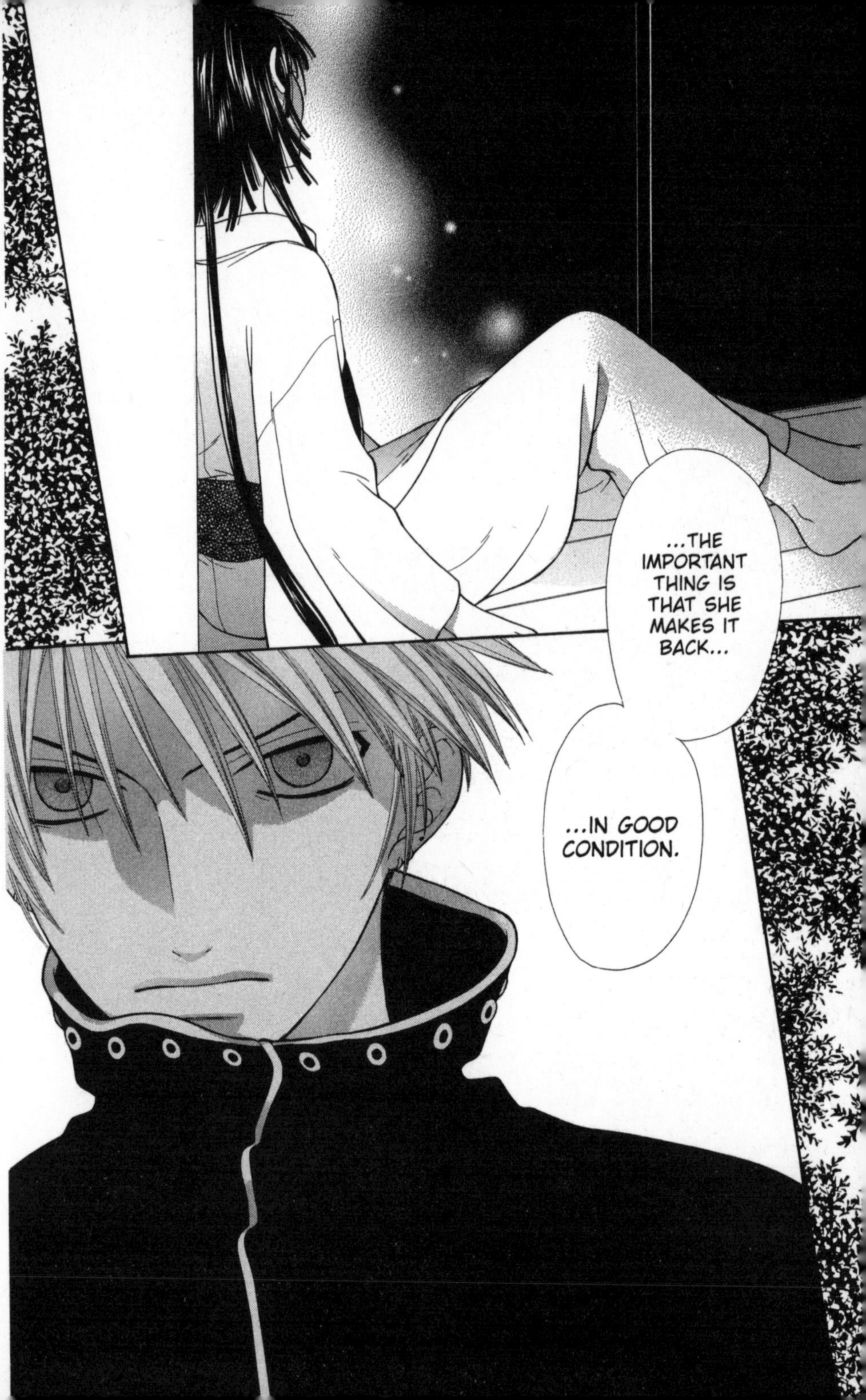
...THE IMPORTANT THING IS THAT SHE MAKES IT BACK...
...IN GOOD CONDITION.

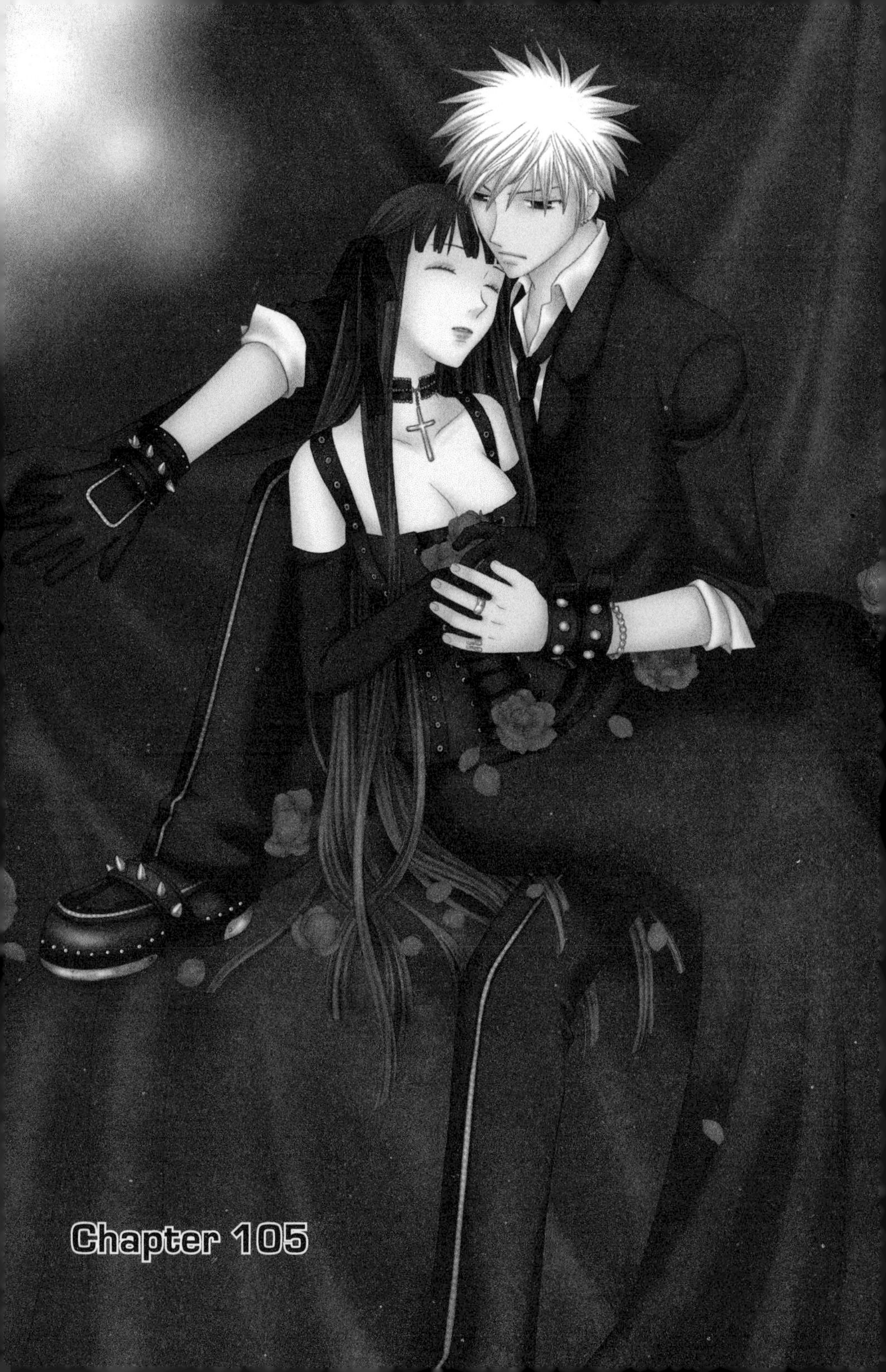

Chapter 105

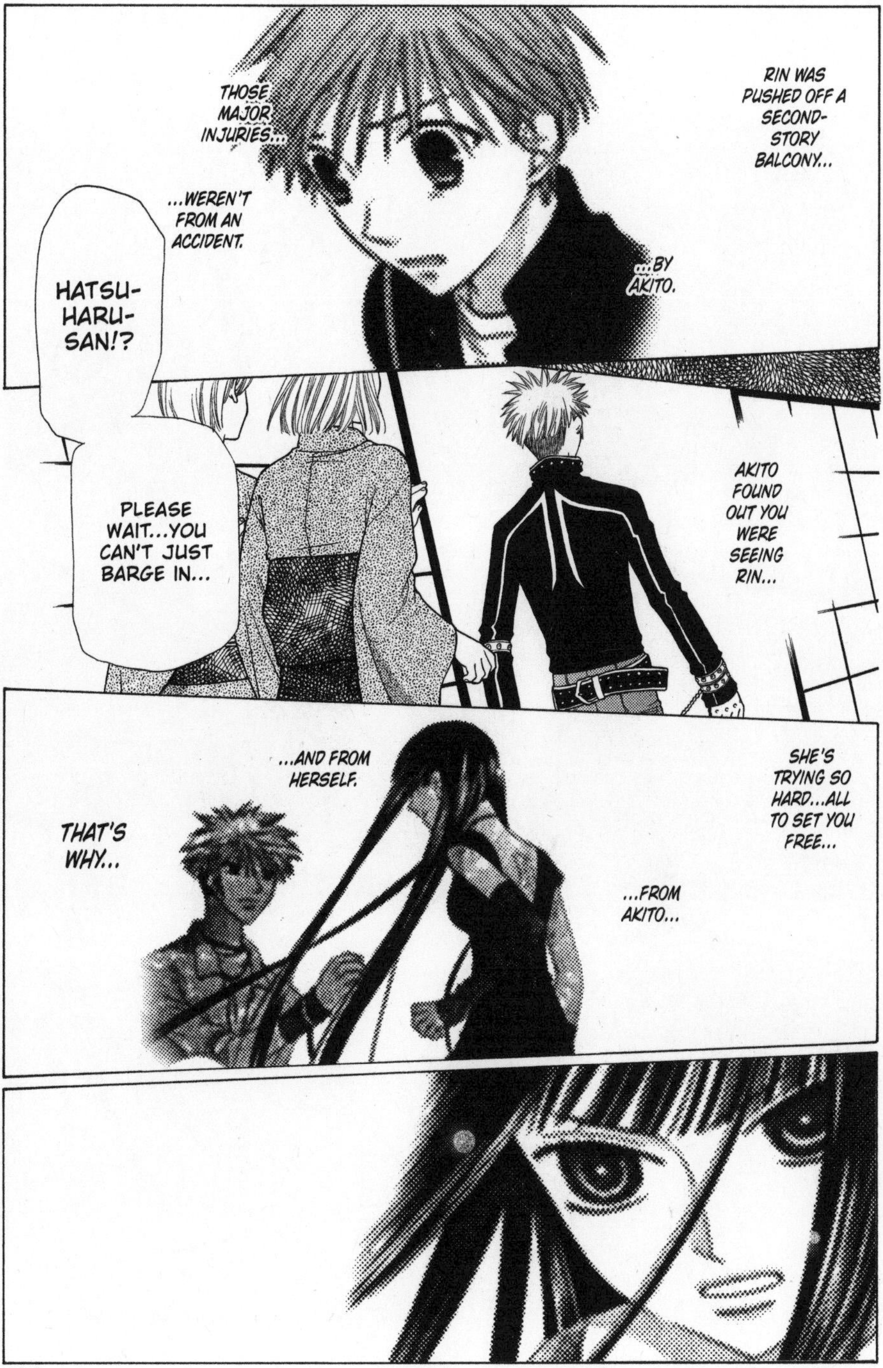
RIN WAS PUSHED OFF A SECOND-STORY BALCONY...
...BY AKITO.
THOSE MAJOR INJURIES...
...WEREN'T FROM AN ACCIDENT.
AKITO FOUND OUT YOU WERE SEEING RIN...
HATSU-HARU-SAN!?
PLEASE WAIT...YOU CAN'T JUST BARGE IN...
SHE'S TRYING SO HARD...ALL TO SET YOU FREE...
...FROM AKITO...
...AND FROM HERSELF.
THAT'S WHY...

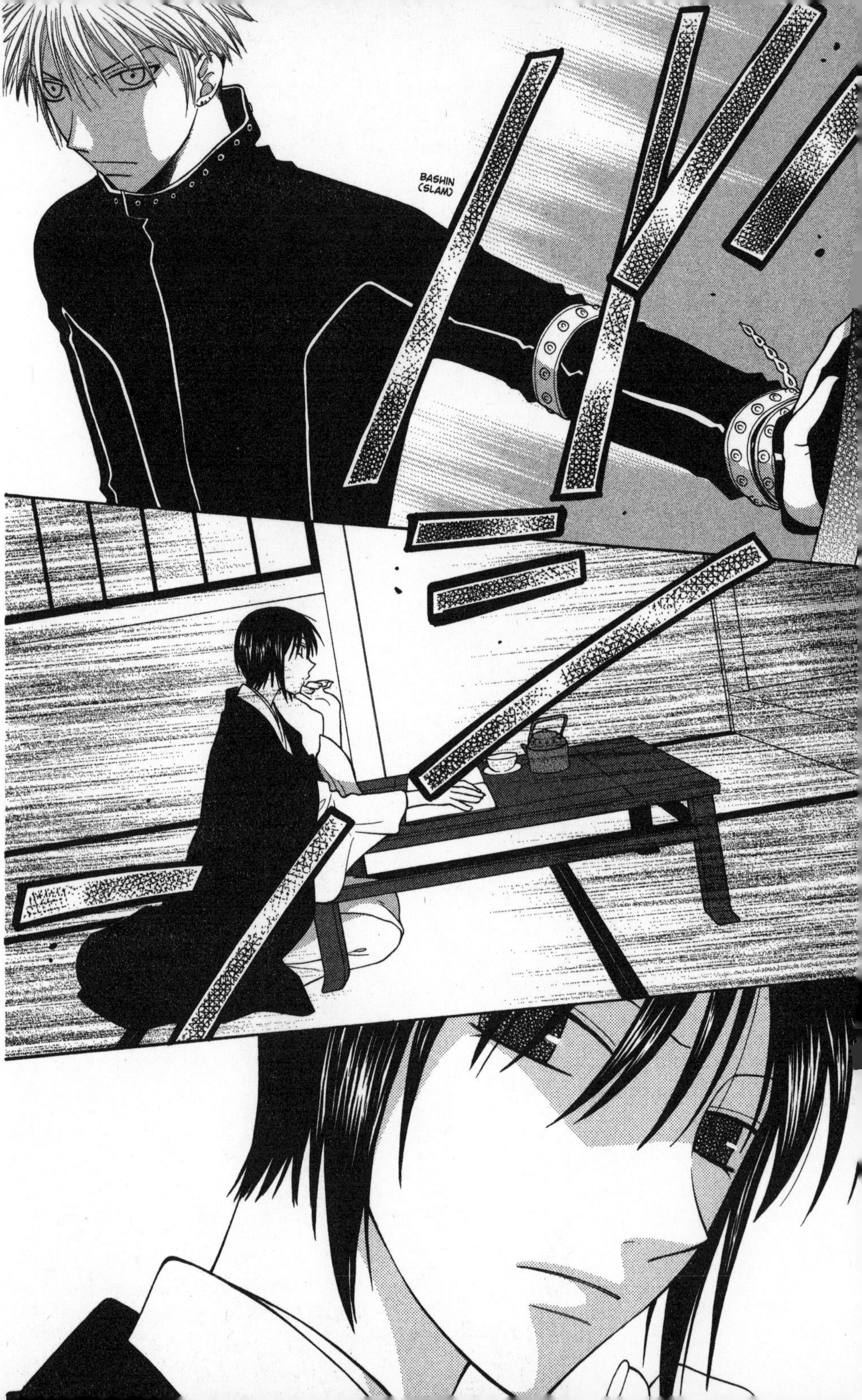
BASHIN
(SLAM)

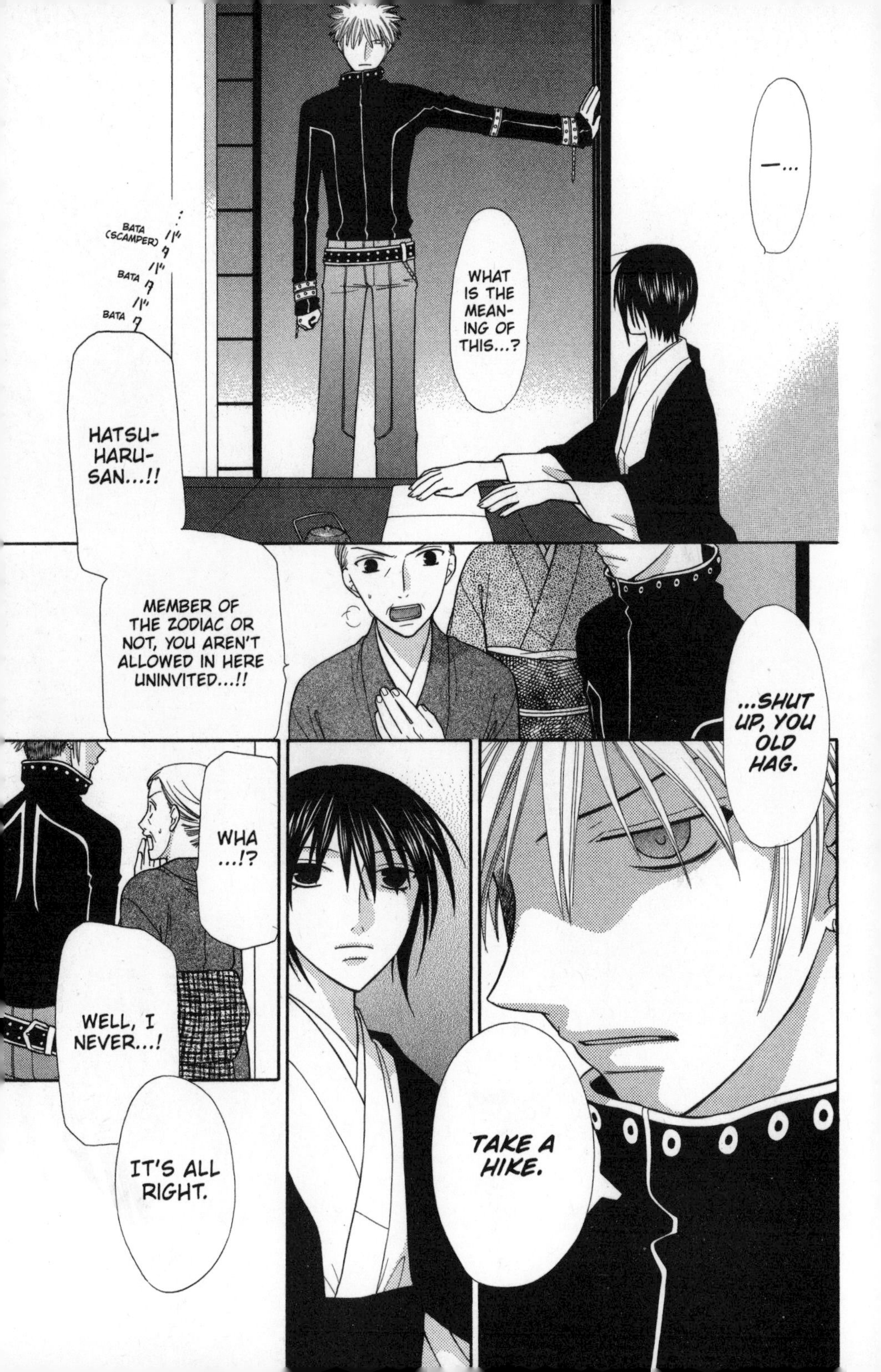
—...
WHAT IS THE MEANING OF THIS...?
BATA (SCAMPER) バタ
BATA バタ
BATA バタ
HATSUHARU-SAN...!!
MEMBER OF THE ZODIAC OR NOT, YOU AREN'T ALLOWED IN HERE UNINVITED...!!
...SHUT UP, YOU OLD HAG.
TAKE A HIKE.
WHA ...!?
WELL, I NEVER...!
IT'S ALL RIGHT.

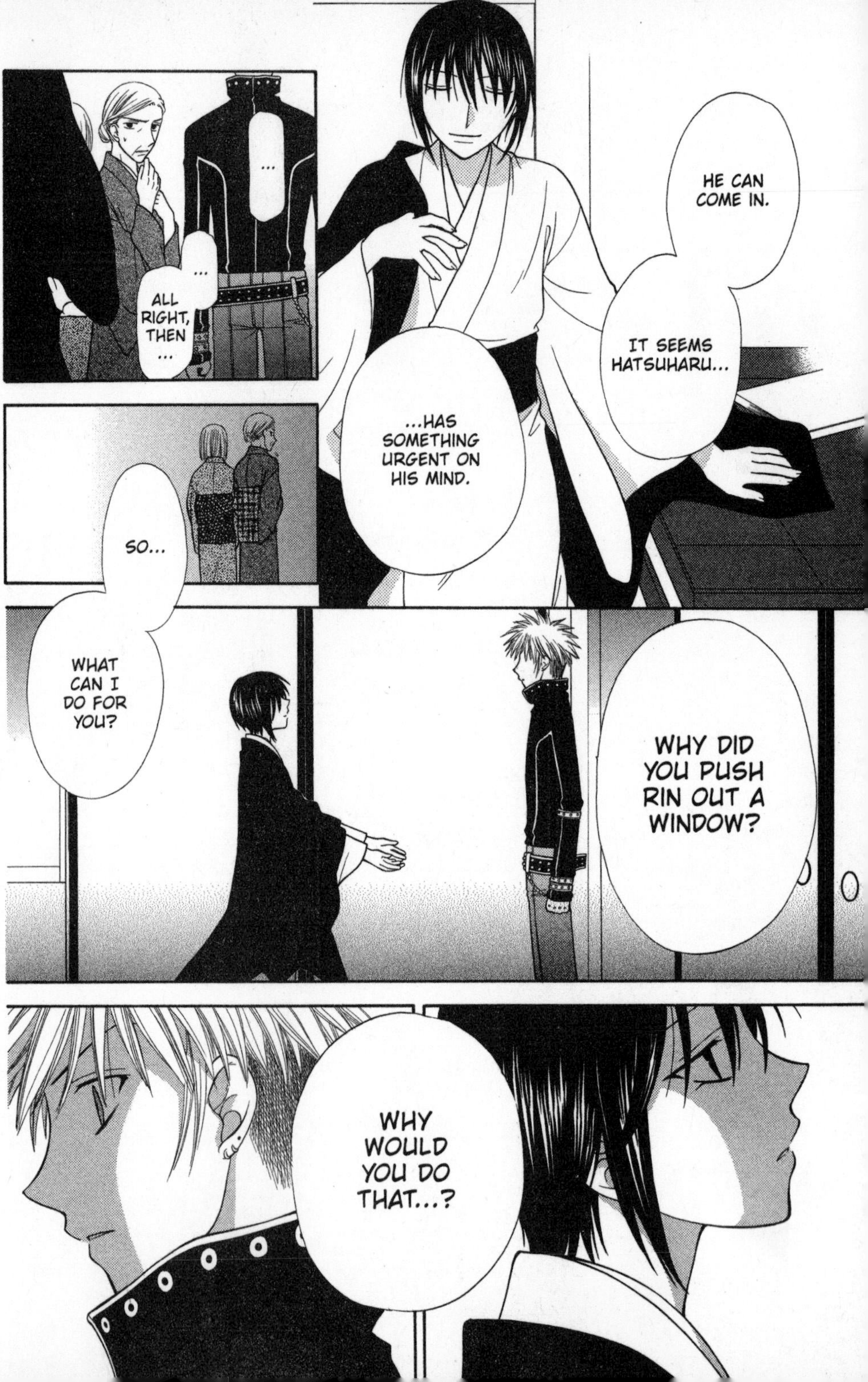
HE CAN COME IN.
IT SEEMS HATSUHARU...
...HAS SOMETHING URGENT ON HIS MIND.
...
... ALL RIGHT, THEN ...
SO...
WHAT CAN I DO FOR YOU?
WHY DID YOU PUSH RIN OUT A WINDOW?
WHY WOULD YOU DO THAT...?

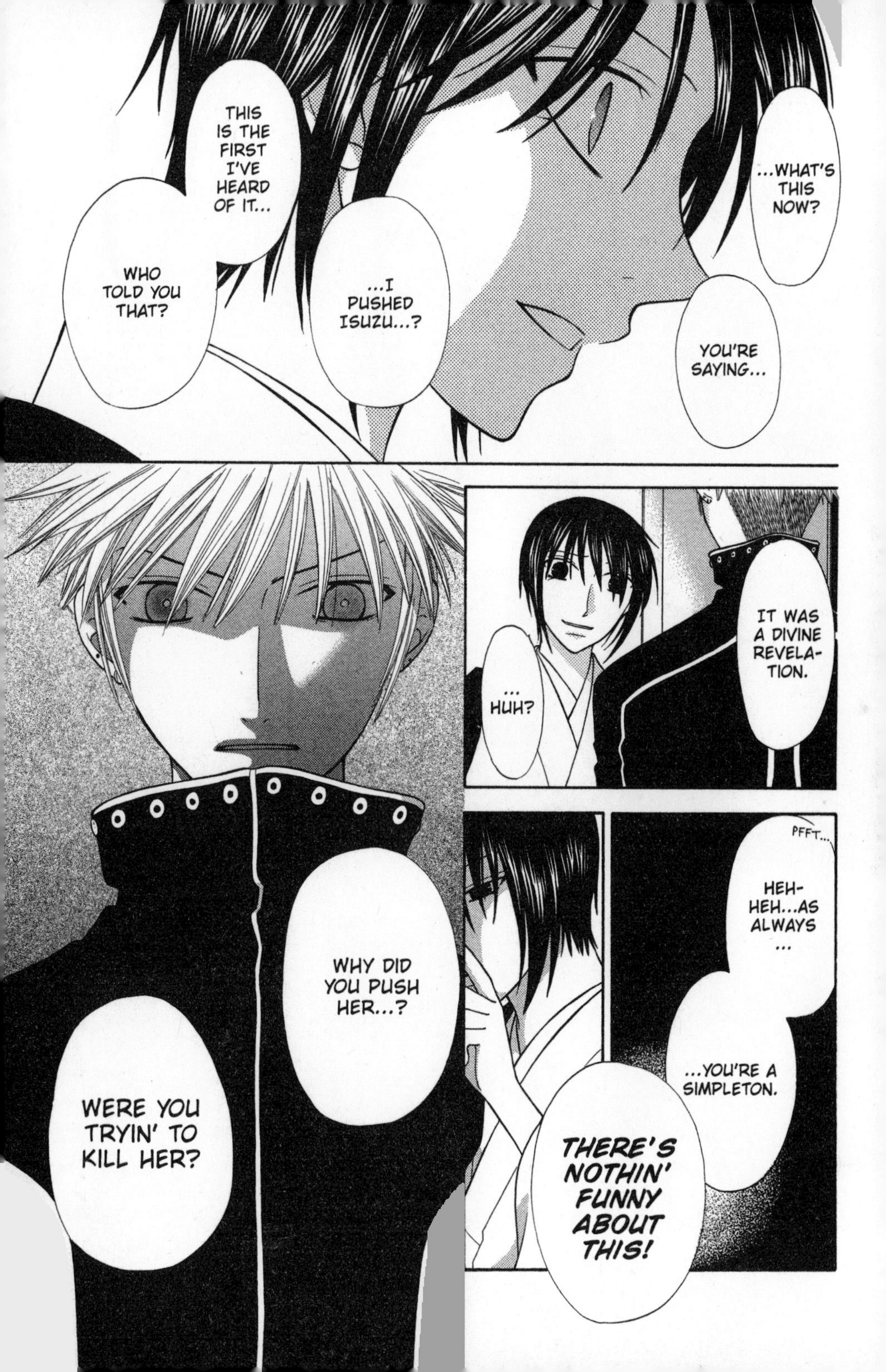
...WHAT'S THIS NOW?
YOU'RE SAYING...
...I PUSHED ISUZU...?
THIS IS THE FIRST I'VE HEARD OF IT...
WHO TOLD YOU THAT?
IT WAS A DIVINE REVELATION.
... HUH?
PFFT...
HEH-HEH...AS ALWAYS ...
...YOU'RE A SIMPLETON.
THERE'S NOTHIN' FUNNY ABOUT THIS!
WHY DID YOU PUSH HER...?
WERE YOU TRYIN' TO KILL HER?

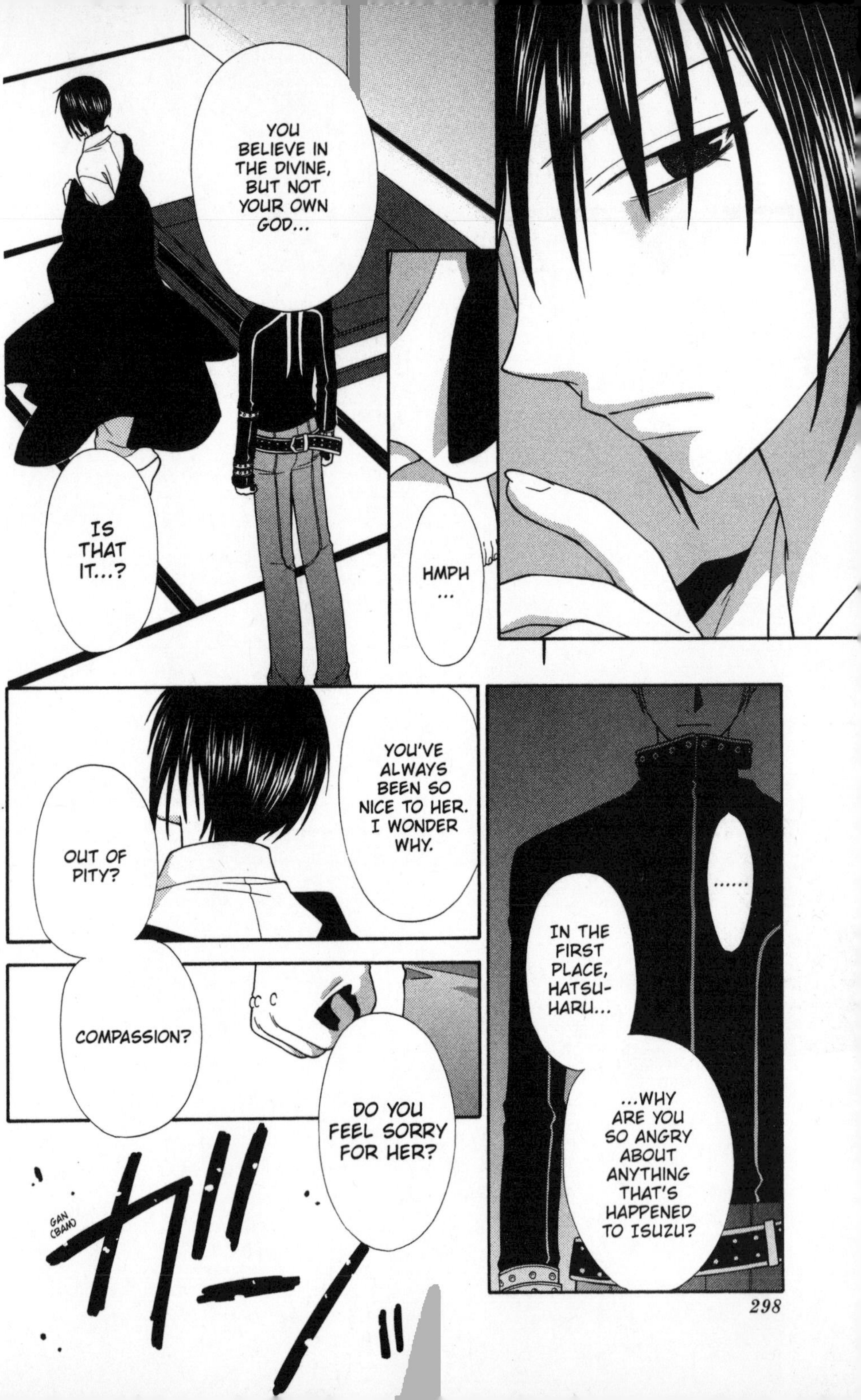
HMPH...
YOU BELIEVE IN THE DIVINE, BUT NOT YOUR OWN GOD...
IS THAT IT...?
......
IN THE FIRST PLACE, HATSU-HARU...
...WHY ARE YOU SO ANGRY ABOUT ANYTHING THAT'S HAPPENED TO ISUZU?
YOU'VE ALWAYS BEEN SO NICE TO HER. I WONDER WHY.
OUT OF PITY?
COMPASSION?
DO YOU FEEL SORRY FOR HER?
GAN (BAM)

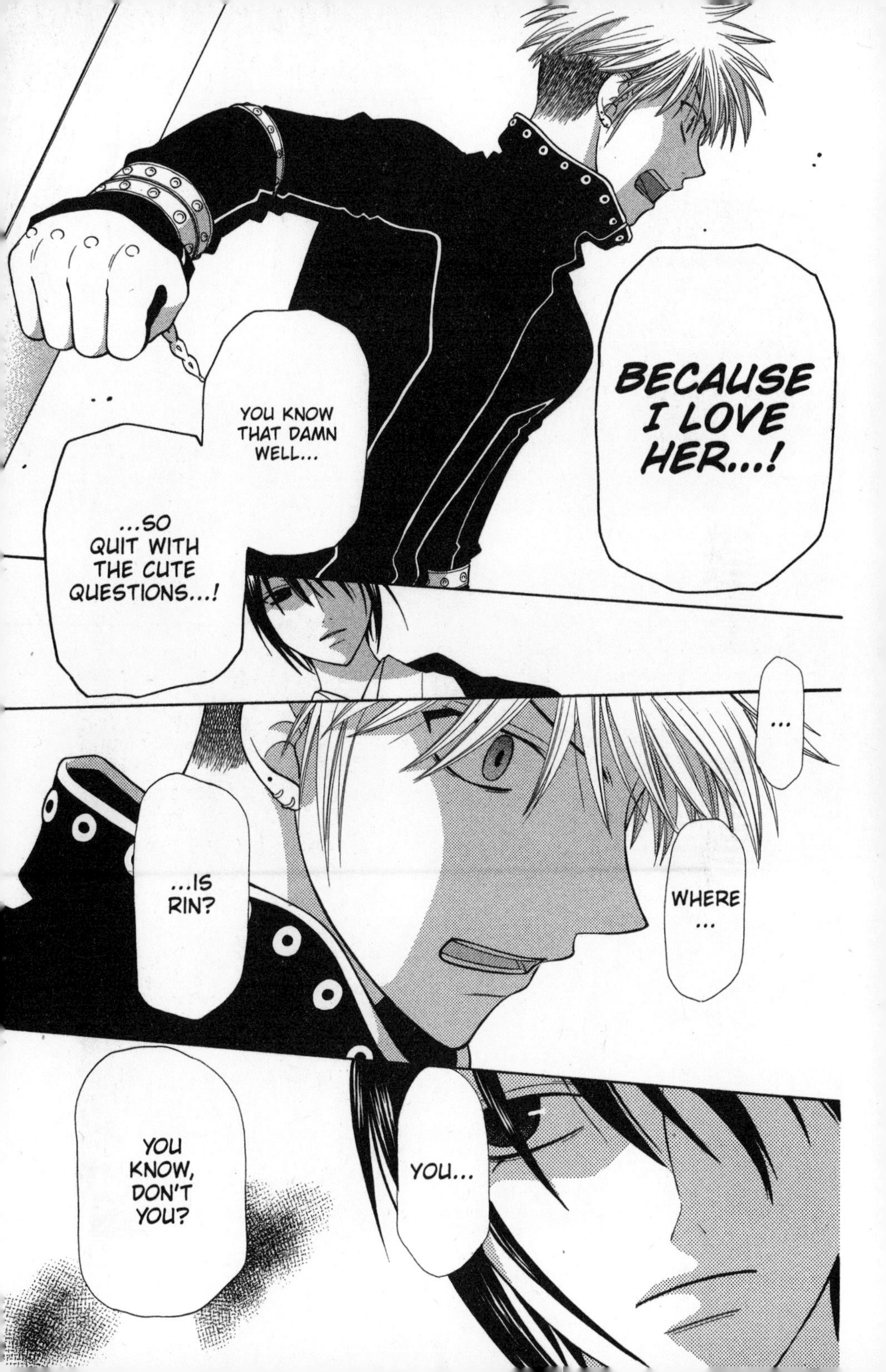
BECAUSE I LOVE HER...!
YOU KNOW THAT DAMN WELL...
...SO QUIT WITH THE CUTE QUESTIONS...!
...
WHERE ...
...IS RIN?
YOU...
YOU KNOW, DON'T YOU?

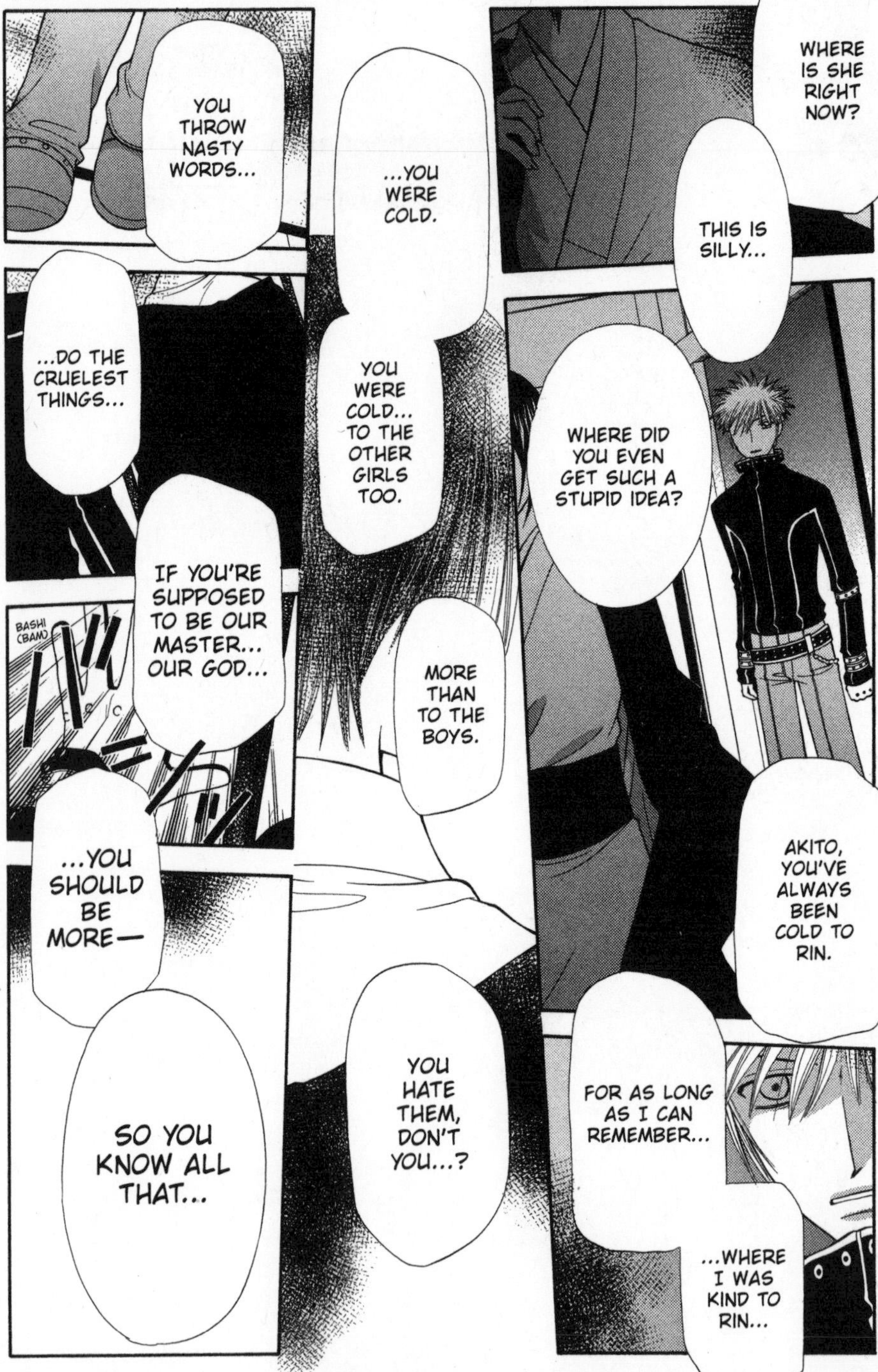
WHERE IS SHE RIGHT NOW?
THIS IS SILLY...
WHERE DID YOU EVEN GET SUCH A STUPID IDEA?
AKITO, YOU'VE ALWAYS BEEN COLD TO RIN.
FOR AS LONG AS I CAN REMEMBER...
...WHERE I WAS KIND TO RIN...
YOU THROW NASTY WORDS...
...YOU WERE COLD.
...DO THE CRUELEST THINGS...
YOU WERE COLD... TO THE OTHER GIRLS TOO.
IF YOU'RE SUPPOSED TO BE OUR MASTER... OUR GOD...
MORE THAN TO THE BOYS.
BASHI (BAM)
...YOU SHOULD BE MORE—
YOU HATE THEM, DON'T YOU...?
SO YOU KNOW ALL THAT...

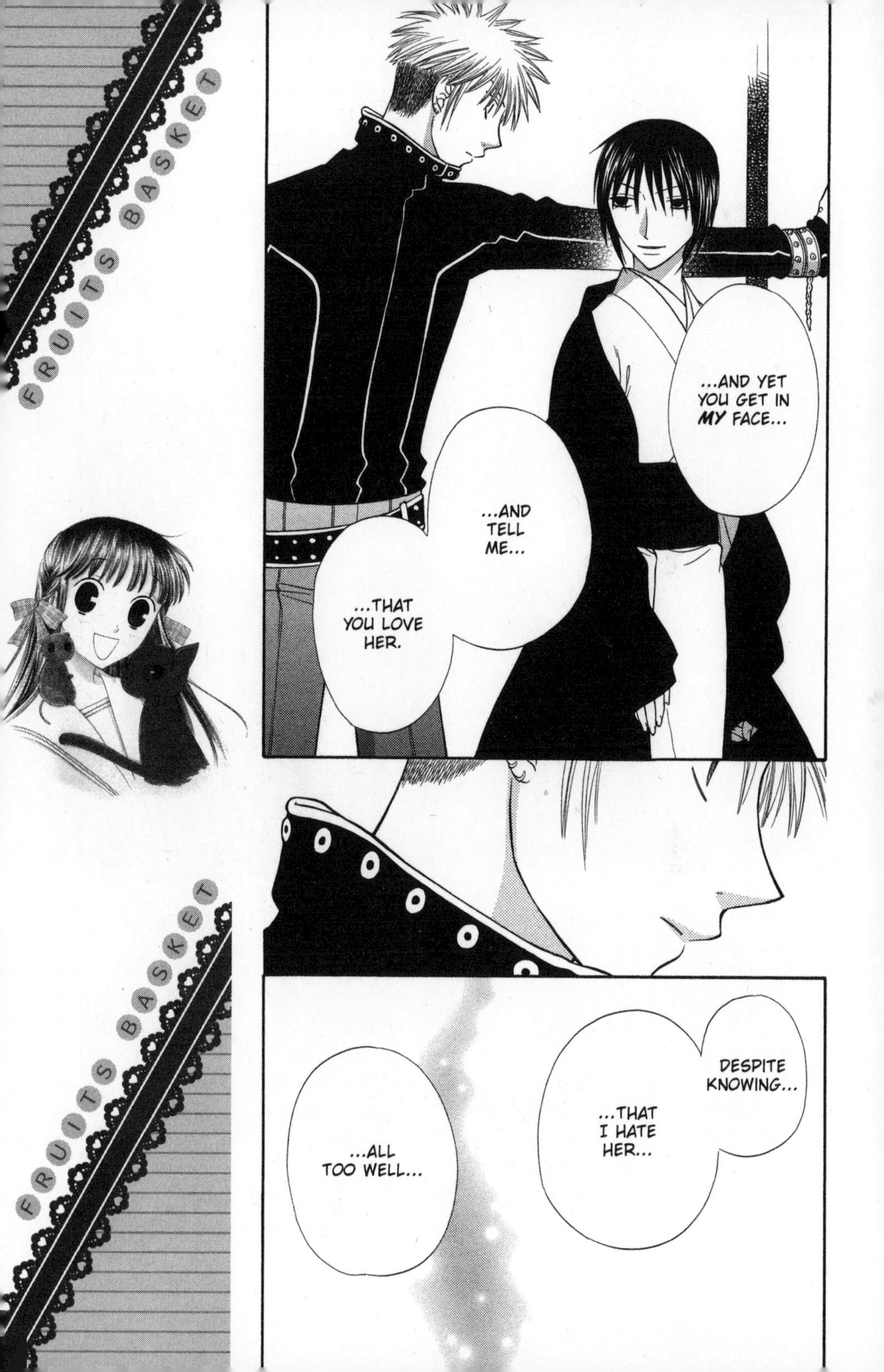
...AND YET YOU GET IN MY FACE...
...AND TELL ME...
...THAT YOU LOVE HER.
DESPITE KNOWING...
...THAT I HATE HER...
...ALL TOO WELL...

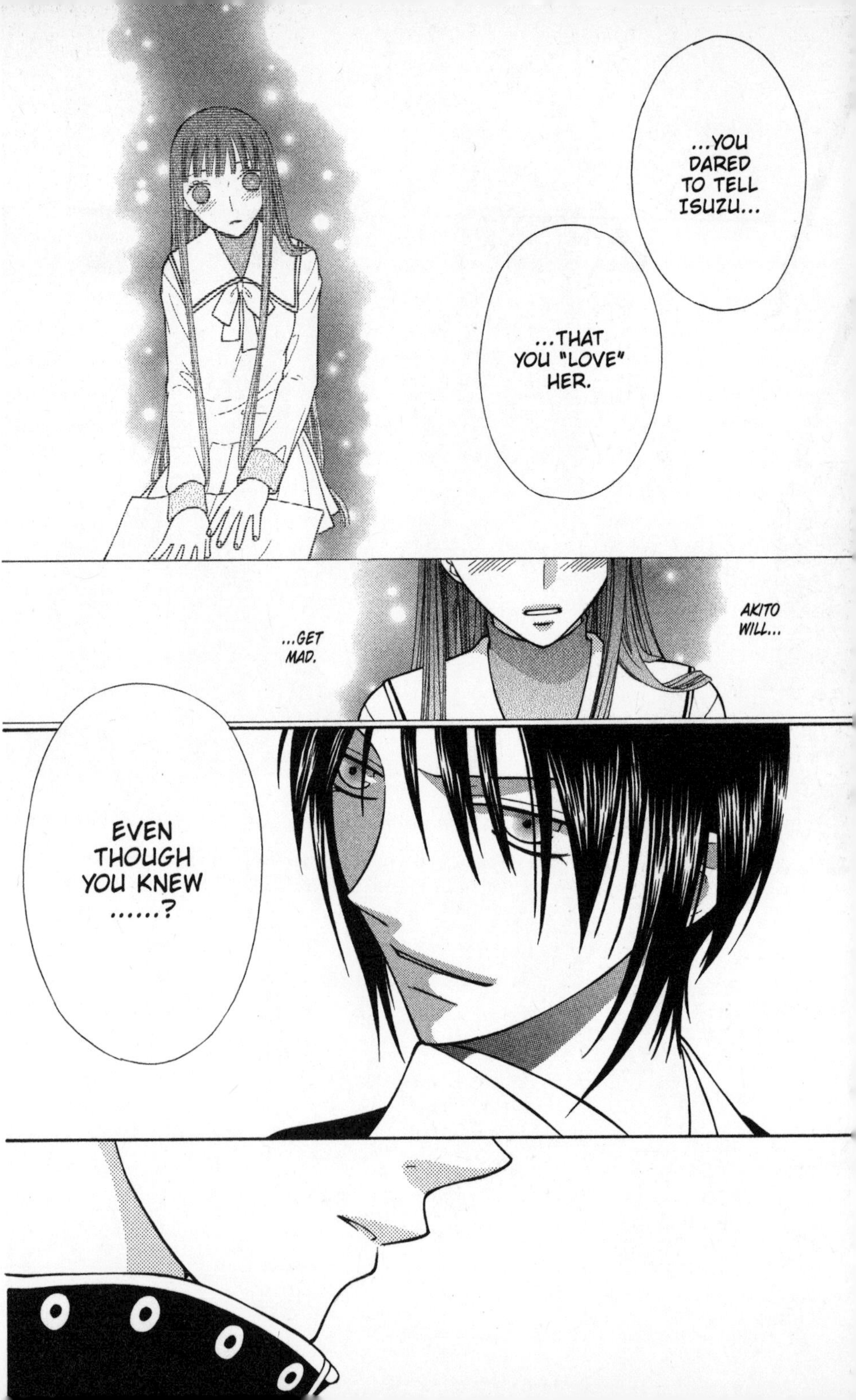
...YOU DARED TO TELL ISUZU...
...THAT YOU "LOVE" HER.
AKITO WILL...
...GET MAD.
EVEN THOUGH YOU KNEW ......?

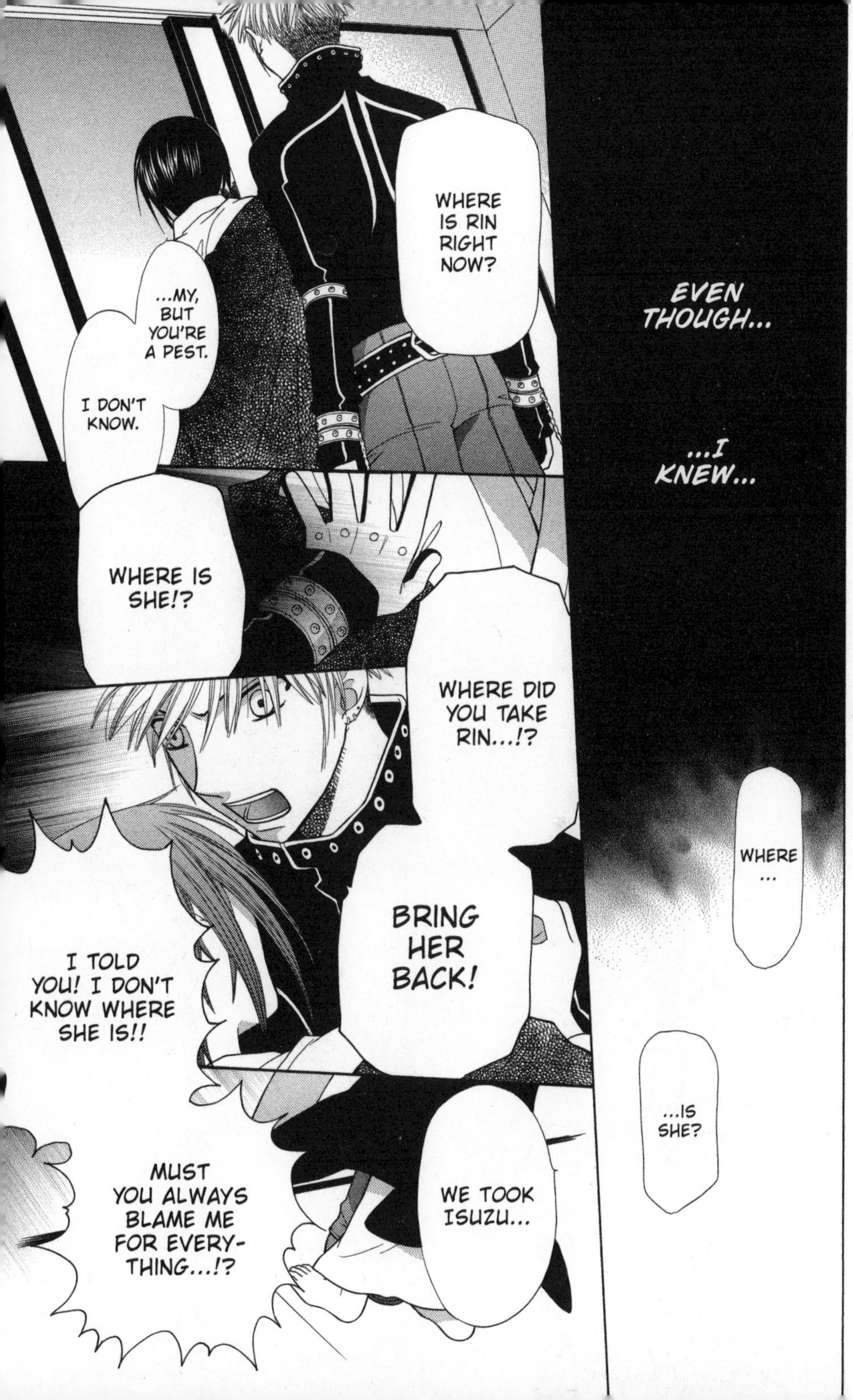
EVEN THOUGH...
...I KNEW...
WHERE...
...IS SHE?
WHERE IS RIN RIGHT NOW?
...MY, BUT YOU'RE A PEST.
I DON'T KNOW.
WHERE IS SHE!?
WHERE DID YOU TAKE RIN...!?
BRING HER BACK!
I TOLD YOU! I DON'T KNOW WHERE SHE IS!!
WE TOOK ISUZU...
MUST YOU ALWAYS BLAME ME FOR EVERY-THING...!?

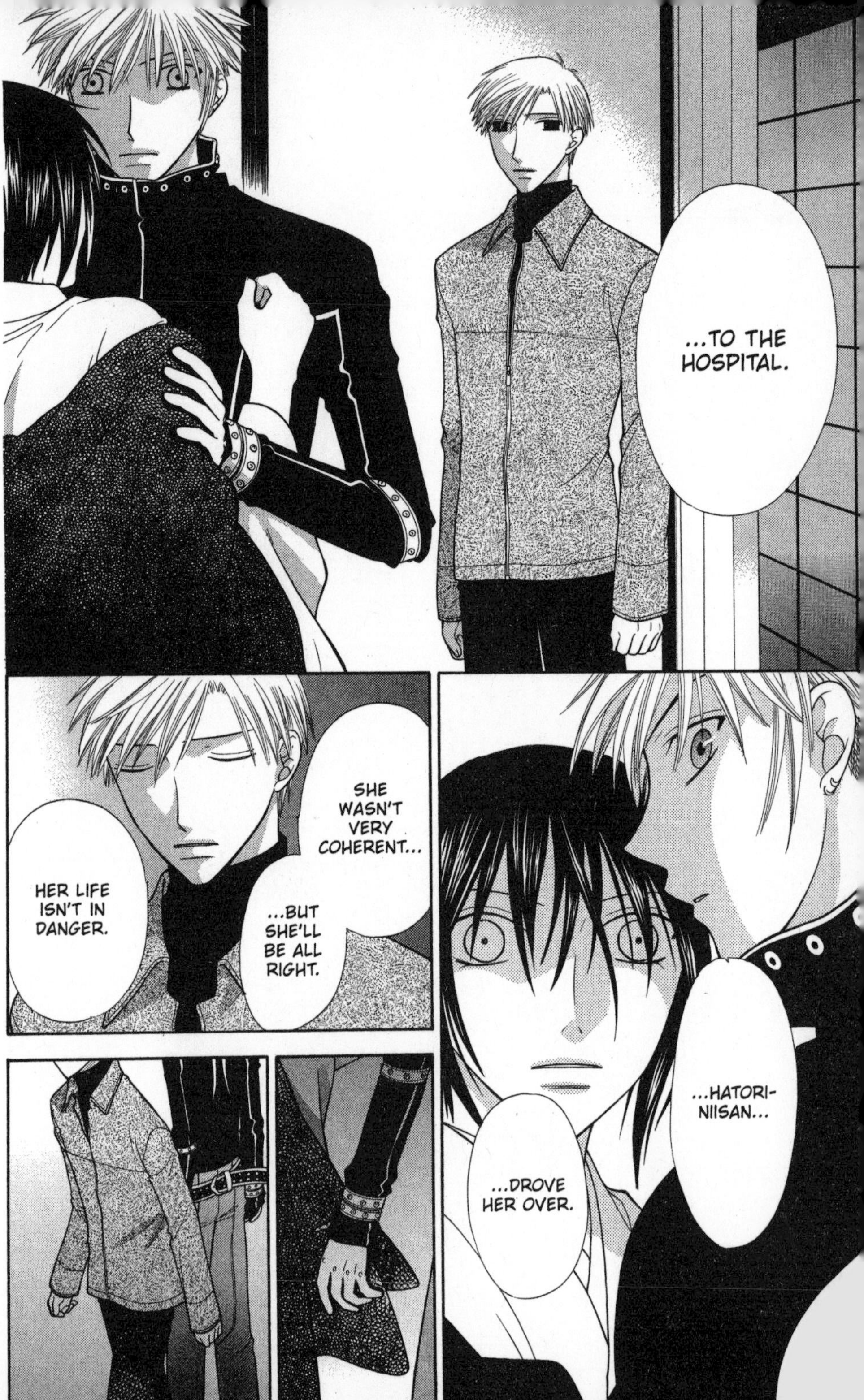
...TO THE HOSPITAL.
...HATORI-NIISAN...
...DROVE HER OVER.
SHE WASN'T VERY COHERENT...
...BUT SHE'LL BE ALL RIGHT.
HER LIFE ISN'T IN DANGER.

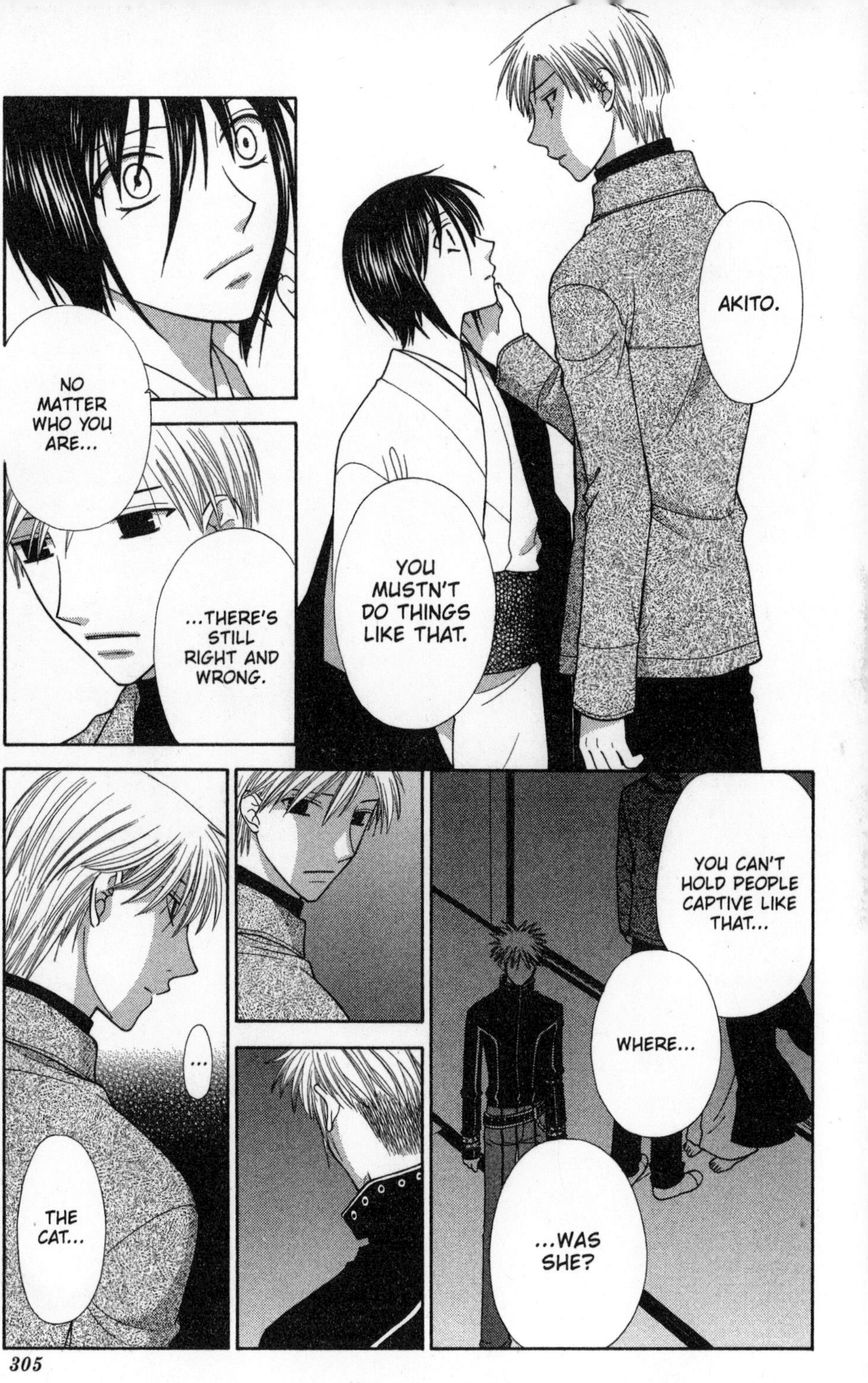

AKITO.
YOU MUSTN'T DO THINGS LIKE THAT.
NO MATTER WHO YOU ARE...
...THERE'S STILL RIGHT AND WRONG.
YOU CAN'T HOLD PEOPLE CAPTIVE LIKE THAT...
WHERE...
...WAS SHE?
...
THE CAT...

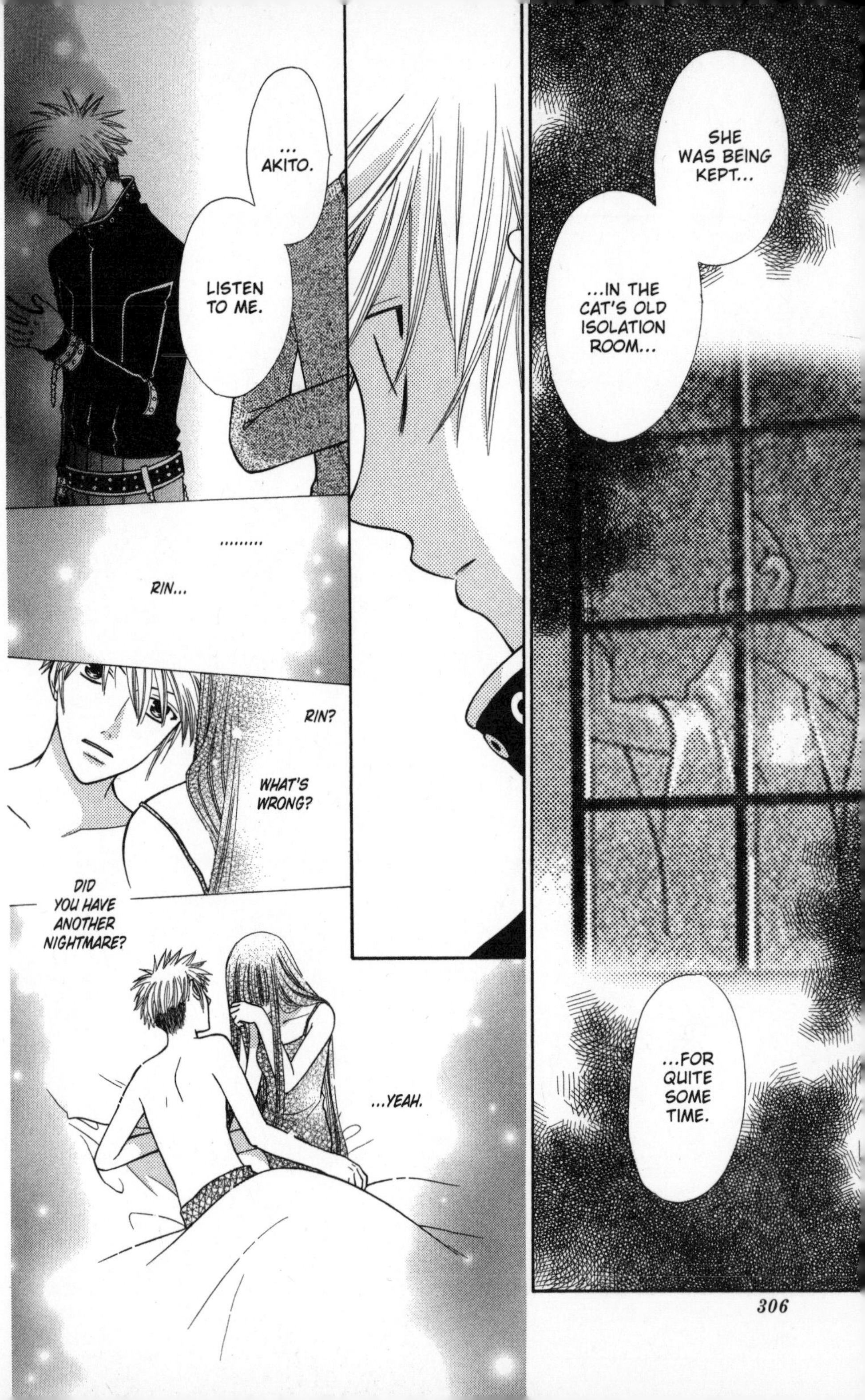
SHE WAS BEING KEPT...
...IN THE CAT'S OLD ISOLATION ROOM...
...FOR QUITE SOME TIME.
...AKITO.
LISTEN TO ME.
....
RIN...
RIN?
WHAT'S WRONG?
DID YOU HAVE ANOTHER NIGHTMARE?
...YEAH.

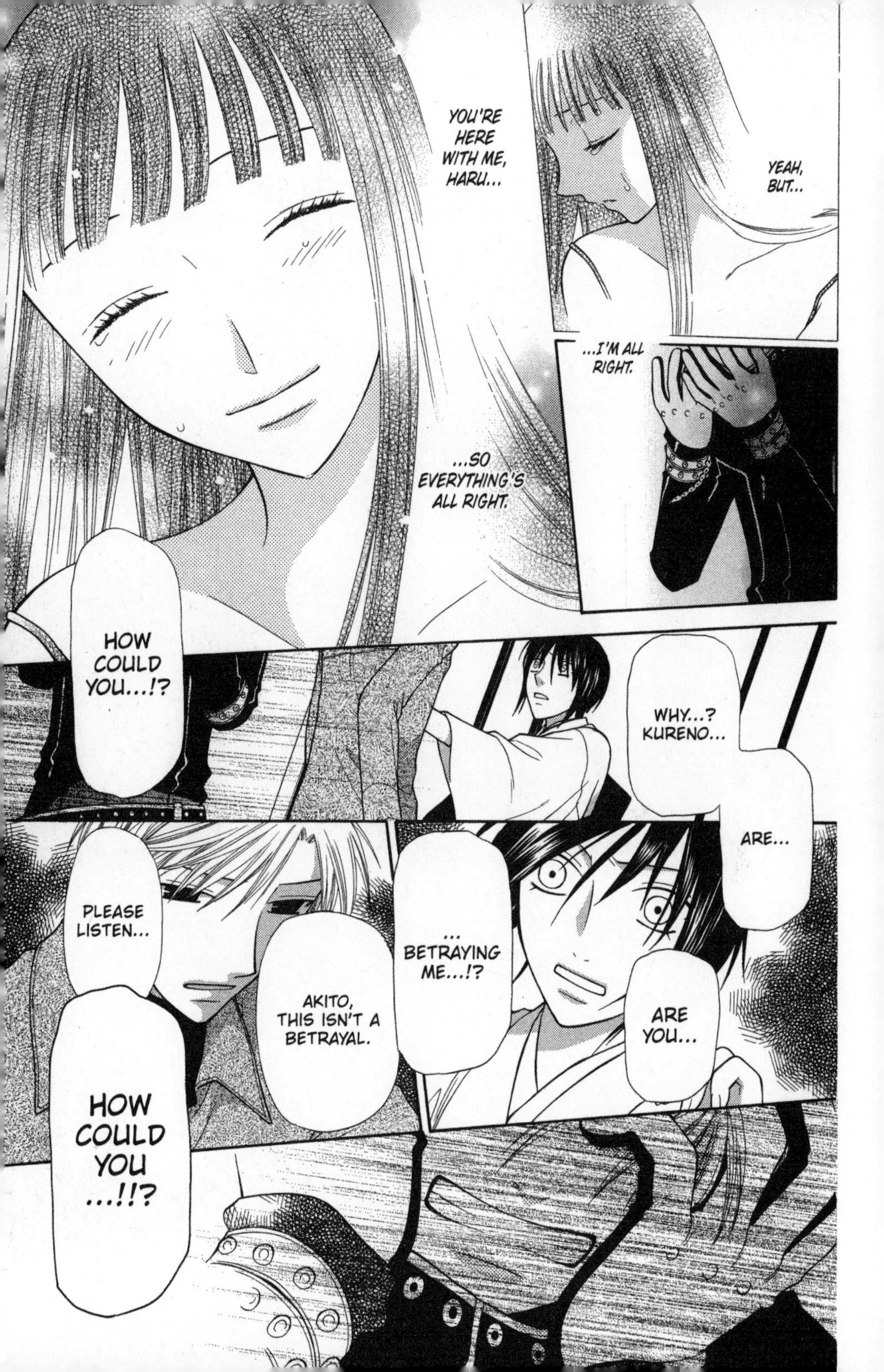
YEAH, BUT...
...I'M ALL RIGHT.
YOU'RE HERE WITH ME, HARU...
...SO EVERYTHING'S ALL RIGHT.
WHY...? KURENO...
HOW COULD YOU...!?
ARE...
ARE YOU...
...BETRAYING ME...!?
AKITO, THIS ISN'T A BETRAYAL.
PLEASE LISTEN...
HOW COULD YOU ...!!?

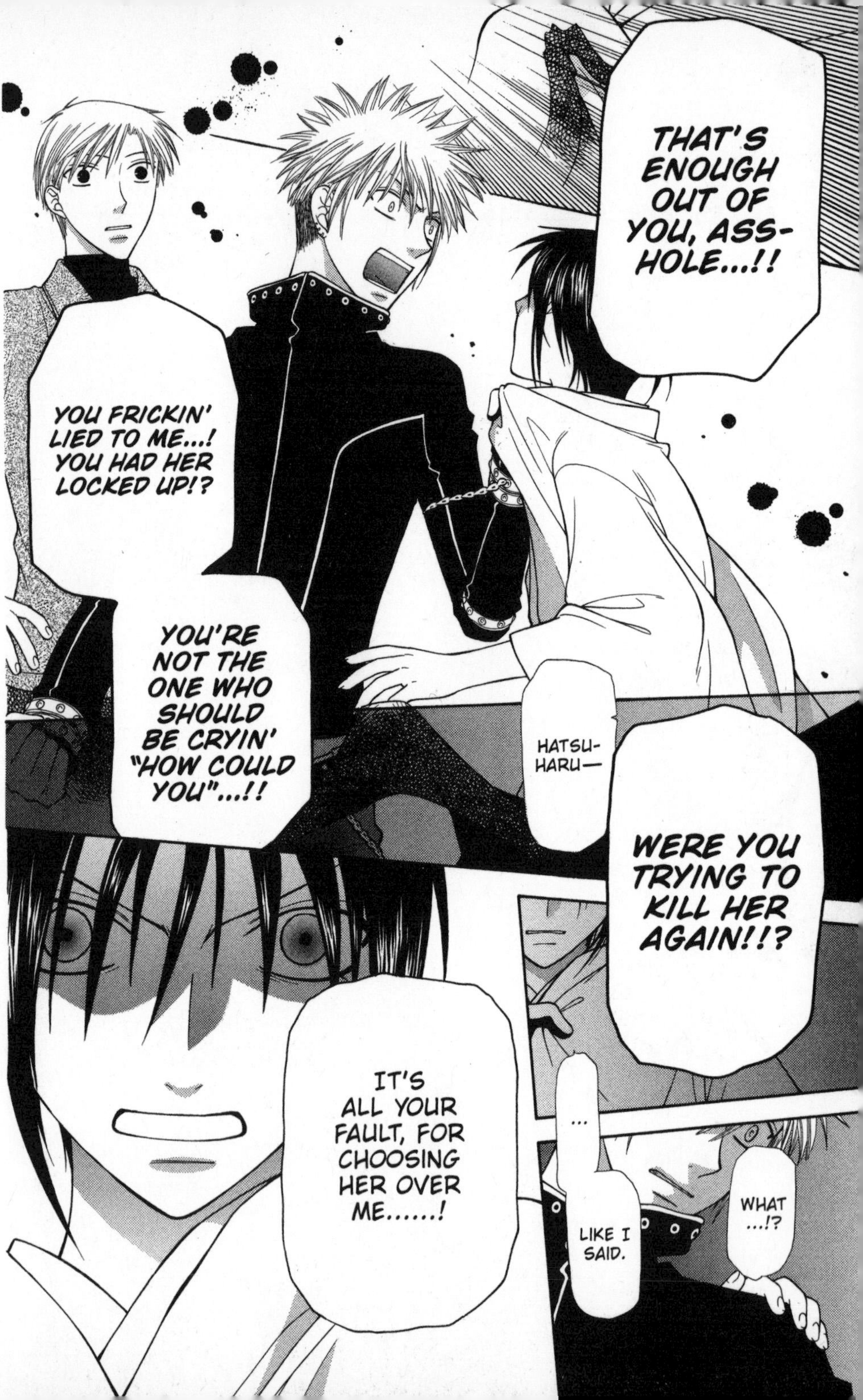
THAT'S ENOUGH OUT OF YOU, ASS-HOLE...!!
YOU FRICKIN' LIED TO ME...! YOU HAD HER LOCKED UP!?
YOU'RE NOT THE ONE WHO SHOULD BE CRYIN' "HOW COULD YOU"...!!
HATSU-HARU—
WERE YOU TRYING TO KILL HER AGAIN!!?
...
WHAT ...!?
LIKE I SAID.
IT'S ALL YOUR FAULT, FOR CHOOSING HER OVER ME......!

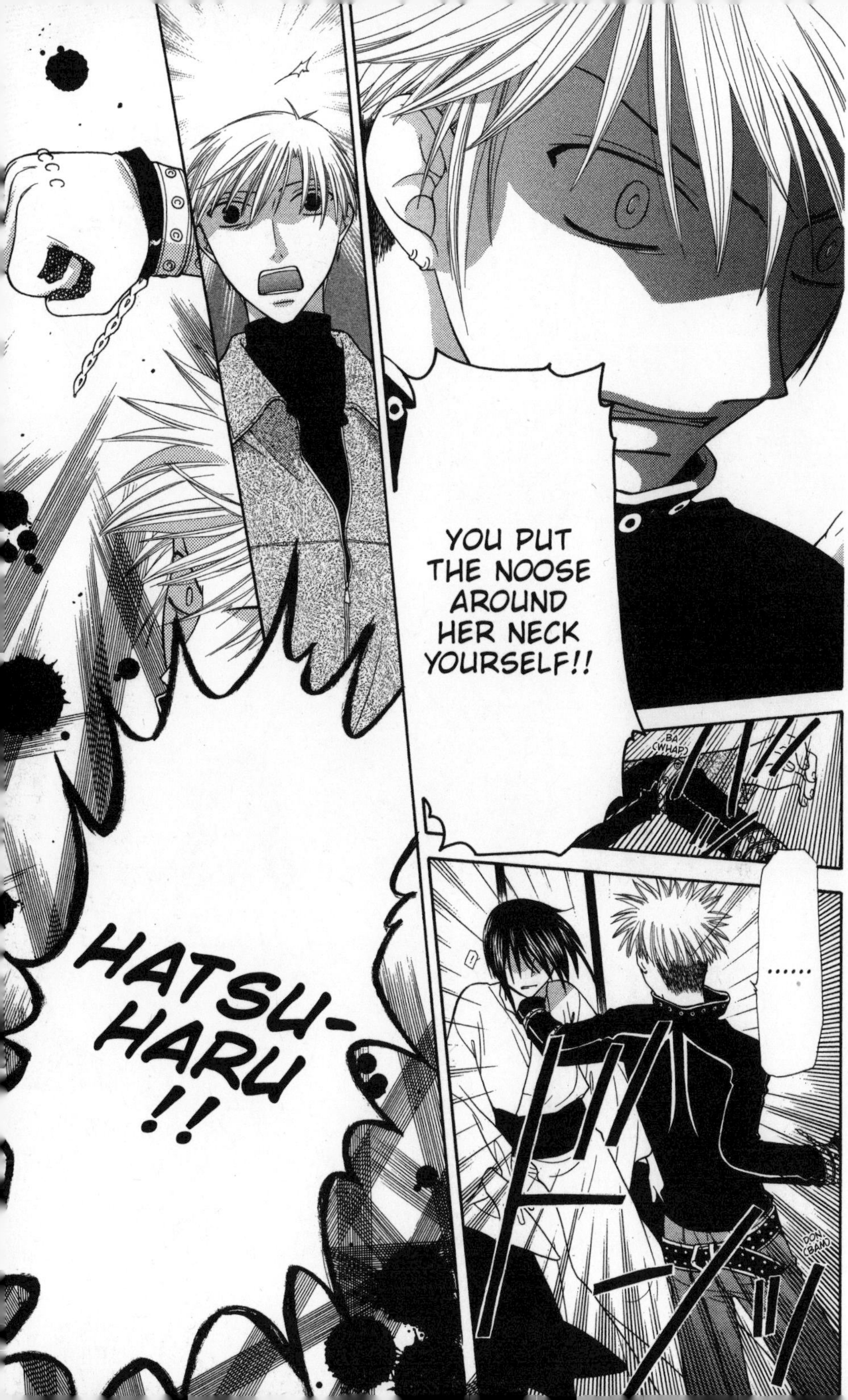
YOU PUT THE NOOSE AROUND HER NECK YOURSELF!!
BA (WHAP)
......
!
DON (BAN)
HATSU-HARU!!

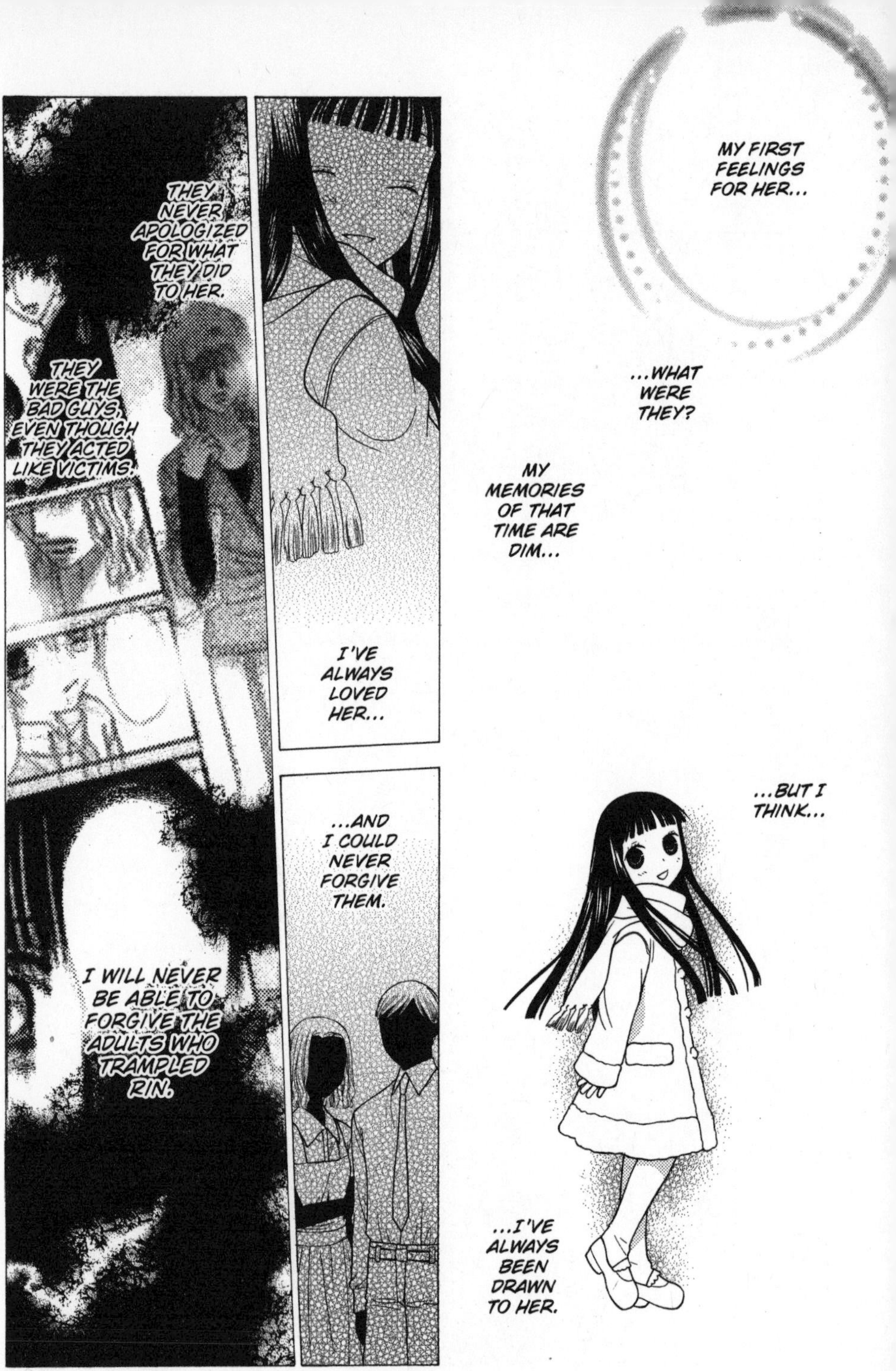
MY FIRST FEELINGS FOR HER...
...WHAT WERE THEY?
MY MEMORIES OF THAT TIME ARE DIM...
...BUT I THINK...
...I'VE ALWAYS BEEN DRAWN TO HER.
I'VE ALWAYS LOVED HER...
...AND I COULD NEVER FORGIVE THEM.
THEY NEVER APOLOGIZED FOR WHAT THEY DID TO HER.
THEY WERE THE BAD GUYS, EVEN THOUGH THEY ACTED LIKE VICTIMS.
I WILL NEVER BE ABLE TO FORGIVE THE ADULTS WHO TRAMPLED RIN.

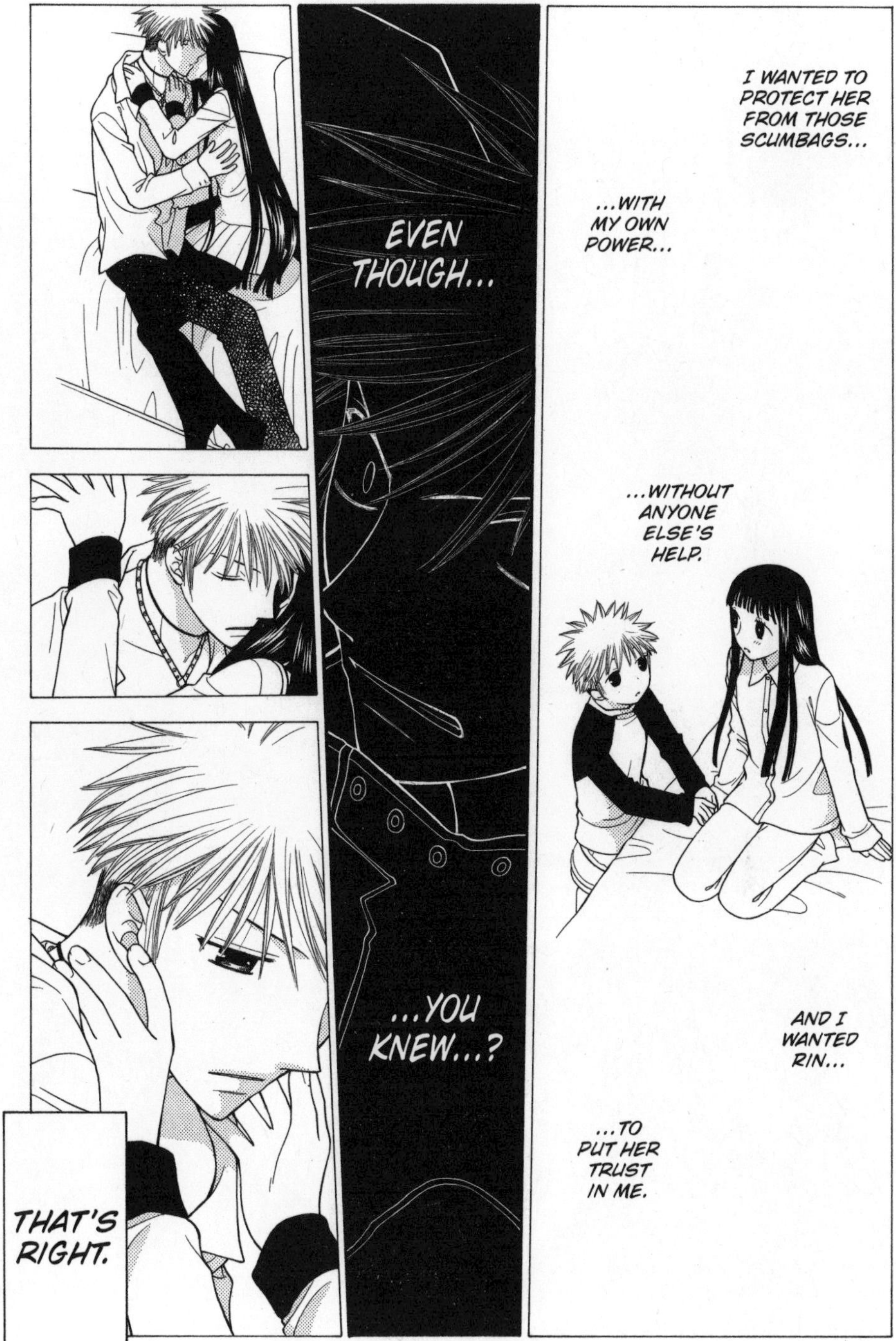
I WANTED TO PROTECT HER FROM THOSE SCUMBAGS...
...WITH MY OWN POWER...
...WITHOUT ANYONE ELSE'S HELP.
AND I WANTED RIN...
...TO PUT HER TRUST IN ME.
EVEN THOUGH...
...YOU KNEW...?
THAT'S RIGHT.

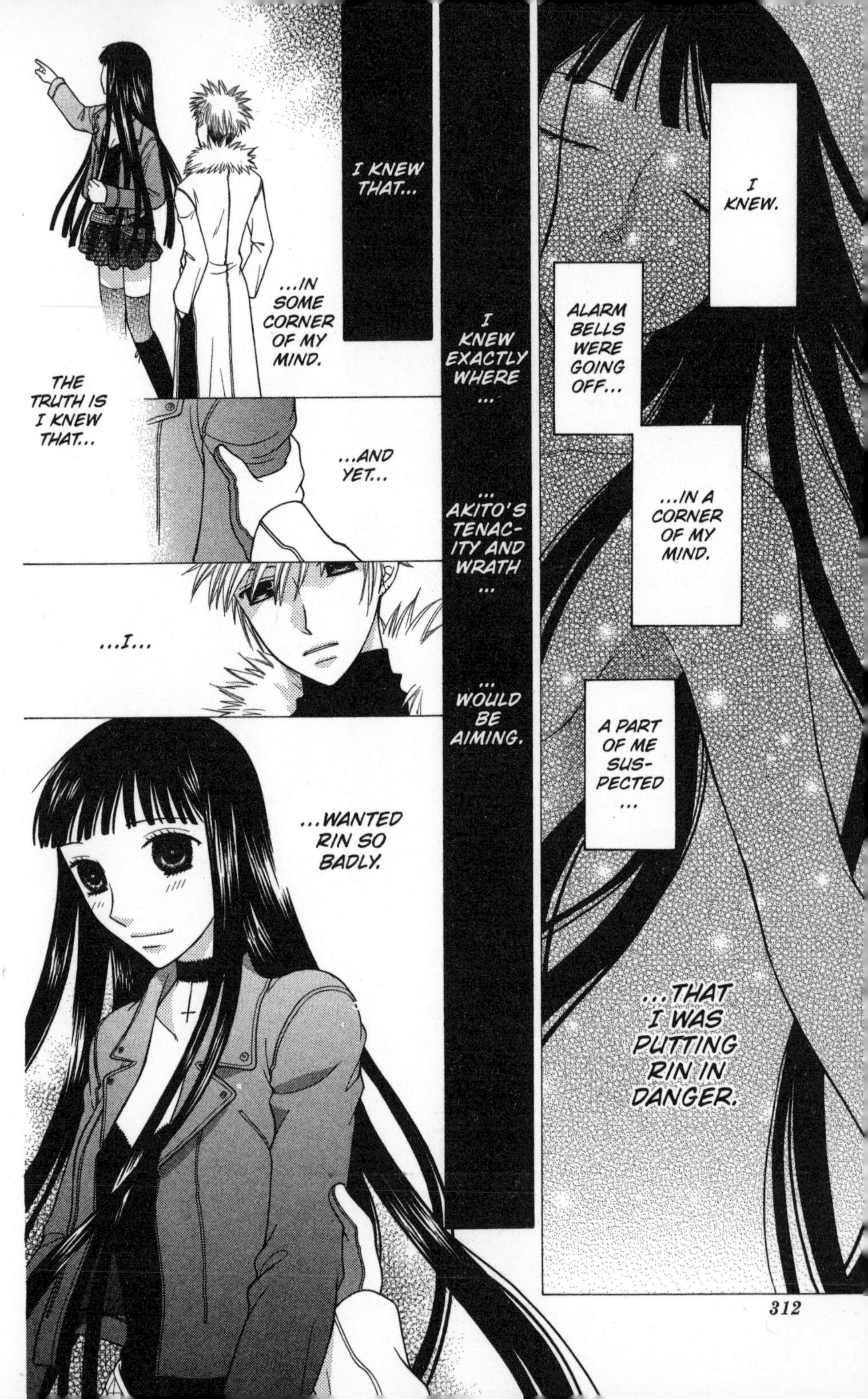
I KNEW.
ALARM BELLS WERE GOING OFF...
...IN A CORNER OF MY MIND.
A PART OF ME SUS-PECTED...
...THAT I WAS PUTTING RIN IN DANGER.
I KNEW EXACTLY WHERE...
...AKITO'S TENAC-ITY AND WRATH...
...WOULD BE AIMING.
I KNEW THAT...
...IN SOME CORNER OF MY MIND.
THE TRUTH IS I KNEW THAT...
...AND YET...
...I...
...WANTED RIN SO BADLY.

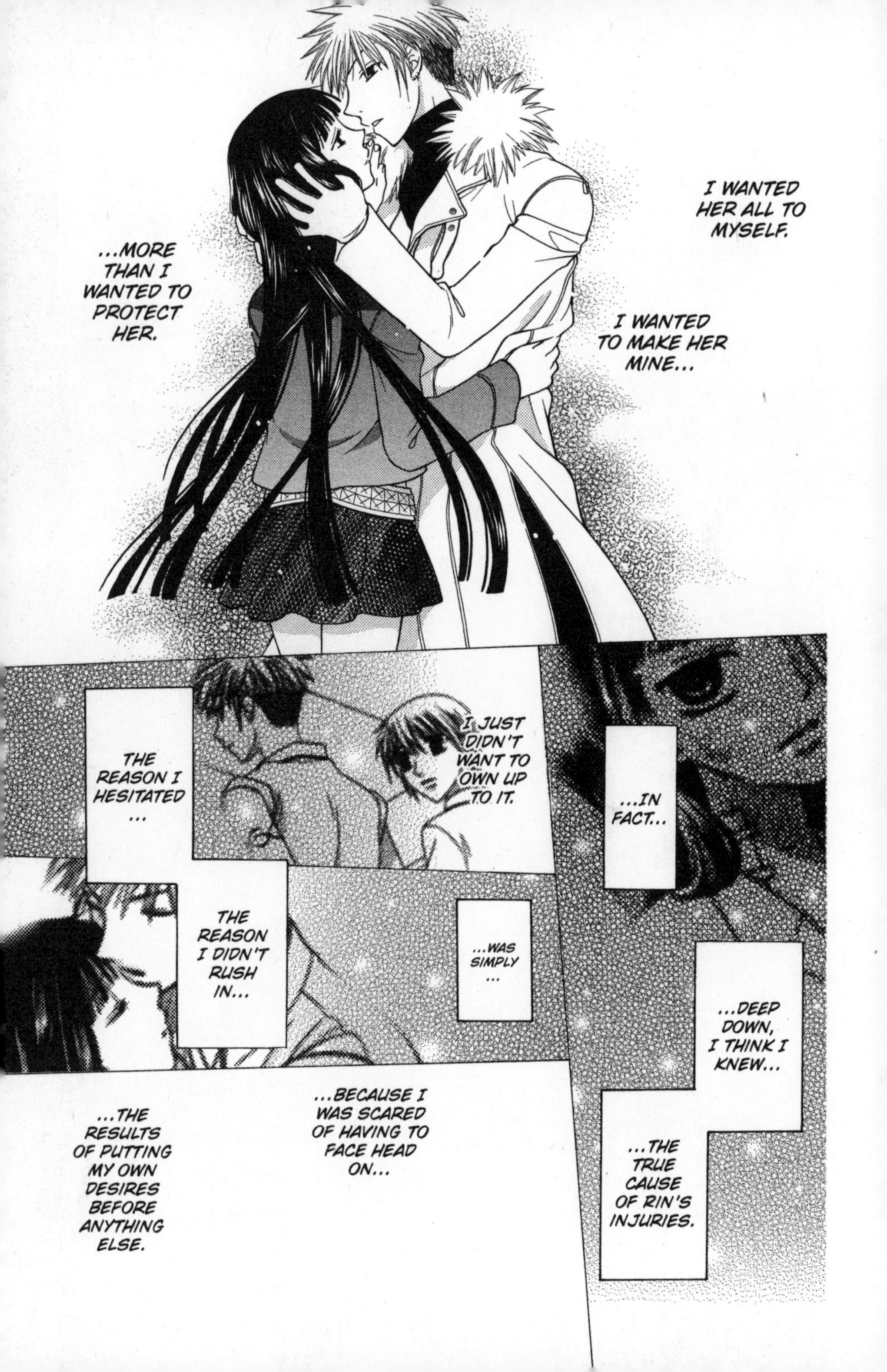
I WANTED HER ALL TO MYSELF.
I WANTED TO MAKE HER MINE...
...MORE THAN I WANTED TO PROTECT HER.
...IN FACT...
...DEEP DOWN, I THINK I KNEW...
...THE TRUE CAUSE OF RIN'S INJURIES.
I JUST DIDN'T WANT TO OWN UP TO IT.
THE REASON I HESITATED...
...WAS SIMPLY...
THE REASON I DIDN'T RUSH IN...
...BECAUSE I WAS SCARED OF HAVING TO FACE HEAD ON...
...THE RESULTS OF PUTTING MY OWN DESIRES BEFORE ANYTHING ELSE.

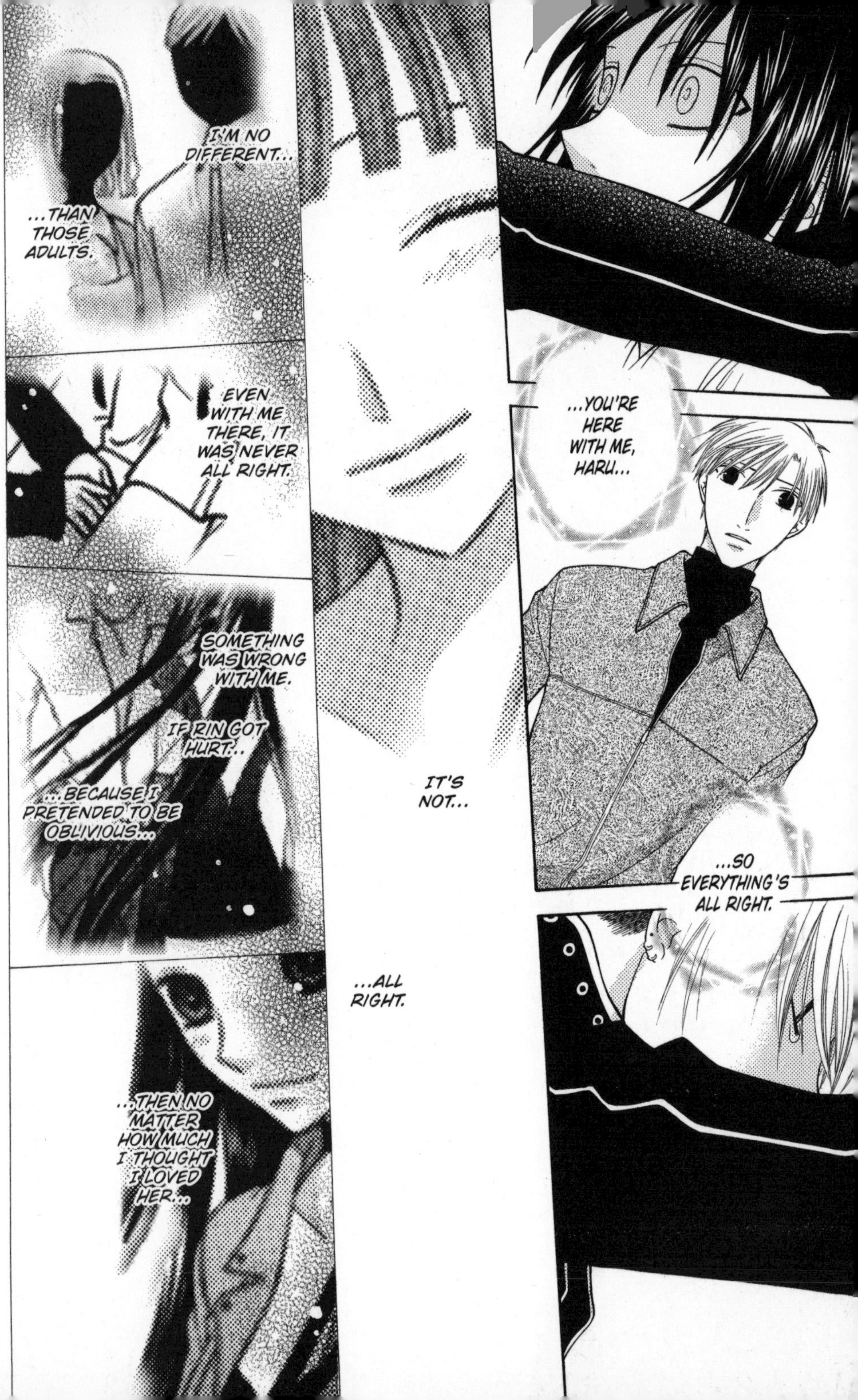
...YOU'RE HERE WITH ME, HARU...
...SO EVERYTHING'S ALL RIGHT.
IT'S NOT...
...ALL RIGHT.
I'M NO DIFFERENT...
...THAN THOSE ADULTS.
EVEN WITH ME THERE, IT WAS NEVER ALL RIGHT.
SOMETHING WAS WRONG WITH ME.
IF RIN GOT HURT...
...BECAUSE I PRETENDED TO BE OBLIVIOUS...
...THEN NO MATTER HOW MUCH I THOUGHT I LOVED HER...

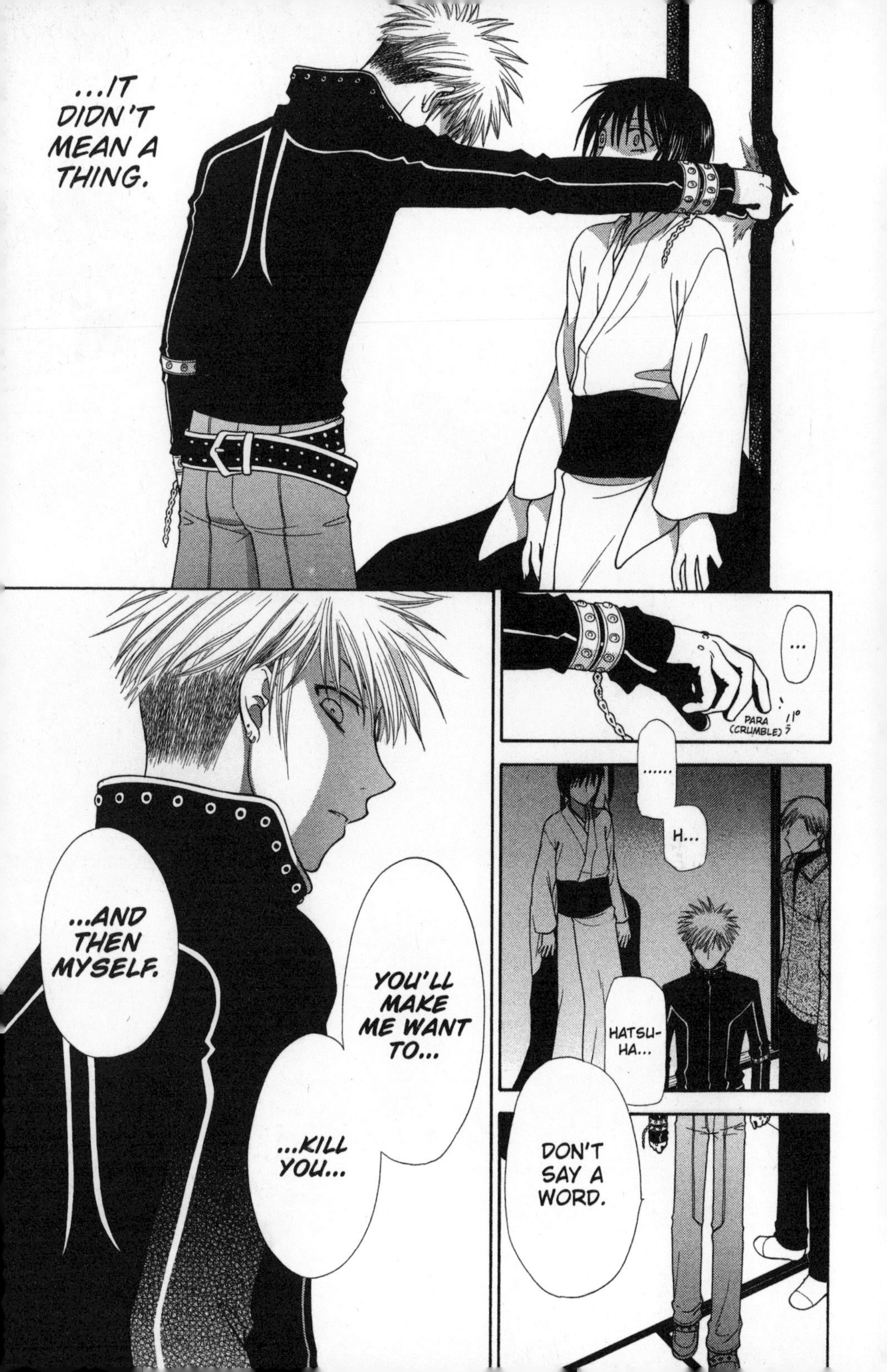
...IT DIDN'T MEAN A THING.
...
PARA (CRUMBLE)
......
H...
HATSU-HA...
DON'T SAY A WORD.
YOU'LL MAKE ME WANT TO...
...KILL YOU...
...AND THEN MYSELF.

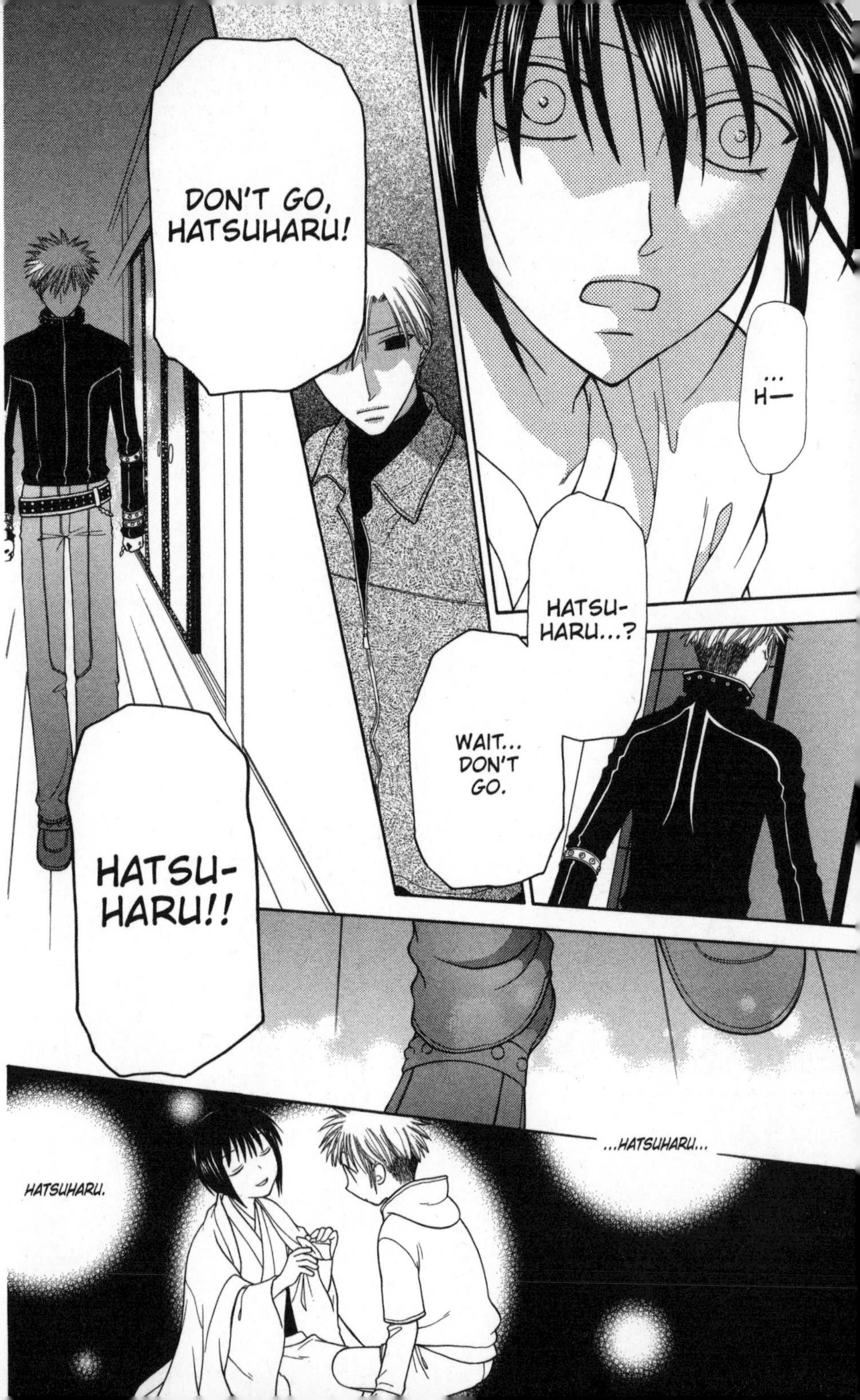

... H—
HATSU-HARU...?
WAIT... DON'T GO.
DON'T GO, HATSUHARU!
HATSU-HARU!!
...HATSUHARU...
HATSUHARU.

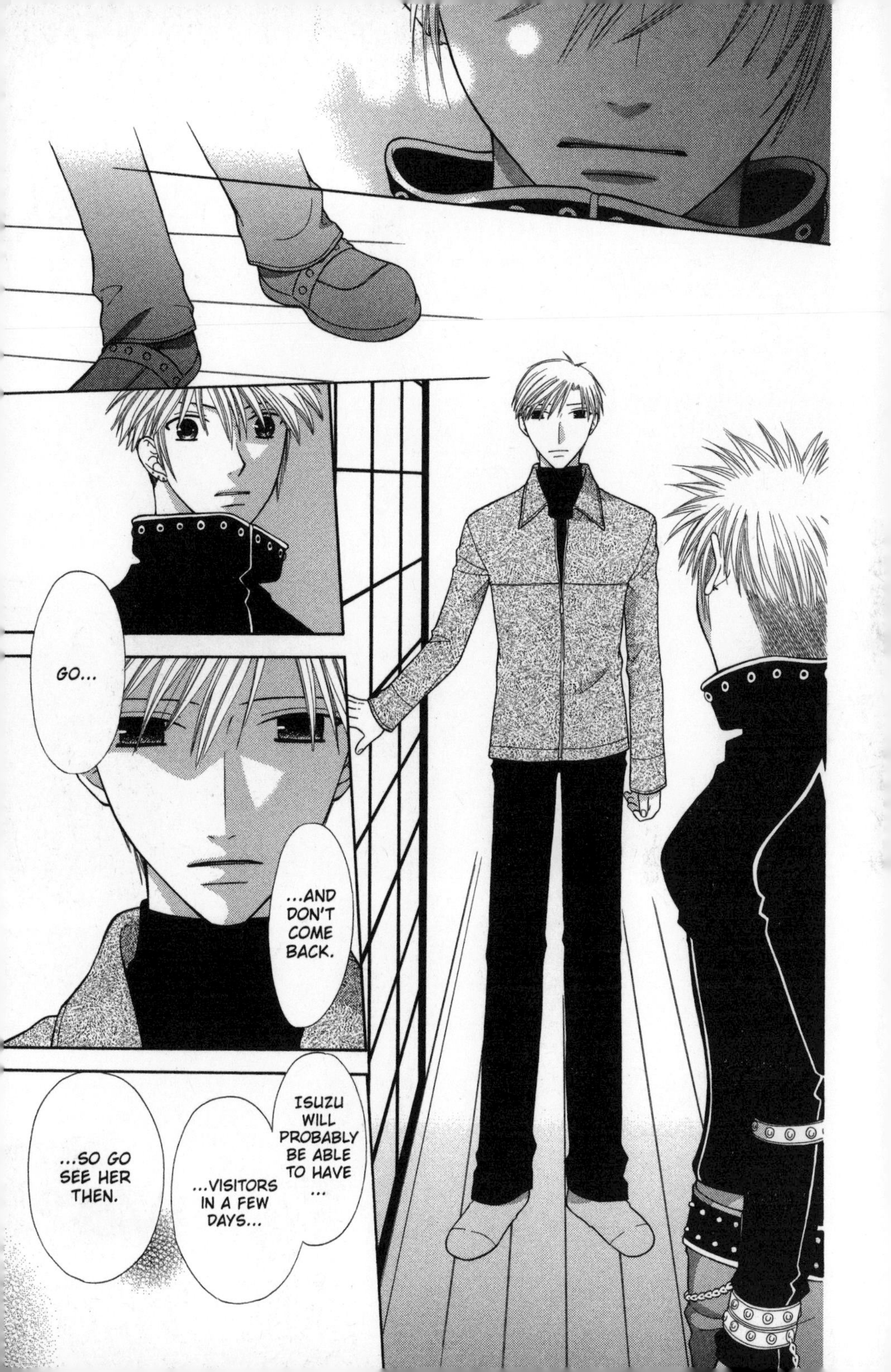

GO...
...AND DON'T COME BACK.
ISUZU WILL PROBABLY BE ABLE TO HAVE ...
...VISITORS IN A FEW DAYS...
...SO GO SEE HER THEN.

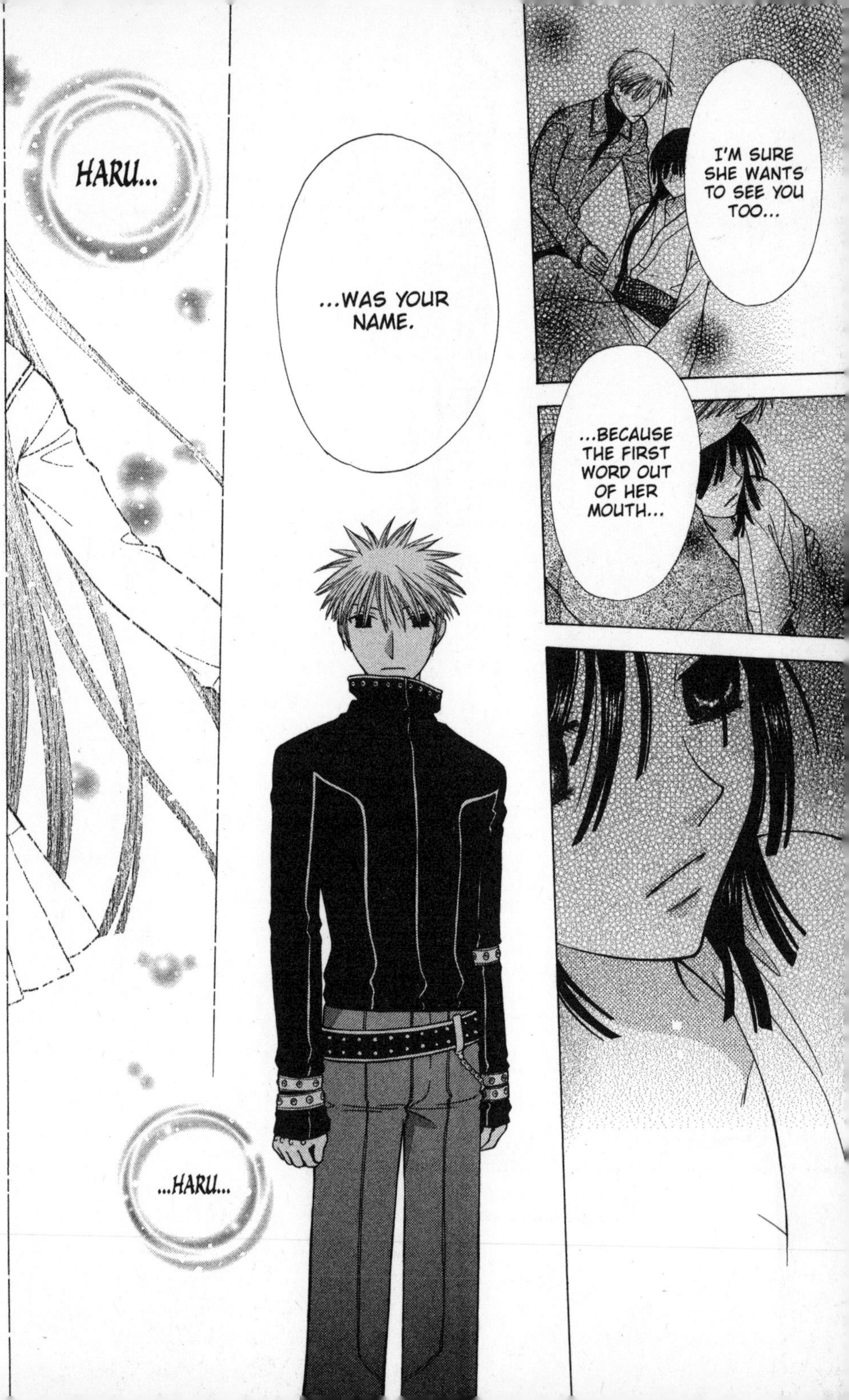
I'M SURE SHE WANTS TO SEE YOU TOO...
...BECAUSE THE FIRST WORD OUT OF HER MOUTH...
...WAS YOUR NAME.
HARU...
...HARU...

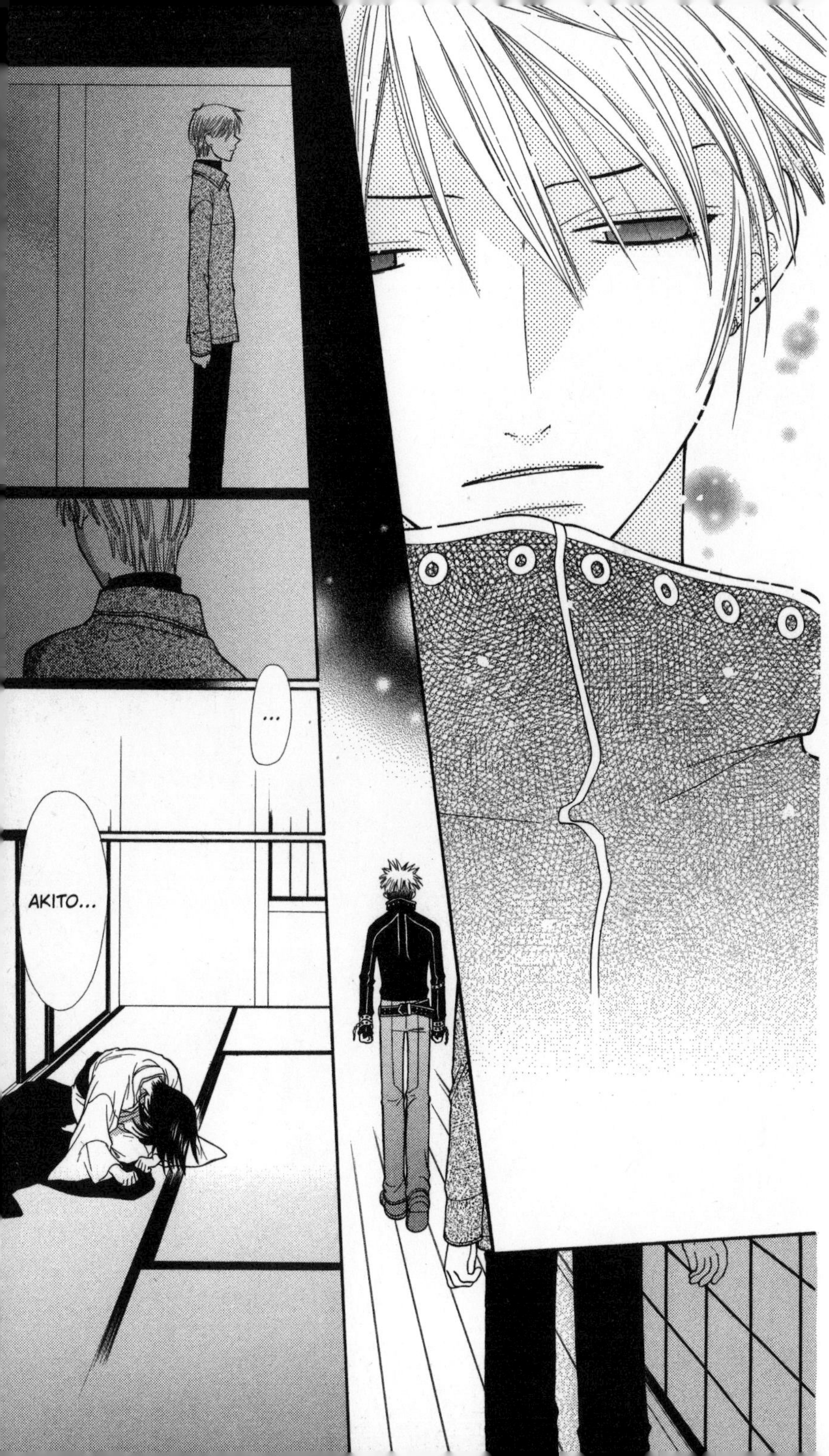
...
AKITO...

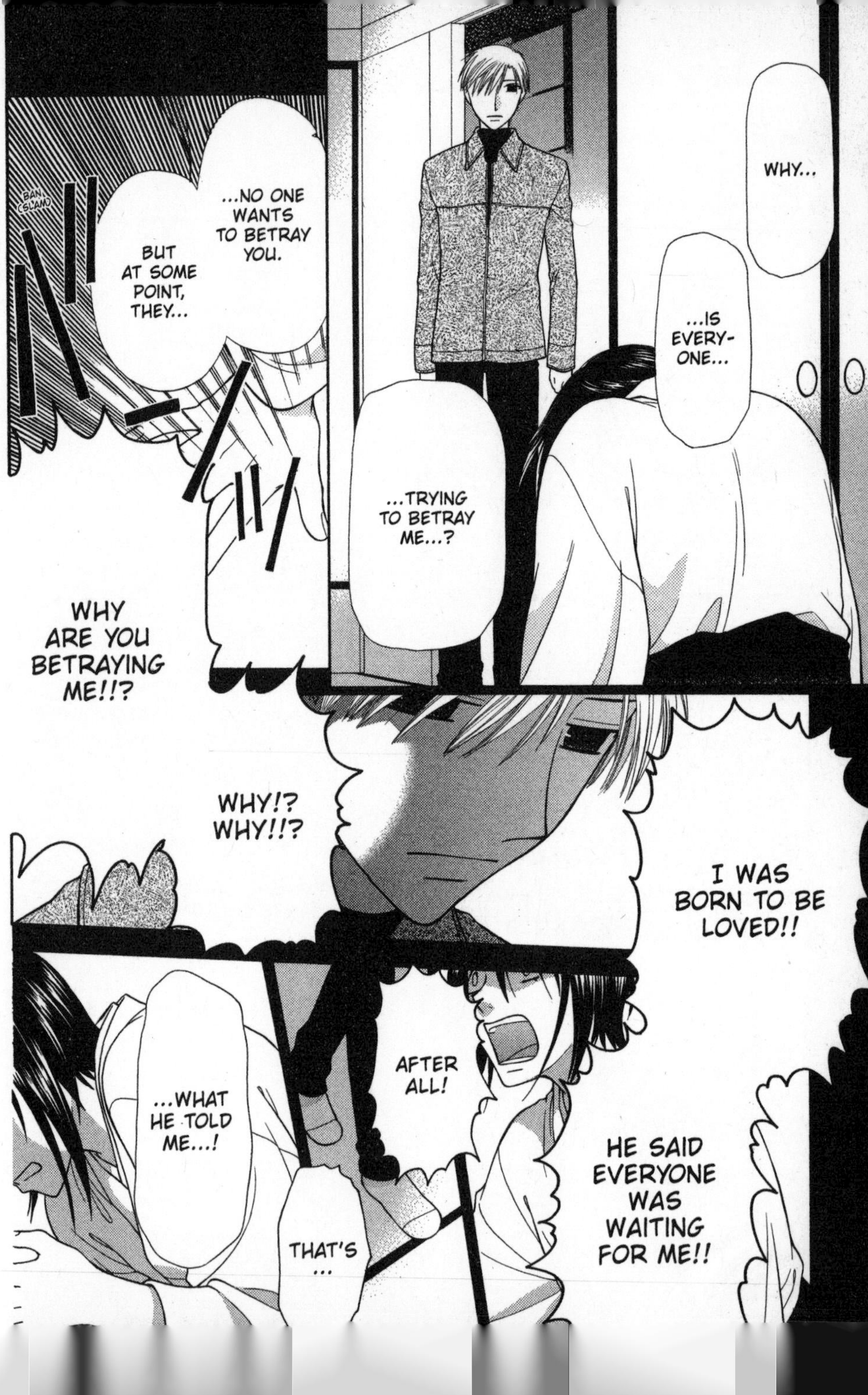
WHY...
...IS EVERYONE...
...TRYING TO BETRAY ME...?
...NO ONE WANTS TO BETRAY YOU.
BUT AT SOME POINT, THEY...
WHY ARE YOU BETRAYING ME!!?
I WAS BORN TO BE LOVED!!
WHY!? WHY!!?
HE SAID EVERYONE WAS WAITING FOR ME!!
AFTER ALL!
THAT'S ...
...WHAT HE TOLD ME...!

HELP ME...

FATHER
...

FATHER
...

FATHER
......

HELP ME.

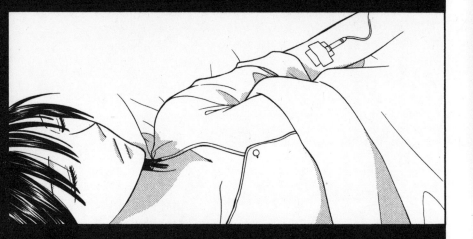

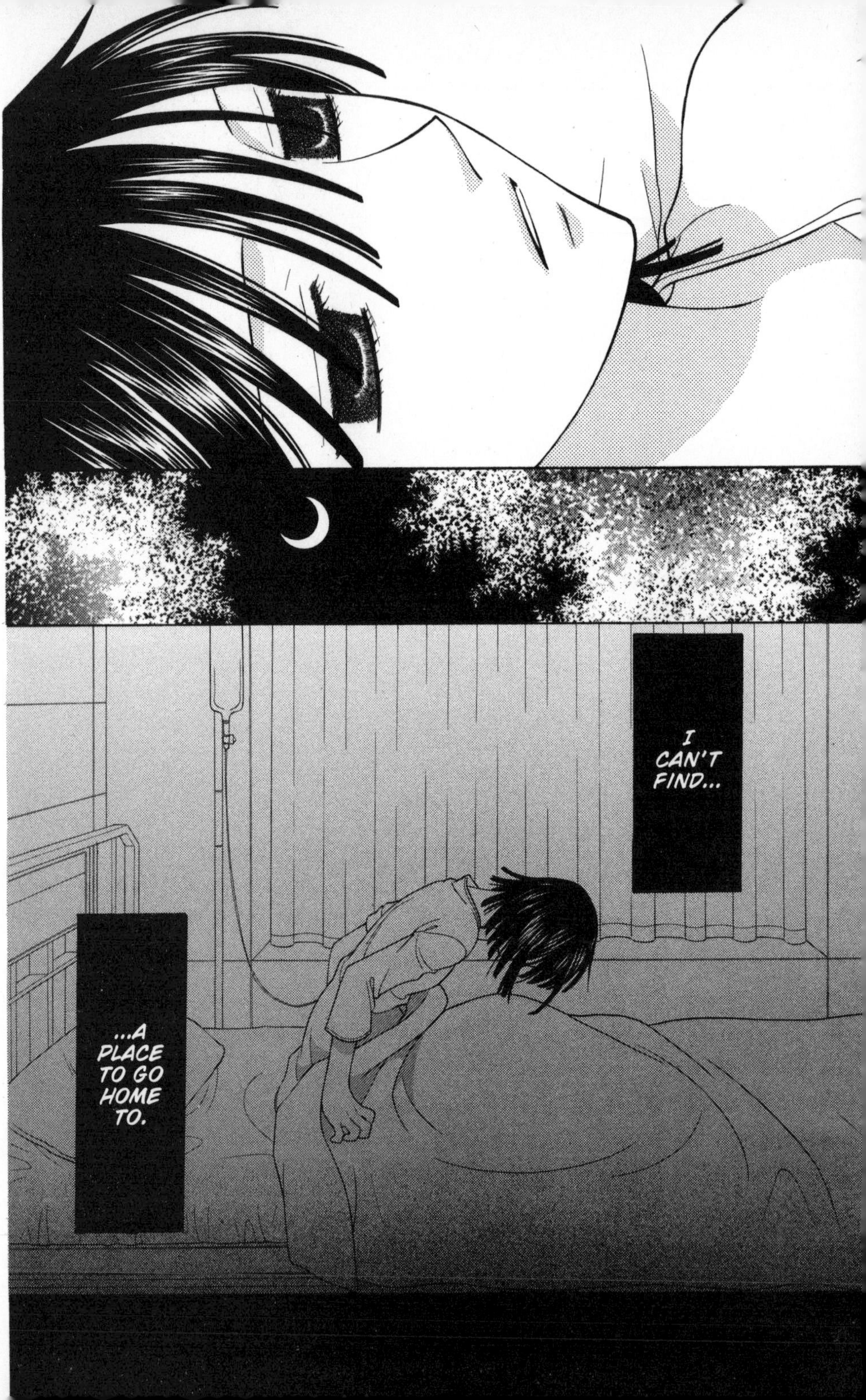
I CAN'T FIND...
...A PLACE TO GO HOME TO.

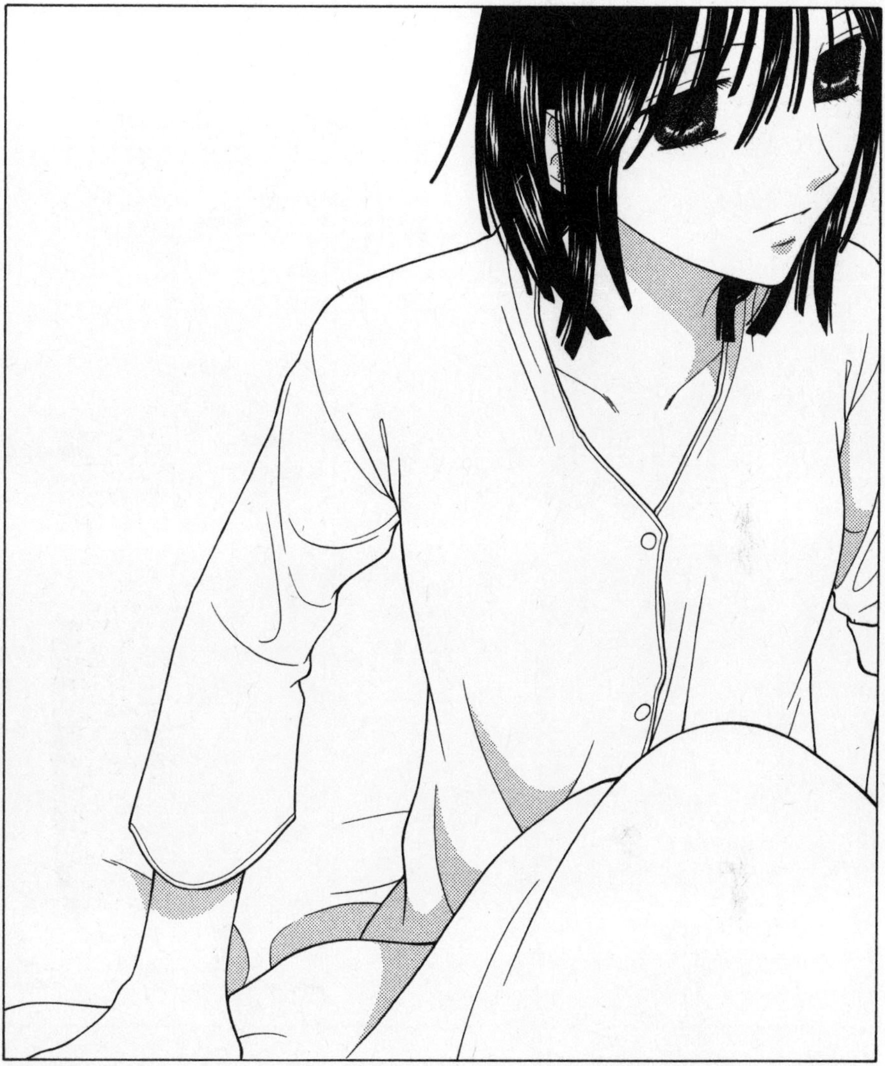

Chapter 106

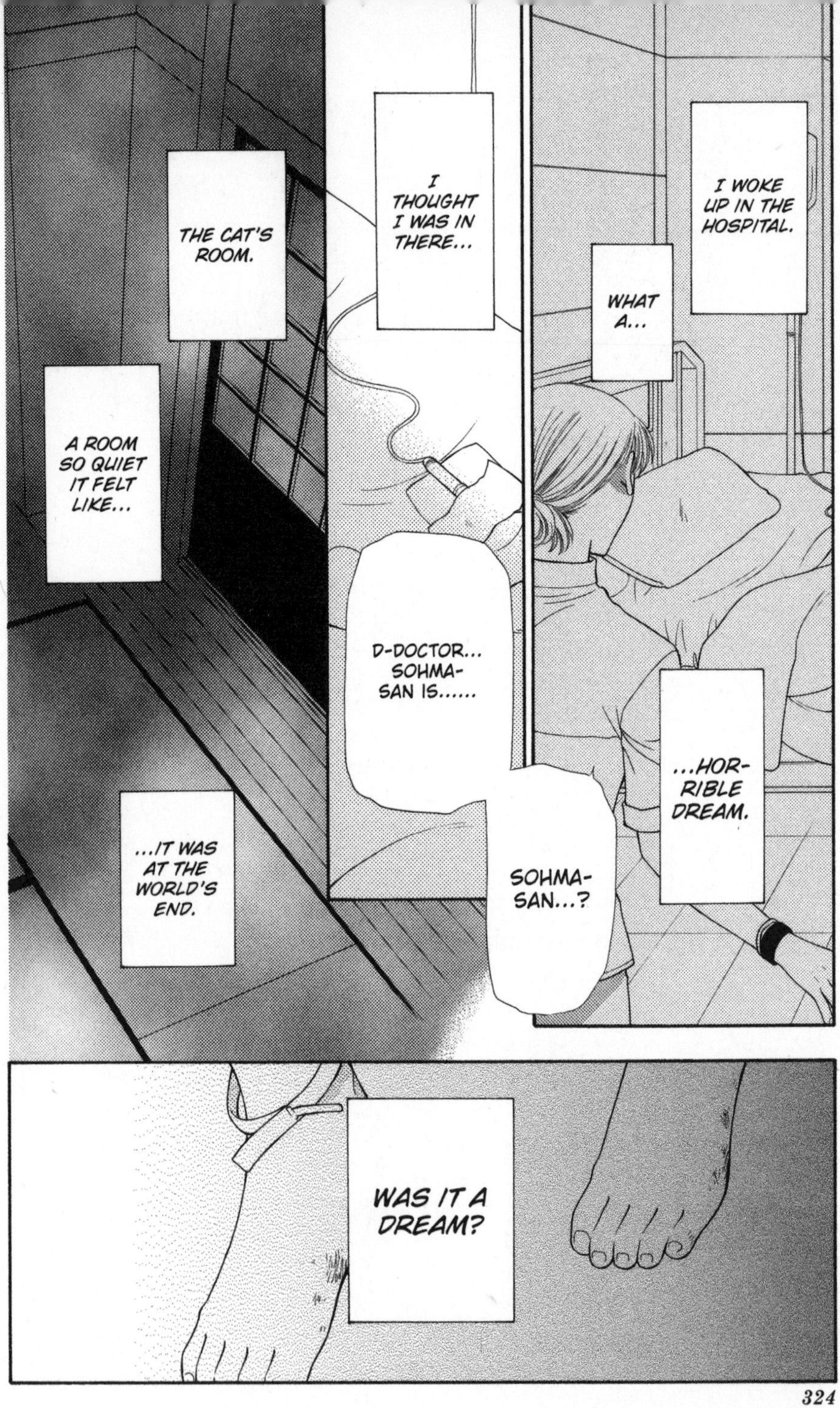
I WOKE UP IN THE HOSPITAL.
WHAT A...
...HOR-RIBLE DREAM.
SOHMA-SAN...?
I THOUGHT I WAS IN THERE...
D-DOCTOR... SOHMA-SAN IS......
THE CAT'S ROOM.
A ROOM SO QUIET IT FELT LIKE...
...IT WAS AT THE WORLD'S END.
WAS IT A DREAM?

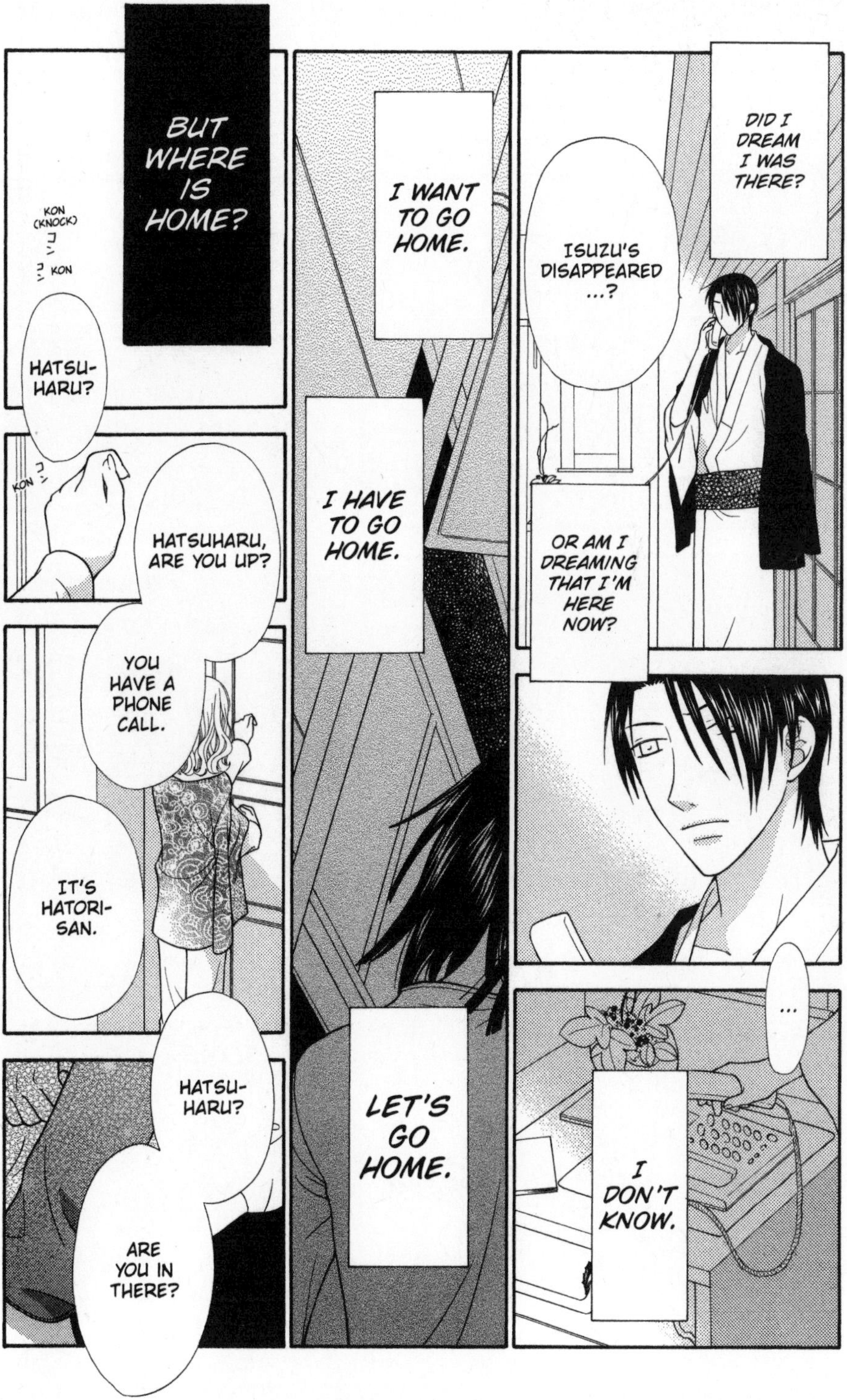
DID I DREAM I WAS THERE?
ISUZU'S DISAPPEARED ...?
OR AM I DREAMING THAT I'M HERE NOW?
...
I DON'T KNOW.
I WANT TO GO HOME.
I HAVE TO GO HOME.
LET'S GO HOME.
BUT WHERE IS HOME?
KON (KNOCK)
KON
HATSU-HARU?
KON
HATSUHARU, ARE YOU UP?
YOU HAVE A PHONE CALL.
IT'S HATORI-SAN.
HATSU-HARU?
ARE YOU IN THERE?

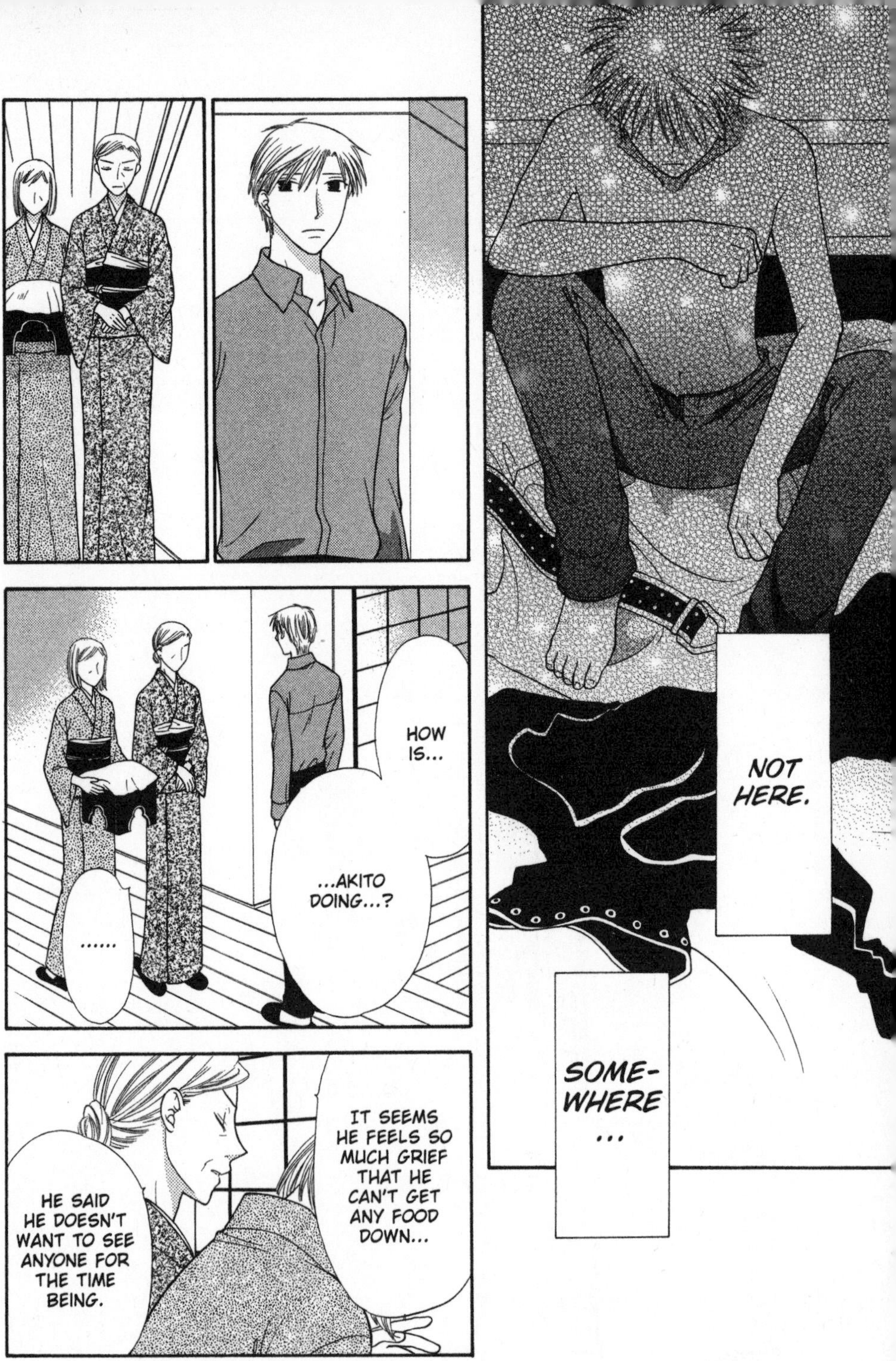

NOT HERE.
SOME-WHERE...
HOW IS...
...AKITO DOING...?
......
IT SEEMS HE FEELS SO MUCH GRIEF THAT HE CAN'T GET ANY FOOD DOWN...
HE SAID HE DOESN'T WANT TO SEE ANYONE FOR THE TIME BEING.

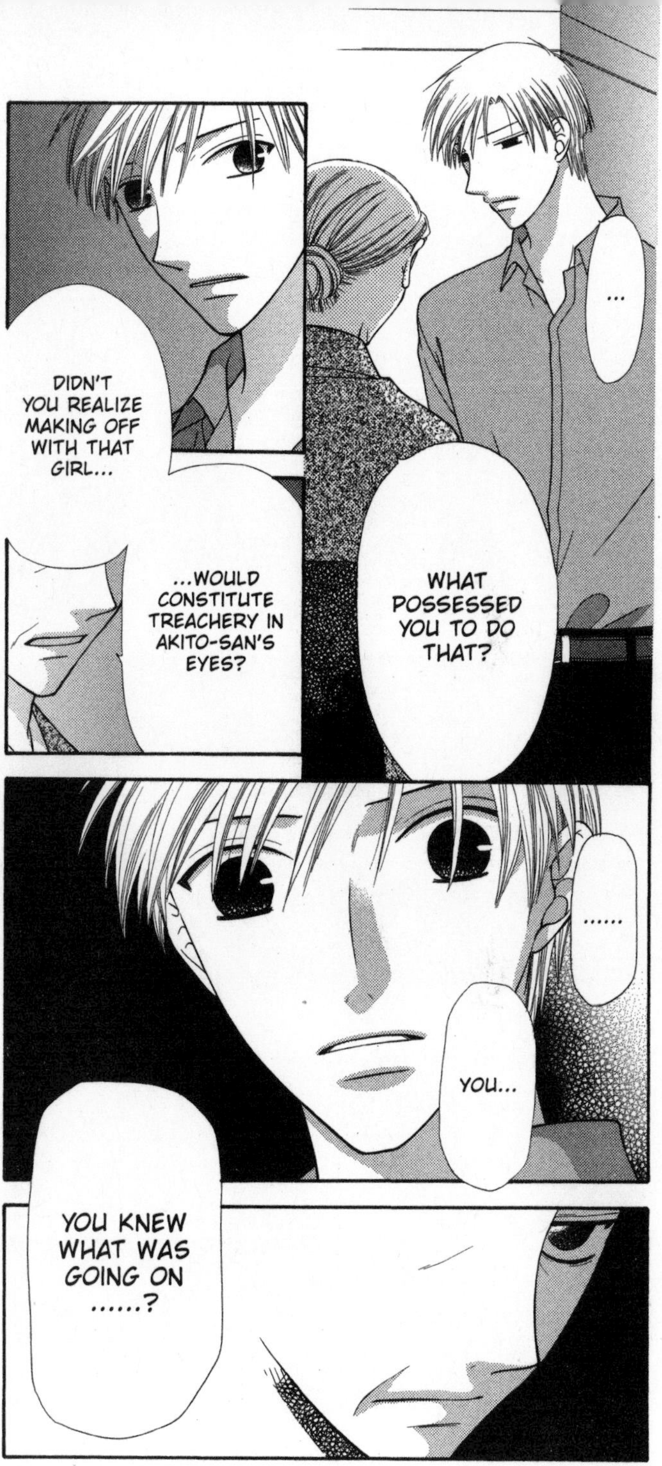
...
WHAT POSSESSED YOU TO DO THAT?
DIDN'T YOU REALIZE MAKING OFF WITH THAT GIRL...
...WOULD CONSTITUTE TREACHERY IN AKITO-SAN'S EYES?
......
YOU...
YOU KNEW WHAT WAS GOING ON ......?

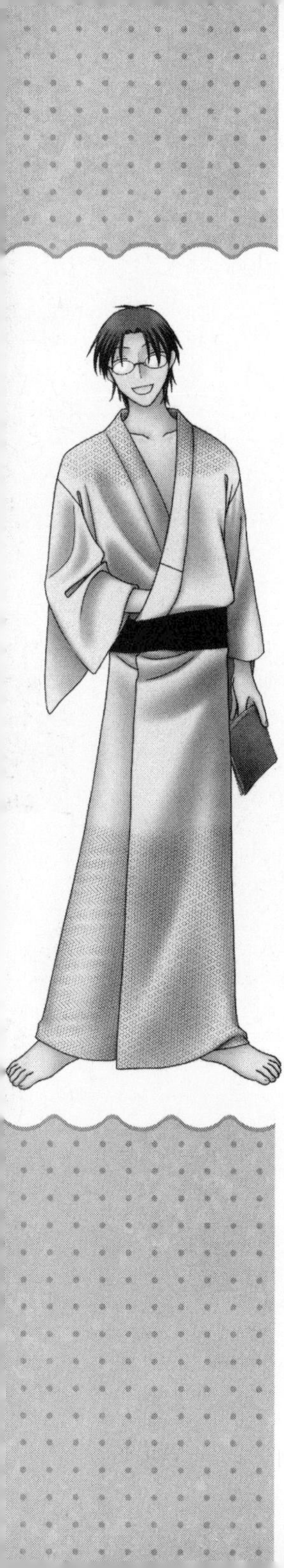

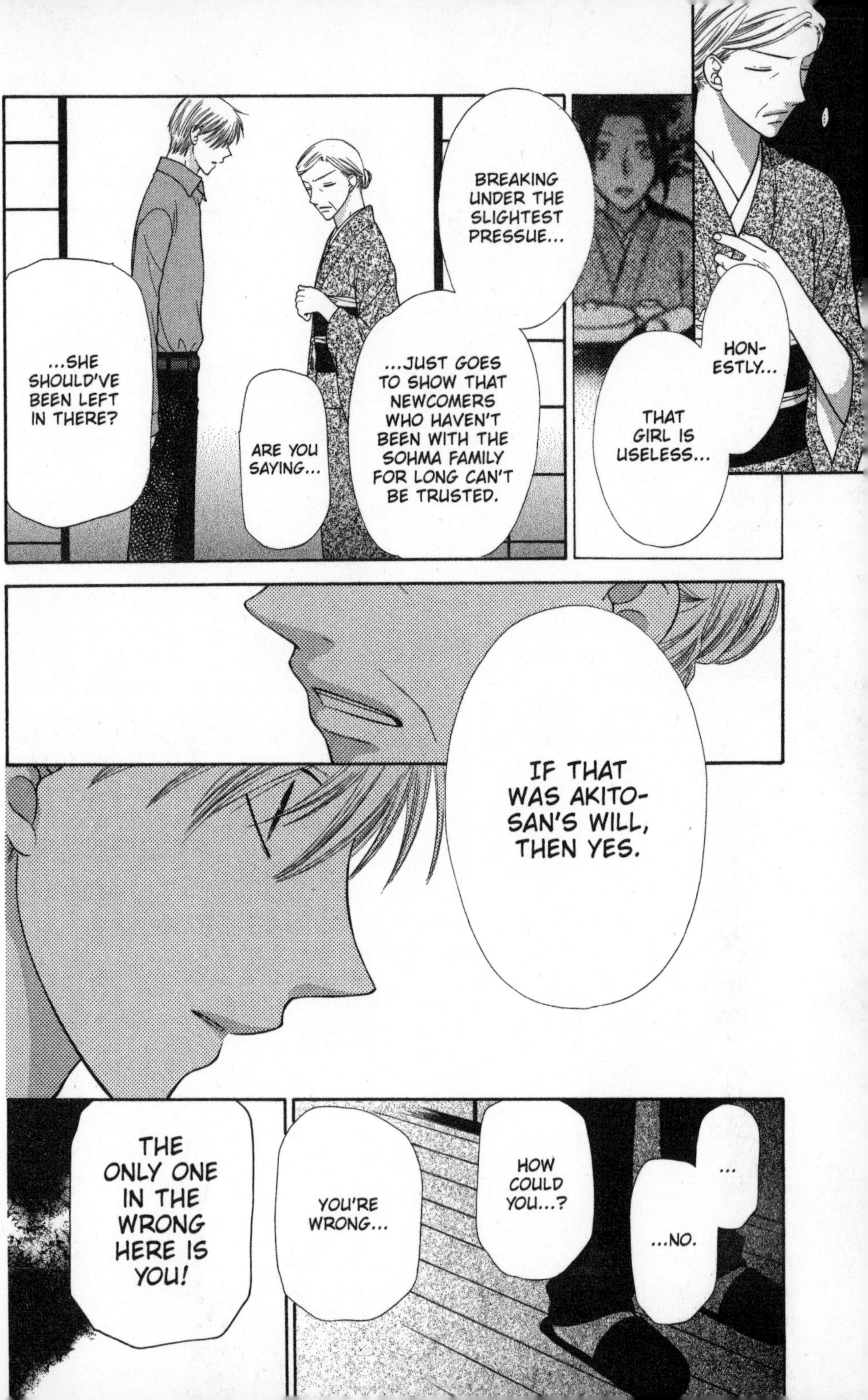
HON-ESTLY...
THAT GIRL IS USELESS...
BREAKING UNDER THE SLIGHTEST PRESSUE...
...JUST GOES TO SHOW THAT NEWCOMERS WHO HAVEN'T BEEN WITH THE SOHMA FAMILY FOR LONG CAN'T BE TRUSTED.
ARE YOU SAYING...
...SHE SHOULD'VE BEEN LEFT IN THERE?
IF THAT WAS AKITO-SAN'S WILL, THEN YES.
...
...NO.
HOW COULD YOU...?
YOU'RE WRONG...
THE ONLY ONE IN THE WRONG HERE IS YOU!

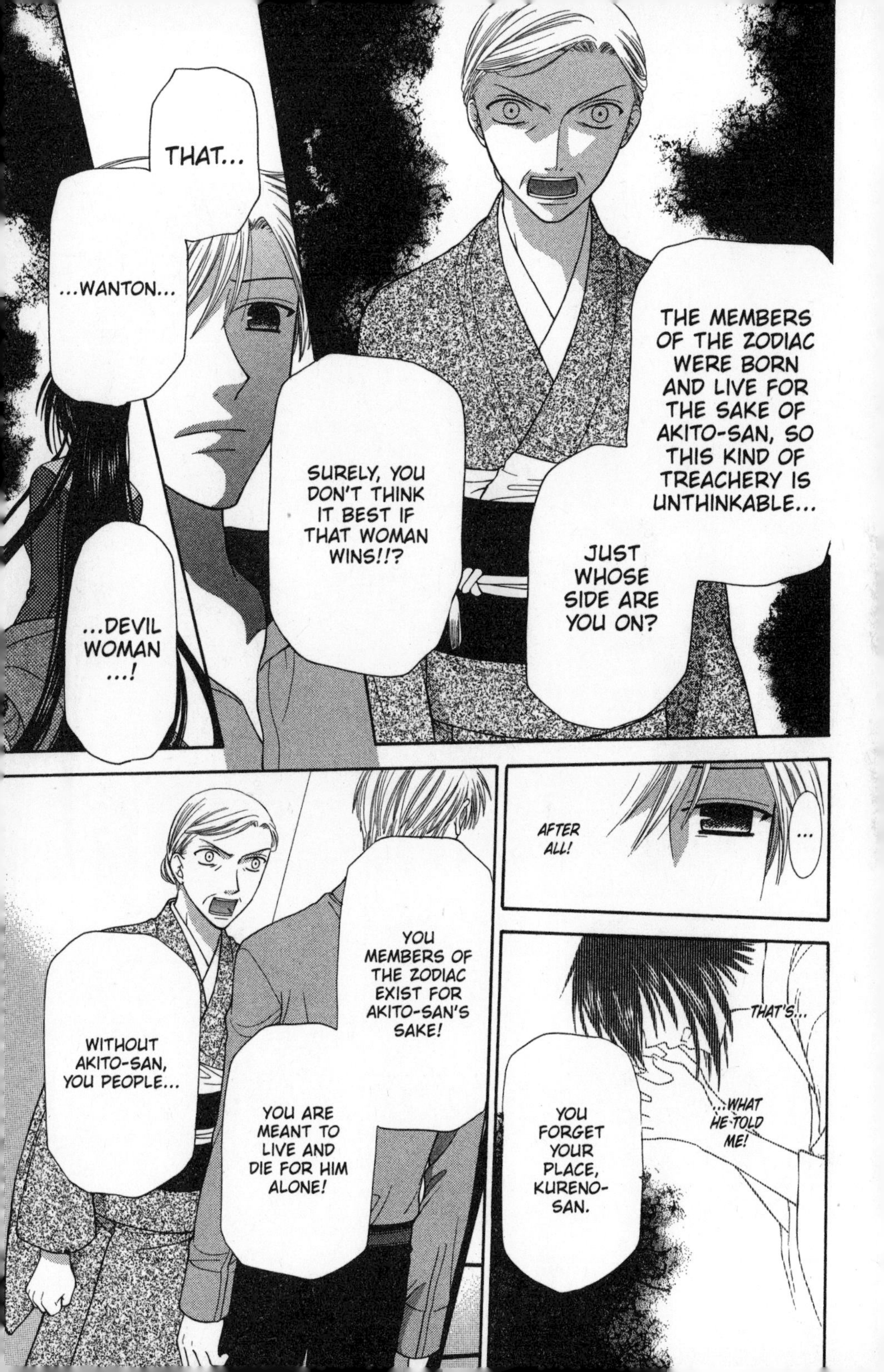
THE MEMBERS OF THE ZODIAC WERE BORN AND LIVE FOR THE SAKE OF AKITO-SAN, SO THIS KIND OF TREACHERY IS UNTHINKABLE...
JUST WHOSE SIDE ARE YOU ON?
SURELY, YOU DON'T THINK IT BEST IF THAT WOMAN WINS!!?
THAT...
...WANTON...
...DEVIL WOMAN ...!
...
AFTER ALL!
THAT'S...
...WHAT HE TOLD ME!
YOU FORGET YOUR PLACE, KURENO-SAN.
YOU MEMBERS OF THE ZODIAC EXIST FOR AKITO-SAN'S SAKE!
YOU ARE MEANT TO LIVE AND DIE FOR HIM ALONE!
WITHOUT AKITO-SAN, YOU PEOPLE...

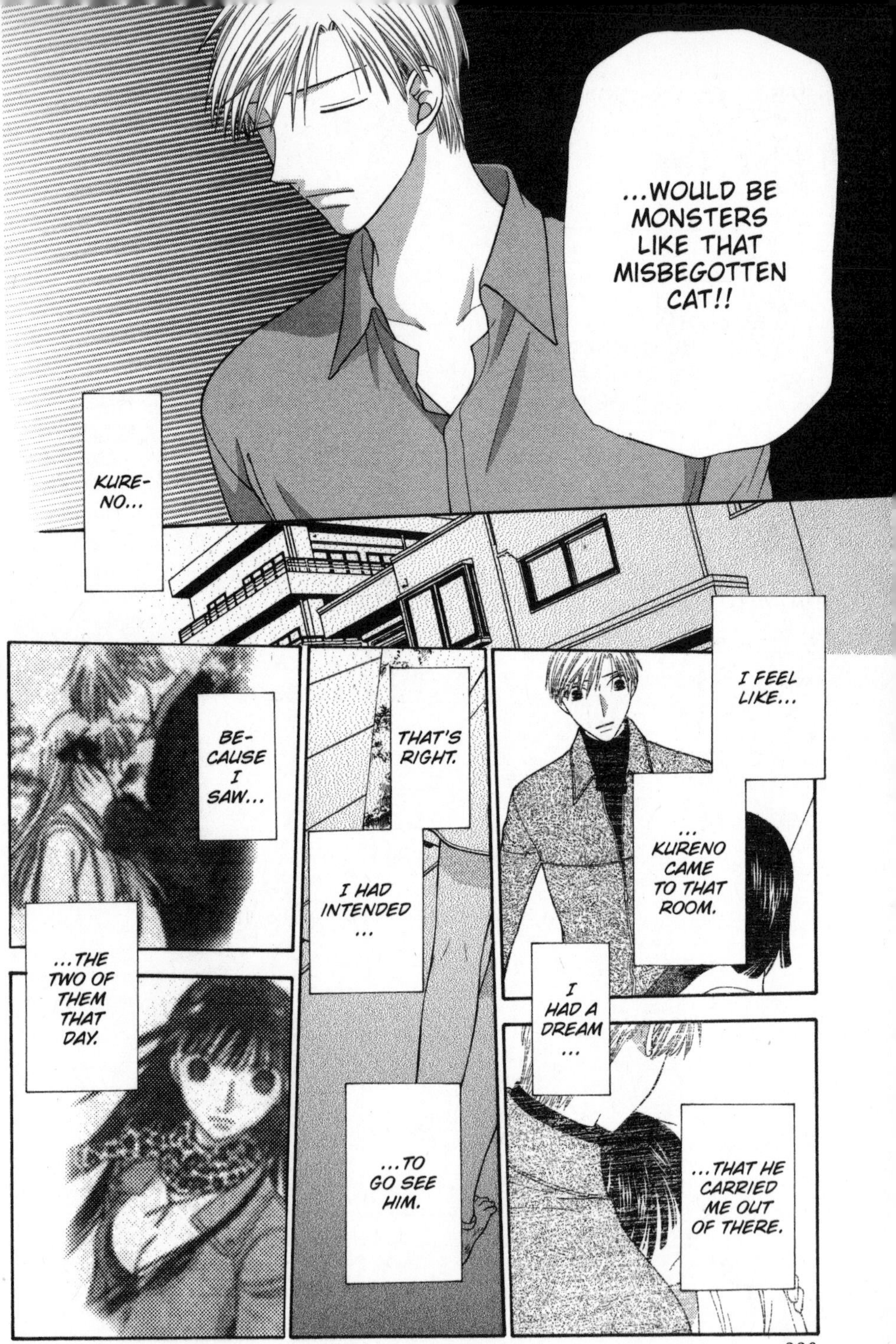
...WOULD BE MONSTERS LIKE THAT MISBEGOTTEN CAT!!
KURE-NO...
I FEEL LIKE...
...KURENO CAME TO THAT ROOM.
I HAD A DREAM...
...THAT HE CARRIED ME OUT OF THERE.
THAT'S RIGHT.
I HAD INTENDED...
...TO GO SEE HIM.
BE-CAUSE I SAW...
...THE TWO OF THEM THAT DAY.

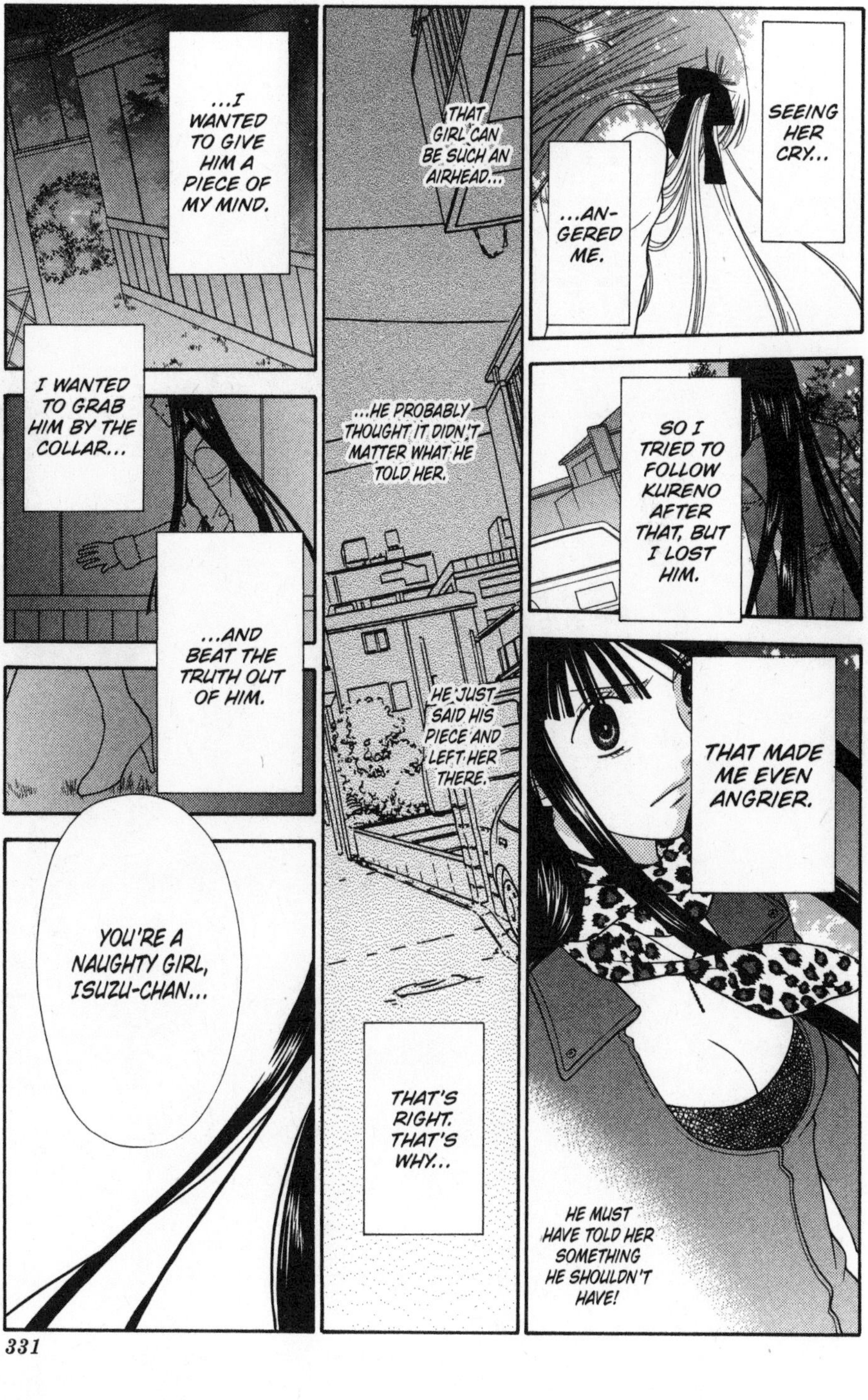
SEEING HER CRY...
...AN-GERED ME.
SO I TRIED TO FOLLOW KURENO AFTER THAT, BUT I LOST HIM.
THAT MADE ME EVEN ANGRIER.
HE MUST HAVE TOLD HER SOMETHING HE SHOULDN'T HAVE!
THAT GIRL CAN BE SUCH AN AIRHEAD...
...HE PROBABLY THOUGHT IT DIDN'T MATTER WHAT HE TOLD HER.
HE JUST SAID HIS PIECE AND LEFT HER THERE.
THAT'S RIGHT. THAT'S WHY...
...I WANTED TO GIVE HIM A PIECE OF MY MIND.
I WANTED TO GRAB HIM BY THE COLLAR...
...AND BEAT THE TRUTH OUT OF HIM.
YOU'RE A NAUGHTY GIRL, ISUZU-CHAN...

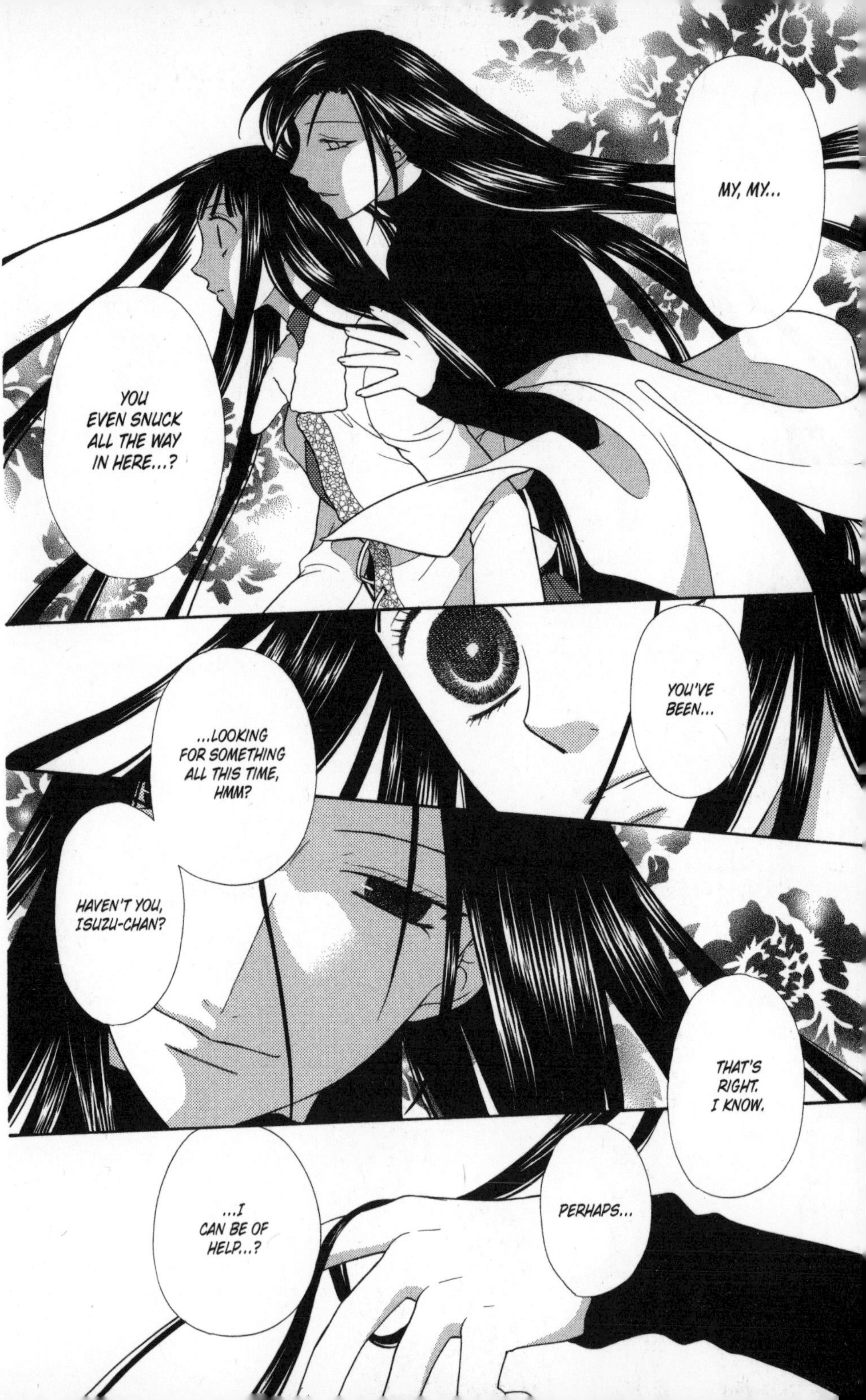
MY, MY...
YOU EVEN SNUCK ALL THE WAY IN HERE...?
YOU'VE BEEN...
...LOOKING FOR SOMETHING ALL THIS TIME, HMM?
HAVEN'T YOU, ISUZU-CHAN?
THAT'S RIGHT. I KNOW.
PERHAPS...
...I CAN BE OF HELP...?

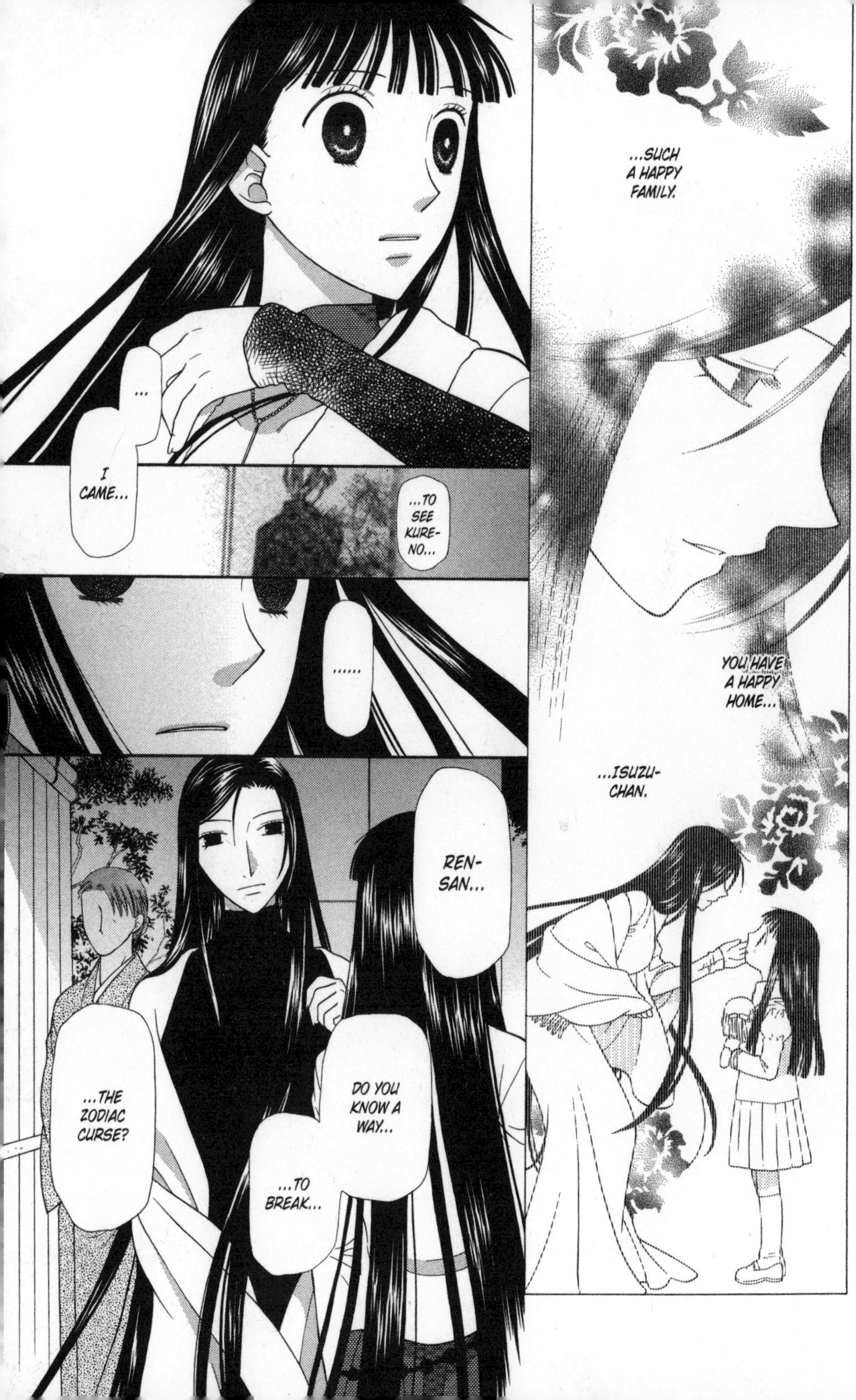
...SUCH A HAPPY FAMILY.
YOU HAVE A HAPPY HOME...
...ISUZU-CHAN.
...
I CAME...
...TO SEE KURE-NO...
......
REN-SAN...
DO YOU KNOW A WAY...
...TO BREAK...
...THE ZODIAC CURSE?

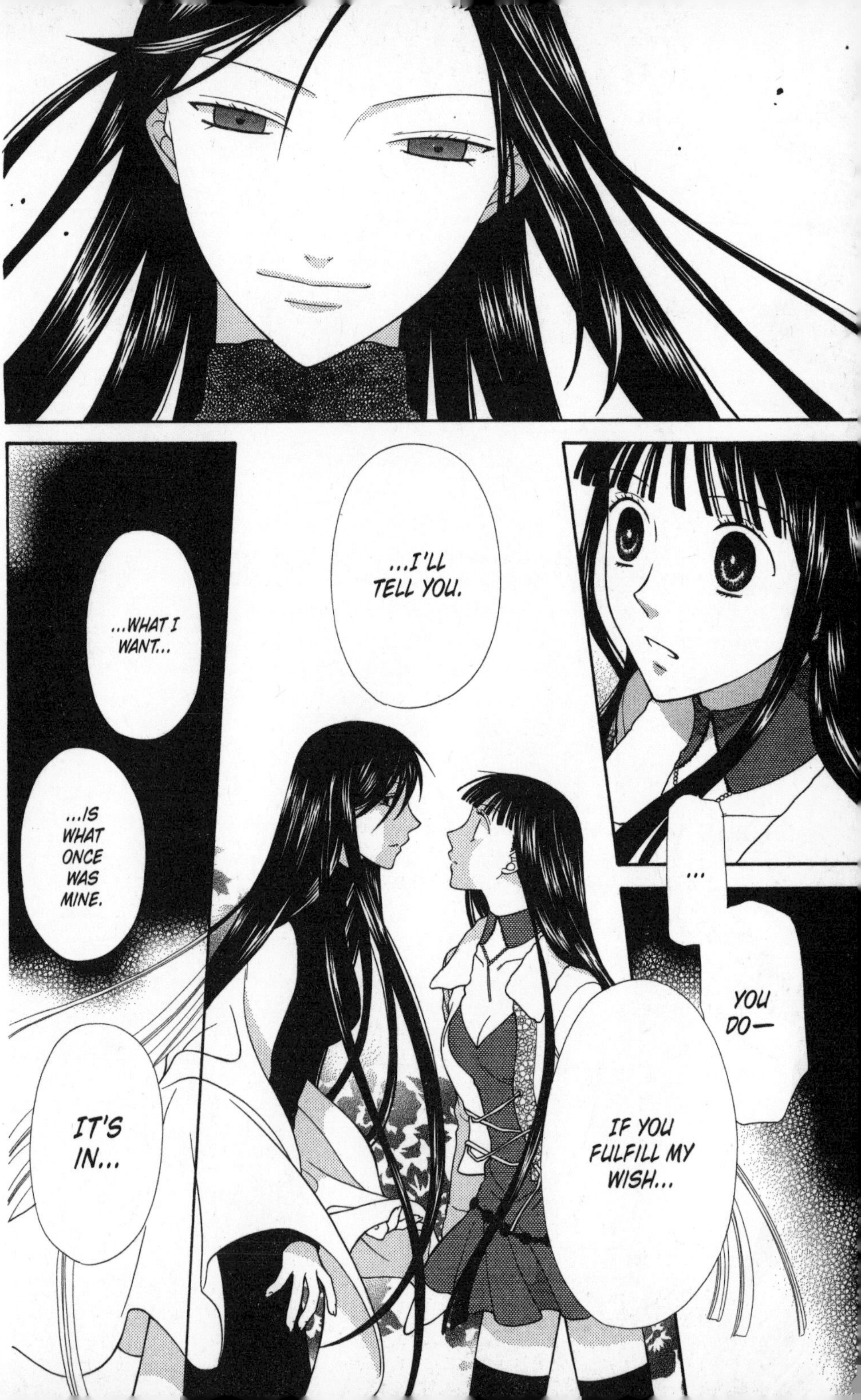
...
YOU DO—
...I'LL TELL YOU.
IF YOU FULFILL MY WISH...
...WHAT I WANT...
...IS WHAT ONCE WAS MINE.
IT'S IN...

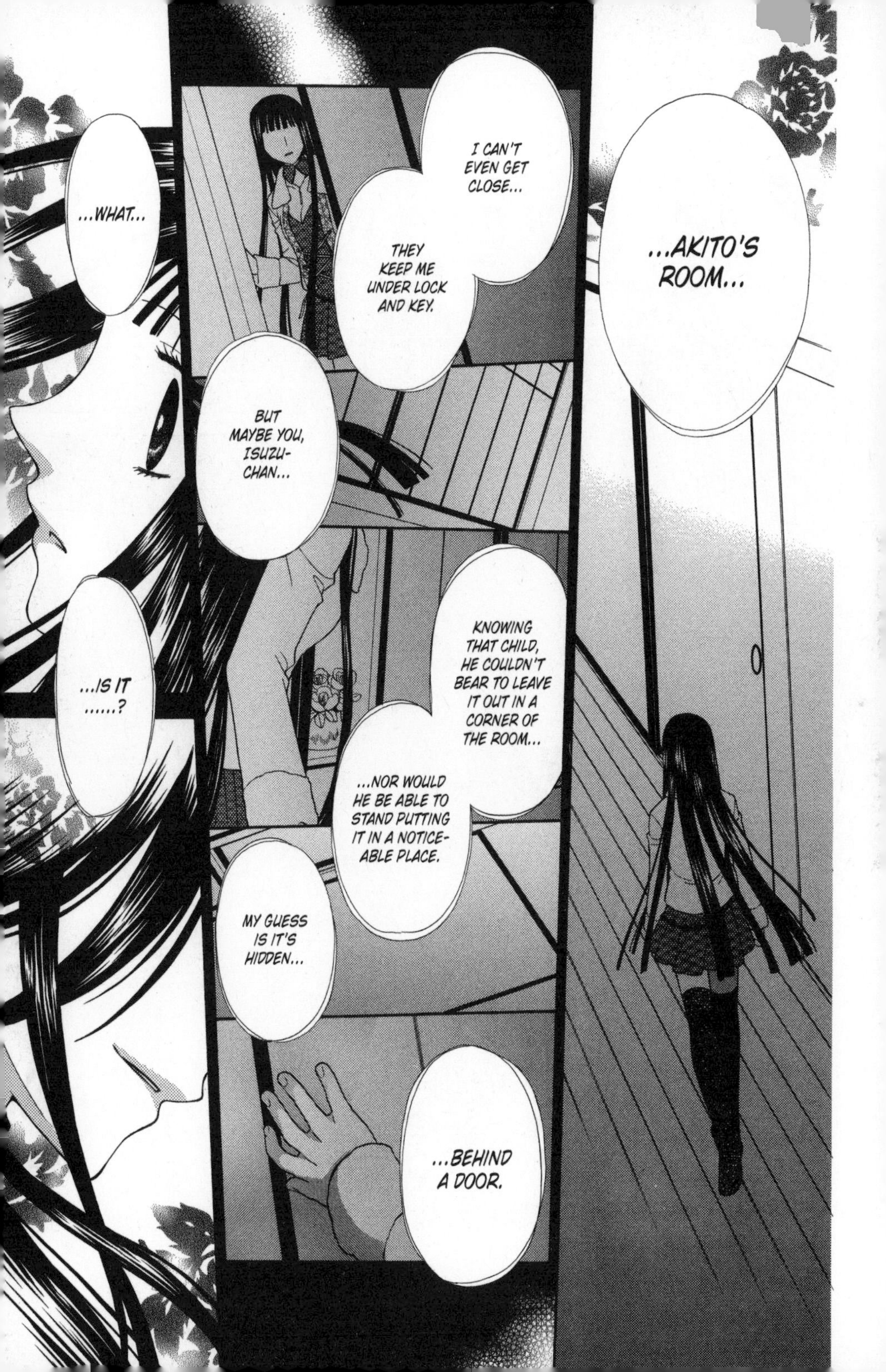
...AKITO'S ROOM...
I CAN'T EVEN GET CLOSE...
THEY KEEP ME UNDER LOCK AND KEY.
BUT MAYBE YOU, ISUZU-CHAN...
KNOWING THAT CHILD, HE COULDN'T BEAR TO LEAVE IT OUT IN A CORNER OF THE ROOM...
...NOR WOULD HE BE ABLE TO STAND PUTTING IT IN A NOTICE-ABLE PLACE.
MY GUESS IS IT'S HIDDEN...
...BEHIND A DOOR.
...WHAT...
...IS IT ......?

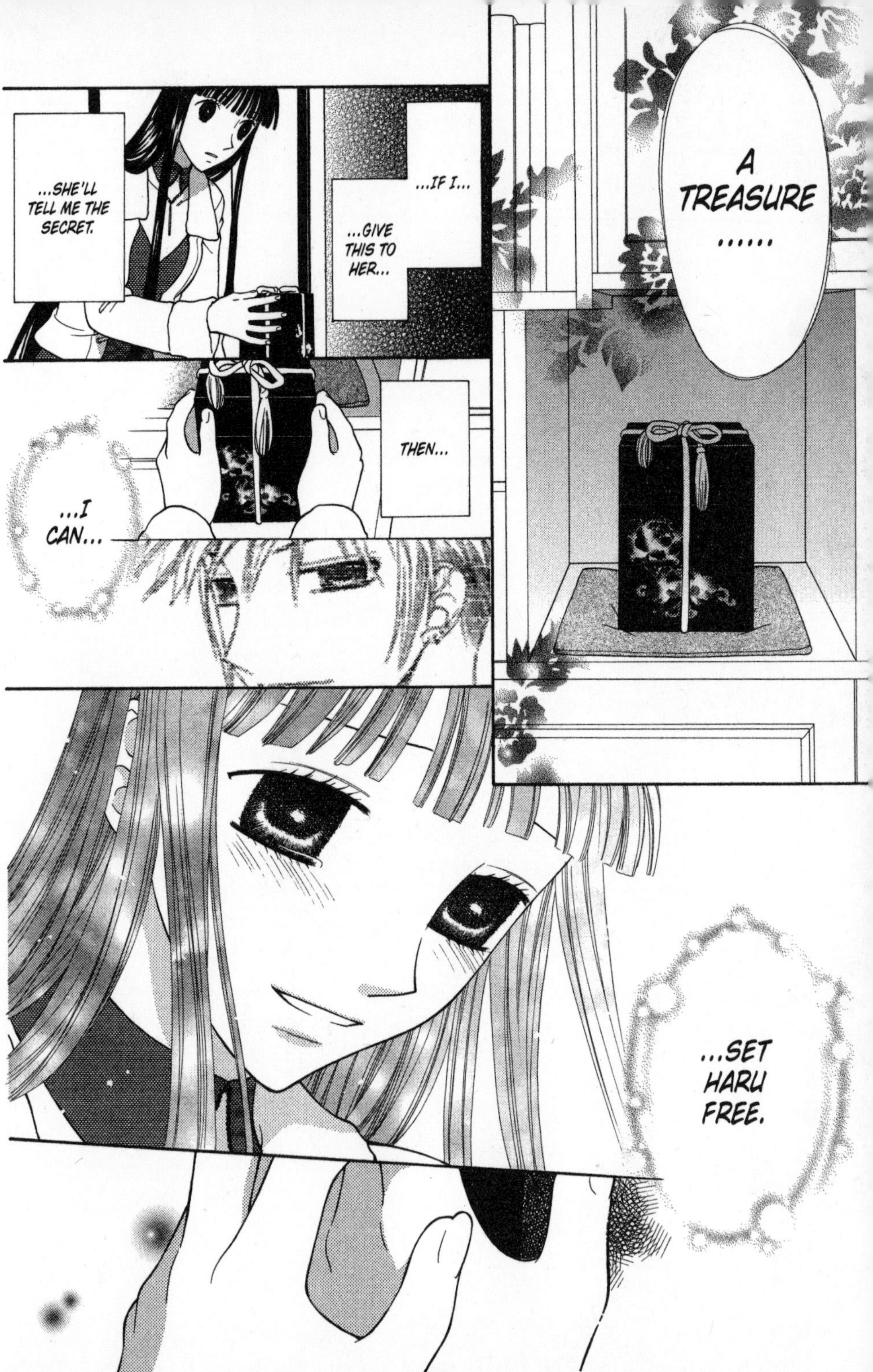
A TREASURE ......
...IF I...
...GIVE THIS TO HER...
...SHE'LL TELL ME THE SECRET.
THEN...
...I CAN...
...SET HARU FREE.

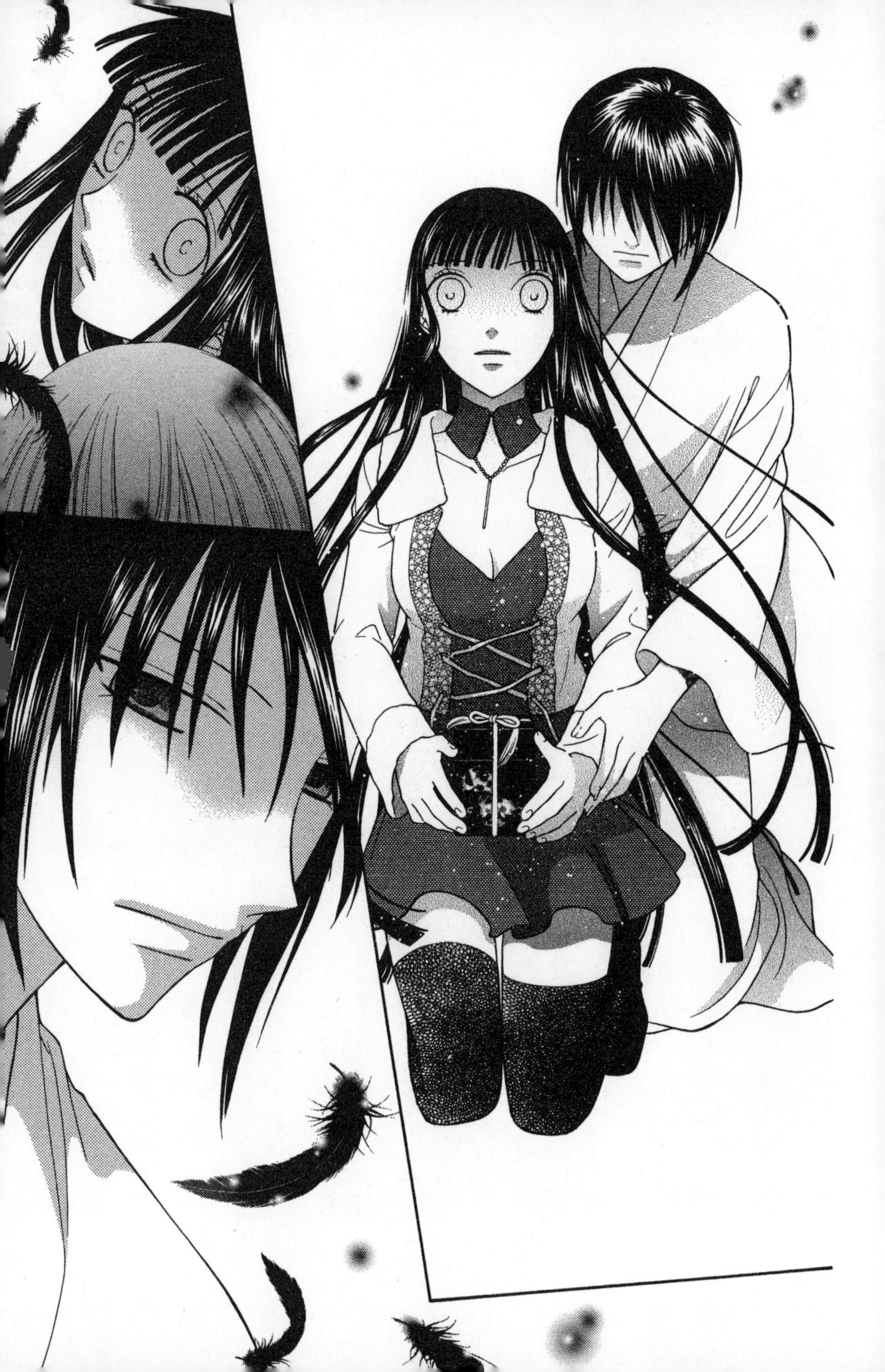

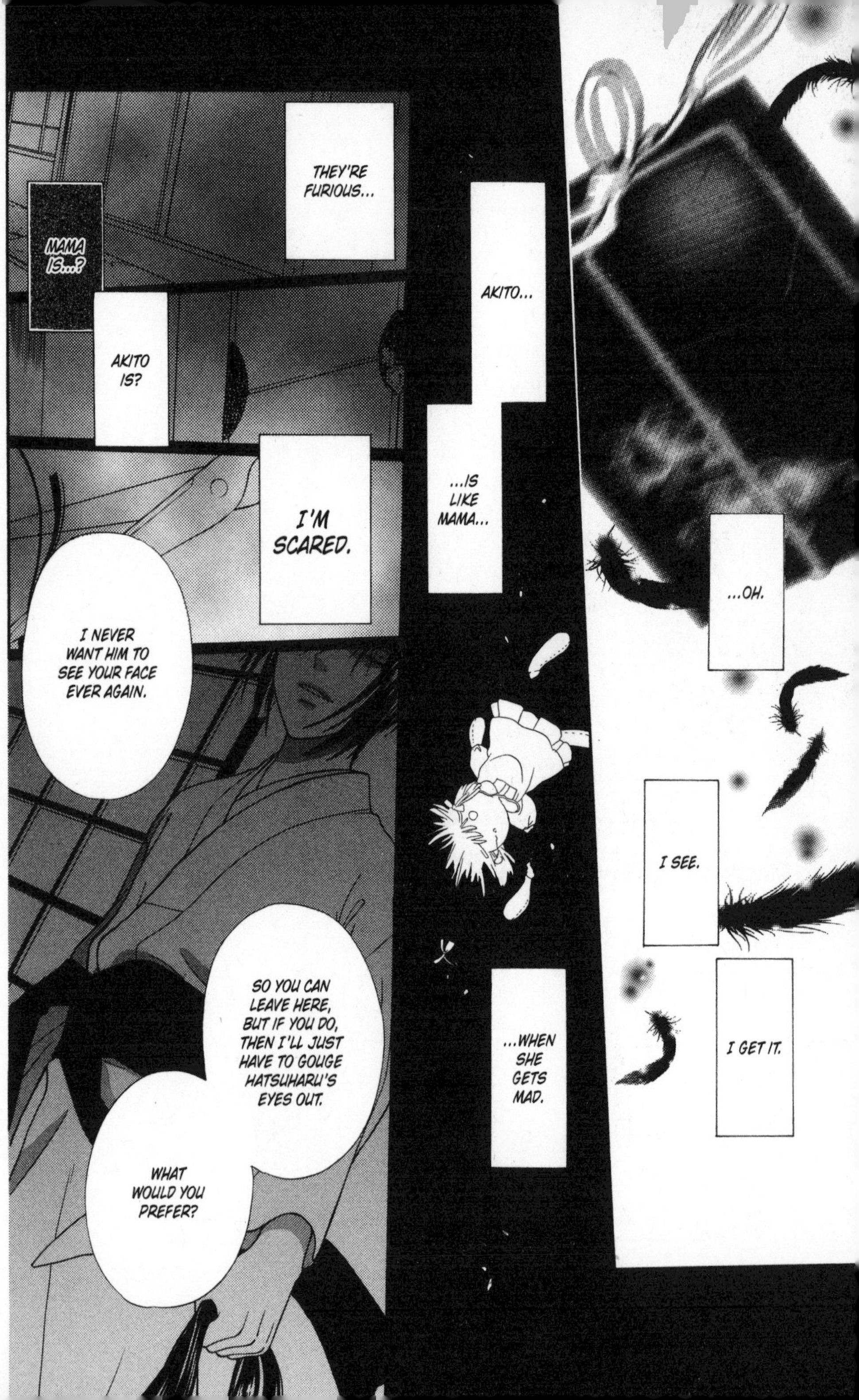
...OH.
I SEE.
I GET IT.
AKITO...
...IS LIKE MAMA...
...WHEN SHE GETS MAD.
THEY'RE FURIOUS...
MAMA IS...?
AKITO IS?
I'M SCARED.
I NEVER WANT HIM TO SEE YOUR FACE EVER AGAIN.
SO YOU CAN LEAVE HERE, BUT IF YOU DO, THEN I'LL JUST HAVE TO GOUGE HATSUHARU'S EYES OUT.
WHAT WOULD YOU PREFER?

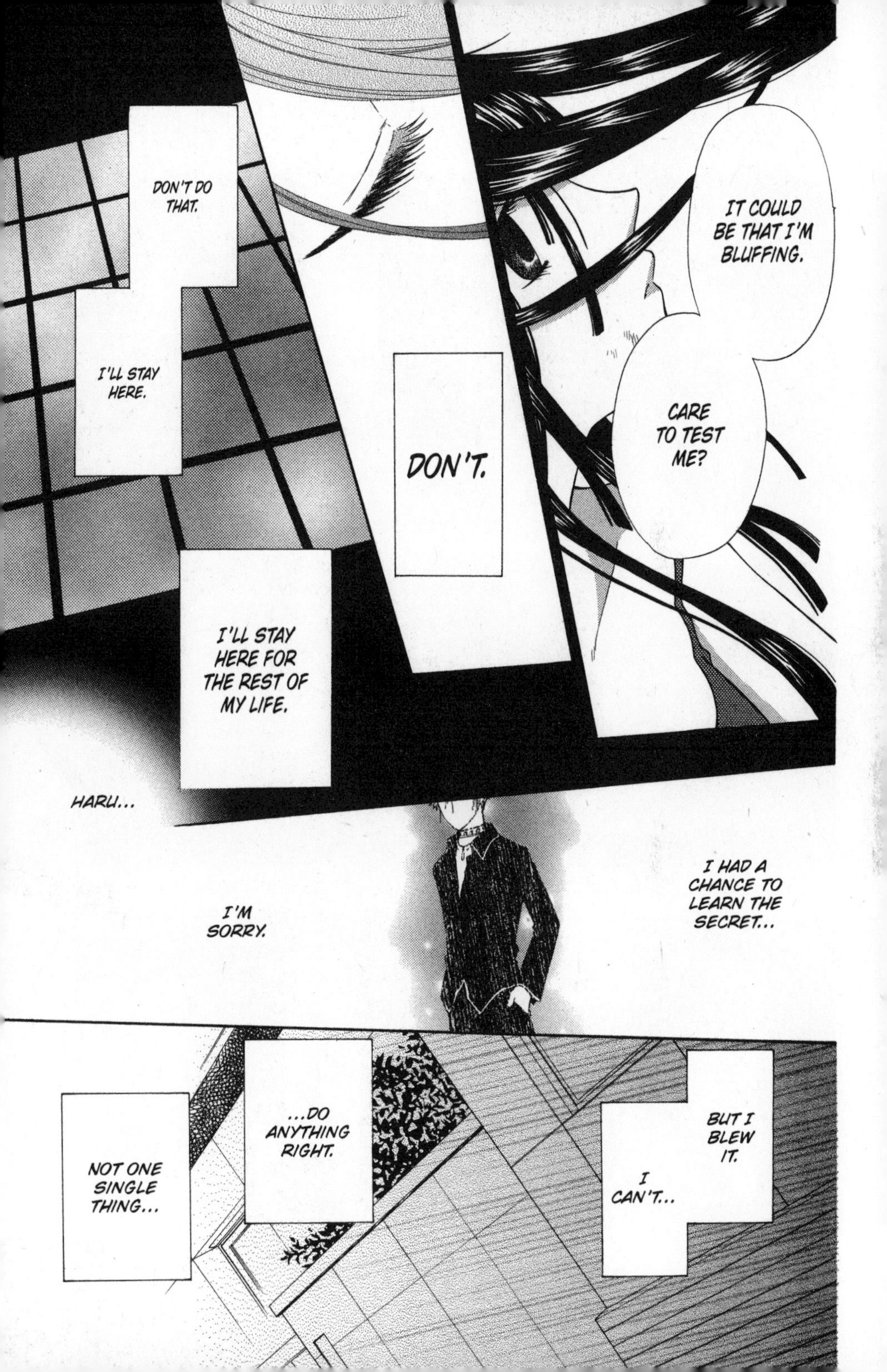
IT COULD BE THAT I'M BLUFFING.
CARE TO TEST ME?
DON'T.
DON'T DO THAT.
I'LL STAY HERE.
I'LL STAY HERE FOR THE REST OF MY LIFE.
HARU...
I'M SORRY.
I HAD A CHANCE TO LEARN THE SECRET...
BUT I BLEW IT.
I CAN'T...
...DO ANYTHING RIGHT.
NOT ONE SINGLE THING...

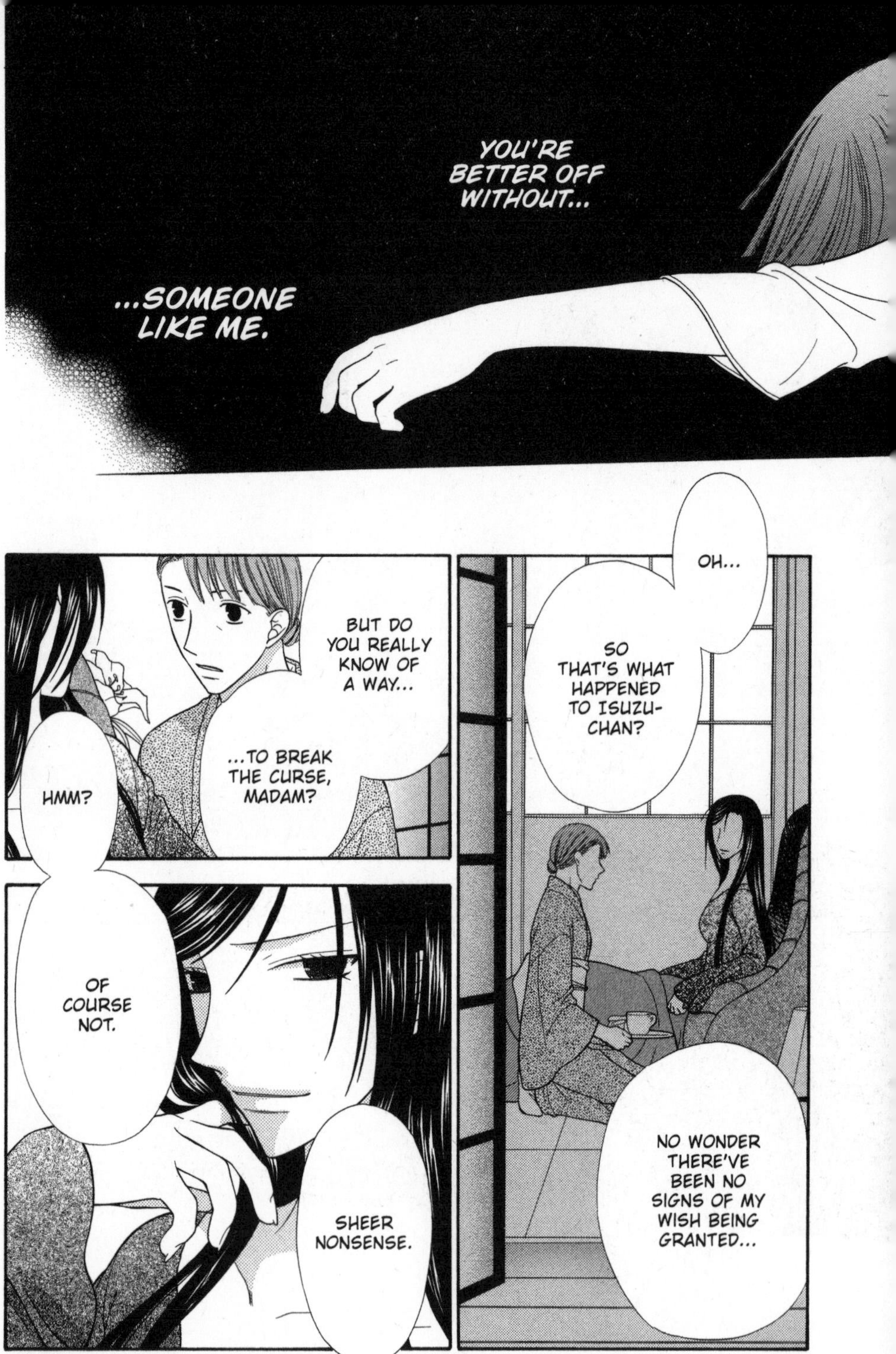
YOU'RE BETTER OFF WITHOUT...
...SOMEONE LIKE ME.
OH...
SO THAT'S WHAT HAPPENED TO ISUZU-CHAN?
NO WONDER THERE'VE BEEN NO SIGNS OF MY WISH BEING GRANTED...
BUT DO YOU REALLY KNOW OF A WAY...
...TO BREAK THE CURSE, MADAM?
HMM?
OF COURSE NOT.
SHEER NONSENSE.

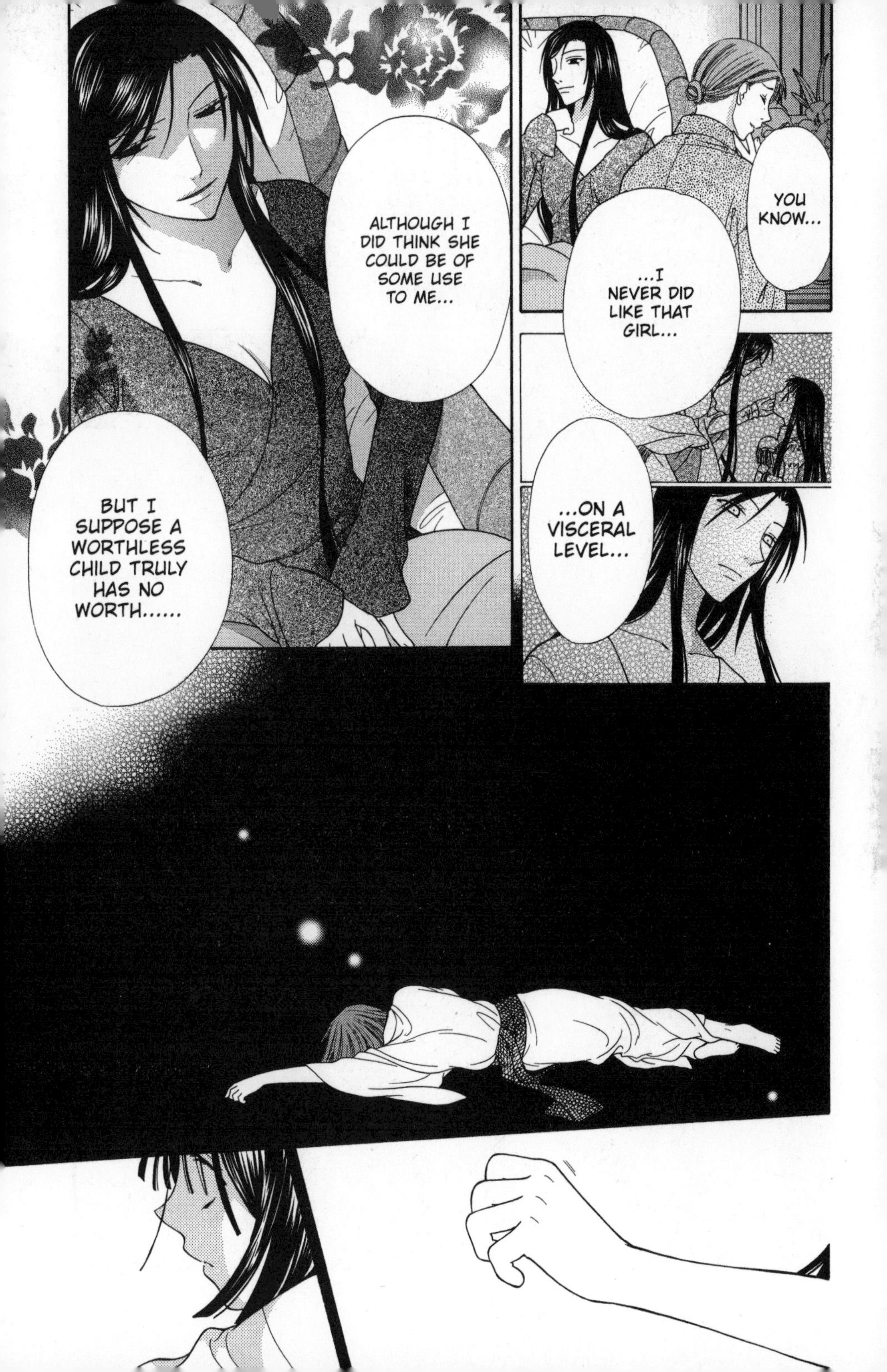
YOU KNOW...
...I NEVER DID LIKE THAT GIRL...
...ON A VISCERAL LEVEL...
ALTHOUGH I DID THINK SHE COULD BE OF SOME USE TO ME...
BUT I SUPPOSE A WORTHLESS CHILD TRULY HAS NO WORTH......

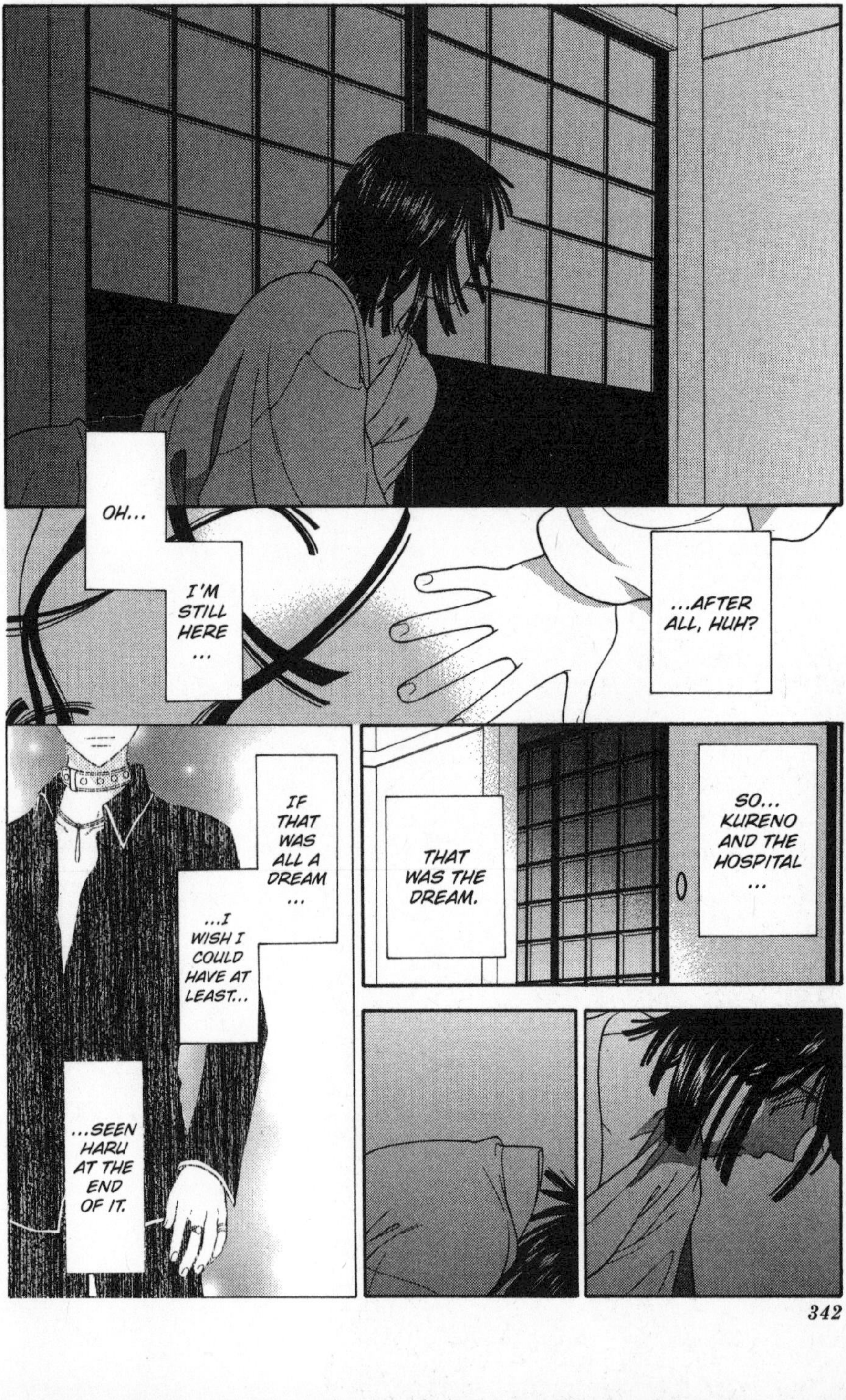
OH...
I'M STILL HERE...
...AFTER ALL, HUH?
SO... KURENO AND THE HOSPITAL...
THAT WAS THE DREAM.
IF THAT WAS ALL A DREAM...
...I WISH I COULD HAVE AT LEAST...
...SEEN HARU AT THE END OF IT.

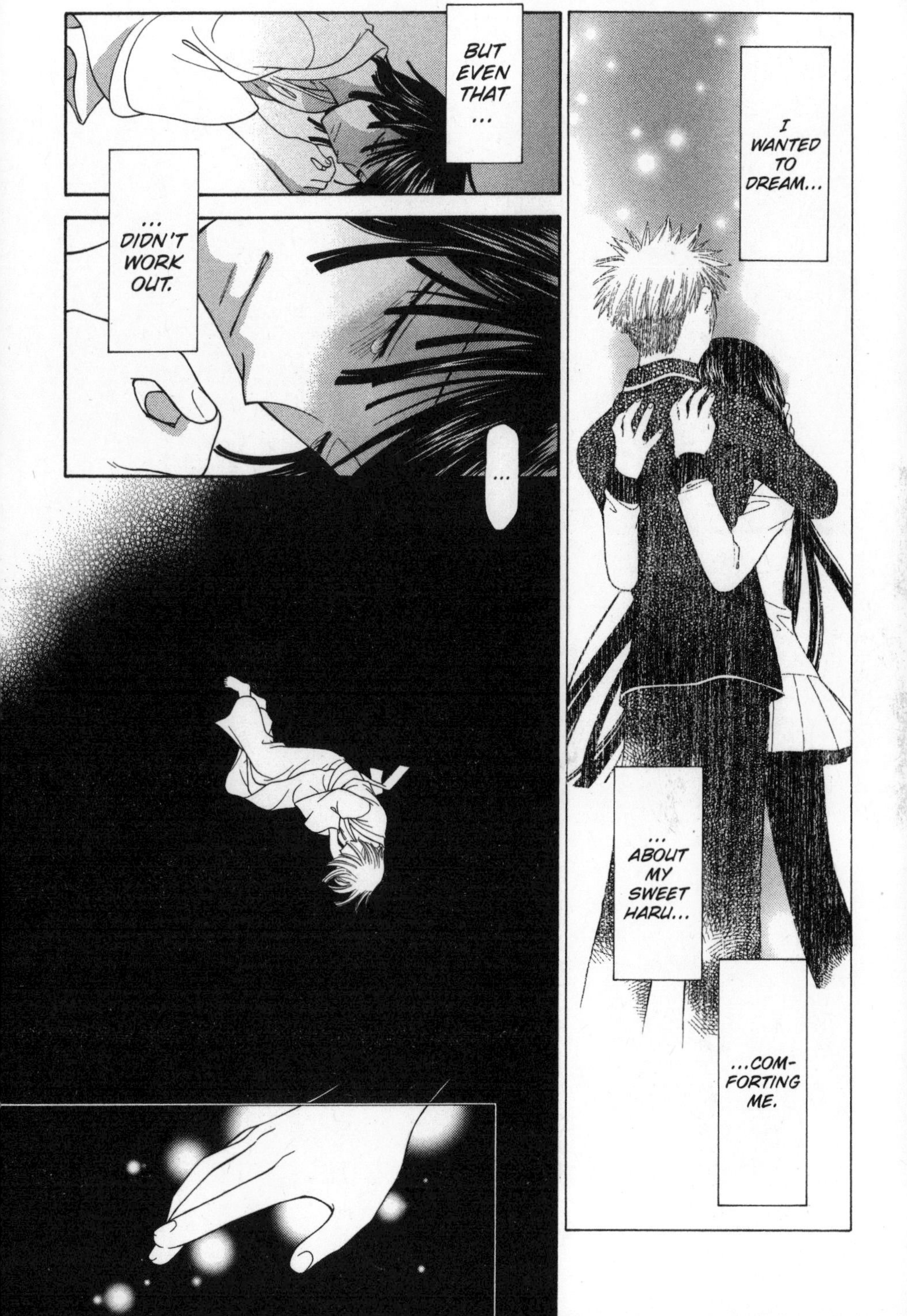
I WANTED TO DREAM...
...ABOUT MY SWEET HARU...
...COMFORTING ME.
BUT EVEN THAT...
...DIDN'T WORK OUT.
...

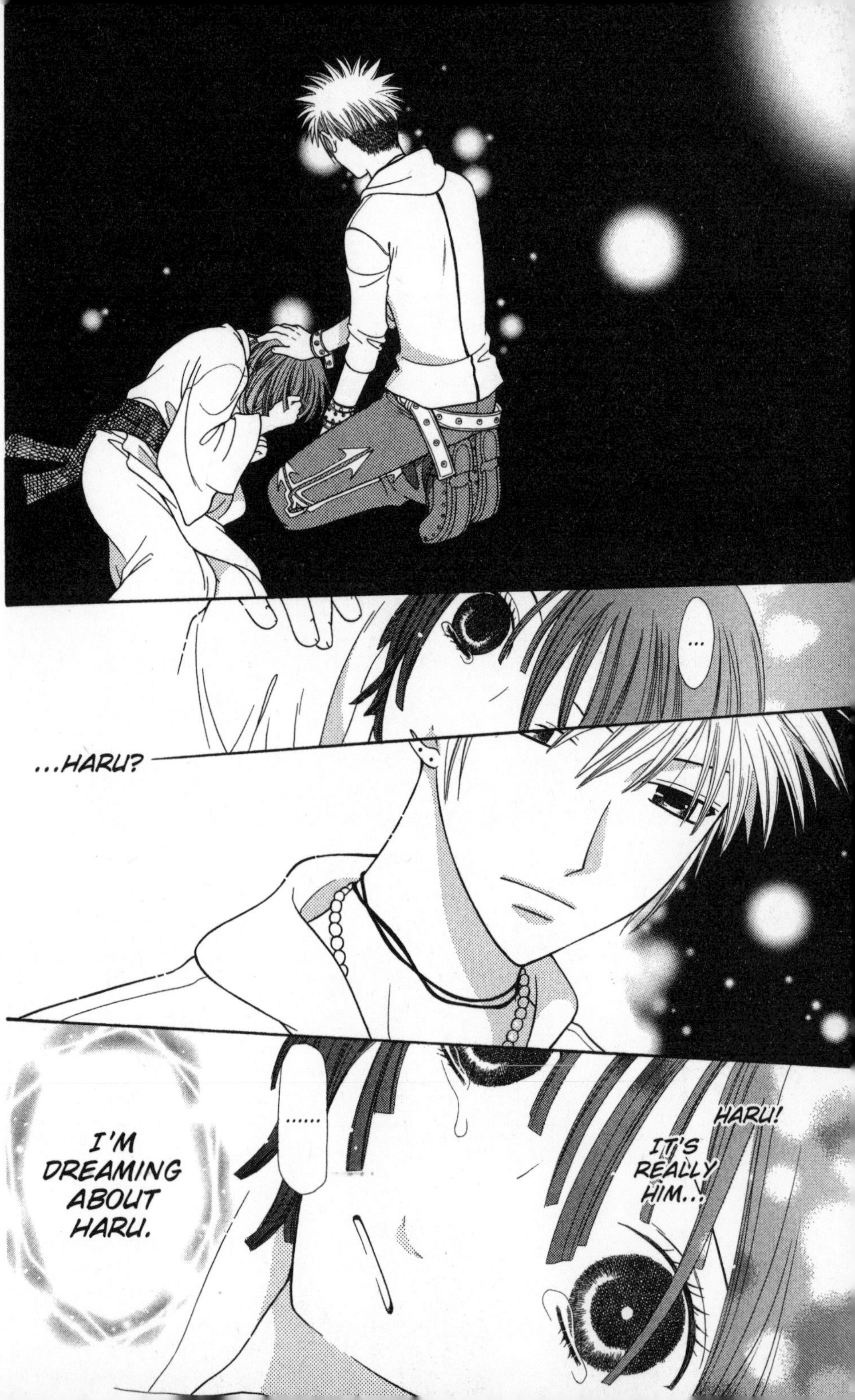
...
...HARU?
HARU! IT'S REALLY HIM...
......
I'M DREAMING ABOUT HARU.

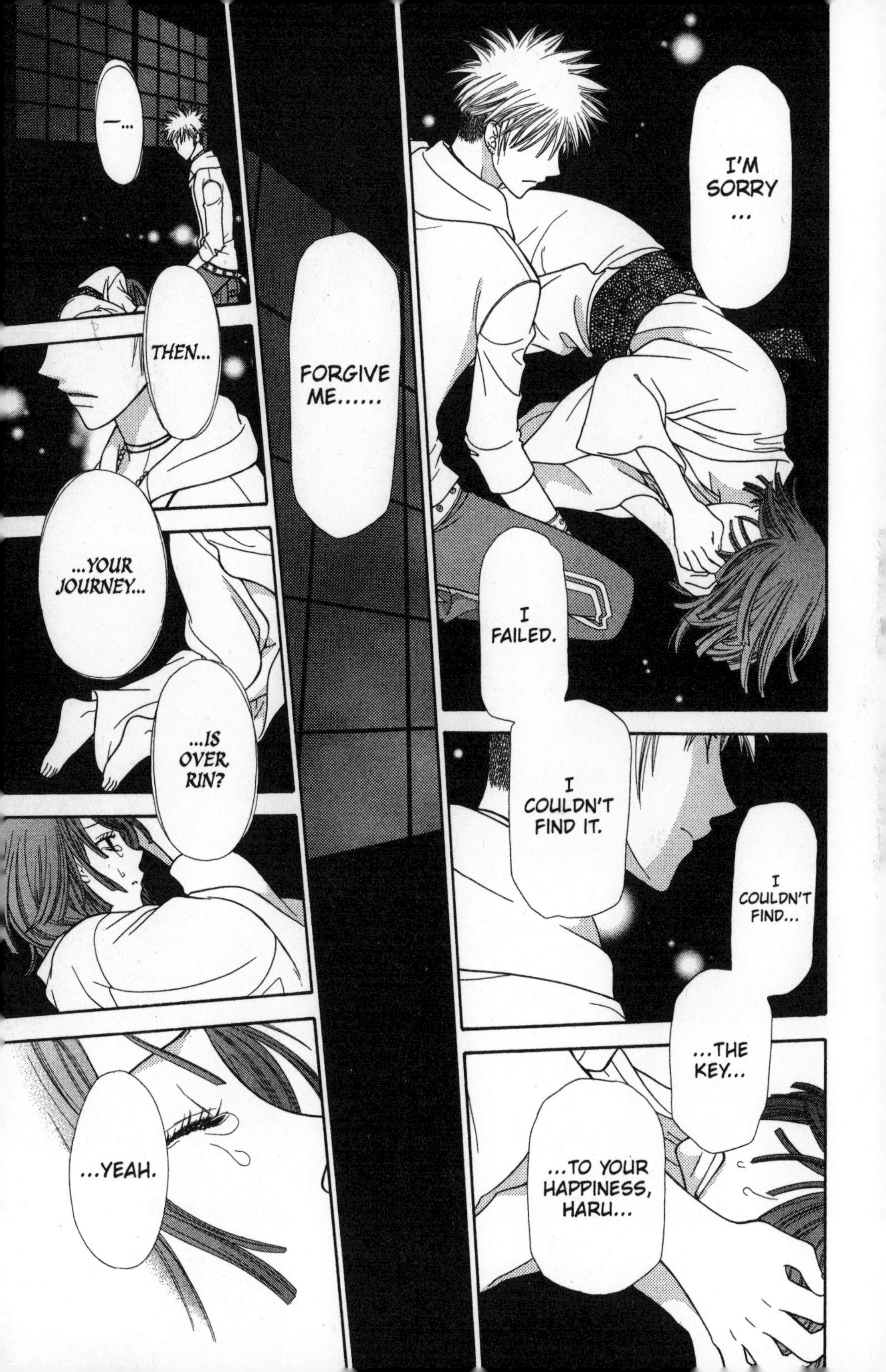
I'M SORRY ...
I FAILED.
I COULDN'T FIND IT.
I COULDN'T FIND...
...THE KEY...
...TO YOUR HAPPINESS, HARU...
FORGIVE ME......
—...
THEN...
...YOUR JOURNEY...
...IS OVER RIN?
...YEAH.

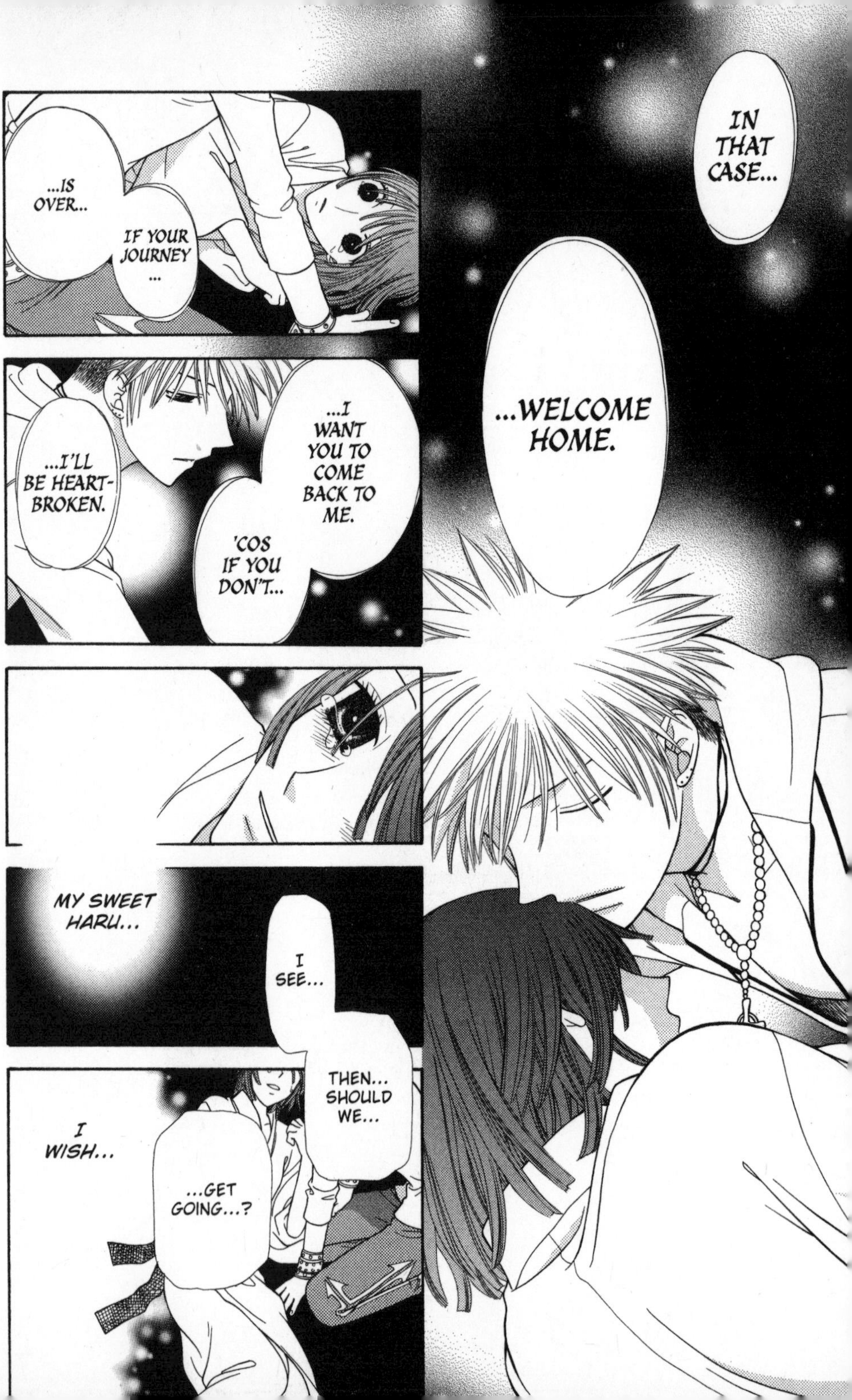
IN THAT CASE...
...WELCOME HOME.
IF YOUR JOURNEY ...
...IS OVER...
...I WANT YOU TO COME BACK TO ME.
'COS IF YOU DON'T...
...I'LL BE HEART-BROKEN.
I SEE...
MY SWEET HARU...
THEN... SHOULD WE...
...GET GOING...?
I WISH...

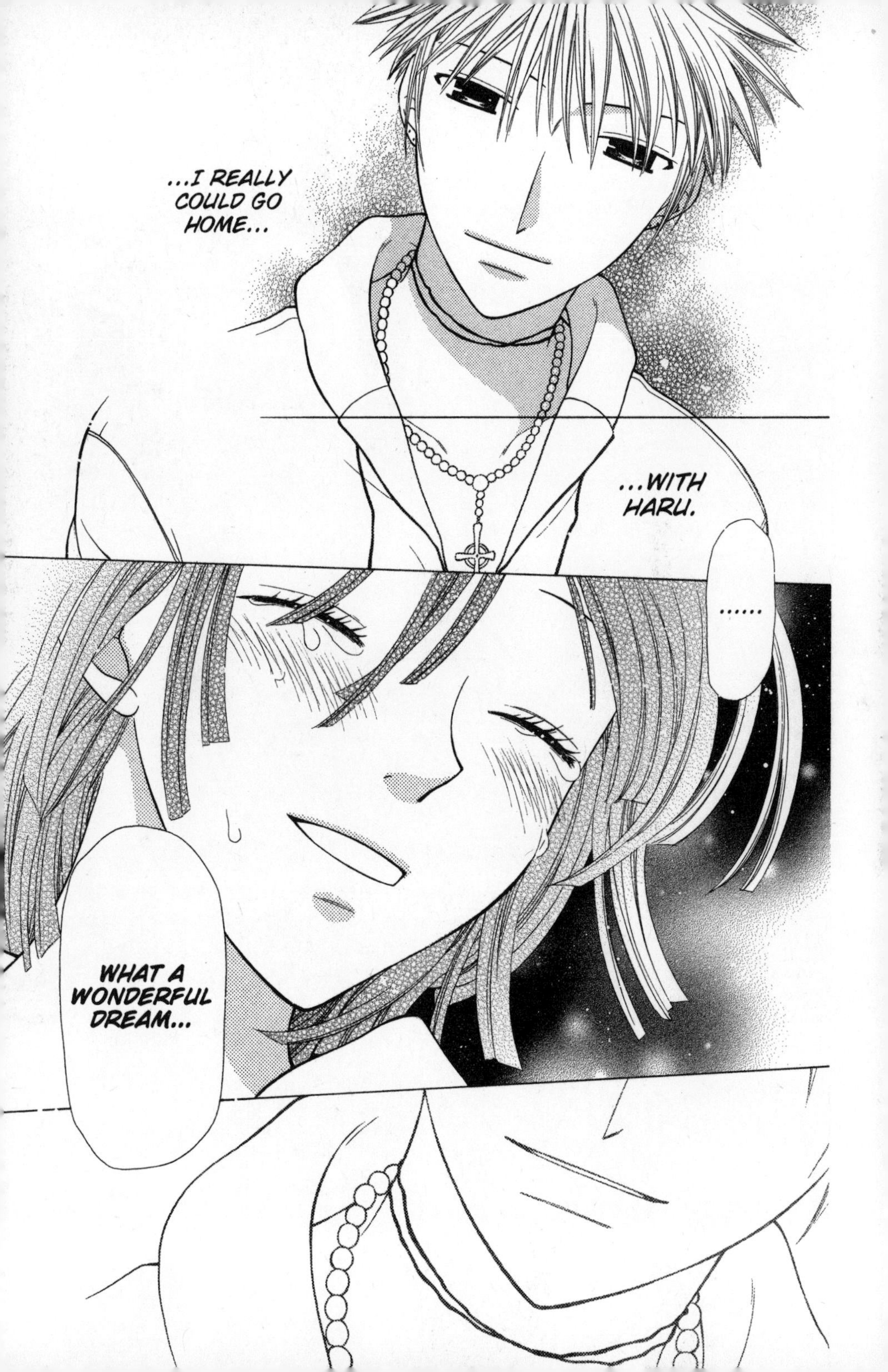
...I REALLY COULD GO HOME...
...WITH HARU.
......
WHAT A WONDERFUL DREAM...

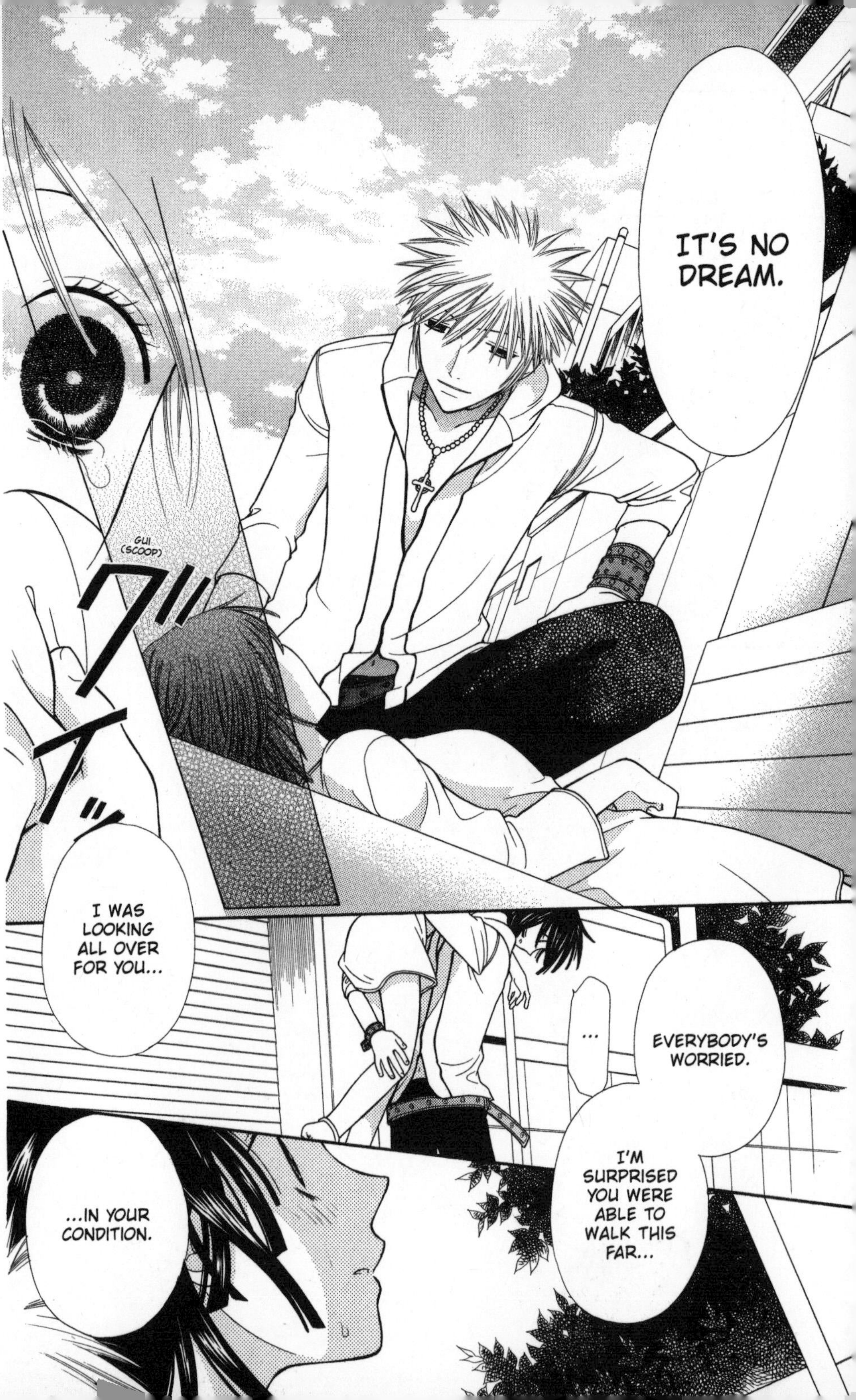
IT'S NO DREAM.
GUI (SCOOP)
グイ
I WAS LOOKING ALL OVER FOR YOU...
EVERYBODY'S WORRIED.
...
I'M SURPRISED YOU WERE ABLE TO WALK THIS FAR...
...IN YOUR CONDITION.

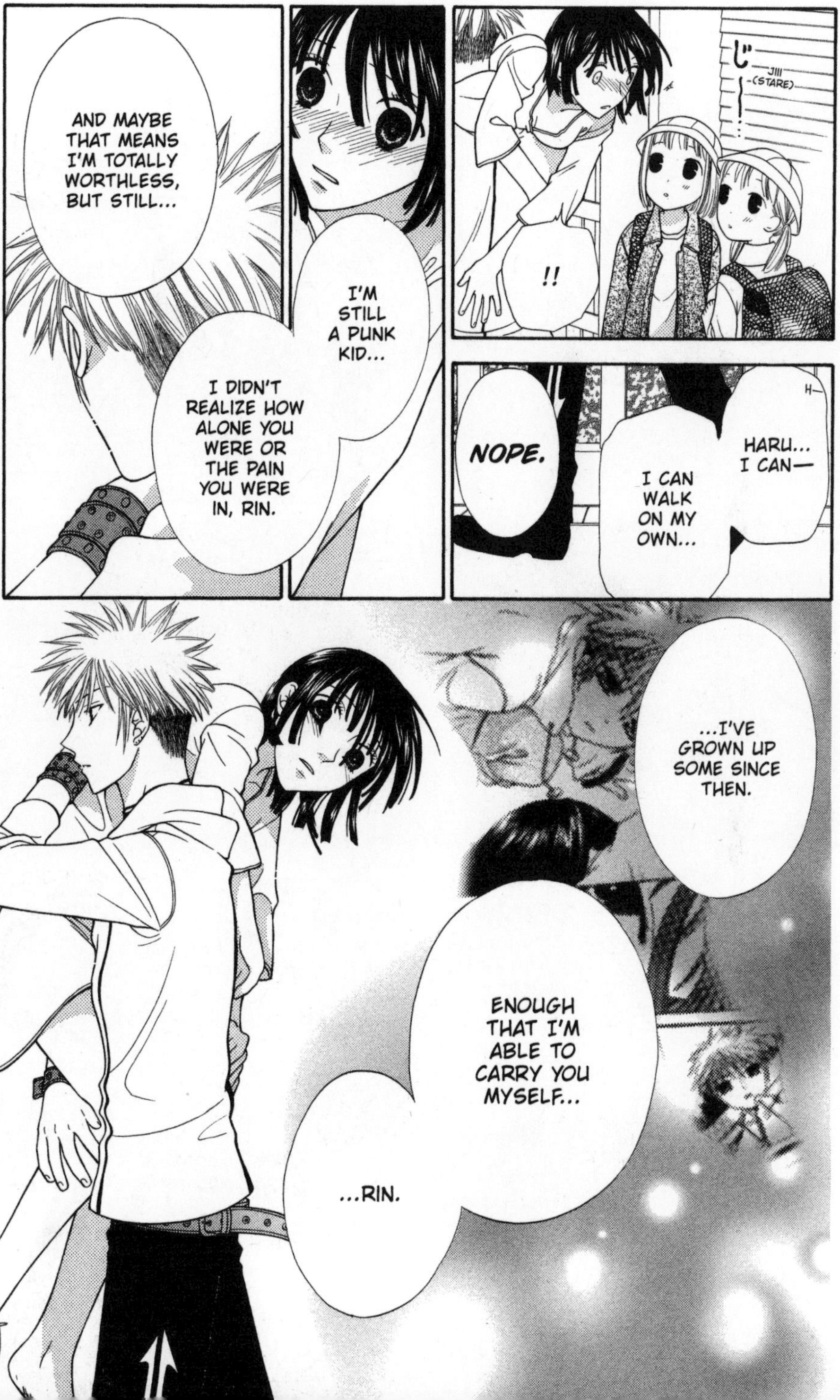
じー
JIII (STARE)
!!
H—
HARU... I CAN—
I CAN WALK ON MY OWN...
NOPE.
I'M STILL A PUNK KID...
I DIDN'T REALIZE HOW ALONE YOU WERE OR THE PAIN YOU WERE IN, RIN.
AND MAYBE THAT MEANS I'M TOTALLY WORTHLESS, BUT STILL...
...I'VE GROWN UP SOME SINCE THEN.
ENOUGH THAT I'M ABLE TO CARRY YOU MYSELF...
...RIN.

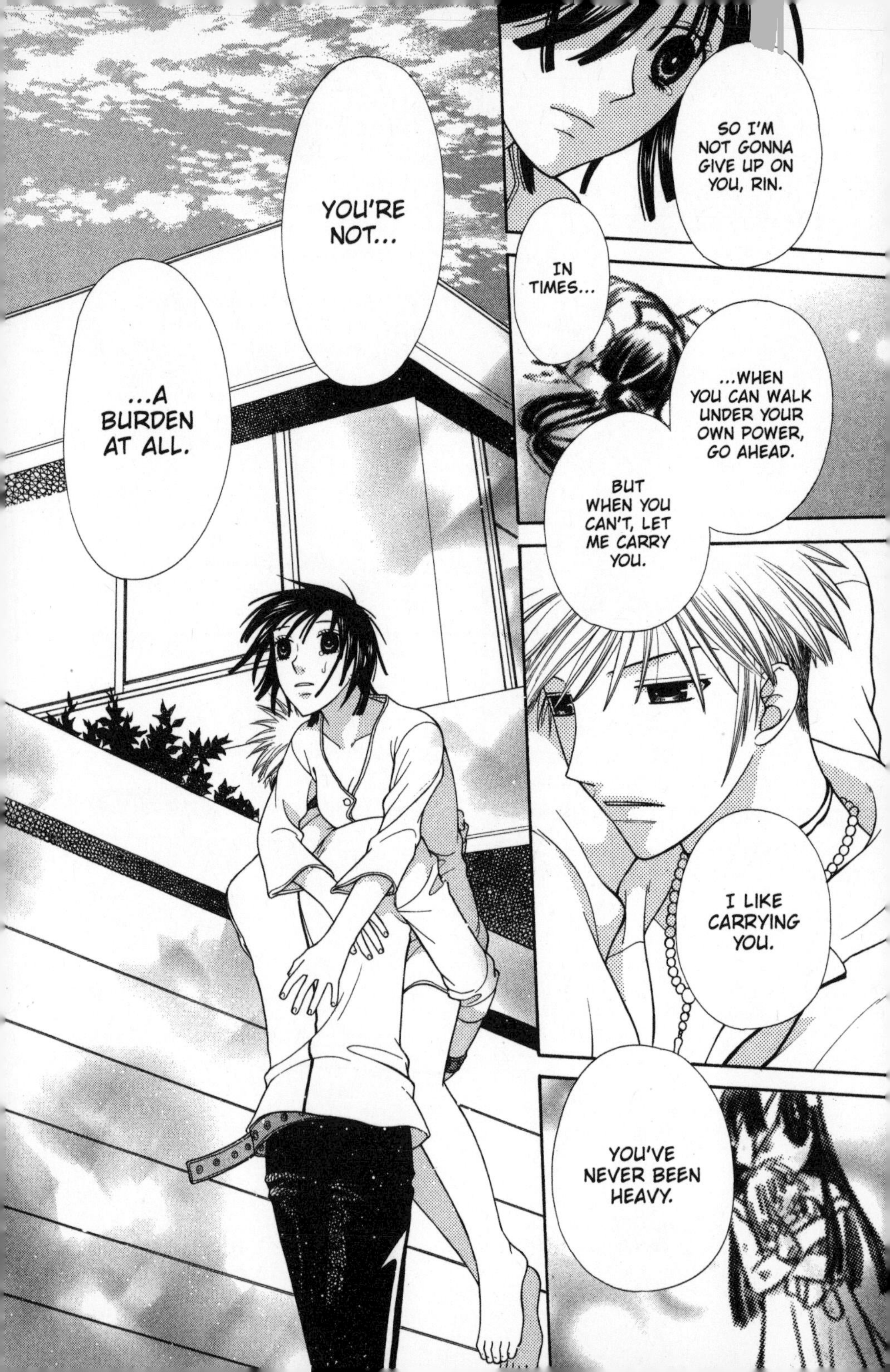
SO I'M NOT GONNA GIVE UP ON YOU, RIN.
IN TIMES...
...WHEN YOU CAN WALK UNDER YOUR OWN POWER, GO AHEAD.
BUT WHEN YOU CAN'T, LET ME CARRY YOU.
I LIKE CARRYING YOU.
YOU'VE NEVER BEEN HEAVY.
YOU'RE NOT...
...A BURDEN AT ALL.

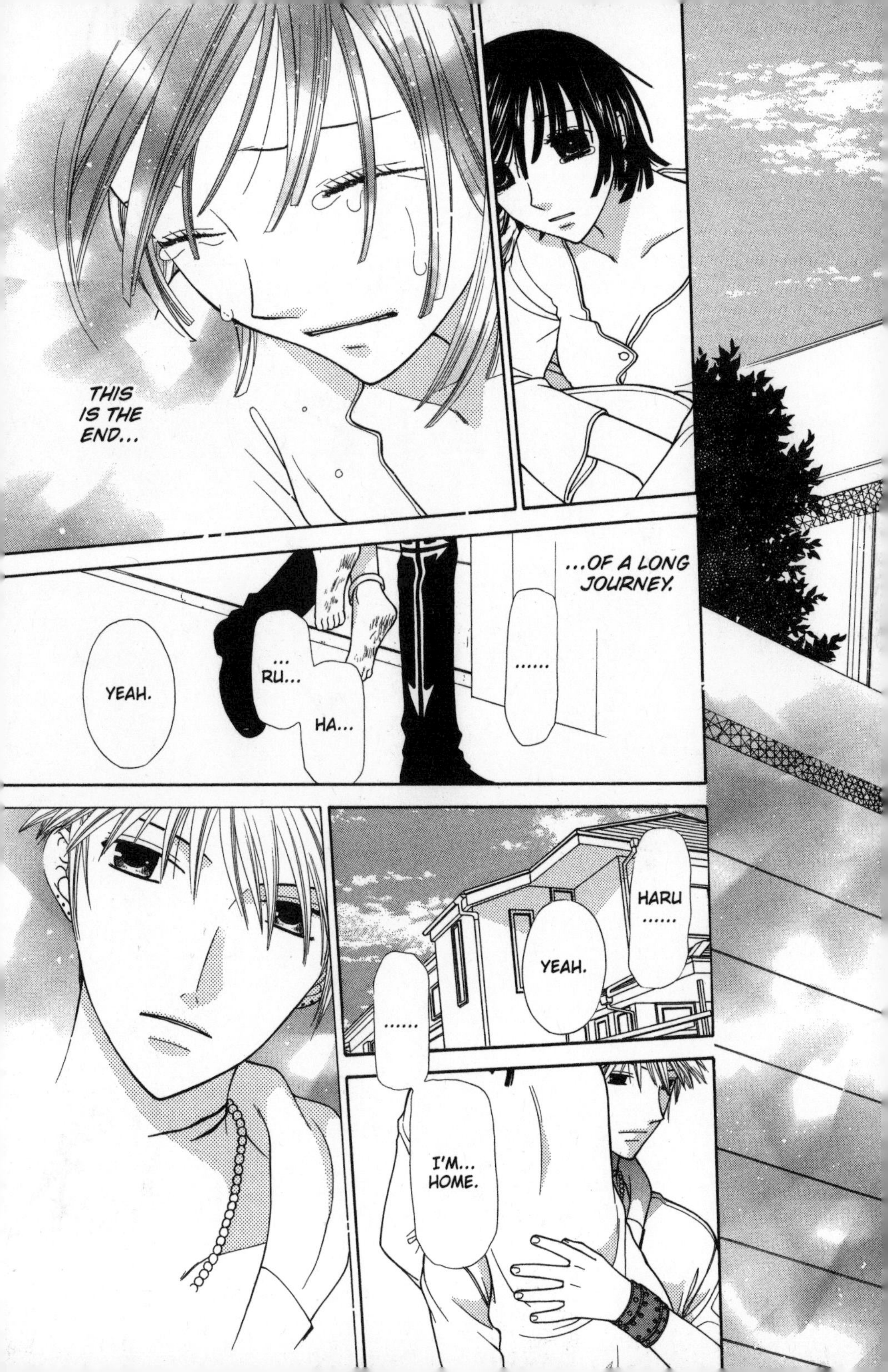
THIS IS THE END...
...OF A LONG JOURNEY.
......
... RU... HA...
YEAH.
HARU ......
YEAH.
......
I'M... HOME.

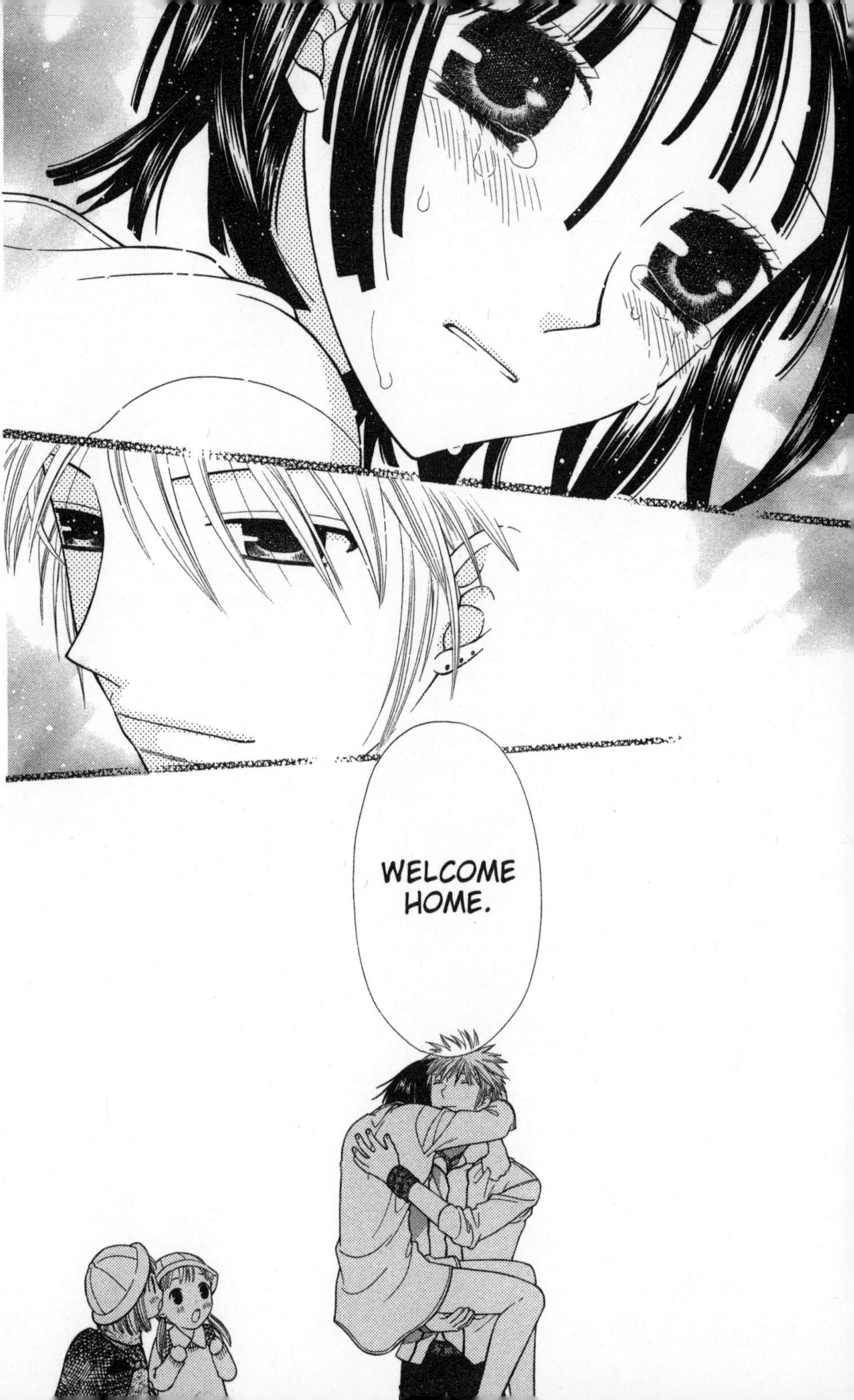
WELCOME HOME.

COLLECTOR'S EDITION

Fruits Basket

COLLECTOR'S EDITION

Fruits Basket

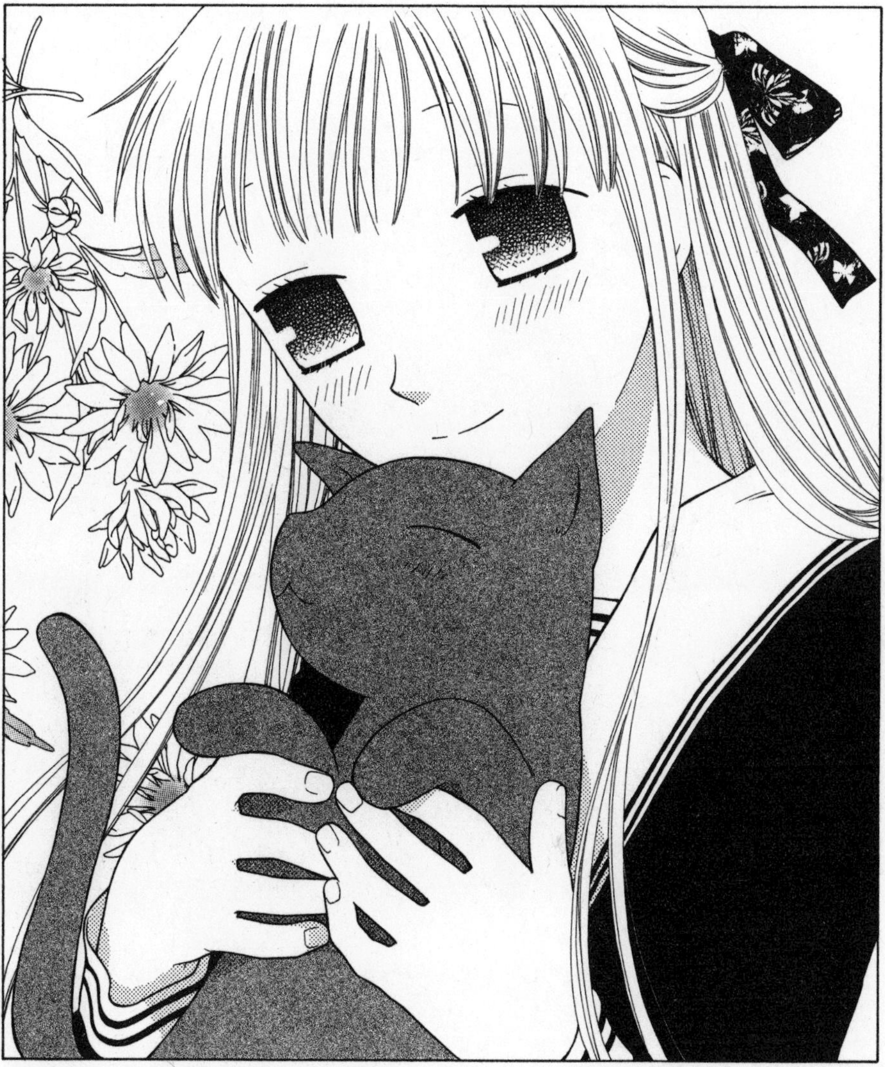

Chapter 107

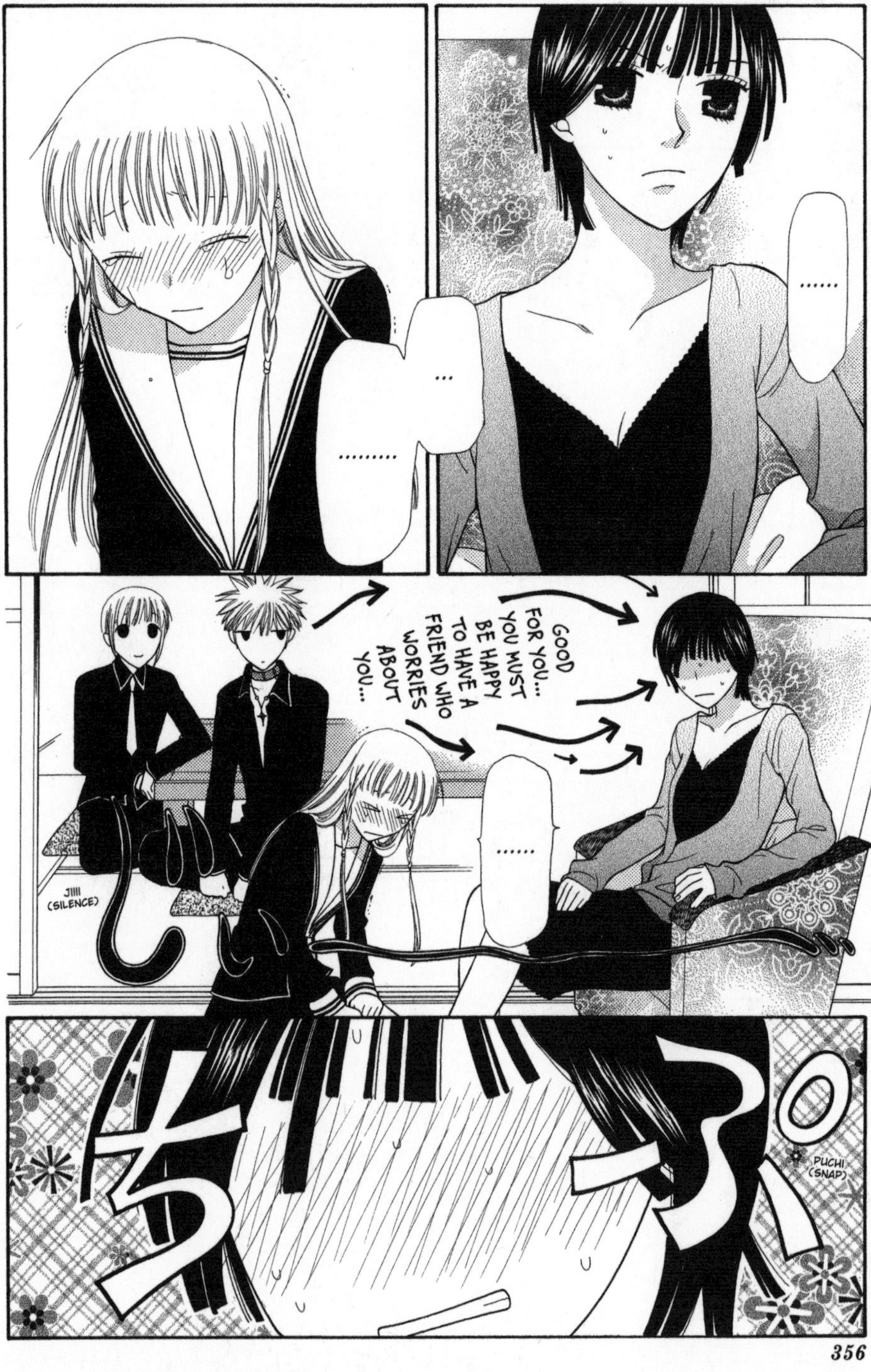
......
...
....
GOOD FOR YOU... YOU MUST BE HAPPY TO HAVE A FRIEND WHO WORRIES ABOUT YOU...
......
JIIII (SILENCE)
PUCHI (SNAP)

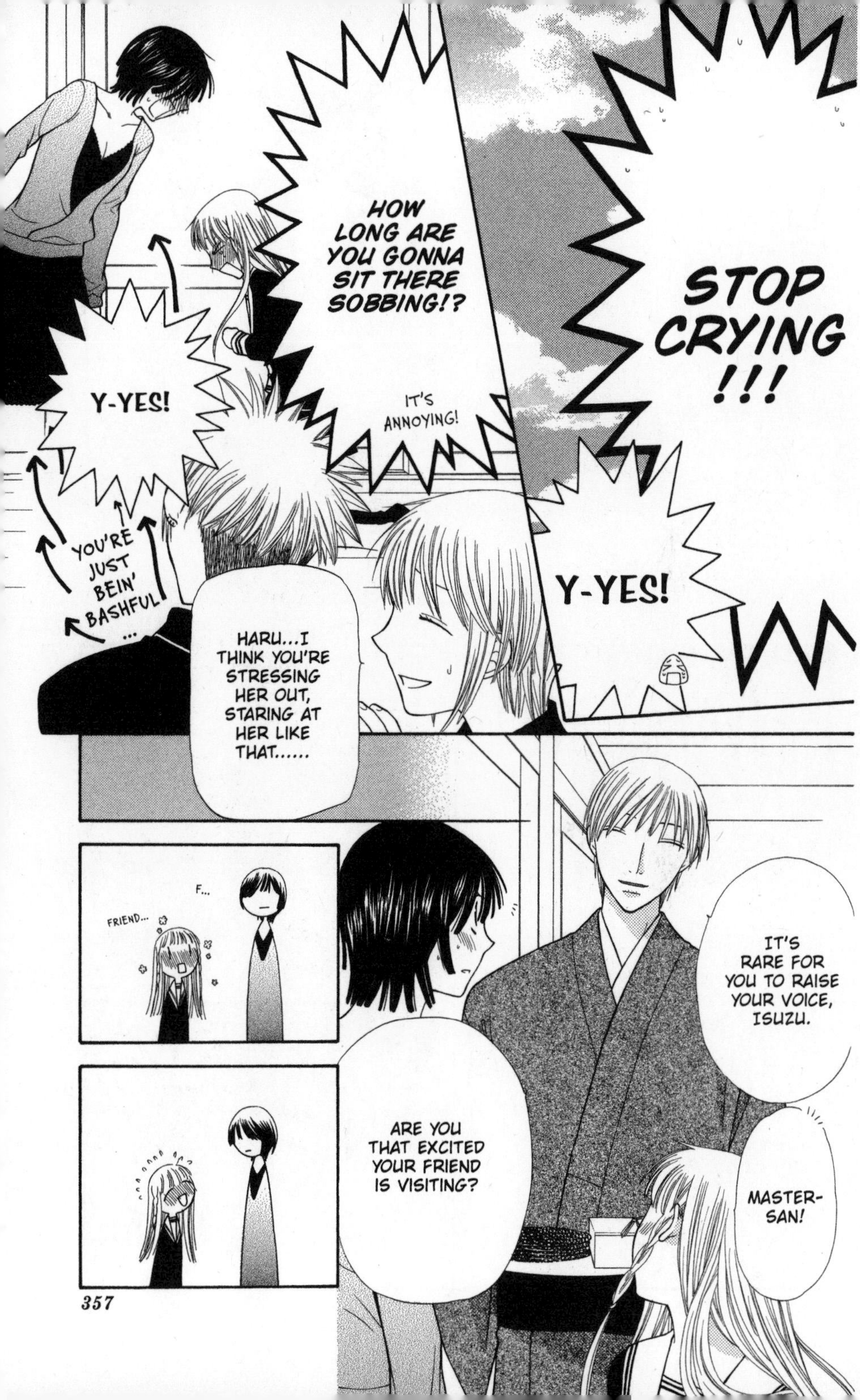
STOP CRYING!!!
Y-YES!
HOW LONG ARE YOU GONNA SIT THERE SOBBING!?
IT'S ANNOYING!
Y-YES!
YOU'RE JUST BEIN' BASHFUL...
HARU...I THINK YOU'RE STRESSING HER OUT, STARING AT HER LIKE THAT......
IT'S RARE FOR YOU TO RAISE YOUR VOICE, ISUZU.
MASTER-SAN!
ARE YOU THAT EXCITED YOUR FRIEND IS VISITING?
F...
FRIEND...

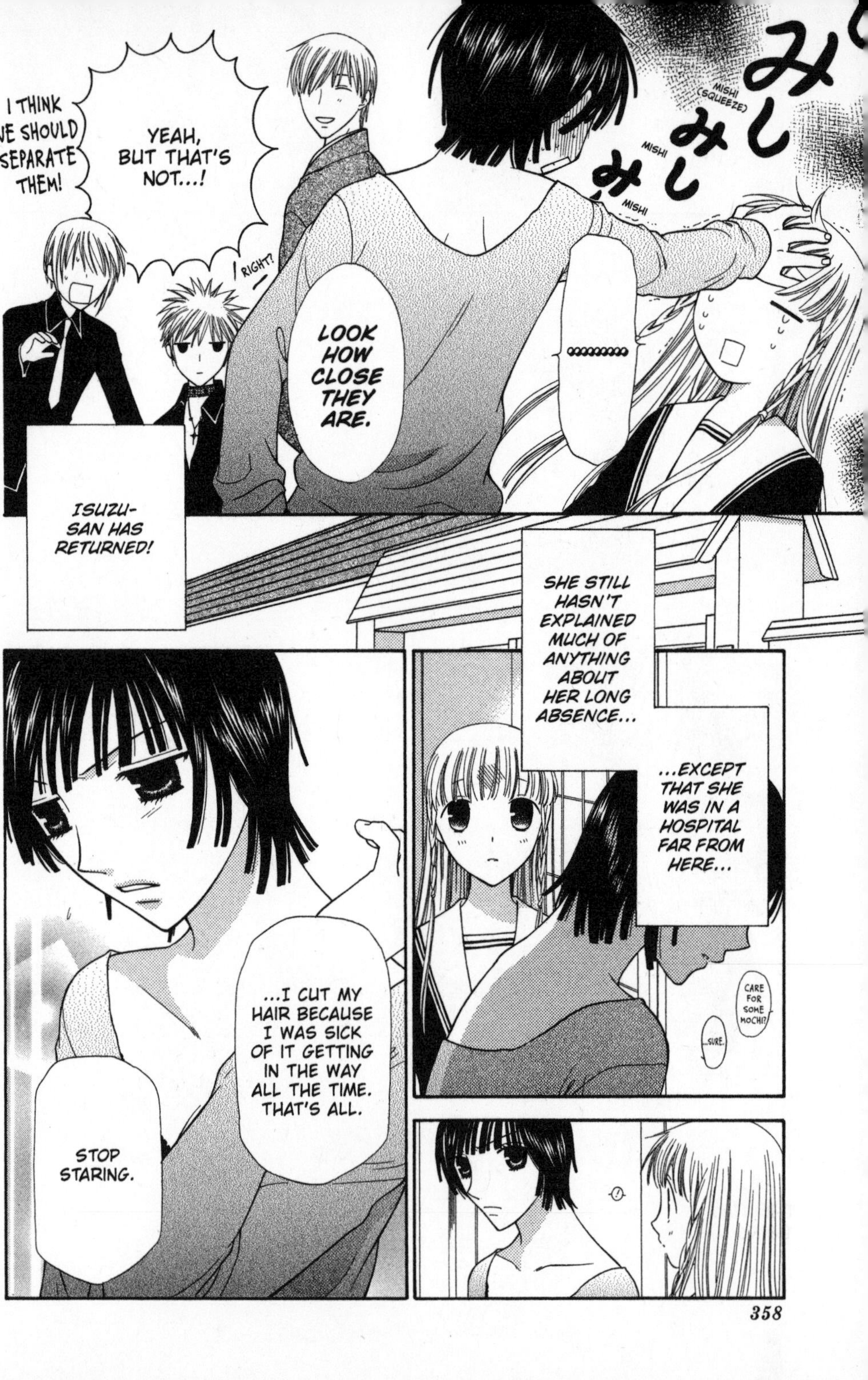
みし
MISHI (SQUEEZE)
みし
MISHI
みし
MISHI
LOOK HOW CLOSE THEY ARE.
RIGHT?
YEAH, BUT THAT'S NOT...!
I THINK WE SHOULD SEPARATE THEM!
ISUZU-SAN HAS RETURNED!
SHE STILL HASN'T EXPLAINED MUCH OF ANYTHING ABOUT HER LONG ABSENCE...
...EXCEPT THAT SHE WAS IN A HOSPITAL FAR FROM HERE...
CARE FOR SOME MOCHI?
...SURE.
!
...I CUT MY HAIR BECAUSE I WAS SICK OF IT GETTING IN THE WAY ALL THE TIME. THAT'S ALL.
STOP STARING.

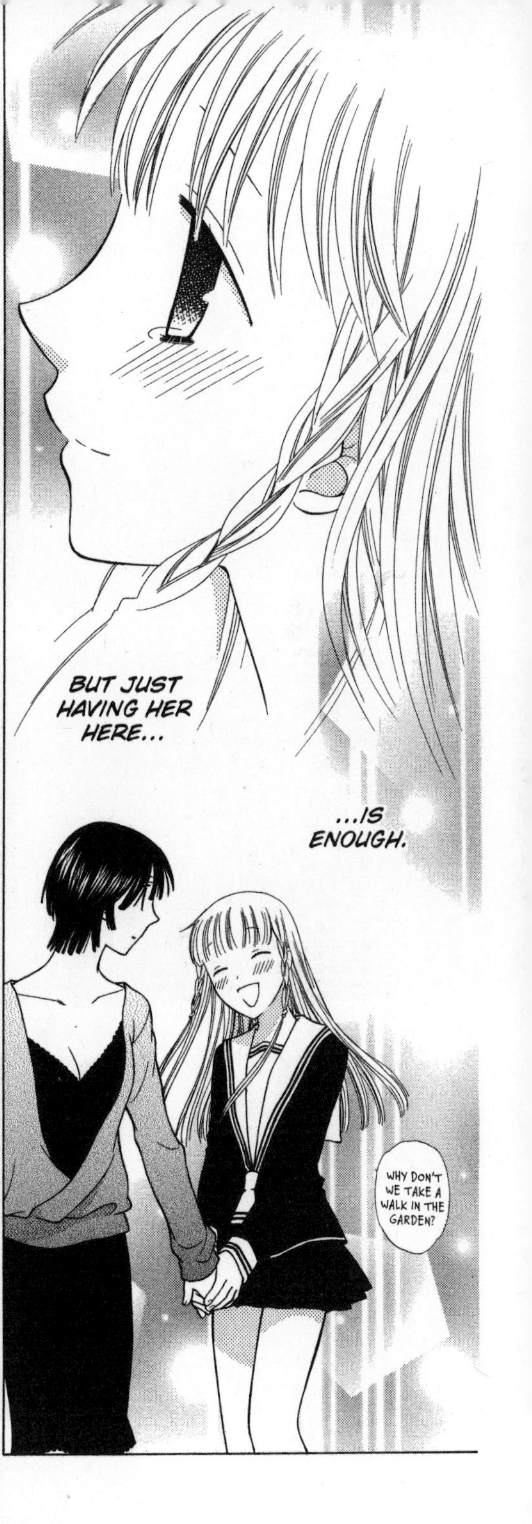
BUT JUST HAVING HER HERE...
...IS ENOUGH.
WHY DON'T WE TAKE A WALK IN THE GARDEN?

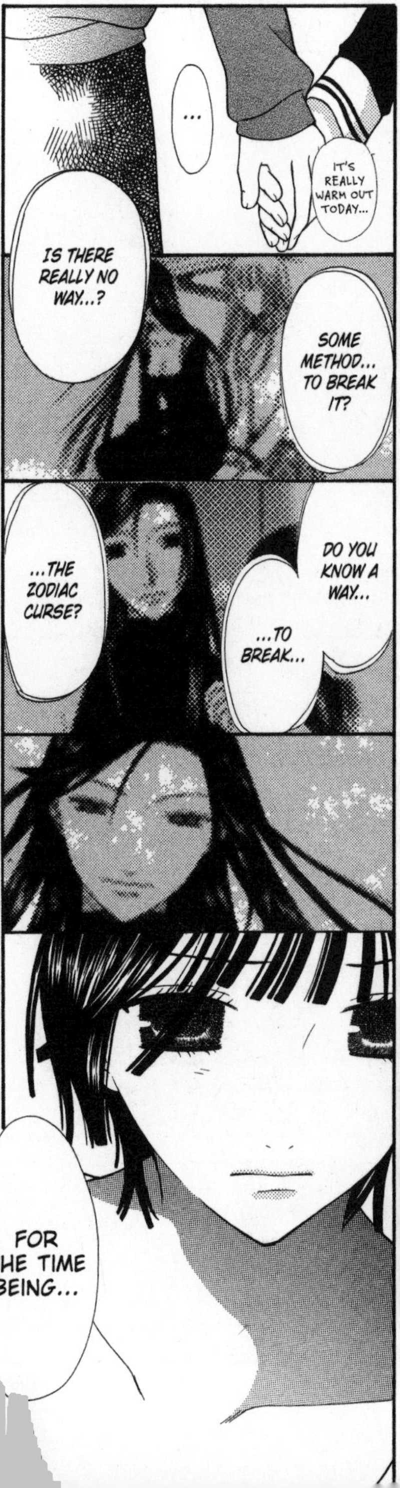
IT'S REALLY WARM OUT TODAY...
...
IS THERE REALLY NO WAY...?
SOME METHOD... TO BREAK IT?
DO YOU KNOW A WAY...
...TO BREAK...
...THE ZODIAC CURSE?
FOR THE TIME BEING...

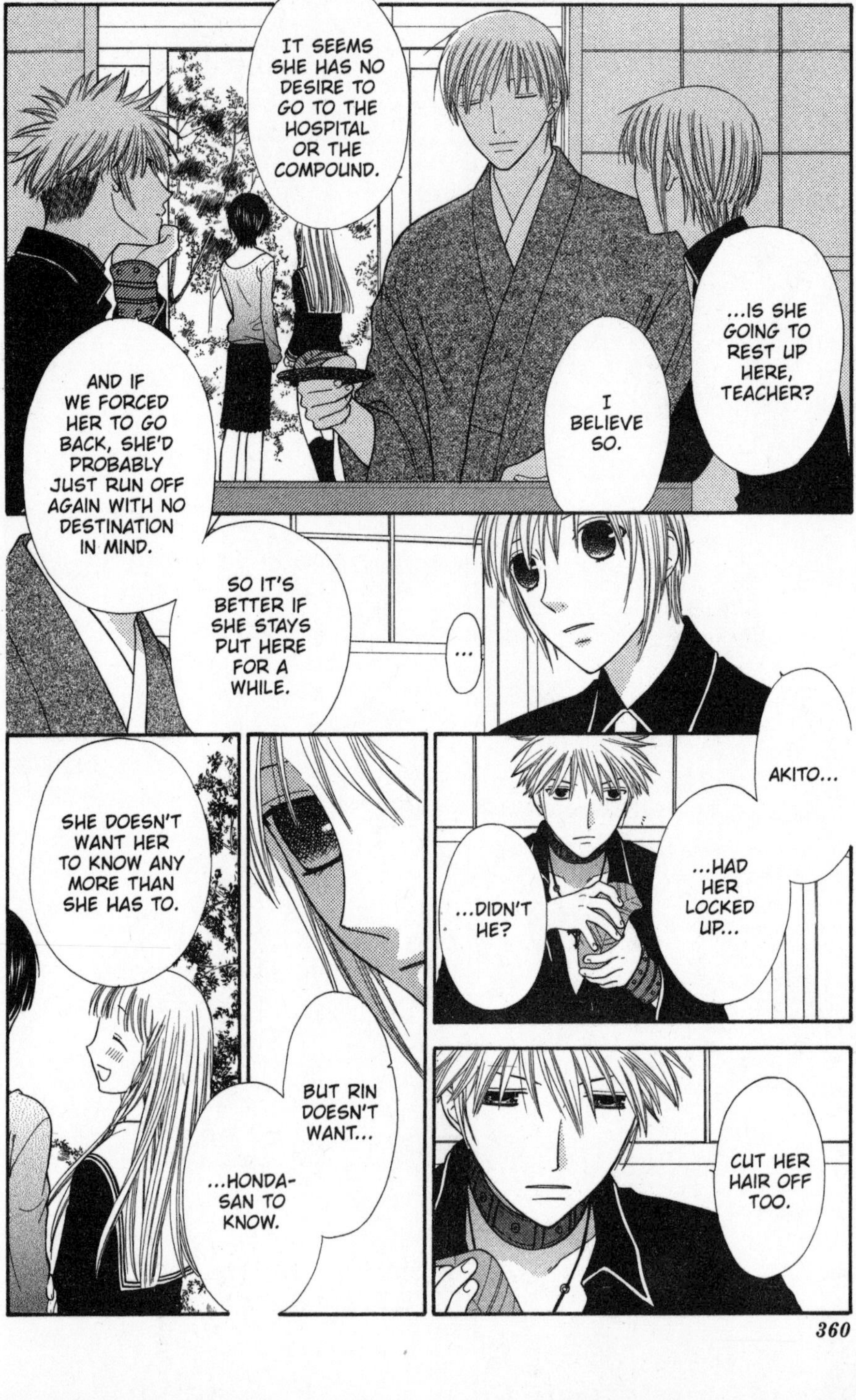
...IS SHE GOING TO REST UP HERE, TEACHER?
I BELIEVE SO.
IT SEEMS SHE HAS NO DESIRE TO GO TO THE HOSPITAL OR THE COMPOUND.
AND IF WE FORCED HER TO GO BACK, SHE'D PROBABLY JUST RUN OFF AGAIN WITH NO DESTINATION IN MIND.
SO IT'S BETTER IF SHE STAYS PUT HERE FOR A WHILE.
...
AKITO...
...HAD HER LOCKED UP...
...DIDN'T HE?
CUT HER HAIR OFF TOO.
BUT RIN DOESN'T WANT...
...HONDA-SAN TO KNOW.
SHE DOESN'T WANT HER TO KNOW ANY MORE THAN SHE HAS TO.

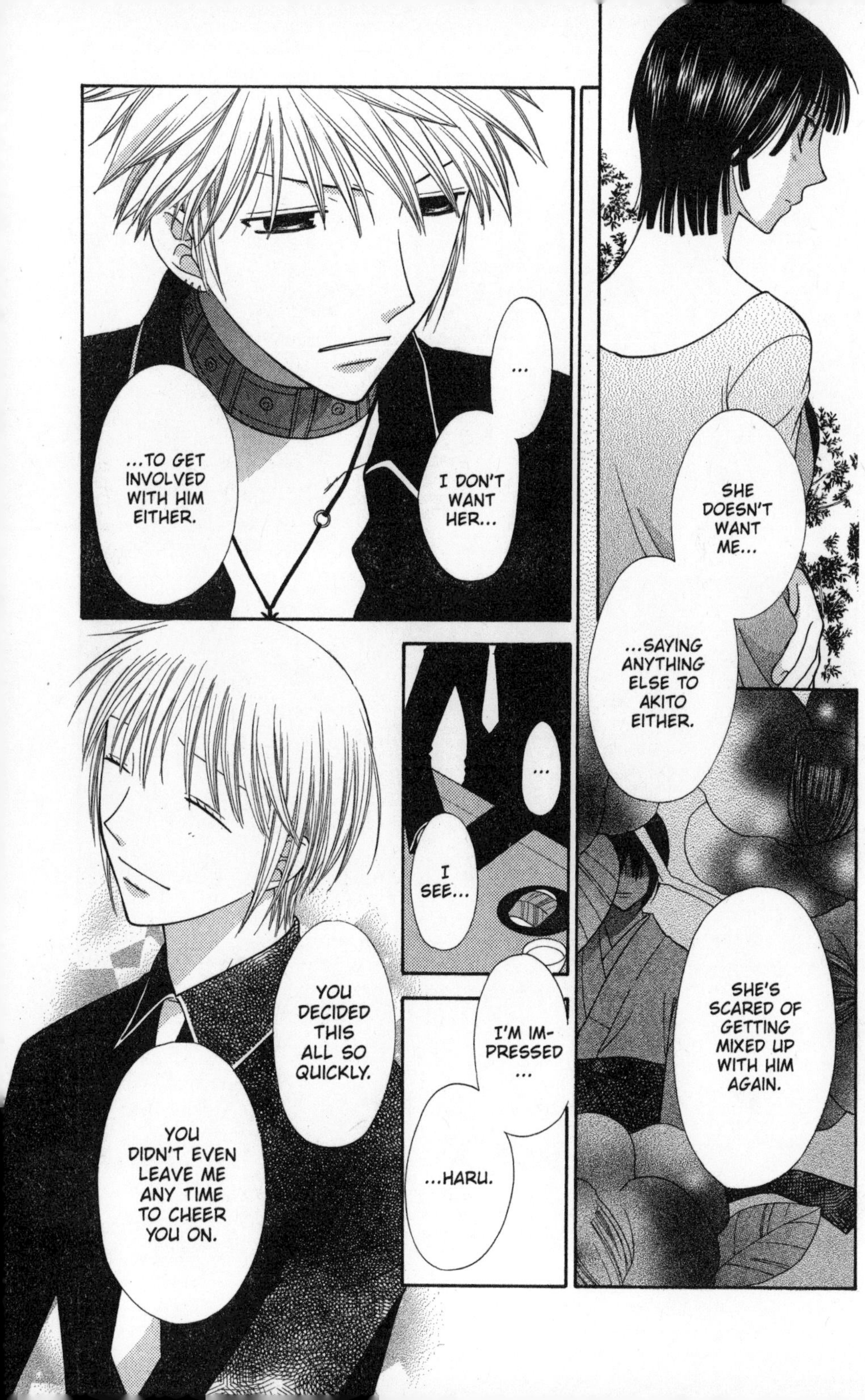
SHE DOESN'T WANT ME...
...SAYING ANYTHING ELSE TO AKITO EITHER.
SHE'S SCARED OF GETTING MIXED UP WITH HIM AGAIN.
...
I DON'T WANT HER...
...TO GET INVOLVED WITH HIM EITHER.
...
I SEE...
I'M IM-PRESSED...
...HARU.
YOU DECIDED THIS ALL SO QUICKLY.
YOU DIDN'T EVEN LEAVE ME ANY TIME TO CHEER YOU ON.

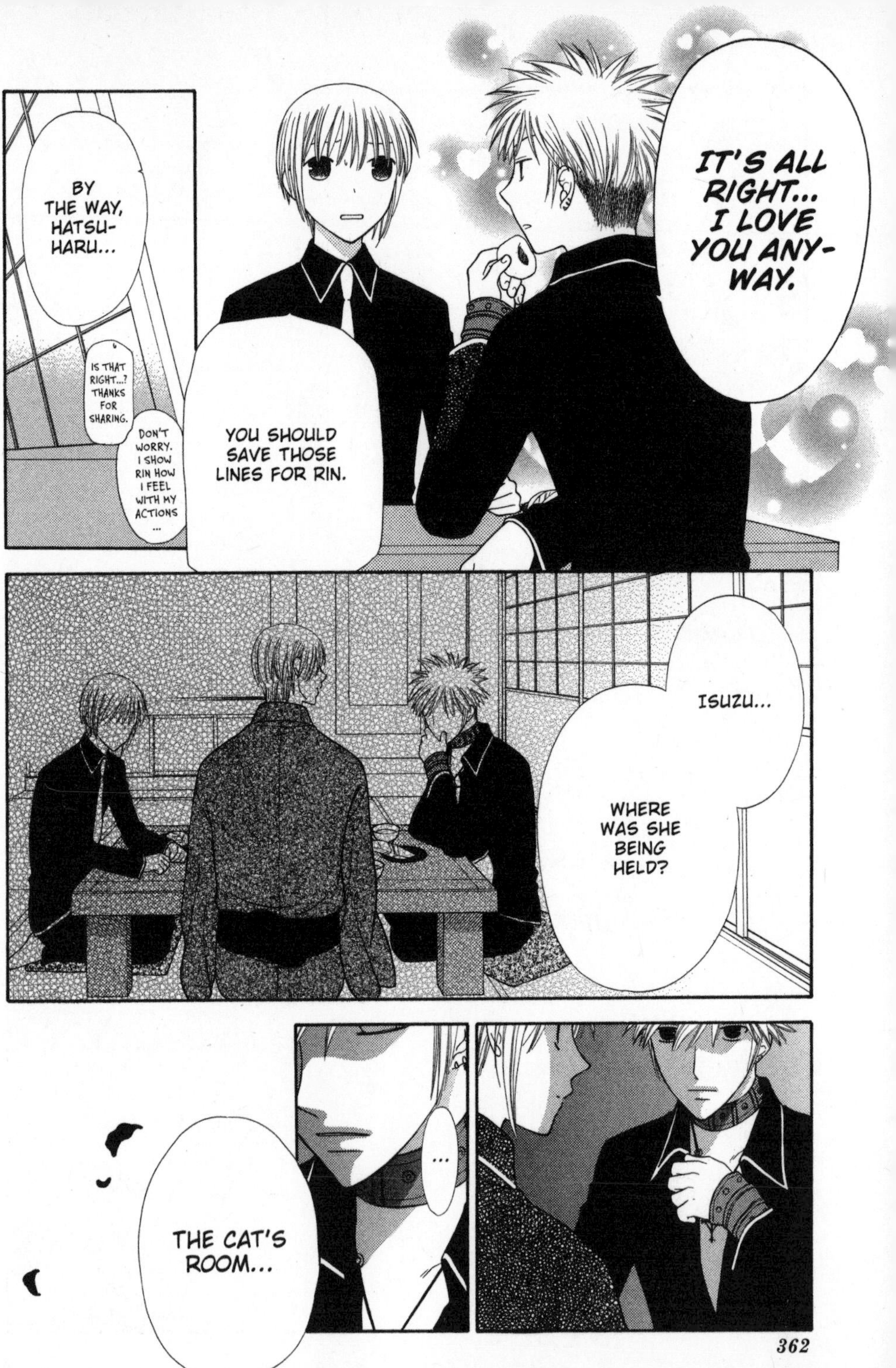
IT'S ALL RIGHT... I LOVE YOU ANYWAY.
YOU SHOULD SAVE THOSE LINES FOR RIN.
DON'T WORRY. I SHOW RIN HOW I FEEL WITH MY ACTIONS...
IS THAT RIGHT...? THANKS FOR SHARING.
BY THE WAY, HATSUHARU...
ISUZU...
WHERE WAS SHE BEING HELD?
...
THE CAT'S ROOM...

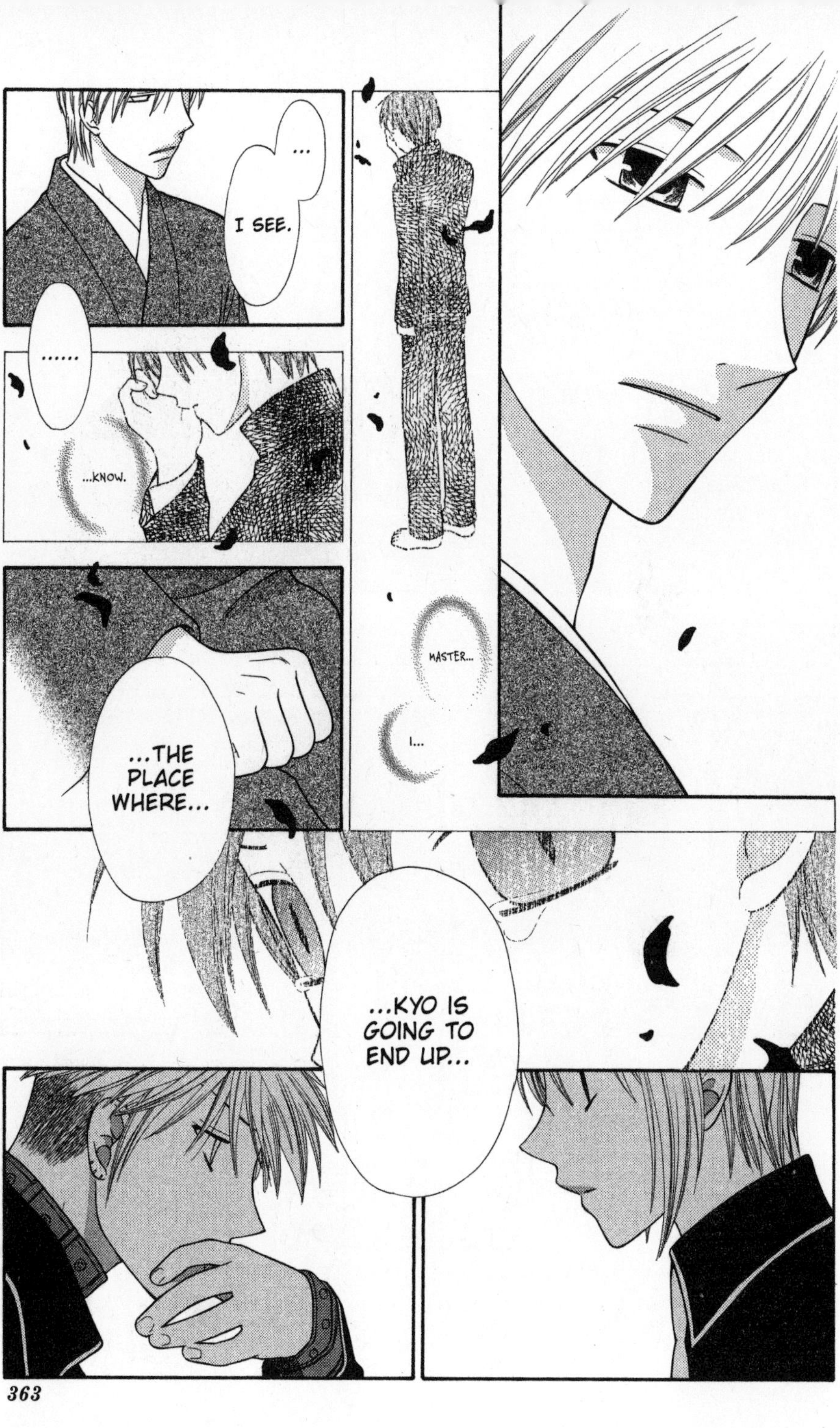
MASTER...
I...
...
I SEE.
......
...KNOW.
...THE PLACE WHERE...
...KYO IS GOING TO END UP...

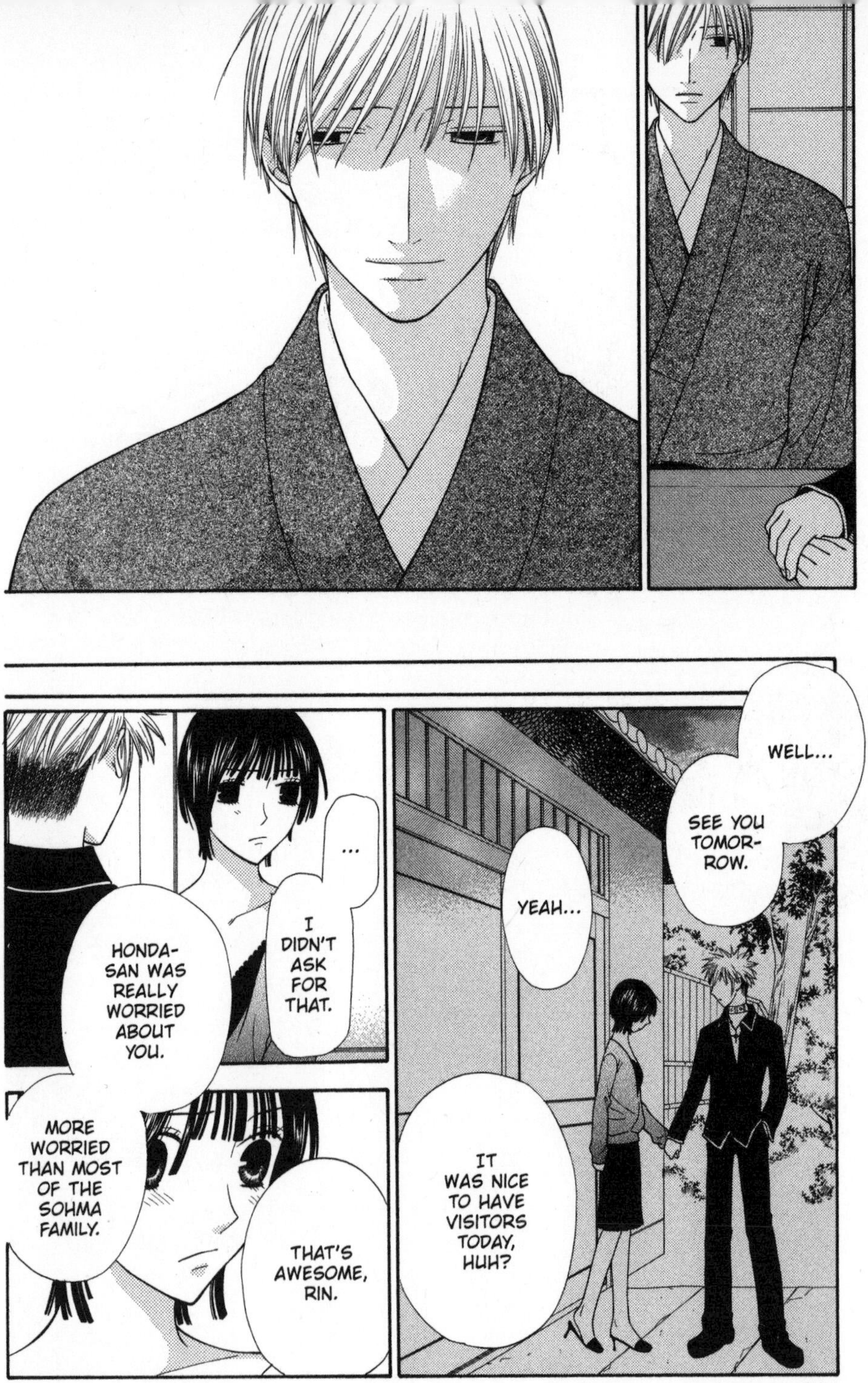
WELL...
SEE YOU TOMORROW.
YEAH...
IT WAS NICE TO HAVE VISITORS TODAY, HUH?
...
I DIDN'T ASK FOR THAT.
HONDA-SAN WAS REALLY WORRIED ABOUT YOU.
MORE WORRIED THAN MOST OF THE SOHMA FAMILY.
THAT'S AWESOME, RIN.

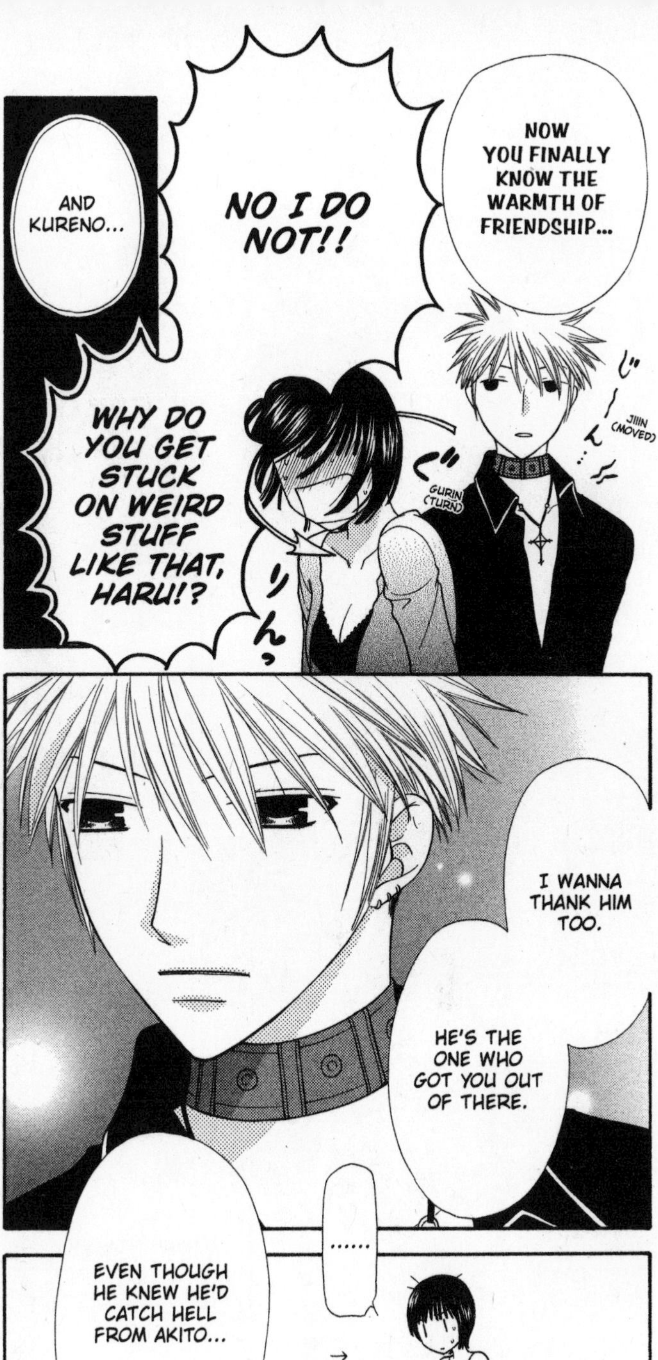
NOW YOU FINALLY KNOW THE WARMTH OF FRIENDSHIP...
じ~ん...
JIIN (MOVED)
NO I DO NOT!!
WHY DO YOU GET STUCK ON WEIRD STUFF LIKE THAT, HARU!?
ぐりん
GURIN (TURN)
AND KURENO...
I WANNA THANK HIM TOO.
HE'S THE ONE WHO GOT YOU OUT OF THERE.
EVEN THOUGH HE KNEW HE'D CATCH HELL FROM AKITO...
......
→ ORIGINALLY WANTED TO BEAT UP KURENO

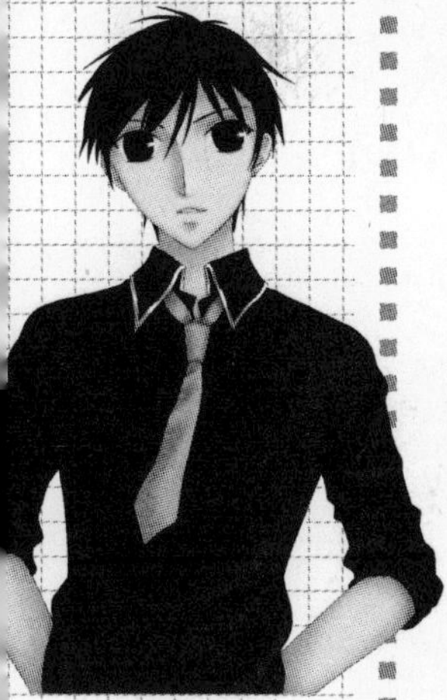

KAKERU MANABE

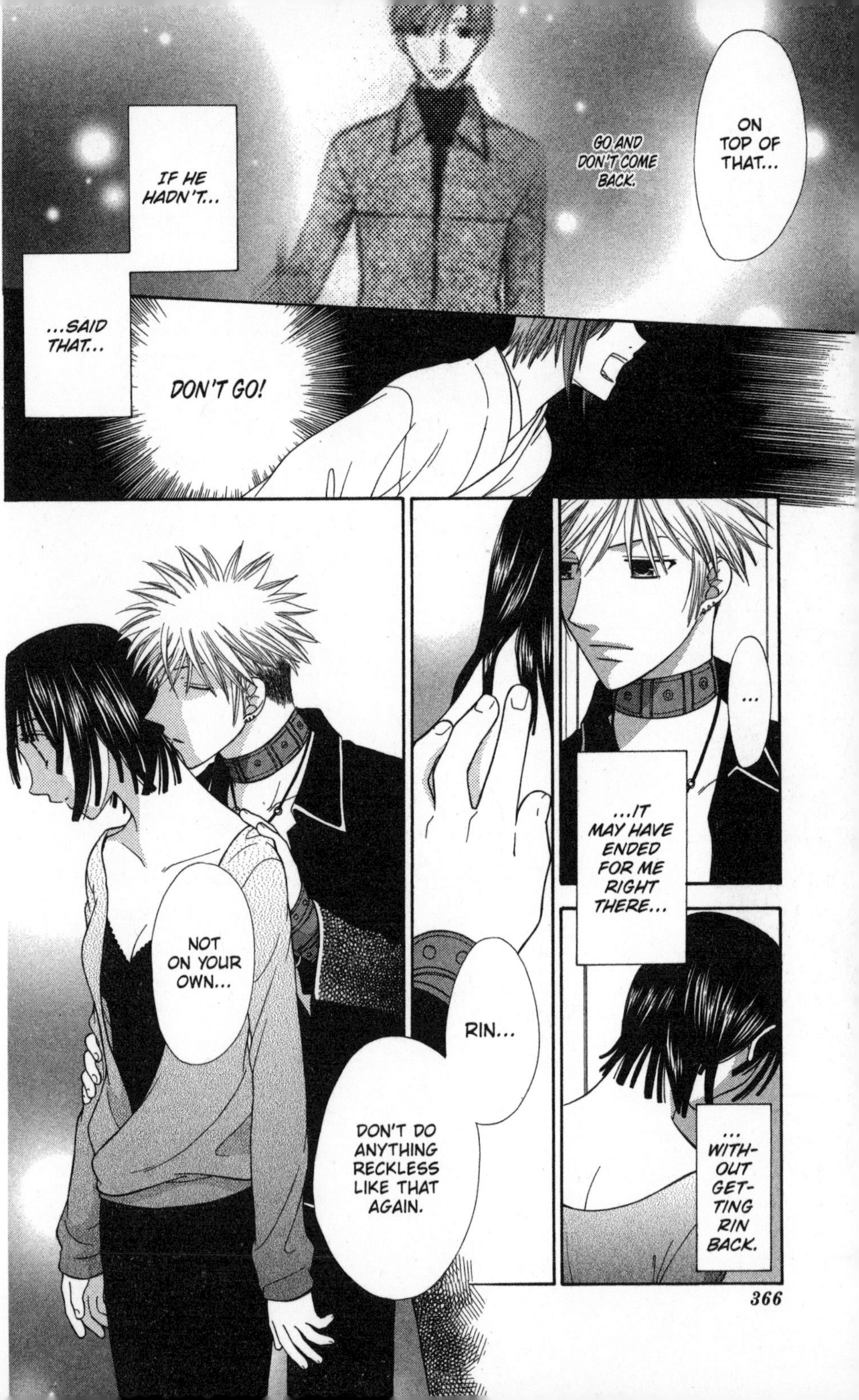
ON TOP OF THAT...
GO AND DON'T COME BACK.
IF HE HADN'T...
DON'T GO!
...SAID THAT...
...
...IT MAY HAVE ENDED FOR ME RIGHT THERE...
...WITHOUT GETTING RIN BACK.
RIN...
DON'T DO ANYTHING RECKLESS LIKE THAT AGAIN.
NOT ON YOUR OWN...

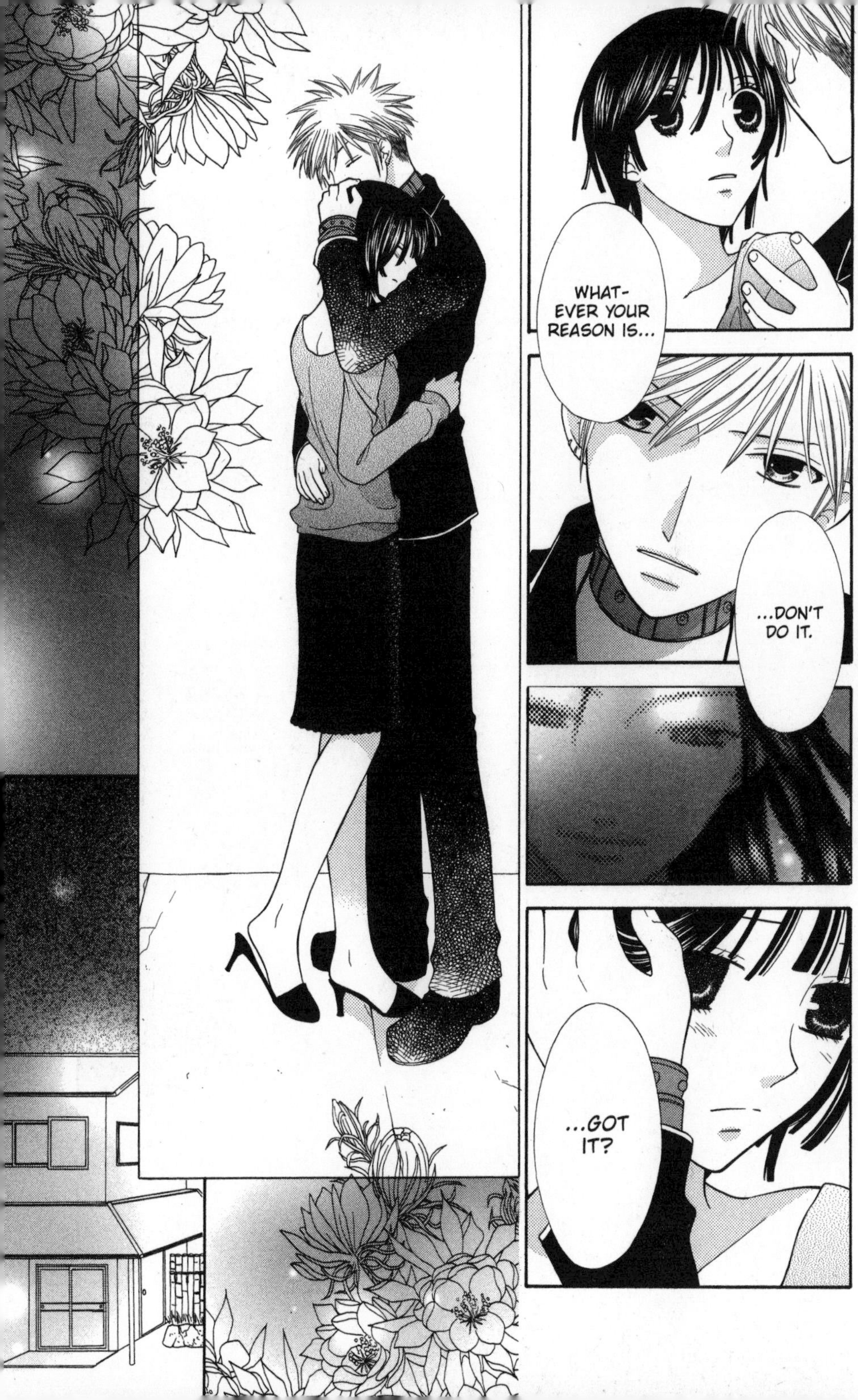
WHAT-EVER YOUR REASON IS...
...DON'T DO IT.
...GOT IT?

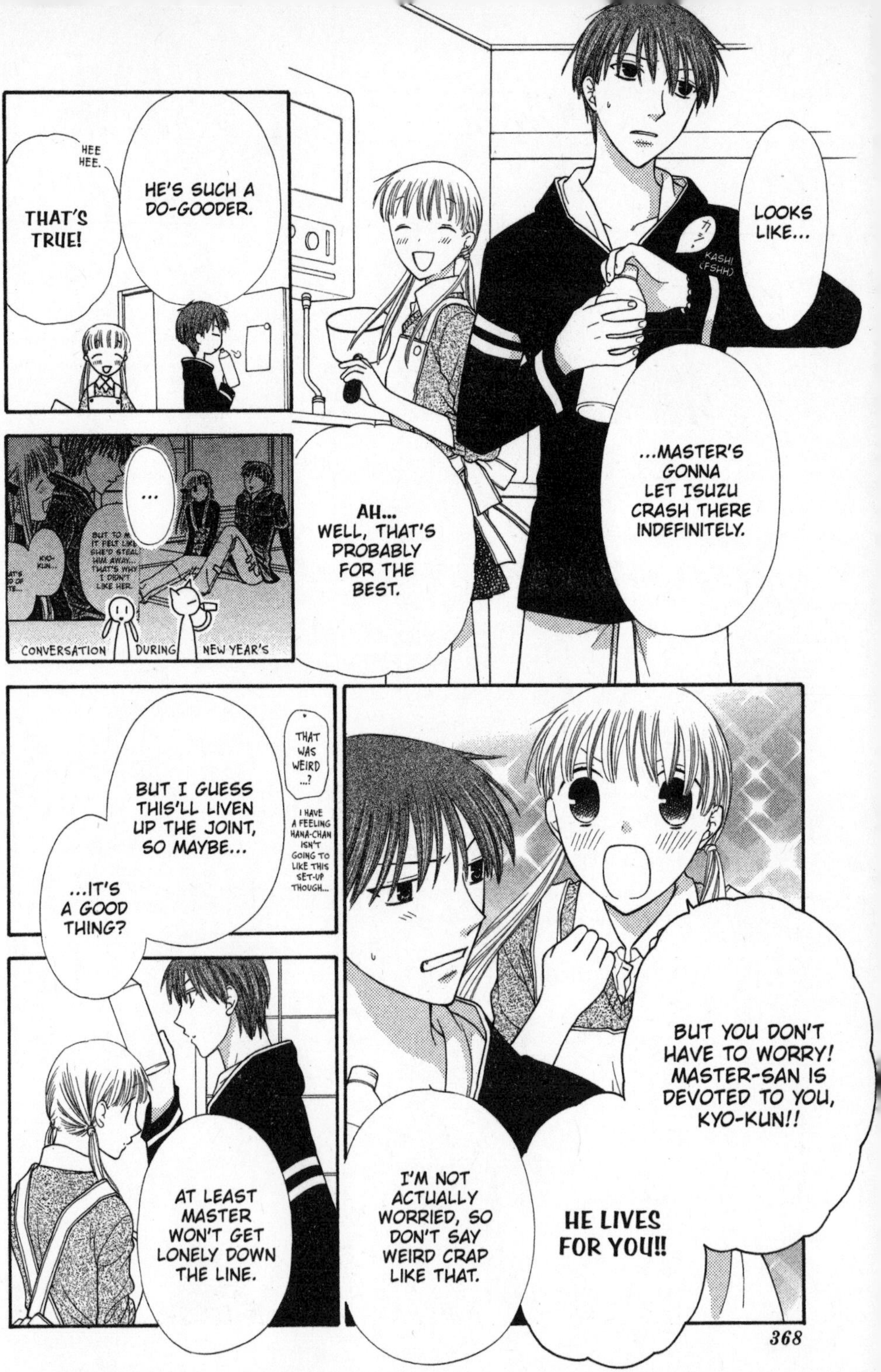
LOOKS LIKE...
KASHI (FSHH)
...MASTER'S GONNA LET ISUZU CRASH THERE INDEFINITELY.
AH... WELL, THAT'S PROBABLY FOR THE BEST.
HE'S SUCH A DO-GOODER.
HEE HEE.
THAT'S TRUE!
...
BUT TO M IT FELT LIKE SHE'D STEAL HIM AWAY... THAT'S WHY I DIDN'T LIKE HER
KYO-KUN...
CONVERSATION DURING NEW YEAR'S
BUT YOU DON'T HAVE TO WORRY! MASTER-SAN IS DEVOTED TO YOU, KYO-KUN!!
HE LIVES FOR YOU!!
I'M NOT ACTUALLY WORRIED, SO DON'T SAY WEIRD CRAP LIKE THAT.
BUT I GUESS THIS'LL LIVEN UP THE JOINT, SO MAYBE...
...IT'S A GOOD THING?
THAT WAS WEIRD...?
I HAVE A FEELING HANA-CHAN ISN'T GOING TO LIKE THIS SET-UP THOUGH...
AT LEAST MASTER WON'T GET LONELY DOWN THE LINE.

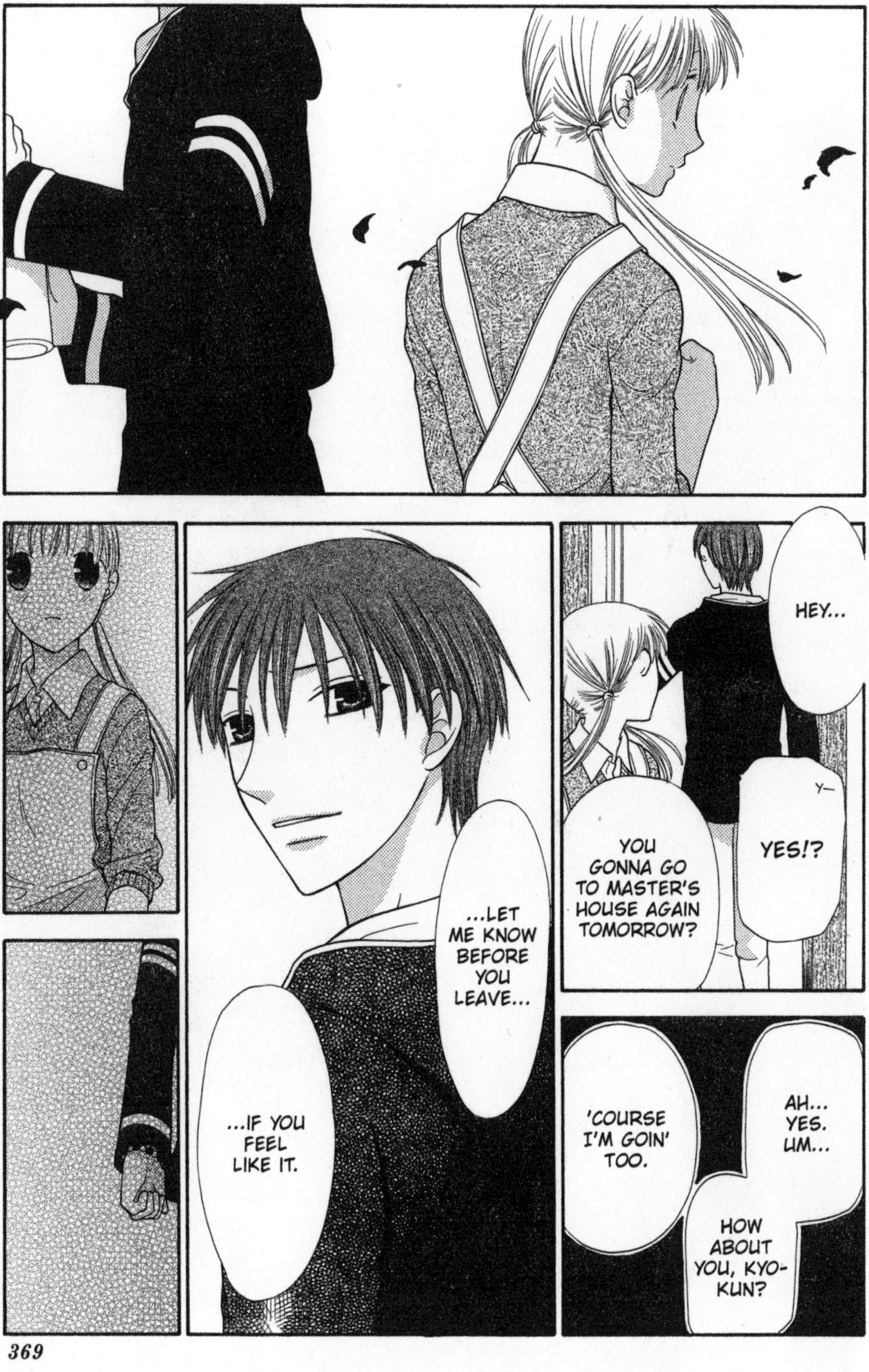
HEY...
Y—
YES!?
YOU GONNA GO TO MASTER'S HOUSE AGAIN TOMORROW?
AH... YES. UM...
HOW ABOUT YOU, KYO-KUN?
'COURSE I'M GOIN' TOO.
...LET ME KNOW BEFORE YOU LEAVE...
...IF YOU FEEL LIKE IT.

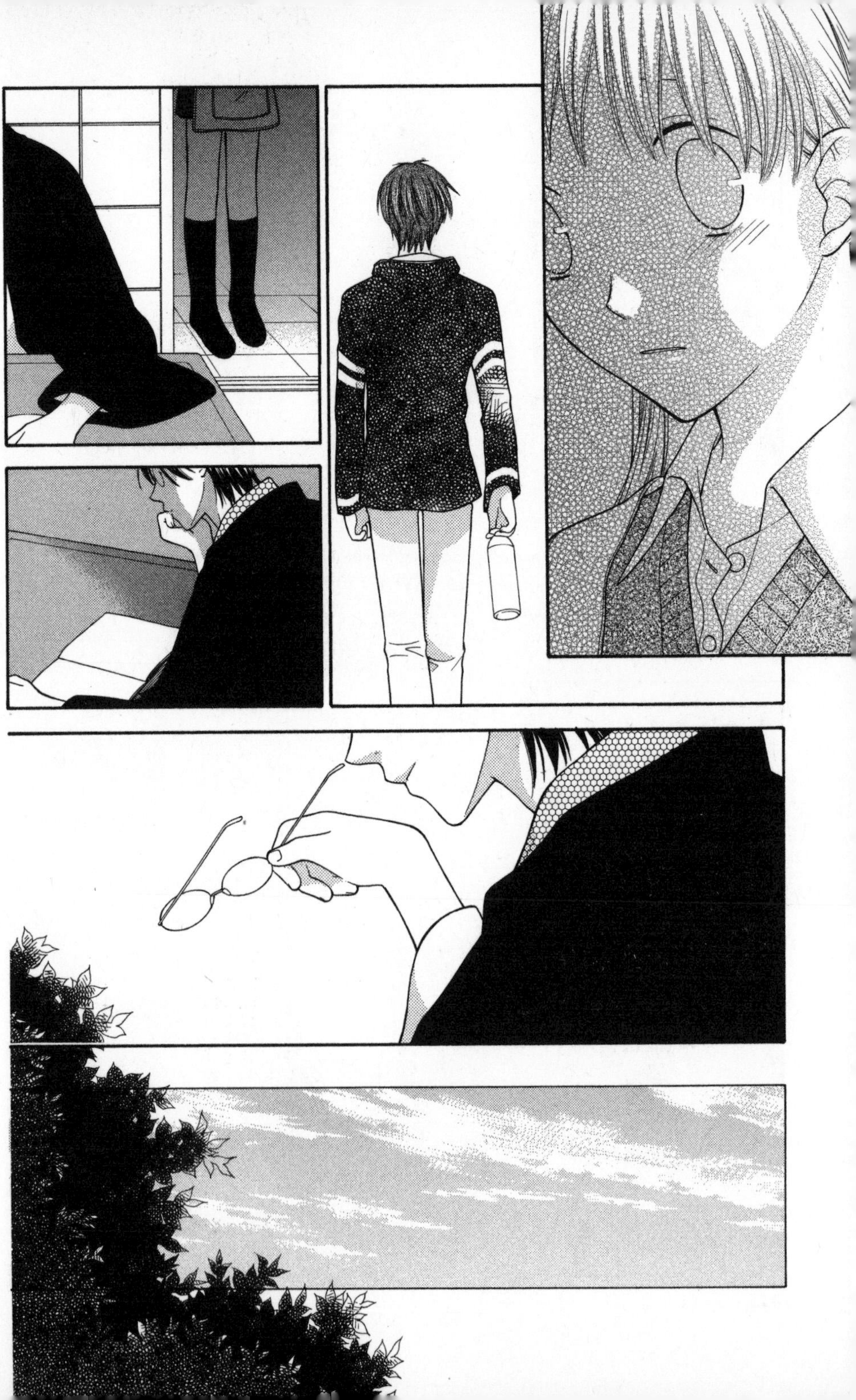

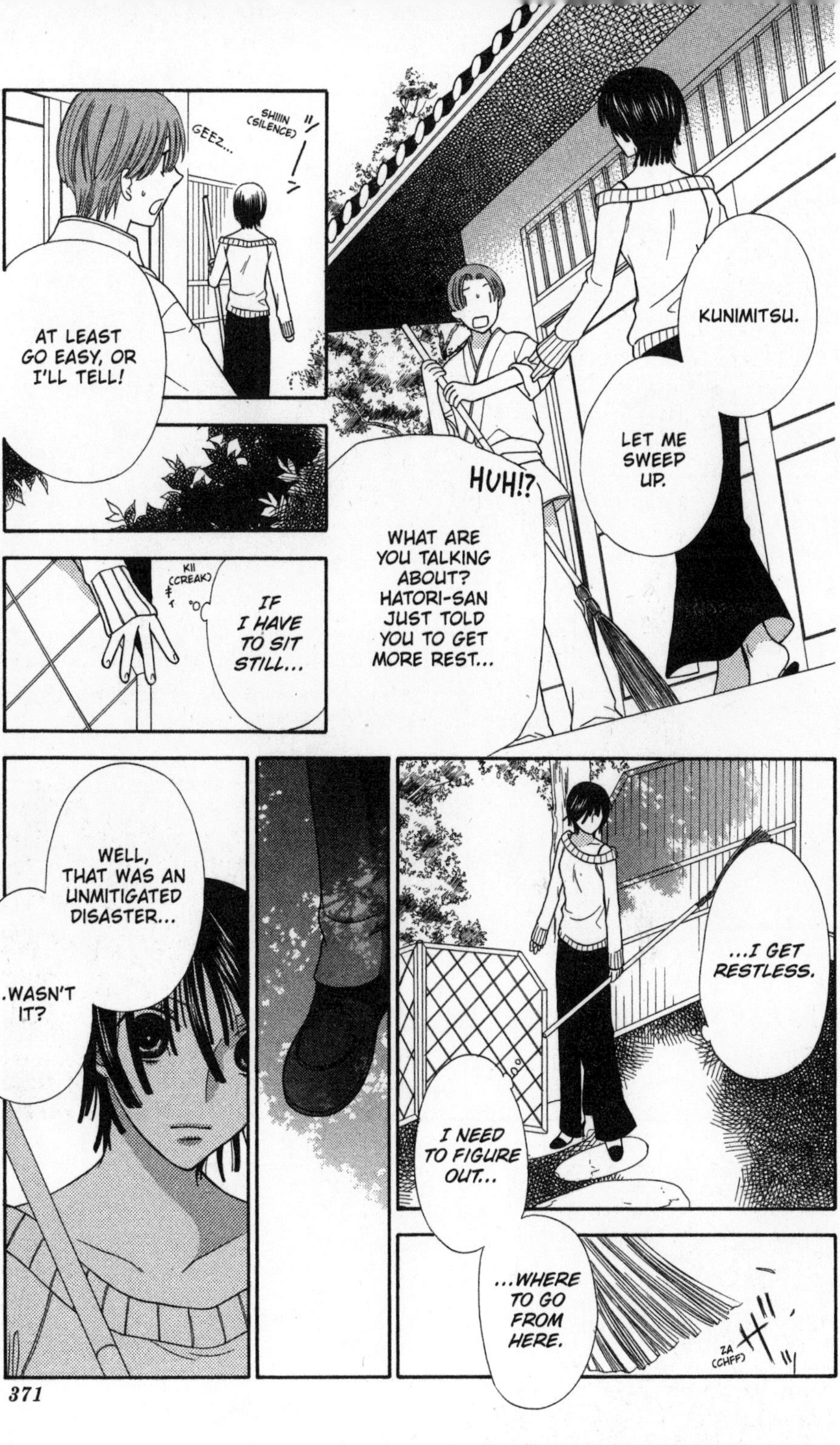
KUNIMITSU.
LET ME SWEEP UP.
HUH!?
WHAT ARE YOU TALKING ABOUT? HATORI-SAN JUST TOLD YOU TO GET MORE REST...
SHIIIN (SILENCE)
GEEZ...
AT LEAST GO EASY, OR I'LL TELL!
KII (CREAK)
IF I HAVE TO SIT STILL...
...I GET RESTLESS.
I NEED TO FIGURE OUT...
...WHERE TO GO FROM HERE.
ZA (CHFF)
WELL, THAT WAS AN UNMITIGATED DISASTER...
...WASN'T IT?

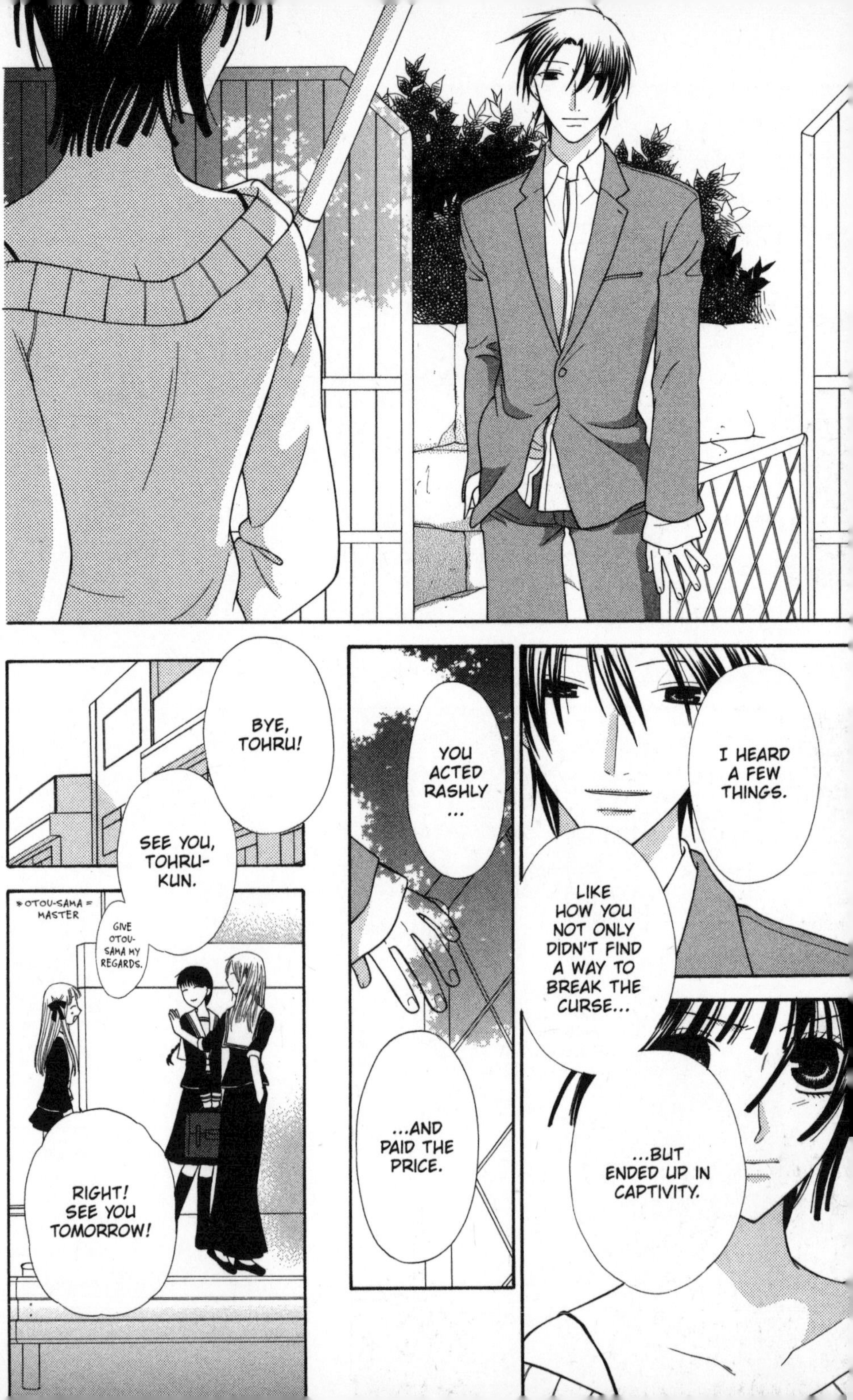
I HEARD A FEW THINGS.
LIKE HOW YOU NOT ONLY DIDN'T FIND A WAY TO BREAK THE CURSE...
...BUT ENDED UP IN CAPTIVITY.
YOU ACTED RASHLY ...
...AND PAID THE PRICE.
BYE, TOHRU!
SEE YOU, TOHRU-KUN.
GIVE OTOU-SAMA MY REGARDS.
*OTOU-SAMA = MASTER
RIGHT! SEE YOU TOMORROW!

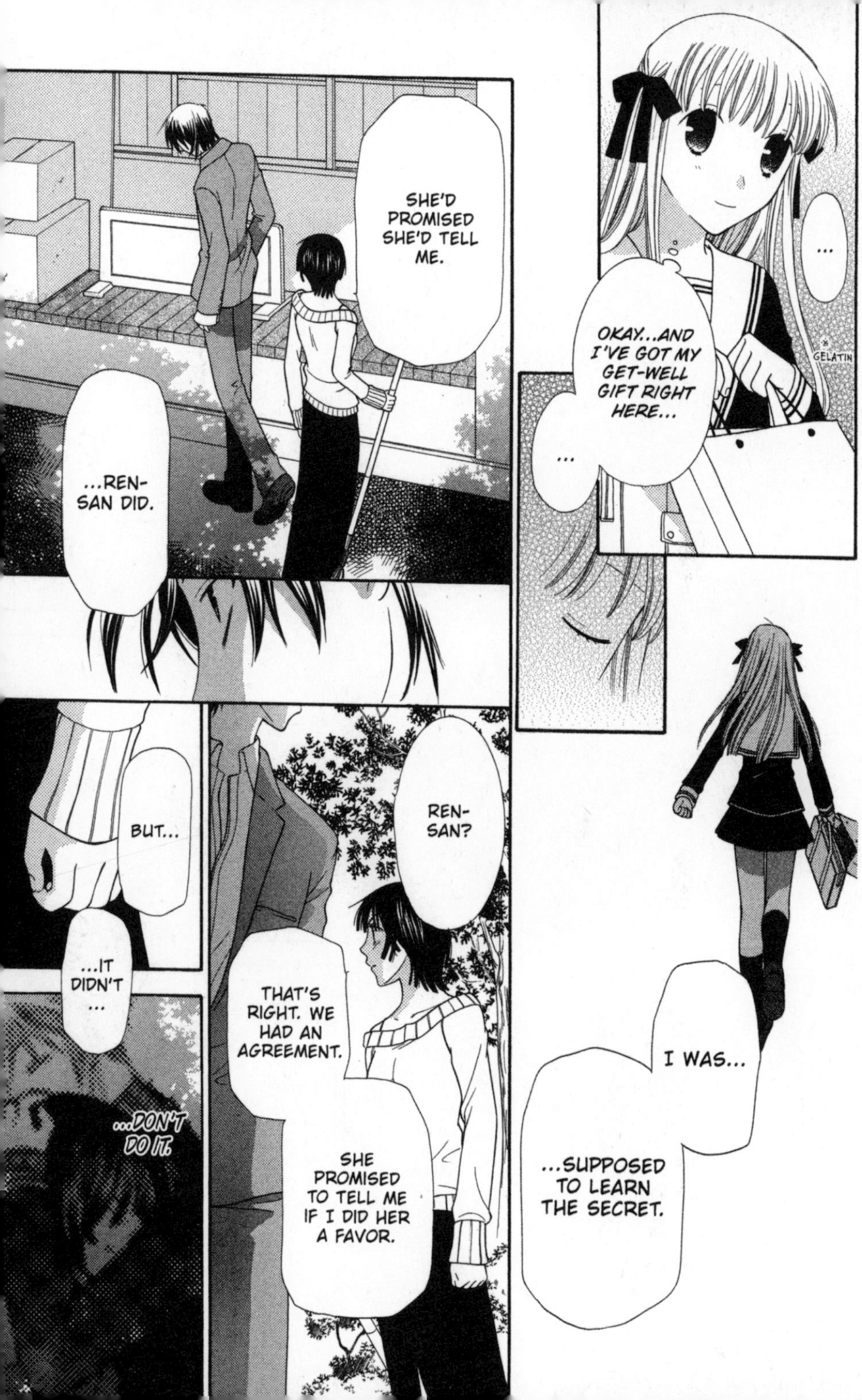
...
OKAY...AND I'VE GOT MY GET-WELL GIFT RIGHT HERE...
* GELATIN
...
I WAS...
...SUPPOSED TO LEARN THE SECRET.
SHE'D PROMISED SHE'D TELL ME.
...REN-SAN DID.
REN-SAN?
THAT'S RIGHT. WE HAD AN AGREEMENT.
SHE PROMISED TO TELL ME IF I DID HER A FAVOR.
BUT...
...IT DIDN'T ...
...DON'T DO IT.

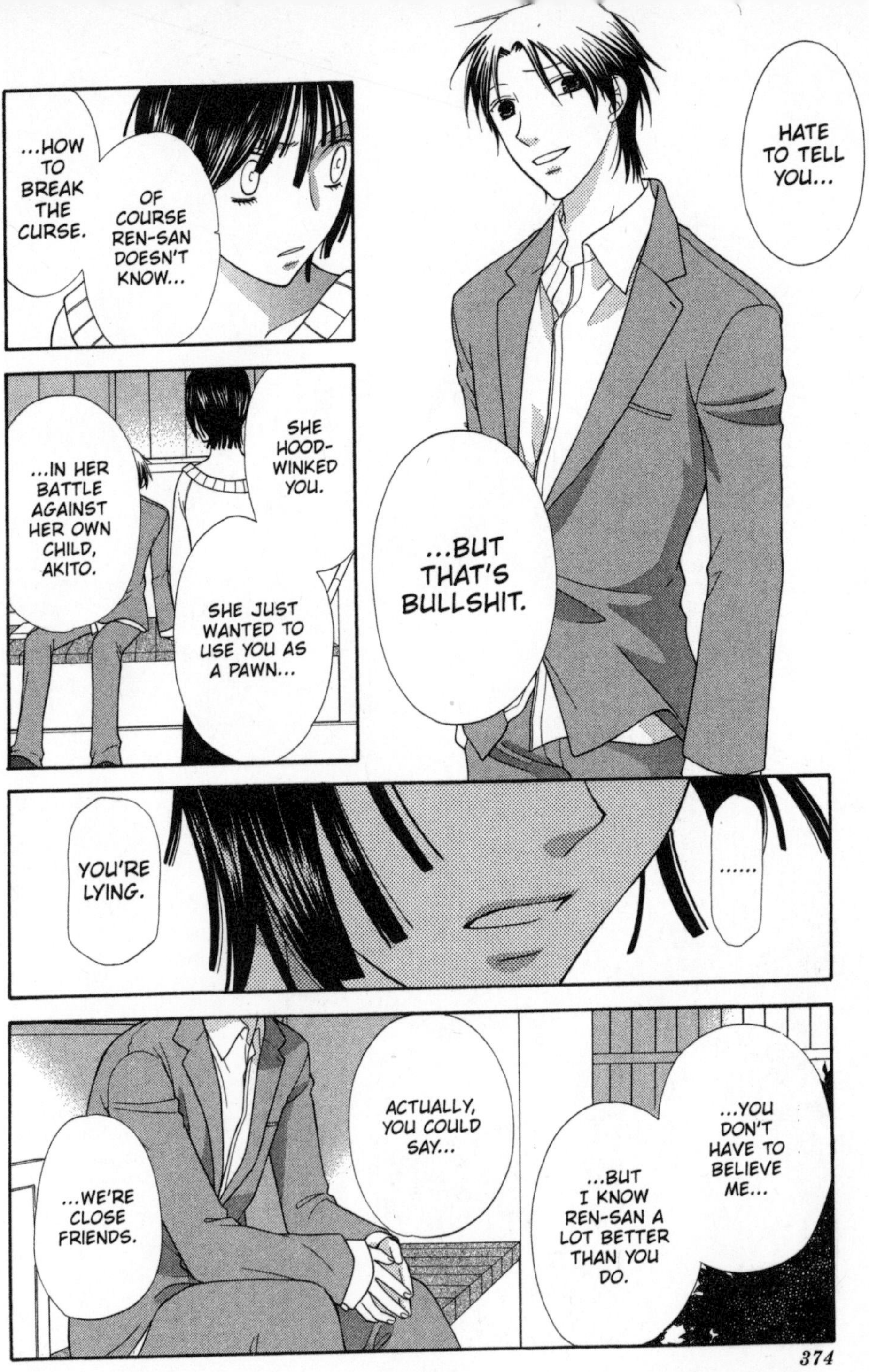
HATE TO TELL YOU...
...BUT THAT'S BULLSHIT.
OF COURSE REN-SAN DOESN'T KNOW...
...HOW TO BREAK THE CURSE.
SHE HOOD-WINKED YOU.
SHE JUST WANTED TO USE YOU AS A PAWN...
...IN HER BATTLE AGAINST HER OWN CHILD, AKITO.
......
YOU'RE LYING.
...YOU DON'T HAVE TO BELIEVE ME...
...BUT I KNOW REN-SAN A LOT BETTER THAN YOU DO.
ACTUALLY, YOU COULD SAY...
...WE'RE CLOSE FRIENDS.

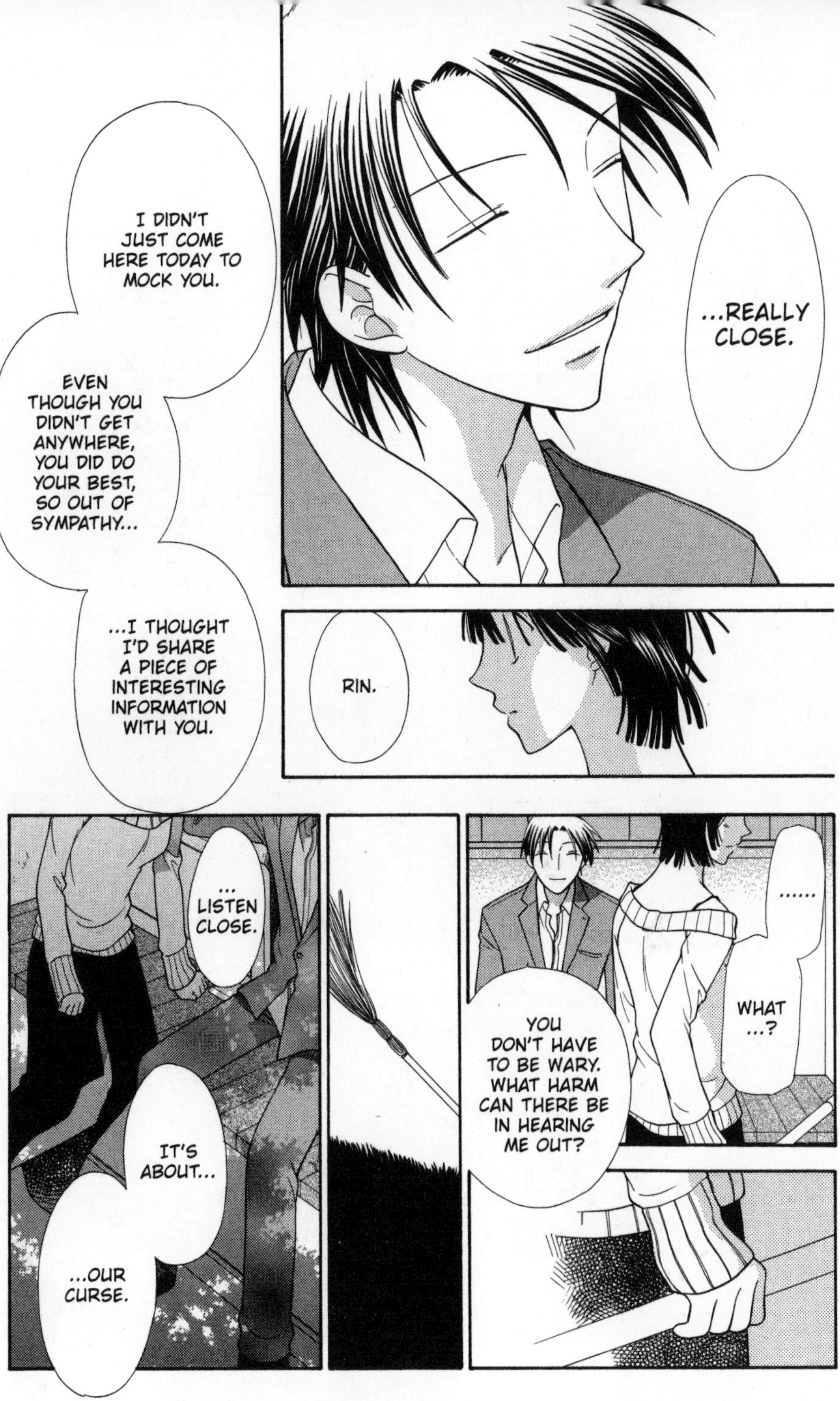

...REALLY CLOSE.
RIN.
I DIDN'T JUST COME HERE TODAY TO MOCK YOU.
EVEN THOUGH YOU DIDN'T GET ANYWHERE, YOU DID DO YOUR BEST, SO OUT OF SYMPATHY...
...I THOUGHT I'D SHARE A PIECE OF INTERESTING INFORMATION WITH YOU.
......
WHAT ...?
YOU DON'T HAVE TO BE WARY. WHAT HARM CAN THERE BE IN HEARING ME OUT?
... LISTEN CLOSE.
IT'S ABOUT...
...OUR CURSE.

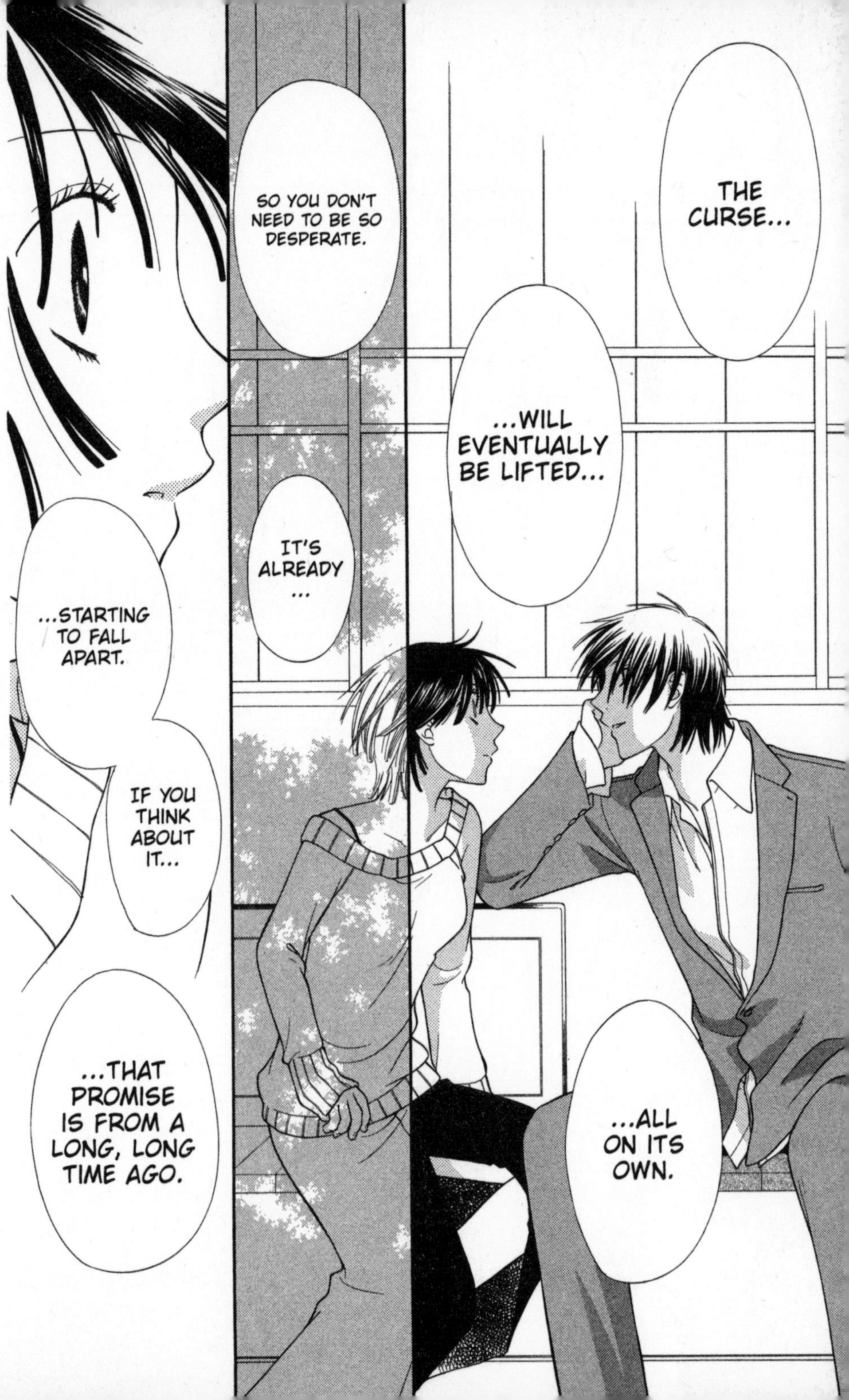
THE CURSE...
...WILL EVENTUALLY BE LIFTED...
...ALL ON ITS OWN.
SO YOU DON'T NEED TO BE SO DESPERATE.
IT'S ALREADY ...
...STARTING TO FALL APART.
IF YOU THINK ABOUT IT...
...THAT PROMISE IS FROM A LONG, LONG TIME AGO.

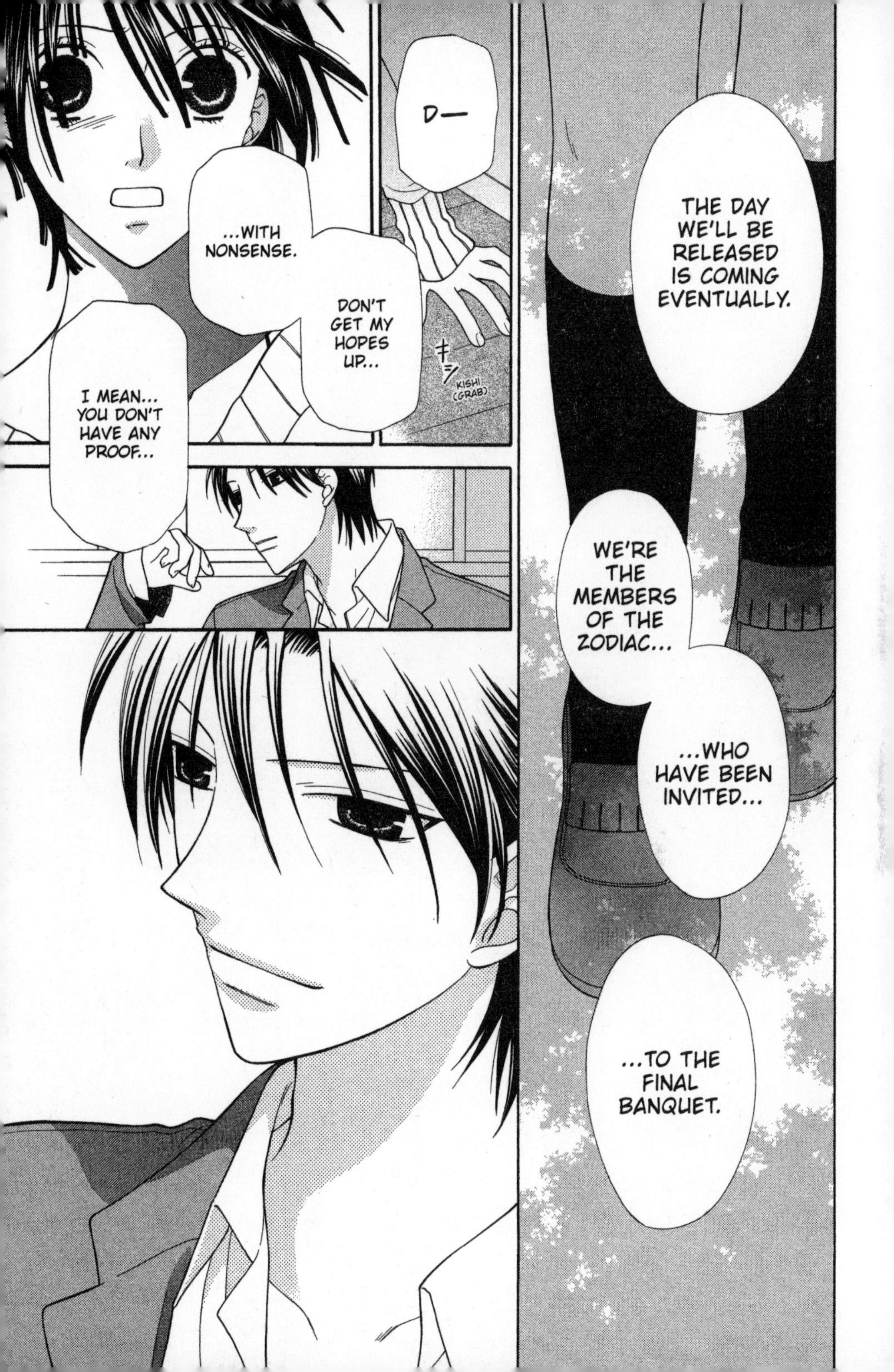
THE DAY WE'LL BE RELEASED IS COMING EVENTUALLY.
WE'RE THE MEMBERS OF THE ZODIAC...
...WHO HAVE BEEN INVITED...
...TO THE FINAL BANQUET.
D—
キシ
KISHI (GRAB)
...WITH NONSENSE.
DON'T GET MY HOPES UP...
I MEAN... YOU DON'T HAVE ANY PROOF...

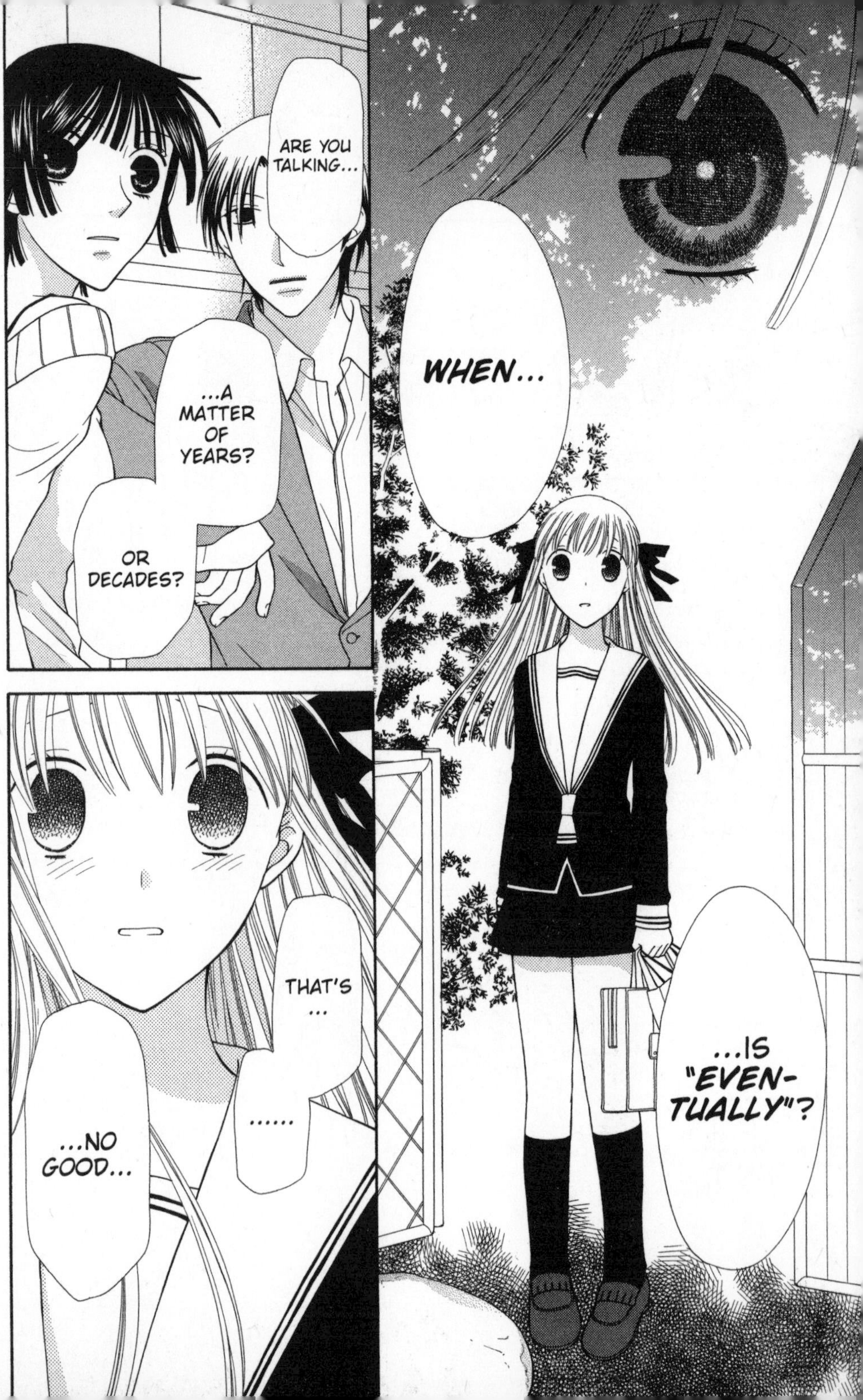
WHEN...
...IS "EVEN-TUALLY"?
ARE YOU TALKING...
...A MATTER OF YEARS?
OR DECADES?
THAT'S ...
......
...NO GOOD...

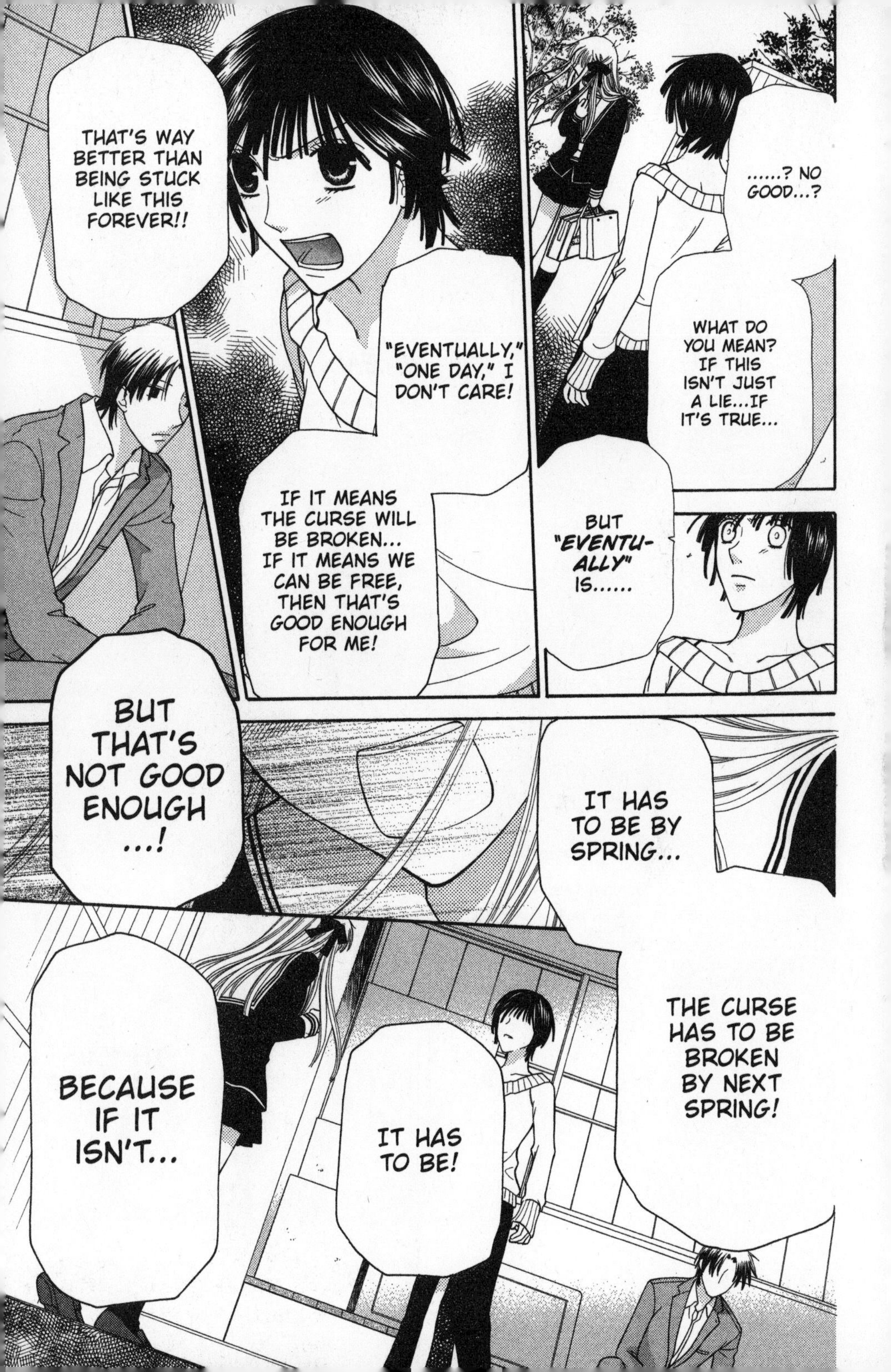

......? NO GOOD...?
WHAT DO YOU MEAN? IF THIS ISN'T JUST A LIE...IF IT'S TRUE...
BUT "EVENTUALLY" IS......
"EVENTUALLY," "ONE DAY," I DON'T CARE!
IF IT MEANS THE CURSE WILL BE BROKEN... IF IT MEANS WE CAN BE FREE, THEN THAT'S GOOD ENOUGH FOR ME!
THAT'S WAY BETTER THAN BEING STUCK LIKE THIS FOREVER!!
BUT THAT'S NOT GOOD ENOUGH ...!
IT HAS TO BE BY SPRING...
THE CURSE HAS TO BE BROKEN BY NEXT SPRING!
IT HAS TO BE!
BECAUSE IF IT ISN'T...

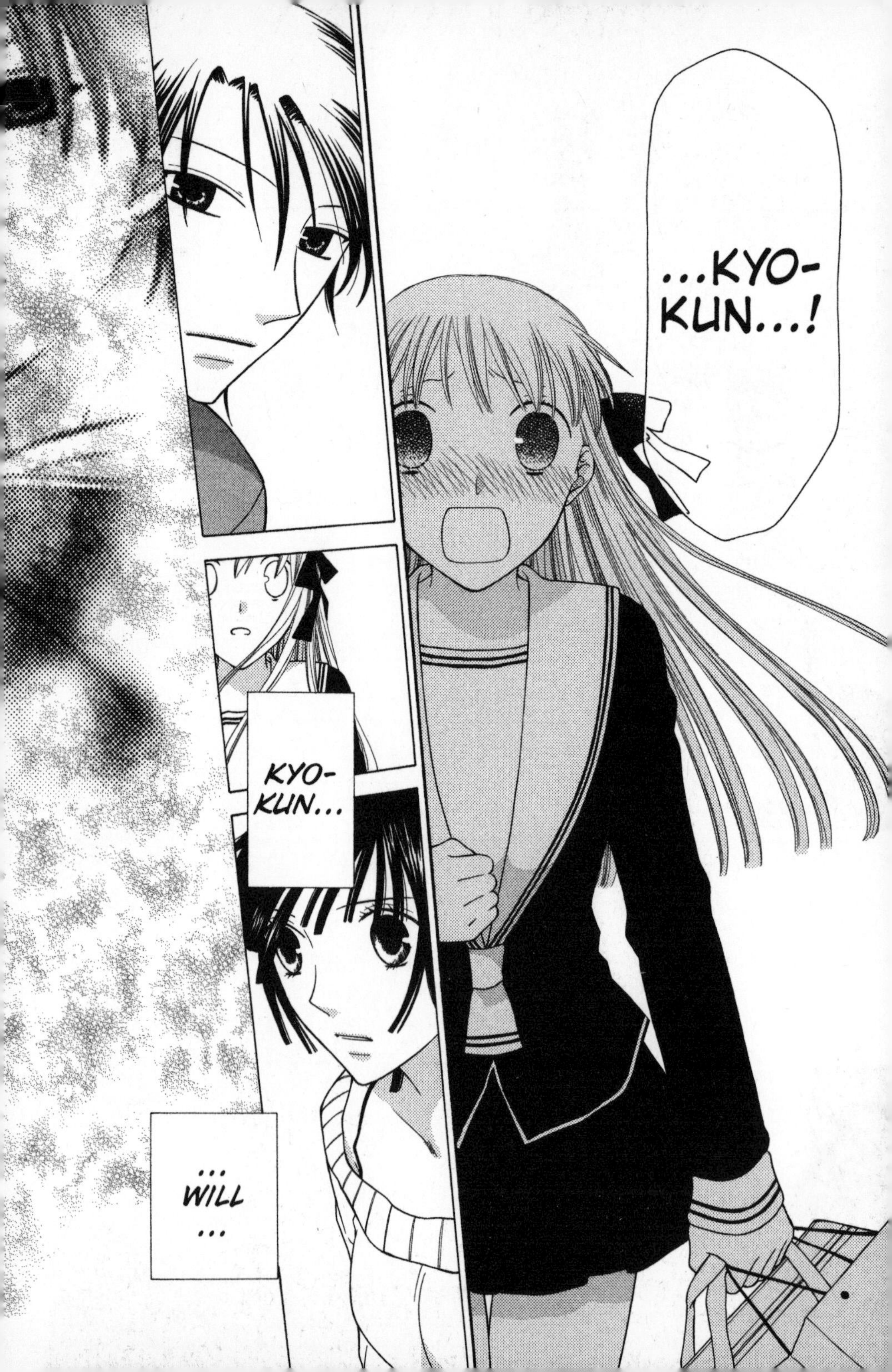
...KYO-KUN...!
KYO-KUN...
...WILL...

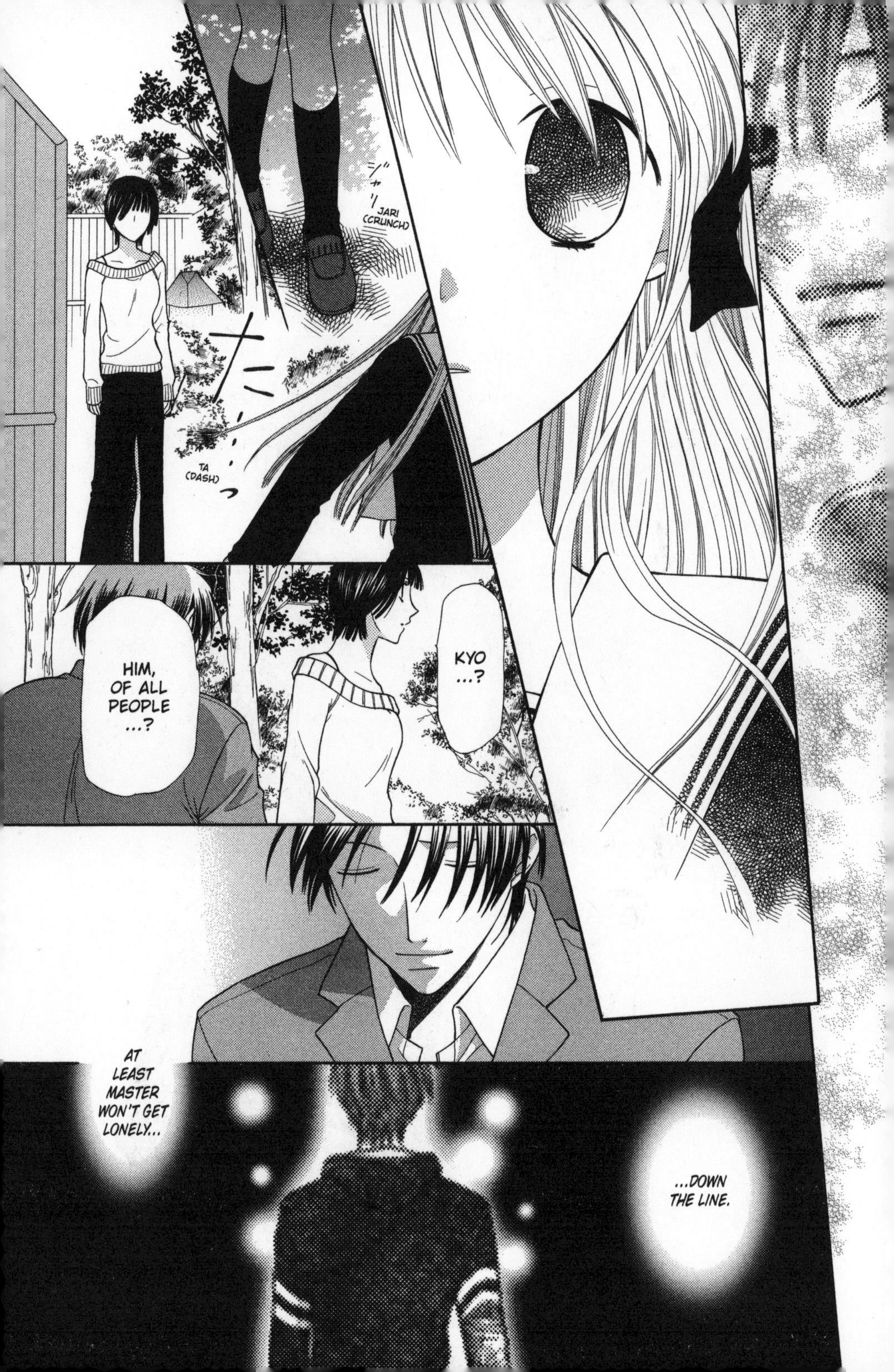
ジャリ
JARI (CRUNCH)
TA (DASH)
KYO ...?
HIM, OF ALL PEOPLE ...?
AT LEAST MASTER WON'T GET LONELY...
...DOWN THE LINE.

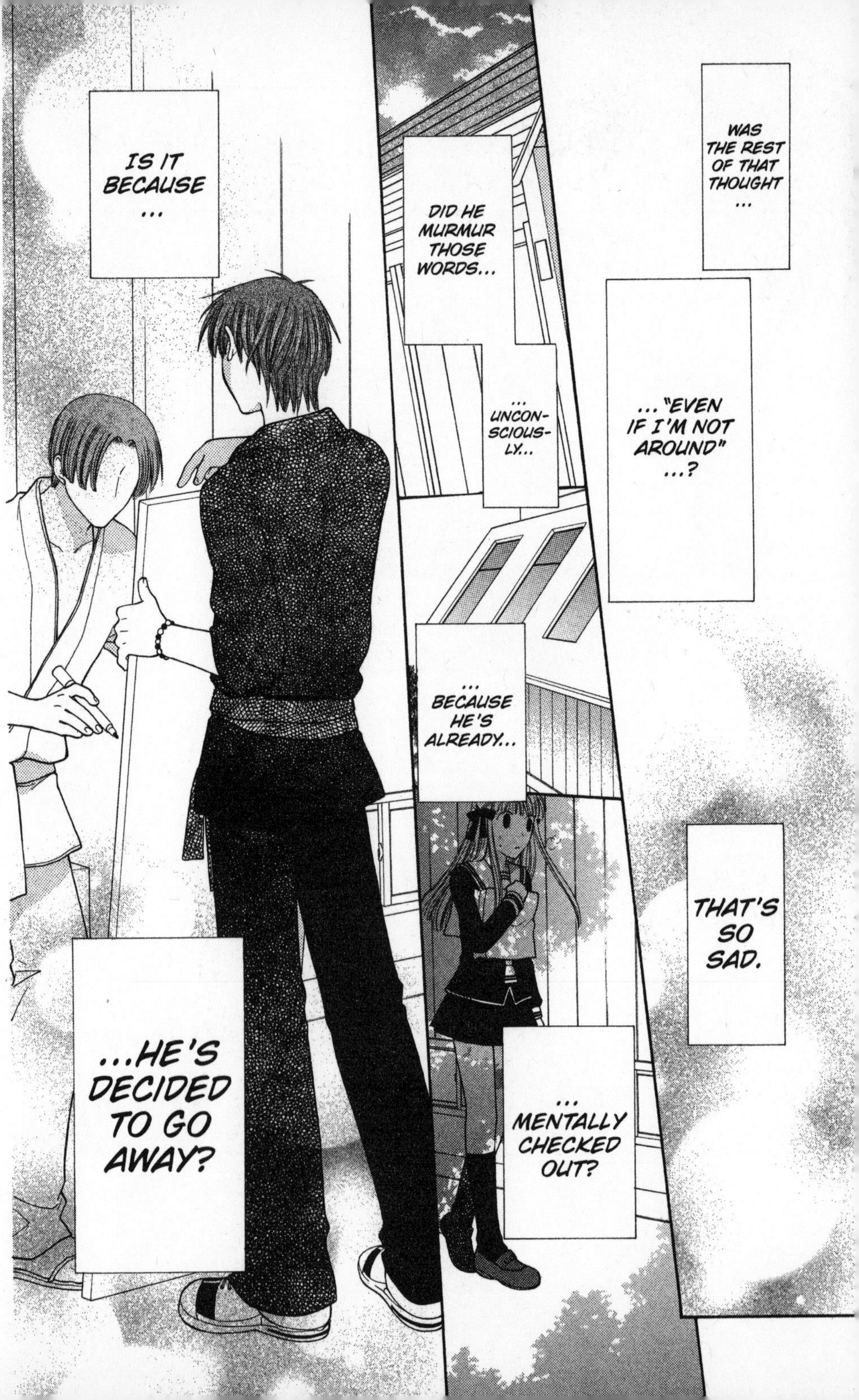

WAS THE REST OF THAT THOUGHT...
..."EVEN IF I'M NOT AROUND"...?
THAT'S SO SAD.
DID HE MURMUR THOSE WORDS...
...UNCONSCIOUSLY...
...BECAUSE HE'S ALREADY...
...MENTALLY CHECKED OUT?
IS IT BECAUSE...
...HE'S DECIDED TO GO AWAY?

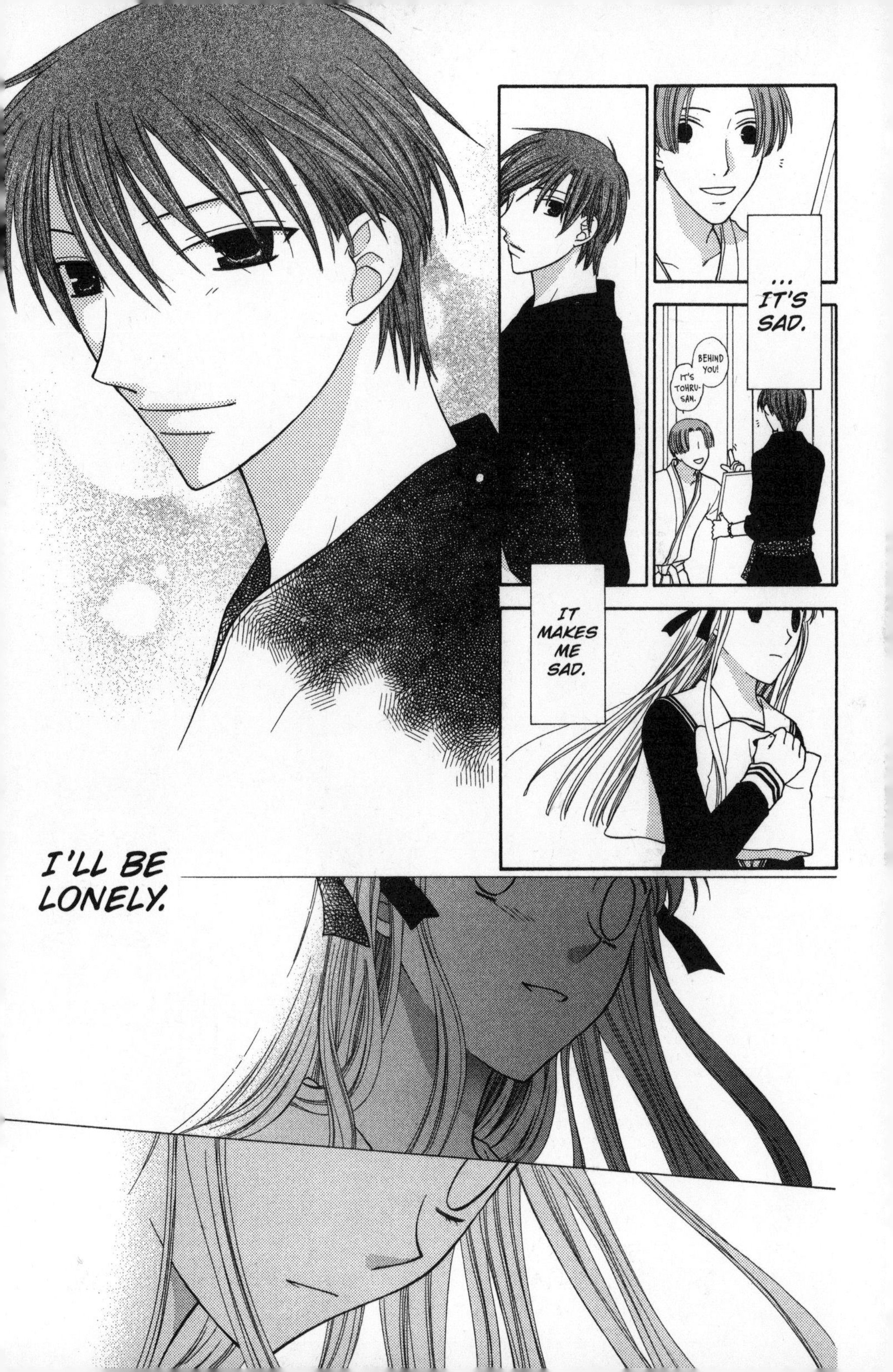
...IT'S SAD.
BEHIND YOU!
IT'S TOHRU-SAN.
IT MAKES ME SAD.
I'LL BE LONELY.

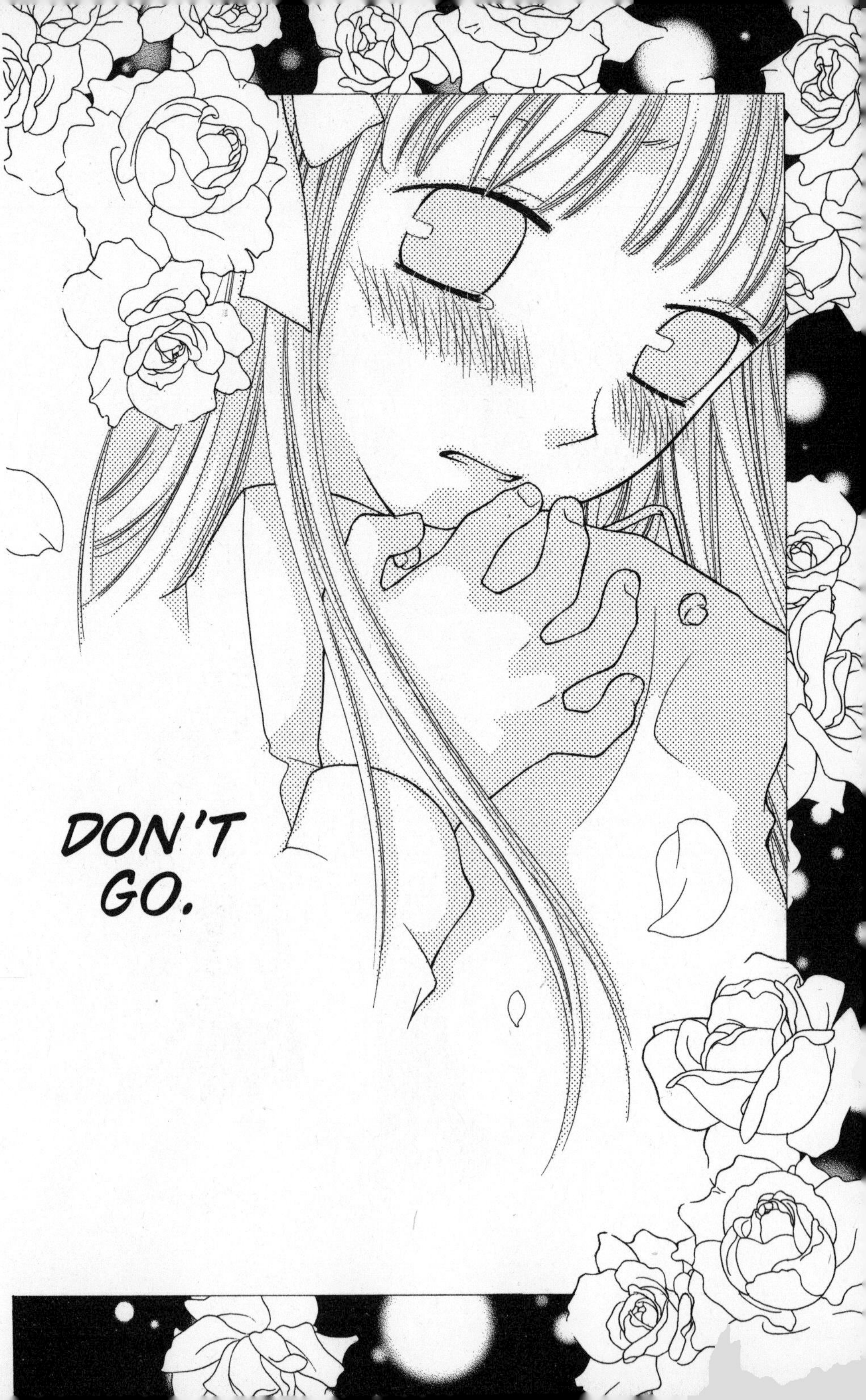
DON'T GO.

FEELING OF GRATITUDE

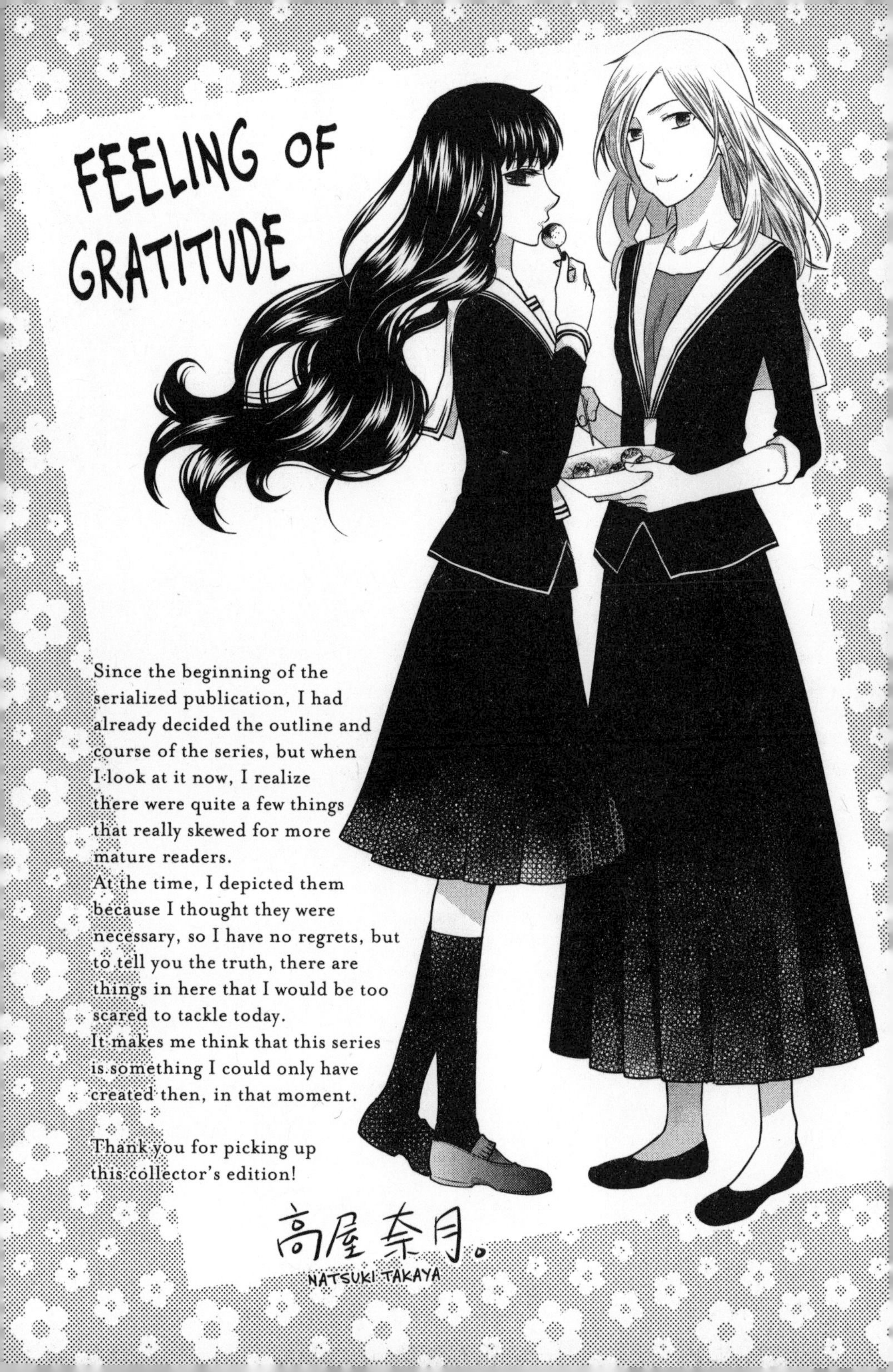

Since the beginning of the serialized publication, I had already decided the outline and course of the series, but when I look at it now, I realize there were quite a few things that really skewed for more mature readers.
At the time, I depicted them because I thought they were necessary, so I have no regrets, but to tell you the truth, there are things in here that I would be too scared to tackle today.
It makes me think that this series is something I could only have created then, in that moment.

Thank you for picking up this collector's edition!

高屋奈月。
NATSUKI TAKAYA

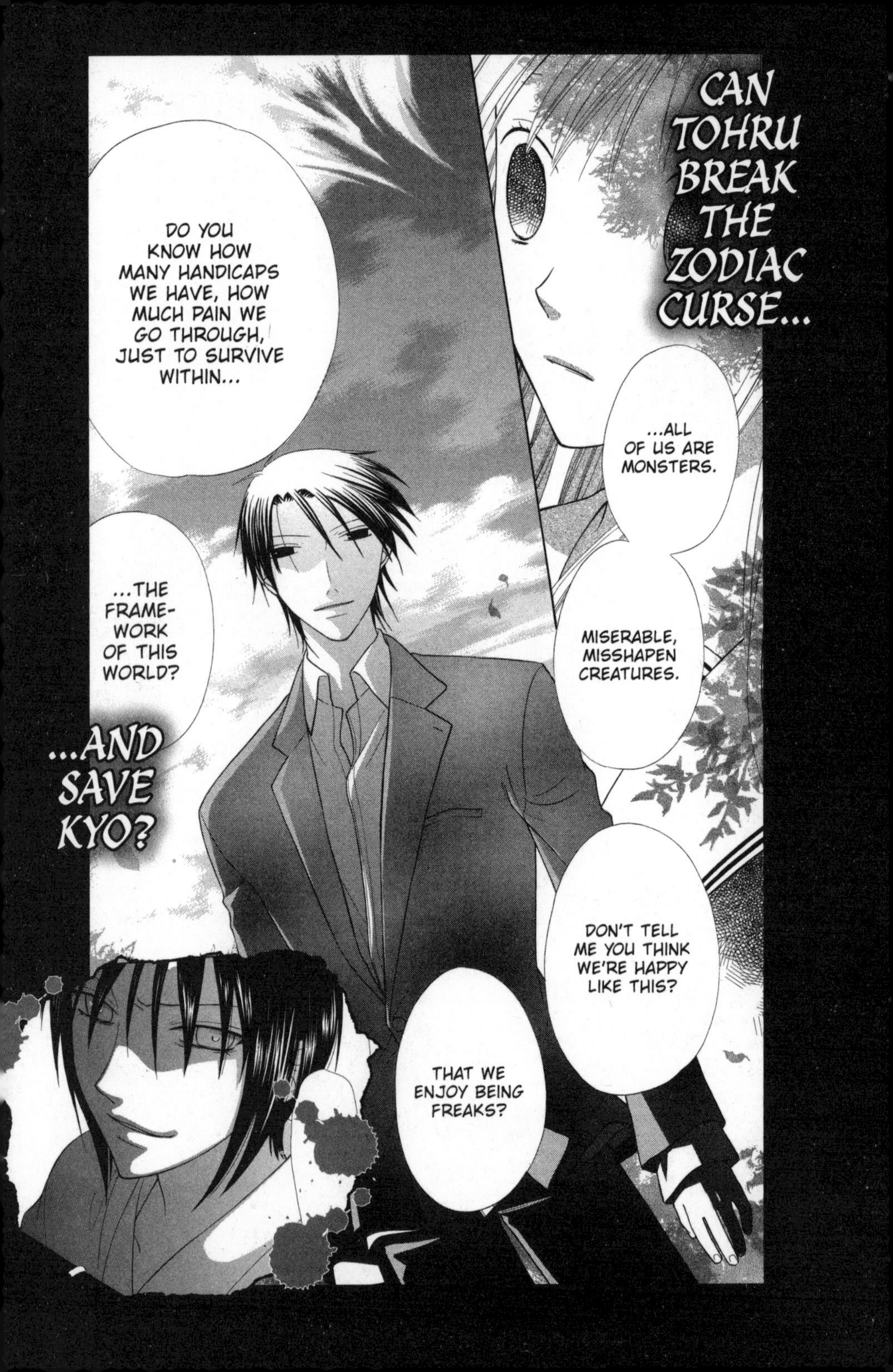
CAN TOHRU BREAK THE ZODIAC CURSE...
...ALL OF US ARE MONSTERS.
MISERABLE, MISSHAPEN CREATURES.
DON'T TELL ME YOU THINK WE'RE HAPPY LIKE THIS?
THAT WE ENJOY BEING FREAKS?
DO YOU KNOW HOW MANY HANDICAPS WE HAVE, HOW MUCH PAIN WE GO THROUGH, JUST TO SURVIVE WITHIN...
...THE FRAME-WORK OF THIS WORLD?
...AND SAVE KYO?

GRADUATION IS COMING SOON!
...FOR JUST A LITTLE LONGER.
AND I THINK ...
I'LL HAVE TO DO SOME-THING.
... WON'T HELP.
TIMES MARCHES ON.
THE END IS COMING...
WHEN THEIR WORLD BREAKS APART, WHERE WILL THE PIECES FALL!?

Fruits Basket 10

COLLECTOR'S EDITION

IN STORES FEBRUARY 2017!!

TRANSLATION NOTES

COMMON HONORIFICS
no honorific: Indicates familiarity or closeness; if used without permission or reason, addressing someone in this manner would constitute an insult.
-san: The Japanese equivalent of Mr./Mrs./Miss. If a situation calls for politeness, this is the fail-safe honorific.
-sama: Conveys great respect; may also indicate that the social status of the speaker is lower than that of the addressee.
-kun: Used most often when referring to boys, this indicates affection or familiarity. Occasionally used by older men among their peers, but it may also be used by anyone referring to a person of lower standing.
-chan: An affectionate honorific indicating familiarity used mostly in reference to girls; also used in reference to cute persons or animals of either gender.
-senpai: A suffix used to address upperclassmen or more experienced coworkers.
-kouhai: A suffix used to address underclassmen or less experienced coworkers.
-sensei: A respectful term for teachers, artists, or high-level professionals.

Page 101
"Da-da-da-duuum!": The opening theme of Beethoven's Fifth Symphony. Often used in a comedic way to indicate something of great import has happened or is about to happen.

Page 174
"He's in his twenties.": Twenty is the age of adulthood in Japan. This is the age celebrated in the annual coming-of-age ceremonies every January and the age at which an individual has the right to drink, smoke, and vote.

Page 177
Nii-san: Nii-san is a respectful term for an older brother but can also be used for an older brother figure, as it is in this situation.

Page 240
Shoe lockers: Japanese students typically have a separate pair of shoes that they wear inside the school building, and these lockers are used to store their "outside" shoes. In manga, they are often multipurpose, used for passing notes, love letters, and Valentine's Day candy.

Page 255
Hiro and Hinata: The kanji characters for *Hiro* are *hi* ("light/lamp") and *ro* ("road/path"), hence "light on the path" as Hiro's mom said. *Hinata* is a word that means "sunny place" or "in the sun."

Page 288
Onee-chan: This term is the familiar form of "older sister" in Japanese and can also be used to refer to older females (in their teens to early twenties) whom one respects or admires.

Page 372
Otou-sama: A very respectful term for a father (or father figure, as in this case).

Fruits Basket

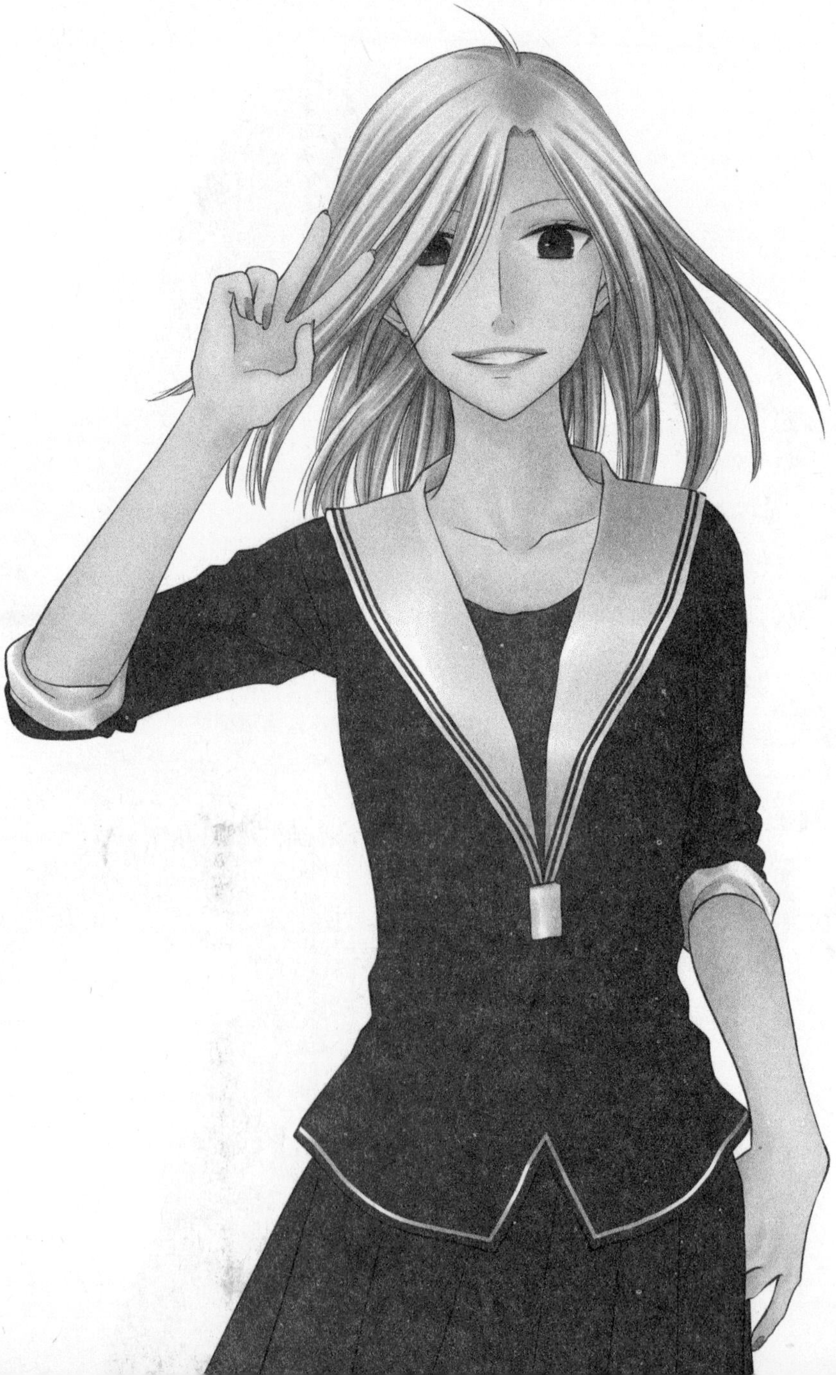

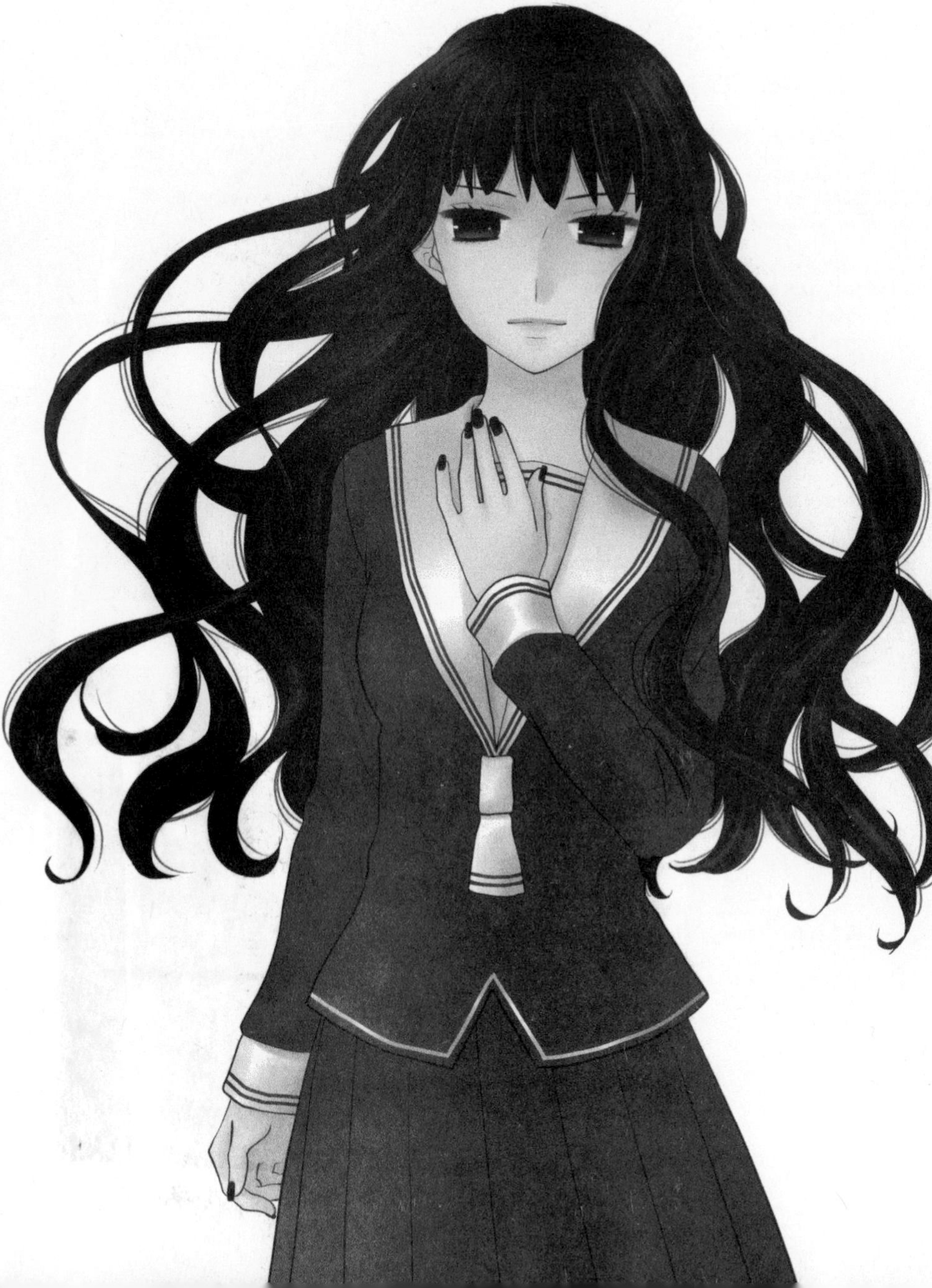

COLLECTOR'S EDITION

Fruits Basket

NATSUKI TAKAYA

Translation: Sheldon Drzka • Lettering: Lys Blakeslee and Katie Blakeslee

Fruits Basket Collector's Edition, Vol. 9 by Natsuki Takaya
© Natsuki Takaya 2016
All rights reserved.
First published in Japan in 2016 by HAKUSENSHA, INC., Tokyo.
English language translation rights in U.S.A., Canada and U.K. arranged with
HAKUSENSHA, INC., Tokyo through Tuttle-Mori Agency, Inc., Tokyo.

English Translation © 2017 by Yen Press, LLC

Yen Press
1290 Avenue of the Amer
New York, NY 10104

Visit us at yenpress.com
facebook.com/yenpress
twitter.com/yenpress
yenpress.tumblr.com
instagram.com/yenpress

First Yen Press Edition:

Yen Press is an imprint
The Yen Press name and

The publisher is not res

Library of Congress Co

ISBN: 978-0-316-5016

10 9 8 7 6 5 4 3

BVG

Printed in the United Sta